TAX, ESTATE, AND LIFETIME PLANNING

FOR MINORS

SECOND EDITION

AMERICAN**BAR**ASSOCIATION
Real Property, Trust and
Estate Law Section

TAX, ESTATE, AND LIFETIME PLANNING

FOR MINORS

SECOND EDITION

Carmina Y. D'Aversa

Editor

AMERICAN**BAR**ASSOCIATION
Real Property, Trust and
Estate Law Section

Cover design by Andrew Alcala

Library of Congress Cataloging-in-Publication Data
Names: D'Aversa, Carmina Y., editor.
Title: Tax, estate, and lifetime planning for minors / edited by Carmina Y. D'Aversa.
Description: Second edition. | Chicago : American Bar Association, [2019] | Includes bibliographical references and index.
Identifiers: LCCN 2019008850 | ISBN 9781641053891 (print)
Subjects: LCSH: Estate planning—United States. | Tax planning—United States. | Inheritance and transfer tax—Law and legislation—United States. | Minors—United States.
Classification: LCC KF750 .T39 2019 | DDC 332.024/016—dc23
LC record available at https://lccn.loc.gov/2019008850

In memory of Jon J. Gallo, Esquire

Contents

Relevant documents and forms are available for download at
http://ambar.org/Minors2e

Preface

Welcome to the second edition of *Tax, Estate, and Lifetime Planning for Minors*. For the second edition, I have added a new chapter dealing with the management of a minor's digital assets. I thank Professor Naomi Cahn and her co-authors for graciously accepting to write this new and highly relevant chapter.

Like the first edition, I envisioned a book that not only presented legal concepts but also supplied the reader with practical information. That is, I wanted the book to serve as a source of "practical wisdom" for those professionals counseling and drafting for families with minors, whether those professionals be busy solo practitioners, first-year associates in estate planning, general practitioners, or lawyers changing their fields of concentration. This book is designed to be that handy desk reference when there is no senior partner available for consultation, when one needs a quick answer, or when one requires a starting point for further research. With the dedication and skill of our contributors, I hope this second edition has achieved its objective.

I also want to extend a warm and heartfelt thank you to each of our contributors. This book truly is a team effort, and would not exist without the commitment and combined effort of our contributors. A special thank you to Jeff Salyards and Amelia Stone of ABA Publishing.

Carmina Y. D'Aversa
Editor

About the Editor

Carmina Y. D'Aversa, JD, LLM (Taxation), focuses her federal and Pennsylvania law practice on international and domestic tax planning and compliance. She formerly was with the International Estate and Gift Tax Group of the Internal Revenue Service. Before joining the Internal Revenue Service in Washington, DC, Ms. D'Aversa was an active member of the Education Committee of the Philadelphia Bar Association's Probate and Trust Law Section. Ms. D'Aversa also served as an elected term member for the Council of the Pennsylvania Bar Association's Real Property, Probate and Trust Law Section; a Chancellor's appointee for the Executive Committee of the Philadelphia Bar Association's Section on Probate and Trust Law; and an adjunct member of the Ethics Committee of the Hospital of the University of Pennsylvania. To date, Ms. D'Aversa has been designated as a Trust and Estate Practitioner (TEP) by the international organization, the Society of Trust and Estate Practitioners (STEP). Ms. D'Aversa authors and co-authors legal articles and publications, and lectures for continuing legal and professional education programs.

About the Second Edition Contributors

Cynthia L. Barrett (retired) practiced law for forty years in Portland, Oregon. She served as president of both the Multnomah Bar Association and the National Academy of Elder Law Attorneys (NAELA). In 2016, the LGBT Bar Association gave her the Leading Practitioner award. Many state and national bar groups have invited Ms. Barrett to present on elder law, special needs trust planning, LGBT planning, and LGBT federal benefits. Most recently, she presented on federal benefits for the LGBT Bar Association's 2018 Lavender Law meeting in New York City.

Svetlana V. Bekman is a senior vice president and senior legal counsel at The Northern Trust Company where she advises the bank on matters relating to trusts, estates, IRAs, and related fiduciary matters. Prior to joining The Northern Trust Company, Ms. Bekman was a partner in the Private Clients Group of Schiff Hardin LLP. Ms. Bekman speaks about and publishes articles and chapters on various aspects of IRAs and other retirement plans. Ms. Bekman received her law degree from the Northwestern University School of Law and served as a clerk to the Honorable Elaine E. Bucklo (U.S. District Court of the Northern District of Illinois).

Kenneth Black III is a graduate of the University of North Carolina and received his Juris Doctorate from the University of Georgia School of Law. He is the coauthor with Harold D. Skipper of the 14th and the centennial 15th edition of *Life Insurance*. He has provided consulting services to major life insurers, national and international life insurance agency operations, and law firms. As an adjunct instructor for many years, he taught courses in business law, risk and insurance principles, life insurance, financial planning, and financial institutions management in the Department of Risk Management and Insurance at Georgia State University. He also has served as guest lecturer in the department's Munich Re International Visiting Fellows Program. He has been a member of the American Risk and Insurance Association (ARIA) and the Asia-Pacific Risk and Insurance Association (APRIA). From 1993 to 2007, he organized and served as the founding president of a private life insurer affiliate of the former Fortis banking and insurance group.

Robert M. Brucken, retired partner at Baker & Hostetler LLP, Cleveland, Ohio, has practiced trust and estate law in Cleveland for almost 60 years, all with this firm. A fellow of the American College of Trust and Estate Counsel, Mr. Brucken also serves as the editor of the *Probate Law Journal of Ohio*, *Merrick-Rippner Ohio Probate* law manual, and the OSBA *Ohio Trust Code Manual*, and is past chair of the Estate Planning, Trust and Probate Law Section of Ohio State Bar Association.

Naomi Cahn is the Harold H. Greene Professor at the George Washington University Law School. She is the author or co-author of numerous books and articles, including family law and trusts and estates casebooks. She is an ACTEC Fellow, a member of the American Law Institute, and a board member of the Donor Sibling Registry. In 2017, she received the Lifetime Achievement in Family Law Award from the University of Illinois Law School.

Katherine Coeyman, a member of the Georgia bar, is an associate with James-Bates-Brannan-Groover-LLP. Katherine graduated cum laude from the University of Georgia School of Law in 2018. While at Georgia Law, she served as the managing editor for the *Journal of Intellectual Property Law* and was a Court-Appointed Special Advocate (CASA). In 2017, she was awarded the State Bar of Georgia Tax Section Outstanding Student Award. Prior to attending law school, Katherine graduated magna cum laude from Clemson University with a Bachelor of Arts in philosophy and graduated with general honors from Clemson's Calhoun Honors College.

Alyssa A. DiRusso is the Whelan W. and Rosalie T. Palmer Professor of Law at the Cumberland School of Law at Samford University in Birmingham, Alabama. She is a member of the American Law Institute, an Academic Fellow of the American College of Trust and Estate Counsel, and a Certified Financial Planner™. Before teaching, she practiced with the Boston law firm of Choate, Hall & Stewart and served as in-house counsel to Bank of America/Fleet National Bank. Among other publications, she is a co-author of the forthcoming textbook *Trusts and Estates: In Focus*. She is grateful for the support of her husband of twenty years, Brian, and their three minors: Jason, Lila, and Kathleen.

Susan N. Gary, the Orlando J. and Marian H. Hollis Professor at the University of Oregon School of Law, received her BA from Yale University and her JD from Columbia University. Before entering academia she practiced with Mayer, Brown & Platt in Chicago, and with DeBandt, van Hecke & Lagae in Brussels. Professor Gary teaches trusts and estates, estate planning, non-profit organizations, and an undergraduate course on law and families. She has written and spoken about the regulation of charities; fiduciary duties, including the prudent investor standard; the definition of family for inheritance purposes; donor intent in connection with restricted charitable gifts; and the use of mediation to manage conflict in the estate planning context. She is a member of the American Law Institute and an Academic Fellow and former Regent of the American College of Trust and Estate Counsel. She has served as a trustee on the University of Oregon's Board of Trustees and on the Council of the Real Property, Trust and Estate Section of the American Bar Association.

Andrew P. Gidiere received his JD from Cumberland School of Law and his LLM in taxation from the Georgetown University Law Center. He was a student extern in the Whistleblower Litigation Office of the Internal Revenue Service. He now practices law in Alabama.

Lisa Milot is an associate professor at the University of Georgia School of Law and of counsel with Ivins, Phillips & Barker in Washington, DC. She teaches and practices in the estate planning area, and her research focus includes the regulation of human bodies.

Matt Savare is a partner in Lowenstein Sandler LLP's Media and Entertainment Group, the Tech Group, and the Blockchain Technology and Digital Assets Group. Matt focuses his practice on media, entertainment, intellectual property, online advertising, privacy, blockchain, and cryptocurrency issues. Prior to joining Lowenstein Sandler, Matt worked for six years for the Department of the Army at Ft. Monmouth, New Jersey, negotiating and drafting contracts for Night Vision equipment and services. Matt received his BA in economics and business management from Drew University, his MA in corporate and public communications from Monmouth University where he graduated valedictorian, and his JD from Seton Hall University where he also graduated valedictorian.

Nancy E. Shurtz, the Bernard A. Kliks Professor at the University of Oregon School of Law, received her BA from the University of Cincinnati, her JD from Ohio State University, and her LLM in taxation from Georgetown University Law Center. Before coming to Oregon she taught at the Wharton School of Business at the University of Pennsylvania. Before that, she practiced with the law firm of Ginsburg, Feldman and Bress in Washington DC. Professor Shurtz teaches in the areas of taxation, estate planning, sustainable business, and women and the law, and has written and spoken extensively in these four areas. Professor Shurtz is currently the book review columnist for the *Estate Planning* magazine and senior editor of the Books & Media Committee of the Real Estate, Trust and Estate Law Section of the American Bar Association.

Thomas J. Striepe is the associate director of Research Services at the University of Georgia School of Law Library. He teaches advanced legal research, business law research and 1L legal research. Prior to joining the University of Georgia School of Law Library he practiced in estate planning and trust administration at Courey, Kosanda & Zimmer. He graduated from the University of Iowa (BAcc, with honors), Arizona State University School of Law (JD, magna cum laude), and the University of Arizona School of Information Resources and Library Science (MLIS).

John Wintermute is a graduate of Seton Hall Law School and was a licensing associate in the Tech Group of Lowenstein Sandler LLP. He is currently serving as a law clerk for the Honorable Madeline Cox Arleo at the U.S. District Court for the District of New Jersey.

CHAPTER 1

Federal Taxes: An Overview

Susan A. Beveridge and Jon J. Gallo,
updated by Katherine F. Coeyman

I. FUNDAMENTAL PRINCIPLES OF FEDERAL TRANSFER TAXATION

This overview deals exclusively with federal law and primarily with U.S. citizens and residents.[1] Some states have enacted separate death tax systems. For further explanation of state systems, please see Chapter 2.

A. Introduction

The Internal Revenue Code[2] (hereinafter Code or IRC) currently taxes transfers of property during lifetime or at death through two interrelated tax systems, the federal gift tax and the federal estate tax, and also via federal generation-skipping transfer (GST) taxation. These transfer taxes have been and continue to be in flux. For example, the Economic Growth and Tax Reconciliation Relief Act of 2001[3] (EGTRRA) initially provided for a gradual phaseout of the estate tax and GST tax (but not the gift tax) between 2002 and 2010.[4] During the 2002 to 2010 period, the federal estate tax exemption increased and the maximum federal estate and gift tax rates decreased.[5] The federal gift tax exemption remained at $1 million.[6] After the phaseout period, the estate tax and the GST tax (but not the gift tax) were scheduled to be abolished for only one year, namely, calendar year 2010. For gifts made and estates of decedents dying after December 31, 2010, EGTRRA provisions would no longer be in effect, and the pre-2002 tax rates and exemption amounts (i.e., a maximum tax rate of 55 percent and exemption amounts of $1 million) would be reinstated.[7]

In 2010, however, Congress, due to economic and political pressures, passed the Tax Relief, Unemployment Insurance Reauthorization and Job Creation Act of 2010 (2010 Act).[8] Instead of repeal in 2010 under EGTRRA, the 2010 Act allowed the estates of those individuals dying in 2010 the option of electing to be subject to the estate tax regime with a $5 million exemption or be subject to a carryover basis regime.[9] The 2010 Act also introduced the concept of portability, as discussed in subsection I.B.3. of this chapter.[10] The American Taxpayer Relief Act of 2012[11] made permanent the exemption provisions of the 2010 Act.[12] These exemption provisions allowed for a reunified exemption of $5 million for years 2010 and 2011 and an inflation adjustment of the $5 million exemption amount thereafter. Set forth in this chapter is an introduction to the federal gift tax, the federal estate tax, and the federal GST tax as affected by the Tax Cuts and Jobs Act[13] as well as some related federal income tax provisions.

B. Unified Credit System

1. Applicable Exclusion Amount

To date, the federal estate and gift tax exemptions are unified. The unified exemption, that is, "applicable exclusion amount," is the fair market value of property a taxpayer may transfer during lifetime or at death without being subject to any federal gift or estate tax. In the case of a surviving spouse,[14] the applicable exclusion amount is the sum of the basic exclusion amount and the deceased spousal unused exclusion amount (DSUE) to be discussed later in subsection I.B.3.[15] Under current law, each taxpayer has a basic exclusion amount of $10 million, indexed for inflation.[16] In 2018, this inflation adjustment results in a basic amount of $11,180,000.[17]

> EXAMPLE
>
> In 2018, a single (never married) individual dies without making lifetime taxable gifts (as described in subsection I.C.). At his death, the fair market value of his gross estate is $11,180,000. No federal estate tax is due. In addition, because the individual's gross estate (including any and all of the individual's lifetime taxable gifts) does not exceed the basic exclusion amount in effect for the year of the individual's death, no federal estate tax return (Form 706[18]) is required to be filed.[19]

2. Applicable Credit Amount

The applicable credit amount is the tentative tax calculated per the rate schedule under Code section 2001(c) on the applicable exclusion amount. Assuming no DSUE, the applicable credit amount is $4,417,800, the tentative tax on $11,180,000 for 2018.[20] Generally, this credit is applied against the federal gift tax due on any taxable gifts a taxpayer makes during his or her lifetime with any remaining credit amount available to reduce the federal estate tax otherwise due upon the taxpayer's death. Since 2013, the unified gift and estate tax rate has remained constant at 40 percent, while the applicable exclusion amount and corresponding basic credit amount have increased as follows:

Calendar Year	Credit Amount	Exclusion Amount	Highest Rate
2013	$2,045,800	$5.25 million	40%
2014	$2,081,800	$5.34 million	40%
2015	$2,117,800	$5.43 million	40%
2016	$2,125,800	$5.45 million	40%
2017	$2,141,800	$5.49 million	40%
2018	$4,417,800	$11.18 million	40%

To reiterate, any use of the taxpayer's applicable exclusion amount and corresponding credit during his or her lifetime reduces the applicable exclusion amount and corresponding credit available at death on a dollar-for-dollar basis.

EXAMPLE

In 2017, a single (never married) individual uses up his entire $5.49 million basic exclusion amount on taxable gifts, and then passes away in 2018 when the basic exclusion amount is $11.18 million. Assuming no statutory increase in the exclusion amount in year of death, the decedent's estate will have an exclusion amount of $5.69 million available at death.

In 2026, the basic exclusion amount is scheduled to revert to $5 million, adjusted for inflation based upon the chained consumer price index,[21] with a corresponding decrease in the applicable credit amount.[22]

PRACTICE NOTE

Given the basic exclusion amount is scheduled to revert to $5 million from $10 million (before inflation adjustments), some practitioners are concerned whether transfers during the interim period (i.e., between December 31, 2017, and January 1, 2026) will be "clawed back." That is, whether an individual or an estate will be subject to federal gift or estate taxation because the increased exclusion amount no longer exists. New Code section 2001(g)(2), added by the Tax Act and Jobs Act, gives the U.S. Treasury the authority to issue regulations. Guidance, as part of the Treasury Department's 2017–2018 Priority Guidance Plan, is expected.[23]

UPDATE TO PRACTICE NOTE

On November 23, 2018, the Internal Revenue Service published proposed regulations (REG-106706-18; 83 F.R. 59343-59348) addressing the impact of the Tax Cuts and Jobs Act's temporary changes to the basic exclusion amount. In attempting to resolve the "clawback" issue, the proposed regulations would amend Regulation section 20.2010-1 by generally allowing a decedent's estate to compute the applicable credit amount using the higher of the basic exclusion amount applicable at date of gift or at date of death. *See* Prop. Reg. § 20.2010-1(c)(2) (Example). This special rule effectively would prevent inappropriate taxation of gifts made during the period of the increased basic exclusion amount.

3. *Portability*

If a decedent's estate did not utilize the entire exemption amount and corresponding credit in determining federal estate tax liability, it was lost. This most often occurred in the event the decedent left his entire estate to his surviving spouse and, thus, solely applied the marital deduction in the estate tax calculation.[24] To ensure full use of the exemption amount, practitioners recommended credit shelter trusts, as discussed in subsection I.D.3. Effective for estates of decedents dying and gifts made after December 31, 2010, portability of the decedent's unused exclusion amount between spouses[25] is allowed.[26] To take advantage of this change, the estate of a married individual must timely file a federal estate tax return to *elect* to allow the decedent's surviving spouse to utilize the DSUE amount.[27] An extension of time, under Regulation section 301.9100-3, solely to elect portability is not available for those estates above the threshold basic exclusion (i.e., already required to timely file a federal estate tax return).[28] Once the due date of the filing of the federal estate tax return, including extensions[29] actually granted, has passed, the election is irrevocable.[30] Generally, the surviving spouse may use the DSUE amount during lifetime for taxable gifts and/or at death for determination of federal estate tax due.[31] Unlike the basic exclusion amount, the DSUE is *not* indexed for inflation.[32] In addition, portability of the GST tax exemption, as discussed in subsection E.3., is *not* available.[33]

EXAMPLE

Mike and Sarah are married.[34] In 2018, when the exclusion amount is $11.18 million, Mike dies with assets of $3.18 million. Mike's estate is below the exclusion amount, and no federal estate tax is due. Nonetheless, Mike's estate must timely file the federal estate tax return if the estate wants to elect to allow Sarah to utilize the DSUE amount of $8 million. Otherwise, the $8 million exclusion amount and corresponding credit is lost.

PRACTICE NOTE

Regardless of the expiration of the statute of limitations for the predeceased spouse's federal estate tax return and the issuance of a closing letter for the predeceased spouse's estate, the Internal Revenue Service has the authority to audit the predeceased spouse's federal estate tax return in order to determine the correct DSUE amount for the estate of the later deceased spouse.[35]

C. The Federal Gift Tax

1. *Taxable Gifts*

Taxable gifts generally are total gifts made during the calendar year less certain exclusions and deductions.[36] Taxable gifts are reported on the federal gift tax return (Form 709[37]), which generally is due at the same time as the donor's federal income tax return.[38] For each succeeding calendar year, the federal gift tax is computed on a cumulative basis.[39]

> **EXAMPLE**
>
> In 2016 (year one), T makes $100,000 of taxable gifts to E. In 2017 (year two), T makes $200,000 of taxable gifts to G. For year one, T files a federal gift tax return showing $100,000 of taxable gifts. For year two, T files a federal gift tax return showing $100,000 of taxable gifts for year one and $200,000 of taxable gifts for year two. For year two, the tentative gift tax (i.e., the gift tax before the application of the applicable credit amount) is the difference between the tentative gift tax computed on the sum of (1) the $100,000 of taxable gifts and (2) the $200,000 of taxable gifts and the tentative tax computed on the $100,000 of taxable gifts. In this scenario, no gift tax is due because of the application of the applicable credit amount available in year one and remaining for year two.

Gifts are not limited to outright transfers. A gift can be a transfer to a trust. A gift also can be in the form of the exercise, release, or lapse of a "general power of appointment" by the holder of the power.[40] For a further discussion of powers of appointment, please refer to Chapter 3.

2. *Annual Exclusion*

A donor may make gifts qualifying for the annual exclusion under Code section 2503(b). The annual exclusion allows for the exclusion of $10,000 per donee from taxable gifts.[41] This dollar amount of $10,000 is indexed for inflation, in multiples of $1,000, beginning in 1999.[42] For 2018, the first $15,000[43] of a gift a donor makes to a donee[44] during the calendar year is excluded from taxable gifts. There is no limit on the number of annual exclusion gifts that the donor may make during the calendar year, nor is there any requirement that the recipients be related to the donor. In addition, an annual exclusion gift need not be given at one time.

> **EXAMPLE**
>
> A donor transfers $5,000 on January 31, 2018, $4,500 on March 8, 2018, and $5,500 on October 22, 2018, to the same donee. The transfers qualify for the annual exclusion of $15,000 per donee.

Only gifts of present interests qualify for the annual exclusion.[45] Transfers of assets considered future interests—that is, interests that the donee or beneficiary cannot enjoy currently—do not qualify for the annual exclusion. The Treasury Regulations provide that "an unrestricted right to the immediate use, possession, or enjoyment of principal or income is a present interest," whereas a future interest, a "legal term," is "limited to commence in use, possession, or enjoyment at some future date or time."[46] An outright transfer constitutes a present interest. Whether a transfer in trust is a present interest or a future interest depends on the rights of the beneficiary. For example, a transfer in trust wherein the beneficiary receives an "immediate interest" in trust income creates a present interest. An interest in trust income is "immediate" if the beneficiary has a current right to trust income.[47] On the other hand, a transfer in trust in which distributions of income are in the discretion of the trustee constitutes a gift of a future interest that would not qualify for the annual exclusion.[48]

EXAMPLE

In 2018, a donor pays a life insurance premium in the amount of $15,000 on a policy owned outright by the donee. This payment qualifies for the donor's annual exclusion.

EXAMPLE

In 2018, a donor transfers $15,000 to a trust for payment of a life insurance premium on a policy owned by the trust. The beneficiary of the trust does not have a present interest in the trust because the trust provisions provide that the trustee has the discretion to distribute income to the beneficiary. The transfer of $15,000 does not qualify for the donor's annual exclusion because the $15,000 is not a gift of a present interest. Certain transfers in trust, however, may qualify for the annual exclusion. Chapter 3 (relating to lifetime gifts to minors) and Chapter 4 (relating to the use of life insurance in planning for minors) explain the trust requirements for qualification of the transfer for the annual exclusion.

No gift tax return need be filed if only annual exclusion gifts are made, unless gift splitting is elected, although there may be good reasons to file anyway.[49] A married couple[50] may elect to split gifts—that is, to treat gifts by one spouse as if the gifts had been made one-half by each of them to a third party. If gift splitting is elected, all gifts must be split—the couple cannot pick and choose which gifts to split.[51] To elect gift splitting, each spouse generally files a gift tax return consenting to the gift split.[52]

PRACTICE NOTE

By gift splitting,[53] a married couple effectively is allowed to double the amount of annual exclusion gifts *each* makes in a calendar year to as many individuals as they want, even though the gift is made entirely out of one spouse's separate property.[54]

The following examples illustrate the interaction of annual exclusion gifts, gift splitting, and/or federal gift tax return filing requirements.

EXAMPLE

In 2018, a donor makes a cash gift of $15,000 to a child and makes no additional gifts to the child (or to any trust for the child's benefit) during the calendar year. This gift utilizes the donor's annual exclusion, and no federal gift tax return need be filed.

EXAMPLE

In 2018, a donor makes a cash gift of $15,000 to each of her two children, totaling $30,000, and makes no additional gifts to either child (or to any trust for either child's benefit) during the calendar year. These gifts utilize the donor's annual exclusions, and no federal gift tax return need be filed.

EXAMPLE

In a community property state, a husband and wife make a cash gift of $30,000 to a child in 2018. Because gifts of community property are treated as being made one-half by each of the husband and the wife, the gift is actually two $15,000 gifts to the child, one by the husband and one by the wife. Assuming neither husband nor wife makes any other gifts to the child (or to any trust for the child's benefit) in that calendar year, the gifts qualify for the husband's and wife's annual exclusion, and no federal gift tax returns need be filed.

EXAMPLE

In a noncommunity property state, a husband makes a cash gift of $30,000 to a child in 2018. This may be reported in either of two ways. First, this may be treated as a gift of $30,000 by the husband to the child, of which $15,000 would qualify for the husband's annual exclusion, and $15,000 would use part of the husband's applicable exclusion amount. This gift would need to be reported on the husband's federal gift tax return because he made gifts over and above his annual exclusion. Alternatively, the husband and wife could "split" the gift. In that case, the gift would be treated as a gift of $15,000 by each of the husband and wife, but federal gift tax returns would need to be filed by each spouse for consent to the gift splitting.

EXAMPLE

In a noncommunity property state, a husband makes a gift of $30,000 to his child, and his wife makes a gift of $300,000 to her sister in 2018. If gift splitting is elected, each spouse is treated as making a gift of $15,000 to the child and $150,000 to the wife's sister. Even though the husband may not desire to utilize his applicable exclusion amount[55] on gifts to his wife's sister, if he wants to split the $30,000 gift with his wife, he also must split the $300,000 gift with her. Either all gifts in a single calendar year must be split, or none.

3. Excluded Transfers under Code Section 2503(e)

In addition to the annual exclusion, the Code excludes certain transfers, referred to as "qualified transfers," from taxable gifts and, therefore, from federal gift taxation. These qualified transfers are:

- Direct payment of tuition by the donor to the educational institution, on behalf of any individual, whether or not related to the donor.[56]

EXAMPLE

On behalf of his child, a donor makes a direct payment to the college for his child's books and housing at college. The payment does not meet the requirements of section 2503(e) because the direct payment is not for tuition.[57]

EXAMPLE

A donor gives his friend $20,000 for payment of tuition at graduate school. The transfer does not meet the requirements of section 2503(e) because the donor did not make the payment directly to the graduate school.[58]

- Direct payment of medical expenses to the medical provider on behalf of an individual, whether or not related to the donor, receiving medical care.[59] These medical expenses include amounts paid for medical insurance but not for expenses reimbursed by the insurer.[60]

EXAMPLE

A donor transfers $600 to her child for payment of her child's medical premiums. The transfer does not meet the requirements of section 2503(e) because there is no direct payment to the insurer.

EXAMPLE

A donor directly pays a medical provider for her child's medical treatment in the amount of $1,000. The insurer reimburses 80 percent of the $1,000 payment. Only $200 (20 percent of $1,000) is a qualified transfer under Code section 2503(e).[61]

The following example illustrates the interrelationship between qualified transfers under section 2503(e), the annual exclusion, and the applicable exclusion amount:

EXAMPLE

In 2018, a donor makes payments totaling $50,000 as follows: An amount of $10,000 is paid directly to his child's grammar school for tuition. Since the amount of $10,000 is paid directly to the educational institution for tuition, $10,000 (constituting the qualified transfer) is excluded from taxable gifts under section 2503(e). The remainder ($40,000) he gives directly to his child. Of this, $15,000 is excluded from being a taxable gift by reason of the annual exclusion. The remaining $25,000 is a taxable gift, which is reported on the donor's federal gift tax return, and utilizes part of the donor's applicable exclusion amount. If this is the first taxable gift the donor has ever made, his applicable exclusion amount remaining for gifts in later years is reduced by $25,000. (Taxable gifts automatically reduce the donor's applicable exclusion amount. The donor does not have the option to pay the gift tax on the $25,000 taxable gift and keep his applicable exclusion amount intact to be used against future taxable gifts during his lifetime or to be used at his death.)

4. *Federal Gift Tax Marital Deduction*

A gift tax marital deduction effectively allows for lifetime transfers between spouses[62] without imposition of federal gift taxation, but only if the donee spouse is a U.S. citizen.[63]

The following example illustrates the mechanics of the applicable exclusion amount and the marital deduction during lifetime:

> **EXAMPLE**
>
> Assuming a married individual's applicable exclusion amount is $11.18 million, a married individual makes taxable gifts of $11.18 million to his children (or others) without being subject to federal gift taxes in 2018. Despite no available applicable exclusion amount, the married donor, in the same year, also may make taxable gifts (i.e., gifts less annual exclusion amounts and any Code section 2503(e) qualified transfers) in any amount to his U.S. citizen spouse without incurring any federal gift tax because of the availability of the gift tax marital deduction.

D. The Federal Estate Tax

1. *Gross Estate*

A federal estate tax is imposed on the "taxable estate" of the decedent. The "taxable estate" is the gross estate less authorized deductions.[64] The decedent's gross estate includes assets in which the decedent held an interest at date of death.[65] These assets typically include what are considered the probate assets passing under the decedent's will (e.g., a fee interest in real estate, a tenant in common interest in real estate, an automobile or other tangible personal property owned solely by the decedent, stock or other intangible personal property owned solely by the decedent, or an insurance policy owned solely by the decedent on the life of another without a beneficiary designation). The gross estate for federal estate tax purposes also may include the following:[66]

- the proceeds of life insurance on the life of the decedent;[67]
- retirement benefits payable to beneficiaries;
- certain annuities;[68]
- the decedent's interest in jointly held property;[69]

- relinquishment of a power under Code sections 2036, 2037, or 2038 (see below) "during the 3-year period ending on the decedent's date of death";[70]
- transfer of a life insurance policy that would have been includable in the decedent's gross estate under Code section 2042, "during the 3-year period ending on the decedent's date of death";[71]
- gift tax paid by the decedent or his or her estate "on any gift made by the decedent or his or her spouse during the 3-year period ending on the date of the decedent's death";[72]
- certain powers or rights over assets held by a decedent at death. These powers or rights are set forth in Code sections 2036, 2037, 2038, and 2041.

Under Code section 2036, the decedent's gross estate includes any interest the decedent transferred (for example, by gift) during his or her lifetime, but (1) of which he or she retained possession or enjoyment; (2) from which he or she retained the right to the income from the asset; or (3) over which he or she retained the right to designate who may possess or enjoy the asset or the income therefrom.

EXAMPLE

During his lifetime, A transfers stocks and bonds to a trust for the benefit of his child, but retains the right to the income from the stocks and bonds for the life of A. The stocks and bonds are included in A's gross estate.[73]

Under Code section 2037, the decedent's gross estate includes property the decedent transferred, but retained a reversionary interest exceeding 5 percent of the value of the property immediately before the decedent's date of death.

EXAMPLE

During his lifetime, B transfers property to a trust. The trust document provides income to his wife for life, remainder payable to B and, if B is not living at his wife's death, to his child or child's estate. Assuming B's reversionary interest immediately before his death exceeds 5 percent of the value of the property, the value of the property, less the wife's outstanding life estate, is included in B's, the decedent's, gross estate.[74]

Under Code section 2038, the decedent's gross estate includes property the decedent transferred but has the power to alter or amend.

EXAMPLE

During his lifetime, C transfers stocks and bonds to a trust for the benefit of his children, but retains the right to designate who should receive the income. Under Code section 2038, the income interest is includable in C's, the decedent's, gross estate.[75]

Under Code section 2041, the decedent's gross estate includes any property over which the decedent held, at his or her death, a "general power of appointment." A general power of appointment, for federal estate tax purposes, is the power to designate that property (typically but not necessarily owned by a trust) to the decedent, the decedent's creditors, the decedent's estate, or creditors of the decedent's estate.[76] Property over which the decedent holds a special power of appointment—that is, one limited by an ascertainable standard—is not included in the decedent's gross estate.[77]

PRACTICE NOTE

Whether a power of appointment is limited by an ascertainable standard is strictly construed. It is prudent to use statutory language or the language set forth in the regulations in drafting a special power of appointment.[78]

2. Federal Estate Tax Deductions

(a) Federal Estate Tax Marital Deduction

The Code also allows for an unlimited[79] marital deduction for property passing at death from the decedent to the surviving spouse,[80] if the surviving spouse is a U.S. citizen.[81] If the surviving spouse is not a U.S. citizen, the deduction is not allowed unless the transfer is to a specialized trust known as a qualified domestic trust (QDOT).[82] Note, however, that the assets qualifying for the marital deduction will be subject to federal estate tax upon the surviving spouse's subsequent death, so the marital deduction delays, but does not eliminate, federal estate tax on the death of the first spouse to die.[83]

(b) Deduction for Administration Expenses

Assuming the requirements of Code sections 2053 and 2054 are met, expenses, indebtedness, certain taxes, and losses of the decedent's estate are deductible on the federal estate tax return. One common example is funeral expenses.[84]

(c) State Death Tax Deduction

A decedent's gross estate may be reduced by state estate, inheritance, legacy, or succession tax paid.[85] At the state level, there has been a recent trend to either eliminate these taxes or to raise their exemption levels, which may be due in part to the repeal of the state death tax credit. Please see Chapter 2 for further discussion of this topic.

3. The Concept of the Credit Shelter Trust

If a married person passes away and the survivor is a U.S. citizen, the simplest way to defer federal estate tax arguably is to leave everything to the survivor, delaying payment of federal estate taxes until the survivor's death. Especially before the introduction of portability and the increased inflation-adjusted exclusion amounts, practitioners, in many cases, determined that doing so actually increased the total estate taxes required to be paid at the survivor's death.

This concept may be illustrated by reference to a hypothetical married couple,[86] each of whom has a net worth of $7.5 million. Suppose that the husband died in 2016, when the exclusion amount was $5.45 million, and the widow dies in 2018, when the exclusion amount is $11.18 million. Assume the husband's executor does not elect portability for his unused exclusion amount. Assume also no taxable transfers by either spouse took place during lifetime.

If the husband left his entire estate to his wife, there would be no estate tax at his death since his estate passed to his surviving U.S. citizen spouse. That is, use of the marital deduction reduced the husband's taxable estate to zero, as reflected in column one of scenario one, which follows. However, at the widow's subsequent death in 2018, her estate would amount to $15 million (assuming no change in value), and her exclusion amount would be $11.18 million, leaving $3,820,000 taxable. Federal estate taxes would be $1.528 million. Note that the husband's exclusion amount (and corresponding credit) was never used at his death nor was the unused amount utilized at the widow's death.

Scenario One

Husband dies in 2016		Wife dies in 2018	
Gross estate	$7,500,000	Gross estate	$15,000,000
Marital deduction	($7,500,000)	Marital deduction	N/A
Taxable estate	$0	Taxable estate	$15,000,000
Tentative estate tax per I.R.C. § 2001(b)(1)	$0	Tentative tax per I.R.C. § 2001(b)(1)	$5,945,800
Unified credit calculated per I.R.C. § 2001(c)	N/A	Unified credit calculated per I.R.C. § 2001(c)	($4,417,800)
Estate tax due	$0	Estate tax due	$1,528,000

In order to avoid estate taxes at his death, the husband only had to leave his wife $2.05 million, which is the amount by which his estate ($7.5 million) exceeded his basic exclusion amount ($5.45 million). He may have left the remaining $5.45 million of assets in trust for his wife. This trust commonly is known as a credit shelter trust or bypass trust. Especially before the availability of the portability election and higher exclusions, the credit shelter trust was a commonly used estate planning tool.

The credit shelter trust could provide the wife with benefits during her lifetime, but would not be treated as part of her taxable estate and would pass to the couple's children tax-free when the wife passed away. At her death, the wife's taxable estate would have amounted to $9.55 million (her

$7.5 million plus the $2.05 million inherited from her husband) rather than the $15 million amount that occurs if the husband leaves his entire estate to his wife. At her death in 2018, the wife's estate tax credit would shelter all of her $9.55 million estate; none of it would have been taxable. Her estate tax liability would have amounted to over $1,528,000 less in taxes than would have occurred had the husband left his entire estate to his wife.[87]

The $2.05 million bequest to the wife could have been outright or in a special trust known as a marital trust. While an outright bequest is simpler, the use of a marital trust for the widow's bequest may offer her protection from creditors, as well as from claims of a future spouse, if any, and can help ensure that the trust property eventually passes to the intended beneficiaries.

Scenario Two

Husband dies in 2016		Wife dies in 2018	
Gross estate	$7,500,000	Gross estate	$9,550,000
Marital deduction	($2,050,000)	Marital deduction	N/A
Taxable estate	$5,450,000	Taxable estate	$9,550,000
Tentative estate tax per I.R.C. § 2001(b)(1)	$2,125,800	Tentative tax per I.R.C. § 2001(b)(1)	$4,165,800
Unified credit calculated per I.R.C. § 2001(c)	($2,125,800)	Unified credit calculated per I.R.C. § 2001(c)	($4,417,800)
Estate tax due	$0	Estate tax due	$0

<u>PRACTICE NOTE</u>

Despite the availability of portability,[88] practitioners, depending on the client's specific circumstances, may continue to recommend use of credit shelter planning or disclaimer trust planning.[89]

4. *Basis Consistency and Reporting*

Generally, the basis of property acquired from the decedent or to whom property passed from the decedent is the property's fair market value on the decedent's date of death or the alternate valuation date, if elected.[90] For property with respect to a federal estate tax return filed after July 31, 2015, consistent basis may be required under Code section 1014(f).[91] That is, the basis of property in the hands of a person inheriting the property from the decedent must not exceed the final value determined for federal estate taxation purposes and, if not determined, the value identified on a statement required under Code section 6035(a).[92] In addition to basis consistency, the estate may be required to satisfy certain reporting requirements, namely,

1. file an information return (i.e., Form 8971,[93] including copies of Schedule A for each beneficiary) with the Internal Revenue Service and
2. furnish a statement (i.e., Schedule A of Form 8971) to each beneficiary who has or will receive property from the estate.[94]

The information return generally is required to be filed with the Internal Revenue Service and the statement is required to be furnished to each beneficiary on or before the *earlier* of (1) thirty days after the due date of the filing of the federal estate tax return (including extensions actually granted) or (2) thirty days after the date the federal estate tax return is filed.[95] Penalties may be imposed for failure to file a timely and complete information return and statements.[96] In addition, accuracy-related penalties under Code section 6662 may be imposed for utilizing a basis inconsistent with the federal estate tax value of the property.[97]

The basis consistency requirement only applies to property includable in the decedent's gross estate for federal estate tax purposes and results in an increased federal estate tax before application of the applicable credit amount.[98]

EXAMPLE

Property qualifying for the marital deduction does not generate estate tax liability and, therefore, is excluded from property subject to the basis consistency requirements of Code section 1014(f).[99] Nonetheless, the basis must be reported pursuant to Code section 6035.[100]

Property excluded from reporting includes:

1. Cash "(other than a coin collection or other coins or bills with numismatic value),"
2. Income in respect of the decedent (as defined in Code section 691),
3. Tangible personal property for which an appraisal is not required under Regulation section 20.2031-6(b) "(relating to valuation of certain household goods and personal effects),"[101] and
4. Property "sold, exchanged, otherwise disposed of (and therefore not distributed to the beneficiary) by the estate in a transaction in which capital gain or loss is recognized."[102]

PRACTICE NOTE

Basis reporting requirements also do not apply to federal estate tax returns solely filed for the portability election or a GST allocation.[103]

E. Federal Generation-Skipping Transfer Tax

1. *Theory of Federal Generation-Skipping Transfer Tax*

As a matter of tax policy, it is Congress's goal to collect either a gift tax or an estate tax once per generation as assets pass from parents to children to grandchildren. From a congressional viewpoint, there is a major problem with the estate and gift tax system: Taxpayers can structure lifetime gifts or bequests at death in a way that only one tax is collected, even though the property "moves down" several generations. For example, a grandparent can make a taxable gift to his or her grandchild at the cost of a single gift tax, even though the property has moved down two generations. A testator could leave property to a trust for his or her descendants at the cost of a single estate tax even though the trust benefits children, grandchildren, and great-grandchildren.

The GST tax is Congress's attempt to collect a tax once per generation. For example, assume that a grandparent makes a taxable gift to his or her grandchild. A GST tax will be imposed *in addition to* the gift tax. The combined cost of both taxes essentially is equal to the total taxes that would have been incurred had the grandparent made a taxable gift to his or her child and the child in turn made a taxable gift to the grandchild. If an estate plan leaves property to a trust for the benefit of children, grandchildren, and great-grandchildren, only one tax will be incurred when the testator passes away. However, on the child's subsequent death, a GST tax will be imposed *as if* the property in the trust were part of the child's estate.

2. Federal Generation-Skipping Transfer Tax Rate

The GST tax is imposed at the highest marginal estate tax rate in effect at the time the property is treated as passing from the child to the grandchild.[104] Currently, the GST tax rate is 40 percent.[105]

3. Federal Generation-Skipping Transfer Tax Exemption

Each individual has a $10 million exemption amount, indexed for inflation, from GST tax.[106] For 2018, the inflation-adjusted amount, like the basic exclusion amount for estate and gift taxes, is $11,180,000.[107] The GST exemption is scheduled to return to $5 million, indexed for inflation, but based upon the chained consumer price index.[108] Portability does *not* apply to an individual's unused GST tax exemption.[109]

4. Mechanics of Federal Generation-Skipping Transfer Tax

The GST tax is imposed on any transfer to a "skip person." A skip person is any individual who is assigned to a generation that is two or more generations younger than the generation of the transferor.[110] For transfers to relatives, generation assignment is based on the family tree. Thus, a child is one generation younger than the transferor. A grandchild is two generations younger than the transferor and hence a skip person. For individuals who are not related to the transferor or to the transferor's spouse, the generation assignment is determined by comparing the date of birth of the transferee to that of the transferor. Nonrelatives who are more than thirty-seven and a half years younger than the transferor are skip persons.[111] A trust is a skip person if all beneficiaries holding a present interest in the trust are skip persons.[112] Thus, a trust exclusively for grandchildren is a skip person, and a transfer to that trust would trigger a GST tax. A trust for children and grandchildren is not a skip person, and a transfer to that trust does not trigger a GST tax. However, a distribution of income or principal from the trust to a grandchild during the life of the child would constitute a taxable distribution subject to the GST tax. Similarly, the death of the child survived by issue (irrespective of whether the trust then terminates or the trust principal is retained in further trust for the grandchildren) constitutes a taxable termination subject to the GST tax. As can be seen from these examples, the GST tax is imposed when benefits actually pass to the grandchildren's generation.

Automatic Allocation. GST tax exemption is allocated automatically to gifts to skip persons, as well as to some trusts in which skip persons have an interest, unless the transferor files a timely federal gift tax return and opts out of the automatic allocation.[113]

II. FUNDAMENTAL PRINCIPLES OF FEDERAL INCOME TAXATION PERTAINING TO MINORS

Two aspects of federal income taxation are commonly relevant to planning for passing wealth to minors: income taxation of the minor and income taxation of irrevocable trusts for the benefit of minors.

A. Federal Income Taxation of Minors

Like adults, minors can be subject to federal income tax. Minors may be taxed at the same rates as other individuals unless the kiddie tax, discussed next, applies. A minor's gross income for federal income tax purposes excludes qualified scholarships and qualified tuition reductions, as defined by Code section 117.

The kiddie tax allows for the unearned income (i.e., dividends, interest, other investment income) over and above an inflation-adjusted threshold amount[114] ($2,100[115] in 2018) of a child who is under the age of nineteen (or, if a full-time student, under the age of twenty-four) to be calculated differently from other individual taxpayers. For tax years before 2018, this unearned income, in effect, was subject to the greater of the child's rate or the parent's or parents' top marginal tax rate.[116] For tax years beginning after December 31, 2017, and before January 1, 2026, this unearned income generally is subject to the income tax rates and brackets applicable to trusts and estates.[117] For tax year 2018, trust and estate income from interest and short-term capital gains is taxed at the following rates:

If interest income and short-term capital gains are . . .	The tax is . . .
Not over $2,550	10% of the taxable income
Over $2,550 but not over $9,150	$255 plus 24% of the excess over $2,550
Over $9,150 but not over $12,500	$1,839 plus 35% of the excess over $9,150
Over $12,500	$3,011.50 plus 37% of the excess over $12,500

Although subject to compressed income thresholds, long-term capital gains and "qualified dividends" are subject to tax at their current favorable rates as follows:[118]

If long-term capital gains and "qualified dividends" are . . .	The tax is . . .
Not over $2,599	0%
Over $2,599 but not over $12,700	15%
More than $12,700	20%

PRACTICE NOTE

The purpose of the kiddie tax is to prevent parents from reducing their income tax by transferring income-producing property to their children and using their children's lower income-tax brackets. In calculating the kiddie tax with the temporary application of the trusts and estate tax rates and brackets, some commentators, however, are finding that the deterrent effect on high income parents may be lessened.[119]

B. Federal Income Taxation of Irrevocable Trusts for the Benefit of Minors[120]

Children are often the beneficiaries of irrevocable trusts created for their benefit by parents or grandparents. The Code essentially divides irrevocable trusts into two categories: non-grantor trusts and grantor trusts. Non-grantor trusts are treated as separate taxpayers for federal income tax purposes. In general, a non-grantor trust pays federal income taxes on its taxable income if that income is not distributed to the beneficiaries during the calendar year. To the extent that its taxable income is distributed to the beneficiaries, such beneficiaries are responsible for the income taxes. Grantor trusts are not treated as separate taxpayers. Instead, all items of income, deduction, and credit are reported on the federal income tax return of the trust's grantor or settlor.

1. Non-Grantor Trusts

Income from assets owned by non-grantor trusts either is taxed to the trust itself or is reported as a deduction to the trust and income to the trust beneficiaries individually, depending on various factors. It often is advantageous to cause the income of a non-grantor trust to be taxed to its beneficiaries in order to take advantage of their income tax brackets.[121] In 2018, a non-grantor trust reaches the maximum 37 percent federal income tax bracket at over $12,500 of taxable income while a single person does not reach that bracket until over $300,000 of taxable income.[122]

A concept unique to federal income taxation of non-grantor trusts is distributable net income, or DNI. In the most general sense, DNI describes the trust's taxable income. To the extent that distributions are made to beneficiaries, DNI is said to be "carried out" by the distribution, with the result that the beneficiary is receiving taxable income. DNI is basically the sum of the trust's ordinary income and tax-exempt income, less various deductions, including amounts distributed to charity. As a general rule, capital gains are not included in DNI and hence are taxed to the trust. However, the trustee may elect to include capital gains in DNI, an action typically associated with a total return trust strategy.[123] Distributions to trust beneficiaries are considered taxable income to the beneficiaries, and deductions to the trust, up to the amount of each beneficiary's share of DNI. The beneficiary's share of DNI is determined by reference to the terms of the trust agreement. Distributions in excess of the beneficiary's share of DNI are neither taxable income to the beneficiary nor deductions to the trust. If distributions to the trust's beneficiaries are less than the trust's DNI, only a portion of the trust's income will be reported by the beneficiaries, and the remainder will be reported by the trust. If distributions to the beneficiaries are equal to or greater than the trust's DNI, all of the trust's income could potentially be reported by the beneficiaries on their individual returns. Exceptions to this general rule exist, of course, so determination of the income tax consequences of any particular distribution should be made by an advisor familiar with all of the subtleties of income taxation of non-grantor trusts.

2. Grantor Trusts

Grantor trusts are irrevocable trusts that are completely valid for state law purposes but that are not recognized as separate taxpayers for federal income tax purposes. Instead, all items of trust income, deduction, and credit are reported on the grantor's personal income tax return, regardless of how or to whom trust income may actually have been distributed. As a general rule, an irrevocable trust is treated as a grantor trust if the grantor (or settlor) retains the power[124] to (1) change beneficiaries, (2) control distributions of income and principal to beneficiaries, (3) deal with the assets of the trust in a nonfiduciary capacity, or (4) utilize trust income or principal for his or her own benefit. An irrevocable trust also may be treated as a grantor trust if a "related or subordinate party"[125] serves as trustee and possesses these powers.

Since the grantor pays the income tax attributable to the grantor trust's taxable income, even though that income is either retained by the trust or distributed to the beneficiaries, the grantor is effectively making a gift to the trust and its beneficiaries. However, payment of the income tax liability may not be treated by the Internal Revenue Service as a gift by the grantor to the trust or its beneficiaries.[126]

Because the grantor and the trust are considered to be one taxpaying entity, sales between the grantor and the trust may not be recognized for federal income tax purposes. This allows the grantor to sell an appreciated asset to a grantor trust without realizing capital gains. Since no gain is recognized, the grantor trust retains the grantor's income tax basis in the property that it purchased. Other transactions between the grantor and the trust that would otherwise be taxable, such as payment of interest or rent, also are ignored for federal income tax purposes.

Irrevocable trusts for minors, including Crummey trusts, often are structured intentionally as grantor trusts in order to maximize the trust's cash flow since the grantor will pay all income taxes attributable to the trust's income.[127] Grantor trusts also are used when the grantor wishes to sell income-producing property to a trust for a minor without realizing capital gains taxes. Such transactions usually are structured as installment sales, and a portion of the property's cash flow is used to debt service the trust's promissory note to the grantor. Finally, a grantor who owns one or more policies of insurance on his or her life may sell those policies in a highly advantageous manner to a grantor trust.[128]

PRACTICE NOTE

Practitioners and taxpayers also must consider the "net investment income" tax under Code section 1411, effective for tax years after December 31, 2012. This tax is *in addition to* the federal income tax. Individuals with net investment income are subject to a 3.8 percent tax if the single individual's modified adjusted gross income[129] is $200,000 (in the case of married filing jointly, $250,000).[130] Generally, estates and certain trusts[131] with undistributed net investment income also are subject to the tax if adjusted gross income[132] is over $12,500 for tax year 2018.[133] Net investment income includes interest; dividends; annuities; royalties and rents, not derived "in the ordinary course of a trade or business"; and "gains from the sale of stocks and bonds."[134]

NOTES

1.   Section 2801 of the Internal Revenue Code provides for a tax on certain gifts and bequests from "covered expatriates." This tax, more akin to an inheritance tax than a transfer tax, is beyond the scope of this chapter.

2.   Section references are to the Internal Revenue Code of 1986, as amended, or to regulations issued thereunder, unless otherwise indicated.

3.   Economic Growth and Tax Relief Reconciliation Act of 2001, Pub. L. No. 107-16 (June 7, 2001).

4.   For a general overview of the earlier history of the federal transfer tax system, see JOINT COMMITTEE ON TAXATION, HISTORY, PRESENT LAW, AND ANALYSIS OF THE FEDERAL WEALTH TRANSFER TAX SYSTEM (JCX-108-07) (Nov. 13, 2007), https://www.jct.gov/x-108-07.pdf.

5.   *See* Economic Growth and Tax Relief Reconciliation Act of 2001, Pub. L. No. 107-16, § 511, § 521. In increasing the estate tax exemption and decreasing the highest estate tax rate, EGTRRA also increased the GST tax exemption and the GST tax rate. *See id.*; I.R.C. § 2641(a)(1).

6.   *See id.* § 521.

7.   *See id.* § 901.

8.   Tax Relief, Unemployment Insurance Reauthorization, and Job Creation Act of 2010, Pub. L. No. 111-312 (Dec. 17, 2010).

9.   Without election of the carryover basis regime, the beneficiaries of the estate generally receive what commonly is referred to as a stepped-up basis (i.e., the fair market value of the property at date of the decedent's death) in the property acquired from the decedent. *See* I.R.C. § 1014(a)(1).

10.   *See* Tax Relief, Unemployment Insurance Reauthorization, and Job Creation Act of 2010, Pub. L. No. 111-312, § 302, § 303, § 304.

11.   American Taxpayer Relief Act of 2012, Pub. L. No. 112–240 (Jan. 2, 2013).

12.   *See id.* § 101.

13.   An Act to provide for reconciliation pursuant to titles II and V of the concurrent resolution on the budget for fiscal year 2018, Pub. L. No. 115-97 (Dec. 22, 2017), informally referred to as the Tax Cuts and Jobs Act.

14.   For federal tax purposes, the terms "husband," "wife," "spouse," "husband and wife," and "marriage" apply to same sex couples if the individuals are lawfully married under state law, regardless of domicile. *See* United States v. Windsor, 570 U.S. 744, 133 S. Ct. 2675 (2013) (in federal estate tax refund case, USSC ruled Defense of Marriage Act's definition of marriage as between a man and a woman is unconstitutional). *See also* Reg. § 301.7701-18 (generally same; also terms "spouse" and "husband and wife," for federal tax purposes, "do not include individuals who have entered into a registered domestic partnership, civil union, or similar formal relationship not denominated as a marriage under the law of the state, possession, or territory of the United States where such relationship was entered into, regardless of domicile."). *See also* I.R.S. Notice 2017-15; 2017-6 I.R.B. 783 (I.R.S. procedures for recalculating remaining applicable exclusion amount and remaining GST tax exemption, discussed in subsection E.3., to the extent allocation of exclusion or exemption were made while the taxpayer was married to a taxpayer of the same sex).

15.   *See* I.R.C. § 2010(c)(2).

16.   *Id.* at § 11061.

17.   Rev. Proc. 2018-18; 2018-10 I.R.B. 392, § 3.35. For tax years beginning after December 31, 2017, the inflation adjustment is based upon the chained consumer price index (CPI) not the traditional CPI. *See* I.R.C. § 1(f)(3); I.R.C. § 2010(c)(3)(B). Thus, adjustments may be in smaller increments. For up-to-date information regarding inflation-adjusted tax items, the reader usually is referred to the applicable Internal Revenue Service revenue procedure issued near the end of each year. Because of the late enactment of the Tax Cuts and Jobs Act in 2017, the Internal Revenue Service issued additional revenue procedures in the beginning of the year 2018 for certain items impacted by the act.

18.   Form 706 and Instructions for Form 706 are available on the IRS website, www.irs.gov.

19.   *See* I.R.C. § 6018(a).

20.   *See* I.R.C. § 2010(c)(1) (cross-referencing I.R.C. § 2001(c)).

21.   *See* note 17.

22.   *See* I.R.C. § 2010(c)(3)(A). *See also* I.R.C. § 2010(c)(3)(C).

23. *See* 2017–2018 Priority Guidance Plan, fourth quarter update (Aug. 17, 2018), *available at* www.irs.gov/pub/irs-utl/2017-2018_pgp_4th_quarter_update.pdf.

24. If the estate passes to a U.S. citizen spouse, the marital deduction must be taken, leaving a net estate of zero and no federal estate tax due. Thus, any credits designed to reduce tax are unnecessary. *See* I.R.C. § 2056(a). *See also* subsection D.3. (calculations) of this chapter.

25. *See* note 14.

26. *See* I.R.C. §§ 2010(a), 2010(c)(2)(B).

27. *See* Reg. §§ 20.2010-2(a)(2), 20.2010-3(a)(2). *See also* Form 706 (rev. Nov. 2018), Part 6. Forms and instructions are available on the IRS website, www.irs.gov.

28. *See* Reg. § 20.2010-2(a)(1). A request for a private letter ruling may not be required for those estates below the threshold basic exclusion amount. *See* simplified method in Rev. Proc. 2017-34; 2017-24 I.R.B. 1282 (June 9, 2017) (reinstating simplified method set forth in earlier revenue procedure for obtaining an extension of time to elect portability for estates below the threshold basic exclusion amount "for a period the last day of which is the later of January 2, 2018, or the second anniversary of the decedent's date of death"). *See also* Rev. Proc. 2018-3, § 6.08, 2018-1 I.R.B. 130 (no ruling if request filed before second anniversary of the decedent's date of death and where IRS provided administrative procedure to seek extension).

29. This extension is the extension typically requested for the late filing of a federal estate tax return required to be filed when the gross estate is above the threshold basic exclusion amount. *See* Reg. § 20.6081-1. *See also* I.R.C. § 6075(a); Reg. § 20.6075-1. *See also* Form 4768, Application for Extension of Time To File a Return and/or Pay U.S. Estate (and Generation-Skipping Transfer) Taxes. Forms and instructions are available on the IRS website, www.irs.gov.

30. *See* Reg. § 20.2010-2(a)(4).

31. *See* Reg. § 20.2010-3(a)(1)(ii).

32. *Compare* I.R.C. § 2010(c)(3).

33. *See* I.R.C. § 2631(c). *See also* I.R.C. §§ 2010(a), 2010(c)(2), 2505.

34. *See* note 14.

35. *See* Estate of Sower v. Commissioner, 149 T.C. No. 11 (2017). *See also* I.R.C. § 2010(c) (5)(B); Reg. §§ 20.2010-2(d), 20.2010-3(d).

36. "Adjusted taxable gifts" is the technical term that the Code uses to refer to gifts made after 1976, "other than gifts which are includible in the gross estate of the decedent." *See* I.R.C. § 2001(b) (flush language).

37. Form 709 and Instructions for Form 709 are available on the IRS website, www.irs.gov.

38. I.R.C. § 6075(b). *See also* I.R.C. § 6019(a).

39. *See* I.R.C. §§ 2502(a), 2001(b). *See also* Reg. § 25.2502-1(a).

40. I.R.C. § 2514.

41. I.R.C. § 2503(b)(1).

42. I.R.C. § 2503(b)(2).

43. *See* Rev. Proc. 2017-58, 2017-45 I.R.B. 489, § 3.37(1) (Oct. 19, 2017).

44. If the donee spouse is a non-U.S. citizen, the annual exclusion of $10,000, indexed for inflation, does not apply. Instead, a $100,000 annual exclusion applies. *See* I.R.C. § 2523(i)(2). Like the $10,000 annual exclusion, this exclusion also is indexed for inflation based upon the chained CPI. *See* note 17. For 2018, the amount is $152,000. *See* Rev. Proc. 2017-58, *supra* note 43, § 3.37(2).

45. I.R.C. § 2503(b)(1).

46. *See* Reg. §§ 25.2503-3(b), 25.2503-3(a).

47. *See* Rev. Rul. 75-506, 1975-2 C.B. 375 (applying language contained in current Regulation section 25.2503-3(a)).

48. *See also* Chapter 3.

49. *See* I.R.C. § 6019. Note that there, however, are reasons to report annual exclusion gifts, including record keeping, commencing the statute of limitations for the value of the asset gifted, and allocating GST tax exemption (mentioned later) for annual exclusion gifts transferred to trusts. *See* Chapter 3 (regarding interaction of GST allocation and annual exclusion gifts). *See also* subsection E.4. of this chapter.

50. *See* note 14.

51. I.R.C. § 2513(a)(2).

52. I.R.C. § 2513(a)(2)-(b); *see* Reg. § 25.2513-2 (regarding "[m]anner and time of signifying consent").

53. Gift splitting is available only if, at the time of the gift, each spouse is a citizen or resident of the United States. I.R.C. § 2513(a)(1). Gift splitting also is not available for an interest in property over which the spouse creates a general power of appointment, as defined in Code section 2514(c), for his or her spouse. *See* I.R.C. § 2513(a)(1); Reg. § 25.2513-1(b)(3).

54. I.R.C. § 2513(a).

55. *Id.*

56. I.R.C. § 2503(e)(2)(A).

57. Reg. § 25.2303-6(b)(2).

58. *See additional examples*, Reg. § 25.2503-6(c), Ex. 1 & 2.

59. I.R.C. § 2503(e)(2)(B).

60. *See* Reg. § 25.2503-6(b)(3).

61. *See additional example*, Reg. § 25.2503-6(c), Ex. 3.

62. *See* note 14.

63. I.R.C. § 2523(a).

64. *See* I.R.C. § 2051.

65. *See* I.R.C. § 2033.

66. This is not an exclusive list.

67. *See* I.R.C. § 2042.

68. *See* I.R.C. § 2039.

69. If the surviving joint tenant is a U.S. citizen spouse, one-half of the value of the jointly held property automatically is excluded from the decedent's gross estate. *See* I.R.C. § 2040(b). The federal estate and gift tax implications of property held in joint tenancy with a non-U.S. citizen spouse are beyond the scope of this chapter. *See* Miriam A. Goodman, *Joint Tenancy with a Noncitizen Spouse: An Estate and Gift Tax Guide for the Perplexed*, PROB. & PROP. (Jan./Feb. 2002).

70. I.R.C. § 2035(a).

71. *Id.*

72. I.R.C. § 2035(b).

73. *See* Reg. § 20.2036-1(a)(ii).

74. Reg. § 20.2032-1(e), Ex. 3.

75. Reg. § 20.2038-1(a)(3).

76. Code section 2041(b)(1) specifically states, "[t]he term 'general power of appointment' means a power which is exercisable in favor of the decedent, his estate, his creditors, or the creditors of his estate." *Id.*

77. I.R.C. § 2041(b)(1)(A).

78. *See* I.R.C. § 2041(b)(1)(A); Reg. § 20.2041-1(c)(2). *See also* Chapter 3.

79. Local law and governing instruments (e.g., will) must be reviewed to determine the effect of taking deductions for certain administration expenses and/or state death taxes on the amount of the marital deduction taken on the federal estate tax return. *See* Reg. § 20.2056(b)(4).

80. *See* note 14.

81. I.R.C. § 2056.

82. I.R.C. § 2056(d).

83. I.R.C. § 2044. In addition, certain distributions from a qualified domestic trust are subject to estate taxation during the life of the surviving spouse. *See* I.R.C. § 2056A.

84. *See* I.R.C. §§ 2053(a)(1), 2053(c)(2). *See also* Reg. § 20.2053-2.

85. I.R.C. § 2058(a).

86. *See* note 14.

87. I.R.C. § 2011(f).

88. *See* subsection 1.B.3. of this chapter.

89. A disclaimer trust may be designed to allow the decedent's gross estate to pass to the surviving spouse with the surviving spouse having the option of disclaiming assets to the credit shelter trust. Disclaimer trust planning is beyond the scope of this chapter. For further information, including the impact of portability on estate planning, see S. Andrew Pharies, *Portability: The Basics and Beyond*, 21 ALI-CLE Est., Plan., Course Materials J. 45 (2015).

90. *See* I.R.C. § 1014(a). *See also* I.R.C. § 2032.

91. *See* I.R.C. § 1014(f), added by the Surface Transportation and Veterans Health Care Choice Improvement Act of 2015, Pub. L. No. 114-41, § 2004(a) (July 31, 2015). Code section 1014(f) applies to property to which a federal estate tax return is filed after July 31, 2015. *See id.* § 2004(d). Note that the basis becomes relevant for federal income tax purposes in calculating depreciation or gain or loss on the sale of the property.

92. *See* I.R.C. § 1014(f)(1).

93. Forms and instructions are available on the IRS website, www.irs.gov.

94. *See* Prop. Reg. § 1.6035-1(a), 1.6035-1(g)(2) and (3). *See also* I.R.C. § 6035(a), added by Pub. L. No. 114-41, *supra* note 91, § 2004(b)(1).

95. *See* Prop. Reg. § 1.6035-1(d)(1). *See also* I.R.C. § 6035(b). The Internal Revenue Service, however, repeatedly delayed the due date for the reporting requirements. *See* Notice 2015-57, 2015-36 I.R.B. 294; Notice 2016-19, 2016-9 I.R.B. 362; T.D. 9757, REG 127923-15 (temporary and proposed regulations); Notice 2016-27, 2016-9 I.R.B. 362. Final regulations eventually provided that "[e]xecutors and other persons required to file or furnish a statement under [Code] section 6035(a)(1) or (2) after July 31, 2015 and before June 30, 2016, need not have done so until June 30, 2016." *See* Reg. § 1.6035-2(a).

96. *See* I.R.C. §§ 6721, 6722. *See also* Prop. Reg. § 1.6035-1(h). Penalties may be waived due to reasonable clause. *See* I.R.C. § 6724.

97. *See* I.R.C. § 6662(a). *See* I.R.C. § 6662(b)(8), (k), added by Pub. L. No. 114-41, *supra* note 91, § 2004(c). *See also* Prop. Reg. § 1.6662-8. Property later discovered or omitted from the federal estate tax return also may be subject to a zero basis. *See* Prop. Reg. § 1.1014-10(c)(3).

98. *See* I.R.C. § 1014(f)(2). *See also* Prop. Reg. § 1.1014-10(b).

99. *See* Prop. Reg. § 1.6035-1(a)(2).

100. *See* Prop. Reg. §§ 1014-10(b)(2), 1.6035-1(b).

101. This property also is excluded from property subject to the basis consistency requirement. *See* Prop. Reg. § 1014-10(b)(2).

102. *See* Prop. Reg. § 1.6035-1(b).

103. *See* Prop. Reg. § 1.6035-1(a)(2).

104. *See* I.R.C. § 2641(a)(1).

105. *See* I.R.C. § 2641(b) (cross-referencing I.R.C. § 2001(c)).

106. *See* I.R.C. § 2631(c) (GST exemption amount same as basic exclusion amount).

107. *See id. See also* note 17.

108. *See* notes 17 and 21.

109. *See* note 33.

110. I.R.C. § 2651. *See also* I.R.C. § 2613(a)(1).

111. *See* I.R.C. § 2613(d)(2).

112. *See* I.R.C. §§ 2613(a)(2)(A), 2613(a)(1).

113. *See* I.R.C. § 2632(a)(2); Reg. § 26.2632-1(b)(1).

114. *See* I.R.C. § 1(g).

115. *See* I.R.C. § 1(g)(4)(A)(ii) (cross-referencing I.R.C. § 63(c)(5)(A)). *Id. See also* Rev. Proc. 2018-18, *supra* note 17, § 3.14(2).

116. *See* I.R.C. § 1(g)(1).

117. *See* I.R.C. § 1(j)(4) (cross-referencing I.R.C. § 1(j)(2)(E)), added by Pub. L. No. 115-97, § 11001(a), *supra* note 13.

118. *See* I.R.C. § 1(j)(4)(A) and (C), added by Pub. L. No. 115-97, § 11001(a), *supra* note 13. *See also* Jonathan Curry, *"More Than Meets the Eye" to TCJA's Kiddie Tax Tweak*, TAX NOTES 1 (June 11, 2018). For tax years beginning January 1, 2019, estates and trust brackets for interest income and short-term capital gains are adjusted for inflation each year based upon the chained consumer price index. *See* I.R.C. § 1(j)(3)(B) (cross-referencing I.R.C. § 1(f)), added by Pub. L. No. 115-97, § 11001(a), *supra* note 13. Public Law 11-97 (i.e., informally referred to as The Tax Cuts and Jobs Act) did not affect rates for long-term capital gains and "qualified dividends," but changed the income thresholds for these items. *See* I.R.C. § 1(h). *See also* I.R.C. § 1(j)(5), added by Pub. L. No. 115-97, § 11001(a), *supra* note 13.

119. *See, e.g.,* Samuel D. Brunson, *Meet the New 'Kiddie' Tax: Simpler and Less Effective*, TAX NOTES (Sept. 3, 2018).

120. What follows is a gross simplification of an extraordinarily complex topic. It is designed to provide the reader with an overview of taxation of trusts and their beneficiaries. Multivolume works could be—and have been—written on this complex topic.

121. For tax years beginning after December 31, 2017, and before January 1, 2026, this strategy may require reconsideration for minor beneficiaries in light of the amendments to the kiddie tax. *See* subsection II.A. of this chapter.

122. *See* Rev. Proc. 2018-18, *supra* note 17, § 3.01. *See also* I.R.C. § 1(j)(2)(E).

123. A total return strategy refers to a trust that provides for distribution to beneficiaries of a fixed annual percentage return, payable without regard to the accounting income of the trust.

124. The grantor trust rules are found in I.R.C. §§ 671–679.

125. Generally, the "related or subordinate party" is the grantor's spouse, if living with the grantor; the grantor's parent; the grantor's issue; the grantor's sibling; or the grantor's employee. *See* I.R.C. § 672(c).

126. Rev. Rul. 85-13, 1985-1 C.B. 184. *But see also* PLR 9444033, subsequently "corrected" by PLR 9543049, and PLR 199922062. *See also* I.R.C. §§ 6110 (b)(1)(A), 6110 (k)(3) (unless otherwise established by regulation, ruling may not be used or cited as precedent). *See also* Rev. Rul. 2004-64, 2004-2 C.B. 7. Depending on the terms of the trust and applicable state law, the trust assets, nonetheless, may be includable in the grantor's gross estate for federal estate tax purposes. *See id.*

127. *Compare* Chapter 4 (irrevocable life insurance trust usually not designed to generate taxable income).

128. *See also* Chapter 4, notes 60–66 and accompanying text.

129. *See* I.R.C. § 1411(d).

130. *See* I.R.C. §§ 1411(a)(1), 1411(b).

131. In the case of a grantor trust, the grantor, not the grantor trust, is subject to the 3.8 percent tax, if applicable. *See* Reg. § 1.1411-3(b)(1)(v).

132. *See* I.R.C. § 1411(a)(2)(i) (cross-referencing § 67(e)).

133. *See* I.R.C. § 1411(a)(2); I.R.C. § 1(e). *See also* Rev. Proc. 2018-18, *supra* note 17, § 3.01. Inflation adjustment is based upon the chained consumer price index. *See* note 17.

134. *See* I.R.C. § 1411(c)(1)(A)(i). *See also* Reg. § 1.1411-4.

CHAPTER 2

State Death Taxes

Robert M. Brucken

I. STATE ESTATE AND INHERITANCE TAXES

Estate and inheritance taxes once were considered to be principally the realm of the states. With the current status of the federal estate tax,[1] they have become the principal taxes again. State death taxes have been with us since the 19th century. Until the escalation of federal expenses and revenues occasioned by World War II, the state taxes were the principal death levy.

A. Historical Overview

In 1924, a partial credit first was allowed against the then relatively new and modest federal estate tax for state death taxes paid, and, in 1926, that credit was expanded to 80 percent of the federal estate tax. Under that arrangement, a state could levy a death tax of 80 percent of the federal tax, and that major share of the total tax would be paid to the state rather than to the federal treasury, with no additional cost to the taxpayer. The results were two: Every state levied that tax to secure this windfall of revenue without additional expense to its taxpayers; and there was thus a substantial uniformity among the state death taxes. Even states with preexisting death taxes levied this tax, which "sponged up" the federal credit, offsetting their existing taxes against it so that in many estates the total of the two taxes was exactly the amount of the federal credit. However, since most preexisting state death taxes were inheritance taxes with but nominal exemptions and modest tax rates, for smaller estates, and only smaller estates, the state tax generally exceeded any federal credit allowed for it. Later some states enacted their own estate taxes with rates exceeding that of the federal credit, so that their larger estates also paid state estate tax exceeding the federal credit for it.

In years 2002 to 2005, the federal credit for state death taxes was phased out. Since many states levied a tax only to the amount of the federal credit, those states lost their death taxes. Other states retained the death taxes that had been imposed before the federal credit was created and were not coupled to the federal credit. Still other states took action to "decouple" their death taxes from the federal credit (or their taxes were by their terms already so decoupled) to continue them as if the federal credit had not been repealed.

B. State Death Taxes

There are now (2018) only eighteen states that levy a death tax. They may be classified into three groups (information current as of the spring of 2018).

1. Inheritance Taxes

Six states levied inheritance taxes before the federal estate tax credit was created and have continued these taxes both during and after the duration of the federal credit regime. An inheritance tax is paid by the estate but is computed separately on the inheritance of each beneficiary, with any exemption and the tax rates proportional to the beneficiary's relationship to the decedent. These taxes tend to be modest on the immediate family (generally a spouse is entirely exempt) but steeper for collateral relatives and steeper yet for nonrelatives. Those six states are the following:

> Iowa: No tax on family, but tax on inheritance by collaterals and nonrelatives
> Kentucky: No tax on family, but tax on inheritance by collaterals and nonrelatives
> Maryland: No tax on family, but tax on inheritance by collaterals and nonrelatives that is credited against estate tax
> Nebraska: Flat tax of 1 percent on inheritance by family, exempts all gifts to spouse and first $40,000 to each child
> New Jersey: No tax on family, but tax on inheritance by collaterals and nonrelatives
> Pennsylvania: Flat tax of 4.5 percent on inheritance by family, exempts only all gifts to spouse and estates of children under age 21 passing to parents

2. Independent Estate Taxes

Three states levy an independent estate tax. Each once had a tax coupled with the federal estate tax credit, but with repeal of that credit the state replaced the credit tax with its own tax. Those three states are the following:

Connecticut: Exemption $2.6 million, rates up to 12 percent (spouse generally exempt), tax is capped at $20 million per estate
Oregon: Exemption $1 million, rates up to 16 percent (spouse generally exempt)
Washington: Exemption $2,193,000, rates up to 20 percent (spouse generally exempt)

3. *Sponge Taxes*

Ten states levy a "sponge" tax, that is, their taxes are decoupled from the state death tax credit previously allowed against federal estate taxes and computed as if the credit still is allowed for these state taxes, so that a state can "sponge up" the amount of the credit for the particular state. Those ten states are the following:

District of Columbia: Exemption $11,180,000 (the federal exemption in 2018), rates up to 16 percent
Hawaii: Exemption $11,180,000 (the federal exemption in 2018), rates up to 16 percent
Illinois: Exemption $4 million, rates up to 16 percent
Maine: Exemption $5.6 million (the former federal exemption), rates up to 12 percent
Maryland: Exemption $4 million, rates up to 16 percent
Massachusetts: Exemption $1 million, rates up to 16 percent
Minnesota: Exemption $2.4 million, rates up to 16 percent
New York: Exemption $5,250,000, rates up to 16 percent
Rhode Island: Exemption $1,537,656, rates up to 16 percent
Vermont: Exemption $2,750,000, rates up to 16 percent

The sponge taxes generally use as their tax rate schedule the former state death tax credit schedule under the Internal Revenue Code, with the rates (after the current applicable exemption) of 80 percent of the federal rates enacted in 1926, which rise from 1.6 percent to 16 percent. The independent estate tax of Oregon also uses this schedule, but those of Connecticut and Washington do not. Inheritance tax rate schedules are more complex, as they depend also on the relationship of the beneficiary to the decedent.

C. Estate Planning Considerations

The estate planning considerations generated by these state taxes may be limited.

First, over half of the states have no tax at all.

Second, for most families the exemptions in the taxing states will be more than sufficient to avoid any state tax. Exemptions (in all states except Nebraska and Pennsylvania) range from lows of $1 million in Massachusetts and Oregon to the exemptions in District of Columbia and Hawaii equal to the federal estate tax exemption ($11,180,000 in 2018).[2] The Joint

Committee on Taxation, as reported in the November 5, 2017, *Washington Post*, estimated that the 2018 federal exemption will result in only 1,800 estates for that year paying any federal estate tax.[3] Note that some state exemptions also make their taxes apply narrowly to only a few decedents like the federal estate tax, and other states apply their taxes broadly to a much larger proportion of their decedents.

Several cautions about these state exemptions: (1) States do not (yet) allow portability[4] of their exemptions between spouses, which would effectively double them for married decedents, as the federal estate tax exemption is now doubled by portability. The state taxes predate federal portability, and adding it once seemed unnecessary because of their once smaller exemptions. With the substantially increased state exemptions now, particularly in the states tracking the federal exemption, states may consider adding portability, doubling the exemptions for married decedents. (2) In several states, deathbed gifts (for example, gifts made within two or three years before death) may be added back to the estate against which the exemption is claimed, making it perhaps less likely that the augmented estate will be wholly within the state exemption amount. (3) These exemptions change regularly. Some are indexed annually for inflation, others are by current law scheduled to increase periodically, and of course states may pass new laws. For an exemption current to the needs of the reader, one should consult the state website (see Appendix 2-A for a list of state websites).

Third, for those whose estates may exceed the applicable state exemption, the low rates may make avoidance more expensive and troublesome than compliance is. For example, the 1 percent rate of Nebraska is surely in that class, and perhaps the 4.5 percent rate in Pennsylvania, too. These rates mitigate the shortage of exemptions in those two states.

Fourth, in the unlikely event that a state death tax appears on the horizon, an obvious mode of avoidance is to move to a nontaxing state; but there are likely other considerations in choosing a place of residence that will be of more importance to citizens.

Fifth, there is at least one consideration to which attention is warranted. The states treat differently the tax status of gifts to spouses. Of course, if there is a spousal exemption, it surely applies to an outright gift. When the spousal gift is in trust, though, one must take care that the trust terms do not attract an unnecessary tax. For example, in some states, a trust for a spouse is taxable unless he or she receives all of the income and there are no other beneficiaries (this is a common federal-format "marital deduction").[5] In others, the actuarial value of a lifetime income interest of the spouse may be tax-free, but not the actuarial value of the "remainder" after the death of the spouse, unless special language is used. Wills and trusts prepared in taxing states presumably are drawn with rules like these in mind; but, if one moves to a new taxing state, his or her will and trust may not comply with the rules of the new state and review is in order.

Similarly, the rules for deduction or exemption for charitable gifts vary from state to state. Not all states follow the federal rules, particularly the inheritance tax states whose laws antedate the federal law.[6] Again, one's planning presumably has been done with these special rules in mind, but a move to a new taxing state should generate a test of compliance with any special requirements of that state.

State death taxes apply not only to estates of their residents, but also to real property situated there even if owned by nonresidents. They do not apply to most personal property of nonresidents. Sometimes the difference between the two types of property is blurred. For example, the owner of a seasonal home situated in a different and taxing state may transfer the home into a partnership, corporation, or LLC, converting the interest in real property into personal property. However, states have in some cases continued to assert their death taxes on such real property by looking through the entity, just as they have always looked through trusts to tax trust interests of nonresidents.

II. STATE GENERATION-SKIPPING TRANSFER TAXES

There also was once a state generation-skipping transfer tax (GST tax) in some states. When the federal GST tax was enacted in 1986, it contained a modest credit against the federal tax for similar state taxes, and many states enacted a GST tax to "sponge up" that credit. In 2001, the federal credit was repealed, effective after 2004. The result was that state GST taxes also disappeared then with the disappearance of the federal credit for them.

III. STATE GIFT TAXES

In the past, some states also have imposed gift taxes. All but Connecticut have repealed their gift taxes as of 2018. The Connecticut gift tax is similar to the federal gift tax, with the same tax base, deductions, and so on, except that the Connecticut lifetime exemption (in 2018) is "only" $2,600,000 (the corresponding federal exemption in 2018 is $11,180,000), and the Connecticut tax rate beyond the exemption is progressive and tops at 12 percent (the federal tax rate is a flat 40 percent).

Appendix 2-A provides a list of the eighteen states with death taxes (in 2018), citing their laws and the state websites where further information is available. Appendix 2-B, in chart form, identifies the type of tax levied by a state, any exemption amount, the state's highest family tax rate, and any separate state marital deduction. For additional resources in chart form, see ACTEC State Death Tax Chart at https://www.actec.org/resources/state-death-tax-chart/.

NOTES

1. The federal transfer tax system is in flux. *See* Chapter 1.
2. *See* Chapter 1 (explaining federal exemption amount).
3. *But see* note 1.
4. *See* Chapter 1 (explaining portability).
5. *See also id.* (explaining federal version of marital deduction).
6. *See, e.g.,* I.R.C. § 2055 (federal estate tax charitable deduction).

APPENDIX 2-A

State Death Tax Resources

Connecticut	Gen. Stat. § 12-340 *et seq.*	www.ct.gov/drs
District of Columbia	Code Sec. 47-3701 *et seq.*	www.cfo.dc.gov
Hawaii	Rev. Stat. § 236D-1 *et seq.*	www.tax.hawaii.gov
Illinois	Comp. Stat. Ch. 35 § 405/1 *et seq.*	www.revenue.state.il.us
Iowa	Code § 450.1 *et seq.*	www.tax.iowa.gov
Kentucky	Rev. Stat. § 140.010 *et seq.*	www.revenue.ky.gov
Maine	Rev. Stat. Tit. 36 § 3401 *et seq.*	www.maine.gov/revenue
Maryland	Tax-Gen Code § 7-101 *et seq.*	www.comp.state.md.us
Massachusetts	Gen. Laws § 65C.1 *et seq.*	www.mass.gov/dor
Minnesota	Stat. § 291.005 *et seq.*	www.taxes.state.mn.us
Nebraska	Rev. Stat. § 77-2101 *et seq.*	www.revenue.state.ne.us
New Jersey	Stat. § 54:33-1 *et seq.*	www.state.nj.us/treasury/taxation
New York	Tax Law § 951 *et seq.*	www.tax.ny.gov
Oregon	Rev. Stat. § 118.005 *et seq.*	www.oregon.gov/dor
Pennsylvania	Stat. Tit. 72 § 9101 *et seq.*	www.revenue.pa.gov
Rhode Island	Gen. Laws § 44-22-1 *et seq.*	www.tax.state.ri.us
Vermont	Gen. Stat. Tit. 32 § 7441 *et seq.*	www.tax.vermont.gov
Washington	Rev Code § 83.100.010 *et seq.*	www.dor.wa.gov

APPENDIX 2-B

State Death Taxes in 2018

	Kind of Tax	Family Exemption	Highest Family Rate	Separate State Marital Deduction
Alabama				
Alaska				
Arizona				
Arkansas				
California				
Colorado				
Connecticut	Estate	2.6M	12%	CGS 12-391(f)(2)
Delaware				
District of Columbia	Sponge	Federal	16%	No
Florida				
Georgia				
Hawaii	Sponge	Federal	15.7%	No
Idaho				
Illinois	Sponge	4M	16%	35 ILCS 405/2(b-1)
Indiana				
Iowa	Collateral inh only	All		
Kansas				
Kentucky	Collateral inh only	All		
Louisiana				
Maine	Sponge	Federal	12%	MRS 36-4062
Maryland	Coll inh, sponge	4M	16%	Tax Gen. Code 7-309
Massachusetts	Sponge	1M	16%	Admin ruling
Michigan				
Minnesota	Sponge	2M	16%	MS 291.03
Mississippi				
Missouri				
Montana				
Nebraska	Inheritance	40K	1% flat rate	NRS 77-2004
Nevada				

(continued on next page)

	Kind of Tax	Family Exemption	Highest Family Rate	Separate State Marital Deduction
New Hampshire				
New Jersey	Collateral inh only	All		
New Mexico				
New York	Sponge	5,250,000	16%	Admin ruling
North Carolina				
North Dakota				
Ohio				
Oklahoma				
Oregon	Estate	1M	16%	ORS 118.016
Pennsylvania	Inheritance	None	4.5% flat rate	72 PS 9113
Rhode Island	Sponge	1,537,656	16%	Admin ruling
South Carolina				
South Dakota				
Tennessee				
Texas				
Utah				
Vermont	Sponge	2,750,000	16%	No
Virginia				
Washington	Estate	2,193,000	20%	WRC 83.100.047
West Virginia				
Wisconsin				
Wyoming				
Total taxing states	**18**			

Kind of tax: "Estate" is a local estate tax; "Sponge" is an estate tax decoupled from the former federal credit; "Inheritance" is a former NY-style inheritance tax; "Collateral inh" is a collateral inheritance tax (on collateral and non-relatives only). Maryland has both a collateral inheritance tax and a sponge tax, where any inheritance tax due is credited against the sponge tax.

Exemptions are for deaths in 2018. The exemption for Nebraska is for each family member. "Federal" is the same as the federal estate tax exemption (as adjusted for inflation), which is $11.18M for 2018.

Rates are highest rates within the family. Inheritance taxes generally charge higher rates for collateral and nonrelatives. Connecticut tax is caped at $20M of tax per estate.

Separate marital deduction is in addition to any federal marital deduction, needed for example because the state exemption sheltering a credit shelter trust is less than the federal exemption for it. An inheritance tax marital deduction is generally a zero rate for the spouse.

Robert M. Brucken
Retired Partner
Baker & Hostetler LLP
Cleveland, Ohio

#609963205

CHAPTER 3

Lifetime Gifts to Minors

Carmela T. Montesano, updated by Andrew P. Gidiere

I. OVERVIEW

Taxpayers wishing to make lifetime, or "inter vivos," gifts to minors[1] must take into consideration the impact of federal estate, gift, and generation-skipping transfer taxes on the gifts.[2] To minimize, if not totally eliminate, the impact of federal transfer taxes, the taxpayers' use of the following exclusions and/or exemptions is essential:

- The federal gift tax annual exclusion allowed under section 2503(b),[3] which, for example, is for gifts made in calendar year 2018, $15,000 *per donee*;[4]
- The *unlimited* federal gift tax exclusion allowed under section 2503(e) for certain qualifying transfers made directly for educational or medical expenses;[5]
- The unified federal tax exemption amount (currently referred to as the "applicable credit amount");[6]
- The annual exclusion from federal generation-skipping transfer tax (GST tax) allowed under section 2642(c);[7] and
- The federal generation-skipping transfer tax exemption (GST tax exemption) from federal GST tax law allowed under section 2631(c).[8]

This chapter discusses each of these in turn, with a particular emphasis on making lifetime transfers to minors.

A key component in making lifetime gifts to minors is utilization by a taxpayer of the federal gift tax annual exclusion allowed under section

2503(b). Accordingly, included in that discussion[9] is a detailed analysis of the following qualifying transfers:

- Outright gifts to minors;[10]
- Transfers made for the benefit of a minor under an applicable state's Uniform Transfers to Minors Act (UTMA) or Uniform Gifts to Minors Act (UGMA);[11]
- Transfers made for the benefit of a minor under section 2503(b) to certain qualifying trusts (a section 2503(b) trust);[12]
- Transfers made under section 2503(c) to certain qualifying trusts for the benefit of a minor under the age of twenty-one (a section 2503(c) trust);[13] and
- Transfers made for the benefit of a minor to a Crummey trust, which is a type of trust named after the leading decision by the Ninth Circuit in *Crummey v. Commissioner*.[14]

Also included is a discussion regarding the advantages and disadvantages of each of the preceding estate planning techniques and, where appropriate, sample drafting language. Examples illustrating the application of each of the governing principles also are included.

II. FEDERAL GIFT TAX CONSIDERATIONS

A. The Federal Gift Tax Annual Exclusion

1. *Overview*

(a)   Statutory Provisions—Section 2503(b)

For calendar year 2018, a taxpayer may make qualifying gifts of up to $15,000 *per donee* without any federal gift tax consequences. This is known as the federal "gift tax annual exclusion." It is allowed under section 2503(b)(1), which provides, in relevant part, as follows:

> [i]n the case of gifts (*other than gifts of future interests in property*) made to any person by the donor during the calendar year, the first *$10,000* of such gifts to such person shall not . . . be included in the total amount of gifts made during such year (emphasis added).

The $10,000 amount set forth in section 2503(b)(1) is adjusted for inflation under section 2503(b)(2) in multiples of $1,000.[15] For calendar years 1982 through 2001, the annual exclusion amount was $10,000. It increased to $11,000 for calendar year 2002,[16] where it remained for calendar years 2003,[17] 2004,[18] and 2005.[19] Increasing in calendar year 2006[20] to $12,000, it remained at $12,000 for calendar years 2007[21] and 2008.[22] In calendar year 2009,[23] the annual exclusion increased to $13,000, where it remained for calendar years 2010,[24] 2011,[25] and 2012.[26] It then increased to $14,000 for calendar year 2013,[27] where it remained for calendar years 2014,[28]

2015,[29] 2016,[30] and 2017.[31] For calendar year 2018, the annual exclusion has increased to $15,000.[32]

Calendar Years	Annual Exclusion
1982 through 2001	$10,000
2002 through 2005	$11,000
2006 through 2008	$12,000
2009 through 2012	$13,000
2013 through 2017	$14,000
2018	$15,000

(b)   Doubling of Annual Exclusion Amount by Married Taxpayers/Gift Splitting

The amount of the annual per donee exclusion from federal gift tax may be doubled by married taxpayers.[33] For example, in calendar year 2018, a husband and wife may make gifts of up to $30,000 *per donee*, without incurring any liability for federal gift taxes and without any federal gift tax consequences. To accomplish this objective:

- Each spouse may individually transfer assets of his or her own; or
- The nondonor spouse may join in the donor spouse's gift by electing to "gift split" with such spouse by signing in the places indicated on the federal gift tax return that the donor spouse is required to file on April 15 of the year following the gifts. Gift splitting applies to *all* gifts made by either spouse in any year. It does not require that the nondonor spouse have assets of his or her own to transfer or that the donor spouse transfer any assets to the nondonor spouse.

(c)   Significance of Making Annual Exclusion Gifts

Utilization by a taxpayer of annual exclusion gifts is a key component in making lifetime gifts to minors for four reasons. First, annual exclusion gifts may be made year after year by a donor to as many different donees as he or she chooses. As discussed earlier, in calendar year 2018, a single donor may transfer up to $15,000 per donee, and married donors[34] may transfer up to $30,000 per donee. Second, the gifts do not require the filing of a federal gift tax return, unless gift splitting is elected.[35] Third, and perhaps most importantly, if properly structured, making annual exclusion gifts does *not* result in the imposition of federal gift tax or reduce a donor's available applicable credit amount and available GST exemption. Hence, these gifts may be made totally outside of the federal transfer tax system and without any federal transfer tax consequences. Thus they form a key component in making lifetime gifts to minors. Finally, all annual exclusion gifts and any appreciation thereon, will, if properly structured, be removed from the donor's gross estate for federal estate tax purposes as of the date of the gift. Hence, gifts of appreciating assets are particularly desirable, especially in connection with the making of lifetime gifts to minors. Accordingly, if properly structured, annual exclusion gifts do not result in the imposition of federal gift tax or utilize any other exemptions or exclusions to which a donor is otherwise entitled and over a period of years may serve to significantly reduce a donor's gross estate for federal estate tax purposes.

(d)   "Present Interest" Requirement

In order to qualify for the *annual per donee* exclusion, section 2503(b)(1) provides that the gift made to the donee must be a gift of a "present interest."[36] A "present interest" in property is defined as "an unrestricted right to the immediate use, possession, or enjoyment of property or the income from property such as a life estate or term certain."[37] It is to be distinguished from a "future interest" in property,[38] which is a legal term, and "includes reversions, remainders, and other interests or estates, whether vested or contingent, and whether or not ported by a particular interest or estate, which are limited to commence in use, possession, or enjoyment at some future date or time."[39]

Generally, outright gifts of cash or property to a minor qualify as gifts of a present interest in property.[40] Similarly, gifts for the benefit of a minor made under a state's UTMA or UGMA also qualify as gifts of a present interest in property.[41] Further, contributions made to a "qualified tuition program" (a section 529 plan) on behalf of any designated beneficiary (other than one's self) are a gift of a present interest in property.[42]

However, gifts made to a trust do *not* generally qualify as gifts of a present interest in property and thus do *not* qualify for the annual exclusion from federal gift tax. Exceptions to this latter rule exist for interests in certain trusts, specifically, the following:

- a section 2503(b) trust,[43]
- a section 2503(c) trust,[44] and
- a Crummey trust.[45]

We will discuss each of these types of transfers in turn, in the sections that follow.

2. Outright Gifts to Minors (and/or to Guardians Appointed by a Court)

(a)   Overview

Outright gifts of cash or property to minors qualify for the annual exclusion from federal gift tax and typically may be easily effectuated, for example, by transferring cash or personal property (e.g., jewelry) directly to a minor or changing the title on a bank book or a deed to real property.

(b)   Planning Considerations

There are, however, many issues raised in connection with making a gift to a minor. While in most states minors may receive property by gift, they may not have the ability to effectively handle the property once they receive it, unless perhaps a guardian is appointed by a court to represent the minor. While transfers to a guardian do generally qualify for the annual exclusion,[46] the appointment of a guardian is in most states both expensive and time-consuming. In most states, once the guardian is appointed by the court, he or she will be required to report directly to the court on a regular basis with regard to the disposition of each asset, obtain court approval for certain transactions, and, in many jurisdictions, post a bond.[47]

In addition, in most states, minors are not able to make a valid will.[48] If a minor should die before attaining the age of majority, then property gifted to him or her will be distributed, in many instances, pursuant to the intestacy statutes then in effect. If one of the donor's primary purposes in making the gift was to remove the property from his or her gross estate for federal estate tax purposes, this will prove problematic if the property is returned to the donor under the state's applicable intestacy statute.

Moreover, and perhaps more importantly, most donors are reluctant to make outright transfers of either cash or property to a minor due to the donee's age and lack of maturity in handling the property. This is often true even once the donee has attained the age of majority. Hence, in most instances, other than transfers of an insignificant amount of cash or personal property (e.g., jewelry or other items of sentimental value), it generally is advisable and/or necessary to find an alternative method of making annual exclusion gifts to minors.

3.   *Gifts Made Pursuant to a State's UTMA or UGMA*

(a)   Overview

Gifts made for the benefit of a minor under a state's UTMA or UGMA[49] qualify as a present interest in property and thus qualify for the annual exclusion allowed under federal gift tax law.

The UTMA and UGMA provide a statutory framework for a donor to transfer property to a custodian for the benefit of a minor. Under these statutes, the custodian typically will hold and dispose of the property for the benefit of the minor in accordance with the applicable state's statute until the *earlier* of:

- the date that the minor attains the stated age of majority, or
- the minor's death.[50]

During the term of the custodianship, the custodian may deliver or pay to the minor, or expend for the minor's benefit, so much of the custodial property as the custodian considers advisable for the use and benefit of the minor, *without* court order and *without* regard to (1) the duty or ability of the custodian personally or of any other person to support the minor, or (2) any other income or property of the minor that may be applicable or available for the support of the minor.[51] Upon the termination of the custodianship, the custodian will transfer the assets outright either to the newly emancipated minor or his or her estate, as the case may be, in "an appropriate manner."[52]

The statutes vary by state but each provides a host of rules regarding the creation, administration, and termination of the custodianships established thereunder. For example, under the New York Uniform Transfers to Minors Act[53] (NY UTMA), detailed provisions are included regarding the following:

- the manner in which custodial property is created and transfers effected;
- the nomination of a custodian;
- the powers of a custodian;
- a custodian's expenses, compensation, and bond;
- accounting by and determination of liability of a custodian;
- care and use of custodial property;
- a custodian's liability to third persons and exemptions of third persons from liability;
- termination of custodianship;
- age of majority; and
- renunciation, resignation, death, or removal of a custodian and designation of a successor custodian.

Hence, the UTMA and UGMA statutes provide a statutory framework for the making of a gift to a minor and contain essentially many of the administrative and dispositive provisions one would normally expect to find in a trust instrument.

(b)   Creation of Custodial Accounts

Gifts made for the benefit of a minor under UTMA and UGMA may be easily effectuated. Typically, transfers may be made directly to a qualified person or entity as custodian for a minor under the applicable state's UTMA or UGMA or pursuant to a written instrument setting forth the same. The specific form of transfer required depends typically upon the nature of the asset transferred.[54]

For example, under the NY UTMA, custodial property is created and a transfer is made in the following instances:[55]

- An uncertificated security or certificated security in registered form is either (1) registered in the name of the transferor, an adult other than the transferor, or a trust company, followed in substance by the words "*as custodian for* _____ *(name of minor) under the New York Uniform Transfers to Minors Act,"* or (2) delivered, if in certificated form, or any document necessary for the transfer of an uncertificated security is delivered, together with any necessary endorsement, to an adult other than the transferor or to a trust company, as custodian, accompanied by a written instrument in substantially the form set forth below;[56]

- Money is paid or delivered, or a security held in the name of a broker, financial institution, or its nominee is transferred, to a broker or financial institution for credit to an account in the name of the transferor, an adult other than the transferor, or a trust company, followed in substance by the words *"as custodian for* _____ *(name of minor) under the New York Uniform Transfers to Minors Act"*;[57]

- The ownership of a life or endowment insurance policy or annuity contract is either (1) registered with the issuer in the name of the transferor, an adult other than the transferor, or a trust company, followed in substance by the words *"as custodian for* _____ *(name of minor) under the New York Uniform Transfers to Minors Act"*; or (2) assigned in a writing delivered to an adult other than the transferor, or to a trust company whose name in the assignment is followed in substance by the words *"as custodian for* _____ *(name of minor) under the New York Uniform Transfers to Minors Act"*;[58]

- An irrevocable exercise of a power of appointment or an irrevocable present right to future payment under a contract is the subject of a written notification delivered to the payor, issuer, or other obligor that the right is transferred to the transferor, an adult other than the transferor, or a trust company, whose name in the notification is followed in substance by the words *"as custodian for* _____ *(name of minor) under the New York Uniform Transfers to Minors Act"*;[59]

- An interest in real property is recorded in the name of the transferor, an adult other than the transferor, or a trust company, followed in substance by the words *"as custodian for* _____ *(name of minor) under the New York Uniform Transfers to Minors Act"*;[60]

- A certificate of title issued by a department or agency of a state or of the United States, which evidences title to tangible personal property, is either (1) issued in the name of the transferor, an adult other than the transferor, or a trust company, followed in substance by the words *"as custodian for* _____ *(name of minor) under the New York Uniform Transfers to Minors Act"*; or (2) delivered to an adult other than the transferor or to a trust company, endorsed to that person followed in substance by the words *"as custodian for* _____ *(name of minor) under the New York Uniform Transfers to Minors Act"*;[61] or

- An interest in *any other type of property* not described immediately above if such transfer is made by a written instrument[62] in substantially the following form:[63]

TRANSFER UNDER THE NEW YORK UNIFORM TRANSFERS TO MINORS ACT

I, _____ (Name of Transferor or Name and Representative Capacity if a Fiduciary) hereby transfer to _____ (Name of Custodian), as custodian for _____ (Name of Minor) under the New York Uniform Transfers to Minors Act, the following:

(Insert Description of the Custodial Property Sufficient to Identify It).

_____   _____
Date   *Signature of Transferor*

I, _____ (Name of Custodian), acknowledge receipt of the property described above as custodian for the minor named above under the New York Uniform Transfers to Minors Act.

_____   _____
Date   *Signature of Custodian*

Thus, a custodial transfer may be effectuated under the NY UTMA for properties delineated in the statute by simple recitation of the key statutory words "*as custodian for* _____ *[name of minor] under the New York Uniform Transfers to Minors Act.*" In the case of properties not specifically listed in the statute, a written instrument in substantially the form set forth above will suffice.

(c)   Selection of Custodian

Typically, a donor is permitted under applicable state law to serve as the custodian under a UTMA or UGMA.[64] The donor should *not*, however, be named as custodian, as this may have adverse federal estate tax consequences should the donor die during the term of the custodianship. Nor should the donor's spouse be named as custodian if he or she is legally obligated to support the minor and applicable state law does not prohibit the use of custodial property to discharge that obligation. Again, in this instance, the appointment of the donor's spouse also may have adverse federal estate tax consequences. Hence, persons who are not legally obligated to support the minor or banks or trust companies are generally the best candidates to serve as custodians.

(d)   Age of Majority

The age of majority varies by state. For example, under the NY UTMA, the term "minor" is defined as "an individual who has not attained the age of twenty-one years."[65] Hence, the age of majority for purposes of the UTMA statute is generally twenty-one, and it is at this age that a custodianship effectuated as a gift during lifetime or at death generally will terminate.[66] However, like many states, New York also has an age eighteen election[67] and, hence, it is at this age that the custodianship will terminate.[68] Some states, such as California, Nevada, and Tennessee, have statutory provisions extending the age for these purposes to twenty-five.[69]

(e)   Standard of Care

A standard of care typically is provided in a UTMA statute. For example, under the NY UTMA, a UTMA custodian is required to observe the standard of care that would be observed by a prudent person dealing with property of another. The custodian is not limited by any other statute restricting investments by fiduciaries and specifically is authorized to delegate investment and management functions in the manner of a trustee.[70] If a custodian has a special skill or expertise or is named custodian on the basis of representations of a special skill or expertise, the custodian is required to use that skill or expertise.[71] However, a custodian, in the custodian's discretion and without liability to the minor or the minor's estate, may retain any custodial property received from a transferor.[72]

(f)   Life Insurance and Endowment Policies

Under the NY statute, a UTMA custodian may invest in or pay premiums on life insurance or endowment policies on

- the life of the minor *only if* the minor or the minor's estate is the sole beneficiary, or
- the life of another person in whom the minor has an insurable interest *only* to the extent that the minor, the minor's estate, or the custodian in the capacity of custodian is the irrevocable beneficiary.[73]

(g)   Requirement that Custodial Property Must Be Kept Separate and Distinct

Typically, custodial property must be kept separate and distinct by the custodian from all other property in a manner sufficient to identify it clearly as custodial property of the minor.[74] For example, under N.Y. law, custodial property consisting of certificated securities may be held on deposit at a stock brokerage firm or a financial institution registered in a street name or nominee name.[75] Custodial property consisting of an undivided interest is so identified if the minor's interest is held as a tenant in common and is fixed.[76] Custodial property subject to recordation is so identified if it is recorded, and custodial property subject to registration is so identified if it is either registered, or held in an account designated, in the name of the custodian, followed in substance by the words *"as a custodian for_____(name of minor) under the New York Uniform Transfers to Minors Act."*[77]

(h)   Records

A custodian is required to keep records of all transactions with respect to custodial property, including information necessary for the preparation of the minor's tax returns, and to make them available for inspection at reasonable intervals by a parent or legal representative of the minor or by the minor if the minor has attained the age of fourteen years.[78]

(i)   Powers of Custodian

A UTMA custodian typically "has all the rights, powers, and authority over custodial property that unmarried adult owners have over their own property, but a custodian may exercise those rights, powers, and authority in that capacity only."[79] Note: This does not relieve a custodian from liability for breach of the standard-of-care provisions[80] otherwise set forth in the statute.

A UGMA custodian typically only has those powers set forth in the statute, but they include the power to invest in prudent investments.[81]

(j)   Federal Income Tax Returns

Generally, a minor must report all custodial income on his or her own federal income tax return.[82] If custodial income is used to discharge a parent's legal obligation of support, the income is taxable to the parent and must be reported on the parent's federal income tax return. For federal income tax purposes, a custodial account is not considered a trust and hence, no fiduciary income tax return is required.

(k)   Planning Considerations

Utilization of custodial accounts to make gifts to minors qualifies for the federal gift tax annual exclusion and is easily effectuated under applicable state law. The UTMA and UGMA statutes provide a statutory framework—an entire body of governing law—within which the gifts may be made and custodial property administered and disposed.

However, as in the case of outright gifts, there are two significant disadvantages in utilization of custodial accounts, especially if the value of the assets transferred thereto are significant.

First, assuming that the donee survives to the age of majority, the custodial assets will be distributed outright to the donee. As in the case of outright gifts, most donors are reluctant to make outright transfers of either cash or property to a minor due to the donee's age and lack of maturity in handling the property.

Second, if a minor should die before attaining the age of majority, then property gifted to him or her will in many instances be distributed pursuant to the intestacy statutes then in effect. This will prove problematic if one of the donor's primary purposes in making the gift was to remove the property from his or her gross estate for federal estate tax purposes and the property is returned to the donor under the state's applicable intestacy statute.

Hence, in most instances (other than transfers of modest values), it is advisable and/or necessary to find an alternative method of making annual exclusion gifts to minors.

4. Transfers to a Section 2503(b) Trust

(a)   Overview

A section 2503(b) trust is an irrevocable trust[83] made by a donor under which the beneficiary is entitled to receive *all* of the income from the trust, either for a fixed term of years or for life. Upon the termination of the income beneficiary's interest in the trust (whether it is a fixed term of years or a life interest), the trust assets are distributed to those persons and in the manner as the donor initially provided in the governing trust instrument.

At the onset, a section 2503(b) trust provides two key advantages over an outright gift to a minor and/or a transfer made for the benefit of a minor under a UTMA or UGMA. First, the property may be retained in trust for the benefit of a minor for as long as the donor desires (including the donee's entire lifetime) and is not thus limited to a predetermined age (e.g., eighteen, or twenty-one, or even twenty-five). Second, upon the death of the donee, the trust assets will pass to those persons and in the manner as the donor specified under the governing trust instrument and not potentially back to the donor under the applicable intestacy statutes.

(b)   Only Actuarial Value of Income Interest Qualifies as a Present Interest

However, not the entire gift to a section 2503(b) trust will qualify for the annual exclusion from federal gift tax. Only the actuarial value of the income interest will qualify as a present interest in the property and, hence, for the annual exclusion from federal gift tax. As the remainder interest is a gift of a future interest, it does not qualify for the annual exclusion allowed under federal gift tax law. Hence, a federal gift tax return must be filed for each year in which a gift is made to a section 2503(b) trust and either a portion of the donor's available exemption amount must be utilized or, if the entire exemption previously has been utilized, a federal gift tax paid. Clearly, this is a significant disadvantage in making a gift to a section 2503(b) trust.

(c)   Determining Actuarial Value

To determine the actuarial value of the income interest, the valuation tables set forth under section 7520 are used. Section 7520(a) provides generally that the value of any annuity, any interest for life or a term of years, or any remainder or reversionary interest is determined under tables prescribed by the secretary of the U.S. Treasury, and by using an interest rate (rounded to the nearest two-tenths of 1 percent) equal to 120 percent of the federal midterm rate in effect under section 1274(d)(1) for the month in which the valuation date falls. As the interest factor under the tables changes monthly, the value in a given month under the tables will vary. The section 7520 rate is published monthly, usually in a revenue ruling.[84] This determination will be required in each month for which a transfer is made to a section 2503(b) trust.

(d)   Income Interest under a Section 2503(b) Trust

The income interest required in a section 2503(b) trust must constitute an absolute right to which the beneficiary is entitled under all circumstances. Hence, a trust where the trustee has discretionary authority to make an income distribution will not qualify.

A spendthrift clause prohibiting a beneficiary from assigning his or her income rights should not prove problematic.[85] However, a spendthrift provision authorizing the trustee to withhold income most likely will render the income interest to qualify as a gift of a future interest as opposed to as a gift of a present interest.[86]

Moreover, the trust must invest in income-producing assets. If a trustee is authorized to invest in non-income-producing assets, this will prevent the income interest from qualifying for the annual exclusion even if the trustee never exercises his or her authority to do so.[87]

(e)   Federal Income Tax Consequences

As all of the income of a section 2503(b) trust must be distributed to the beneficiary, the beneficiary is taxable on that income for federal income tax purposes. The trust, however, is a separate taxpayer. It must have its own employer identification number and file its own federal income tax returns. It is taxable on any capital gains and losses and all other items allocable under federal income tax law to trust corpus. As in the case of a gift under a UTMA or UGMA, the grantor of a section 2503(b) trust also will be taxable on any income used by the trustee to discharge the grantor's legal obligation of support for any income beneficiary.[88] Finally, as the section 2503(b) trust is not permitted to accumulate income, its tax reporting will be simpler than that for a section 2503(c) trust[89] or a Crummey trust,[90] both of which are discussed later in the chapter.

(f)   Principal Distributions under a Section 2503(b) Trust

Principal generally may be distributed under a section 2503(b) trust, *but only to* the income beneficiary. Neither the income nor the principal of the trust may be expended to, or for the benefit of, another beneficiary. Hence, a section 2503(b) trust must be established for either one beneficiary or multiple beneficiaries where each has a separate and distinct share that is fixed and ascertainable. A "pot" trust or discretionary trust for multiple beneficiaries will not suffice.

Moreover, if the trustee is required to make principal distributions, these distributions will reduce the value of the income interest and accordingly the portion of any gift that will qualify as a present interest in property for purposes of the annual gift tax exclusion.

(g)   Selection of Trustee

Generally, the grantor of a section 2503(b) trust *may* serve as trustee. As a section 2503(b) trust is required to distribute all of its income, the grantor may serve as trustee without violating the grantor trust rules for purposes of federal income tax law[91] or cause inclusion of the assets in the grantor's gross estate for federal estate tax purposes if the grantor should die during the term of the trust. However, these rules are applicable generally *if and only if*

- the trustee does not have the authority to distribute principal; or
- if the trustee does have the authority to distribute principal, the authority is limited to an ascertainable standard that is clearly set forth in the governing trust instrument (i.e., the power to make a distribution for a beneficiary's "health," "support," maintenance," and "education").[92]

A third party also may serve as trustee and need not be an independent party, even if he or she is given broad discretion to make principal distributions without regard to an ascertainable standard. Hence, a related or subordinated party (other than the grantor) may serve as trustee under these circumstances.

5. *Transfers Made to a Section 2503(c) Trust*

(a)   Overview

A section 2503(c) trust is an irrevocable trust made in accordance with the statutory provisions set forth in section 2503(c), which is entitled *"Transfer for the benefit of minor."* A transfer to a section 2503(c) trust qualifies as a present interest in property and thus qualifies for the federal gift tax annual exclusion.

(b)   Statutory Provisions—Section 2503(c)

Section 2503(c) provides, in relevant part, that "[n]o part of a gift to an individual who has not attained the age of twenty-one years on the date of such transfer shall be considered a gift of a future interest in property for purposes of subsection (b) *[which allows for the annual per donee exclusion from federal gift tax]* if the property and the income therefrom":

- may be expended by, or be for the benefit of, the donee before his or her attaining the age of twenty-one years, and
- will to the extent not so expended:
- pass to the donee on his or her attaining the age of twenty-one years, and

- in the event the donee dies before attaining the age of twenty-one years, be payable to the estate of the donee or as he or she may appoint under a general power of appointment as defined in section 2514(c).[93]

Hence, under this statutory provision, a section 2503(c) trust is an irrevocable trust created for the benefit of a single beneficiary (as opposed to multiple beneficiaries) who has not yet attained the age of twenty-one, if the following three statutory criteria are met:

1. The trust principal and income may be expended by, or for the benefit of, the donee before his or her attainment of the age of twenty-one years. To meet this requirement, the trustee must be given broad discretionary power and no "substantial restrictions" may be placed thereon.[94] The power of the trustee to make discretionary distributions of *both* income and principal to a donee is one of the key advantages of a section 2503(c) trust over a section 2503(b) trust.

2. To the extent that the property is not so expended, it will pass to the beneficiary upon his or her attainment of age twenty-one.[95]

3. If the beneficiary should die before his or her twenty-first birthday, the assets will be includable in his or her gross estate for federal estate tax purposes either because:
   - the assets are payable to his or her estate under the provisions of the governing trust instrument, or
   - he or she is given a general power of appointment over the assets under the governing trust instrument.

If the assets are made payable to the beneficiary's estate, the assets will be included in the beneficiary's gross estate for federal estate tax purposes. However, as in the case of outright gifts, if a minor does not have the capacity to make a valid will under applicable state law and he or she should die before attaining the age of majority, then property gifted to the minor will in many instances be distributed pursuant to the intestacy statutes then in effect. As in the case of outright gifts, this will prove problematic if one of the donor's primary purposes in making the gift was to remove the property from his or her gross estate for federal estate tax purposes and the property is returned to the donor under the state's applicable intestacy statute.

This potential result may be avoided by the use of a general power of appointment. Either a power of appointment exercisable by the donee by will or a power of appointment exercisable by the donee during his or her lifetime will satisfy the condition that the donee be given a power of appointment.[96] If the minor is given a power of appointment exercisable by will or is given a power of appointment exercisable during a lifetime, the fact that under local law a minor is under a disability to execute a will or to exercise an inter vivos power does not cause the transfer to fail to satisfy the conditions of section 2503(c).[97]

Hence, a section 2503(c) trust may grant the donee a testamentary general power of appointment[98] and then provide for alternate takers in the event that the power is not exercised. This will result in the assets being included in the donee's gross estate for federal estate tax purposes as is required by the statute and, at the same time, avoid the possibility that the assets will be returned to the donor.

If these three criteria are met, the *entire* value of a gift made to a section 2503(c) trust will qualify for the annual exclusion from federal gift tax. Unlike a section 2503(b) trust, no portion of the gift constitutes a future interest, even though the beneficiary cannot control the funds until age twenty-one. The reason for this is that section 2503(c) carves out a special statutory exclusion for these transfers.

(c)   Donee Election to Extend Trust's Term beyond Age Twenty-One

Pursuant to Treasury Regulations, a donee may elect to extend the term of a section 2503(c) trust upon reaching age twenty-one.[99] No further requirements are mandated by the regulations. However, in order for the donee to extend the term of a section 2503(c) trust, the donee should be given notice of what is essentially a right of withdrawal over the trust assets. Notice should be given in writing and the period of time in which the donee has the power to withdraw the assets should be reasonable.[100] While this permits the trust term to be extended beyond age twenty-one, there is, of course, no guarantee that the beneficiary will make this election.

The Internal Revenue Service (IRS) has sanctioned a section 2503(c) trust where the trust term continued until the donee attained age thirty-three, unless the donee withdrew the funds within a reasonable period of time after attaining age twenty-one.[101]

(d)   Federal Income Tax Consequences Where Beneficiary Elects to Extend Term

If the beneficiary does elect to extend the term of a section 2503(c) trust, he or she will be treated for federal income tax purposes as having withdrawn and recontributed the assets to the trust. This will make the beneficiary the owner of the trust for federal income tax purposes under section 677(a). At this juncture, the trust will no longer be a separate taxpayer and the beneficiary will be taxable on all trust income.[102]

Further, the beneficiary's power to withdraw the trust assets is a general power of appointment under section 2514(a). This should not prove problematic for federal gift tax purposes so long as the beneficiary retains the right to vary the ultimate recipients by will or under a testamentary power of appointment.

(e)   Selection of Trustee

The donor should *not* be named as trustee of a section 2503(c) trust. This may have adverse federal estate tax consequences should the donor die during the term of the trust.[103]

In addition, it also is not advisable to have the donor's spouse be named as trustee if the donor's spouse is legally obligated to support the minor. Under these circumstances, the trust assets will be includable in the gross estate of the donor's spouse as property subject to a general power of appointment.[104] If the beneficiary becomes emancipated and the legal obligation of support lapses, it is still problematic as this may be construed as the lapse of a general power of appointment and constitute a taxable gift for federal gift tax purposes under section 2514. Moreover, under this scenario, the donor's spouse may be treated as the grantor of the trust, and power to control the income and principal of the trust by the donor's spouse may be viewed as a power to control the enjoyment of the property for federal estate tax purposes. Hence, if the donor's spouse were to die during the term of the trust, the assets would be includable in the his or her gross estate.[105]

Note: Persons who are not legally obligated to support the minor or banks or trust companies are generally the best candidates to serve as custodians.

(f)   Federal Income Tax Return

A section 2503(c) trust is a separate taxpayer for federal income tax purposes and must have its own employer identification number and file its own federal income tax return. Unlike a section 2503(b) trust, it is a complex trust because it can accumulate or distribute net income. This will complicate the filing of both its federal income tax return and its estimated federal income tax obligations.[106] While this makes the reporting more involved, it also provides the trustee with the opportunity to time distributions, that is, selecting between the trust and the donee depending upon the nature of the assets, the age of the donee,[107] and the available deductions.

As in the case of a gift under a UTMA or UGMA or a section 2503(b) trust, the grantor of a section 2503(c) trust will be taxed on any income used by the trustee to discharge the grantor's legal obligation of support for any income beneficiary. Consideration should be given by the draftsperson to including a clause in the governing trust instrument requesting, but not requiring, that the trustee not make any distributions that would discharge the grantor's legal obligation of support to the beneficiary.

6. *Transfers Made to a Crummey Trust*

(a)   Overview

A Crummey trust is an irrevocable trust under which a beneficiary has a power for a limited period of time, typically thirty to sixty days, to withdraw any gift made by a donor thereto or the value of any gift. Upon the expiration of this limited period of time, the trust assets are no longer subject to the donee's power of withdrawal and are held, administered, and disposed of by the trustee in accordance with the provisions otherwise set forth in the governing trust instrument.

As in the case of a section 2503(b) trust, the beneficiary may have an interest in the trust either for a fixed term of years or for life. Similarly, upon the termination of the income beneficiary's interest in the trust (whether it is a fixed term of years or a life interest), the trust assets are distributed to those persons and in the manner as the donor initially provided in the governing trust instrument.

Unlike the section 2503(b) trust, however, the *entire* value of the gift made to a Crummey trust will qualify as a present interest in property and, thus, for the annual exclusion from federal gift tax because the beneficiary has the right to withdraw the entire gift made to the trust, even though this power of withdrawal is limited in time. The use of this type of withdrawal power to qualify a gift to a trust for the annual exclusion was first approved by the Court of Appeals for the Ninth Circuit in *Crummey v. Commissioner*,[108] and was accepted by the IRS in 1973.[109] Hence, the name Crummey trust. Interestingly, in that decision, the beneficiary was a minor who could not exercise the withdrawal power without the appointment of a guardian, a guardian was never appointed, and the power was never exercised and had a limited duration.

(b) Notice and Duration of Withdrawal Right

In order to qualify for the annual exclusion, the beneficiary *should* be given written notice[110] of the existence of the withdrawal power and of any gift made thereto in any calendar year and an adequate period of time in which to determine whether to exercise his or her power. While the U.S. Tax Court has approved a period of fifteen days, the IRS has for the most part regularly approved a period of thirty days. Practitioners tend to use a window of thirty to sixty days.

When the beneficiary is a minor, written notification of the existence of the withdrawal power and of any gift made thereto in any calendar year should be made to the minor's parent or guardian, who may in turn make the determination regarding the exercise of the minor's withdrawal power; provided, however, that if the parent or guardian is the donor of the trust, he or she should not serve in this capacity as there is a possibility that this would cause inclusion in the donor's gross estate for federal estate tax purposes.[111]

(c) Advantages

There are a host of significant advantages in the utilization of a Crummey trust.

First, as in the case of a section 2503(b) trust, the property may be retained in trust for the benefit of a minor for as long as the donor desires (depending on applicable state law) and is not limited to a predetermined age.

Second, upon the death of the donee, the trust assets will pass as the donor directed under the governing trust instrument and not potentially back to the donor under the applicable intestacy statutes.

Third, unlike a section 2503(b) trust, the trustee may be authorized to make income (and principal) distributions in its discretion as opposed to requiring mandatory distributions of income and then investing in income-producing properties. This provides the trustee with greater flexibility in the administration of the trust and is typically more in accord with the donor's intent in providing for the beneficiary.

Fourth, a Crummey trust may be created for multiple beneficiaries. This is a key advantage. It allows the donor to make gifts to one trust for the benefit of a class of beneficiaries (e.g., children or grandchildren or issue) and to provide for after-born and after-adopted members of the class. It also provides for one trust as opposed to a host of trusts, which reduces the administration and tax reporting requirements in connection therewith.

Fifth, a Crummey trust may be a separate taxpayer for federal income tax purposes, in which event it would have its own employer identification number and file its own federal income tax return.[112] However, some portion of the trust income may be taxed directly to the withdrawal power holders. This provides the trustee with planning opportunities in terms of timing distributions and selecting between the trust and its donees, depending upon the nature of the assets, the age of the donee,[113] and the available deductions.

(d)   Disadvantages

The disadvantages of a Crummey trust are as follows:

First, the beneficiary may, in fact, exercise his or her power to withdraw the assets. This should not typically be a significant issue, as the gifts to a Crummey trust normally are designed for and limited by the annual exclusion amount and in making gifts, donors are permitted to exclude one or more beneficiaries as they may wish.

Second, a Crummey trust is typically a separate taxpayer for federal income tax purposes, and must have its own employer identification number and file its own federal income tax return. Unlike a section 2503(b) trust, it is a complex trust because it can accumulate or distribute net income. This in turn will complicate the filing of both its federal income tax return and its estimated federal income tax obligations.[114] In addition, as in the case of a gift under a UTMA or UGMA or a section 2503(b) or section 2503(c) trust, the grantor of a Crummey trust will be taxed on any income used by the trustee to discharge the grantor's legal obligation of support for any income beneficiary.[115]

Third, and perhaps most significantly, is that, while the IRS has acknowledged that the use of a Crummey withdrawal power will serve to qualify a gift to a trust for the annual exclusion from federal gift tax, it has imposed over the years numerous technical requirements and formalities on the withdrawal powers, which makes the drafting of a Crummey trust much more complex and involved than in the case of either a section 2503(b) trust or a section 2503(c) trust, both of which are essentially drafted under the applicable provisions of the Internal Revenue Code. For example, there are a host of rules regarding the time period in which the withdrawal period may be exercised,[116] the manner in which notice must be given,[117] and that notice may not be waived[118] or be illusory.[119]

Moreover, the Crummey power of withdrawal is a general power of appointment for federal gift tax purposes. If the beneficiary does not exercise his or her power to withdraw the addition to the trust within the given time period, the power "lapses" and the gifted assets then constitute a portion of the trust assets to be held, administered, and disposed of by the trustee under the provisions of the governing trust instrument. The lapse of a Crummey power of withdrawal is a taxable event under section 2514(e)[120]—as the Crummey power holder does not elect to withdraw the funds, he or she is deemed under federal gift tax law to be making a taxable gift to the remainder beneficiaries. This "deemed" gift does not qualify as a present interest for purposes of the annual exclusion from federal gift tax and is, thus, a gift of a future interest. Hence, the Crummey power holder is required to file a federal gift tax return in each year in which a gift is made and either pay federal gift tax or use a portion of his or her available exemption amount.

To avoid the "lapse" result, the Crummey power typically is limited to the greater of $5,000 or 5 percent of the value of the trust assets from which the power could be satisfied in accordance with the safe harbor provisions set forth in section 2514(e)[121] or drafted so as to constitute either a power coupled with testamentary control or a "hanging power." This leads to both complexities in drafting a Crummey trust and numerous additional record-keeping requirements for the trustee.

In addition, the federal income taxation of a Crummey trust is not definitive, especially in terms of the Crummey power holder. For example, the IRS ruled in a 1981 revenue ruling[122] that a minor beneficiary who possessed a Crummey withdrawal power is taxable as the owner of a portion of the trust under section 678. In that ruling, the minor was entitled to all of the trust income, which is not typically the case in a Crummey trust. It is not clear how to determine what portion of a Crummey trust is taxable to the holder of the withdrawal power under current law.

Fourth, utilization of a Crummey trust imposes upon the trustee additional reporting and record-keeping requirements. Existing law and the terms of the Crummey trust require the trustee to make a reasonable effort to notify the trust's lifetime beneficiaries of any gifts that are made to the trust and their right to withdraw their appropriate share of the gift amount. Hence, the trustee should provide each beneficiary with written notification *each and every time* a gift is made to the trust.[123] In addition, in connection with each gift, the trustee should maintain a separate list in each calendar year summarizing the following key information:

- the date of any gift;
- the name, address, telephone number(s), and Social Security number of the donor(s);

- the amount of the gift;
- the nature of the gifted asset;
- a statement indicating whether the donor(s) has made any other previous gifts to the trust or to the withdrawal beneficiaries in any given calendar year;
- a statement as to whether the donor has excluded any beneficiary under the trust from participating in the gift;
- a statement as to whether the donor has created any separate trusts for the benefit of one or more of the withdrawal beneficiaries and, if so, whether the beneficiary has a withdrawal power under that instrument (if so, the instrument must be reviewed to achieve the desired tax consequences);
- whether the donor will be filing a federal gift tax return and/or utilizing any portion of his or her available exclusion amount of GST exemption (discussed in section III. of this chapter);
- if the donors are married,[124] whether they will be electing "gift splitting" for the calendar year;
- a summary of all withdrawal powers that are exercised;
- a summary of all withdrawal powers that are not exercised and lapse, the date that they lapse, and whether any powers "hang" into the future years;
- the value of the trust assets immediately prior to the addition of the gift; and
- any and all other related information.

B. The Unlimited Federal Gift Tax Exclusion Allowed under Section 2503(e) for Direct Transfers to Certain Educational Organizations or Persons Who Provide Medical Care

1. Overview

The *unlimited* federal gift tax exclusion is set forth under section 2503(e).[125] Under this statutory provision, a "qualified transfer" will *not* be treated as a transfer of property by gift for purposes of federal gift tax law.[126] This exclusion is available *in addition to* the $15,000 annual per donee exclusion from federal gift tax allowed under section 2503(b).[127] Furthermore, this exclusion is permitted without regard to the relationship between the donor and the donee.[128]

The term "qualified transfer" is statutorily defined under section 2503(e) as "any amount paid *on behalf of an individual*

- as tuition *to* an educational organization described in section 170(b)(1)(A)(ii)[129] for the education or training of such individual, or
- *to* any person who provides medical care (as defined in section 213(d))[130] with respect to such individual as payment for such medical care."[131]

As the language highlighted above states, a critical component of quali-fying as a section 2503(e) expense is that the transfer be made *directly* to the educational organization described in section 170(b)(1)(A)(ii) or to the person providing medical care (as defined in section 213(d)). It may *not* thus be made directly to the donee. Examples set forth in Treasury Regulations illustrate the operation of these principles:

EXAMPLE 1

Assume that A transfers $100,000 to a trust, the provisions of which state that the funds are to be used for tuition expenses incurred by A's grandchildren. A's transfer to the trust is a completed gift for federal gift tax purposes and is not a direct transfer to an educational organization and does not qualify for the unlimited exclusion from gift tax under section 2503(e).[132]

EXAMPLE 2

C was seriously injured in an automobile accident in 1982. D, who is unre-lated to C, paid C's various medical expenses by checks made payable to the physician. D also paid the hospital for C's hospital bills. These medical and hospital expenses were types described in section 213 and were not reimbursed by insurance or otherwise. Because the medical and hospital bills paid in 1982 for C were medical expenses within the meaning of section 213, and since they were paid directly by D to the person rendering the medical care, they are not treated as transfers subject to gift tax.[133]

EXAMPLE 3

Assume the same facts as in Example 2 except that instead of making the payments directly to the medical service provider, D reimbursed C for the medical expenses, which C had previously paid. The payments made by D to C do *not* qualify for the exclusion under section 2503(e) and are subject to the gift tax on the date the reimbursement is received by C to the extent the reimbursement and all other gifts from D to C during the year of the reimbursement exceed the amount of the section 2503(b) annual exclusion.[134]

EXAMPLE 4

A contribution made to a section 529 plan does no qualify for the section 2503(e) exclusion.[135]

2. Planning Considerations

As in the case of the $15,000 annual per donee exclusion from federal gift tax, gifts qualifying as a section 2503(e) expense do *not* require the filing of a federal gift tax return, the payment of gift tax, or the utilization of a tax-payer's available exclusion amount for federal estate and gift tax purposes. These gifts may be made year after year and are, unlike the annual per donee exclusion permitted under section 2503(b), unlimited.

Moreover, utilization of this section 2503(e) provides a wonderful opportunity for a donor to make gifts for the educational and medical needs of a minor, without the formalities and administrative burdens and costs typically associated with gifts made under a UTMA or UGMA, a section 2503(b) trust, a section 2503(c) trust, or a Crummey trust under section 2503(b). No written instruments are needed, other than for the donor to write a check directly to the educational institution or medical care provider. For example, a grandparent may provide for the private education of his or her minor grandchildren by simply writing a check to the educational institution in question for the minor's tuition as it becomes due.

3. IRS Authority for Prepayment of Tuition Expenses

There is IRS authority for the prepayment of tuition expenses.[136]

EXAMPLE

Beginning in 1994, an decedent had entered into a series of tuition payment arrangements with a private school providing classes for preschool through 12th grade (School). Under the arrangements, School sent Decedent an invoice covering tuition for her two grandchildren, Grandchild 1 and Grandchild 2, for multiple future years. In this instance, the Decedent made the following payments:

February 16, 1994	$18,015 for tuition for 1994–1995
June 1, 1994	$49,395 for tuition for 1995–1996, 1996–1997, and 1997–1998
February 16, 1995	$20,000 for tuition for 1998–1999
July 30, 1996	$94,000 for tuition for 1999–2000, 2000–2001, 2001–2002, 2002–2003, and 2003–2004

Grandchild 1 and Grandchild 2 were students at School during the years the above payments were made by Decedent. With the exception of the February 1994 payment, all payments were for tuition for years other than the year in which the payment was made. Beginning with the June 1994 payment, Decedent and School entered into written agreements regarding the payments. Under the agreements, the payments were to be applied in payment of tuition for Grandchild 1 and Grandchild 2 for specified years. *The payments were not refundable.* If, for example, the grandchildren ceased to attend School, then School would retain the funds. Furthermore, *Decedent and Father, the parent of Grandchild 1 and Grandchild 2, agreed that if the cost of tuition at School increased, with respect to any year, then School would be paid the additional funds necessary to cover the increase in tuition cost.* Father provided a letter to School confirming his agreement to pay any tuition increase not paid by Decedent.

In Technical Advice Memorandum 199941013, the IRS determined that, under the preceding facts, the payments were made directly to an educational organization to be used exclusively for the payment of specified tuition costs for designated individuals. It ruled that "the payments constituted an 'amount paid on behalf of an individual as tuition to an educational organization . . . for the education or training of such individual,' for purposes of section 2503(e)(2)." The IRS stated that this "is in contrast to the situation presented in [Regulation] section 25.2503-6(c), Example 2, where the payments were not made to an educational organization in payment of specific tuition costs for a designated individual." Accordingly, it concluded that the decedent's payments qualify as qualified transfers under section 2503(e).

To qualify for this exclusion, the following rules, as set forth in the following paragraphs 4 and 5, are applicable:

4. *Definition of Educational Organization; Meaning of Tuition*

An educational organization described under section 170(b)(1)(A)(ii) is one that normally maintains a regular faculty and curriculum and normally has a regularly enrolled body of pupils or students in attendance at the place where its educational activities are regularly carried on.[137] The unlimited section 2503(e) exclusion is permitted for tuition expenses of full-time or part-time students *paid directly to* the qualifying educational organization providing the education.[138] No unlimited section 2503(e) exclusion is permitted for amounts paid for books, supplies, dormitory fees, board, or other similar expenses that do not constitute direct tuition costs.[139] There is no requirement that the educational organization be in the United States.[140]

5. *Definition of Medical Care*

Medical care is defined generally under section 213(d)(1) as amounts paid for (1) the diagnosis, cure, mitigation, treatment, or prevention of disease, or for the purpose of affecting any structure or function of the body; (2) transportation primarily for and essential to medical care; (3) qualified long-term care services (as defined in section 7702B(c)); or (4) insurance (including amounts paid as premiums under part B of title XVIII of the Social Security Act, relating to supplementary medical insurance for the aged) covering medical care or for any qualified long-term care insurance contract (as defined in section 7702B(b)).[141]

Hence, for these purposes, qualifying medical expenses are limited to those expenses defined in section 213(d) (section 213(e) prior to January 1, 1984) and include expenses incurred for the diagnosis, cure, mitigation, treatment, or prevention of disease, or for the purpose of affecting any structure or function of the body or for transportation primarily for and essential to medical care.[142]

In addition, the unlimited section 2503(e) exclusion from the federal gift tax includes amounts paid for medical insurance on behalf of any individual.[143] The unlimited section 2503(e) exclusion from the federal gift tax does not apply to amounts paid for medical care that are reimbursed by the donee's insurance.[144] Thus, if payment for a medical expense is reimbursed by the donee's insurance company, the donor's payment for that expense, to the extent of the reimbursed amount, is not eligible for the unlimited exclusion from the gift tax and the gift is treated as having been made on the date the reimbursement is received by the donee.[145]

C. Utilization of the Federal Exemption Amount

As a result of the 2017 Tax Cuts and Jobs Act, each individual has a $10 million lifetime federal estate and gift tax exemption (i.e., "applicable exclusion amount"),[146] indexed for inflation.[147] Under this law, the previous exemption amount of $5 million is doubled.[148] The inflation adjustment, however, is tied to the chained consumer price index (CPI) instead of the previously utilized CPI, allowing for the inflation-adjusted amount of the exemption to increase, on a yearly basis, at a relatively slower pace.[149] For calendar year 2018, the unified exemption is $11.18 million.[150] The $10 million exemption amount is scheduled to revert back to the $5 million amount, but tied to the *chained* CPI, for tax years beginning after December 31, 2025.[151] This exemption corresponds to a credit known as the "applicable credit amount," formerly "unified credit."[152]

As a matter of accepted and competent practice, taxpayers were encouraged to utilize their lifetime exemption from federal gift tax.[153] To date, the federal transfer system is in flux, and may call into doubt the continued utility of making these gifts. However, utilization of this exemption during lifetime will remain a viable estate planning tool for taxpayers and practitioners alike who believe that the federal estate tax will ultimately persist.[154]

III. FEDERAL GST TAX CONSIDERATIONS

A. Annual Exclusion from Federal GST Tax

Section 2642(c) provides a special rule for the treatment of certain direct skips[155] that are "nontaxable gifts" within the meaning of section 2642(c)(3). Under section 2642(c)(3), the term "nontaxable gift" means any transfer of property to the extent the transfer is *not* treated as a taxable gift by reason of

- section 2503(b) (taking into account the application of section 2513),[156] or
- section 2503(e).[157]

Section 2642(c)(3) provides specifically that, in the case of a direct skip that is a "nontaxable gift," the inclusion ratio shall be zero.[158] This rule does *not* apply, however, to any transfer made *to a trust* for the benefit of an individual *unless*

- during the life of the individual, no portion of the corpus or income of the trust may be distributed to (or for the benefit of) any person other than the individual; and

- if the trust does not terminate before the individual dies, the trust assets will be includable in the gross estate of the individual.[159]

That is, the federal GST annual exclusion set forth under section 2642(c) provides that a gift that is exempt from federal gift tax because of either (1) the federal gift tax annual exclusion allowed under section 2503(b) (which is, for gifts made in 2018, $15,000 per donee) or (2) the *unlimited* federal gift tax exclusion allowed under section. 2503(e) for certain qualifying transfers made directly for educational or medical expenses also is exempt from federal GST tax, *if* the gift is a direct skip gift to a skip person or to a trust. If the transfer is *to a trust*,[160] however, it must meet the following requirements:

- the trust is created for the benefit of *one* skip person,
- during the life of the skip person, no portion of the corpus or income of the trust may be distributed to (or for the benefit of) any person other than the skip person, and
- if the trust does not terminate before the death of the skip person, the assets are includable in his or her gross estate for federal estate tax purposes.

Accordingly, a typical section 2503(c) trust or a Crummey trust established for the benefit of a single beneficiary and utilizing the format of testamentary control (whether by distribution of the assets to the beneficiary's estate or the possession by the beneficiary of a testamentary general power of appointment) will qualify for the annual exclusion from both federal gift and GST tax.

In addition, a transfer that qualifies under section 2503(e) will have an inclusion ratio of zero and no GST exemption will be required. However, a typical section 2503(b) trust or a Crummey trust utilizing the format of the 5 & 5 exclusion or of a hanging power[161] will qualify for the annual exclusion from federal gift, but will *not* qualify for the annual exclusion from federal GST tax.[162] If a transfer qualifies for the federal gift tax annual exclusion, but not for the federal GST annual exclusion, a federal gift tax return must be filed and GST exemption allocated to the trust if an inclusion ratio of zero is desired.

B. Federal GST Tax Exemption

For calendar year 2018, the federal GST tax exemption allowed under section 2631(c) is $11.18 million.[163] Like the federal gift and estate tax exemption, the federal GST exemption is scheduled to revert to $5 million, with inflation adjustments per the chained CPI.[164] As in the case of the federal estate and gift tax exemption, utilization of the GST exemption will remain a viable estate planning tool for taxpayers and practitioners alike who believe that the federal estate tax and GST tax will ultimately persist.

NOTES

1.   For purposes of this chapter, a minor shall mean any individual who has not attained the age of majority in the state in which he or she is domiciled. The "age of majority" is generally the age at which a person acquires all of the rights and responsibilities of being an adult, including, for example, the capacity to make a valid will. In most states, the age of majority is eighteen. In some states, it is different ages for different purposes. Accordingly, the laws of each state must be carefully reviewed to determine the age of majority for the specific purposes sought.

2.   For a more general discussion regarding federal estate, gift, and generation-skipping transfer taxes, see Chapter 1. Note: A discussion of any applicable state taxes, if any, is beyond the scope of this chapter and must be carefully reviewed before the implementation of any gift-giving program. *See also* Chapter 2. Section 2801 of the Internal Revenue Code provides for a tax on certain gift and bequests from "covered expatriates." This tax, more akin to an inheritance tax than a transfer tax, is beyond the scope of this chapter.

3.   All references are to the Internal Revenue Code of 1986, as amended, and regulations thereunder unless otherwise indicated.

4.   Section 2503(b) is entitled "Exclusions from gifts." For greater discussion regarding section 2503(b), see subsection II.A. in this chapter.

5.   Section 2503(e) is entitled "Exclusion for certain transfers for educational expenses or medical expenses." For greater discussion regarding section 2503(e), see subsection II.B. in this chapter.

6.   Section 2505 is entitled "Unified credit against gift tax." *See also* section 2010(a). For greater discussion regarding sections 2505 and 2010, see subsection II.C. in this chapter.

7.   Section 2642(c) is entitled "Treatment of certain direct skips which are non-taxable gifts." For greater discussion regarding section 2642(c), see subsection III.A. in this chapter.

8.   Section 2631(c) is entitled "GST exemption amount." For greater discussion regarding section 2631(c), see subsection III.B. in this chapter.

9.   For greater discussion, see subsection II.A. in this chapter.

10.   For greater discussion, see subsection II.A.2. in this chapter.

11.   For greater discussion, see subsection II.A.3. in this chapter.

12.   For greater discussion, see subsection II.A.4. in this chapter.

13.   For greater discussion, see subsection II.A.5. in this chapter.

14.   397 F.2d 82 (9th Cir. 1968). For greater discussion, see subsection II.A.6. in this chapter.

15.   Section 2503(b)(2), entitled "Inflation adjustment," provides that, in the case of gifts made in a calendar year after 1998, the $10,000 figure will be increased by an amount equal to $10,000 multiplied by a cost-of-living adjustment. If the adjusted amount is not a multiple of $1,000, the amount is rounded to the next lowest multiple of $1,000. *See id.* For tax years beginning after December 31, 2017, the inflation adjustment no longer is tied to the consumer price index (CPI) but instead to the chained CPI. *See* § 2503(b)(2)(B) (cross-referencing new § 1(f)). *See also* An Act to provide for reconciliation pursuant to titles II and V of the concurrent resolution on the budget for fiscal year 2018, Pub. L. No. 115-97, § 11002(a), replacing § 1(f) (Dec. 22, 2017), informally referred to as the Tax Cut and Jobs Act. For up-to-date information regarding inflation-adjusted tax items, the reader is referred

to the applicable IRS Revenue Procedure usually issued near the end of each year that contains inflation-adjusted tax items for the following tax year.

16. Rev. Proc. 2001-59, § 3.19(1), 2001-2 C.B. 623 (Dec. 7, 2001).
17. Rev. Proc. 2002-70, § 3.24(1), 2002-2 C.B. 845 (Oct. 30, 2002).
18. Rev. Proc. 2003-85, § 3.26(1), 2003-2 C.B. 1184 (Nov. 19, 2003).
19. Rev. Proc. 2004-71, § 3.28(1), 2004-2 C.B. 970 (Nov. 19, 2004).
20. Rev. Proc. 2005-70, § 3.28(1), 2005-47 I.R.B. 1 (Oct. 28, 2005).
21. Rev. Proc. 2006-53, § 3.32(1), 2006-2 I.R.B. 996 (Nov. 9, 2006).
22. Rev. Proc. 2007-66, § 3.32(1), 2007-45 I.R.B. 970 (Oct. 18, 2007).
23. Rev. Proc. 2008-66, § 3.30(1), 2008-45 I.R.B. 1107 (Oct. 16, 2008).
24. Rev. Proc. 2009-50, § 3.30(1), 2009-45 I.R.B. 617 (Oct. 15, 2009).
25. Rev. Proc. 2010-40, § 3.21(1), 2010-46 I.R.B. 663 (Oct. 28, 2010).
26. Rev. Proc. 2011-52, § 3.31(1), 2011-45 I.R.B. 701 (Oct. 20, 2011).
27. Rev. Proc. 2012-41, § 3.19(1), 2012-45 I.R.B. 539 (Oct. 18, 2012).
28. Rev. Proc. 2013-35, § 3.34(1), 2013-47 I.R.B. 537 (Oct. 31, 2013).
29. Rev. Proc. 2014-61, § 3.35(1), 2014-47 I.R.B. 860 (Oct. 30, 2014).
30. Rev. Proc. 2015-53, § 3.35(1), 2015-44 I.R.B. 615 (Oct. 21, 2015).
31. Rev. Proc. 2016-55, § 3.37(1), 2016-45 I.R.B. 707 (Oct. 25, 2016).
32. Rev. Proc. 2017-58, at § 3.37(1), 2017-45 I.R.B. 489 (Oct. 19, 2017). With the application of the chained CPI, it is expected that the inflation adjustments will take place at a slower place. *See* note 15.
33. *See* Chapter 1, note 14.
34. *See* note 33.
35. §§ 6019, 2513.
36. § 2503(b)(1), which provides, in relevant part: "[i]n the case of gifts (*other than gifts of future interests in property*)."
37. Reg. § 25.2503-3(b).
38. § 2503(b)(1); Reg. § 25.2503-3, entitled "Future interests in property."
39. Reg. § 25.2503-3(a). Note: "The term has no reference to such contractual rights as exist in a bond, note (though bearing no interest until maturity), or in a policy of life insurance, the obligations of which are to be discharged by payments in the future. But a future interest or interests in such contractual obligations may be created by the limitations contained in a trust or other instrument of transfer used in effecting a gift." *Id.*
40. For greater discussion, see subsection II.A.2. in this chapter.
41. For greater discussion, see subsection II.A.3. in this chapter.
42. *See* § 529(c)(2)(A), which provides: "For purposes of chapters 12 and 13— (A) In general. *Any contribution to a qualified tuition program on behalf of any designated beneficiary—(i) shall be treated as a completed gift to such beneficiary which is not a future interest in property,* and (ii) shall *not* be treated as a qualified transfer under section 2503(e)" (emphasis added). Note: Section 529(c)(2)(B) further provides: "[i]f the aggregate amount of contributions . . . during the calendar year by a donor exceeds the limitation for such year under section 2503(b), such aggregate amount shall, at the election of the donor, be taken into account for purposes of such section ratably over the 5-year period beginning with such calendar year." Hence, a donor may under this statutory provision use up to five years' worth of his or her available annual exclusion from federal gift tax in one year. The donor must elect accelerated annual exclusion treatment for the five-year spread gift by checking the box at the top of page 2 of the federal gift tax return (IRS Form 709, which is available on

the IRS website, www.irs.gov). If a donor elects accelerated annual exclusion treatment under section 529(c)(2)(B), he or she must keep adequate records with regard to the same. As for the federal estate tax consequences of a 529 plan, no amount is includable in the gross estate of any individual by reason of an interest in a qualified tuition program. § 529(c)(4)(A). However, in the case of a donor who makes the accelerated annual exclusion election and who dies before the close of the five-year period, his or her gross estate will include the portion of the contributions properly allocable to periods after the date of death of the donor. § 529(c)(4)(C). *See also* Chapter 5.

43. For greater discussion, see subsection II.A.4. in this chapter.

44. For greater discussion, see subsection II.A.5. in this chapter.

45. For greater discussion, see subsection II.A.6. in this chapter.

46. *See, e.g.*, Rev. Rul. 54-400, 1954-2 C.B. 319. In this ruling, the IRS states: "An unqualified and unrestricted gift to a minor, with or without the appointment of a legal guardian, is a gift of a present interest; and disabilities placed upon minors by State statutes should not be considered decisive in determining whether such donees have the immediate enjoyment of the property or the income therefrom within the purport of the Federal gift tax law." It further states: "In the case of an outright and unrestricted gift to a minor, the mere existence or nonexistence of a legal guardianship does not of itself raise the question whether the gift is of a future interest. *Cf.* Rev. Rul. 54-91, C.B. 1954-1, 207, involving a gift in trust for the benefit of a minor. It is only where delivery of the property to the guardian of a minor is accompanied by limitations upon the present use and enjoyment of the property by the donee, by way of a trust or otherwise, that the question of a future interest arises." *See also* Rev. Rul. 55-408, 1955-1 C.B. 113; Messing v. Comm'r, 48 T.C. 502 (1967).

47. Individual state law regarding guardianships of a minor's property must be consulted. *See also* Chapters 6 and 9.

48. For example, in New York, a domiciliary must be eighteen years old to make a will. *See* N.Y. Est. Powers & Trusts Law § 3-1.1.

49. UGMA was first adopted by the National Conference of Commissioners on Uniform State Laws in 1956 and subsequently revised in 1966. It was adopted in some form by each of the fifty states and the District of Columbia. Then, in 1983, UTMA legislation was adopted by the National Conference of Commissioners on Uniform State Laws. Essentially all states have adopted UTMA, although UGMA does remain in force in some states. For a state-by-state comparison of the UTMA and UGMA, see Chapter 9, Appendix 9-C.

50. *See, e.g.*, N.Y. Est. Powers & Trusts Law § 7-6.20.

51. *See, e.g.*, N.Y. Est. Powers & Trusts Law § 7-6.14(a).

52. *See, e.g.*, N.Y. Est. Powers & Trusts Law § 7-6.20.

53. N.Y. Est. Powers & Trusts Law §§ 7-6.1 to 7-6.26.

54. A key difference in the UGMA and UTMA statutes is with regard to the nature of the properties that may be transferred. The UGMA statutes typically apply *only* to gifts of cash, cash equivalents, life insurance policies, and securities, whereas the UTMA statutes generally allow a custodian to take title to real estate and tangible personal property as well as any other property interest not specifically delineated in its statutes.

55. N.Y. Est. Powers & Trusts Law § 7-6.9.

56. N.Y. Est. Powers & Trusts Law § 7-6.9(a)(1).
57. N.Y. Est. Powers & Trusts Law § 7-6.9(a)(2).
58. N.Y. Est. Powers & Trusts Law § 7-6.9(a)(3).
59. N.Y. Est. Powers & Trusts Law § 7-6.9(a)(4).
60. N.Y. Est. Powers & Trusts Law § 7-6.9(a)(5).
61. N.Y. Est. Powers & Trusts Law § 7-6.9(a)(6).
62. N.Y. Est. Powers & Trusts Law § 7-6.9(a)(7).
63. N.Y. Est. Powers & Trusts Law § 7-6.9(b).
64. *See, e.g.*, N.Y. Est. Powers & Trusts Law §§ 7-6.3, 7-6.9.
65. N.Y. Est. Powers & Trusts Law § 7-6.1(k).
66. N.Y. Est. Powers & Trusts Law § 7-6.20(a). Note: The termination provisions set forth under N.Y. Est. Powers & Trusts Law § 7-6.20(a) are applicable only with regard to transfers effectuated either under N.Y. Est. Powers & Trusts Law § 7-6.4, captioned "Transfer by gift or exercise of power of appointment," or N.Y. Est. Powers & Trusts Law § 7-6.5, captioned "Transfer authorized by will or trust." *Id.*
67. N.Y. Est. Powers & Trusts Law § 7-6.21, entitled "Age eighteen election." This section provides that "Notwithstanding the foregoing sections of this part, if with respect to any gift made pursuant to 7-6.9, the designations of the custodian contains, in substance, the phrase, 'until age eighteen,' then all records of the custodian with respect to such gift shall contain such phrase, and the gift shall be administered under this part as if the word 'eighteen' were substituted for the word 'twenty-one' wherever such word appears in paragraphs (a) and (k) of section 7-6.1 [which is entitled 'Definitions' and defines the term 'minor'] and in section 7-6.20 [which is entitled 'Termination of Custodianship']." Section 7-6.9, entitled "Manner of creating custodial property and effecting transfer; designation of initial custodian; control," is discussed in subsection II.A.3.b. at greater length. Acknowledging the limitations imposed by the required disbursement at age twenty-one to a UTMA beneficiary, the Trust, Estates & Surrogate's Courts Committee of the New York City Bar Association supports the New York State Bar Association's proposal to amend N.Y. Estates, Powers and Trust Law section 7.6.1 and 7-6.20 by "explicitly allow[ing] a custodian to use custodial assets to fund a trust that satisfies the requirements of § 2503(c) of the Internal Revenue Code for the benefit of the minor," consistent with "a number of states." *See* Committee Report: Report in support of proposed amendments to New York's Uniform Transfers to Minors Act (Mar. 9, 2016), *available at* https://www.nycbar.org/member-and-career-services/committees/reports-listing/reports/detail/report-in-support-of-proposed-amendments-to-new-yorks-uniform-transfers-to-minors-act. For further discussion pertaining to the §2503(c) trust, see subsection II.A.5.
68. N.Y. Est. Powers & Trusts Law §§ 7-6.20 and 7-6.21. *See also* note 67.
69. *See, e.g.*, Cal. Prob. Code §§ 3900–3925, 6341–6349 (1990, Supp. 1996); Nev. Rev. Stat. § 167.010–167.100; Tenn. Code Ann. §§ 35-7-201 to 35-7-226, respectively. *See also* the state-by-state comparison chart on the UTMA and UGMA in Chapter 9, Appendix 9-C. *See also* note 67.
70. N.Y. Est. Powers & Trusts Law § 7-6.12(b).
71. *Id.*
72. *Id.*
73. N.Y. Est. Powers & Trusts Law § 7-6.12(c).

74. *See, e.g.*, N.Y. Est. Powers & Trusts Law § 7-6.12(d).
75. *Id.*
76. *Id.*
77. *Id.*
78. *See, e.g.*, N.Y. Est. Powers & Trusts Law § 7-6.12(e).
79. *See, e.g.*, N.Y. Est. Powers & Trusts Law § 7-6.13(a).
80. *See, e.g.*, N.Y. Est. Powers & Trusts Law § 7-6.13(b).
81. Although the powers granted to a UTMA custodian exceed those granted to a UGMA custodian, both have greater powers in terms of administering and disposing of the asset than a guardian. Moreover, unlike a guardian, a custodian is not required to post surety, obtain court approval to enter into a transaction, or provide periodic accountings to a court.
82. In establishing a custodial account, the minor's Social Security number is to be used as the identification number. Parents, however, may elect to report the child's unearned income on the parents' federal income tax return. *See* § 1(g)(7). *See also* Form 8814 (Parents' Election to Report Child's Interest and Dividends), available on the IRS website, www.irs.gov. *See also* IRS website, https://www.irs.gov/taxtopics/tc553. Apparently, this election no longer may be available for tax years beginning after December 31, 2017, and before January 1, 2026, because the child's tax is not calculated at the parent's rate for those tax years. *See* Chapter 1.
83. As in the case of all trusts, applicable state law must be consulted for all rules regarding or pertaining to an express (i.e., written) trust, including, for example, the creation, funding, administration, termination, and execution thereof. A discussion of these formalities is beyond the scope of this chapter and must be carefully reviewed before the implementation of making any such gifts.
84. *See, e.g.*, Rev. Rul. 2018-28, 2018-45 I.R.B. 1 (Oct. 16, 2018), Table 5. This table contains the federal rate for determining the present value of an annuity, an interest for life or for a term of years, or a remainder or a reversionary interest in November 2018 for purposes of section 7520.
85. *See, e.g.*, Rev. Rul. 54-344, 1954-2 C.B. 319.
86. *See, e.g.*, PLR 8347090, PLR 8248008, and Rev. Rul. 85-35, 1985-1 C.B. 328. *But see* §§ 6110 (b)(1)(A), 6110 (k)(3) (unless otherwise established by regulation, ruling may not be used or cited as precedent).
87. *See, e.g.*, Reg. § 20.7520-3(b)(2)(v).
88. § 677(a).
89. For greater discussion, see subsection II.A.5. in this chapter.
90. For greater discussion, see subsection II.A.6. in this chapter.
91. §§ 671–677. *See also* Chapter 1.
92. §§ 2041, 2514.
93. Section 2514(c) defines the term "general power of appointment" for federal gift tax purposes. It provides, in part, that the term "general power of appointment" means a power that is exercisable in favor of the individual possessing the power, his estate, his creditors, or the creditors of his estate; except that a power to consume, invade, or appropriate property for the benefit of the possessor, which is limited by an ascertainable standard relating to the health, education, support, or maintenance of the possessor, shall not be deemed a general power of appointment. § 2514(c)(1).
94. Reg. § 25.2503-4(b)(1).

95. The governing trust instrument may, however, contain a provision allowing the donee to elect to extend the trust's term beyond age twenty-one. *See* subsection II.A.5.c. in this chapter.

96. Reg. § 25.2503-4(b). However, if the transfer is to qualify for the annual exclusion, there must be no "restrictions of substance" (as distinguished from formal restrictions of the type described in paragraph (g)(4) of § 25.2523(e)-1) by the terms of the instrument of transfer on the exercise of the power by the donee. *Id. See* Reg. § 25.2523(e)-1(g)(4). ("If the power is in existence at all times following the transfer of the interest, limitations of a formal nature will not disqualify the interest. Examples of formal limitations on a power exercisable during life are requirements that an exercise must be in a particular form, that it must be filed with a trustee during the spouse's life, that reasonable notice must be given, or that reasonable intervals must elapse between successive partial exercises. Examples of formal limitations on a power exercisable by will are that it must be exercised by a will executed by the donee spouse after the making of the gift or that exercise must be by specific reference to the power.")

97. *Id.*

98. A testamentary general power of appointment is one exercisable by the possessor at death. Section 2041(b)(1) defines the term "general power of appointment" for federal estate tax purposes. It provides, in part, that "[t]he term 'general power of appointment' means a power that 'is exercisable in favor of the decedent, his estate, his creditors, or the creditors of his estate.'" While both an inter vivos power and testamentary power are permitted under the regulations to section 2503(c) trust, use of a testamentary power is typically preferable in terms of control of the assets.

99. Reg. § 25.2503-4(b)(2).

100. For an analogous matter, see the discussion in subsection-II.A.6.b. in this chapter regarding a "Crummey power."

101. *See, e.g.,* Rev. Rul. 74-43, 1974-1 C.B. 285.

102. *See, e.g.,* PLR 8142061. *But see* §§ 6110(b)(1)(A), 6110(k)(3) (unless otherwise established by regulation, ruling may not be used or cited as precedent).

103. A trustee's power to control income and principal distributions is a power to control beneficial enjoyment over the trust assets under federal estate tax law. *See* §§ 2036, 2038.

104. *See* § 2041.

105. *See* §§ 2036, 2038.

106. For compliance requirements pertaining to estimated federal income tax payments for estates and trusts, see Form 1041-ES, available on the IRS website, www.irs.gov.

107. For example, the trustee may plan around the "kiddie tax" rules, which tax unearned income distributed to a beneficiary before he or she is nineteen (or, if a full-time student, under age twenty-four) at the marginal income tax rate of the beneficiary's parents. *See* § 1(g). Note: This type of planning with regard to the "kiddie tax" rules may be utilized in any instance involving a distribution to a minor beneficiary. For tax years beginning after December 31, 2017, and before January 1, 2026, the child's unearned income, however, may be subject to federal income tax rates and brackets applicable to trusts and estates, generally eliminating the disparity between how a child's unearned income and trust income is taxed for federal income tax purposes. *See* § 1(j)(4). *See also* Chapter 1.

108. Crummey v. Commissioner, 397 F.2d 82 (9th Cir. 1968).

109. Rev. Rul. 73-405, 1973-2 C.B. 321.

110. Written notice is not technically required, but it is highly prudent and certainly customary among estate planning practitioners to do so. In order for the withdrawal power to create a present interest in property as is required under applicable law, the beneficiary *must* be aware of both the existence of the power and of any gift against which it may be exercised. *See, e.g.*, Rev. Rul. 81-7, 1981-1 C.B. 474. (*Held*, that a trust provision giving a legally competent adult beneficiary the power to demand corpus does *not* qualify a transfer to the trust as a present interest eligible for the federal gift tax annual exclusion if the donor's conduct makes the demand right illusory and effectively deprives the donee of the power.) Also, at least one court has held that the requirement that a trustee give notice to the holders of Crummey powers is more than a mere tax formality. *See, e.g.*, Karpf v. Karpf, 481 N.W.2d 891 (Neb. 1992). Typically, written notification is required in the instrument and is key in the event of an audit.

111. *See* §§ 2036 and 2038.

112. A Crummey power is often utilized in irrevocable life insurance trusts. The trust may have to file its own federal income tax return, depending upon the amount and kind of income produced. If the only asset owned by the trust is one or more life insurance policies, then the trust will not have any reportable income. In that case, the trust would file a federal income tax return (IRS Form 1041) for the trust showing zero income. If the trust does have income, then pursuant to section 677(a)(3), the income is taxable to the donor to the extent it is used to pay the life insurance premiums. Accordingly, the trustee may be required to file a federal income tax return (IRS Form 1041) and state informational income tax return for the trust if it has taxable income. IRS forms and instructions are available on the IRS website, www.irs.gov.

113. For example, the trustee may plan around the "kiddie tax" rule. *See* note 107.

114. However, as discussed earlier, while this makes the reporting more involved, it also provides the trustee with the opportunity to time distributions, that is, selecting between the trust and the donee depending upon the nature of the assets, the age of the donee, and the available deductions. *See also* note 106.

115. Consideration should be given by the draftsperson to including a clause in the governing trust instrument requesting, but not requiring, that the trustee not make any distributions that would discharge the grantor's legal obligation of support to the beneficiary. Note: The provision may not be included in a section 2503(b) trust.

116. As discussed previously, while the Tax Court has approved a period of as little as fifteen days, the IRS has for the most part regularly approved a period of thirty days. *See, e.g.*, Estate of Cristofani, 97 T.C. 74 (07/29/1991), *acq. in result only* 1992-1 C.B. 4, 1996-1 C.B. 1 and PLR 200130030 and PLR 200011058, respectively. Note: Practitioners tend to use a thirty- to sixty-day window.

117. *See* note 110.

118. *See, e.g.*, TAM 9532001. In TAM 9532001, a decedent and her spouse created a trust for the benefit of their nine grandchildren. The terms of the trust provided that the grandchildren had a right of withdrawal over the initial contribution to the trust. Each of the grandchildren/beneficiaries of the trust, in statements signed by them on the date of creation of the trust, waived their right to withdraw the initial gift and receive any further notices regarding their right of withdrawal as to future

gifts. The IRS ruled that the immediate use, possession, or enjoyment of property is clearly restricted if the donee does not know of its existence. Accordingly, a donee must have current notice of any gift in order for that gift to be a transfer of a present interest. Because of the waiver by the grandchildren of their right to receive notice regarding their right of withdrawal as to future gifts as well as the lack of proof that any current notice was given to the grandchildren regarding any gifts after the initial gift, all transfers to the trust after the initial transfer were transfers of a future interest.

119. *See, e.g.,* Estate of Eleanor T.R. Trotter v. Comm'r., T.C. Memo 2001-250 (2001). In this decision, a taxpayer created an irrevocable trust for the primary benefit of her grandchildren and their issue, with a contingent interest in her husband. The only asset transferred to the trust was a condominium in which the decedent resided. A Crummey power was given to the beneficiaries, but never exercised by them. In this case, the Tax Court rejected the estate's position that the Crummey powers negated any implied understanding between the decedent and her family members that she could reside in the condominium until her death. The court stated:

> The numerous indicia discussed above are equally supportive of an implied understanding that the withdrawal rights would not be exercised, an interpretation buttressed by the awareness that the beneficiaries were decedent's grandchildren (and three of the five were minors). We cannot blind ourselves to the reality of the family relationships involved, and the estate has failed to show that the withdrawal rights were anything more than a paper formality without intended economic substance. In addition, such construction is strengthened still further by fact that the trust's having been funded solely with a single piece of real estate would have made any attempt to effectuate a withdrawal complex and burdensome at best. While it is not entirely clear from the document how the provision would operate in this circumstance, we doubt that any beneficiary would seriously have contemplated forcing the trustee to . . . sell the home so that he or she could collect $10,000.

In TAM 200341002, the IRS ruled that that there was a legal impediment prohibiting the withdrawal powers granted to charities from ever becoming effective. The IRS stated:

> Here, Trust purportedly gave the charities the option of either withdrawing the funds from each contribution, or allowing the funds to remain in the trust subject to distribution to Decedent's relatives for private noncharitable purposes with the possibility of the charities receiving a distribution on Decedent's death. In view of the strict prohibition on the use of a charity's property for private purposes and the fiduciary obligations imposed on a charity and its directors, it is doubtful that any officer or director of a charity could properly participate in this kind of gamble, where funds charity purportedly controls are to be set aside for private utilization until some future date.

***

Indeed, as noted earlier, the charities, in the aggregate, were granted 44 separate withdrawal rights, none of which were ever exercised. Further, as discussed previously, in some cases, the Notification letter was sent to the charities before the transfer was made, such that the withdrawal period expired before the date of the transfer. In other cases, the Notification letter did not accurately describe the amount subject to withdrawal or was undated, so it was unclear when the withdrawal period commenced. The failure to make any of the withdrawals coupled with the haphazard execution of the notification procedure, without any adverse comment from the charities, evidence that at least the charities understood that they were legally precluded from actively participating in this withdrawal arrangement that allowed funds to enure for private purposes.

120. Section 2514(e), captioned "Lapse Of Power," provides that "[t]he lapse of a power of appointment created after October 21, 1942, during the life of the individual possessing the power shall be considered a release of such power. The rule of the preceding sentence shall apply with respect to the lapse of powers during any calendar year only to the extent that the property which could have been appointed by exercise of such lapsed powers exceeds in value the greater of the following amounts: (1) $5,000, or (2) 5 percent of the aggregate value of the assets out of which, or the proceeds of which, the exercise of the lapsed powers could be satisfied." This exclusion from the lapse rule typically is referred to in estate tax parlance as the "5 & 5 exception."

121. Specifically, taking into consideration the 5 & 5 exception to the lapse rule set forth in section 2514(e). For the provisions of section 2514(e), *see supra* note 120.

122. Rev. Rul. 81-6, 1981-1 C.B. 385.

123. Copies of withdrawal right notification letters that are sent to beneficiaries, and copies of these letters, if any, after they have been signed by the trust beneficiaries should be retained by the trustee. If they were sent via certified mail, return receipt requested, or in some other manner that provides the trustee with the date the letters were sent, the receipts should be attached to these letters and retained as well. These signed (and thus acknowledged) letters may be needed in the event of a federal gift tax audit or in the event of a federal estate tax audit at the time of the donor's death.

124. *See* note 33.

125. § 2503(e), entitled "Exclusion for certain transfers for educational expenses or medical expenses."

126. § 2503(e)(1). *See also* Reg. § 25.2503-6, entitled "Exclusion for certain qualified transfer for tuition or medical expenses," which provides, in subpart (a), in part, as follows: "Section 2503(e) provides that any qualified transfer after December 31, 1981, shall not be treated as a transfer of property by gift for purposes of chapter 12 of subtitle B of the Code. *Thus, a qualified transfer on behalf of any individual is excluded in determining the total amount of gifts in calendar year 1982 and subsequent years.*" (Emphasis added.)

127. Reg. § 25.2503-6(a).

128. § 2503(e)(2). Note: The statute provides that a qualified transfer means "any amount paid on behalf of an individual" as opposed to "*to* an individual."

129. Section 170(b)(1)(A)(ii) provides as follows: "an educational organization which normally maintains a regular faculty and curriculum and normally has a

regularly enrolled body of pupils or students in attendance at the place where its educational activities are regularly carried on."

130. Medical care is defined generally under section 213(d)(1) as amounts paid for (1) the diagnosis, cure, mitigation, treatment, or prevention of disease, or for the purpose of affecting any structure or function of the body, (2) transportation primarily for and essential to medical care referred to in the immediately preceding clause, (3) qualified long-term care services (as defined in section 7702B(c)), or (4) insurance (including amounts paid as premiums under part B of title XVIII of the Social Security Act, relating to supplementary medical insurance for the aged) covering certain medical care or for any qualified long-term care insurance contract (as defined in section 7702B(b)). In the case of a qualified long-term care insurance contract (as defined in section 7702B(b)), special rules are provided. Additional rules are set forth in section 213(d)(2) regarding "amounts paid for certain lodging away from home treated as paid for medical care." *See also* Reg. § 25.2503-6(b)(3), which provides, in part, as follows: "For purposes of paragraph (b)(1)(ii) of this section, qualifying medical expenses are limited to those expenses defined in section 213(d) (section 213(e) before January 1, 1984) and include expenses incurred for the diagnosis, cure, mitigation, treatment or prevention of disease, or for the purpose of affecting any structure or function of the body or for transportation primarily for and essential to medical care. In addition, the unlimited exclusion from the gift tax includes amounts paid for medical insurance on behalf of any individual. The unlimited exclusion from the gift tax does not apply to amounts paid for medical care that are reimbursed by the donee's insurance. Thus, if payment for a medical expense is reimbursed by the donee's insurance company, the donor's payment for that expense, to the extent of the reimbursed amount, is not eligible for the unlimited exclusion from the gift tax and the gift is treated as having been made on the date the reimbursement is received by the donee."

131. § 2503(e)(2) (endnotes, bullets, and emphasis added). Note: The statute provides that a qualified transfer means "any amount paid on behalf of an individual" as opposed to "to an individual."

132. Reg. § 25.2503-6(c), Example 2.

133. Reg. § 25.2503-6(c), Example 3.

134. Reg. § 25.2503-6(c), Example 4.

135. *See* note 42.

136. TAM 199941013.

137. § 170(b)(1)(A)(ii); Reg. § 25.2503-6(b)(2).

138. Reg. § 25.2503-6(b)(2).

139. *Id.*

140. *See, e.g.,* Reg. § 25.2503-6(c), Example 1 ("In 1982, A made a tuition payment directly to a foreign university on behalf of B. A had no legal obligation to make this payment. The foreign university is described in section 170(b)(1)(A)(ii) of the [Internal Revenue] Code. A's tuition payment is exempt from the gift tax under section 2503(e) of the [Internal Revenue] Code.") *See also* Rev. Rul. 82-143, 1982-2 C.B. 220.

141. § 213(d)(1). In the case of a qualified long-term care insurance contract (as defined in section 7702B(b)), special rules are provided. Additional rules are set forth in section 213(d)(2) regarding "[a]mounts paid for certain lodging away from home treated as paid for medical care." Moreover, section 213(d) provides a host of other statutory rules, including, for example, definitions of the terms "prescribed

drug" and "physician," and special rules regarding children of divorced parents, insurance contracts, cosmetic surgery, eligible long-term care premiums, and certain payments to relatives that are treated as not-paid-for medical care.

142. Reg. § 25.2503-6(b)(3). *See also* note 131.

143. *Id.*

144. *Id.*

145. *Id.*

146. Since 2010, the term "applicable exclusion amount" is the sum of the "basis exclusion amount" and any "deceased spousal unused exclusion (DSUE) amount." Thus, an individual, assuming certain requirements are met, may utilize the unused exemption amount of a predeceased spouse for purposes of federal estate and gift taxation. *See* Pub. L. No. 111-12 (Tax Relief, Unemployment Insurance Reauthorization, and Jobs Creation Act), § 303(a), codified at § 2010(c)(2). *See also* Chapter 1 (explaining requirements and mechanics of DSUE amount). For discussion of the general use of the applicable exclusion amount and the corresponding credit at death, see Chapter 1. For the definition of "spouse" for federal tax purposes, *see* Chapter 1 at note 14.

147. An Act to provide for reconciliation pursuant to titles II and V of the concurrent resolution on the budget for fiscal year 2018, Pub. L. No. 115-97, § 11061, codified at § 2010(c)(3)(C) (Dec. 22, 2017), informally referred to as the "Tax Cut and Jobs Act."

148. *See id.*

149. *See id.*, § 11002(d)(1)(CC), codified at § 2010(c)(3)(B)(ii) (cross-referencing § 1(f)(3)).

150. Rev. Proc. 2018-18; 2018-10 I.R.B. 392, § 3.35. For up-to-date information regarding inflation-adjusted tax items, the reader usually is referred to the applicable Internal Revenue Service revenue procedure issued near the end of each year. Because of the late enactment of the Tax Cuts and Jobs Act in 2017, the Internal Revenue Service issued additional revenue procedures in the beginning of the year 2018 for certain items impacted by the act. The DSUE amount is *not* indexed for inflation. *See* § 2010(c)(3)(B). *See also* note 146.

151. *See* § 2010(c)(3).

152. *See* § 2505, entitled "Unified credit against gift tax." *See also* § 2010(a). Generally, unused exemption during lifetime corresponding credit can be used at death. *See* Chapter 1.

153. For federal income tax planning purposes, practitioners may recommend transfer of appreciated assets at death rather than during lifetime, thus avoiding a carryover basis in the hands of a beneficiary and, instead, allowing for a "step up" in basis at death. *See* § 1014. *See also* Chapter 1. When the beneficiary later sells the inherited property with a step up in basis, gain from the sale may be reduced or eliminated for federal income tax purposes.

154. Practitioners may be concerned whether transfers will be subject to "claw back," resulting in federal gift or estate taxation, because of the scheduled reduction of the exemption amount. Proposed regulations, for the most part, have eliminated this concern. *See* Chapter 1.

155. A direct skip is a transfer subject to federal gift or estate tax of an interest in property to a "skip person." § 2612(c)(1). A "skip person" is statutorily defined as (1) a natural person assigned to a generation that is two or more generations below the generation assignment of the transferor or (2) a trust if (A) all interests in such

trust are held by skip persons or if (B) there is no person holding an interest in such trust and, at no time after such transfer, may a distribution (including distributions on termination) be made from such trust to a non-skip person. Section 2613(a). A "non-skip person" is statutorily defined as "any person who is *not* a skip person." § 2613(b).

156. Section 2513 is entitled "Gift by husband or wife to third party" and sets forth the rules regarding gift splitting. For greater discussion, see subsection II.A.1.b. in this chapter.

157. *See also generally* § 2611(b)(1), which provides that the term "generation-skipping transfer" does not include any transfer that, if made inter vivos by an individual, would not be treated as a taxable gift by reason of § 2503(e).

158. § 2642(c)(1). The "inclusion ratio" is a fraction reflecting the amount of GST exemption allocated to a transfer. If all GST exemption is allocated to a transfer, the inclusion ratio is zero.

159. § 2642(c)(2).

160. As opposed to an outright gift.

161. In general, a "hanging power" is a type of Crummey withdrawal power that lapses in each year to the greatest extent possible under a 5 & 5 power. Hanging powers are useful for trusts with multiple Crummey holders. They are, however, complex both in terms of drafting and administering.

162. *See generally* Reg. § 26.2642-1(d), Example 3.

163. Section 2631(c), entitled "GST exemption amount," provides, in relevant part, that "the GST exemption amount for any calendar year shall be equal to the *basic* exclusion amount under section 2010(c) for such calendar year." Thus, the GST exemption does *not* include a DSUE amount.

164. *See* note 149 and accompanying text.

CHAPTER 4

The Role of Life Insurance in Planning for Minors

INTRODUCTION*

The most common use of life insurance in planning for minors is to provide funds for the children's support and education if the parents pass away while the children are still minors. If the parents are divorced or separated, insurance may be used as surety for child support payments. In larger estates, parents often maintain insurance on their lives in order to provide liquidity to pay estate taxes without the need to sell assets like the family home. Slightly less common is the purchase of insurance on the children's lives, usually as an investment.

Life insurance products constantly are evolving as insurance companies attempt to create policies that can compete with other financial instruments. To avoid professional liability, a lawyer who is advising parents or guardians concerning life insurance needs to take into consideration both the financial condition of the insurer and the type of insurance that is being offered.

Part I of this chapter provides the expertise and perspective of an insurance expert. Part II of the chapter identifies selected issues in life insurance planning and compliance.

---

*Jon J. Gallo, Esquire, originally prepared materials contained in the introduction of this chapter.

PART I: FACTORS IN SELECTING LIFE INSURANCE POLICIES[1]

Kenneth Black III

The selection and acquisition of life insurance is commonly an integral part of an estate plan designed for the benefit of minors. Life insurance policies, being complex, highly differentiated financial instruments, generally are fully understood only by professionals whose full-time occupation is devoted to their analysis and placement. It is unreasonable to expect an attorney whose required expertise and responsibilities in the estate planning process are so much broader to possess the same level of insight as an insurance professional. Yet, the client frequently looks to his or her attorney for life insurance advice when developing the plan. The purpose of this section is to provide the estate planning practitioner with the ability to identify the essential issues involved in the acquisition and ownership of life insurance and to provide careful guidance in the process. This section will discuss issues affecting (1) the selection of an insurance advisor, (2) the selection of a financially strong insurer, (3) life insurance contract formation, (4) term life insurance, (5) cash value life insurance, (6) selection of appropriate policies and amounts, (6) policy illustrations, and (7) ongoing policy management.

A. Selecting an Insurance Advisor

1. *Licensing*
Insurance producers—called agents and brokers—are sales people licensed by individual states, contracted to sell one or more insurer's products, and are paid a commission expressed as a percentage of the policy premium. State licensing requires the passing of an examination and meeting character requirements. Producers account for more than 90 percent of new individual life insurance sales and virtually all cases in which planning is complex, as with estate planning. Producers selling securities-oriented variable policies (to be discussed later in this section) also must hold a federal license from the Financial Industry Regulatory Authority (FINRA), requiring additional examinations.

2. *Professional Designations*
Professional designations and society memberships do not guarantee fair and competent service. They do, however, indicate a level of knowledge necessary to acquire the designation and a professional career commitment. The oldest and most widely recognized life insurance–oriented designation

is the chartered life underwriter (CLU®), granted by The American
To earn the CLU® designation, a candidate must (1) pass eight ι
tions touching on life insurance fundamentals, planning, and uses;
three years of qualified, full-time experience; (3) meet an ethics requiɾᴄᴍent;
and (4) agree to comply with the College's Code of Ethics. Individuals holding this designation can be presumed to be knowledgeable about life insurance and its uses. The American College also offers the chartered financial
consultant (ChFC®) reflecting expertise in broader personal financial issues,
as does the certified financial planner (CFP®) designation offered by the
College for Financial Planning.[3]

Individuals holding the CLU® designation often affiliate with the Society
of Financial Service Professionals (SFSP).[4] (Attorneys, accountants, financial planners, and other financial professionals may belong as well.) Members are expected to subscribe to the Code of Professional Conduct of the
Society of Financial Service Professionals. The Code sets forth standards of
(1) fairness, (2) competence, (3) integrity, and (4) diligence.

3. Sources of Information about Producers

Resources are available to seek information about producers. Although
detailed information about individual complaints often is deemed to be con-
fidential, state insurance departments provide information about whether
any complaints have been filed against an agent and also the agent's licensing qualifications. Information pertaining to agents licensed to sell variable
policies (to be discussed later in this section) can be sought from the Financial Industry Regulatory Authority (FINRA).

> #### EXAMPLE
>
> Under "Broker Check Reports" on FINRA's website (www.finra.org), one can
> locate a range of information about registered firms and brokers, including
> individual credentials, current registrations, exams passed, previous employ-
> ment, and client disputes. To reiterate, there are no services equivalent to
> those offered by FINRA for agents not involved with variable products.

> #### PRACTICE NOTE
>
> Appendix 4-A to this part of the chapter provides a questionnaire that can
> be used for evaluating producers (i.e., insurance agents and brokers).

B. Selecting an Insurer with Financial Strength

1. The Special Nature of Insurance Obligations

The obligations of a life insurer to its policy owners differ from ordinary
commercial obligations in ways amplifying the importance of the financial strength of the insurer. First, life insurance contracts can be very long
term, lasting for decades. It seldom is important to consider the financial
condition of a party to a contract for these long periods of time. Second,

the insurer's promise to pay at some indeterminate time in the future is the only thing of value the insurer offers. That is, the insurer's promise is value-less until honored.

An insurer's financial strength largely is measured by the amount of capital (i.e., assets exceeding liabilities) it holds. Capital exists as a safety margin in the event an insurer's expenses are greater than what were forecast when premiums were set. The more capital a company holds, the safer are its promises to policy owners. However, the less capital an insurer holds, the greater will be its profits. This tension between shareholder and policy-holder interests demands careful attention from prospective policy owners.

2. Rating Agencies

Although a number of rating agencies exist, the Securities and Exchange Commission (SEC) has designated the four most important rating agencies as Nationally Recognized Statistical Rating Organizations (NRSROs). These rating agencies are A.M. Best, Fitch Ratings, Moody's Investors Service, and Standard & Poor's.

A.M. Best.[5] A.M. Best has been publishing financial information about insurance companies for more than a century—longer than any other rating agency. It published ratings briefly in the 1930s, and has continuously since 1976. It also rates more U.S. life insurers than any other rating agency, numbering about 1,000. Ratings are reviewed periodically, but, not less frequently than once a year, and can be changed at any time. Insurers pay an annual fee to be rated by Best.

Fitch Ratings.[6] Fitch rates more than 300 U.S. life insurers, each for a fee. If an insurer requests a rating, Fitch will make the rating public even if the insurer disagrees with the rating.

Moody's Investors Service.[7] Moody's rates about 200 U.S. life insurers. Insurers pay an annual fee to be rated.

Standard & Poor's (S&P).[8] About 350 life insurers requesting ratings are rated by S&P. A few dozen life insurers, not requesting ratings, also are rated based solely on publicly available information, with the rating designated as "pi."

3. Rating Agency Reports and Categories

While the content and format of each rating agency's reports differ, these reports include similar types of information. Quantitative and qualitative analysis and remarks are included about the insurer's investments, liquidity, capitalization, profitability, financial flexibility, and other related financial and operational elements. Various financial data and ratios also are provided. While the information provided in rating agency reports can be valuable, the complexity of the information can limit its usefulness. Accordingly, the agencies have developed a sort of shorthand summary of its results in the form of rating categories ranked by letter grade.

Table 4.1 Rank Orders of Ratings and Categories for Four Rating Agencies

Rank Number	Best	Fitch	Moody's	S&P
1	A++	AAA	Aaa	AAA
2	A+	AA+	Aa1	AA+
3	A	AA	Aa2	AA
4	A–	AA–	Aa3	AA–
5	B++	A+	A1	A+
6	B+	A	A2	A
7	B	A–	A3	A–
8	B–	BBB+	Baa1	BBB+
9	C++	BBB	Baa2	BBB
10	C+	BBB–	Baa3	BBB–
11	C	BB+	Ba1	BB+
12	C–	BB	Ba2	BB
13	D	BB–	Ba3	BB–
14	E	B+	B1	B+
15	F	B	B2	B
16		B–	B3	B–
17		CCC+	Caa1	CCC+
18		CCC	Caa2	CCC
19		CCC–	Caa3	CCC–
20		CC	Ca	CC
21		C	C	R

Each rating agency has its own rating categories, resulting in ratings from agency-to-agency of similar nomenclature but dissimilar import. For example, an A+ rating from Best is its second highest rating, but it is Fitch's and S&P's fifth highest rating. Table 4.1 lists each of the four rating agencies' categories along with a rank number. The rank number indicates where each rating ranks among those of each rating firm. Equivalent rank numbers do not mean equivalence of ratings. Insurers receiving ratings shown in the shaded area fall into the rating agencies' "vulnerable" category. Insurers receiving ratings that do not appear in the shaded area are considered "secure."

Clearly, higher ratings are preferred to lower. Regrettably, other things are not always the same, and it is worth remembering that ratings are opinions and not guarantees or assurances of financial strength. A lower-rated insurer may offer better underwriting or more flexible or competitive products or superior advice and ongoing service. As the rating agencies themselves often stress, small differences in ratings, especially between adjacent categories, mean only slight perceived differences in financial strength.

PRACTICE NOTE

Great caution, however, should be exercised in dealing with life insurers whose ratings from one or more agencies fall within the vulnerable category or have no rating from any of the major agencies. A vulnerable rating or no rating does not mean that the company necessarily is about to fail or that it is in financial difficulty. Nonetheless, the failure rate of companies that have vulnerable ratings or no ratings has been considerably higher than those rated in the secure category. Insurers in financial difficulty often withdraw their ratings, if permitted by the rating agency.

4. Comdex Scoring

Many advisors also secure the Comdex number in their review. Comdex is a composite index of ratings, expressed as the average percentile of a company's rating (i.e., the proportion of rated insurers that are rated lower).[9] While not itself a rating, the Comdex number gives an insurer's standing, on a scale of 1 to 100, in relation to other rated insurers. Thus, a Comdex of 90 means that the composite of the insurer's ratings places it in the 90th percentile of rated companies (i.e., 10 percent are rated higher and 90 percent lower).

PRACTICE NOTE

Comdex scores are available at www.ebixlife.com/vitalsigns/. The EbixExchange sells its Comdex scores; however, Internet searches often will produce a "free look" from sites that republish the scores.

C. Life Insurance Contract Formation

1. Contract Elements

One should be aware that life insurance agreements differ substantially from ordinary arms-length commercial contracts. Among other distinguishing features, these agreements are, first, contracts of utmost good faith. That is, each party is entitled to rely in good faith on the representations of the other, and each is under an obligation not to attempt to deceive the other. As a consequence, the applicant is under an affirmative legal obligation to provide complete and true information in the application. Any failure to comply with this requirement could render the policy worthless. Second, life insurance contracts are conditional in that the insurer's obligation to pay depends upon the policy owner's payment of premiums and furnishing proof of death at the time of a claim. Third, life insurance contracts are contracts of adhesion, the provisions of which are fixed by the insurer, and must be adhered to by the policy owner. Thus, ambiguities in a life insurance contract generally are construed against the insurer.

The contract law elements of capacity, offer and acceptance, and valuable consideration also have nuanced meanings in the context of a life insurance contract.[10]

- **Capacity.** Although contracts generally can be entered into only by those having attained eighteen years of age, most states allow older minors (typically age fifteen) to enter into life insurance contracts.
- **Offer and acceptance.** Submission of the application with the first premium is an "offer," and issuance of the policy is the "acceptance." Submission, without the premium, is an invitation to the insurer to make an offer. After submission of the application with or without the premium, the insurer may issue a conditional receipt providing coverage during the period of time passing from the submission of the application to the issuance of the policy. Underwriting (see the following subsections relating to underwriting) of the proposed insured takes place during this period of time. The conditional receipt provides that the insurer is considered to have made an offer conditional upon determination of the proposed insured's acceptability (i.e., insurability), and the applicant accepts the conditional offer by payment of the premium. The insurance becomes effective as of the date of the conditional receipt or, if later, the time of the physical examination, provided that the proposed insured is found insurable. The acceptability or insurability requirement is objective. That is, the standard is whether the proposed insured would have been accepted under the insurer's ordinary business practice had the proposed insured lived. Most U.S. insurers use this type of receipt.
- **Legal consideration.** The insurer's legal consideration is its promise to pay benefits, and the insured's legal consideration is the truth of the representations made in the application, again emphasizing the importance of a full and true application.

2. Parties to the Contract

Most commercial contracts have two principal parties. The life insurance contract typically has three. First, ownership of the policy and the authority to exercise rights under the policy belong to the *policy owner*. Second, the person whose life is the subject of the policy is the *insured*. Third, the person or entity entitled to payment of the policy death benefit is the *beneficiary*. The insured must be a natural person. The policy owner and beneficiary may be a corporation, LLC, trust, or other legal entity. In the case of a natural person, the policy owner and insured are often the same. In the case of a trust, the policy owner and beneficiary are often the same. Within the context of family estate planning, section II of this chapter explains the important role of trusts as policy owners and as beneficiaries.

3. *Underwriting: Application*

Insurers do not approve applications without a careful examination of the health and insurability of the proposed insured. The insurer has five primary sources of information: (1) the policy application, (2) the physical exam, (3) attending physician statements (APS), (4) the inspection report, and (5) the Medical Information Bureau (MIB).

> PRACTICE NOTE
>
> Clients can become upset or uncomfortable about aspects of the process, so it is best practice for an attorney to make the client aware in advance of what to expect.

Underwriting is the process the insurer undertakes to select (i.e., accept or reject) applicants and to determine the appropriate policy premium. The areas of principal concern to insurers are (1) the insured's health; (2) the family health history; (3) the insured's alcohol and drug usage, including smoking; (4) the insured's occupation; (5) the insured's sports and avocations; (6) the insured's aviation and military service; and (6) the insured's financial status and condition.

The life insurance application is the most important and critical source of information in the underwriting process. It typically is comprised of two parts. The first part elicits financial, lifestyle, and administrative information about the proposed insured, including

- past addresses;
- occupation;
- gender;
- date of birth;
- current coverage and current applications for life and health insurance with other insurers, any history of refused applications or policies issued with a rating, and whether existing insurance will be replaced;
- driving record;
- past and planned private aviation activities;
- avocations;
- foreign travel; and
- net worth and earned and unearned income.

The second part of the application is for recording the insured's answers to questions about his or her health, including

- illnesses, injuries, diseases, and surgeries during the past ten or so years;
- physician consultations during the previous five or so years;

- alcohol, tobacco, and drug use; and
- the medical history of parents and siblings, including their current health and the causes and dates of any deaths.

It typically is completed by a medical or paramedical examiner.

Insurers seek to minimize the time required to complete an application to ease the process for the agent, proposed insured, and/or applicant. Thus, inquiries are limited to information essential to making an informed underwriting decision. The medical questions contained in the second part of the application may be condensed for younger insureds and for those seeking smaller amounts of insurance.

4. *Underwriting: Physical Examination*

A medical exam is required if the requested insurance amount is comparatively large or if additional information is needed about the insured's health status. The examiner may be a physician or, for lesser amounts of insurance and to minimize costs, a paramedic. The examination typically includes height, weight, chest, and abdomen measurements; a blood profile and test measuring exposure to the HIV virus; and a urinalysis, including testing for nonprescription drug and possible tobacco usage. A regular physical exam might include all of these items plus an examination of the condition of the heart, lungs, and nervous system. For larger life policies, more detailed information involving complete blood and urine testing, electrocardiograms, pulmonary function tests, and chest x-rays often are requested.

5. *Underwriting: Attending Physician Statements*

When the amount of insurance applied for is sufficiently large or if the individual application or the medical examiner's report reveals conditions or situations, past or present, about which more information is desired, the insurer may order APS, which provide physician reports of the proposed insured's condition and treatment. APS may reveal additional health conditions or the names of additional physicians not reported in the application.

PRACTICE NOTE

Physicians are not authorized to disclose patient information without a specific authorization from the patient. Thus, every insurance application includes an authorization to be signed by the proposed insured.

6. *Underwriting: Inspection Report*

For larger amounts of insurance, insurers obtain an "inspection report," an industry term for a consumer report used by underwriters and prepared by an inspection company. The inspection report is intended to verify and/ or supplement mainly nonmedical information provided by a proposed insured. Most insurers obtain these reports from an "independent inspection company," an industry term for a consumer reporting agency. The independent inspection company collects and sells information about an individual's employment history, driving record, financial situation, creditworthiness, character, personal characteristics, mode of living, and other possibly relevant "personally identifiable information."

If the amount of insurance is large, a more careful and detailed report—an "investigative consumer report"—may be obtained, particularly regarding financial information. To obtain the necessary information for the investigative consumer report, the investigator may interview the proposed insured's employer, neighbors, banker, accountant, business associates, and others who may be able to contribute the information desired. Insurers also utilize telephone interviews of proposed insureds to replace or supplement inspection reports.

7. Underwriting: Medical Information Bureau (MIB)

Another source of information regarding insurability is an industry-sponsored data base of personal information maintained by the MIB in the United States and Canada.[11] The MIB is a membership-sponsored corporation responsible for collecting "personally identifiable information" about individuals who have applied for life or health insurance from member companies and who have certain medical and/or other conditions that might affect their insurability.

PRACTICE NOTE

MIB procedures and some state privacy laws require the individual to be informed in writing, before the individual's completion of an insurance application, of the insurance company's reporting of information to the MIB. In addition, these procedures and state laws require MIB to secure the proposed insured's authorization for MIB's release of the proposed insured's information to the insurer.

D. Insurance Policy Features

There are two fundamental approaches to life insurance offered by insurers. The first is *term insurance*, which provides only the payment of a death benefit if the insured dies before the end of a specified period of coverage. The second is *cash value life insurance*, which, in addition to a death benefit, offers a savings element called the *cash value* or *account value*. Term insurance becomes increasingly expensive (and eventually unavailable) as the insured ages because of dramatic increases in the probability of death. Traditionally, the purpose of cash value life insurance is to combine an increasing savings element with a decreasing term life insurance benefit so that the sum of the two equals a stated death benefit over the "whole of life."[12] The building of the cash value is referred to as "prefunding of mortality." This cash value/death benefit pattern is reflected in Figure 4.1.

In Figure 4.1, the policy, with a death benefit of $1,000,000, is issued to the insured at age thirty-five. Note as the insured ages, the cash value of the policy increases while the term component of the policy decreases. At age

Figure 4.1 The Increasing Cash Value and Decreasing Term Insurance of a Traditional Whole Life Policy

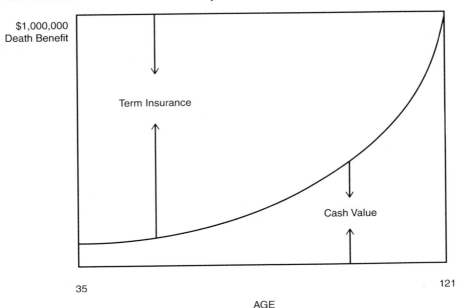

121, the policy endows (i.e., the policy reserves equal the face amount of the policy).[13] The basic structure of the *traditional whole life policy (WL)* is inflexible in the sense that the premium, death benefit, and cash value, prospectively, are fixed and do not change.

The second major type of cash value life insurance is *universal life insurance (UL)*. UL, unlike WL, allows (1) flexibility to change premiums and the death benefit over time and (2) the insurer's determination of the cash value. Unlike the WL cash value, which is fixed, the UL insurer credits the cash value with interest based on how the insurer's investments have performed at the end of each crediting period.

1. *Term Insurance*

Term life insurance furnishes protection for a limited number of years, at the end of which the policy expires, meaning that it terminates with no value. The face amount of the policy is payable only if the insured dies during the stipulated term. If the insured survives the stipulated term, nothing is paid. Term policies may be issued for as short a period as one year, but customarily provide protection for a set number of years, such as ten or twenty, or to a stipulated age, such as seventy-five or eighty.

Initial premium rates are lower for term life insurance than for cash value life insurance products issued on the same basis. A typical term policy provides for no cash value. Premiums for term coverage, however, escalate rapidly over time. Three features applicable to many term life policies deserve special attention: renewability, convertibility, and reentry.

Distinguishing Features and Options of Term Insurance

- Term insurance is temporary insurance providing coverage for a period of time or term.
- Term insurance provides pure insurance protection without buildup of cash value.
- Term insurance generally is the least expensive form of life insurance in the early years.
- Term insurance is renewable or not renewable.
- If renewable, term insurance may become more expensive with each renewal because it is age-based.
- A conversion option to exchange a term policy for a cash value policy may be available.
- A reentry feature may be available.

(a) Term Insurance Renewability

Most one-year and five-year term policies and many ten-year policies are *renewable*. That is, the policy owner may continue the policy for a limited number of additional periods of protection merely by paying a higher renewal premium. This renewal option allows the policy owner, at each interim term period, to continue the policy without reference to the insured's health or other insurability conditions at renewal time. Companies often limit the age (generally to age seventy-five or eighty in the United States) as to when these term policies may be renewed.

The premium, although level for each interim period, increases with each renewal and is based on the insured's attained age at renewal time. A scale of guaranteed future premium rates is contained in the insurance contract. Some policies, however, have indeterminate premiums, which allow the company to charge rates lower than those guaranteed in the policy.

PRACTICE NOTE

The extra cost of renewable term insurance often is offset by the increased flexibility and security of being able to maintain coverage if the insured becomes uninsurable for any reason.

(b) Term Insurance Convertibility

Most term insurance policies include a *conversion feature*, which affords the policy owner the option to exchange the term policy for a cash value insurance contract without evidence of insurability. The period during which conversion is permitted often is shorter than the maximum duration of the policy. The conversion privilege increases the flexibility of term life insurance.

At the time a term policy is purchased, a policy owner may have preferred a cash value policy but, because of budget considerations, decided on low-premium term coverage. After issuance, circumstances may have changed, enabling the policy owner to purchase an adequate amount of cash value insurance. The conversion feature permits the policy owner to exchange the term policy for a cash value policy that is more compatible with his or her present goals.

If the insured is insurable at standard rates, however, there may be no direct financial advantage in exercising the conversion privilege. Instead, the insured may want to reenter the marketplace and shop carefully, despite recognizing the time and inconvenience of doing so has value.

(c) Term Insurance Reentry

Some insurers include a *reentry* feature in their term policies, which allows policyholders to pay lower premiums than the guaranteed renewal premium, if insureds can demonstrate they meet continuing insurability criteria. These term policies are referred to as "reentry term" because insureds may be able to reenter the select group periodically, if the insured resubmits evidence of satisfactory health and insurability to the insurer. Reentry term policies have two sets of premiums, namely, select and ultimate. The select rates are lower and apply to those insureds who recently have been underwritten. Once the benefit of recent underwriting begins to diminish, those insureds are charged the higher ultimate rates.

For those insureds who fail to take advantage of the reentry provision or who fail to qualify for reentry because of insurability problems, ultimate rates are charged thereafter. An individual who cannot qualify for select rates usually will be unable to qualify for a new policy and, therefore, higher ultimate rates may be the only option if he or she wishes to continue insurance coverage.

E. Cash Value Life Insurance Features

There are a wide variety of cash value policies available. Almost all are some sort of variation of traditional whole life (WL) or universal life (UL). For estate planning purposes, the most relevant cash value policies are (1) participating WL, (2) generic UL, (3) no lapse guarantee UL, (4) variable UL, and (5) equity index UL.

The performance of participating WL, generic UL, and no lapse guarantee UL depend on the performance of the insurer's general account investment portfolio. By regulation, the insurer's investments are limited to high-quality fixed income, bonds, and mortgages. As a result, the investment results are both very safe and relatively low yielding. Variable UL and equity index UL were developed to allow policy owners who were seeking higher returns and were willing to tolerate more risk to participate in the stock and other investment markets.

1. *Whole Life Insurance (WL)*

The traditional WL policy features fixed, scheduled premiums, guaranteed cash values, and guaranteed death benefit. These features are inflexible in that they generally cannot be changed. If a change is permitted, such as a reduced death benefit, the premium and cash values also will be reduced proportionately accordingly.

Insurers offering a WL policy, with long-term guarantees implicit in a policy with fixed benefits, may be vulnerable to competition from UL policies, because insurers credit the UL policies once actual results are known. Nonetheless, insurers offering participating WL policies effectively price their products by reducing the effective cost in the form of a dividend declared at the end of each policy year and payable to the policy owner. The dividend can be (1) received in cash, (2) applied to the next premium, or (3) left to accumulate with the insurer.

There are two additional dividend options that are common in the estate planning context. Each option is designed to reduce the overall cost of the insurance. Dividends can be used to purchase one-year term insurance, which supplements the basic WL policy and, thus, allows for a smaller death benefit and lowers the cost the basic policy. Dividends also may be used to purchase paid-up additions (i.e., incrementally small amounts of death benefit), which are fully paid for life.

PRACTICE NOTE

Use of one-year term and paid-up additions can be used eventually to eliminate the need to pay any premium *assuming the dividends are paid as illustrated* (see later discussion of illustrations). In the past, during times of high interest rates, so-called *vanishing premium* policies were sold based on an assumption of continued high interest rates. Policy owners, however, learned that interest rates can fall as fast as they can rise and, as a result, the anticipated dividends were essentially unrealistic and could not be paid as illustrated. The vanishing premium reappeared and became the subject of extensive litigation. Illustration practices and a lower interest rate environment make

---

Distinguishing Features of Traditional WL Insurance

- Traditional WL insurance provides guaranteed death benefit and a guaranteed cash value in exchange for fixed, level premiums for the life of the insured.
- Barring insolvency of the insurance company, the insured will have insurance coverage as long as the premium is paid when due.
- In comparison to other forms of cash value insurance, WL insurance may be the most expensive.

the issue less relevant, but care should be taken when planning depends heavily on illustrated dividends.

2. Universal Life Insurance (UL)

Universal life (UL) policies differ significantly from WL policies. First, UL policies are flexible, in that the premium and death benefit can be changed, within certain limits, at the option of the policy owner. Second, the death benefit and premiums are not bundled. That is, either can be changed while the other remains the same within prescribed limits. Third, the UL policy is transparent, in that the internal policy mechanics are reported periodically to the policy owner. Finally, the UL cash value account is not fixed but is a residual sum after accounting for expenses and credits. The basic accounting structure for a UL policy is as follows:

Beginning Account Value

+ Premiums Paid

− Policy expenses

− Mortality Expense

+ Cash Value Credits

_____

Ending Account Balance

As long as the ending account balance remains positive, the policy remains in force, whether a premium has been paid or not. The policy owner has the option to change the premium and face amount at any time subject to two limitations. First, decreases in the face amount are limited relative to the existing cash value and premiums. Second, death benefit increases may require new underwriting and proof of insurability.

Policy expenses (based on policy size) and mortality charges (based on the amount of the death benefit) usually are guaranteed not to exceed specified limits, and actual charges customarily are considerably less than the guaranteed maximum. Similarly, the interest credits are guaranteed at a specified minimum rate, and customarily a significantly higher amount actually is credited.

PRACTICE NOTE

Both frequency and amount of premium payments are flexible as long as the cash value of the generic UL policy is able to cover mortality and expenses each month. However, if the cash value of the generic UL policy is allowed to drop to this low a level, the future contributions required to keep the policy in effect will be substantially similar to the cost of annually increasing term insurance and the cost of maintaining the policy may become prohibitive. Moreover, if the cash value is allowed to drop below the level necessary to keep a generic UL policy in force, the policy terminates and a new policy must be purchased with the premiums based on the then-age of the insured.

(a) No Lapse Guarantee Universal Life Insurance (NLGUL)

Provided the minimum continuance premium is timely paid, NLGUL guarantees a minimum death benefit to a certain age or for life, even if the account value becomes depleted before that time. Not all UL policies are labeled as such but, if a UL policy provides this option, whether at an additional premium or not, it will remain in force to a certain age or for life and the policy is an NLG contract.

PRACTICE NOTE

The great advantage of NLGUL policies is lifetime guaranteed insurance coverage can be purchased with a low premium outlay in comparison to that required for most other lifetime guarantee policies such as WL.

(b) Variable Universal Life Insurance (VUL)

VUL insurance policies permit their owners to control their policies' investment allocations and, thereby, determine the levels of risk that they are willing to assume. VUL policy owners may select from a menu of funds from the insurer's separate account offerings. Separate accounts are effectively mutual funds in which assets are held separate from the insurer's general account assets. Policyholders may change funds as they wish, altering the risk/return profile of their policies, subject to insurer administrative requirements. The performance of the selected funds determines the "cash value credits" in the accounting structure previously outlined. The policy's separate account investment risks are borne totally by the policyholder, a characteristic not found in WL and generic VL insurance. In contrast, WL and generic VL policies provide a minimum guaranteed interest crediting rate. Separate account assets are not subject to the claims of general creditors in the event of an insurer's insolvency offering the policy owner additional protection.

(c) Equity Index Universal Life Insurance (EIUL)

EIUL is a UL variation with the same operational characteristics and platform as generic UL products, but with an interest crediting rate tied to (1) the insurer's general account-based products or (2) one or more equity indexes, such as the S&P 500 index. The policy owner selects the account value amounts to be exposed to each crediting mechanism. The EIUL cash or account value, backed by the insurer's general account assets, is divided into two or more policy accounts: a fixed account and one or more index accounts. The policyholder selects the funds to be included in each account. The fixed account crediting rate, typically the same as with the insurer's other UL policies, is influenced by the investment returns in the insurer's general account. The index account is the portion of the EIUL cash or account value for which the crediting rate is determined by changes in an equity index, subject to the "growth floor" (i.e., a guaranteed minimum crediting rate) and the "growth cap" (i.e., a maximum crediting rate). The "growth floor" limits the loss the account can suffer in a down market.[14]

On the other hand, the "growth cap" limits the amount of gain credited to the account in a rising market.[15]

F. Selecting the Appropriate Policy and Amount

1. Policy Type

Selecting the appropriate policy type involves both the subjective temperament of the client and the nature of the insurance need. Important client considerations include (1) the ability to pay premiums, (2) personal risk tolerance, and (3) personal financial discipline. The nature of the insurance need is characterized by (1) the duration of the need and (2) the changing pattern, if any, over time.

(a) Term Insurance

Term insurance can be useful for persons with modest incomes and high insurance needs, a common family situation. Risk management principles suggest that the family unit should be protected against catastrophic losses. If current family income does not permit the option of purchasing cash value life insurance in adequate amounts, the individual arguably should purchase term insurance. Parents who have careers to establish and have temporarily limited income arguably should use their resources primarily to establish their careers and, therefore, opt for term insurance in preference to cash value insurance. It also can be said with little reservation that where the insurance need is definitely temporary, term insurance will be appropriate and, where the insurance need is definitely lifelong, term insurance probably is inappropriate.

(b) Whole Life Insurance

For individuals whose life insurance need is expected to extend for fifteen or more years and who are interested in accumulating savings via life insurance, WL, like UL, can be an attractive option. Interest credited on cash values generally enjoys favorable income tax treatment, rendering the policy a potentially attractive means of accumulating savings.

By leveling premium payments, WL outlays can be relatively modest. For many individuals whose careers are just beginning, the premium payment required for an adequate amount of WL insurance, however, may be too great, given other priorities. Rather than reduce the insurance amount to what is affordable, good risk management principles argue for placing primary emphasis on the insurance needed to cover the potential loss, with secondary emphasis on product type. The only effective choice may be to purchase term insurance.

(c) Universal Life Insurance

In thinking about how UL can fit into a financial plan, it is sometimes suggested that one think of UL not as a generic type of life insurance but as a flexible platform or shell, allowing it to become whatever generic type of life insurance the customer wishes. Because the policyholder, not the insurer, determines the magnitude of premium payments, the policyholder thereby determines the size and rate of the cash value buildup and, therefore, the policy's generic type (e.g., term, WL insurance). Because of this premium flexibility, policyholders can effectively design their own policies to reflect their own needs and changing financial circumstances. Like WL and its regular, mandatory premium payments, the flexibility afforded by UL also requires strict financial discipline.

Three variations of UL may be considered. These variations are NLGUL, VUL, and EIUL. Despite the low cost of long-term coverage associated with NLGUL, there is a risk—because of rigidity and complexity and perhaps because of policyholder naivety or ignorance—that the policyholder (and possibly agent) may fail to understand fully the purpose, nature, and risks of the policy; that is, the product may be unsuitable for the customer. As compared to standard UL, NLGUL policies typically have *heavy surrender charges for the first ten to twenty policy years*. Because NLGUL products have *modest or nonexistent cash values*, many advisors urge clients to think of NLGUL products as term insurance.

Like generic UL, VUL policies require financial discipline. VUL policies are potentially useful for those persons who desire to treat their life insurance policy cash values more as an investment than a savings account. Thus, the policy is more suitable for those with greater investment savvy and understand the volatility and long-term nature of equity markets. At the same time, some VUL policies have been criticized because of having, what some consider, excessive charges. One of the strengths of the life insurance industry historically has been its investment guarantees. With variable insurance products, consumers are largely foregoing these guarantees.

While the basic mechanics of an EIUL policy may seem relatively straightforward, the details—of which there are many—prove to be complex. These policies can be misunderstood if not explained thoroughly. They require careful monitoring and service, and the details affecting the interest crediting rate can seem bewildering. Nonetheless, EIUL policies occupy an important place between traditional UL policies and variable UL policies. They can be considered as providing much of the protection of a traditional UL policy with some of the return potential of a variable UL policy, as illustrated in Figure 4.2.

(d) Second-to-Die Policies

"Second-to-die" life insurance, also called "survivorship life insurance" and "last to die" life insurance, insures two lives and pays proceeds only at the second death. This feature generally is available with any of the general types of insurance discussed in this section. The second-to-die option often can prove attractive. First, the proceeds of the second-to-die policy can be used to pay any federal estate taxes due at the death of a surviving spouse.[16] Second, the premium cost of a second-to-die policy is considerably lower than the total premium for two individual policies insuring one life each.

Figure 4.2 Risk/Return Profiles of Three Universal Life Policies

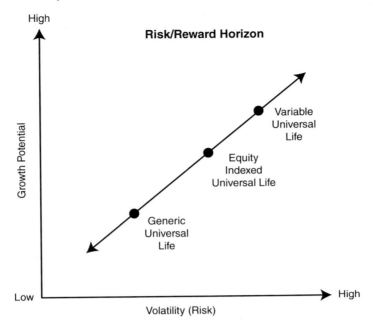

PRACTICE NOTE

If the life insurance proceeds are necessary after the death of a spouse (i.e., necessary to replace the earning capacity of the first spouse to die), a single policy may be appropriate.

2. *Policy Amount*

(a) First Step: Identifying the Need

The first step in the determination of policy amount is to identify the need. Some needs are identified easily. For example, the amount of cash needed to liquidate a mortgage obligation is a routine determination. The need to provide a regular income for beneficiaries in the event of the death of the insured often arises, and requires a more complex evaluation. There are two basic philosophical views of determining an appropriate amount. The *capital liquidation* approach assumes both the death benefit principal and interest are liquidated over the course of the beneficiary's life. The *capital retention* approach assumes the beneficiary will receive only interest on the death benefit capital. The *capital liquidation* approach has the advantage of a lower cost, but it introduces the necessity of estimating the number of years the beneficiary or beneficiaries may live. Thus, the approach introduces the element of longevity risk into the calculation. The *capital retention* approach is the more expensive option, but it provides a more secure income for beneficiaries. It also may be attractive to those with estate philanthropic motives in that the retained capital could be left to secondary beneficiaries (e.g., a charity) after the financial lifetime care and death of primary beneficiaries.

With either approach, it is necessary to capitalize the income need, that is, to identify the amount of capital required to produce the desired level of income. With each approach, it also is necessary to make an assumption about the interest rate available for the investment of death benefit proceeds. In the *capital liquidation* approach, the present value of all future income needs is calculated using the available interest assumption as the discount rate. In the *capital retention* approach, the required annual income simply is divided by the assumed interest rate to determine the necessary death benefit. In addition to income requirements, the total insurance need will include one-time cash requirements at death (e.g., funeral expense, debts taxes, etc.) and any inheritances.

EXAMPLE

It is determined that Jane requires an annual income of $100,000. Jane's life expectancy is twenty-five years. In addition, it is expected that Jane can invest safely at 4 percent.

Under the capital liquidation approach, Jane will need an insurance death benefit of $1,562,207.99 (i.e., death benefit equal to the present value of a ten-year annuity at 4 percent).[17]

Under the capital retention approach, Jane will need an insurance death benefit of $2,500,000 ($100,000/.04).

(b) Second Step: Identification of Resources

The second step in the determination of the insurance need is to identify resources available at death. The three most important are (1) liquid savings in taxable or tax-advantaged accounts, (2) existing personal life insurance, and (3) life insurance provided by others. Employers often provide group term coverage to employees, but the amount rarely exceeds $50,000 and coverage typically ends when employment terminates. Some employers provide plans allowing the purchase of additional limited amounts through payroll deductions. In some cases, it may be advantageous to utilize this resource. Highly compensated corporate employees often have nonqualified supplemental executive retirement plans, funded with life insurance, providing a significant death benefit. Modest amounts of government death benefits are provided through Social Security.

G. Policy Illustrations

The prospective life insurance buyer often desires a competitive evaluation of a recommended policy. This evaluation usually involves an illustration of possible future policy values. Illustrations can serve other purposes, including demonstration of (1) how the various policy elements work together, (2) how different funding and coverage levels might affect future policy values, and (3) how the proposed policy fits into financial plans. The agent or broker, presenting the illustrations, will have the resources to produce multiple scenarios at the request of the client. Illustrations that target specific goals can be prepared.

EXAMPLE 1

By way of illustration, the agent can show the premium required to produce a given cash value at a specified age while maintaining the death benefit.

EXAMPLE 2

By way of illustration, the agent can show the minimum amount of premium required to maintain a policy in force until a given age.

Policy illustrations include *assumptions* about four *experience* factors affecting policy performance. These four *experience* factors are (1) mortality (i.e., the rate of death of insureds), (2) investment results, (3) expenses, and (4) persistency (i.e., the number of policy owners who do not surrender).

After the four *experience* factors are identified, life insurance policies generally are priced only retrospectively. In the case of UL, the retrospective nature is explicit, because results are credited to the policy at the end of each period. In the case of participating WL, retrospective results are reflected in the amount of the dividend. In both cases, the insurer guarantees minimum credits it will make without regard to actual experience. Table 4.2 includes an abbreviated version of a UL policy illustration.

The illustrated policy is based on the assumption that an annual premium of $21,313 is paid for ten years. The results of three different interest rate scenarios are provided. At the guaranteed rate of 3 percent, the illustration presents a policy that will fail before the end of the fifteenth year. That is, the premium of $21,313 for ten years is not enough to support a $1,000,000 death benefit. The cash value also will reduce to zero before age sixty-five. By contrast, the policy, at the assumed rate of 5.45 percent, remains viable at age seventy, with a significant and growing cash value that will carry it to age ninety-five or beyond.[18] Special rules apply to VUL illustrations. Illustrations can employ hypothetical assumptions about investment returns, but one illustrated result must be based on a 0 percent return and none can exceed 12 percent annually.

Table 4.2 Abbreviated UL Policy Illustration

| Yr. | Age | Cumulative Premium Outlay | Guaranteed 3.00% | | Nonguaranteed | | | |
| | | | | | Intermediate | | Illustrated 5.45% | |
			Cash Value	Death Benefit	Cash Value	Death Benefit	Cash Value	Death Benefit
5	55	$106,565	$22,591	$1,000,000	$56,200	$1,000,000	$91,558	$1,000,000
10	60	213,130	35,805	1,000,000	123,139	1,000,000	218,480	1,000,000
15	65	213,130	0	1,000,000	0	1,000,000	324,437	1,000,000
20	70	213,130	—	—	—	—	451,046	1,000,000

PRACTICE NOTE

Like the foregoing illustration, the majority of policies sold today contain nonguaranteed policy elements, also called "current assumptions." Illustrations prepared for these policies, therefore, contain both guaranteed and nonguaranteed values. Illustrations containing nonguaranteed values do not suggest or promise those values will be realized.

1. Illustration Comparison

Life insurance policy costs can vary greatly. Consumers often erroneously equate a policy's cost with its premium. The premium is a measure of the annual outlay for a policy, not its cost. Cost includes all elements of a policy (i.e., premiums, death benefits, cash values, and dividends), not just premiums. The true cost of life insurance to any individual can be determined only ex post (i.e., only after the contract terminates by death, maturity, or surrender). It is virtually impossible to estimate a policy's competitiveness ex ante—before policy termination—without relying on current illustrated values and comparing them with competing policies, particularly for policies containing nonguaranteed policy elements.

2. Almost Identical Characteristics

Policy comparisons should be based on as many identical characteristics of the policies and the proposed insured and scenarios as feasible. All illustrations should be run assuming the same insured characteristics. Thus, the same sex, age, and smoking and health status should be assumed for each, although doing so sometimes can be challenging, as insurers may use different definitions for terms such as age, smoker status, and preferred risk.

3. Stress Test

Illustrations should be stress tested. A stress test involves running illustrations with reduced crediting rates and/or at less favorable charges to provide an idea of potential downside policy performance. It is useful for managing policyholder expectations.

PRACTICE NOTE

One should be wary of a highly competitive policy illustration that is based on current assumptions and yet is unable to demonstrate performance under slightly less favorable assumptions. It is best to subject different policy proposals to the same stress test in order to identify the policy that is least sensitive to the hypothetical changes proposed in the different policy proposals. In that way, the policy with superior value can be discovered.

4. Track Record of Insurer

The track record, reputation, and intentions of an insurer often provide the greatest comfort regarding illustrated policy value sustainability. Seasoned advisors and producers who service in-force policies should have an understanding of which insurers treat their policyholders well. Some insurers have a questionable reputation regarding in-force policy performance and service, while others have quite positive reputations.

5. *Regulated*

Consumers and their advisors can take some comfort in the fact that illustrations generally are regulated. Life insurers are required to appoint an illustration actuary who must make certain annual certifications to the state insurance regulator and the insurer's board of directors regarding the insurer's practices and compliance with regulations.

H. Ongoing Policy Management

Once a cash value policy has been issued, it requires monitoring for two reasons. First, policy performance must be evaluated regularly to ascertain whether the policy is meeting expectations and, thus, remains suited to its purpose. Second, cash value policies offer significant lifetime benefits in addition to death benefits and, as a client's circumstances change, it is possible the lifetime benefits could become more attractive or appropriate than the death benefit.

1. *Policy Performance*

(a) Annual Reviews

Annually, on the date of the policy's anniversary, insurers provide policy reports to policyholders. An annual report contains (1) the beginning and ending policy year values, including the surrender value; (2) the account or cash value; and (3) the death benefit. Transactions affecting any policy cash flows and values also are shown, including premium payments, withdrawals, loans, and loan interest due and paid. Dividends paid are shown for participating WL policies. For UL policies, annual reports show actual mortality charges assessed, assessed expense charges, and interest credited to account values during the policy year. Relevant interest crediting rates also typically are shown. For variable policies, the report also shows policy value detail by fund or account.

Annual reviews consist of comparing the current policy values and elements against those illustrated in the previous policy illustration. The previous illustration may be the one provided at the time the policy was sold—called *as-sold illustrations* in industry jargon—or an updated illustration (i.e., *in-force illustration*) at some later period. The objective of the comparison is to determine whether the policy remains on track to meet the policyholder's insurance goals.

The annual review should reveal whether values are sufficient or insufficient to meet the client's objectives. In the case of WL policies, performance generally will depend on whether dividends are being paid as projected, particularly where dividends are used to enhance the policy cash value or death benefit. In the case of UL policies, performance generally will depend on whether the interest crediting rate and planned future premiums appear to be sufficient to maintain coverage in the amount and for the term required.

When the policy values reflect underperformance, the policy owner can (1) make additional premium payments on UL policies and WL policies where dividends have been used to reduce premium outlays; (2) reduce the future death benefit; or (3) replace the policy if the insured remains insurable and market alternatives are attractive. In some cases, the best course of action may be to do nothing, because (1) the insured may no longer be insurable, (2) the policy owner may be unable to make additional premium payments, or (3) the policy owner may prefer to continue to monitor the policy with an expectation the policy values will improve.

When policy values exceed what is necessary to maintain policy performance as was expected when the policy was originally acquired, the policy owner may consider (1) reducing future premium payments; (2) increasing future death benefits; or (3) taking withdrawals from the policy as discussed below. The policy owner also simply may make no changes if there is a reasonable expectation inflation or other factors will make an increased death benefit appropriate.

2. *Securing Lifetime Policy Benefits*

If the purpose of life insurance ownership no longer exists, the policy owner may wish to surrender the policy and receive the cash value. The procedure to surrender is simple. The policy owner simply completes the company's form, and the cash will be paid. In addition to a full surrender of the policy, other options include (1) partial surrenders, (2) policy loans, and (3) accelerated death benefits in the case of a living insured with a terminal illness. Care should be taken to account for the federal income tax treatment of each of these options, as generally discussed in the following subsection.

In addition to a full surrender of the policy, owners of UL policies can make withdrawals from the policy account value while either keeping the face amount constant or reduced. Policy owners of many WL policies can make a partial surrender of the cash value, which also will cause an automatic reduction in the death benefit.

Both UL and WL policies offer policy loan provisions allowing the owner to borrow a sum from the insurer based on the security of the policy cash value and death benefit. The interest rate generally will be variable, and can be paid in cash or paid through a loan. The amount of the loan will reduce the net death benefit.

PRACTICE NOTE

Excessive loan amounts, approaching the total cash value, can cause the mandatory surrender of a policy.

Accelerated death benefits (sometimes called "terminal illness coverage") provide that a specified maximum percentage, from 25 to 100 percent, of the policy's face amount can be paid if the insured is diagnosed as having a terminal illness, usually subject to a specified overall maximum payment, such as $250,000. Most insurance contract provisions require the insured to have a maximum of one year to live, unless state law mandates otherwise. The insurer requires satisfactory evidence the insured suffers from a terminal illness, including (1) certification by a physician, (2) hospital or nursing home records, and, possibly, (3) a medical examination (paid by the insurer).

(a) Federal Income Taxation of Lifetime Policy Benefits[19]

Surrenders, partial surrenders, and withdrawals generally are not included in the policy owner's taxable income unless exceeding the basis in the policy.[20] The excess is taxable as ordinary income.[21] The basis in the policy generally is the total of premiums paid, less dividends and prior withdrawals to the extent the dividends and prior withdrawals were excludable from federal gross income.[22] Accelerated death benefits may be treated federal income tax-free if certain requirements are met including certification by a physician stating the insured has an "illness or physical condition which can reasonably be expected to result in death in twenty-four months or less after the date of certification."[23]

NOTES

1.   Part I of this chapter is drawn substantially from *The Advisor's Guide to Life Insurance* by Harold D. Skipper and Wayne Tonning (Chicago: American Bar Association 2013) and *Life Insurance*, 15th edition by Harold Skipper, Kenneth Black, Jr., and Kenneth Black, III (Atlanta, GA: Lucretian, LLC 2015). *The Advisor's Guide* is published in cooperation with the Real Property, Trust and Estate Law Section of the American Bar Association and focuses specifically on practice matters of importance to client advisors. *Life Insurance* continues the discussion and broadens the range of topics with in-depth theoretical and practical analysis.

2.   *See* www.theamericancollege.edu.

3.   *See* www.cffp.edu.

4.   *See* https://national.societyoffsp.org.

5.   *See* www.ambest.com.

6.   *See* www.fitchratings.com.

7.   *See* www.moodys.com.

8.   *See* www.standardandpoors.com/ratings.

9.   www.ebixlife.com/vitalsigns/.

10.   The life insurance contract also must have a legal purpose. Accordingly, a life insurance contract is enforceable only if the beneficiary has an insurable interest. That is, the beneficiary must have a substantial economic interest in the continued life, health, or bodily safety of the insured person or a substantial interest engendered by love and affection.

11. *See* www.mib.com.

12. If the insured is alive, the policy *endows* at age 121 and the death benefit is paid. Before a recent life insurance regulatory change, the endowment age was ninety-five.

13. *Id.*

14. This "growth floor" is not available for an insured's variable universal life insurance account.

15. In contrast, theoretically unlimited gains may be available in the case of a variable universal life insurance policy.

16. Federal estate taxes may be due at the death of the surviving spouse resulting from the use of the marital deduction at the death of the predeceased spouse. *See* Chapter 1 (proper use of marital deduction allows for deferral, not elimination, of federal estate tax; calculations). To avoid inclusion of the life insurance in the gross estate for federal estate tax purposes, it is prudent to utilize an irrevocable life insurance trust (ILIT). *See* Part II of this chapter.

17. The formula, utilized in this example to determine present value, is:

$$\text{Present Value (PV)} = \text{P (Period Payment)}\left[\frac{1 - (1 + r(\text{rate per period})^{-n(\text{number of periods})}}{r(\text{rate per period})}\right].$$

Imputing the hypothetical numbers, the calculation is:

$$100,000\left[\frac{1 - (1 + 0.4)^{-04}}{.04}\right].$$

18. A full illustration would include additional scenarios and specificity.

19. If an insurance policy constitutes a modified endowment contract (MEC), these federal income tax consequences generally do not apply.

20. *See* I.R.C. § 72(e).

21. *See generally* Barr v. Comm'r, T.C. Memo 2009-250.

22. *See* I.R.C. § 72(e)(6).

23. *See* I.R.C. § 101(g)(4)(A). *See also* §§ 101(g)(1)(A), 101(g)(1)(B)(ii). *See also* subsection C.3. of Part II of this chapter (pertaining to amendments to I.R.C. § 101).

APPENDIX 4-A

Life Insurance Agent Questionnaire

Agents are expected to conduct themselves with fairness, competence, integrity, and diligence. Please respond to the following questions touching on each of these four areas.

Fairness

A. What is the justification for your recommendation regarding the:
   i. Amount of insurance?
   ii. Type of policy?
   iii. Policy funding technique?
   iv. Beneficiary?
   v. Policy ownership arrangement?
   vi. Insurance company?
B. Did you review multiple insurers and products, including policy performance comparisons? Which ones and why did you eliminate them?
C. With what life insurance companies do you place most of your business and why?
D. Are you free to place business with insurers not affiliated with your primary insurer? If not, explain why the client should be satisfied with your primary insurer.

Competence

A. What is your educational and professional background, including professional designations?
B. What do you consider your area of expertise?
C. For how many years have you worked full-time in the life insurance business, and for how many years have you devoted most of your time in your area of expertise?
D. What are the qualifications and experience of your support staff?
E. What continuing professional development activities have you undertaken in the past three years, including pursuit of any professional designations?
F. To what professional organizations do you belong? What positions have you occupied within them?

Integrity

    A.   Do you or your firm have a written and enforced confidentiality policy and accompanying guidelines? If so, please supply respective copies of the same.

    B.   Do you or your firm have a written and enforced ethics policy and accompanying guidelines? If so, please supply respective copies of the same.

    C.   Has any client ever sued you or registered any complaints against you with any professional society, government regulatory agency (including any state insurance department), or the Financial Industry Regulatory Authority (FINRA)? If so, explain the circumstances.

Diligence

    A.   What is your understanding of the client's financial needs, goals, and circumstances?

    B.   What is your policy regarding working with other professionals? With how many have you worked in the previous year and what is their expertise?

    C.   What is the platform/administrative "setup" on which you provide ongoing policy service and how do you monitor policy and insurer performance, including treatment of in-force policies and insurer financial strength?

    D.   Explain the source of any leverage you have with insurers in connection with policy negotiation and pricing and re-pricing.

    E.   What have been the first-year lapse rates on the business you have written in each of the preceding three years?

Adapted from Harold D. Skipper and Wayne Tonning, *The Advisor's Guide to Life Insurance* (Chicago; American Bar Association, 2013), Appendix 1.

APPENDIX 4-B

Compiled List of Sources*

BOOKS

Lawrence Brody et al., *Due Diligence of Trust-Owned Life Insurance* (ABA Real Property, Probate and Trust Law Section 2018).

Harold Skipper & Wayne Tonning, *The Advisor's Guide to Life Insurance* (ABA Real Property, Probate and Trust Law Section 2013).

Harold Skipper, Kenneth Black, Jr., & Kenneth Black, III, *Life Insurance,* 15th ed. (Atlanta, GA: Lucretian, LLC 2015).

WEBSITES

General, History

- The Insurance Forum, www.theinsuranceforum.com/pages/bi0413.html

Professional designations

- The American College, www.theamericancollege.edu
- College for Financial Planning, www.cffp.edu
- Society of Financial Service Professionals, https://national.societyoffsp.org

Licensing and sources of information about agents and brokers

- Financial Industry Regulatory Authority, www.finra.org
- State insurance department websites (e.g., www.dfs.ny.gov/insurance/dfs_insurance.htm)

---

*This list is not exhaustive.

Rating agencies and Comdex scores

- Best, www.ambest.com
- Comdex scores, www.ebixlife.com/vitalsigns
- Fitch, www.fitchratings.com
- Moody's, www.moodys.com
- Standard and Poor's, www.standardandpoors.com/ratings

Underwriting

- Medical Information Bureau, www.mib.com

PART II: SELECTED ISSUES IN LIFE INSURANCE PLANNING AND COMPLIANCE

Originally prepared by Jon J. Gallo

A. Federal Estate Taxation of Life Insurance

1. *"Incidents of Ownership"*

Parents with large estates may acquire life insurance to protect their minor children without taking into account the federal estate tax laws.[1] If the life insurance policy is owned by a parent and payable for the benefit of the minor, the proceeds may be subject to federal estate tax when the insured parent passes away. Insurance on the life of the insured is includable in the insured's gross estate for federal estate tax purposes if the insured either possessed any "incidents of ownership" or if the proceeds are payable to or for the benefit of the insured's estate.[2] "Incidents of ownership" pertain to the insured or the estate's rights to the economic benefits from the policy, including but not limited to, the power (1) to change the beneficiary, (2) to surrender or cancel the policy, (3) to assign the policy, (4) to revoke an assignment, (5) to pledge the policy for a loan, and/or (6) to obtain from the insurer a loan against the policy's surrender value.[3] It does not matter whether the insured owned the policy individually or in a fiduciary capacity. Accordingly, if insurance is held by a custodian under the Uniform Transfers to Minors Act, the insured should not serve as the custodian to avoid retaining "incidents of ownership" in the transferred policy.[4] Likewise, the insured should avoid serving as trustee of an irrevocable trust in which the insured transferred the insurance policy.[5]

(a) Power to Remove and Replace the Trustee

An irrevocable trust for children is the preferred means of owning life insurance. If insurance is owned by an irrevocable trust and the parent is informed that he or she cannot serve as trustee, the parent typically will want to retain the right to change the trustee. In 1979, the Internal Revenue Service (IRS), in Revenue Ruling 79-353,[6] determined that the grantor's retention of the right to remove a corporate trustee of an irrevocable trust and appoint another corporate trustee without cause would result in federal gross estate inclusion under sections 2036 and 2038 of the Internal Revenue Code (Code).[7] Later, in Technical Advice Memorandum 8922003, the IRS, maintaining "the rationale" of Revenue Ruling 79-353 to be pertinent, determined that a decedent's retention of the power to replace a trustee (with someone other than himself) was tantamount to a decedent's "reservation of a trustee's powers to exercise the incidents of ownership" in an insurance policy held by a trustee.[8] However, in *Estate of Wall v. Commissioner*,[9] the U.S. Tax Court refused to follow Revenue Ruling 79-353.[10] In response to *Estate of Wall*, the IRS released Revenue Ruling 95-58,[11] which revoked Revenue Rulings 79-353[12] and 81-51[13] and modified Revenue Ruling 77-182.[14] In so doing, the IRS determined that a grantor did not retain discretionary control over trust income despite the grantor's power to remove the trustee and appoint an individual or corporate *successor* trustee that was not related or subordinate to the grantor (within the meaning of Code section 672(c)).[15] It should be noted that the successor trustee was named in the trust document and not a new replacement. *General* takeaways that may be gleaned from later IRS rulings applying Revenue Ruling 95-58 include:

- A grantor may have the power to remove and appoint an individual or corporate *successor* trustee that is *not* related or subordinate to the decedent (within the meaning of Code section 672(c)) without triggering federal gross estate inclusion under Code sections 2036 and 2038.[16]
- A beneficiary may have the power to remove and replace a corporate trustee so long as the trustee appointed by the beneficiary is *not* related or subordinate to the beneficiary (within the meaning of Code section 672(c)), without causing federal gross estate inclusion under Code section 2041 for the estate of the beneficiary.[17]
- A grantor's power to remove a trustee *for cause* and replace the trustee with someone *other than the grantor or insured* may *not* trigger federal estate inclusion under Code section 2042.[18]

Of course, in each of the foregoing instances, the initial, successor, and replacement trustee should *not* be the grantor or insured.

2. Three-Year Rule

Life insurance is one of the few areas where the three-year rule of Code section 2053 may apply.[19] Life insurance proceeds may be includable in the insured's gross estate for federal estate tax purposes if any incident of ownership actually is transferred by the insured by gift within three years of his or her death.[20] Thus, the insured must survive the transfer of an existing life insurance policy to an irrevocable life insurance trust by at least three years to avoid inclusion of the policy in his or her federal gross estate. If the insurance trust or other transferee thereafter pays any of the premiums, includability is limited to that portion of the insurance proceeds equal to the ratio of premiums paid by the insured to total premiums paid.[21]

PRACTICE NOTE

For each policy identified on the federal estate tax return, IRS Form 712 (Life Insurance Statement) must be filed with the return.[22] According to the form's instructions, "[t]he statement must be made, on behalf of the insurance company that issued the policy, by the officer of the company having access to the records of the company."[23] Two of the inquiries requiring a response on Form 712 are:

- whether there were any transfers of the policy within the three years before the death of the decedent and, if so,
- the date (including month, day, and year) of the assignment or transfer.

B. Federal Gift Taxation of Life Insurance

Generally, the transfer of all ownership rights in a life insurance policy to a third party, including an insurance trust, is a taxable gift measured by the fair market value (i.e., replacement value) of the policy at date of gift.[24] If the policy is term insurance, apparently the gift is measured by the unused portion of the premium.[25] Under Regulation section 25.2512-6, if the policy is a whole life policy in existence for some time and further premiums are to be paid, the value of the gift is the interpolated terminal reserve (which is similar to but not exactly the same as the cash surrender value of the policy) at the time of the gift, plus the unused portion of the last premium and dividend accumulations, less outstanding policy loans.[26] For a newly purchased policy, the fair market value is its cost (e.g., the premiums actually paid).[27] If the insured is uninsurable at the time of the transfer, the fair market value (i.e., replacement value) of the policy may be substantially higher than the amount computed pursuant to Regulation § 25.2512-6(a).[28] Under these conditions, a facts-and-circumstances test is employed. For example, in *Estate of Pritchard v. Commissioner*,[29] the decedent assigned insurance policies upon his life to his wife for their cash surrender value one month before he died of cancer. The estate argued that the policies had been transferred for full and adequate consideration and hence were not included in the decedent's gross estate for federal estate tax purposes. In rejecting the estate's argument, the U.S. Tax Court found that, based upon the special facts of the case, including the imminence of the insured's death and uninsurability of the insured at time of transfers, the cash surrender value of a fully paid-up policy "was wholly inadequate as a measure of [the policies'] worth at the time of the transfers" and replacement cost "would be only helpful as a criterion of the minimum value to be placed on the policies."[30] Instead, the court accepted the face amount of the policies as better reflecting the value of the policies near the insured's date of death.

PRACTICE NOTE

The latest amendments to Regulation section 25.2512-6 date back to 1974, when the types of life insurance primarily were term or whole life.[31] Consequently, the regulation may not provide sufficient guidance in valuing current products, and one is left with a facts-and-circumstance approach in valuing ever-changing insurance products.[32]

A gift of a present interest in property is eligible for the annual exclusion under Code section 2503(b).[33] According to Treasury Regulations, a present interest in property is "an unrestricted right to the immediate use, possession, or enjoyment of property or the income from property."[34] An outright gift of an insurance policy to an individual is a gift of a present interest. Whether a transfer of an insurance policy to a trust is a gift of a present interest generally depends on the terms of the trust and the current rights allowed under the transferred policy. To illustrate, example 2 of Regulation section 25.2503-3(c) provides:

> C transfers certain insurance policies on his life to a trust created for the benefit of D. Upon C's death, the proceeds of the policies are to be invested and the net income therefrom paid to D during his lifetime. Since the income payments to D will not begin until after C's death[,] the transfer in trust represents a gift of a future interest in property against which no exclusion is allowable.

In addition, if a trust provides for discretionary payments of income and/ or principal, the transfer to the trust may constitute a gift of a future interest in property unless Crummey demand powers are implemented properly, as discussed in Chapter 3. In contrast, if the trust document provides that all of the trust income is to be paid to a beneficiary for life; the trust document further precludes accumulation of trust income; and the life insurance policy allows for dividends, the transfer of the policy to the trust may constitute a gift of a present interest.[35]

C. The Irrevocable Life Insurance Trust

1. General

Proper ownership of the insurance policy is vital if the proceeds are to avoid federal estate taxation at the parent's death. In addition, there are drawbacks to having insurance proceeds paid outright to a child:

- Doing so may be inconsistent with the best interests of the child because the child may be a minor or an individual lacking in financial sophistication and unable to invest the proceeds wisely. If the child is a minor, a guardianship or custodianship will be necessary to administer the insurance proceeds during minority.[36] Of course, if a guardianship would be necessary for other assets, this is not a major issue.
- The insurance proceeds may be subject to the claims of the child's creditors and, depending on state law, possibly to the claims of an ex-spouse.

The federal tax-favored solution to these drawbacks is usually an irrevocable life insurance trust. An irrevocable life insurance trust is both the owner and beneficiary of one or more life insurance policies. Upon the death of the parent/insured, the trustee invests the insurance proceeds and administers the trust for the children.

PRACTICE NOTE

An irrevocable life insurance trust also may provide for the proceeds to be held for the benefit of the insured's spouse for his or her life and then paid to the children immediately after the insured's spouse's death or until the children reach a specific age.

If the insured transfers an existing policy to the insurance trust, the insurance will be removed from the insured's gross estate for federal estate tax purposes *only if* the insured survives the date of the transfer by not less than three years.[37] If the insured dies within this three-year period, the transfer will be ignored and the proceeds will be included in the insured's gross estate. If possible, one should avoid transferring existing insurance to an insurance trust. It is preferable that the trustee of the insurance trust be the original applicant and owner of the insurance in order to create a paper trail.

PRACTICE NOTE

If the insured's spouse is also a beneficiary of the trust, it may be prudent to include a back-up marital trust, qualifying for the marital deduction, so that, if the insurance proceeds are includable in the insured's gross estate pursuant to the three-year rule under Code section 2035, a marital deduction can be taken, reducing the value of the insured's gross estate for federal estate tax purposes at the insured's death and allowing for deferral of federal estate taxation until the death of the insured's spouse.[38]

Insurance trusts may be *funded* or *nonfunded*. A funded life insurance trust owns both one or more insurance contracts and income-producing assets. The income from the assets is used to pay some or all of the premiums. Funded insurance trusts may not be commonly used for two reasons: (i) the additional federal gift tax cost of transferring income-producing assets to the trust, not qualifying for the annual exclusion,[39] may be cost-prohibitive, and (ii) the grantor trust rule of Code section 677(a)(3) causes the grantor to be taxed on the trust's income. Customarily, unfunded insurance trusts own one or more policies of insurance and are funded by annual gifts from the grantor. To qualify these gifts for the annual exclusion under Code section 2503(b), the trust document allows for implementation of Crummey powers, as discussed in Chapter 3.

PRACTICE NOTE

To avoid discontinuation of funding the trust during a grantor's possible incapacity, the grantor may want to expressly allow his agent or attorney-in-fact under a durable power of attorney to make gifts to the trust.[40]

To provide the estate with liquidity at the death of the insured and, at the same time, shield the insurance proceeds from federal estate tax, the trust document customarily provides for the trustee to be authorized, but *not required*, to either purchase assets from or loan insurance proceeds to the insured's estate. If the trustee is required to make these purchases or loans, the death benefit may be includable in the insured's gross estate under Code section 2042.[41] Especially given the flux of the federal transfer tax, the insurance trust instrument, although irrevocable, also should include provisions allowing for flexibility. These provisions may include the power of an independent trustee to terminate the trust and distribute trust assets to the beneficiaries or to a new trust. The trust document, however, should prohibit exercise of the termination power during the exercise of a Crummey power or its lapse.[42]

2. Purchasing a Life Insurance Policy

If new insurance will be owned by the insurance trust, the trust should be established *before* the original application is submitted to the carrier, and the trustee should be the original applicant. If at all possible, selection of the policy and related discussions with the insurance agent should be conducted by the trustee without the involvement of the insured/settlor, whose involvement should be limited to executing the trust, executing the insurance application, and funding the trust. The trust should give the trustee broad investment discretion and should *not require* the purchase of insurance on the settlor's life. However, the trustee should be given the authority to purchase life insurance and exercise all incidents of ownership. Some commentators believe that it is preferable that the term "insurance trust" not be used in the trust's title.

As discussed earlier and in contrast to the purchase of a policy by an independent trustee,[43] the transfer of an existing insurance policy to an insurance trust is treated as a gift to the beneficiaries of the trust.[44] Transfers, including transfers of cash, to an insurance trust usually are made to qualify for the federal gift tax annual exclusion through the use of a Crummey demand clause, which is discussed in Chapter 3.[45] A transfer also will result in taxable income to the owner if the insurance policy is subject to a loan in excess of basis.[46]

PRACTICE NOTE

If a transfer to the trust exceeds the amount eligible for the annual exclusion under Code section 2503(b) or the grantor wants to elect gift splitting with his or spouse,[47] the grantor must file Form 709, United States Gift (and Generation-Skipping Transfer) Tax Return along with a Form 712.[48] The grantor also will want to file Form 709 to make an allocation or an election out of an automatic allocation, as the circumstances require, of his or her federal generation-skipping transfer tax (GST) exemption (as discussed in subsection C.4. of Part II of this chapter).[49]

3. Transferring an Existing Policy

Sometimes it is simply impractical for an insurance trust to acquire new insurance on a parent's life. The parent may be uninsurable or the cost of new insurance may be too high.[50] In either case, there is no alternative but to transfer existing insurance policies to the insurance trust. Specific provisions of Code section 101(a) may offer a means of avoiding the three-year rule of Code section 2035 when an existing insurance policy is transferred to a grantor trust. Code section 101(a)(2) establishes what is commonly known as the "transfer-for-value" rule, which is intended to deter speculation on people's lives through buying and selling insurance policies. The transfer-for-value rule provides that, if the owner of a life insurance policy purchased the policy from an earlier owner, the entire insurance proceeds are no longer exempt from federal income tax at the death of the insured.[51] Instead, the proceeds (excluding the sum of (1) the actual consideration paid for the policy and (2) the premiums or other amounts paid by the transferee after the transfer) may be taxable income to the new owner.[52]

Exceptions to the transfer-for-value rule may be used to avoid the three-year rule when transferring an existing insurance policy to a grantor trust. Under Code section 102(a)(2)(B), the transfer-for-value rule does not apply if the new owner acquired the policy through a transaction in which the new owner retains the transferor's income tax basis in the policy.[53] If the insurance trust is structured as a grantor trust under Code sections 674–678 so that the insured is treated as the owner of the trust for federal income tax purposes, a sale to the trust by the insured of a policy on his or her life for fair market value not only removes the transaction from the three-year rule, but also takes advantage of the transfer-for-value rule exception under Code section 101(a)(2)(B) for federal income tax purposes. On a number of occasions, the IRS has determined that the settlor of an insurance trust that *authorizes, but not requires* the trustee to use income realized by the trust to pay premiums is the owner of the entire trust for purposes of Code section 677(a)(3).[54]

The transfer-for-value rule also can be used when the terms of an existing insurance trust are no longer acceptable to a client. The transfer-for-value rule does not apply if the party acquiring the insurance policy is the insured.[55] Suppose a client created an insurance trust for his minor children and has now decided that the terms of the trust are no longer appropriate. One alternative would be for the client to purchase the policy from the existing insurance trust for fair market value and transfer it to a new insurance trust with acceptable terms. Because the insured purchased the policy, the transfer-for-value rule does not apply, although the three-year period of Code section 2035 will begin to run with respect to the transfer to the new insurance trust. A better alternative would be for the client to establish a new irrevocable insurance trust that also is a grantor trust under Code section 677(a)(3) and make a gift of cash to the new trust sufficient to allow it to purchase the insurance policy from the existing trust. Since the insured is the owner of the new insurance trust under the grantor trust rules, the insured is treated as acquiring the policy, and the transfer-for-value exception under Code section 101(a)(2)(A) will apply.[56] In addition, the policy, acquired for full value, is not a gift, making the three-year rule of Code section 2035 inapplicable.

<u>PRACTICE NOTE</u>

> When a change in trust ownership of a policy is contemplated, the trustee of the new insurance trust immediately should change the beneficiary of the policy from the trustee of the existing trust to the trustee of the new trust.[57]

Clients need not transfer the policy back to a trust. Under Code section 101(a)(2)(B), the transfer-for-value rule also does not apply if the party acquiring the insurance policy is a partner of the insured, a partnership in which the insured is a partner, or a corporation in which the insured is a shareholder or officer.[58] Thus, the sale of life insurance policies owned by the trustee of a grantor trust to a limited partnership in which the insured is a limited partner may fall within the exception to the transfer-for-value rule under Code section 101(a)(2)(B).[59]

2017 Tax Cuts and Jobs Act: New Code section 101(a)(3)[60] may warrant consideration when reviewing the federal income tax consequences associated with the foregoing suggested strategies. In addition, the information reporting requirements under new Code section 6050Y,[61] if applicable, may be an additional factor in deciding whether to engage in these strategies.

Pursuant to new Code section 101(a)(3), the exceptions contained in Code section 101(a)(2) (i.e., Code sections 101(a)(2)(A) and (B)) do *not* apply in the case of a "reportable policy sale" occurring after December 31, 2017. "[T]he term 'reportable policy sale' means the acquisition of an interest in a life insurance contract directly or indirectly, if the acquirer has no substantial family, business, or financial relationship with the insured apart from the acquirer's interest in such life insurance contract." "For purposes of the preceding sentence, the term 'indirectly' applies to the acquisition of an interest in a partnership, trust, or other entity that holds an interest in the life insurance contract."

According to Notice 2018-14,[62] the IRS and the U.S. Department of the Treasury expect to propose amendments to Regulation section 1.101-1 to reflect the addition of new Code section 101(a)(3). The definition of "reportable policy sale" will be addressed further in proposed regulations under new Code section 6050Y. The term will include viatical settlements.[63]

Effective for "reportable policy sales" occurring after December 31, 2017, and for reportable death benefits paid after December 31, 2017,[64] new Code section 6050Y requires information reporting:

- on the acquirer and the issuer in the case of the acquisition (or notice of the acquisition) of an existing life insurance contract in a 'reportable policy sale,' and
- on each person who makes a payment (the 'payor') of reportable death benefits.[65]

The IRS and the U.S. Department of the Treasury expect to issue proposed regulations clarifying "which parties are subject to the reporting requirements and other definitional issues," as explained in Notice 2018-41.[66] IRS forms and instructions ultimately will be available.

4. Generation-Skipping Transfer Trust

Insurance trusts frequently are drafted to take advantage of the settlor's exemption from the federal generation-skipping transfer (GST) tax and, therefore, shield the insurance proceeds from federal estate taxation at the death of the beneficiaries of the insurance trust.

The GST tax imposes a tax on outright gifts and transfers in trust to or for beneficiaries two or more generations younger than the donor, such as grandchildren. The GST tax will be imposed if the transfer avoids incurring a gift or estate tax at each generation level. Each transferor is allowed an exemption from the GST tax.[67] For 2018, the exemption is $11.18 million, the same amount as the currently unified federal gift and estate tax basic exclusion amount.[68] The GST exemption may be applied against lifetime gifts or against transfers at death.[69] Transfers covered by the federal gift tax annual exclusion normally are exempt from the GST tax.[70] In the case of federal gift tax annual exclusions obtained through the use of Crummey powers, however, the annual exclusion transfer is GST tax exempt only if (1) during the beneficiary's lifetime, distributions may not be made to anyone, but the particular beneficiary; and (2) the trust assets will be included in the beneficiary's estate if the beneficiary dies before termination of the trust.[71] In a nutshell, this limitation requires that no person other than the particular power holder has an interest in that particular power holder's share of the trust. This is not the case in a typical irrevocable life insurance trust; thus, annual exclusion transfers to an irrevocable life insurance trust will be subject to GST tax requiring allocation of GST exemption.

A life insurance trust may be drafted to take advantage of the settlor's GST tax exemption. A typical example of a GST insurance trust is one providing that the insurance proceeds are to be invested and the net income therefrom is to be paid to the insured's children for their lives. Upon the death of the last of the insured's children to die, the principal of the trust is either retained in further trust for the insured's grandchildren or distributed to them outright. Under the Economic Growth and Tax Reconciliation Relief Act of 2001[72] (EGTRRA) definition, the foregoing trust constitutes a GST trust, allowing for automatic allocation of GST exemption to transfers to the trust unless a properly filed Form 709, United States Gift (and Generation-Skipping Transfer) Tax Return, indicates an election to opt out of the automatic allocation.[73]

The irrevocable life insurance trust is an extremely efficient means of leveraging the GST tax exemption. If all transfers to an irrevocable insurance trust are exempt from the GST tax through use of the settlor's or transferor's GST tax exemption, the trust will be wholly removed from the federal GST tax system. Since the trust itself would be exempt, proceeds of insurance attributable to policies owned by the trust also would be removed from the federal GST tax system.

Generation-skipping life insurance trusts customarily have the following characteristics:

- The child receives income in the discretion of the third-party trustee during minority. Typically, adult children receive the net income from the trust. In addition, the child may utilize principal if needed to provide for the child's health needs and support.

- Upon the child's death, the trust is either distributed outright to the child's children or retained in further trust for the child's children until they reach a designated age(s). The trust documents also may provide for a *limited testamentary power of appointment*, exercisable by the child *only* after his or her death. By virtue of this limited power, the child could adjust certain trust provisions. For example, the limited power could allow the child to name his or her spouse as a successor income beneficiary of the trust; change the ages at which principal will be distributed to the child's children; or change the proportions in which the trust will be distributed.[74]

Utilizing the GST tax exemption in this manner offers two important advantages:

- Any appreciation in the value of the assets owned by the generation-skipping trust will escape all transfer taxes when the children die and will instead pass tax free to the grandchildren.

- The assets of the irrevocable trust generally will be protected from the claims of creditors and, to some degree, from claims of ex-spouses. For example, if the trust property is left to the children via the insured's will, the property, depending on state law, will be subject to these claims.

5. *Frequently Asked Questions*

(1) Who should be the trustee?
A third party other than the insured must serve as trustee. If the insured serves as a trustee of the insurance trust, the insured will be deemed to possess "incidents of ownership" in the policy.[75] The insured may retain the authority to remove the third-party trustee and appoint a successor individual or corporate trustee provided that the successor is *not* related or subordinate to the insured within the meaning of Code section 672(c).

(2) Who should not be the trustee?
For federal estate tax purposes, the insured should *not* be the trustee. If the life insurance trust includes second-to-die life insurance, neither the insured nor the spouse of the insured should be a trustee. As a general matter, anyone who has contributed to the trust should not be the trustee because of possible federal estate tax inclusion under Code sections 2036 and 2038.[76] In fact, the trust instrument expressly may prohibit the appointment of those persons as follows:

> **Notwithstanding any provision of this trust instrument, the grantor, donor or insured are ineligible to serve as trustee or co-trustee hereunder.**[77]

(3) Should the beneficiary of the trust be appointed trustee or co-trustee? Generally, the sole current beneficiary of the life insurance trust should not be designated as the sole trustee. For federal estate tax purposes, the beneficiary of the trust should not serve as co-trustee if:

- the beneficiary contributed property to the trust,
- the beneficiary is an insured under any life insurance policy owned by the trust,
- state law or the trust instrument provides that the beneficiary has the discretionary power to sprinkle income or principal among the trust beneficiaries. (Along with the federal estate tax consequences under Code section 2041,[78] this power also may cause federal gift tax consequences for the trustee/beneficiary if he or she exercises the power in favor of another beneficiary and the trustee/beneficiary, for example, has a remainder interest in the trust.[79] Accordingly, the trust instrument must be drafted to prohibit the trustee/beneficiary's participation in the power, or the discretionary power must be limited by an ascertainable standard.[80])

(4) Should the insured have the power to change the trustee?
The insured should have the power to remove and replace the trustee in order to provide flexibility. However, for federal estate tax purposes, the drafter of the trust document must tailor the power to satisfy certain IRS requirements. For example, the insured may have the power to remove the trustee and replace the trustee with a successor trustee if the trustee appointed by the insured is *not* related or subordinate to the insured (within the meaning of Code section 672(c)).

(5) Who should be named the owner and beneficiary of the policy in the trust document?
The trustee of the insurance trust should be named as the owner and beneficiary of the policy. The following example illustrates the proper designation. Note the trustee is designated instead of merely the trust.

EXAMPLE 1

John Smith is serving as trustee of the Jones Irrevocable Trust of 2004. The beneficiary of the trust is Mary Jones, a minor child. John Smith is applying for insurance on the life of Mary's father, Fred Jones. The proper owner and beneficiary of the policy is "John Smith, as Trustee of the Jones Irrevocable Trust of 2004." Mary Jones should not be named as the beneficiary, since doing so would result in payment of the death benefit directly to her, bypassing the insurance trust.

(6) Who should purchase the life insurance policy?
The trustee should purchase the life insurance policy. In completing the life insurance contract application, the trustee (not the insured) should be identified as the owner and the beneficiary of the life insurance policy. These precautions are to avoid the three-year rule of Code section 2035.

(7) How should the trust document provide for estate liquidity?

To provide estate liquidity and yet prevent inclusion in the grantor's federal gross estate, the trust document must permit, but *not require*, the trustee to purchase assets, at fair market value, from the grantor's estate or to make loans, for adequate consideration, to the grantor's estate. Allowing for estate liquidity is especially helpful if federal estate tax is due at the death of the grantor. Note the trustee is not the grantor.

NOTES

1.   Note the federal transfer tax system is in flux. For example, the exemption of $10 million, indexed for inflation ($11.18 million for calendar year 2018), will revert to $5 million, indexed for inflation, after December 31, 2025. *See* Chapter 1. The inflation adjustment is based upon the chained consumer price index. *See id. See also* Jonathan Curry, *Life Insurance's Role in Estate Tax Planning Now in Flux*, 159 TAX NOTES 231 (Apr. 9, 2018) (commentator believes "clients should continue to treat their insurance policy as insuring against pre-[Tax Cuts and Jobs Act] estate tax exemption amount").

2.   *See* § 2042. *See also* Reg. § 20.2042-1. Section references are to the Internal Revenue Code of 1986, as amended, or to regulations issued thereunder, unless otherwise indicated.

3.   Reg. § 20.2042-1(c)(2). "Incidents of ownership," however, do not include the right, upon termination of employment, to convert the insured's group term life insurance policy to an individual policy when no evidence of insurability is required. *See* Snead v. Comm'r, 78 T.C. 43 (1982), *acq.*, 1984-2 C.B. 194; Rev. Rul. 84-130, 1984-2 C.B. 194 (modifying in part Rev. Rul. 69-64, 1969-1 C.B. 221).

4.   *See* Chapters 3 and 9.

5.   *See* Reg. § 20.2042-1(c)(4); Rose v. United States, 511 F.2d 259 (5th Cir. 1975); Estate of Fruehauf, 50 T.C. 915 (1968), *aff'd*, 427 F.2d 80 (6th Cir. 1970); Estate of Skifter v. Comm'r, 468 F.2d 699 (2d Cir. 1972).

6.   1979-2 C.B. 325 (as modified by Rev. Rul. 81-51, 1981-1 C.B. 458).

7.   *See* Rev. Rul. 79-353 (decided under Code sections 2036(a)(2) and 2038(a)(1)), *supra* note 6. *See also* Chapter 1 (explaining operation of Code sections 2036 and 2038).

8.   *See* TAM 8922003 (decided in favor of the taxpayer on other grounds). *But see* § 6110(b)(1)(A), 6110(k)(3) (unless otherwise established by regulation, technical advice memorandum cannot be used or cited as precedent).

9.   101 T.C. 300 (1993).

10.   *See* note 6.

11.   1995-2 C.B. 191.

12.   *See* note 6.

13.   1981-1 C.B. 458.

14.   1977-1 C.B. 273.

15.   Revenue Ruling 95-58 also was in response to *Estate of Vak v. Comm'r*, 973 F.2d 1409 (8th Cir. 1992, *rev'g* T.C. Memo 1991-503).

16.   Revenue Ruling 95-58, *supra* note 15, and accompanying text.

17.   *See* PLR 9607008 (no general power of appointment over trust income and principal by virtue of beneficiary's power to remove and replace corporate trustee).

But see § 6110(b)(1)(A), 6110(k)(3) (unless otherwise established by regulation, ruling cannot be used or cited as precedent).

18. *See* PLR 9832039 (retention of right to remove trustee for cause is not incident of ownership). *But see* § 6110(b)(1)(A), 6110(k)(3) (unless otherwise established by regulation, ruling cannot be used or cited as precedent). *See also* Sebastian V. Grassi, Jr., *Drafting a Flexible Irrevocable Life Insurance Trust*, 31 ACTEC J. 208, 215 (2005) (referencing PLR 9832039 and PLR 9607008).

19. *See* § 2035. *See also* Chapter 1.

20. *See* § 2035(a), (d).

21. Estate of Silverman v. Comm'r, 61 T.C. 338 (1973), *aff'd*, 521 F.2d 574 (2d Cir. 1975); TAM 9128008. *But see* § 6110(b)(1)(A), 6110(k)(3) (unless otherwise established by regulation, technical advice memorandum cannot be used or cited as precedent).

22. Forms and instructions are available on the IRS website, www.irs.gov.

23. *See* Form 712, Life Insurance Statement (rev. Apr. 2006) at 3. *See also* Reg. § 20.6018-4(d) ("For every policy of life insurance listed on the [federal estate tax] return, the executor must procure a statement on Form 712 by the company issuing the policy and file it with the return.")

24. *See* Reg. § 25.2512-1. *See also* Guggenheim v. Rasquin, 312 U.S. 254 (1941).

25. *See generally* Reg. § 25.2512-6(a).

26. *See id.*

27. Reg. § 25.2512-6(a), Example (1).

28. *See* United States v. Ryerson, 312 U.S. 260 (1941).

29. 4 T.C. 204 (1944).

30. *Id.* at 208.

31. *See* T.D. 6334, 23 F.R. 8904, Nov. 15, 1958 (as amended by T.D. 6542, 26 F.R. 549, Jan. 20, 1961). Revised by T.D. 6680, 28 F.R. 10872, Oct. 10, 1963 (as amended by T.D. 7319, 39 F.R. 26723, July 23, 1974). *See also* Richard L. Harris, *Life Insurance Policy Valuation*: Schwab v. Commissioner—*Common Sense Prevails* at 1, https://www.americanbar.org/content/dam/aba/publishing/rpte_ereport/2014/June/te_alert.authcheckdam.pdf.

32. *See* Harris, *supra* note 31 (referencing Schwab v. Comm'r., 136 T.C. 120 (2011), *aff'd*, 715 F.3d 1169 (2013)).

33. *See also* Rev. Rul. 76-490, 1976-2 C.B. 300 (monthly premium payments by employer are indirect gifts of present interests by the insured employee where group term policy was irrevocably assigned to trust by insured employee). *But see* Rev. Rul. 79-47, 1979-1 C.B. 312 (monthly premium payments by employer are gifts of future interests where the trustee, holding the irrevocably assigned group term policy, was required to retain the insurance proceeds in trust after the insured's death and, thereafter, pay income to trust beneficiaries).

34. *See* Reg. § 25.2503-3(b).

35. *See* Tidemann v. Comm'r, 1 T.C. 968 (1943) (given the trustee has no authority to accumulate dividends, right to dividends with respect to insurance policy is a gift of a present interest to trust beneficiaries).

36. *See* Chapter 9 (explaining advantages and disadvantages of custodianships, guardianships, and trusts). *See also* Chapter 3.

37. *See* § 2035.

38. *See* Chapter 1, note 14 (regarding definitions of spouse and marriage for purposes of federal taxes).

39. *See* Chapters 1 and 3 (explaining operation of annual exclusion).

40. Sebastian V. Grassi Jr., *Drafting Life Insurance Trusts after the 2001 Tax Act*, 24 Mɪᴄʜ. Pʀᴏʙ. & Esᴛ. Pʟᴀɴ J. 22, 28 (2004) (referencing Estate of Casey v Comm'r, 948 F.2d 895 (4th Cir. 1991); Estate of Gaynor v Comm'r, T.C. Memo. 2001-206; TAM 9736004; TAM 9342003). *See also* Estate of Sylvia v. United States, 10 Fed. Appx. 833 (Fed. Cir. 2001); Estate of Pruitt v. Comm'r, T.C. Memo 2000-287.

41. Requiring the trustee to make purchases of estate assets or loans to the estate may be tantamount to the insurance proceeds being receivable by the executor. *See* Reg. § 20.2042-1(b). *See also* § 2042(1).

42. For this and other considerations and drafting tips, see Sebastian V. Grassi Jr., *Drafting a Flexible Irrevocable Life Insurance Trust*, 31 ACTEC J. 208 (2005).

43. *See* subsection C.5. (Frequently Asked Questions) of Part II of this chapter (discussing selection of trustee).

44. *See* subsection B of Part II of this chapter (discussing federal gift taxation of life insurance).

45. *See id.*

46. Simon v. Comm'r, 285 F.2d 422 (3rd Cir. 1961).

47. *See* note 38.

48. *See* Chapter 1 (explaining the annual exclusion and gift splitting). *See also* Chapter 1, note 49 (explaining reasons for filing federal gift tax return despite no formal requirement). Form 712 does not require specifically filing the form with a federal gift tax return, but instructions to Form 709 indicate otherwise. *See* 2018 Instructions for Form 709 at 10. Forms and instructions are available on the IRS website, www.irs.gov.

49. *See* section III of Chapter 3. *See also* section C.4. of Part II of this chapter.

50. The insured also may want to transfer an employer group term policy to the insurance trust. The "assignability of the policy must be permitted by state law and under the terms of the insurance certificate itself." Lawrence L. Bell, *Group Term Life Insurance Benefits: A Forgotten Planning Tool*, 7 J. Rᴇᴛɪʀᴇᴍᴇɴᴛ Pʟᴀɴ. 15, 15 (2004). An allowable, initial assignment of the policy triggers the three-year rule of Code section 2035. In contrast, the automatic annual renewal of a group term life insurance policy, not requiring proof of insurability, may not be treated as a new transfer of the policy and, therefore, may not trigger the three-year rule. *See* Rev. Rul. 82-13, 1982-1 C.B. 132.

51. Generally, life insurance proceeds, by reason of the insured's death, are exempt from federal income taxation. *See* § 101(a)(1).

52. *See* § 101(a)(2). *But see, e.g.*, § 101(a)(2)(A) (exception).

53. *See* § 101(a)(2)(A).

54. *See, e.g.,* PLR 8103074, PLR 8126047, PLR 8118051. *But see* § 6110(b)(1)(A), 6110(k)(3) (unless otherwise established by regulation, ruling cannot be used or cited as precedent).

55. *See* § 101(a)(2)(B).

56. *See* Rev. Rul. 2007-13, 2007-1 C.B. 684 (Feb. 16, 2007) (transfer to grantor trust is transfer to grantor within meaning of Code section 101(a)(2)(B) and, therefore, net proceeds from life insurance policies are excludable from gross income).

57. *See* Example 1 (providing example of naming trustee of specific trust), Q5 of subsection C.5. (Frequently Asked Questions) of Part II of this chapter.

58. § 101(a)(2)(B). *See, e.g.*, PLR 9843024. *But see* § 6110(b)(1)(A), 6110(k)(3) (unless otherwise established by regulation, ruling cannot be used or cited as

precedent). *See also* Sebastian V. Grassi, Jr., *Transfer for Value Rule and Life Insurance Proceeds*, 32 ACTEC J. 314 (2007).

59. *See generally* PLR 9843024 (with caveats). *See also* I.R.C. § 6110(b)(1)(A), 6110(k)(3) (unless otherwise established by regulation, ruling may not be used or cited as precedent). To date, the IRS will not issue determination letters for the questions: (1) "[w]hether there has been a transfer for value for purposes of [Code section] 101(a) in situations involving a grantor and a trust when (i) substantially all of the trust corpus consists or will consist of insurance policies on the life of the grantor or the grantor's spouse, (ii) the trustee or any other person has a power to apply the trust's income or corpus to the payment of premiums on policies of insurance on the life of the grantor or the grantor's spouse, (iii) the trustee or any other person has a power to use the trust's assets to make loans to the grantor's estate or to purchase assets from the grantor's estate, and (iv) there is a right or power in any person that would cause the grantor to be treated as the owner of all or a portion of the trust under [Code sections] 673 to 677" and (2) "[w]hether, in connection with the transfer of a life insurance policy to an unincorporated organization, (i) the organization will be treated as a partnership under [Code sections] 761 and 7701, or (ii) the transfer of the life insurance policy to the organization will be exempt from the transfer for value rules of [Code section] 101, when substantially all of the organization's assets consist or will consist of life insurance policies on the lives of the members." Rev. Proc. 2019-3, § 3.01(14) and (15), 2019-1 I.R.B. 130 (January 2, 2019).

60. An Act to provide for reconciliation pursuant to titles II and V of the concurrent resolution on the budget for fiscal year 2018, Pub. L. No. 115-97, § 13522, codified at § 101(a)(3) (Dec. 22, 2017), informally referred to as the Tax Cuts and Jobs Act.

61. *Id.* at § 13520, codified at § 6050Y.

62. Notice 2018-41, 2018-20 I.R.B. 584. Notice 2018-41 is available at https://www.irs.gov/pub/irs-drop/n-18-41.pdf.

63. Notice 2018-41, sec. 2.A. The term "reportable policy sale" is defined in Code section 6050Y(d)(2) by a cross-reference to new Code section 101(a)(3)(B).

64. Despite the statutory effective dates, Notice 2018-41 provides that reporting under Code section 6050Y will not be required until final regulations are issued. *See* Notice 2018-41, sec. 1 (cross-referencing sec. 3.A.iv.). In addition, "[f]or reportable policy sales and payments of reportable death benefits occurring after December 31, 2017, and before the date final regulations under [Code section] 6050Y are published in the Federal Register, the [U.S. Department of the] Treasury and the IRS intend to allow additional time after the date final regulations are published to file the [information] returns and furnish the written statements required by [Code section] 6050Y." Notice 2018-41, sec. 1.

65. *See* Notice 2081-41, *supra* note 62, sec 2.B.

66. *See id.*, sec 3.A.

67. § 2631(a).

68. § 2631(c) (cross-referencing § 2010(c)). *See also* Rev. Proc. 2018-18, 2018-10 I.R.B. 392, § 3.35. *See also* Chapter 1.

69. If a husband and wife, as defined under Regulation section 301.7701-18, elect gift split treatment, each may allocate his or her individual GST exemption to their respective one-half portion of the gift. *See generally* PLR 201811002; Reg. § 26.2632-1(b)(4)(iii), Example 5. *See also* Chapter 1 (describing general requirements for gift splitting and definition of husband and wife).

70. § 2642.

71. § 2642(c)(2).

72. Economic Growth and Tax Relief Reconciliation Act of 2001, Pub. L. No. 107-16 (June 7, 2001).

73. *See* Pub. L. No. 107-16 § 561(a), codified at I.R.C. § 2632(c)(1) and (3)(B). *See also* Reg. § 26.2632-1(b)(2). Forms and instructions are available on the IRS website, www.irs.gov.

74. Practitioners must assess the possible GST tax consequences of a limited power that allows for trust property to pass to the third generation along with assessing the availability of GST exemption. *See* subsection C.4. of Part II of this chapter.

75. *See* Reg. § 20.2042-1(c)(4). If the trust holds second-to-die insurance, it generally is not advisable for either of the two insured spouses to be trustee for federal estate tax purposes. *See* subsection F.3.(d) of Part I of this chapter (explaining second-to-die insurance policy).

76. *See* Chapter 1.

77. William S. Huff, *How to Draft the Irrevocable Life Insurance Trust*, 9 ALI-ABA COURSE MATERIALS J. 7, 49 (1984).

78. *See* Chapters 1 and 3.

79. *See generally* Reg. § 25.2511-1(g)(1) (transfer of beneficial interest is a gift).

80. *See* Chapters 1 and 3. *See also* Reg. § 25.2511-1(g)(2). *See also* Georgiana J. Slade, *Personal Life Insurance Trusts (Portfolio 807-2nd)*, BLOOMBERG, at A-73, https://www.bna.com/life-insurance-trusts-p2857/ (last visited Dec. 21, 2018).

CHAPTER 5

Approaches to Funding Education

Originally prepared by Aen Walker Webster,
Christopher P. Cline, and Laura A. Baek[1]

With rising tuition costs outpacing the rate of inflation, education expenses can claim an ever greater portion of net worth. Paying for the education of younger family members, therefore, is an increasingly popular way to benefit future generations while reducing the donor's potential federal estate tax liability at little or no federal gift tax cost.[2] Many options are available, and the best method for a particular client depends on the situation and individual needs of the client and client's family.

This chapter explores the various education funding options available to clients at various levels of income and wealth. The discussion is divided into three sections: (1) direct funding of the education costs by the donor, (2) gifts for the benefit of the student, and (3) payment of education costs by the student.[3]

I. DONOR DIRECTLY FUNDS EDUCATION COSTS

A. "Qualified Transfer" under Code Section 2503(e)

1. General

The most straightforward method of funding education costs is to make payments of tuition directly to the educational organization as the tuition comes due or through prepayment. Generally, payment of tuition directly to an "educational organization," as described in Internal Revenue Code[4]

(Code) section 170(b)(1)(A)(ii),[5] is a "qualified transfer"[6] under Code section 2503(e), not subject to federal gift taxation. Direct payment of tuition to the educational organization can be made on behalf of a family member or non-relative, regardless of relationship or age, and can be unlimited in amount. The tax advantage associated with Code section 2503(e), however, applies only to *tuition* paid directly to the educational organization. For example, it does not include payments made for room and board, books, transportation, and other fees. The term "educational organization," for purposes of Code section 2503(e), is not limited to a higher education institution, but can be a primary or secondary school as well.

2. *Federal Gift Tax and GST Tax Consequences*

Direct tuition payments to an "educational organization" are not transfers subject to federal gift taxation under Code section 2503(e) nor subject to the generation-skipping transfer (GST) tax under Code section 2642(c). As stated earlier, these tuition payments can be unlimited in amount and do not require a relationship between the donor and the student. Generation assignment is not a factor, as an excludable payment of tuition also is *not* treated as a transfer subject to the GST tax. Further, these direct payments do not reduce the donor's available annual exclusion under Code section 2503(b)[7] for the year of payment with respect to that particular student. For example, if the donor makes a qualified payment under Code section 2503(e), the donor also can make annual gifts to the student or to a life insurance trust for the benefit of the student, up to the donor's annual exclusion amount per donee.[8]

3. *Tuition Must Be Paid Directly to the Educational Organization*

As stated earlier, tuition payments may be made as they come due or, assuming certain requirements are met (as discussed in subsection I.B. of this chapter), may be prepaid. Either way, payment *must* be made directly to the educational organization, not to the student or a trust, to qualify under Code section 2503(e).

EXAMPLE

A transfers $100,000 to a trust, the provisions of which state that the funds must be used only for tuition incurred by A's grandchildren. A's transfer to the trust is not a direct transfer to an "educational organization" and, therefore, the transfer is not a "qualified transfer" under Code section 2503(e).[9]

Because the donor does not pay tuition directly to the educational organization, funds contributed to a state or institution-sponsored 529 plan (discussed in subsection I.D. of this chapter) or other prepaid tuition intermediary also will not constitute a qualified payment under Code section

2503(e). Making payments directly to the educational organization on a current basis, nonetheless, has some advantages. Because the funds are applied directly, the donor need not be concerned whether the student has unfettered control of or indirect access to the funds. In addition, except in the case of prepayments (discussed next), the donor generally does not have to worry about forfeiting amounts paid if the student dies, is expelled, or drops out. If the donor does not like how the student's education is progressing (or if an unforeseen event arises), the donor simply does not have to write the next check.

B. Prepayment of Tuition

1. General

Before choosing to make a prepayment of tuition, the donor must determine whether the student's chosen school has a prepayment program in place. Even if there is no formal program, many schools are willing to accept prepayments. Assuming the school is willing to adopt a prepayment plan or already has a plan in effect, this is an excellent way to remove large amounts of money from the donor's gross estate for federal estate tax purposes. In addition, the donor can lock in current tuition prices and can make large tuition payments while hedging the risk that the donor will die before the student graduates.

2. Prepaid Tuition Must Be Nonrefundable and Subject to Forfeiture

In a 1999 Technical Advice Memorandum, the Internal Revenue Service (IRS) concluded that prepaid tuition constitutes a "qualified transfer" under Code section 2503(e) if the prepayment arrangement: (1) does not allow a refund *and* (2) provides for the donor's forfeiture of payments if the student ceases to attend the school.[10] Based on the ruling, it appears that a donor may not credit the unused portion of the prepaid tuition to a sibling attending the same school. As will be shown later, this lack of transferability is in contrast to the transferability of the beneficiary's interest in 529 plans.

PRACTICE NOTE

Before recommending the prepayment method to a client, practitioners should advise the client of the consequences of the prepayment plan in the event the student, for example, may (1) transfer to a different school, (2) be expelled, (3) die, or (4) become incapacitated. Some education organizations permit application of the unused funds to tuition of a relative. In most cases, however, surplus prepayments are forfeited. In any event, the 1999 Technical Advice Memorandum[11] suggests that application of the unused prepayment to other students may disqualify the payment for favorable federal gift tax treatment under Code section 2503(e).

3. *Federal Gift and Estate Tax Consequences*

The prepayment method may have the same federal gift tax consequences as the "pay as you go" method discussed earlier. In some circumstances, tuition prepayment also can be an effective means to reduce federal estate tax exposure for clients who are near the end of their lives.

EXAMPLE

In May 2018, Anne B., an eighty-seven-year-old grandmother, learns that she is not likely to live longer than six months. She has been in the habit of making current tuition payments for her grandchildren as the bills come due. In the final weeks of her life, Anne prepays the secondary school, college, and graduate school tuitions, totaling $150,000, for three of her grandchildren. By prepaying tuition for those grandchildren whose educational organizations so permit and who are unlikely to change schools before graduation, Anne B. successfully removes over $150,000 from her estate at no federal gift tax cost, without depleting her applicable exclusion amount,[12] and with no adverse consequence under Code section 2035.[13] This example assumes the prepayment is nonrefundable and subject to forfeiture.

PRACTICE NOTE

A direct payment of tuition, whether current or by prepayment, may be appropriate for an attorney-in-fact. Many powers of attorney expressly authorize the attorney-in-fact to make gifts. In some states, an attorney-in-fact may not make gifts on behalf of the principal absent a specific authorization. Carefully consider including in powers of attorney an authorization with respect to tuition payment (as well as qualified payments to providers of medical care)[14] under Code section 2503(e).

C. U.S. Saving Bonds

1. *General*

Savings bonds may be used by people within the qualifying income range to fund higher education expenses of their dependents. These bonds, which include Series EE (issued between 1989 and 2011) and Series I, generally defer recognition of interest income until the bonds are redeemed.[15] For example, qualifying taxpayers may apply the full face amount of Series EE bonds to pay tuition or fees for higher education without ever recognizing the interest income that constitutes at least one-half of the face value of the Series EE matured bond. This federal income tax advantage begins to phase out, however, at specified income levels. Drawbacks to this method include (1) the relatively low income ceiling, discussed later; (2) the inability to gift the bonds without recognizing the interest for federal income tax purposes; and (3) the inability to use the bonds to pay for the education of students other than usually the holder's dependents.

2. Federal Income Tax Treatment

For federal income tax purposes, qualifying donors generally may exclude from gross income the interest accrued on a "qualified United States savings bond" to the extent the proceeds are used to pay for "qualified higher education expenses" of the donor, the donor's spouse, or a dependent of the donor.[16] A "qualified United States savings bond" is one issued (1) after 1989, (2) at a discount,[17] and (3) to an individual who has reached the age of twenty-four before the date of issue.[18] "Qualified higher education expenses" include tuition and fees required to enroll in or attend an "eligible educational institution."[19] This means of funding is not available for secondary or primary education directly. "Qualified higher education expenses," however, include contributions to a 529 plan or to a Coverdell Education Savings Account (discussed later).[20] Given that these plans currently allow for payment of secondary or primary education expenses, contributions of the proceeds to these education savings devices indirectly may serve to pay for secondary or primary education.

Coordination with Education Tax Benefits. Use of savings bond proceeds and distributions form 529 plans and Coverdell education savings accounts (discussed later) to pay for "qualified higher education expenses" requires coordination. That is, the amount of "qualified higher education expenses" taken into account in determining federal income tax-free distributions from 529 plans or Coverdell education savings accounts may reduce the amount of "qualified higher education expenses" taken into account in determining whether qualified bond interest proceeds are federal income tax-free.[21] In addition, the federal income tax exclusion of accrued bond interest from gross income may be reduced by the amount of the "qualified higher education expenses" taken into account for purposes of the Lifetime Learning Credit (discussed later).[22]

Practitioners should be aware that the federal income tax benefits associated with these bonds are available only to taxpayers within a certain modified adjusted gross income (MAGI) limit.[23] By way of example, for tax year 2018, the interest exclusion begins to phase out for single taxpayers with MAGI of $79,550 ($119,300 for married taxpayers filing jointly) and is completely phased out at $94,550 ($149,300 for married taxpayers filing jointly).[24] Further, if the taxpayer is married, the exclusion applies only if the taxpayer files a joint income tax return.[25]

3. Federal Gift Tax Consequences

The purchase of a savings bond should not trigger federal gift tax consequences if the bond is held in the donor's name. If the bond, held in the donor's name is redeemed *and* the proceeds are used to pay tuition directly to the educational organization, the payment may constitute a "qualified transfer" under Code section 2503(e).

Generally, bonds are nontransferable and cannot be gifted from a donor to a third person. However, bonds may be purchased in the name of the person receiving the bond (i.e., not the donor). In this instance, the purchase is treated as a gift for federal gift tax purposes, but may qualify for the annual exclusion under Code section 2503(b).

PRACTICE NOTE

It is possible to register the bond in either the name of the purchaser or the intended beneficiary. However, given the requirement that the holder must have reached the age of twenty-four years before the date of issue in order to qualify for tax-favored treatment, it is wise to name the purchaser in order to receive the federal income tax benefits.[26]

D. 529 Plans

1. General—The Various Types of Plans Available

529 plans are available to clients at all income levels to fund higher education and, currently, education at "an elementary or secondary public, private, or religious school."[27] It is important to be familiar with the various types of plans available as well as the tax consequences of owning—and being the beneficiary of—these plans.

529 plans are available as either (1) state-sponsored or (2) institution-sponsored plans, which are sponsored by a group of educational institutions (discussed in further detail later). State-sponsored plans are creatures of state statute, which set forth the requirements of the plan in accordance with Code section 529. Each state sponsoring a 529 plan can fine-tune the terms of its respective plan, so long as the federal requirements are satisfied. There are two basic types of state-sponsored plans: prepaid tuition plans and college savings accounts. Each plan is treated the same for federal tax purposes.

Tax Cuts and Jobs Act of 2017. With the modifications made by the Tax Cuts and Jobs Act[28] to the definition of "qualified higher education expenses" (discussed later), some state legislatures are authorizing the implementation of 529 plans designed solely to meet the needs of the donor who wants to save for a student's elementary or secondary education.[29]

2. *State-Sponsored Prepaid Tuition Plans*

Prepaid tuition plans allow the donor to purchase tuition credits or certificates on behalf of a designated beneficiary. The tuition credits or certificates entitle the beneficiary to the waiver or payment of "qualified higher education expenses" at a participating educational institution.[30] Specifically, a donor may buy a certain amount of tuition related to credit hours. The cost of the credits or certificates is based on the price of tuition of in-state public institutions of higher education at the time the donor contributes the funds into the account. When the beneficiary attends a participating school (i.e., an in-state school), the credits or certificates are used to pay tuition and other educational expenses. Thus, a prepaid tuition plan enables the donor to lock in tuition at today's rates to avoid the risk of market fluctuation or negative (or minimal) rates of return on amounts invested to pay for education expenses in the future.

However, under the prepaid tuition program, the donor must be relatively certain the beneficiary will attend an in-state school. If the beneficiary enrolls in an out-of-state school (or a nonparticipating school), the credits are refunded in cash according to a formula used to determine the equivalent in-state public tuition amount. This may result in a smaller return on the investment because the cost of education expenses at a nonparticipating school may not compare to the initial purchase of credits or certificates. Another disadvantage is that most prepaid tuition plans are available only to state residents.

Not all states offer a prepaid tuition plan. In addition, a number of the plans may be closed to new investment.[31] However, in states where these plans are still available and open, for a donor who is risk-averse and interested in paying for a child's education with certainty, and if the child in question is certain to attend an in-state school, a prepaid tuition plan may be an option to consider.

3. *Institution-Sponsored Prepaid Tuition Plans*

Eligible educational institutions also may partner with one another and establish an institution-sponsored plan. This program is similar in nature to the prepaid tuition plan in that the donor buys credits or certificates that can be used in the future to pay for educational expenses at any one of the participating institutions. As with all types of 529 plans, the program must provide that (1) amounts are held in a "qualified trust" and (2) the program has received a ruling or determination from the IRS that the program satisfies the requirements for a "qualified tuition program" under Code section 529.[32] The Private College 529 Plan (originally named "Tuition Plan Consortium") is an example of an institution-sponsored plan in which nearly 300 independent colleges and universities from at least thirty-seven states (and the District of Columbia) share a plan that beneficiaries may use at any one of the participating institutions.[33]

4. *State-Sponsored College Savings Accounts*

The most popular type of state-sponsored plan is the college savings account.[34] Under this type of plan, the donor chooses among a variety of investment options offered by a given plan. The contributed money grows federal income tax-free in the account and may be withdrawn in the future to pay for "qualified higher education expenses" at any "eligible educational institution." Therefore, the college savings account is a more straightforward investment tool without the restrictions of a prepaid tuition plan. Because of the overwhelming popularity of these accounts, the balance of this section emphasizes the tax treatment and practitioner points applicable to college savings accounts, although many of the same rules discussed later also apply to state-sponsored prepaid tuition plans and institution-sponsored plans.

5. *Income Tax Treatment of Contributions, Distributions, and Refunds*

(a) Contributions and distributions

Contributions to a 529 plan may be made only in cash,[35] and the contributions are not deductible for federal income tax purposes. Depending on the donor's state of residence, the donor may be able to deduct a limited amount of the contribution for state income tax purposes.[36] The real tax benefits associated with a 529 plan, however, are realized when the funds are withdrawn from the account and used to pay for "qualified higher education expenses"[37] of the designated account beneficiary.[38] In that case, the assets invested in the plan grow tax-free. That is, the income accrued in the account is not subject to federal[39] income tax and, depending on state law, not subject to state[40] income tax. If funds are distributed, but are not used for "qualified higher education expenses," the portion of the distribution attributable to the earnings is subject to federal income tax and a 10 percent penalty.[41] However, the penalty generally may be waived if the distributions are made by reason of the beneficiary's death, disability, receipt of a scholarship, or attendance at a military academy.[42]

ABLE Account. New Code section 529(c)(3)(C)(i)(III), added by the Tax Cut and Jobs Act,[43] provides that a distribution from a 529 plan made between December 22, 2017, and January 1, 2026, is not subject to federal income tax and a 10 percent penalty if, within *sixty* days of the distribution, the distributed amount is transferred to an ABLE[44] account of (1) the designated beneficiary of that 529 plan or (2) a family member[45] of that designated beneficiary.[46] The IRS and the U.S. Department of the Treasury expect to issue proposed regulations, consistent with Code requirements, providing that distributions will be federal income tax-free if two requirements are met:

1. The distributed amount must be transferred to the ABLE account within *sixty* days after withdrawal of the distributed amount from the 529 plan.
2. Excluding any contributions of the ABLE beneficiary's compensation to the ABLE account, the distributed amount and any other contributions cannot exceed an amount equal to the annual gift tax exclusion[47] for the taxable year.[48]

Additional proposed regulations, designed to protect the ABLE beneficiary's eligibility for certain public benefits[49] and from inadvertent federal income taxation, are expected to:

1. require a 529 plan to prohibit the direct transfer of any amount that would cause the limit, equal to the annual exclusion amount for a calendar year, to be exceeded.[50]
2. prohibit a qualified ABLE program from accepting certain contributions in *excess* of the limitations applicable to ABLE accounts.[51]

In the case of direct transfers, regulations also will provide any excess contribution rejected by a qualified ABLE program and returned to a 529 plan will *not* be deemed a new contribution to the 529 plan.[52] Before the issuance of the proposed regulations, "taxpayers, beneficiaries, and administrators of 529 and ABLE programs may rely on the rules described in [the notice]."[53]

<u>PRACTICE NOTE</u>

> Before the issuance of the proposed regulations, the IRS "encourages the 529 plan beneficiary (in the case of a rollover) or the 529 plan (in the case of a direct transfer) to contact the qualified ABLE program before contributing any funds to the ABLE account to ensure that the limit . . . will not be exceeded."[54]

(b) Refunds

For tax years beginning after December 31, 2014, the Protecting Americans From Tax Hikes (PATH) Act of 2015[55] added Code section 529(c)(3)(D), generally allowing for refunds of amounts used for "qualified higher education expenses" to be excluded from gross income for federal income tax purposes if recontributed to the 529 plan account, of which the individual is a beneficiary, no later than *sixty* days after the date of the refund.[56] Note that Code section 529(c)(3)(D) may be relevant in the event a beneficiary decides, for any reason, to discontinue class enrollment during an academic semester. The IRS and the U.S. Department of the Treasury are expected to issue proposed regulations providing that the entire recontributed amount is treated as principal, thus eliminating the administrative burden of determining the earnings portion of the recontributed amount.[57] The regulations also are expected to provide for the recontributed amount to *not* count as a contribution on behalf of the beneficiary.[58]

Evolving Definition of "qualified higher education expenses" under Code section 529

"Qualified higher education expenses" are:

- "Tuition, fees, books, supplies, and equipment required for the enrollment or attendance" of a beneficiary at an "eligible education institution"[59]
- Room and board for students who are enrolled at least half-time[60]
- In the case of a special needs beneficiary, "special needs services incurred in connection with enrollment or attendance at an eligible education institution"[61]
- Expenses for the purchase of certain computer or peripheral equipment, certain computer software, or internet access and related services used primarily by the beneficiary during years enrolled at an eligible education institution[62]

Note: Code section 529 specifically provides that "expenses for computer software designed for sports, games, or hobbies" are not included, "unless the software is predominantly educational in nature."[63]

- For distributions after December 31, 2017, "expenses for tuition in connection with enrollment or attendance at an elementary or secondary public, private, or religious school," limited to *$10,000* per beneficiary during the taxable year, regardless of the number of accounts for the beneficiary[64]

Note: In Notice 2018-58,[65] the U.S. Treasury Department and the IRS "intend to issue regulations defining the term 'elementary or secondary' to mean kindergarten through grade 12 as determined under [s]tate law and consistent with the definition applicable for Coverdell education accounts in [Code section] 530(b)(3)(B)."[66]

"Qualified higher education expenses" do *not* include expenses related to home schooling.[67]

PRACTICE NOTE

Use of 529 plans as income tax deferral investment vehicles for purposes other than saving for "qualified higher education expenses" is discouraged. The Pension Protection Act of 2006[68] granted regulatory authority to the Secretary of the U.S. Treasury to prevent abuse and ensure that qualified tuition plans are used for their intended purpose, namely, as savings vehicles for education expenses and not, for example, as investment accounts for retirement.[69] To date, in January 2008, the IRS and the U.S. Treasury Department announced they will propose a general anti-abuse rule, applicable to 529 accounts "established or used for purposes of avoiding or evading transfer tax or for other purposes inconsistent with Code section 529."[70] The anti-abuse rule may be applied retroactively.[71] In requesting comments to its proposal, the IRS explained:

> The anti-abuse rule generally will deny the favorable transfer tax treatment under [Code] section 529 if contributions to those accounts are intended or used for purposes other than providing for the [qualified higher education expenses] of the [designated beneficiary] (except to the extent otherwise allowable under section 529 or the corresponding regulations). The IRS and the [U.S.] Treasury Department anticipate that the anti-abuse rule will generally follow the steps in the overall transaction by [(1)] focusing on the actual source of the funds for the contribution, [(2)] the person who actually contributes the cash to the section 529 account, and [(3)] the person who ultimately receives any distribution from the account. If it is determined that the transaction, in whole or in part, is inconsistent with the intent of [Code] section 529 and the regulations, taxpayers will not be able to rely on the favorable tax treatment provided in [Code] section 529. The anti-abuse rule will include examples . . . that provide clear guidance to taxpayers about the types of transactions considered abusive.[72]
>
> The IRS and the [U.S.] Treasury Department intend to monitor transactions involving [Code] section 529 accounts. If concerns regarding abuse continue, the IRS and the [U.S.] Treasury Department will consider adopting broader rules including, for example, rules [(1)] limiting the circumstances under which a [qualified tuition program] may permit [account owners] to withdraw funds from accounts; [(2)] limiting the circumstances under which there may be a change in [designated beneficiary]; and [(3)] limiting the circumstances under which the [account owner] may name a different [account owner]. These rules may be adopted in addition or as an alternative to the general anti-abuse rule.[73]

6. *Income Tax Treatment of Account Changes, Rollovers, and Changes in Beneficiary Designation*

The flexibility generally offered by the 529 plan is a main attraction. This method is available to any client because there are no income limits for account ownership. Furthermore, the donor has some flexibility in choosing the accounts, changing the investment strategy, or changing the designated beneficiary.

There is no federal requirement of state residency in order to establish a college savings account. The same may not be true on the state level.[74] Assuming no state residency requirement, individuals may establish a plan in any one of the states' programs. Some states offer a variety of invest-ment choices for 529 plans, offering several mutual funds, while other states' investment choices are more limited.[75] Generally, a donor may choose from among different types of investment options available under the different types of plans offered by various states. For tax years begin-ning before December 31, 2014, Code section 529 prohibited the donor or the designated beneficiary from directing the investment of any contri-bution under a plan.[76] For tax years beginning after December 31, 2014, Code section 529 allows a change in investment "no more than two times per calendar year."[77]

If the donor is interested in a wider array of investment choices offered under a different state's 529 plan than one in which the donor currently contributes, the donor may rollover an account to the new state's 529 plan without incurring federal tax if certain requirements are met, includ-ing completing the transfer within *sixty* days.[78] If a beneficiary attends a school in a different state from the one in which the donor contributes, or the donor changes beneficiaries to another family member,[79] a federal income tax-free rollover also may be made, assuming certain requirements are met.[80]

Practice Note

Some states impose residency restrictions, which may preclude the rollover, while other states require the refund of any state income tax deduction (if applicable), or charge fees for nonresident account owners.[81]

Most 529 plans (especially college savings plans) allow the donor to des-ignate any individual as beneficiary, including the donor and individuals not related to the donor.[82] The donor also may change the beneficiary des-ignation of a 529 plan at any time. However, in order for the beneficiary change to be federal income tax-free, the new beneficiary must be a "mem-ber of the family"[83] of the prior beneficiary.[84] Accordingly, if the new benefi-ciary is not a member of the family of the prior beneficiary, the change will be treated as a distribution for federal income tax purposes.

For purposes of Code section 529, the phrase "member of the family" is defined to include (1) a son or daughter, or a descendant of either; (2) a stepson or stepdaughter; (3) a brother, sister, stepbrother, or stepsister; (4) the father or mother of the designated beneficiary, or an ancestor of either; (5) a stepfather or stepmother; (6) a son or daughter of a brother or sister; (7) a brother or sister of the father or mother of the designated beneficiary; (8) a son-in-law, daughter-in-law, father-in-law, mother-in-law, brother-in-law, or sister-in-law; (9) the spouse of any of the aforementioned individuals; (10) the spouse of the designated beneficiary; or (11) a first cousin of the designated beneficiary.[85] "For purposes of determining who is a member of the family, a legally adopted child of an individual shall be treated as the child of such individual by blood."[86] The terms "brother" and "sister" include siblings by the half blood.[87]

UPDATE

The IRS and the U.S. Treasury Department expect to develop rules specifically to address potential misuse of section 529 accounts by an account owner who:

(1) "withdraws part or all of the funds from a section 529 account for the AO's [account owner's] own benefit,"
(2) "transfers control of the account to a new AO," or
(3) "names himself or herself (or the AO's spouse) as the designated beneficiary."[88]

Concerns are a contributor may want to avoid federal gift tax by making contributions of the annual exclusion amount ($15,000 per donee for 2018)[89] to *multiple* accounts having the *same* account owner and, thereafter, the account owner withdraws the funds without the contributor owing federal gift tax. An additional concern is the federal tax implications of transactions (2) and (3) described immediately above.[90]

Accordingly, proposed rules may include:

(1) "limiting account owners to individuals"[91] and
(2) "making the account owner liable for [federal] income tax on the entire amount of funds distributed for the AO's benefit except to the extent that the AO can substantiate that the AO made the contributions to the section 529 account and, therefore, has an investment in the account within the meaning of [Code] section 72."[92]

To date, no final regulations have been issued.

7. Federal Gift and GST Tax Consequences

Contributions to a 529 plan are treated as gifts of present interests from the donor to the designated beneficiary.[93] Because the 529 plan transfer is a present-interest gift, the transfers are available for the annual exclusion under Code section 2503(b), as well as the GST exclusion under Code section 2642(c).[94] Therefore, in 2018 (and not until the annual exclusion increases)[95] the first $15,000 of contributions per beneficiary avoids both federal gift taxation and GST taxation without using any of the donor's applicable credit amount.

In addition, donors may "front-load" contributions by making a lump-sum contribution up to five times the available annual exclusion amount in a single calendar year. The excluded gift then is taken into account ratably over a five-year period.[96] That is, a donor can contribute $75,000 per beneficiary in 2018 without incurring gift tax or GST tax, and without reducing his or her available applicable exclusion amount.[97] Front-loading requires the donor to make an election on the federal gift tax return, Form 709, United States Gift (and Generation-Skipping Transfer) Tax Return.[98] The IRS also expects to clarify the manner in which the election may be made by the following proposed rule:

> Rule 1. The election must be made on the last . . . Form 709 filed on or before the due date of the return, including extensions actually granted, or, if a timely return is not filed, on the first gift tax return filed by the donor after the due date. The election, once made, will be irrevocable, except that it may be revoked or modified on a subsequent return that is filed on or before the due date, including extensions actually granted.[99]

To date, final regulations have not been issued.

The following example demonstrates the mechanics of front-loading contributions.

EXAMPLE

In Year 1, when the annual exclusion under Code section 2503(b) is $15,000, P makes a contribution of $85,000 to a 529 plan for the benefit of P's child, C. P elects under Code section 529(c)(2)(B) to account for the gift ratably over a five-year period beginning with the calendar year of contribution. P is treated as making an excludible gift of $15,000 in each of Years 1 through 5 and a taxable gift of $10,000 in Year 1. In Year 3, when the annual exclusion is increased to $16,000, P makes an additional contribution for the benefit of C in the amount of $10,000. P is treated as making an excludible gift of $1,000 under Code section 2503(b). The remaining $9,000 is a taxable gift in Year 3.[100]

Without front-loading, a married[101] donor can contribute up to $30,000 in 2018 per beneficiary, provided that both spouses make the gift split election on their respective federal gift tax returns.[102] If both gift splitting and front-loading are elected by the donor, up to $150,000 per beneficiary in 2018 may not be subject to federal gift and GST taxation.[103]

PRACTICE NOTE

While front-loading contributions is a great benefit, it also means that the donor can make no further annual exclusion gifts for the next five years to that beneficiary, which could interfere with existing annual exclusion gift techniques, such as funding insurance trusts.[104]

Generally, distributions from a 529 plan account are not treated as taxable gifts.[105] However, if a donor changes the beneficiary, and the new beneficiary is (1) not a member[106] of the prior beneficiary's family and (2) not assigned to the same generation as (or a higher generation than) the prior beneficiary, the change may be treated as a transfer subject to federal gift.[107] In addition, if the new beneficiary is at least two generation levels below the generation assignment of the prior beneficiary, the transfer may be subject to GST taxation.[108] To date, in January 2008, the IRS and the U.S. Treasury Department announced they expect to propose a rule that would address the assignment of federal gift and GST liability in the event of a taxable change of a designated beneficiary. Specifically, the IRS and the U.S. Treasury Department explained:

> In order to assign the tax liability to the party who has control over the account and is responsible for the change of any beneficiary, the forthcoming notice of proposed rulemaking will provide that a change of DB [designated beneficiary] that results in the imposition of any tax will be treated as a deemed distribution to the AO [account owner][109] followed by a new gift. Therefore, the AO will be liable for any gift or GST tax imposed by the change of the DB, and the AO must file gift and GST tax returns if required.[110]

According to the advance notice, the foregoing position is consistent with the 1998 proposed regulation section 1.529-3(c)(1), treating "a change of DB to a new DB who is not a member of the family of the former DB as a distribution to the AO, provided the AO has the authority to change the DB."[111]

PRACTICE ALERT

With the exception of a general anti-abuse rule, "[t]he IRS and the [U.S.] Treasury Department anticipate that the proposed rules will generally apply *prospectively* to all section 529 accounts, namely, after the effective date of final regulations.[112] Transition rules will be provided if necessary."[113] To date, final regulations have not been issued. Nonetheless, it should be noted that the aforementioned position, in part, relies on a proposed regulation. The proposed regulations, in turn, state that taxpayers may rely on the proposed regulations.[114] Query whether the account owner, not the designated beneficiary, of a 529 plan *currently* has potential federal gift and GST tax liability and return filing responsibilities in the case of the account owner's change of beneficiary under the IRS proposal.[115]

8. *Federal Estate Tax Consequences*

The assets in the 529 plan generally are not included in the gross estate of any individual for federal estate tax purposes.[116] One exception to this general rule applies to donors who elect to front-load contributions to a 529 plan using the five-year spread rule. Specifically, if the donor front-loads the contributions and dies before the close of the fifth year, then the portion of the five-year spread contributions, allocable to the period after the donor's death, will be included in the donor's gross estate for federal estate tax purposes.[117] Another statutory exception occurs in the case of amounts distributed on account of the death of a designated beneficiary, requiring inclusion in the designated beneficiary's gross estate for federal estate tax purposes.[118] In January 2008, the IRS proposed rules for determining the federal estate tax consequences of specific circumstances arising from the death of the designated beneficiary and during administration. The rules are as follows:

> **Rule 1.** If the AO [account owner] distributes the entire 529 account to the estate of the deceased DB [designated beneficiary] within 6 months of the death of the DB, the value of the account will be included in the deceased DB's gross estate for federal estate tax purposes.
>
> **Rule 2.** If a successor DB is named in the section 529 account contract or program and the successor DB is a member of the family of the deceased DB and is in the same or a higher generation (as determined under [Code] section 2651) as the deceased DB, the value of the account will *not* be included in the gross estate of the deceased DB for [f]ederal estate tax purposes.
>
> **Rule 3.** If *no* successor DB is named in the section 529 account contract or program, but the AO names a successor DB who is a member of the family of the deceased DB and is in the same or a higher generation (as determined under [Code] section 2651 as the deceased DB, the value of the account will *not* be included in the gross estate of the deceased DB for [f]ederal estate tax purposes.
>
> **Rule 4.** If *no* successor DB is named in the section 529 account contract or program, and the AO does not name a new DB but instead withdraws all or part of the account, the AO will be liable for the [federal] income tax on the distribution, and the value of the account will *not* be included in the gross estate of the deceased DB for federal estate tax purposes.
>
> **Rule 5.** If, by the due date for filing the deceased DB's [federal] estate tax return, the AO has a llowed funds to remain in the section 529 account without naming a new DB, the account will be deemed to terminate with a distribution to the AO, and the AO will be liable for the [federal] income tax on the distribution. The value of the account will *not* be included in the gross estate of the deceased DB for [f]ederal estate tax purposes.[119]

As stated earlier, no final regulations have been issued.

PRACTICE NOTE

Descent or distribution of the account is determined by the account's successorship designation or, if no such designation is in place, then according to the dispositive provisions in the account owner's will. If the will makes no specific disposition of the account, then it will pass as part of the residue of the owner's estate. In order to avoid unexpected disposition of 529 plans owned at death, it is important to address these assets specifically in the owner's will or other documents with testamentary effect. Absent specific disposition, the 529 plans would pass as part of the residue of the owner's estate. Even for clients who do not have yet 529 plans in place, it may be prudent to add a clause to their estate planning documents directing any 529 plans to the beneficiaries designated.

9. *Asset Protection*

Generally, a donor's creditors have no access to completed gifts to third parties as long as there was no fraudulent conveyance.[120] Unlike the typical completed gift situations, however, a donor, as an account owner, may re-acquire funds contributed to a 529 plan for the benefit of a third party Nonetheless, federal bankruptcy law excludes 529 plans, under certain circumstances, from the owner's bankruptcy estate if the designated beneficiary of the account is a child, stepchild, grandchild, or stepgrandchild of the owner/debtor.[121] Federal bankruptcy law further limits the amount of a 529 plan that may be excluded.[122] State law also may determine the ability of creditors (whether of the donor, owner or the beneficiary) to reach assets of a 529 plan.[123] State law and the provisions of each plan's governing document should be consulted.

PRACTICE NOTE

State law may differ as to whether the donor, owner, and/or a beneficiary of an account is protected from creditors. Other limitations, including limiting creditor protection to a state's own program, may be imposed.

10. *State Fund Variations and Planning*

Although the 529 plan is a creature of federal statute, the number of options and amount of flexibility in a plan may be subject to the design of a particular state's plan. As a result, there can be wide variation in the ways a donor can structure his or her investments inside the plan. Some of the factors that change from state to state include:

- contribution limits;
- investment options;
- ability to hold gifts from multiple donors in one account;
- ability of a trust to fund or own an account;
- ability of UTMA or other custodian to fund or own account;
- portfolio choice of investment depending upon the age of the beneficiary; and
- administrative fees.

The proper choice of a particular state can have a huge impact on the overall investment return. The federal tax advantages of a 529 plan, in the abstract, will provide very small advantage if the state's choice of investments is limited, and these available investments have high administrative fees associated with them.

PRACTICE NOTE

The lawyer who does not want to provide investment advice should be careful to find his or her client an investment advisor qualified to analyze the choices. The lawyer also should make certain that the advisor does not charge a separate annual fee to review the fund because that additional cost will further erode any tax-favored investing inside the plan.

11. Coordination with Other Funding Methods

One of the opportunities that estate planners and their clients often would like to pursue is transferring 529 plans to the trustees of trusts or to Uniform Transfers to Minors Act (UTMA) or Uniform Gifts to Minors Act (UGMA) accounts[124] for the beneficiaries of the plan. The short answer is that either option is available, but whether it is advisable is a different matter.

The more useful of the two options is the creation of a 529 plan by the trustee of a trust. Apparently, the Code and proposed regulations allow the trustee of a trust to establish a plan,[125] and most states allow trustees to be account owners. Note, however, that the designated beneficiary of the plan is not the trust, but rather an individual (and not more than one) designated by the trustee because the designated beneficiary of a 529 plan must be an individual under the Code. This restriction may be tax-disadvantaged, as discussed later.

Use of a trustee, rather than an individual with no fiduciary obligations, to own a 529 plan can have several advantages:

- The succession of owners (the trustees) can be specified in the trust agreement.
- Nonqualified distributions, even to the account owner, would have to be held in trust and not used for the account owner's personal benefit.
- Additional creditor protection can be created through the presence of a spendthrift clause in the governing instrument of the trust.

PRACTICE ALERT

Establishment of a trust or a UTMA/UGMA custodial account to purchase and hold 529 plan accounts and Coverdell Education Savings accounts (discussed later) also may serve to protect either type of accounts from classification as marital property, subject to equitable distribution, in the event of divorce of the minor's parents.[126]

There are, of course, disadvantages as well. Chief among these is the loss of the annual exclusion because the gift of cash (used by the trustee to establish the 529 plan) is not made to the individual designated beneficiary.[127] This also means that the front-loading of five years' worth of annual exclusion gifts is lost.[128] As with any trust, there could be adverse federal income tax and transfer tax consequences if the trustee makes distributions to a beneficiary whom the trustee already has a legal obligation to support. Further, the trustee may be subject to investment restrictions imposed by state law (though these investment restrictions may be overridden by properly drafted trust provisions).

The case for UTMA and UGMA ownership of 529 plans seems even more tenuous. It seems that most plan sponsors allow a custodian under either a state's UTMA or UGMA act to establish a 529 plan account.[129] As the custodian must, like all donors, contribute cash, capital gains tax liability can be incurred if the custodian has to sell appreciated assets to generate that cash. Yet, at first blush, the idea seems to have merit. The custodian creates an investment vehicle that generates no federal income tax liability. However, much of the flexibility that makes 529 plans attractive is lost to the custodian. If a custodian were to change the beneficiary of the plan, he or she would have breached his or her fiduciary obligation to the minor for whose benefit the custodial assets are held. Further, upon the minor reaching the age at which the custodial account is to terminate, the custodian must give the assets to the minor by making the minor the account owner or, otherwise, the custodian again breaches his or her fiduciary obligations.[130] The custodian also may face breach of fiduciary duty claims because the minor would have to pay the penalty for any nonqualified withdrawals. The custodian may argue that the income tax savings during the time the investments were held in the 529 plan outweigh the penalty, but that would be a question of proof in court.

PRACTICE NOTE

In light of these issues, it seems that the only appropriate use for custodial ownership of a 529 plan is in the situation where the minor is relatively young (and therefore the federal income tax-free investment feature will generate a more significant benefit) and the amount of cash transferred to the plan is almost certain to be used before the minor reaches the age of account termination.

UPDATE (TRUSTEE AS CONTRIBUTOR)

In January 2008, the IRS and U.S. Treasury Department questioned whether entities other than an individual can contribute to a 529 plan. After reviewing the 1998 proposed regulation adoption of the definition of "person" contained in Code section 7701 and further considering gift tax regulation section 25.2511-1(h)(1),[131] the IRS and U.S. Treasury Department "believe[d] it may be possible to interpret [Code] sections 529(b)(1) (providing that "a person" makes contributions to a 529 plan) and 529(c)(2)(A) (treating a contribution as a completed present-interest gift) consistently without limiting the class of permissible contributors to individuals by providing *special rules* for contributions made by corporations, partnerships, estates, trusts, and other entities." The IRS and U.S. Treasury Department provided an example of a special rule, based upon the aforementioned gift tax regulation, as follows:

> [A] contribution by a person other than an individual may be treated as a separate gift by each beneficiary, member, shareholder, partner, etc., in an amount representing that individual's allocable share of the contribution.[132]

The IRS and U.S. Treasury Department, thereafter, concluded that the forthcoming notice will follow the 1998 proposed regulation approach of utilizing the definition of "person" found in Code section 7701(a)(1).[133]

The IRS and U.S. Treasury Department, nonetheless, welcomed comments regarding, among other matters, "whether the definition of 'person' under [Code] section 529(b)(1) should be limited to individuals" and "whether the complexity of any special rules would outweigh the benefit of allowing non-individual contributors[,]" in the case of determining both federal transfer and income tax consequences.[134]

Later, in March 2008, the IRS again invited comments in response to its concerns and the foregoing proposed approach. It also welcomed comments "regarding the potential income tax consequences when contributions are made by non-individuals, such as a trust or estate, and whether the complexity of any special rules would outweigh the benefit [, raising these specific questions:

> (1)] if a trust makes contributions to a [Code] section 529 account, how should the trust treat the contributions to and distributions from the account for income tax purposes?
>
> [(2)] If the trustee of the trust is the [account owner], would the income tax treatment be the same?"[135]

These uncertainties also may constitute disadvantages in a trust holding 529 plans.

UPDATE (UTMA OR UGMA ACCOUNT AS CONTRIBUTOR)

In January 2008, the IRS and the U.S. Treasury Department observed that the 1998 proposed regulations did not address the situation of UTMA and UGMA accounts making contributions to a 529 plan for the benefit of the minor, distinguishing the situation from a 529 account established with a qualified tuition program as a UTMA or UGMA account.[136] Regarding the first circumstance, the IRS expressed concern that the minor, as beneficial owner of a UTMA or UGMA account, may be funding a 529 plan for his or her own education expenses, albeit not contrary to any express statutory prohibition, but not contemplated by the transfer tax provisions of Code section 529. The IRS, nonetheless, recognized that "section 529 accounts provide an efficient method for [UTMA and UGMA] accounts to provide for the . . . education expenses of their minor beneficiaries."[137] Accordingly, the IRS concluded that it expects to allow contributions to 529 plans by UTMA and UGMA accounts for the benefit of their minor beneficiaries but, in order to "ensure consistent transfer and income tax treatment under [Code] section 529 for these accounts and accounts created by persons for the benefit of other [designated beneficiaries,] special rules will apply in cases of a subsequent change of [designated beneficiary]."[138] These special rules are as follows:

> [T]he change of the DB [designated beneficiary] from the contributor to any other person will be deemed to be a distribution to the

contributor followed by a new contribution (as described in [Code] section 529(c)(2)) of the account balance by the contributor to a new [Code] section 529 account for the new DB.[139]

It is anticipated that the deemed distribution to the contributor, followed by the new contribution of the account balance to a new . . . 529 account for the new DB, will be treated as a rollover (as described in [Code] section 529(c)(3)(C)) and thus will not be subject to [federal] income tax or the 10-percent [penalty] imposed by [Code] section 529(c)(6) if the new DB is a member of the family of the former DB.[140]

The new contribution by the contributor will be treated in the same way for transfer tax purposes as all other contributions to . . . 529 accounts under [Code] section 529(c)(2). If the change of DB in these situations results in any [federal] gift and/or GST tax, the contributor will be liable for the tax and must file [federal] gift and/or GST tax returns. However, the contributor may elect to take advantage of the special 5-year rule under [Code] section 529(c)(2)(B).[141]

12. Frequently Asked Questions

Q: What factors should I consider when selecting a 529 plan?

A: When choosing between the various 529 plans available, many individuals immediately focus on the plans sponsored by their state of residency. While the individual may qualify for a state income tax deduction for a limited amount of the contribution, if allowed by state law, it is important to weigh other factors in the equation. Each plan, whether sponsored by a state or institution, is managed by an independent financial institution. At a minimum, it is important to analyze the reputation of the financial institution as well as the past investment performance of the plan. One also must take into account the amount of fees imposed by the financial institution, which could be a significant factor in the overall financial performance of the plan.

Q: How do I designate a successor owner for a 529 plan?

A: The easiest way is to indicate the successor owner on the 529 plan application form. Most plans have a section on the application form allowing the applicant to designate a successor owner. If no successor designation is on file with the plan sponsor, or if all successors named predecease the owner, the plan would default to the estate of the owner, and would pass according to the dispositive provisions of his or her will, either by specific bequest or as part of the residue of the estate. In the absence of a will, assets in the plan would pass on the owner's death according to the laws of intestate succession in the state of the owner's domicile at death. Once the initial designation is made and filed, it is prudent to seek confirmation from the plan sponsor. In addition, practitioners should take the opportunity to confirm the beneficiary designation with the client and the plan sponsor whenever the estate plan is updated.

Q: How do I change a beneficiary for a 529 plan?

A: Account owners can change the designation of a beneficiary by contacting the plan administrator. As discussed previously, the change generally should not have negative federal income tax consequences if the new beneficiary is a member of the family of the previous beneficiary. However, federal transfer tax liability may occur if the new beneficiary is assigned to a generation that is one or more generations below that of the previous beneficiary.

E. Coverdell Education Savings Accounts

1. General

Formerly known as Education IRAs, Coverdell Education Savings Accounts (Coverdell ESAs) are trusts or custodial accounts[142] used to save for the "qualified education expenses" of a designated beneficiary. The annual contribution amounts for Coverdell ESAs are limited, and the federal income tax benefits are available only to individuals within certain income limits.

2. Contributions

Like contributions to a 529 plan, contributions to a Coverdell ESA must be made in cash, and are not deductible for federal income tax purposes.[143] Excluding rollovers (discussed later), Coverdell ESA contributions are limited to $2,000 annually per designated beneficiary. The amount of the permitted annual contribution begins to phase out when the donor's MAGI[144] exceeds $95,000 for single taxpayers ($190,000 for married taxpayers filing jointly), and completely is phased out at $110,000 for single taxpayers ($220,000 for married taxpayers filing jointly).[145]

Military death benefits. The annual contribution limit may not apply in the case of a donor who receives and contributes up to the full amount of a military death gratuity[146] or Servicemembers' Group Life Insurance payment[147] to a Coverdell ESA.[148] Under Code section 530(b)(9), either contributed military death benefit is treated as a federal income tax-free rollover if made within *one* year of the respective date of receipt of the benefits. These military benefit amounts are reduced by any contributions of these amounts to a Roth individual retirement account (IRA)[149] or another Coverdell ESA.[150] The annual limit on the number of rollovers (as discussed later) also does not apply.[151]

3. Federal Income Tax Treatment of Contributions, Distributions, and Change of Beneficiary; Limitation on Contributions

While the Coverdell ESA contribution is not deductible, funds from the account used to pay for the beneficiary's "qualified education expenses" are not subject to federal income taxation. For purposes of the Coverdell ESA, "qualified education expenses" include "qualified higher education expenses" as defined in Code section 529(e)(3)[152] and "qualified elementary and secondary education expenses" as defined in Code section 530(b)(3)(A).[153] If the funds are used for these expenses, the income earned in the account, along with the principal amount of the contribution, generally are exempt from federal income tax.[154]

Definition of "qualified education expenses" under Code section 530

"Qualified education expenses" are:

- "qualified higher education expenses" as defined in Code section 529(e)(3)[155]
- "qualified elementary and secondary education expenses"[156]

"Qualified elementary and secondary expenses" are defined further as:

- "expenses for tuition, fees, academic tutoring, special needs services in the case of a special needs beneficiary, books, supplies, and other equipment which are incurred in connection with the enrollment or attendance of the designated beneficiary of the [Coverdell ESA] as an elementary or secondary school student at a public, private, or religious school,"[157]
- "expenses for room and board, uniforms, transportation, and supplementary items and services (including extended day programs) which are required or provided by a public, private, or religious school in connection with such enrollment or attendance,"[158] and
- expenses for the purchase of any computer technology or equipment or Internet access and related services, if such technology, equipment, or services are to be used by the beneficiary and the beneficiary's family during any of the years the beneficiary is in school.[159] These expenses do *not* include "expenses computer software designed for sports, games, or hobbies unless the software is predominantly educational in nature."[160]

If the funds in a Coverdell ESA are not used to pay the beneficiary's "qualified education expenses," or if the distribution amount exceeds the current "qualified education expenses," the earning portion of the withdrawn funds are subject to federal income taxation and a 10 percent penalty.[161] The 10 percent penalty generally may be waived if the beneficiary dies, becomes disabled, receives a scholarship, or attends a military academy.[162]

Comparison Chart (Current as of October 2018)

	529 Plan	**Coverdell ESA**
Code section	529	530
Income limitations	None	Phase-outs: · $95,000–$105,000 (single) · $190,000–$220,000 (married filing jointly)
Other contribution limitations	Only cash*	· Only cash* · No contribution after date beneficiary attains age *eighteen, except* in case of a special needs designated beneficiary (DB) · *Except* in case of a rollover, including contribution of certain military death benefits, aggregate contributions for the taxable year cannot exceed *$2,000*.
Coordination of contributions	A donor can contribute to a 529 plan and a Coverdell ESA in the same year for the same DB.	A donor can contribute to a 529 plan and a Coverdell ESA in the same year for the same DB.
Federal gift tax treatment of contributions	· A contribution is a completed gift, and eligible for the annual exclusion. · Election for five-year spread period is available (front-loading).	· A contribution is a completed gift, and eligible for the annual exclusion. · Election for five-year spread period is available (front-loading).
Federal GST tax treatment of contributions	If the contribution qualifies for the gift tax annual exclusion, the contribution generally is *not* subject to GST tax.	If the contribution qualifies for the gift tax annual exclusion, the contribution generally is *not* subject to GST tax.
Federal income tax-free distributions	Distributions for "qualified higher education expenses"** are *not* subject to federal income tax.	Distributions for "qualified education expenses," that is, · "qualified higher education expenses"** under Code section 529 and · "qualified elementary and secondary expenses"** are *not* subject to federal income tax.
Coordination of distributions with other tax benefits	"Qualified higher education expenses"** are reduced by American Opportunity and Lifetime Learning Credits (discussed later).	"Qualified education expenses"** are reduced by American Opportunity and Lifetime Learning Credits (discussed later).
Deemed distribution at a certain age of DB	Not applicable	Amounts remaining in the Coverdell ESA must be distributed within thirty days after the DB reaches *thirty* years, *except* in the case of a special needs DB.

* If clients do not have cash readily available to contribute to a 529 plan or Coverdell ESA and, instead, the client incurs capital gains in order to gain access to cash, this method of funding may not be appealing. Further, it may reduce the amount of the client's potential contribution to the extent sale proceeds must be used to pay capital gains tax.

** *See* notes 59–67 and accompanying text for definitions. As stated earlier, "qualified higher education expenses" include "expenses for *tuition* in connection with enrollment or attendance at an *elementary or secondary* public, private, or religious school," for distributions after December 31, 2017. *See* note 64. As also stated earlier, the IRS and the U.S. Treasury Department intend to issue regulations defining the term "elementary or secondary" so that the term is consistent for purposes of Code sections 529 and 530.

	529 Plan	Coverdell ESA
Federal income tax penalty for taxable distribution	*Ten percent* penalty imposed on payment or distributions from a 529 plan not used for "qualified higher education expenses"** and included in gross income for federal income tax purposes.	*Ten percent* penalty imposed on payment or distributions from Coverdell ESA not used for "qualified education expenses"** and included in gross income for federal income tax purposes.
Federal income tax treatment of a refund of QHEE	Refund is tax-free if recontributed to a 529 plan, of which the individual is a beneficiary, no later than *sixty* days after date of refund.	
Federal income tax treatment of a rollover	A rollover is a taxable distribution *unless*: · The new DB is the same DB or a "member of the family" of the DB. · The rollover occurred within *sixty* days of distribution or payment. · No more than *one* rollover *per year* occurred. · Effective for distributions after December 22, 2017, and before January 1, 2026, the distribution or payment, subject to certain limitations, is to an ABLE account.	A rollover is a taxable distribution *unless*: · The new DB is the same DB or a "member of the family" of the DB, and the DB has not attained age *thirty* as of the date of the distribution or payment. · The rollover occurred within *sixty* days of distribution or payment. · No more than *one* rollover *per year* occurred, *except* for military death benefit contributions (treated as a rollover).
Federal income tax treatment of a change in DB	A change in DB is *not* a taxable distribution if the new DB is a "member of the family" of the former DB.	A change in DB is *not* a taxable distribution if the new DB is a "member of the family" of the former DB *and* has not attained age *thirty* as of the date of the change.
Federal gift tax treatment of a change of DB or a rollover to the account of a new DB	Federal gift tax applies *unless* the new DB is: · a "member of the family" of the former DB *and* · assigned to same or higher generation as the former DB.***	Federal gift tax applies *unless* the new DB is: · a "member of the family" of the former DB *and* · assigned to same or higher generation as the former DB.****
Federal GST tax treatment of a change of DB or a rollover to the account of a new DB	Federal GST tax applies if the new DB is at least two generations below the generation assignment of the former DB.***	Federal GST tax applies if the new DB is at least two generations below the generation assignment of the former DB.****
Federal estate tax treatment of 529 plan	· Generally included in the DB's gross estate. · Generally excluded from the donor's gross estate unless the donor dies during five-year spread period.	· Generally included in the DB's gross estate. · Generally excluded from the donor's gross estate unless the donor dies during five-year spread period.

** *See* notes 59–67 and accompanying text for definitions. As stated earlier, "qualified higher education expenses" include "expenses for *tuition* in connection with enrollment or attendance at an *elementary or secondary* public, private, or religious school," for distributions after December 31, 2017. *See* note 64. As also stated earlier, the IRS and the U.S. Treasury Department intend to issue regulations defining the term "elementary or secondary" so that the term is consistent for purposes of Code sections 529 and 530.
*** *See also* notes 107–108 and accompanying text.
**** *See also* notes 180–181 and accompanying text.

While there is no requirement that the designated beneficiary be related to the owner, no contributions can be made to a Coverdell ESA after the date the beneficiary attains *eighteen* years of age.[163] In addition, any remaining balance in the account *at the time the beneficiary reaches the age of thirty* is deemed to be distributed within *thirty* days after that date (or, if earlier, within *thirty* days of the date the beneficiary dies).[164] The deemed distribution will result in federal income tax on the earnings portion of the distribution, as well as a 10 percent penalty to the beneficiary.[165] Before 2002, if a donor contributed to both a Coverdell ESA and a 529 plan on behalf of the same beneficiary in the same tax year, the contributions were subject to a 6 percent excise tax.[166] This excise tax was repealed for contributions made after 2001.[167] Any change in the beneficiary is not treated as a distribution (and therefore, not subject to federal income taxation) if the new beneficiary is a member of the family[168] of the prior beneficiary and has *not attained age thirty* as of the date of the change.[169]

Special needs beneficiary. The eighteen-year and thirty-year age limitations do not apply in the case of a special needs beneficiary.[170]

4. Rollovers

There is no federal income tax imposed on a rollover from one Coverdell ESA to another so long as the rollover takes place within *sixty* days of the payment or distribution[171] and other requirements are met. These additional requirements are: the rollover must be for (1) the same designated beneficiary or (2) for the benefit of a new beneficiary who is a member of the prior beneficiary's family and (3) if not a special needs beneficiary, the beneficiary is under age *thirty*.[172] If the foregoing requirements are not met, the rollover will be treated as a distribution subject to federal income tax and a 10 percent penalty.[173] With the exception of certain military death benefit contributions (described earlier), only one rollover is permitted in each twelve-month period.[174]

PRACTICE NOTE

The statutory language set forth in sections 529 and 530 does not specify whether a Coverdell ESA owner may roll amounts over to a section 529 plan, and vice versa. However, Notice 2001-81[175] indicates that amounts in a Coverdell ESA may be rolled over to a section 529 plan federal income tax-free. That is, the Notice provides that final 529 regulations will clarify how a rollover to a 529 plan may be executed. To date, final section 529 regulations have not been issued. The 2018 Instructions for Form 5498-ESA (Coverdell ESA Contribution Information form in which distributions from a Coverdell ESA are reported) indicate that a rollover may be made from "certain U.S. Savings Bonds or another Coverdell ESA."[176]

5. *Federal Gift and GST Tax Consequences of Contributions, Distributions, and Change of Beneficiary*

Contributions to Coverdell ESAs are treated in the same fashion as 529 plan contributions for federal gift tax purposes (i.e., contributions are treated as completed present-interest gifts from the donor to the beneficiary).[177] Accordingly, contributions to Coverdell ESAs may qualify for the annual gift tax exclusion and also not be subject to GST taxation.[178] Similar to 529 plans, the Code provides that, if contributions to a Coverdell ESA exceed the annual exclusion amount under Code section 2503(b), the donor may elect to take the contribution amount into account ratably over a five-year period (i.e., front-load the contribution).[179] However, in operation, the ability to front-load generally may be irrelevant to Coverdell ESA donors, as the $2,000 limitation is significantly lower than the annual exclusion amount (which for 2018 is $15,000).

Generally, distributions from a Coverdell ESA are not treated as taxable gifts.[180] However (similar to beneficiary changes under a 529 plan, discussed earlier), if a donor changes the beneficiary and the new beneficiary is not a "member of the family" of the prior beneficiary and not a generation below the prior beneficiary, a taxable gift has occurred.[181] Further, if the new beneficiary is at least two generation levels below the generation assignment of the prior beneficiary, the change in beneficiary may result in imposition of GST tax.[182]

6. *Federal Estate Tax Consequences*

The Coverdell ESA account is not included in the donor's gross estate for federal estate tax purposes.[183] Instead, the amount distributed on account of the death of the designated beneficiary is included in the beneficiary's gross estate for federal estate tax purposes.[184]

PRACTICE NOTE

The actual succession of the account is determined by the beneficiary designation on file with the plan provider or, if there is no designation on file, by the dispositive provisions of the donor's will.

F. Traditional and Roth Individual Retirement Accounts (IRAs)

1. *General*

Distributions from traditional and Roth IRAs may be used to fund education. For federal income tax purposes, contributions to Roth IRAs are limited by an individual's adjusted gross income (AGI), and are not deductible. Contributions to traditional IRAs generally are not subject to income limits, but their deductibility may be affected by an individual's participation in an employer-sponsored plan.

2. *Federal Income Tax Treatment*

Contributions to a traditional or Roth IRA must be made from compensation.[185] Contributions to a traditional IRA are deductible by the IRA owner,[186] whereas contributions to a Roth IRA are nondeductible.[187] The investments held in either type of IRA grow federal income tax-free.[188] However, distributions from traditional IRAs are includable in gross income for federal income tax purposes,[189] whereas distributions from Roth IRAs generally are excludable from gross income.[190]

The maximum annual contribution to all of an individual's traditional and Roth IRAs cannot exceed $5,000, indexed for inflation.[191] For tax years 2017 and 2018, the maximum annual contribution to all of an individual's IRAs cannot exceed $5,500.[192] Individuals who are age fifty or older may make additional catch-up contributions.[193]

A Roth IRA is subject to limits based on the IRA owner's income (both for unmarried and married IRA owners). Specifically, the maximum contribution amount for a Roth IRA is gradually phased out once an owner has an AGI[194] level of $95,000 ($150,000 for married filing jointly) and is completely phased out at an AGI level of $110,000 ($160,000 for married filing jointly).[195] In contrast to contributions to the traditional IRA, contributions to the Roth IRA are allowed even after the Roth IRA owner attains age seventy and a half.[196]

For traditional IRAs, if an owner or spouse also actively participates in an employer-sponsored retirement plan, deductible contributions are reduced according to income ranges.[197] For example, in 2018, the deductible amount is reduced if the AGI[198] of an IRA contributor (also an active participant) exceeds $63,000 ($101,000 for married filing jointly). The tax deduction is no longer available for the active participant whose AGI exceeds $73,000 ($121,000 for married filing jointly).[199] For the IRA contributor who is not an active participant but is married to someone who is an active participant, the deduction is phased out if the married couple's income is between $189,000 and $199,000.[200]

3. *IRA Distributions and Qualified Higher Education Expenses*

Generally, a 10 percent penalty is imposed on distributions from either type of IRA before the owner reaches age fifty-nine and a half.[201] However, there are exceptions to this general rule.[202] One exception is an IRA owner is not subject to the 10 percent penalty on distributions to the extent the distributions "do not exceed the qualified higher education expenses of the taxpayer for the taxable year."[203] It is important to note that the IRA distribution must occur in the same year as the tuition payment in order to avoid the penalty. It also is important to coordinate the amount of the distribution with the amount of the expenses so that the distribution amount does not exceed amount of the "qualified higher education expenses."[204] In order to qualify for the "qualified higher education expenses" exception, the expenses must be for education furnished to the IRA owner, the IRA owner's spouse, or any child or grandchild of the IRA owner or the IRA owner's spouse.[205] "Qualified higher education expenses" have the same meaning as defined for 529 plans.[206]

G. Other Tax Breaks for Education

1. General

Practitioners should be aware of the various credits available for individuals who pay their own higher education expenses or those of their spouse or dependents. These tax credits, identified in the next subsection, are available only to individuals whose income is below certain limits.

2. American Opportunity Tax Credit and Lifetime Learning Credit

Within limitations, individuals are allowed to take the American Opportunity Tax Credit (AOTC) (formerly named the Hope Scholarship Credit) and the Lifetime Learning Credit (LLC) for "qualified tuition and related expenses"[207] incurred by themselves, their spouses, or their dependents.[208] In order to take advantage of the AOTC, the student must be attending an "eligible educational institution"[209] for at least half of a normal full-time schedule.[210] Unlike the AOTC, the LLC is not subject to the degree, workload, or year of study requirement.[211]

The AOTC currently is limited to $2,500[212] per year and is available for expenses incurred for the first four years of undergraduate education for each "eligible student."[213] Forty percent of the credit is refundable unless the taxpayer is subject to the kiddie tax.[214] The availability of the AOTC is gradually phased out for taxpayers with MAGI[215] between $80,000 and $90,000 (and $160,000 to $180,000 for married taxpayers filing jointly).[216] In contrast, the LLC is limited to $2,000 per year,[217] and the student may be enrolled for as little as one course to qualify for the LLC.[218] The course may be taken "to acquire or improve job skills."[219] The LLC is nonrefundable.[220] The availability of the LLC is gradually phased out for taxpayers with MAGI[221] between $57,000 and $67,000 (and $114,000 to $134,000 for married taxpayers filing jointly) in 2018.[222] Neither credit is available for married individuals filing individually.[223] Neither credit is allowed to a taxpayer who is claimed as a dependent on another taxpayer's return.[224] Both credits cannot be claimed in the same tax year with respect to the same student.[225] However, a taxpayer may elect both credits in the same tax year for different students.

> EXAMPLE
>
> In 2018, Jane pays $5,000 of qualified tuition for Dependent Mary and $5,000 of qualified tuition for Dependent Helen. Jane's MAGI[226] is $50,000. Mary is a full-time student in her first year of post-secondary schooling. Helen attends college, but does not attend on a full- or part-time basis. Jane elects the AOTC with respect to Mary. Jane may not claim an LLC for Mary. Jane may, however, claim the LLC for Helen.

The AOTC also is disallowed in the case of a student who is convicted of a federal or state felony drug offense before the end of the taxable year for which the pertinent academic period ends.[227] If a taxpayer fraudulently claims the AOTC or recklessly or intentionally disregards rules and regulations in claiming the AOTC, the AOTC is disallowed for a ten-year period and a two-year period, respectively.[228] Additional substantiation to claim the AOTC in a current taxable year may be required if the taxpayer, in any prior taxable year, was disallowed the AOTC as the result of deficiency procedures.[229] The 10 percent penalty for excess distributions from 529 plans or Coverdell ESAs may be waived if the excess contribution is caused by an education credit.[230]

PRACTICE NOTE

As a result of the coordination with other tax-favored education funding methods, practitioners are advised to run the numbers to determine which method results in the largest tax savings to the taxpayer.

Comparison Chart[231] (Current as of October 2018)

	AOTC	LLC
Code section	25A	25A
Maximum tax credit or tax benefit	$2,500	$2,000
Refundable?	Forty percent of credit is refundable unless taxpayer is a child subject to kiddie tax.	The LLC is not refundable.
Income limitations	No credit is allowed if MAGI exceeds $90,000 ($180,000 in the case of a joint return). MAGI is *not* adjusted for inflation.	No credit is allowed if MAGI exceeds $67,000 ($114,000 in the case of a joint return). MAGI is adjusted for inflation.
Eligible if married filing separately?	No	No
Dependent status	A taxpayer cannot elect the credit if taxpayer is claimed as a dependent on someone else's federal income tax return.	A taxpayer cannot elect the credit if taxpayer is claimed as a dependent on someone else's federal income tax return.
Identification requirements	To claim the credit, the taxpayer must provide the name of the student and the student's identification number. There also are additional requirements for identifying the student. *See* § 25A(g)(B).	To claim the credit, the taxpayer must provide the name of the student and the student's identification number.
Election?	Yes	Yes
IRS form and instructions	Form 8863 and instructions	Form 8863 and instructions

	AOTC	LLC
"Qualified tuition and related expenses" eligible for credit or deduction	Tuition and fees, and *course materials* required for enrollment or attendance of: · taxpayer, · taxpayer's spouse, or · taxpayer's dependent at an "eligible education institution"	Tuition and fees required for enrollment or attendance of: · taxpayer, · taxpayer's spouse, or · taxpayer's dependent at an "eligible education institution"
Expenses ineligible for credit or deduction	· student activity fees, · athletic fees, · insurance expenses, or · other expenses *unrelated* to an individual's academic course of instruction, or · expenses with respect to any course or other education involving sports, games, or hobbies, *unless* the course or other education is part of the individual's degree program	· student activity fees, · athletic fees, · insurance expenses, or · other expenses *unrelated* to an individual's academic course of instruction, or · expenses with respect to any course or other education involving sports, games, or hobbies, *unless* the course or other education is part of the individual's degree program
Coordination of expenses with other allowances	Expenses must be reduced by: · a qualified scholarship, · an educational assistance allowance, and · a payment for the student's educational expenses (excluding by gift or inheritance) that is excludable from gross income under any U.S. law	Expenses must be reduced by: · a qualified scholarship, · an educational assistance allowance, and · a payment for the student's educational expenses (excluding by gift or inheritance) that is excludable from gross income under any U.S. law
Number of years credit or deduction is allowed	Credit is allowed only for *first four* years of postsecondary education years.	Credit is allowed for *unlimited* years.
Enrollment or number of courses	Student must be enrolled at least one academic period during the tax year.	Non-degree courses (if part of a postsecondary degree program or taken to acquire or improve job skills) or degree courses are eligible for the credit.
Payee statement Requirement (Form 1098-T)	For tax years beginning after June 29, 2015, no credit generally is allowed unless taxpayer receives payee statement under Code section 6050S(d).	For tax years beginning after June 29, 2015, no credit generally is allowed unless taxpayer receives payee statement under Code section 6050S(d).
Other limitations	· Disallowance of credit if student is convicted of felony drug offense. · Restrictions on taxpayers who improperly claimed AOTC in prior years	Not applicable Not applicable
Coordination between credits	Both credits cannot be claimed in the *same* tax year for the *same* student.	Both credits cannot be claimed in the *same* tax year for the *same* student.

II. DONOR MAKES GIFT FOR BENEFIT OF CHILD

A. Custodial Accounts

1. General

Donors also can provide funds to pay education costs through custodial gifts to minors under the applicable Uniform Gifts to Minors Act (UGMA) or, more common, Uniform Transfers to Minors Act (UTMA).[232] Both UGMA and UTMA accounts are relatively inexpensive to establish and are easily maintained. Unlike trusts, custodial accounts require no formal accounting or independent annual income tax reporting. The donor transfers money or property to a custodian for the benefit of the designated minor. A UTMA account can hold a wide variety of property, whereas a UGMA account can hold only securities, money, insurance policies, and annuity contracts.[233] Each account may benefit only one minor. Although bound by the "prudent person" investment standard, the custodian has the discretion to accumulate or distribute income or principal for the minor's benefit.[234]

A common issue for clients is the choice of custodians. Many clients wish to act as custodians of accounts they create. However, a donor who acts as custodian and who dies during the term of the account risks full federal gross estate inclusion of the account assets.[235]

The biggest disadvantage of UGMA and UTMA accounts is the account must terminate when the minor reaches the statutory age of termination. This age varies from state to state, but is typically either eighteen or twenty-one. Recent trends in most states are to raise the maximum age of termination.[236] Once the beneficiary reaches the age of termination, the beneficiary controls the use of the funds and neither the custodian nor the donor has any power to direct the funds to be used for educational purposes.[237]

2. Federal Income Tax Treatment

The property held in a UTMA account is held by a custodian in a fiduciary capacity and is invested in for the benefit of the child. Generally, the "kiddie tax" will apply to the child's unearned income if (1) the child has not reached nineteen years of age at the close of the taxable year or (2) the child is a full-time student under the age of twenty-four.[238] Unearned income includes dividends, interest, and other investment income over and above an inflation-adjusted threshold amount[239] ($2,100[240] in 2018). Before the passage of the Tax Cuts and Jobs Act[241] in 2017, the child's unearned income was subject to the greater of the child's rate or the parent's or parents' top marginal tax rate.[242] For tax years after December 31, 2017, and before January 1, 2026, the child's unearned income generally is subject to the income tax rates and brackets applicable to trusts and estate.[243] Long-term capital gains and "qualified dividends" are subject to current favorable rates, but with modified income thresholds.[244] To the extent the investment income of the UTMA is used by the custodian for the support of the child, the income will be included in the gross income of the parent or person legally obligated to provide support to the child.[245]

3. *Federal Gift Tax Consequences*

Transfers to UTMA accounts qualify for the annual gift tax exclusion under Code section 2503(b). Therefore, in 2018, a donor may transfer up to $15,000 per donee[246] ($30,000 for a married[247] donor, if gift splitting[248] is elected) to the UTMA account without federal gift tax consequences.[249]

4. *Federal Estate Tax Consequences*

As mentioned earlier, if the donor acts as custodian of the account and the donor dies while serving as custodian, the account assets are included in the donor's gross estate for federal estate tax purposes. If the donor designates someone else other than the donor (and excluding someone who is legally obligated to support the minor) to be custodian of the account, the property generally will be includable in the minor's gross estate if the minor dies before the account terminates.[250]

5. *Coordination with Other Funding Mechanisms*

UTMA custodians can invest cash in 529 accounts on behalf of the minor.[251] Thus, if the UTMA account holds assets (e.g., mutual funds, stocks, bonds) other than cash, the assets must be sold or exchanged, possibly resulting in negative federal income tax consequences. Given the contribution limitations of a Coverdell ESA, investment in a Coverdell ESA by a UTMA custodian or qualification of the custodial account as a Coverdell ESA may be impractical. In fact, some financial institutions are no longer accepting applications to open a Coverdell ESA or allowing the establishment of a new Coverdell ESA by way of an account transfer.[252]

B. Trusts

1. *General*

The trust can be an education funding mechanism, most attractive to wealthier clients generally. Trusts are a more expensive option because, in addition to initial transaction costs, they require ongoing "care and feeding" throughout the term of existence, which includes administrative costs, legal fees, accountant fees, and possibly fiduciary and custodial fees. The two types of trusts optimal for education funding are (1) the Code section 2503(c) trust and (2) a trust that includes so-called Crummey[253] withdrawal powers. Gifts to both types of trusts qualify for the gift tax annual exclusion as they are gifts of present interests.[254] Code section 2503(c) trusts allow for a one-time withdrawal of all of the trust property by the beneficiary at age twenty-one. The Crummey trust, on the other hand, generally grants annual withdrawal rights, but only for a limited time (often thirty days) and only over the assets contributed to the trust that year.[255]

2. *Federal Income Tax Treatment*

These trusts may be treated either as grantor or non-grantor trusts depending on the way the trust is drafted.[256] Generally, income generated from a grantor trust is included in the gross income of the grantor for federal income tax purposes, allowing trust assets to grow federal income tax-free. The income of non-grantor trusts is subject to federal income tax at a compressed rate schedule.[257] Therefore, the assets in a non-grantor trust do not grow tax-free. If the income in a non-grantor trust actually is distributed or required to be distributed to the beneficiary, distributable income may be taxed to the beneficiary at the beneficiary's rate.[258]

3. The Effects of Transfer

While a properly drafted trust may provide asset protection to the donor or student from creditor's claims, the donor must be willing to relinquish dominion and control over the assets transferred to the trust.[259] The transfer of the assets by the donor must be considered complete to remove the property from the donor's gross estate for federal estate tax purposes. Many clients are unwilling to relinquish control over the investment and distribution of assets that will be held beneficially for their children.

4. Coordination with 529 Plans

A donor may want to use both the trust and other education funding methods. For example, as discussed earlier, many 529 plans allow trusts to be the account holder. In that case, it is important to ensure that the trust is drafted to allow the trustee to invest in a 529 plan.[260] Otherwise, the applicable prudent investor rule may not permit the investment. As already discussed, use of a trust may provide additional asset protection, but may eliminate the ability to front-load contributions to avoid federal gift tax consequences as a result of the limitations applicable to annual exclusion gifts to trusts.[261]

III. STUDENT FUNDS EDUCATION COST

A. Financial Aid, Scholarship Concerns, and Student Loans

Many students financing their own education rely on financial aid. Aid may be in the form of direct aid from the government or institution, grants, student loans, or scholarships.

An above-the-line federal income tax deduction[262] of up to $2,500 is available to a taxpayer who pays interest on a "qualified education loan."[263] Generally, the lender must not be related to or be an employer of the debtor.[264] In order to take this deduction, the taxpayer may not be claimed as a dependent on someone else's federal income tax return.[265] The deduction may be claimed by an individual who makes payments on a qualified loan as long as the individual is married to the student or claims the student as a dependent on his or her income tax return.[266] If the individual is married, he or she must file jointly in order to claim the deduction.[267] For taxable years beginning in 2018, the deduction, however, is phased out for individuals with MAGI[268] of $65,000 to $80,000 ($135,000 to $165,000 for married individuals filing jointly).[269]

The sources of financial aid are beyond the scope of this discussion.[270] Nonetheless, some of the education funding methods discussed may affect the student's qualification for financial aid. For example, 529 prepaid tuition plans reduce the student's need for financial aid dollar-for-dollar, and a college savings plan typically is considered an asset of the account owner with 50 percent of the earnings portion attributable to the student.[271] When determining who should be the owner of a 529 account, one should consider naming someone other than the student, and perhaps even someone other than the parent, for financial aid qualification purposes. Further, while the earnings in a 529 plan are taxed upon withdrawal if not used for qualified expenses, the 10 percent penalty is waived if the student receives a qualified scholarship.[272]

B. 529 Plans and Coverdell ESAs

Students can create 529 plans and Coverdell ESAs for their own benefit. The main attraction of these accounts is the federal income tax-free growth of the assets or, as in the case of 529 prepaid tuition plans, the ability to lock in future tuition prices. Therefore, the sooner the student establishes the account the better. It is important to understand (1) how each device works; (2) the associated advantages and disadvantages; as well as (3) the potential age, (4) residency, and (5) income level restrictions associated with each investment vehicle to determine which one is most suitable for the student's needs.

C. Family Loans

Some students also may have the option of borrowing from friends or relatives to finance their education by entering into a loan agreement at rates more favorable than commercial lending rates. This option will be particularly attractive in periods of low interest rates. Students able to fund education through this method can either enter into each loan transaction as the next installment of tuition comes due or borrow a lump sum up front and invest the money in an investment vehicle with a rate of return higher than the interest rate on the loan. Unfortunately, as stated earlier, the student loan interest deduction of Code section 221 is not available to the student if the lender is related to the student.[273] The statute governing these loans for federal tax purposes is Code section 7872. Among other things, the lender will be deemed to recognize interest income at the applicable federal rate whether or not the interest is paid.

These loans should have interest rates no lower than the applicable federal rate (Code section 1274(d) rate) for the month when the loan is made. In general, the Code section 1274(d) rate is lower than the rate available for commercial borrowing. This method can generate costs including legal fees to prepare the promissory note and any related loan documents. This transaction must be deemed to be conducted at arm's length. Otherwise, the loan proceeds, or the interest accruing thereon, may be treated as a gift between the lender and student. The interest rate should not be set below the applicable federal rate in effect at the time at which the transaction is entered. Furthermore, the student must actually make the interest and principal payments as required by the terms of the promissory note on a timely basis.

If the applicable federal rate declines after the promissory note has been executed, the parties should be careful when considering refinancing. Generally, this will entail amending or restating the note to reduce the interest rate and should include some consideration for the lender such as a shorter maturity date or some acceleration of principal repayment. If done improperly, the reduced amount of interest may be deemed a gift by the lender to the debtor. Thus, the reduced interest rate cannot be the only change to the terms of the loan.

IV. CONCLUSION

The field of saving for education provides an embarrassment of riches. As these materials have shown, there are a bewildering number of choices available to clients, with no readily available one-size-fits-all approach. However, a few rules of thumb can probably be derived from the preceding discussion.

First, consider the ages of the students for whom savings are being made. A student near college age is not a very good candidate for the 529 plan because the contributed amounts will not remain in the plan long enough for the federal income tax-free savings benefit to outweigh the potential drawbacks (e.g., higher administrative costs, fewer investment choices, possible penalty). Instead, direct tuition payment, which is perhaps the most effective option, should be considered first, with any excess going to the student to pay for other expenses under the annual exclusion amount.

Second, the level of family wealth will to a large extent dictate the choice of education funding vehicle. If the parent or grandparent has significant wealth and intends to make large lifetime gifts, the use of a trust for those gifts probably is appropriate because the use of a trust allows the most flexibility of distribution and asset management. This is particularly true if the donor intends to use assets of a family business that will be held until the child reaches college age and then liquidated to pay for the education.

Third, the giving of multiple generations should be considered. There may be tools available to the parents that are unavailable to grandparents, and use of both the grandparents' and parents' tools may provide the greatest savings potential. For example, if the parents' MAGI is below the thresholds described earlier, they may be able to use the AOPC or LLC. At the same time, the grandparents (if they have the means to do so) could be contributing to a 529 plan or Coverdell ESA.

Fourth, a "layering" approach may be appropriate. For example, if the state in which a parent resides offers a state income tax deduction for contributions up to a certain amount (assume $1,000 for the sake of discussion), the parent may want to give the first $1,000 of the funds he or she has earmarked for education savings to that state's 529 plan. Next, he or she might consider transferring the next $2,000 of education funding money to a Coverdell ESA because that vehicle can offer greater investment choice and lower fees, and distributions from it can be used for private elementary and secondary education as well as college. This second strategy assumes the Tax Cuts and Jobs Act amendment to the definition of "qualified higher education expenses" under Code section 529 is not in effect.[274] The donor, nonetheless, may want to proceed with this approach because of (1) the other identified factors, that is, greater investment choices and lower fees, (2) the $10,000 limitation imposed on qualified expenses for elementary and secondary education under Code section 529,[275] and (3) a state's 529 plan does not permit distributions for elementary and secondary education. After those first two contributions are made, the balance of the education savings assets should be transferred to the state's 529 plan with the greatest investment choices and lowest administrative cost.

Regardless of the method or methods chosen, however, the overriding goal of the lawyer advising clients who are saving for education first is to explain the range of options available, and then to help the client determine which of those options is most consistent with the client's estate and income tax planning needs.

A. Resources for Further Information

- www.collegesavings.org
- www.finaid.org
- www.irs.gov
- www.savingforcollege.com
- www.treasurydirect.gov
- Laura L. Monagle, Financial Aid for Students: Online Resources, Congressional Research Service R43108 (June 12, 2018), *available at* https://fas.org/sgp/crs/misc/R43108.pdf.

NOTES

1. Also contributing to the original chapter while employed by Buchanan Ingersoll, P.C. was Christopher E. Condeluci. This chapter, nor any of the chapters in this book, necessarily reflect the views of the Internal Revenue Service.

2. For calendar year 2018, the currently unified federal estate and gift tax exemption for a U.S. citizen or domiciliary, indexed for inflation, is $11.18 million. *See* Chapter 1 (explaining mechanics of the exemption). One, however, must be cognizant of the state of flux of the federal transfer tax system in making estate and

gift plans. For example, the exemption is scheduled to revert to $5 million, indexed for inflation, for years beginning January 1, 2026. *See id.* After 2017, the inflation adjustment is tied to the chained consumer price index. *See id.*

3.   Because the individual funding the costs could be a grandparent, parent, relative, or friend, the individual is referred to, in most instances, as the "donor." Furthermore, because of the variety of possible relationships, the individual who actually will benefit from the education funds is referred to primarily as the "student."

4.   Section references are to the Internal Revenue Code of 1986, as amended, or to regulations issued thereunder, unless otherwise indicated.

5.   *See* § 2503(e)(2)(A) (cross-referencing § 170(b)(1)(A)(ii)). To qualify under Code section 170(b)(1)(A)(ii), the "educational organization" must be "an educational organization that normally maintains a regular faculty and curriculum and normally has a regularly enrolled body of pupils or students in attendance at the place where its educational activities are regularly carried on." Apparently, the educational organization, if meeting the Code definition, may be domestic or foreign. *See* Chapter 3, note 140.

6.   Code section 2503(e) statutorily refers to an exclusion from taxable gifts as a "qualified transfer." A "qualified transfer" is not treated as a transfer of property by gift for federal gift tax purposes and, thus, is not subject to federal gift taxation. *See* § 2503(e)(1). *See also* Chapter 1 (explaining mechanics of "qualified transfer"). For purposes of this chapter, "qualified transfer," "qualified payment," "excludable payment," and "2503(e) exclusion" may be used interchangeably.

7.   *See* Chapter 1 (explaining the annual exclusion under Code section 2503(b)).

8.   *See also* Chapters 1, 3, and 4.

9.   Reg. § 25.2503-6(c), Example (2).

10.   TAM 199941013 (distinguishing example 6 of Regulation section 25.2503-6(c)). *But see* § 6110(k)(3) (unless otherwise established by regulations, "written determination" cannot be used or cited as precedent); § 6110(b)(1)(A) ("written determination" includes "technical advice memorandum").

11.   *See* note 10.

12.   *See* Chapter 1 (explaining applicable exclusion amount).

13.   *See* Chapter 1 (explaining Code section 2035).

14.   *See* § 2503(e)(2)(B). *See also* Chapters 1 and 3.

15.   Beginning on September 1, 2004, holders of Series EE bonds no longer could continue to defer federal income tax on interest income by converting to Series HH bonds.

16.   *See* §§ 135(a), 135(c)(2)(A).

17.   Although the Series I bond is not issued at discount, IRS publications treat the bond as a "qualified United States savings bond." *See, e.g.,* 2018 IRS Form 8815 and accompanying instructions. Forms and instructions are available on the IRS website, www.irs.gov.

18.   *See* § 135(c)(1).

19.   *See* § 135(c)(2). "Qualified higher education expenses" do not include "expenses with respect to any course or other education involving sports, games, or hobbies other than as part of a degree program." *See* § 135(c)(2)(B). The term "eligible education institution" has the same meaning as set forth in Code section 529(e) (5). *See* § 135(c)(3) (cross-referencing § 529(e)(5)). *See also* note 37.

20.   *See* § 135(c)(2)(C).

21.   *See* § 135(d)(2)(B) (cross-referencing §§ 529(c)(3)(B) and 530(d)(2)).

22.   *See* § 135(d)(2)(A) (cross-referencing § 25A).

23.   § 135(b)(2). MAGI is calculated on a worksheet provided in the instructions to Line 9 of 2018 IRS Form 8815. Form 8815 and accompanying instructions are available on the IRS website, www.irs.gov.

24.   *See* § 135(b)(2)(B). *See also* Rev. Proc. 2018-18, § 3.18, 2018-10 I.R.B. 392. For tax years beginning after December 31, 2017, the inflation adjustment is based upon the chained consumer price index (CPI), not the traditional CPI. *See* § 135(b)(2)(B)(ii) (cross-referencing § 1(f)(3)). For up-to-date information regarding inflation-adjusted tax items, the reader usually is referred to the applicable IRS revenue procedure issued near the end of each year. Because of the late enactment of the Tax Cuts and Jobs Act in 2017 (P.L. 115-97), the IRS issued additional revenue procedures in the beginning of the year 2018 for certain items impacted by the act. *See also* note 27 (providing formal name of Tax Cuts and Jobs Act).

25.   § 135(d)(3).

26.   *See* note 18 and accompanying text.

27.   *See* An Act to provide for reconciliation pursuant to titles II and V of the concurrent resolution on the budget for fiscal year 2018, Pub. L. No. 115-97, § 11032(a)(1), codified at § 529(c)(7) (Dec. 22, 2017), informally referred to as the "Tax Cuts and Jobs Act." *See also id.* at § 11032(a)(2), codified at § 529(e)(3)(A). These statutory modifications are effective for distributions made after December 31, 2017. *See also* notes 64–67 and accompanying text.

28.   *See* note 27 (providing formal name of Tax Cuts and Jobs Act).

29.   One example is the Louisiana STARTK12 program. *See* www.startsaving. la.gov/savings/index.jsp. According to the website, the program will "allow families to save for tuition expenses related to the attendance at any Louisiana school that provides any or all of kindergarten through twelfth grade." At the time of this writing, the program is not fully operational because of software development issues.

30.   § 529(b)(1)(A)(i). *See also* Prop. Reg. § 1.529-2(a)(1), 1.529-2(c)(1).

31.   *See, e.g.,* Virginia Prepaid 529™ Program. For a list of prepaid tuition programs, see https://www.cappex.com/hq/articles-and-advice/financial-aid/saving-for -college/List-of-State-Prepaid-Tuition-Plans.

32.   § 529(b) (flush language).

33.   *See* www.privatecollege529.com/OFI529/?action=participating-schools-section.

34.   *See* § 529(b)(1)(A)(ii). Prop. Reg. § 1.529-2(a)(2), 1.529-2(c)(2).

35.   § 529(b)(2). A 529 plan may accept payment by check, money order, credit card, or similar methods. *See* Prop. Reg. § 1.529-2(d).

36.   For example, New York generally allows an annual deduction of up to $5,000 for individuals or heads of household and up to $10,000 for married couples filing jointly. *See* N.Y. Tax Law § 612(c)(32). Other states permitting a state income tax deduction include, but are not limited to, Georgia, Idaho, Michigan, Mississippi, Oklahoma, Oregon, and Virginia. As stated earlier, however, many states afford a deduction only to state residents. Practitioners are advised to determine whether the state in which their client establishes a 529 plan permits a deduction for contributions and whether the availability of the deduction is contingent on state residency.

37.   See § 529(e)(3) (defining "qualified higher education expenses" for enrollment or attendance at an "eligible education institution"). *See also* notes 59–67 and accompanying text (providing evolving definition of "qualified higher education expenses" for purposes of § 529). An "eligible education institution," having the same meaning for purposes of Code section 135(c)(3), is defined as "an institution which is described in section 481 of the Higher Education Act of 1965 (20 U.S.C. 1088), as in effect on the date of the enactment of this paragraph [i.e., Code section 529(e)(5)(A)],"

and "which is eligible to participate in a program under title IV of such Act." *See* § 529(e)(5). *See also* note 19. These "institutions generally are accredited post-secondary educational institutions offering credit toward a bachelor's degree, an associate degree, a graduate level or professional degree, or another recognized post-secondary credential. Certain proprietary institutions and post-secondary vocational institutions also are eligible institutions. The institution must be eligible to participate in Department of Education student aid programs." Prop. Reg. § 1.529-1(c) (defining "eligible education institution").

38. Before 2004, the earnings portion of the withdrawn funds from institution-sponsored plans, despite being used for "qualified higher education expenses," was subject to federal income taxation. *See* § 529(c)(B)(iii).

39. *See* § 529(c)(3).

40. Practitioners should confirm that the particular state in question follows the federal treatment of income accruing in 529 plan accounts.

41. *See* § 529(c)(6) (cross-referencing § 530(d)(4)).

42. *See* § 529(c)(6) (cross-referencing § 530(d)(4)(B)). *See also* Prop. Reg. § 1.529-2(e)(ii), (iii). As in the case of Coverdell Education Savings accounts (discussed later), the 10 percent penalty may be waived for the beneficiary's cost of attendance of "advance education" at the U.S. Military Academy, the U.S. Naval Academy, the U.S. Air Force Academy, the U.S. Coast Guard Academy, or the U.S. Merchant Marine Academy. *See* § 529 (c)(6). *See also* § 530(d)(4)(B)(iv).

43. *See* Pub. L. No. 115-97, *supra* note 27, § 11032(a)(1), codified at § 529(c)(7).

44. *See* § 529A. The Stephen Beck, Jr. Achieving a Better Life Experience Act of 2014 (ABLE Act), part of the Tax Increase Prevention Act of 2014 (P.L. 113-295), created the original Code § 529A. *See also* Chapter 7.

45. Regulations are expected to be issued specifying the more limited definition of "member of the family," as defined in Code section 529A(e)(4), is not to be utilized. *See* Notice 2018-58, § IV, 2018-33 I.R.B. 305 (July 30, 2018). *See* § 529(e)(2). *See also* notes 85–87 and accompanying text.

46. *See* Pub. L. No. 115-97, *supra* note 27, § 11025(a), codified at § 529(c)(3)(C)(i)(III).

47. Apparently, this amount, statutorily measured in terms of the annual exclusion and allowed under Code section 529A(b)(2)(B)(i), is *in addition to* the annual gift tax exclusion amount allowed under Code section 2503(b). *See* § 529A(b)(2)(B)(i) (cross-referencing § 2503(b)). *See also* Chapter 1 (explaining annual exclusion).

48. *See* Notice 2018-58, § IV, *supra* note 45; 2018-33 I.R.B. 305.

49. "For more information on the effect of ABLE accounts on the beneficiary's eligibility for public benefits," Notice 2018-88 refers the reader to "the preamble of the Notice of Proposed Rulemaking (80 FR 35602) published in the Federal Register on [June 22, 2015]." *See* Notice 2018-88, *supra* note 45, note 4. *See also* Chapter 7.

50. *See also* § 529A(b)(2)(B)(i) (cross-referencing § 2503(b)).

51. *See* Notice 2018-58, *supra* note 45, § IV.

52. *Id.*

53. *See id.* § VI.

54. *Id.* § IV.

55. Pub. L. No. 114-113, *Division Q.*

56. In the case of a refund received after December 31, 2014, and before December 18, 2015, the recontribution must be made no later than *sixty* days after December 18, 2015 (i.e., the date of enactment of Code section 529(c)(3)(D)). *See id.* § 302.

57. *See* Notice 2018-58, *supra* note 45, § III.

58. *See id.*
59. § 529(e)(3)(A)(i).
60. *See* § 529(e)(3)(B) (cross-referencing § 25A(b)(3)).
61. § 529(e)(3)(A)(ii).
62. § 529(e)(3)(A)(iii) (cross-referencing §§ 168(i)(2)(B) and 197(e)(3)(B)).
63. § 529(e)(3) (flush language).
64. § 529(c)(7), 529(e)(3) (flush language).
65. 2018-33 I.R.B. 305.
66. *See* Notice 2018-58 *supra* note 45, § V.
67. Final passage of the Tax Cuts and Jobs Act rejected the Conference Report version of the definition of "qualified higher education expense," which included home schooling expenses. *See* H. Rept. 115-466, § 11032(a)(7)(B).
68. Pub. L. No. 109-280.
69. *See* Pub. L. No. 109-280, § 1304(f), codified at § 529(f). *See also* Joint Committee on Taxation, Technical Explanation of H.R. 4, As Passed By The House On July 28, 2006, And As Considered By The Senate On August 3, 2006, JCX-38-06 (Aug. 3, 2006) at 369. *See also* Advance Notice of Proposed Rulemaking regarding Guidance on Qualified Tuition Programs under Section 529, REG-117127-05(ANPR); 73 F.R. 3441–3446. (Jan. 18, 2008); Announcement 2008-17, 2008-9 I.R.B. 512 (Mar. 3, 2008).
70. Advance Notice, *supra* note 69, overview (Jan. 18, 2008). *But see* ACTEC comments (step-transaction and sham-transaction doctrines sufficient to address most abuse involving Code 529) *available at* www.americanbar.org/content/dam/aba/publications/rpte_ereport/2008/april/section529submission.authcheckdam.pdf.
71. Advance Notice of Proposed Rulemaking, *supra* note 69, overview (Jan. 18, 2008). *Accord*, Announcement, *supra* note 69, overview.
72. *See id.*
73. *See id.*
74. For a web-based resource, see www.savingforcollege.com/compare_529_plans/?plan_question_ids[]=47&page=compare_plan_questions.
75. Many states offer the option of static investment portfolios or age-based investment portfolios that become more conservative as the beneficiary nears the age of eighteen.
76. Pub. L. No. 104-188, title I (Small Business Job Protection Act of 1996), § 1806(b)(1)(5). *See also* Prop. Reg. § 1.529-2(g) (selection among different investment strategies only available at time of initial contribution establishing the account). *But see* Notice 2001-55, 2001-2 I.R.B. 299 (Sept. 10, 2001) (IRS will permit a change in investment options *once* per year *and* on the change in the designated beneficiary of the account), modified by Notice 2009-1, 2009-2 I.R.B. 248 (Dec. 23, 2008) (allowing change in investment options *twice* per year *and* on the change in the designated beneficiary of the account).
77. Pub. L. No. 113-295, div. B, title I (Achieving a Better Life Experience Act of 2014), § 105(a)(1), amending § 529(b)(4). Note the statutory language does not require "a change in the designated beneficiary of the account" as required by earlier IRS notices. *See* note 76.
78. Section 529(c)(3)(C)(i)(I); Prop. Reg. § 1.529-3(a)(2). Only one rollover can be made in any twelve-month period. *See* § 529(c)(3)(C)(iii). Notice 2001-81, 2001-2 C.B. 617 (Dec. 7, 2001), implies that amounts in a Coverdell ESA may be rolled over to a 529 plan. *See id.* at § c(2).

79. *See* notes 85–87 and accompanying text.

80. *See* § 529(c)(3)(C)(i)(II).

81. *See, e.g., Plan Disclosure Booklet and Savings Trust Agreement*, at 24, Georgia Path2College 529 Plan (July 2, 2018), *available at* https://www.path2college529.com /documents/ga_disclosure.pdf.

82. By contrast, prepaid tuition plans usually impose beneficiary age or residency requirements.

83. *See* § 529(c)(3)(C)(ii). *See also* notes 85–87 and accompanying text.

84. § 529(c)(3)(C)(ii).

85. § 529(e)(2) (cross-referencing § 152 (d)(2)(A)–(G)). *See also* Prop. Reg. § 1.529-1(c).

86. Prop. Reg. § 1.529-1(c).

87. *See id.*

88. Advance Notice, *supra* note 69, § II.B. *Accord*, Announcement, *supra* note 69, § II.B.

89. *See* Chapter 1.

90. *See id.*

91. This rule also is being considered in the context of trust ownership. *See* notes 131–134 and accompanying text.

92. *See id.*

93. § 529(c)(2)(A)(i); Prop. Reg. § 1.529-5(b)(1). A contribution is not treated as a "qualified transfer" under Code section 2503(e). *See* § 529(c)(2)(A)(ii). *See* Chapter 1 (explaining "qualified transfer").

94. *See* Chapter 3 (explaining GST exclusion).

95. The annual exclusion is indexed for inflation. *See* Rev. Proc. 2017-58, § 3.37(1), 2017-45 I.R.B. 489 (Oct. 19, 2017). For tax years beginning after December 31, 2017, the inflation adjustment is based upon the chained consumer price index (CPI), not the traditional CPI. *See* § 2503(b)(2)(B) (cross-referencing § 1(f)(3)). For 2018, the change in indexes did not affect the inflated-adjusted amount. *See also* Chapter 1.

96. Prop. Reg. § 1.529-5(b)(2).

97. *See* § 529(c)(2)(B). *See also* Chapter 1 (explaining applicable exclusion amount).

98. *See* § 529(c)(2)(B). *See also* Prop. Reg. § 1.529-5(B)(2)(iii). *See also* Estate of Beyer v. Comm'r, T.C. Memo 2016-184 at 147–48 (federal gift tax liability when no election taken on federal gift tax return). Forms and instructions are available on the IRS website, www.irs.gov.

99. Advance Notice, *supra* note 69, § III(A). *Accord*, Announcement, *supra* note 69, § III(A).

100. Prop. Reg. 1.529-5(B)(2)(v) (example). The taxable gift may be sheltered by the donor's applicable credit amount, resulting in no federal gift taxation. *See* Chapter 1 (explaining applicable credit amount).

101. *See* Chapter 1, note 14 (definition of "husband and wife" and "marriage" for federal tax purposes).

102. Prop. Reg. § 1.529-5(b)(2). *See also* Chapter 1 (explaining gift splitting).

103. *See* Prop. Reg. § 1.529-5(b)(2)(ii). *Accord*, Advance Notice, *supra* note 69, § III.A, Rule 3 (Five-year front-load election "may be made by a donor and the donor's spouse with respect to a gift considered to be made by one-half by each spouse under [Code] section 2513."); Announcement, *supra* note 69, § III.A, Rule 3.

104. *See* Chapter 4.

105. § 529(c)(5)(A).

106. *See* § 529(e)(2). *See also* notes 85–87 and accompanying text.

107. *See* § 529(c)(5)(B). *See also* Prop. Reg. § 1.529-5(b)(3)(ii) (regardless of whether new beneficiary is a member of the family of prior beneficiary, taxable gift occurs "if the new beneficiary is assigned to a lower generation that the old beneficiary, as defined in [Code] section 2651"). *See also* note 181 and accompanying text.

108. *See* § 529(c)(5)(B). *See also* Prop. Reg. § 1.529-5(b)(3)(ii) (providing that if the new beneficiary is at least two generations below the old beneficiary, GST tax consequences will result). *See also* note 182 and accompanying text.

109. Code section 529 does not include a definition of account owner. Proposed regulation section 1.529-1(c), however, provides the following definition:

> Account owner means the person who, under the terms of the [qualified tuition program] or any contract setting forth the terms under which contributions may be made to an account for the benefit of a designated beneficiary, is entitled to select or change the designated beneficiary of an account, to designate any person other than the designated beneficiary to whom funds may be paid from the account, or to receive distributions from the account if no such other person is designated.

According to the Advance Notice of Proposed Rulemaking of January 18, 2008,

> The definition of account owner in [the proposed regulation] was included to reflect practices used at that time to facilitate the establishment of accounts for minor beneficiaries. In practice, the [account owner] retains control over the selection of the DB and has personal access to the funds in the account.

Id. at § II.A. *Accord*, Announcement, *supra* note 69, § II.A.

110. *See* Advance Notice, *supra* note 69, § II.A. *Accord*, Announcement, *supra* note 69, § II.A.

111. *Id.*

112. Advance Notice, *supra* note 69, overview. *Accord*, Announcement, *supra* note 69, overview.

113. *See* note 112.

114. REG-106177-97, no. 55; 63 F.R. 45019–45032.

115. In response, The American College of Trust and Estates Counsel suggested a different approach. That is, a taxable change of a DB should be treated as a transfer by the old DB, but, because of the old DB's lack of control over the 529 account, "the DB should incur liability for the transfer only to the extent the DB consents." "To the extent, the DB does not consent, liability should be imposed on the [account owner], who has possession of the assets that are subject to the deemed transfer." ACTEC comments available at www.americanbar.org/content/dam/aba/publications/rpte_ereport/2008/april/section529submission.auth checkdam.pdf.

116. § 529(c)(4)(A); Prop. Reg. § 1.529-5(d)(1).

117. § 529(c)(4)(C); Prop. Reg. § 1.529-5(d)(2).

118. § 529(c)(4)(B).

119. Advance Notice, *supra* note 69, § II.E. (Rules 1–5) (emphasis added); *accord*, Announcement, *supra* note 69, § II.E. (Rules 1–5) (emphasis added).

120. *See generally* Uniform Voidable Transaction Act, available at www.uniform laws.org/HigherLogic/System/DownloadDocumentFile.ashx?DocumentFileKey =58b5d88d-a3b9-b3bf-873d-8787811656b1&forceDialog=.

121. *See* 11 U.S.C. § 521(b)(6)(A).

122. *See* 11 U.S.C. § 521(b)(6)(B) and (C). For greater detail, *see* Osborne, Johnson, Gopman & Lancaster, *Wealth Protection Planning under the Bankruptcy Abuse Prevention and Consumer Protection Act of 2005*, 30 TAX MGMT. EST., GIFTS & TR. J. 5 (Sept. 2005). *See also* Phillip F. Manns, Jr. & Timothy M. Todd, *Higher Education Savings and Planning: Tax and Nontax Considerations*, 5 TEX. A&M REV. 343 (Winter 2018).

123. *See, e.g.,* COLO. REV. § 23-3.1-307.4 (limited to state's own savings program); FLA. STAT. § 222.22; VA. CODE ANN. § 23.1-707(F) (limited to state's own programs and to contributor, purchaser or beneficiary).

124. *See* Chapter 9 (regarding state variations of UTMA and UGMA).

125. *See* § 529(b)(1)(A); Prop. Reg. § 1.529-1(c) (defining "account owner"). *See also* note 109.

126. *See* Berens v. Berens, 818 S.E.2d 155 (N.C. App. 2018) (money in 529 plans established by divorced parents is not a completed gift to the designated beneficiaries under state law and, therefore, is marital property subject to equitable distribution); Rathkamp v. Danello, No. COA17-760 (N.C. App. 2018) (unpublished opinion) (Coverdell education saving accounts not completed gifts, but marital property, under state law).

127. *See* § 529(e)(1) (defining "designated beneficiary").

128. *See* subsection I.D.7. of this chapter (explaining front loading).

129. *See, e.g.,* NY 529 College Savings Plan, https://www.nysaves.org/home/faqs-other-questions.html#owner (UTMA/UGMA custodian can be account owner of 529 plan).

130. *See* Chapters 3 and 9 (pertaining to termination of custodial accounts).

131. Regulation § 25.2511-1(h)(1) reads:

> The following [is an example] of [a transaction] resulting in taxable gifts and . . . it is assumed that the transfers were not made for an adequate and full consideration in money or money's worth:
>
> > A transfer of property by a corporation to B is a gift to B from the stockholders of the corporation. If B himself is a stockholder, the transfer is a gift to him from the other stockholders but only to the extent it exceeds B's own interest in such amount as a shareholder. A transfer of property by B to a corporation generally represents gifts by B to the other individual shareholders of the corporation to the extent of their proportionate interests in the corporation. However, there may be an exception to this rule, such as a transfer made by an individual to a charitable, public, political or similar organization which may constitute a gift to the organization as a single entity, depending upon the facts and circumstances in the particular case.

132. Advance Notice, *supra* note 69, § II.C. *Accord*, Announcement, *supra* note 69, § II.C.

133. *Id.*

134. *Id.*

135. Announcement, *supra* note 69, § II.C.

136. *See* note 129 and accompanying text.

137. Advance Notice, *supra* note 69, § II.D. *Accord*, Announcement, *supra* note 69, § II.D.

138. *Id.*

139. *Id.*

140. *Id.*

141. *Id.* These special rules also would apply when a contributor establishes a 529 account, names him- or herself as a designated beneficiary, and subsequently changes the designated beneficiary. *Id.* For comments in response to the Advance Notice of Proposed Rulemaking, see www.americanbar.org/content/dam/aba/publi cations/rpte_ereport/2008/april/section529submission.authcheckdam.pdf.

142. *See* § 530(b)(1)(B) (bank trustee); § 530(g) (requirements for treatment of custodial account as trust). *See also* Notice 97-57, § 3, 1997-2 C.B. 308 (Oct. 15, 1997) (An IRS approved nonbank trustee or custodian of individual retirement account is approved automatically by the IRS to be trustees or custodians of Education IRAs). For list of approved nonbank trustees and custodians, *see, e.g.*, Announcement 2011-59; 2011-37 I.R.B. 335.

143. § 530(b)(1)(A)(i).

144. *See* § 530(c)(2) (defining "MAGI").

145. § 530(c)(1).

146. *See* 10 U.S.C. § 1477.

147. *See* 38 U.S.C. § 1967.

148. *See* § 530(b)(9) (cross-referencing 10 U.S.C. § 1477 and 38 U.S.C. § 1967).

149. *See* § 530(b)(9)(A)(ii) (cross-referencing § 408A(e)(2)).

150. *See id.*

151. *See* § 530(b)(9)(B).

152. *See* § 530(b)(2)(A)(i).

153. § 530(b)(2)(A) (cross-referencing §§ 529(e)(3) and 530(b)(3)).

154. § 530(d)(2)(A).

155. *See* § 530(b)(2)(A)(i) (cross-referencing § 529(e)(3)).

156. *See* § 530(b)(2)(A)(ii).

157. *See* § 530(b)(3)(A)(i), 530(b)(3)(B) (defining "school"). *See also* note 66 and accompanying text.

158. *See* § 530(b)(3)(A)(ii). *See also* § 530(b)(3)(B) (defining "school").

159. *See* § 530(b)(3)(A)(iii). *See also* § 530(b)(3)(B) (defining "school").

160. *See* § 530(b)(3)(A) (flush sentence).

161. § 530(d)(1), 530(d)(4).

162. § 530(d)(4)(B).

163. § 530(b)(1)(A)(ii).

164. § 530(b)(1)(E). Divorce or death of a designated beneficiary does not trigger a taxable distribution. *See* § 530(d)(7) (cross-referencing § 220(f)(7) and (8)). For treatment of a Coverdell ESA account at death, see Code section 220(f)(8).

165. §§ 530(d)(8), 530(d)(1), (4).

166. *See* Taxpayer Relief Act of 1997, Pub. L. No. 105-34, § 213(d)(2), codified at former § 4973(e)(1)(B). *See also* Notice 97-60, 1997-42 C.B. 310, § 3, Q & A 22, Q & A 6 (Oct. 27, 1997).

167. *See* Economic Growth and Tax Relief Reconciliation Act of 2001, Pub. L. No. 107-16, § 401(g)(2)(D) codified at § 4973(e)(1)(B).

168. "Member of the family" has the same meaning as defined in Code section 529(e)(2).

169. § 530(d)(6).

170. *See* § 530(b)(1) (flush sentence).

171. *See* § 530(d)(5).

172. *See* § 530(d)(5) (cross-referencing § 529(e)(2), defining "member of the family"). *See also* notes 85–87 and accompanying text.

173. *See* § 530(d)(5) (cross-referencing § 530(d)(1)), 530(d)(6). *See also* § 530(b)(1) (flush sentence).

174. *See* § 530(d)(5).

175. 2001-2 C.B. 617 (Dec. 7, 2001).

176. 2018 Instructions for Form 5498-ESA at 1. Forms and instructions are available on the IRS website, www.irs.gov. The instructions further acknowledge that "[t]he contribution of military death gratuity to a Coverdell ESA is a rollover contribution." *See also* subsection I.E.2. of this chapter.

177. § 530(d)(3) (cross-referencing § 529(c)(2)).

178. §§ 2503(b), 2642(c)(2). *See also* Chapter 1.

179. § 530(d)(3) (cross-referencing § 529(c)(2)).

180. § 530(d)(3) (cross-referencing § 529(c)(2),(4),(5)). *See also* § 529(c)(5)(A).

181. § 530(d)(3) (cross-referencing § 529(c)(2),(4),(5)). *See also* § 529(c)(5)(B). *See also* Prop. Reg. § 1.529-5(b)(3)(ii) (regardless of whether new beneficiary is a member of the family of prior beneficiary, taxable gift occurs "if the new beneficiary is assigned to a lower generation than that of the old beneficiary, as defined in [Code] section 2651").

182. *See* Prop. Reg. § 1.529-5(b)(3)(ii) (providing that if the new beneficiary is at least two generations below the old beneficiary, GST tax consequences will result). *See also* § 529(c)(5)(B)(i) (cross-referencing § 2651).

183. § 530(d)(3) (cross-referencing § 529(c)(4)).

184. *Id.* Given the statutory cross-reference to estate tax rules of Code section 529 in Code section 530(d)(3), the estate tax inclusion rules contained in subsection II.E. of the Advance Notice of Rulemaking pertaining to Guidance on Qualified Tuition Programs Under Section 529 may be relevant for the deceased beneficiary of a Coverdell ESA. *See* note 119 and accompanying text.

185. Compensation generally includes earned income, and "does not include any amount received as a pension or annuity" nor "any amount *received as* deferred compensation." *See* § 219(f)(1) (cross-referencing § 401(c)(2) (defining "earned income")). Alimony is *not* treated as compensation for IRA contribution purposes if the divorce or separation instrument is executed after December 31, 2018, or if the instrument, executed on or before December 31, 2018, is modified after December 31, 2018, and the modification expressly provides that the amendments made by section 11051 of Public Law 115-97 (informally known as the Tax Cuts and Jobs Act) apply. *See* Pub. L. No. 115-97, *supra* note 27, § 11051, codified at § 291(f)(1). Before the amendments by the Tax Cuts and Jobs Act, Code section 291(f)(1) cross-referenced Code section 71. *See* § 219(f)(1). Section 11051 of Public Law 115-97 eliminated Code section 71, which allowed for the inclusion of "alimony or separate maintenance payments" in gross income for federal income tax purposes.

186. § 219(a).

187. § 408A(c)(1); Reg. § 1.408A-1, Q&A-2. For contributions of military death benefits, see Code section 408A(e) (treatment of contribution as a "qualified rollover contribution"). *See also* note 149 and accompanying text.

188. *See* § 408(e)(1); Reg. § 1.408A-1, Q&A-1(b); Reg. § 1.408A-1, Q&A-2.

189. § 408(d)(1).

190. § 408A(d)(1).

191. § 219(b)(1), 219(b)(5)(A), 219(b)(5)(c) (cross-referencing § 1(f)(3)). The $5,000 amount is indexed for inflation in increments of $500 for years beginning

after 2008. For tax years beginning after December 31, 2017, the inflation adjustment is tied to the chained consumer price index (CPI) instead of the traditional CPI. *See* Pub. L. No. 115-97, *supra* note 27, § 11002(a), codified at § 1(f)(3). *See also* www.bls.gov (explaining indexes). Consequently, inflation adjustments are expected to rise in smaller increments.

192. *See* § 219(b). *See also* Notice 2017-64, 2017-45 I.R.B. 486 (Oct. 19, 2017).

193. § 219(b)(5)(B). The maximum catch-up contribution is $500 until 2005, increasing to $1,000 in 2006 and thereafter.

194. § 408A(c)(B)(i) (defining "AGI").

195. § 408A(c)(3)(A). *See generally* Reg. § 1.408A-3, Q&A-3(b).

196. § 408A(c)(4).

197. *See* § 219(g).

198. § 219(g)(3)(A) (defining "AGI").

199. § 219(g). *See also* Notice 2017-64, 2017-45 I.R.B. 486 (Oct. 19, 2017).

200. *See* note 199.

201. *See* § 72(t)(1).

202. *See, e.g.,* Disaster Tax Relief and Airport and Airway Extension Act of 2017, Pub. L. No. 115-63, § 502(a) (providing relief for taxpayers impacted by Hurricanes Harvey, Irma, and Maria and California wildfires; "qualified hurricane distribution" of up to $100,000 not subject to 10 percent penalty). *See also* Tax Cuts and Jobs Act, Pub. L. No. 115-97, *supra* note 27, § 11028(a)-(b) ("qualified 2016 hurricane distribution" not subject to 10 percent penalty).

203. § 72(t)(2)(E), effective for "distributions after December 31, 1997, added by Pub. L. No. 105-34, § 203. Generally, distributions for "qualified higher education expenses" are nonetheless includable in income. *See* § 61(a)(9) (before amendments under Pub. L. No. 115-97, *supra* note 27); § 61(a)(8) (after amendments under Pub. L. No. 115-97, *supra* note 27); § 408(d)(1).

204. In fact, according to IRS 2018 Publication 590-B (Distributions from Individual Retirement Arrangements (IRA)), the IRA distribution does not have to be used to pay the expenses as long as the distributed amount "isn't more than the qualified higher education expenses for the year for education furnished at an eligible educational institution." *Id.* at 23. That appears to be consistent with the statutory language of Code section 172. *But see* Martinez et al. v. Comm'r, T.C. Memo. 2016-182 (taxpayer failed to show 529 plan distribution was "*used* for educational expenses"). Publications are available on the IRS website, www.irs.gov.

205. § 72(t)(7).

206. *See* § 72(t)(2)(E). *See also* § 72(t)(7)(A) (cross-referencing § 529(e)(3)).

207. *See* § 25A(f)(1). "Qualified tuition and related expenses" include tuition and fees required for the enrollment or attendance of the taxpayer, the taxpayer's spouse, or any claimed dependent. *See* § 25A(f)(1)(A). Fees qualifying for the credits are "fees for books, supplies, and equipment used in a course of study, but only if the fees must be paid to the 'eligible educational institution' for the enrollment or attendance of the student at the institution." *See* Reg. § 1.25A-2(d)(ii). In addition, expenses that relate to any course of instruction or other education that involves sports, games, or hobbies are not "qualified tuition and related expenses" unless the course or other education is part of the student's degree program. *See* § 25A(f)(1)(B). "Qualified tuition and related expenses" do not include "student activity fees, athletic fees, insurance expenses, or other expenses unrelated to the individual's academic course of instruction." *See* § 25A(f)(1)(C). *See also* Reg. § 25A-2(d). For purposes of determining the AOTC, "qualified tuition and related expenses" also include course materials. *See* § 25A(f)(1)(D).

208. § 25A(a). The taxpayer elects to claim the credits by completing and submitting Form 8863 with the taxpayer's federal income tax return (i.e., Form 1040). *See* IRS Publication 970 (Tax Benefits for Education For use in preparing 2018 Returns) at 22, 31. *See also* Reg. § 1.25A-1(d) (election made by "attaching" Form 8863 to return). Publications, forms, and instructions are available on the IRS website, www.irs.gov. The taxpayer may elect *not* to have the credits apply to an individual's "qualified tuition and related expenses" in any taxable year. *See* § 25A(e)(1). This option may assist in coordinating tax benefits. *See, e.g.*, note 22 and accompanying text.

209. *See* § 25A(f)(2) (defining "eligible education institution"; same statutory language as Code section 529 (e)(5)).

210. § 25A(b)(3).

211. *See* § 25A(c).

212. The $2,500 amount equals the first $2,000 of "qualified tuition and related expenses" plus 25 percent of the next $2,000 of these expenses per "eligible student." *See* § 25A(b)(1). An "eligible student" is "with respect to an academic period, a student who . . . is carrying at least ½ the normal full-time work load for the course of study the student is pursuing." *See* § 25A(b)(3)(B). For the definition of "academic period," see Regulation section 1.25A-2(c).

213. § 25A(b)(1); Reg. § 1.25A-3(a)(1).

214. § 25A(i) (cross-referencing § 1(g)). *See also* subsection II.A.3. (pertaining to kiddie tax) of this chapter and Chapter 1.

215. § 25A(d)(3) (cross-referencing §§ 911, 931, and 933) (defining "MAGI").

216. § 25A.

217. § 25A(c)(1); Reg. § 1.25A-4(a)(2). The credit is limited to $2,000 for 2003 and tax years thereafter. The $2,000 amount equals 20 percent of "qualified tuition and related expenses" paid by the taxpayer during the tax year and not exceeding $10,000. *See* Reg. § 1.25A-4(a)(2).

218. Notice 97-60, 1997-2 CB 310 (Oct. 27, 1997).

219. *See* Reg. § 1.25A-2(d)(5).

220. § 25A(d)(2).

221. *Id.*

222. § 25A(d)(2); Reg. § 1.25A-1(c)(1). *See also* Rev. Proc. 2017-58, *supra* note 95, § 3.04. For tax years beginning after December 31, 2017, the inflation adjustment is tied to the chained CPI index. For 2018, this inflation adjustment apparently is not impacted by the application of the new index. *See* § 25A(h) (cross-referencing § 1(f)(3)). *See also* note 24.

223. *See* § 25A(g)(6). *See also* Reg. § 1.25A-1(g).

224. *See* § 25A(g)(3)(A).

225. § 25A(c)(2)(A).

226. *See* notes 215 and 221.

227. *See* § 25A(b)(2)(D). *See also* Reg. § 1.25A-3(d)(iv).

228. *See* § 25A(b)(4)(A).

229. *Id.*

230. A taxpayer also has the option of *not* electing to apply either credit with respect to the "qualified tuition and related expenses" of an individual for any taxable year. *See* § 25A(e). *See also* note 208.

231. This chart is an adaptation of an outdated chart at one time available on the IRS website at www.eitc.irs.gov/other-refundable-credits-toolkit/compare-education-credits-and-tuition-and-fees-deduction/compare. The chart compared the education

credits and the above-the-line federal income tax deduction no longer available for the amount of "qualified tuition and related expenses" for the attendance of the taxpayer, the taxpayer's spouse, or the taxpayer's dependent at an "eligible educational institution" under currently terminated Code section 222. For taxable years beginning after December 31, 2017, the Bipartisan Budget Act of 2018 terminated the deduction. *See* Pub. L. No. 115-123, Bipartisan Budget Act of 2018, § 40203(a), amending Code § 222(e) by striking "December 31, 2016" and inserting "December 31, 2017."

232. *See* Chapter 9.

233. *Id.*

234. *See* Chapter 9, notes 21–23 and accompanying text.

235. *See* Chapter 3.

236. *See* Chapter 9.

237. *See also* Chapter 3.

238. *See* § 1(g)(2)(A).

239. *See* § 1(g).

240. *See* § 1(g)(4)(A)(ii) (cross-referencing § 63(c)(5)(A)). *Id. See also* Rev. Proc. 2018-18, *supra* note 24, § 3.14(2). For tax years beginning after December 31, 2017, the inflation adjustment is tied to the chained CPI index. *See* note 24.

241. For formal name of Tax Cuts and Jobs Act, see note 27.

242. *See* § 1(g).

243. *See* I.R.C. § 1(j)(4) (cross-referencing I.R.C. § 1(j)(2)(E)), added by Pub. L. No. 115-97, § 11001(a), *supra* note 27. *See also* Rev. Proc. 2018-18, *supra* note 24, § 3.01. If the beneficiary's income is less than $200,000, the beneficiary will not be subject to the net investment income tax of 3.8 percent. *See* § 1411(b)(3), 1411(a)(1). *See also* Samuel D. Brunson, *Meet the New Kiddie Tax: Simpler and Less Effective*, TAX NOTES (Sept. 3, 2018).

244. *See* I.R.C. § 1(j)(4)(C), 1(j)(5), added by Pub. L. No. 115-97, § 11001(a), *supra* note 27. *See also* I.R.C. § 1(h). For tax rates and corresponding brackets and income thresholds, *see* Chapter 1, note 118 and accompanying text.

245. *See* Rev. Rul. 56-484, 1956-2 C.B. 23.

246. *See also* Chapter 1.

247. *See* note 101.

248. *See* Chapter 1 (explaining gift splitting).

249. *See also id.*

250. *See* Rev. Rul. 59-357, 1959-2 C.B. 212. *See also* Rev. Rul. 70-348; 1970-2 C.B. 193 (inclusion in donor's gross estate when custodian had resigned and donor is *successor* custodian at date of successor custodian's death). *See also* Chapter 3.

251. *But see* notes 131–135 and accompanying text.

252. *See, e.g., Education Savings Accounts (ESAs)*, Vanguard, https://personal .vanguard.com/us/whatweoffer/college/vanguardesa.

253. Crummey trusts are named after the case of Crummey v. Comm'r, 397 F.2d 82 (1968).

254. A third type of trust, formed under Code section 2503(b), qualifies for the annual exclusion, but is not optimal for education funding because accrued income must be distributed to the beneficiary, hindering the growth potential of the trust assets. *See* Chapter 3 (discussing types of trusts).

255. *See also* Chapters 1 and 3.

256. The grantor trust rules are set forth in Code sections 671–678. If federal transfer taxes are a concern, these rules, designed to defeat income shifting, can add

considerably to estate planning options, generally magnifying the benefit of gifts in trust while depleting the donor's estate. *See also* Chapter 1.

257. *See* § 1(e). *See* § 1(j)(2)(E) (for tax years beginning after December 31, 2017, and before January 1, 2026). *See also* Rev. Proc. 2018-18, *supra* note 24, § 3.01, 2018-10 I.R.B. 392. The income, above a certain threshold, also may be subject to the net investment income tax. *See* Chapter 1, notes 132–134 and accompanying text.

258. *See* Chapter 1 and subsection II.A.3. of this chapter. For tax years after December 31, 2017, and before January 1, 2026, a minor child's unearned income may be taxed at substantially the same marginal rates applicable to estates and trusts. *See* notes 242 and 243 and accompanying text.

259. *See* §§ 2036, 2038.

260. *But see* notes 136–141 and accompanying text.

261. Richard M. Horwood & Lauren J. Wolven, *New Choices in Education Funding—Do You Know the ABCs?* 27 Tax Mgmt. Est. Gifts & Tr. J. 01 (January 10, 2002).

262. *See* § 62(a)(17).

263. *See* § 221. A "qualified education loan" is "indebtedness incurred by the tax-payer solely to pay qualified higher education expenses." § 221(d)(1). For purposes of § 221, "qualified higher education expenses" generally are expenses "at an eligible education institution, reduced by the sum of . . . (A) the amount excluded from gross income under [Code] sections 127 [(referring to expenses paid by employer for employee's educational assistance)], 135, 529, or 530 by reason of such expenses, and (B) the amount of any scholarship, allowance, or payment described in [Code] section 25A(g)(2)." § 221(d)(2). An "eligible educational institution" has the same meaning as set forth in Code section 25A(f)(2), "except [the term] shall also [include] an institution conducting an internship or residency program leading to a degree or certificate awarded by an institution of higher education, a hospital, or a health care facility which offers postgraduate training." *Id.* (flush sentence).

264. § 221(d)(1).

265. § 221(c).

266. § 221(d)(1)(A).

267. § 221(e)(2).

268. *See* § 221(b)(2)(C) (defining "MAGI").

269. *See* § 221(b)(2)(B), 221(f). *See also* Rev. Proc. 2017-58, *supra* note 95, § 3.28. For tax years beginning after December 31, 2017, the inflation adjustment is tied to the chained CPI index. For 2018, this inflation adjustment apparently is not impacted by the application of the new index. *See* § 221(f)(1) (cross-referencing § 1(f)(3)). *See also* note 24.

270. For additional information, see subsection V. of this chapter.

271. Saving for College through Qualified Tuition (Section 529) Programs, Congressional Research Service Reports No. RL31214 (Dec. 17, 2001); Horwood & Wolven, *supra* note 233. *See also* http://www.finaid.org.

272. *See* §§ 529(c)(6), 530(d)(4)(B). *See also* Prop. Reg. § 1.529-2(e)(ii), (iii).

273. § 221(d)(1).

274. *See* note 264 and accompanying text.

275. *Id.*

CHAPTER 6

Planning for the Daily Care of a Minor in the Event of an Adult's Incapacity or Death

Naomi R. Cahn and Alyssa A. DiRusso

Most children grow up in their families of origin with at least one of their parents. Where and with whom the child will live, who can legally provide for the child's emotional and psychological needs, and who can choose the child's school are decisions typically left to parents.

When parents are unable to make those decisions themselves, the estate plan or other preparatory documents should address who can act as a guardian with legal rights and responsibilities for the children. One guardian may have authority over both financial and personal care, but the functions can be bifurcated. If a binding designation of a guardian is not made by a parent, then a court will make the designation. In accordance with either common law or the governing statute, a court typically will consider the best interest of the child standard and choose the "next of kin."[1]

A guardian of the person is given legal responsibility for the health and welfare of another person (her ward), because the ward is presumed unable to care for herself. The guardian has both physical and legal control over the minor, including medical and personal decisions concerning the child's welfare. The guardian is responsible for food, clothing, and shelter for her ward. A conservator (sometimes called a guardian of the estate; see Chapter 9) is a fiduciary who is responsible for the financial aspects of the child's property. Many states have integrated their adult and minor guardianship laws.[2]

While they are alive, parents are presumed to be the legal guardians for their children, and if one dies or has had his/her parental rights terminated, then the surviving parent becomes the sole legal guardian.[3] As this chapter shows, parents can delegate some of their caretaking responsibilities while they are still competent. When parents are incapacitated or die, then the legal guardian can act for the child. In the absence of adoption, however, the legal guardian is not the parent and must receive an explicit delegation of legal authority from either the court or a statute. Adoption, like guardianship, is a statutory creation. Unlike guardianship, however, adoption provides the adoptive parents with the same rights as biological parents and terminates the legal relationship between the child and her biological parents and their family.[4] A legal guardian is more limited in the rights she can exercise, and the appointment of a guardian does not terminate the child's relationship with her biological family members.[5]

There are three different methods by which parents can provide for the personal guardianship of their children: (1) by will, (2) by petition, or (3) through another statutorily created mechanism, such as standby guardianships. A guardianship by will only comes into effect when both parents are dead, and, generally, the selection of the last surviving parent controls. The other two means of creating long-term guardianships can occur while one (or both) parents are living.

In addition to these primary methods of guardianship, statutes may provide for more limited delegations of authority, such as the right of a nonparent to consent to medical care. A guardian's authority is defined by the statutory grant, so a guardian appointed pursuant to a medical guardianship statute is limited to making health care decisions under the statute.

States have developed variations of these three methods. Additionally, the Uniform Law Commission drafted a Uniform Guardianship and Protective Proceedings Act (UGPPA) in 1982 that subsequently was amended in 1989 and 1997.[6] In turn, that act substantially was revised in 2017 as the Uniform Guardianship, Conservatorship, and Other Protective Arrangements Act.[7] The Uniform Probate Code (UPC), adopted in almost twenty states, also has provisions for testamentary appointment of a guardian, and the UPC has incorporated the 1997 version of the UGPPA as Article V.[8]

This chapter discusses who may need a guardian, the various temporary and long-term methods of providing caretaking for a child when the parents are incapacitated or dead, suggestions on how to choose a guardian, and coordination of documents implementing the various methods.[9]

I. DEFINITION OF MINOR

While guardianships are useful for anyone who is legally "incompetent," they generally terminate if and when the incompetency ends. The definition of "minor" varies from state to state but always includes unemancipated children younger than eighteen (although the age is higher in a few states, including Nebraska, Alabama, and Mississippi).[10]

A child may petition a court for emancipation earlier than the age of majority, and upon marriage, a child also typically is assumed to be emancipated, terminating the guardianship. Emancipation is a legal procedure through which a minor, after making the proper showing to the court, is able to have most or all of the disabilities of minority removed and can assume the legal rights incident to adult status. Almost half of the states have statutory procedures authorizing emancipation, while it remains a common law doctrine in the other states. Emancipation generally is based on a showing that the minor lives separately from her parents and is supporting herself, or has entered into the armed forces. Courts also may have discretion to confer emancipation when this is in the best interests of the child.

II. TESTAMENTARY GUARDIANSHIP OF THE PERSON

When one parent dies, the surviving parent becomes the custodian of the child, regardless of what the deceased parent's will provides.[11] It is only when the surviving parent dies, or in situations when both parents die at once, that a testamentary guardianship comes into play.

Generally, parents who still are married create similar estate plans, choosing the same guardian, regardless of which spouse dies first. In the event parents are no longer together, or disagree on a nominee, conflicting appointments can be problematic. Most state statutes provide that the appointment of the last parent to die controls.[12] Most states provide that, if the legal parent is living, that parent has custody of the child.[13] Louisiana is the only state that explicitly addresses this, providing that after a divorce or judicial separation, only the parent who has custody has a right to appoint a "tutor."[14]

At common law, a parent had no right to appoint a testamentary guardian for a surviving child under her will.[15] Therefore, testamentary guardianship is a creation of state statute.[16] While all states recognize a parent may nominate a guardian for his or her child in a will, that nomination is not binding on the probate court in all states.

A. Selection and Appointment of Testamentary Guardian

The most common way for a parent to appoint a guardian for a child to serve after the death of the parent is through a testamentary appointment in a will.[17] Notably, the parent should have the capacity to designate a testamentary guardian at the time of signing.[18] In many states, a testamentary guardian nominated by a parent generally shall be entitled to serve as the child's guardian, with some limitations.[19] In other states, the court considers a request in a will, but also considers other factors, with the judge making the ultimate decision.[20]

The UPC allows for the appointment of a guardian by will or other writing. The appointment may be for an existing or future child, and can set limitations on the guardian's powers.[21]

In several states, guardians nominated by will are automatically entitled to receive letters of guardianship. For example, Maryland grants a particularly generous power of guardian appointment to parents and does not require "[t]he guardian . . . be approved by or qualify in any court."[22] New Jersey likewise recognizes a testamentary appointment[23] and allows the appointment to become effective after the guardian posts bond, if required.[24] The court only becomes involved in determining the minor's best interest if someone brings action and provides notice to the guardian.[25]

Other states give some deference to a parent's nomination of testamentary guardian, yet ultimately vest power with the probate court to select a guardian in the best interest of the child. For example, Indiana's statute provides that "[t]he court shall appoint as guardian a qualified person or persons most suitable and willing to serve."[26] The court must have "due regard" for designations under a durable power of attorney,[27] a "request contained in a will or other written instrument,"[28] a request by the minor child, if at least age fourteen,[29] the familial relationship between the guardian and the minor child,[30] and the "best interest" of the minor and the minor's property.[31] In some states, the court will use its power to disrupt the testamentary nomination only in unusual circumstances.[32]

In many states, the opinions of an older child for whom the guardian is being appointed are considered in selecting a guardian. In most states where a child's opinions are considered, the minor must be at least fourteen years old to have input, but in Colorado,[33] Connecticut,[34] and Texas,[35] children twelve and older have a voice. Generally, a minor objecting to the appointment of a particular guardian must file a written objection with the court before the acceptance or within thirty days after notice of the acceptance.[36]

When minors are fourteen or over, the UPC (incorporating UGPPA) requires deference to their choice of guardian, unless the appointment is not in the best interest of the child.[37] Moreover, minors fourteen and over (and in some states, including Colorado and Texas, twelve or over) as well as a limited group of interested others, can object to the guardian nominated by a parent in a will.[38]

If the parents have not appointed a guardian or the appointed guardian declines to accept the appointment, then courts typically will choose a relative who is the "next of kin." Parents with partners who have not legally adopted the children can try to protect the surviving partner's ability to serve as a guardian, but courts do not always respect these testamentary choices. Native American families also may face additional challenges.[39]

B. Commencement of Testamentary Guardianship

States vary as to how a guardianship becomes effective, but generally require an affirmative written statement from the guardian. In some states, such as Oregon, there must be a court order appointing the guardian, the guardian must accept, and then the court will issue "letters of guardianship," which provide notice that the guardianship is effective.[40]

In other states, guardians need file only an acceptance with the court in order for the guardianship to be effective. Once the appointment is effective, guardians typically do not have to file reports with the court concerning the health and welfare of their wards, although the will can provide otherwise. However, the UGPPA (as discussed earlier, incorporated in Article 5 of the UPC)[41] and some states require the guardian to submit reports to the court concerning the health and welfare of the minor.

The parent's appointment of the guardian generally becomes effective upon the parent's death.[42] The initiation of the guardian's right to act begins with him or her filing an acceptance of appointment.[43] After the guardian's appointment is effective, the guardian must file this notice of acceptance within thirty days.[44] The acceptance (along with a copy of the will or other appointing instrument) generally is filed in the probate court handling the administration of the parent's estate.[45] The guardian of an orphaned child gives notice of his or her acceptance to the child, if age fourteen or older, and to anyone who had care and custody of the child.[46] Before the court's confirmation of the appointment, people entitled to notice (including the child if age fourteen or older) have a right to terminate the appointment by filing a written objection with the court.[47]

C. Testamentary Guardian's Responsibilities and Obligations

Guardians typically take physical custody of the minor, decide where the child will live, make educational and medical decisions, and decide on religious training.[48] Because they function as the parent, they also may consent to the minor's marriage or adoption in the majority of states.[49] As guardians of the person, however, they do not have the same financial responsibility as parents; guardians are not legally obligated to provide from their own funds for the minor. Guardians may receive money payable for the support of the minor under the terms of any statutory benefit or insurance system or any private contract, devise, or trust. A minority of states permit guardians to petition the court for reasonable compensation for their services as guardian.[50] Additionally, guardians are not liable to third persons by reason of the parental relationship for acts of the minor.[51]

D. Termination of Testamentary Guardianship

The guardianship typically ends when the child is no longer a minor.[52] In addition, the child or another person may petition the court for removal of the guardian, and the court will hold a hearing.[53] A guardianship may be terminated or modified in the best interests of the ward.[54] In some states, such as Connecticut, in recognition of the seriousness of the petition, the guardian is entitled to representation in removal proceedings.

E. Benefits and Drawbacks of Testamentary Guardianships

By nominating a guardian, a parent can exercise control over the future of the minor and can indicate her choices concerning the future care of the minor. Designating a guardian is a standard part of estate planning.

On the other hand, there are several uncertainties associated with testamentary guardians. First, the parent cannot be certain in all states that the court will accept the nomination because the appointment only takes effect once the will is probated. To overcome this uncertainty, Colorado, Hawaii, and a few other states allow for court confirmation of the appointment before the parent's death in certain limited circumstances. In California, parents can request that the court appoint a joint guardian who will serve concurrently with the parent during her lifetime and who assumes sole responsibility when the parent dies.[55] This option is available, however, only if the parent has a "terminal condition."[56]

Second, if the other parent is still living and is not legally incapacitated, then the testamentary appointment largely is irrelevant. Although divorced parents may believe they can use a testamentary guardianship to preclude the other parent from obtaining custody, this belief generally is inaccurate. The surviving parent, so long as her rights have not been legally terminated, typically is presumed to be the guardian regardless of the circumstances of the divorce and the provisions of the testamentary instrument. However, a few states (South Dakota, Indiana, and Vermont) involve the court in deciding whether the surviving parent gets guardianship when the parents are divorced.[57] (And, as mentioned earlier, Louisiana only gives the custodial parent the right to appoint a guardian.[58]) Fourth, testamentary guardians only assume power after the death of the testator, not upon her incapacity.

III. STANDBY GUARDIANSHIP

Unlike more conventional forms of guardianship, a standby guardian can be appointed before the death or incapacity of parents. Although states typically have been suspicious of inter vivos guardianship appointments, the rise in single mothers and the AIDS epidemic led states to develop improved mechanisms for confirming the parents' choice of standby guardian while the parents still are alive.[59] A traditional inter vivos guardianship *transfers* custody and most other parental rights to a third party upon court approval of the guardianship.[60]

Rather than displacing parental authority completely at the time of the guardianship petition, standby guardians in some states can exercise authority at the same time. The 1997 federal Adoption and Safe Families Act[61] encouraged states to adopt procedures for standby guardianships, and more than half of the states now have standby guardianship statutes (see Appendix 6-B).[62]

Standby guardianship statutes vary, but often have the following four general attributes:[63]

- First, they provide a process for designating a person to act as a standby guardian either by filing a petition in court, or through nominating such a person, affirmed by a subsequent petition and court hearing. At least one state allows for such designations through a power of attorney.[64]

- Second, most states allow the parent to designate a standby guardian regardless of the parent's physical health; in a minority of jurisdictions, parents only can use the standby guardianship process if they have a terminal or chronic illness, or are at significant risk of such a diagnosis.
- Third, the noncustodial parent typically has some role, either through (1) a requirement for that person's consent or through (2) a requirement of notice of any hearing regarding a guardian's appointment.
- Fourth, a standby guardian does not assume authority until the happening of a triggering event, such as the parent's extended hospitalization or death. Some states require that a physician certify the existence of the triggering event.

A court approves the guardianship.[65]

In addition to their use in cases of parental incapacity, standby guardianships can provide a useful bridging authority between the death of a parent and the probate of a will and appointment of a longer-term guardian.[66]

IV. PARTIAL DELEGATION: EDUCATIONAL AND MEDICAL CONSENTS

Medical and educational consent laws authorize caregivers to make a specific set of limited decisions on behalf of a child upon the consent of the parent or guardian. Like powers of attorney, but unlike formal guardianships, delegations can be achieved without court involvement, and statutes often include the forms. The delegation generally must be in writing, although some states may permit oral consent. These delegations sometimes are limited to relative caregivers or to caregivers with whom the child resides, may be limited in duration, and are generally quite limited in the scope of delegation; they generally allow the caregiver the right to make the decision concurrently with the parent.[67]

These laws basically allow caregivers, who do not have legal custody of a child, to consent to a child's medical treatment and enroll them in school.[68] Unlike testamentary or standby guardianships, these partial delegations even may not require parental consent. Several states have statutes establishing who can give educational and medical consent if a parent or other guardian is unavailable and establishing priority between them.

In California, a parent may authorize another person who is caring for the child to consent to medical and dental care.[69] In other jurisdictions, the caregiver can choose the child's school. In Louisiana, a caregiver with whom a child resides can, on her own initiative, execute a form that is valid for up to one year authorizing her to make educational and medical decisions with respect to the child, so long as she has made reasonable efforts to notify the parents of her plans.[70] Louisiana also allows for "Provisional Custody by Mandate," by which a parent can authorize another person "to provide for the care, custody, and control of a minor child" for up to one year.[71] In some states, parents can delegate authority to another person for purposes of consenting to the immunization of a minor.[72] In many states, parents may delegate medical decisions to officials of schools or daycare facilities when a child needs emergency care and the parents cannot be reached, and parents frequently are asked to make such delegations.[73]

V. TEMPORARY AND LIMITED DELEGATION OF PARENTAL POWERS

There are a variety of other mechanisms with different names that states have adopted to allow parents and other legally recognized caregivers the ability to delegate some or all of their parental powers and responsibilities to another for a limited period of time.[74] For example, temporary guardians can be appointed while another guardianship is ongoing, to replace a guardian, or under other circumstances.[75] The UGPPA allows for a "limited guardianship" restricting the powers of a guardian for the purpose "of developing self-reliance of a ward or for other good cause."[76]

VI. POWERS OF ATTORNEY

Although powers of attorney typically are used for business purposes or health care decision making, in a growing number of states, powers of attorney can be used for the care of a minor. The UGPPA provides: "A parent or guardian of a minor or incapacitated person, by a power of attorney, may delegate to another person, for a period not exceeding six months, any power regarding care, custody, or property of the minor or ward, except the power to consent to marriage or adoption."[77] This provision is in effect in at least sixteen states, and other states, including Ohio, similarly recognize the ability of a principal to delegate parental authority through a power of attorney.[78]

Benefits of the power of attorney include that they relatively are easy to execute and can be fairly simple documents, but a primary drawback is that powers of attorney do not create guardianships and are limited in duration.[79]

VII. CHOOSING THE GUARDIAN

The issue of whom to choose as the guardian can be complex, creating conflict between parents, requiring choices among family members, and involving evaluations concerning a guardian's ability to make the best decisions financially and psychologically for the child. While it may be useful to name one person as both guardian of the person and conservator of the minor's estate, there may be considerations, such as financial abilities and aptitudes, which might counsel against naming the same person. On the other hand, if different people are chosen for each guardianship, they will need to coordinate their decision making.

Although the parents may want to choose a couple to act as co-guardians, if that couple then divorces, guardianship decision making would become more complicated. It also is important to name at least one alternate, in case the nominated guardian is unable or unwilling to serve at the necessary time. And it is, of course, critical that the parents ascertain that their chosen guardian is willing to serve. Parents also may leave non-binding instructions as to their wishes concerning the child's upbringing. Particularly where the minor will inherit significant assets, the parents may pair the guardianship nomination with the establishment of a trust, delegating financial management to the trustee rather than the guardian.

The primary questions for parents in choosing a guardian are:

- Who will provide the best care for my children?
- Will the guardian respect my choices concerning the child's upbringing?
- How comfortable are my child, the guardian, and the guardian's family with each other?
- If there are multiple siblings, can a guardian provide for all of them, or must siblings be separated?

Additional considerations in choosing a guardian include:

- Living situation (is there enough space in the guardian's residence?)
- Presence of other children
- Religious upbringing
- Location and community
- Familial relationship
- Financial sophistication
- Relationship to your child

As children grow older, the parents may want to revisit the guardianship decision and to discuss the decision with their children. Recall that the guardian only will serve for children under the age of majority.

Parents also can change the person designated to be a guardian. For testamentary guardians, the parents may execute a new will or a codicil to an existing will. For the other guardianships, the parents will need to sign a new writing with the name of the replacement guardian.

Providing for the care of a minor in the event of parental incapacity or death is a core component of estate planning, requiring counseling and careful consideration of the appropriate person to make the specific types of decisions required.

VIII. COORDINATION OF DOCUMENTS

In sum, estate plans always should include the appointment of a guardian to take effect when both parents die. Although some states allow this to be done outside of a will in another signed writing, the best method is to provide for a testamentary guardian in a will. Executing a will is a comparatively simple act that does not require court involvement until after the parent's death. As they draft their wills, parents can coordinate so that they nominate the same person to serve as guardian (although, of course, after one parent dies, the other is free to change his or her will to nominate someone else). A testamentary guardian assumes authority only after the death of the parent, and, although there is generally a presumption that a court will approve the guardian nominated in the will, there is no guarantee, in most states, that the parent's choice ultimately will be selected.

Standby guardianships, which are authorized in some states, are most useful for parents who believe that they will be incapacitated within a short period of time. Standby guardians can exercise their authority while the parent is still alive and allow for the parent to have more participation in the selection of the guardian. An estate plan could include both a standby guardian nomination and a testamentary nomination. The parent probably will want to choose the same person to ensure continuity of care and to prevent any conflict.

If a parent wants to delegate authority immediately, then the traditional inter vivos guardianship may be appropriate, rather than solely a testamentary nomination.

The other forms of delegation provide far more limited authority to the caregiver. If a child is not living with a parent, then the parent may want to allow the child to go to school in the place where the child is living through an educational consent. If the parents are concerned that they may not be available to consent to medical care, such as when they are planning a trip, then executing a medical consent might be appropriate. Or, if a parent is not married to his or her partner, then these forms can give limited power to the partner to act on behalf of the minor.

IX. APPENDICES

This chapter includes the following additional resources:

Appendix 6-A. Comprehensive state chart indicating which of the previously described caregiving authorizations are available in each state and listing the applicable statutory citations to be consulted.

Appendix 6-B. Individual state charts that offer greater detail about the options available in that state.

Appendix 6-C. Internet resources listing a variety of websites providing forms, links, or other information that may be valuable to a practitioner.

NOTES

1.   *See, e.g.,* Huval v. Jacobs, 548 S.E. 2d 437, 439 (Ga. Ct. App. 2001) (statutory preference for appointing "next of kin" is not absolute where next of kin is "not 'unobjectionable'"); Jefferson v. Dixon, 573 So. 2d 769, 772 (Miss. 1990) (construing statute calling for appointment of guardian among next of kin unless that person is unsuitable).

2.   ABA Commission on Law and Aging, *Relationship Between Adult and Minor Guardianship Statutes,* http://www.americanbar.org/content/dam/aba/administrative /law_aging/Relationship_of_adult_and_minor_guardianship_provisions.auth checkdam.pdf.

3.   *E.g.,* CONN. GEN. STAT. § 45a-606 (LexisNexis, LEXIS through 2015 legislation with exceptions); R.I. GEN. LAWS § 33-5-4 (LexisNexis, LEXIS through Chapter 122 with exceptions of 2015 Sess.); Tenn. Code Ann. § 34-1-102(c) (LexisNexis, LEXIS through 2015 Regular Sess.).

4.   In states that have adopted the Uniform Probate Code, there is a limited exception for stepparent adoptions that permits inheritance by the child from a biological parent. *See* UNIF. PROB CODE § 2-114(b) (2014).

5.   *See* Joyce E. McConnell, *Securing the Care of Children in Diverse Families: Building on Trends in Guardianship Reform,* 10 YALE J. L. & FEMINISM 29, 33 (1998).

6.   Guardianship, Conservatorship, and Other Protective Arrangements Act, UNIF. LAW COMM. (2017), https://www.uniformlaws.org/viewdocument/final-act-no -comments-1?CommunityKey=2eba8654-8871-4905-ad38aabbd573911c&tab=library documents.

7.   Unif. Law Comm., Legislative Fact Sheet (2017), https://www.uniformlaws .org/committees/community-home?CommunityKey=2eba8654-8871-4905-ad38 -aabbd573911c.

8.   *See* UNIF. PROB. CODE §§ 5-101 to -505 (2014). The UPC has been enacted in seventeen states and the U.S. Virgin Islands. ULC, Legislative Fact Sheet— Probate Code (2015), https://my.uniformlawsorg/committees/community-home ?CommunityKey=a539920d-c477-44b8-84fe-b0d7b1a4cca8.

9.   This chapter focuses on guardianships when a parent is incapacitated or dies. Where parents have abused or neglected a child, the state also may assume guardianship over the child.

10.   Unlike Alabama and Nebraska where the age of majority is nineteen, Mississippi's age of majority is twenty-one. ALA. CODE § 26-1-1 (LexisNexis, LEXIS through 2015 Regular and First Spec. Sess.); NEB. REV. STAT. ANN. § 43-2101 (LexisNexis, LEXIS through the 2015 104th First Sess.); MISS. CODE ANN. § 1-3-27 (LexisNexis, LEXIS through 2015 Regular Sess.).

11.   *E.g.,* CONN. GEN. STAT. § 45a-606 (LexisNexis, LEXIS through 2015 legislation with exceptions) ("The father and mother of every minor child are joint guardians of the person of the minor, and the powers, rights and duties of the father and the mother in regard to the minor shall be equal. If either father or mother dies or is removed as guardian, the other parent of the minor child shall become the sole guardian of the person of the minor.").

12.   *See, e.g.,* COLO. REV. STAT. § 15-14-202(7) (LexisNexis, LEXIS through 2015 First Regular Sess. of Seventieth Gen. Assembly); MASS. GEN. LAWS ANN. ch. 190B, § 5-202 (LexisNexis, LEXIS through Act 85 of 2015 Legis. Sess.).

13.   *See* McConnell, *supra* note 5, at 64–65; *see generally,* 755 ILL. COMP. STAT. 5/11-5 (LexisNexis, LEXIS through Pub. Act 99-20 of 2015 Legis. Sess.) (stating in

Illinois, for example, a surviving parent whose parental rights have not been terminated and who is willing, may serve as a guardian for the child); MINN. STAT. § 524.5-204 (LexisNexis, LEXIS through Act Chapter 80 of 2015 Regular Sess. with exceptions) (stating Minnesota follows a similar rule in that the court may appoint a guardian if in the child's best interest and both parents are dead or the parental rights have been terminated); GA. CODE ANN. § 29-2-4 (LexisNexis, LEXIS through 2015 Regular Sess.) (Georgia only allows the testamentary appointment to control if there is not another living parent.).

14.   LA. CIV. CODE ANN. art. 258 (LexisNexis, LEXIS through 2015 legislation with exceptions).

15.   *E.g.,* Copp v. Copp, 20 N.H. 284, 285–86 (1850) ("The common law made various provisions for the tuition and protection of infants, and the care of their estates, but did not recognize the right of a parent to make any testamentary disposition of the guardianship of his children."). *See also* L.S. Tellier, Annotation, *Function, Power, and Discretion of Court Where There is Testamentary Appointment of Guardian of Minor,* 67 A.L.R. 2d 803, 805 (1959) ("Under the early common law a man could not control or affect the guardianship of his children by will.").

16.   Tellier, *supra* note 15 (In view of the fact that testamentary guardianships are statutory in origin and nature it is not surprising that questions as to the place and function of the courts in the situation where a guardian of minors has been named in a will are usually referable to the provisions of the governing statutes, construed in the light of the particular circumstances presented by the individual case.).

17.   Under the UPC, the UGPPA, and in some states, a parent also can select a guardian through an "other signed writing," which includes durable powers of attorney and other specific documents for appointing guardians.

18.   *See* Koshenina v. Buvens, 130 So. 3d 276 (Fla. Dist. Ct. App. 2014).

19.   Sarah M. Johnson, *Planning Considerations in Naming a Guardian for a Minor Child,* WEALTH STRATEGIES J. (Sept.15, 2008, 3:24 AM), \http://www.wealthstrategies journal.com/articles/2008/09/planning-considerations-in-nam.html.   (discussing limitations which include, for example, if the nominee is not within the child's best interest).

20.   *Id.* For an extensive state-by-state description of the orientation of states toward parental selection or court selection, *see* Alyssa A. DiRusso & S. Kristen Peters, *Parental Testamentary Appointments of Guardians for Children,* 25 QUINNIPIAC PROB. L.J. 369 (2012).

21.   UNIF. PROBATE CODE § 5-202(a) (2014) ("A guardian may be appointed by will or other signed writing by a parent for any minor child the parent has or may have in the future. The appointment may specify the desired limitations on the powers to be given to the guardian.").

22.   MD. CODE ANN., EST. & TRUSTS § 13-701 (LexisNexis, LEXIS through 2015 legislation). However, if no guardian is appointed, the court may choose. *Id.* § 13-702. Additionally, the guardian need not file bond or papers. *Id* § 13-703.

23.   N.J. STAT. ANN. § 3B:12-13 (LexisNexis, LEXIS through 2015 216th Second Annual Sess.).

24.   *Id.* § 3B:12-16.

25.   *Id.* § 3B:12-17.

26.   IND. CODE § 29-3-5-4 (LexisNexis, LEXIS through 2015 First Regular Sess. of 119th Gen. Assembly, P.L. 1-259).

27. *Id.* § 29-3-5-4(1).

28. *Id.* § 29-3-5-4(2) (noting this is a "request," not an appointment).

29. *Id.* § 29-3-5-4(3).

30. *Id.* § 29-3-5-4(5).

31. IND. CODE § 29-3-5-4(7) (LexisNexis, LEXIS through 2015 First Regular Sess. of 119th Gen. Assembly, P.L. 1-259).

32. In Idaho, the presumption was strengthened in a challenge to testamentary guardianship—giving the challenging party the burden of proving that the testamentary guardian "was unfit or unqualified" instead of the "best interests" standard. *In re Doe,* 224 P.3d 499, 507 (Idaho 2009).

33. COLO. REV. STAT. § 15-14-203(2) (LexisNexis, LEXIS through 2015 First Regular Sess. of Seventieth Gen. Assembly).

34. CONN. GEN. STAT. § 45a-596(b) (LexisNexis, LEXIS through P.A. 14-235 of 2014 Regular Sess.).

35. VERNON'S TEXAS STAT. § 1104.054 (LexisNexis, LEXIS through 2015 Regular Sess.) ("Selection of Guardian by Minor").

36. *See, e.g.,* ALA. CODE § 26-2A-72 (LexisNexis, LEXIS through 2015 Regular and First Spec. Sess.). Although many states have a thirty-day timeframe, there are some minor variations. *See, e.g.,* MICH. COMP. LAWS § 700.5203 (LexisNexis, LEXIS through 2015 Pub. Act 130) (stating Michigan requires the minor to file the objection before the appointment is accepted or within twenty-eight days after and such objection does not preclude a court appointment).

37. *See* UNIF. PROB. CODE § 5-206 (2014); DiRusso & Peters, *supra* note 20, at 383–85.

38. *See* UNIF. PROB CODE § 5-203 (2014).

39. Appointing testamentary guardians may be complicated for Native American families by the Indian Child Welfare Act. *See* Amina McKoy, Comment, *The Battle of Wills: The Impact of the Indian Child Welfare Act on Parents Who Make Testamentary Appointments of Guardianship for Their Indian Children,* 28 J. JUV. L. 148 (2007).

40. OR. REV. STAT.§125.310 (LexisNexis, LEXIS through 2015 Regular Sess. with exceptions).

41. *See generally* Unif. Guardianship & Protective Proceedings Act (1997), https://www.uniformlaws.org/viewdocument/final-act-no-comments-35?CommunityKey=d716e47d-f50b-4b68-9e25-dd0af47a13b7&tab=librarydocuments (1997). See *also* note 8 and accompanying text.

42. Unif. Prob. Code § 5-202(c) (stating that the appointment is subject to certain limitations, the appointment of the guardian becomes effective upon the first to occur of the parent's death, incapacity, or inability to care for the child (as determined by a physician)).

43. Unif. Prob. Code § 5-202(d).

44. *Id.*

45. Unif. Prob. Code § 5-202(d)(1)(2014).

46. Unif. Prob. Code § 5-202(d)(2).

47. *See* Unif. Prob. Code § 5-203.

48. Unif. Prob. Code § 5-208.

49. Unif. Prob. Code § 5-208(b)(4).

50. Unif. Prob. Code § 5-209.

51. Unif. Prob. Code § 5-209(b).

52. Under the Uniform Probate Code, guardianship terminates "upon the minor's death, adoption, emancipation or attainment of majority or as ordered by the court." Unif. Prob. Code § 5-210(a).

53. Unif. Prob. Code § 5-318.

54. *Id.*

55. CAL PROB. CODE § 2105(f) (LexisNexis, LEXIS through Chapter 428 of 2015 Legis. Sess.).

56. *Id.*

57. DiRusso & Peters, *supra* note 20, at 386–87.

58. *See* note 14 and accompanying text.

59. *See* McConnell, *supra* note 5, at 38–39.

60. *See* Pamela Laufer-Ukeles & Ayelet Blecher-Prigat, *Between Function and Form: Towards a Differentiated Model of Functional Parenthood,* 20 GEO. MASON L. REV. 419, 474 (2013); *see, e.g., In re* V.K.S., 63 P.3d 1284 (Utah Ct. App. 2003); *but see In re* Markham, 795 S.W.2d 931, 933 (Ark. Ct. App. 1990); Styck v. Karnes, 462 N.E.2d 1327, 1329–30 (Ind. Ct. App. 1984).

61. Pub. L. No. 96-272.

62. *Standby Guardianship,* CHILD WELFARE INFORMATION GATEWAY (2015), https:// www.childwelfare.gov/topics/systemwide/laws-policies/statutes/guardianship / (information and summary of state standby guardianship procedures).

63. This description is drawn from *Standby Guardianship, supra* note 62.

64. *Id.* at 2 (Tennessee permits power of attorney use.) Florida has two options: a standby guardian and a preneed guardian. The standby guardian is pre-approved by the court through a hearing *before* the triggering event; the "preneed" guardian is appointed through the typical standby guardian process. FLA. STAT. §§ 744.304– 744.3046 (LexisNexis, LEXIS through 2015 legislation with exceptions).

65. Koshenina v. Buvens, 130 So. 3d 276, 281 (Fla. Dist. Ct. App. 2014) ("[T]he court shall appoint any standby or preneed guardian, unless the court determines that appointing such person is *contrary* to the best interests of the ward.").

66. Note also that the UPC allows appointment of an emergency guardian or temporary substitute guardian in lieu of a standby guardianship. *See* Unif. Probate Code § 5-312 (emergency guardian) and § 5-313 (temporary substitute guardian).

67. Laufer-Ukeles & Blecher-Prigat, *supra* note 60, at 474 (citing TEX. FAM. CODE ANN. §§ 34.001–.009).

68. *Id.*

69. "The parent, guardian, or caregiver of a minor who is a relative of the minor and who may authorize medical care and dental care under Section 6550, may authorize in writing an adult into whose care a minor has been entrusted to consent to medical care or dental care, or both, for the minor." CAL. FAM. CODE § 6910 (Lex-isNexis, LEXIS through Chapter 428 of 2015 Legis. Sess.).

70. LA. REV. STAT. § 9:975 (LexisNexis, LEXIS through 2015 legislation with exceptions) ("Non-legal custodian; consent for certain services; affidavit, form").

71. LA. STAT. ANN. § 9:951-954 (LexisNexis, LEXIS through 2015 legislation with exceptions).

72. *See* Carolyn McAllaster, Carol Suzuki, & Jeffrey Selbin, *Issues in Family Law for People with HIV, in* AIDS AND THE LAW 393, at 453 n.341 (3d ed. Supp. David W. Webber, ed. 2004).

73. *See, e.g.,* OHIO REV. CODE ANN. § 3313.712 (LexisNexis, LEXIS through 131st Gen. Assembly Legis.).

74. *E.g.*, ALA. CODE § 26-2A-71 (LexisNexis, LEXIS through 2015 Regular and First Spec. Sess.) (allowing temporary delegation of up to one year).

75. *See, e.g.,* Unif. Guardianship & Protective Proceedings Act § 204 (d)(temporary guardian can be appointed based upon a showing of "immediate need" and that the appointment is in the minor's best interests); MICH. COMP. LAWS ANN. § 700.5213 (LexisNexis, LEXIS through 2015 Pub. Act 130).

76. Unif. Guardianship & Protective Proceedings Act § 206(b).

77. *Id.* § 105.

78. McAllaster et al., *supra* note 72, at 451–52. They list the following states, which vary in the length of time that the delegation is accurate: Alabama, Alaska, Arizona, Colorado, Idaho, Indiana, Maine, Michigan, Minnesota, Montana, Nebraska, New Jersey, New Mexico, North Dakota, Oregon, and Utah. *Id.*

79. Unif. Guardianship & Protective Proceedings Act § 105 & cmt.

APPENDIX 6-A

Comprehensive State Chart

Availability of Child Care Options

STATE-BY-STATE Statutory Reference

Originally prepared by Julia Belian (2005), substantial updating and revision from Karen Goff, Sarah Gelfand, Naomi Cahn, Alyssa DiRusso, and Others

Empty blocks indicate that these issues are not addressed in statutes reviewed, although comparable arrangements may be possible under a different option. The chart is designed to provide guidance; please consult state-specific statutory compilations for additional information rather than relying solely on the charts and summaries in Appendices 6-A and 6-B.

State	Guardianship of Person	Standby Guardianship	General Delegation of power	Examples of Educational Consent	Examples of Medical Consent
Alabama	26-2A-70 et seq.		26-2A-7		
Alaska	13.26.030 et seq.		13.26.020		
Arizona	14-5201 et seq.		14-5104, 14-5107		
Arkansas	28-65-201 et seq.	28-65-221			20-9-602
California	Prob. Code 1500 et seq.	Prob. Code 2105		Fam. Code 6550, 6552	Fam. Code 6550, 6552
Colorado	15-14-201 et seq.	15-14-202(2)	15-14-105		25-4-1704
Connecticut	45a-596 et seq.	45a-624		10-253(d)	
Delaware	12-3901 et seq.	13-2361 et seq.		14-202	13-707, 708
District of Columbia	21-101 et seq.	16-4801 et seq.	21-2301		16-4901
Florida	744.101 et seq.	744.304, 744.3046			765.2035, 743.0645
Georgia	29-2-1 et seq.	29-2-9	19-9-120		31-9-2

State	Guardianship of Person	Standby Guardianship	General Delegation of power	Examples of Educational Consent	Examples of Medical Consent
Hawaii	560:5-201 et seq.	560:5-202(b)	560:5-105	302A-481 et seq.	577-28
Idaho	15-5-201 et seq.		15-5-104		39-4504
Illinois	755-5/11-1 et seq.	755-5/11-5.3	755-5/11-5.4		
Indiana	29-3-5-1 et seq.	29-3-3-7	29-3-9-1		16-36-1-5
Iowa	633.551 et seq.	633.560			
Kansas	59-3051 et seq.	59-3074			38-135 et seq.
Kentucky	387.020 et seq.			27A.095	27A.095
Louisiana	Civ. Code art. 250 et seq.			La. Rev. Stat. 9:975	La. Rev. Stat. 9:975, and 40:1159.4
Maine	18-A, 5-201 et seq.		18-A, 5-104		
Maryland	13-701 et seq.	13-901 et seq.		7-101	18-4A-01, 20-105 et seq.
Massachusetts	190B, 5-201 et seq.	190B, 2-202(c)	190B, 5-103	201F, 1 et seq.	201F, 1 et seq.
Michigan	700.5201 et seq.		700.5103		
Minnesota	524.5-201 et seq.	257B.01–257B.10	524.5-211		
Mississippi	93-13-7 et seq.				41-41-3
Missouri	475.045 et seq.	475.046	475.024	431.058 et seq.	431.058 et seq.
Montana	72-5-201 et seq.		72-5-103	20-5-501 et seq.	40-6-501 et seq.
Nebraska	30-2605 et seq.	30.2608(c)	30-2604		
Nevada	Sec. 34 et seq.	Sec. 153			129.040
New Hampshire	463:1 et seq.				
New Jersey	3B:12-13 et seq.	3B:12-67 et seq.	3B: 12-39		
New Mexico	45-5-201 et seq.		45-5-104		24-10-2
New York	SCPA 1710 et seq.	SCPA 1726			Pub. Health 2504
North Carolina	35A-1213 et seq.	35A-1370 et seq.		115C-366	32A-34
North Dakota	30.1-27-01 et seq.		30.1-26-04		23-12-13
Ohio	2111.01 et seq.	2111.121	3109.52 et seq.	3313.64(11)	

State	Guardianship of Person	Standby Guardianship	General Delegation of power	Examples of Educational Consent	Examples of Medical Consent
Oklahoma	tit. 30, 2-101 et seq.			tit. 70, 1-113	tit. 10A, 1-3-101
Oregon	125.300 et seq.			109.575	109.575
Pennsylvania	20-2519, 5111 et seq.	23-5602 et seq.			11-2513
Rhode Island	33-5-4, 33-15.1-1 et seq.				
South Carolina	21-21-25 et seq.			59-63-32	
South Dakota	29A-5-201 et seq.				
Tennessee	34-1-101 et seq.	34-1-119	34-6-301 et seq.	34-6-304 et seq.	
Texas	Est. Code 1001.001 et seq.				Fam. Code 32.001 et seq.
Vermont	14-2621 et seq.				
Virginia	64.2-1700 et seq.	16.1-349 et seq.			54.1-2969
Washington	11.88.080 et seq.	11.88.125			
West Virginia	44-10-1 et seq.	44A-5-1 et seq.			
Wisconsin	54.01 et seq.	48.978			
Wyoming	3-2-101 et seq.	3-2-108			3-2-202

APPENDIX 6-B

Individual State Charts

ALABAMA

	Testamentary Guardian of the Person (Ala. Code §§ 26-2A-70 et seq.)	General Delegation of Power (Ala. Code § 26-2A-7)
Who Can Appoint?	Parent of an unmarried minor.[80] Court under some circumstances. 26-2A-70, 26-2A-71, 26-2A-73.	Custodial parent or guardian of a minor. 26-2A-7.
How?	Will, or other writing signed by parent and attested by at least two witnesses. 26-2A-71.	By properly executed power of attorney. 26-2A-7.
Objection by Minor?	Minor fourteen or older may prevent the appointment by filing a written objection before, or within thirty days after receiving notice of acceptance.[81] 26-2A-72.	
Court Role?	Where nominee fails to accept, or minor objects, the court shall appoint person nominated by minor over fourteen, unless finds contrary to best interest. 26-2A-76.	
For What Purpose?	Powers and responsibilities of a parent regarding ward's health, support, education, or maintenance; consent to medical treatment. 26-2A-78.	Delegate any power regarding health, support, education, or maintenance except power to consent to marriage or adoption for a period not exceeding one year. 26-2A-7.
When Takes Effect?	If both parents are dead or incapacitated or the surviving parent has no parental rights, appointment becomes effective when guardian files acceptance in court. 26-2A-71.	
How Terminate?	Upon death, resignation,[82] or removal[83] of guardian or minor's death, adoption, marriage, or majority. 26-2A-79.	
Guardian Compensation	Guardian is entitled to reasonable compensation only as approved by the court or conservator appointed for the estate of the ward. 26-2A-78.	

80. An effective appointment by the parent who dies or became incapacitated later in time has priority. § 26-2A-71.
81. Objection does not preclude appointment by the court of the parental nominee. § 26-2A-72.
82. Resignation of guardian does not terminate guardianship until it has been approved by the court. § 26-2A-79.
83. Any person interested in the welfare of the ward may petition for removal of a guardian on the ground that it would be in the best interest of the ward. § 26-2A-81.

ALASKA

	Testamentary Guardian of the Person (Alaska Stat. §§ 13.26.030 et seq.)	General Delegation of Power (Alaska Stat. § 13.26.020)
Who Can Appoint?	Parent of unmarried minor.[84] Court under some circumstances. 13.26.035, 13.26.045.	Parent or guardian of a minor. 13.26.020.
How?	By will. 13.26.035.	By properly executed power of attorney. 13.26.020.
Objection by Minor?	Minor 14 or older may prevent appointment by filing a written objection with the court before, or within 30 days after notice, of guardian's acceptance.[85] 13.26.040.	
Court Role?	Court may appoint guardian if testamentary guardian failed to accept within 30 days, or minor objects. Court may appoint any adult in best interest of minor with priority to adult family members. Court shall appoint person nominated by minor over 14 unless not in best interest of minor.13.26.045, 13.26.055.	
For What Purpose?	Guardian has powers and responsibilities of a parent, including facilitating ward's education, social, or other activities and authorizing medical treatment. 13-26-070.	Delegate any powers regarding care, custody, or property of the minor, except the power to consent to marriage or adoption for a period not exceeding one year. 13.26.020.
When Takes Effect?	If both parents are deceased or the surviving parent is adjudged incapacitated, the appointment takes effect upon filing acceptance. 13.26.035.	
How Terminate?	Upon the death, resignation,[86] or removal[87] of guardian or upon minor's death, adoption, marriage, or attainment of majority. 13.26.075.	
Subsidization Guardianship	Procedures relating to subsidized guardianships for hard-to-place children governed in 25.23.200 through 240, and 13.26.062.	

84. If both parents are deceased, an effective appointment by the parent who died later has priority. § 13.26.035.
85. Objection does not preclude appointment by the court of the testamentary nominee. §1 3.26.040.
86. Resignation of guardian does not terminate guardianship until it has been approved by the court. § 13.26.075.
87. Any person interested in the welfare of the ward, or the ward, may petition court for removal on the ground that it would be in the best interest of the minor. § 13.26.085.

ARIZONA

	Testamentary Guardian of the Person (Ariz. Rev. Stat. §§ 14-5201 et seq.)	General Delegation of Power (Ariz. Rev. Stat. § 14-5104)	General Delegation of Power (Ariz. Rev. Stat. § 14-5107)
Who Can Appoint?	Parent of unmarried minor.[88] Court under some circumstances. 14-5201, 5202, 5204.	Parent or guardian of minor. 14-5104.	Military member who is a parent or guardian of a minor. 14-5107.
How?	By will. 14-5202.	Properly executed power of attorney. 14-5104.	By power of attorney. 14-5107.
Objection by Minor?	Minor 14 or over may prevent appointment by filing a written objection before, or within 30 days after notice, of guardian's acceptance. 14-5203.		
Court Role?	Court may appoint guardian if testamentary guardian fails to accept or if minor objects to appointment. Court may appoint person nominated by minor over 14, unless contrary to best interests of minor.[89] 14-5204, 5206.		
For What Purpose?	Powers and responsibilities of a custodial parent regarding the ward's support, care and education; can consent to medical care. 14-5209.	May delegate any powers regarding care, custody or property of the minor child, except power to consent to marriage or adoption, for a period not exceeding six months. 14-5104.	May delegate any powers the parent or guardian has regarding care, except power to consent to marriage or adoption, for a period not exceeding one year. 14-5107.
When Takes Effect?	If both parents are dead or the surviving parent is adjudged incapacitated, it becomes effective upon filing the guardian's acceptance with court. 14-5202.		
Guardian Compensation?	Reasonable compensation, but only as approved by order of court or conservator if appointed for the estate of the ward. 14-5209.		
How Terminate?	Upon death, resignation[90] or removal[91] of guardian or on minor's death, adoption, marriage or attainment of majority. 14-5210.		

88. If both parents are dead, an effective appointment by the parent who died later has priority. § 14-5202.
89. Before court may appoint a guardian, a criminal background investigation shall be conducted in order to determine the applicant's suitability as a guardian. § 14-5206.
90. Resignation of guardian does not terminate guardianship until approved by the court. § 14-5210.
91. Any person interested in the welfare of a ward, or ward over fourteen may petition for removal of a guardian. § 14-5212.

ARKANSAS

LEXIS current through 2014 Second Extraordinary Session and the Nov. 2014 election

	Testamentary Guardian of the Person (Ark. Code Ann. §§ 28-65-201 et seq.)	Standby Guardian (Ark. Code Ann. § 28-65-221)	Examples of Medical Consent (Ark. Code Ann. § 20-9-602)
Who Can Appoint?	Court. 28-65-204.	Court. 28-65-221.	
How?	Court shall appoint guardian most willing to serve, having due regard to: any request contained in a will or other written instrument by the parent; any request made by a minor 14 or older; the relationship by blood or marriage to the minor. 28-65-204.	Without surrendering parental rights, any parent who is chronically ill or near death may have standby guardian appointed by the court. 28-65-221.	Subject to conditions and exceptions, parent, person in loco parentis, guardian, adult sibling, or grandparent may consent, orally or otherwise, to medical care for minor. 20-9-602.
Minor Substitution?	When a minor turns 14, guardian may be removed on petition of the ward to have another person appointed. If person is suitable, qualified, and in best interest, that person shall be appointed. 28-65-219.		
For What Purpose?	Care, maintenance, protection, training, education with some decisions requiring court approval. 28-65-301, 302.		Authorization to consent to any surgical, or medical treatment or procedure that may be suggested by a physician. 20-9-602.
When Takes Effect?		Standby guardian's authority would take effect upon: the death of the parent; the mental incapacity of the parent; physical debilitation and con-sent of the parent. 28-65-221.	
How Terminate?	If guardian dies, resigns, or is removed, court may appoint substitute. Guardianship terminated by ward's death, marriage, majority (with conditions), or court order. 28-65-220, 28-65-401.		

CALIFORNIA

LEXIS current through Chapter 62 of the 2015 Session

	Testamentary Guardian of the Person (Cal. Prob. Code §§ 1500 et seq.)	Standby Guardian (Cal. Prob. Code § 2105)	Examples of Educational Consent (Cal. Fam. Code §§ 6550, 6552)	Examples of Medical Consent (Cal. Fam. Code §§ 6550, 6552)
Who Can Appoint?	Court may appoint although parent may nominate. 1500, 1514.	Court. 2105.	Caregiver, 18 years or older. 6550.	Caregiver, who is a relative.[92] 6550.
How?	Upon petition by relative of minor or other person, the court may appoint a guardian. 1510, 1514.	Appoint the custodial parent and a person nominated by the custodial parent as joint guardians. 2105.	Authorization affidavit (lines 1–4). 6550, 6552.	Authorization affidavit (lines 1–8). 6550, 6552.
For What Purpose?	Same authority as custodial parent including care, custody, control, education, and medical care. 2108, 2351, 2352, 2353.	If a custodial parent has been diagnosed as having a terminal condition. 2105.	Enroll in school, and consent to school-related medical care. 6550.	Same rights to authorize medical care and dental care for minor that are given to guardians. 6550.
When Takes Effect?	Nomination is effective when made, except a written nomination may provide that it only becomes effective upon the occurrence of an event (such as death of person making nomination). 1502.	Same as testamentary guardian. 1502.	Upon authorizing consent, except that decision shall be superseded by any contravening decision of the parent. 6550.	Upon authorizing consent, except that decision shall be superseded by any contravening decision of the parent. 6550.
How Terminate?	Terminates upon majority, death, adoption or emancipation of ward, or by court order. 1600, 1601.		If minor stops living with the caregiver. 6550.	If minor stops living with the caregiver. 6550.

92. *See also* CAL. FAM. CODE § 6910. Parent, guardian, or relative caregiver under section 6550 may authorize in writing another adult to consent to medical or dental care.

COLORADO

LEXIS reflects changes through June 1, 2015

	Testamentary Guardian of the Person (Colo. Rev. Stat. §§ 15-14-201 et seq.) with Standby Clause (Colo. Rev. Stat. § 15-14-202(2))	General Delegation of Power (Colo. Rev. Stat. § 15-14-105)	Examples of Medical Consent (Colo. Rev. Stat. § 25-4-1704)
Who Can Appoint?	Parent or guardian, or court. 15-14-201.	Parent or guardian. 15-14-105.	Parent or legal guardian. 25-14-1704.
How?	By will or other signed writing. 15-14-201, 15-14-202. Upon petition of a parent and a finding that the parent will likely become unable to care for the child within two years, the court may confirm the selection of a guardian and terminate the rights of others to object. Minor 12 or older must consent. 15-14-202(2).	By power of attorney. 15-14.105.	May delegate authority to consent verbally or in writing to a stepparent, adult relative of first or second degree of kinship, or an adult childcare provider who has care and control of the minor. 25-4-1704. In the case of verbal designation of authority, the person authorized to consent must confirm in writing at time of consent. 25-4-1704.
Objection?	Until court confirmation, a minor 12 or older or person other than guardian may object.[93] 15-14-203.		
Court Role?	Court may appoint if parental appointee fails to accept. Court shall appoint guardian nominated by minor 12 or older unless not in best interest of minor. 15-14-204, 15-14-206.		

93. Court can still appoint the person selected or can appoint temporary guardian. § 15-14-203.

	Testamentary Guardian of the Person (Colo. Rev. Stat. §§ 15-14-201 et seq.) with Standby Clause (Colo. Rev. Stat. § 15-14-202(2))	General Delegation of Power (Colo. Rev. Stat. § 15-14-105)	Examples of Medical Consent (Colo. Rev. Stat. § 25-4-1704)
For What Purpose?	Except as otherwise limited by the court, guardian has the duties and powers of a parent regarding the ward's support, care, education, health, and welfare. 15-14-207, 15-14-208.	Any power regarding care, custody, or property of minor except consent to marriage or adoption for period not exceeding twelve months. 15-14-105.	To authorize immunization of minor. Must provide accurate health information about the minor to health care provider. 24-4-1704. Person may not consent to immunization of minor if he/she has actual knowledge that the parent or guardian has expressly refused to give consent. 24-4-1704.
When Takes Effect?	Upon the death of the appointing parent; upon an adjudication that parent is an incapacitated person; or upon written determination by a physician that the parent is no longer able to care for the child, and acceptance by guardian and court confirmation of the appointment. 15-14-202.		
Compensation?	Guardian entitled to reasonable compensation as approved by the court. 15-14-209.		
How Terminate?	Upon the minor's death, adoption, emancipation, attainment of majority, or as ordered by the court, or upon guardian's death, resignation, or removal. 15-14-112, 15-14-210.		

CONNECTICUT

LEXIS current through P.A. 14-235 (all Legislation of the 2014 Regular Session)

	Testamentary Guardian of the Person (Conn. Gen. Stat. §§ 45a-596 et seq.)	Standby Guardian (Conn. Gen. Stat. § 45a-624)	Examples of Educational Consent (Conn. Gen. Stat. § 10-253(d))
Who Can Appoint?	Parent of unmarried minor.[94] 45a-596.	Parent/guardian may designate.[95] 45a-624.	
How?	By will or other signed writing.[96] 45a-596.	Designation shall be in signed writing and dated by principal and two witnesses. If both parents are alive, both must consent to designation. 45a-624, 45a-624a.	Nonresident children living permanently with relatives or nonrelatives, without pay, are entitled to all free school privileges. School board may require documentation. 10-253(d).
Minor Substitution?	Minor over 12 may apply for substitution of guardian to supersede previously appointed guardian. 45a-596.		
For What Purpose?		Care, control, education, welfare. 45a-624d, 45a-604.	Cannot be for sole purpose of obtaining school accommodations. 10-253(d).
When Takes Effect?	When guardian's written acceptance is filed in court.[97] 45a-596.	Takes effect upon the occurrence of a contingency, including mental incapacity, physical debilitation or death of principal. 45a-624.	
How Terminate?		Authority and obligations shall cease when specified contingency no longer exists or after expiration of one-year period, whichever is sooner. 45a-624d.	

94. Mandatory appointment of parent's testamentary choice of a guardian; presumption that best interests of child served by the appointment may be rebutted only by showing such appointment would be detrimental to the child. Bristol v. Brundage, 589 A.2d 1 (Conn. App. Ct. 1991).

95. Standby authority ceases ninety days after death of principal unless court appoints standby as guardian. § 45a-624e.

96. If two or more instruments contain an appointment, the latest effective appointment made by the last surviving parents has priority. § 45a-596.

97. If court finds necessary for protection of minor, it may require guardian to furnish a probate bond. § 45a-596.

DELAWARE

LEXIS current through 80 Del. Laws, Ch. 79

	Testamentary Guardian of the Person (Del. Code Ann. tit. 12 §§ 3901 et seq.)	Standby Guardian (Del. Code Ann. tit. 13 §§ 2361 et seq.)	Examples of Educational Consent (Del. Code Ann. tit. 14 § 202)	Examples of Medical Consent (Del. Code Ann. tit. 13 §§ 707, 708)
Who Can Appoint?	Court. 3901.	Court. 2365.	Court. 14-202(e)(2).	No appointment provided for.
How?	Sole surviving parent of minor may name guardian (in written declaration or will) who shall be appointed if there is no cause to the contrary. 3902. When there is no designation by parent, minor 14 or over may choose guardian.[98] 3902. If under 14, court may appoint according to its discretion. 3902.	Upon petition of any parent, custodian, or guardian, that documents significant risk of petitioner's death, incapacity, or debilitation with two years. 2365, 2366, 2367.	If child seeks to be considered resident of a school district based on residence of anyone other than parent, court must give signed order appointing as the child's guardian the resident with whom he/she is residing and guardian must complete the "Care-givers School Authorization." 14-202(e)(2).	Consent to minor's medical care may be given by (1) parent or guardian (2) married minor for self (or by spouse if minor unable to consent) (3) minor 18 or more (4) minor parent for child (5) any person serving as temporary custodian of minor for treatment of life threatening disease (6) relative acting pursuant to an Affidavit of Establishment of Power to Relative Caregivers to Consent to Medical Treatment of Minor. 13-707, 13-708.
For What Purpose?	Same powers of care, maintenance and treatment as a parent including establishing abode, education and medical care. 3922.	To enable parents, custodian, or guardian with progressive chronic or terminal illness to plan for interim or permanent care of child. 2361.	Caregiver author-ized to act in place of parent for child's education decisions (including special education) and will be contacted by school regarding truancy, discipline, and school-based medical care. 14-202(f)(3).	Consent to the perfor-mance upon or for any minor by any licensed medical, surgical, dental, psychological or osteopathic practitioner or nurse of any lawful medical treatment. 13-707.

98. When guardian is appointed by court for minor under fourteen and there is no written designation by the minor's parent, the minor can choose another person as guardian upon reaching fourteen and court shall appoint that person if there is no just cause to the contrary. § 3902.

	Testamentary Guardian of the Person (Del. Code Ann. tit. 12 §§ 3901 et seq.)	Standby Guardian (Del. Code Ann. tit. 13 §§ 2361 et seq.)	Examples of Educational Consent (Del. Code Ann. tit. 14 § 202)	Examples of Medical Consent (Del. Code Ann. tit. 13 §§ 707, 708)
When Takes Effect?		Effective upon death, incapacity, or debilitation of parent, custodian or guardian, subject to earlier date on written consent of petitioners. 2362(10), 2367(d), 2368.		
How Terminate?	Court may remove guardian for any sufficient cause. Guardian may be allowed to resign. Upon removal, resignation or death of guardian, court may appoint a successor guardian. Guardian-ship automatically terminates when minor attains age of 18 years. 3908, 3909.	Petitioner may revoke, or guardian may renounce. 2368(g) and (h). Terminates on guardian's death, adoption or majority of child, or as ordered by court. 2370, 2332.		

DISTRICT OF COLUMBIA

LEXIS current through permanent laws effective as of April 23, 2015

	Testamentary Guardian of the Person (D.C. Code §§ 21-101 et seq.)	Standby Guardianship (D.C. Code § 16-4801 et seq.)	General Delegation of Power (D.C. Code § 21-2301)	Examples of Medical Consent (D.C. Code § 16-4901)
Who Can Appoint?	When one parent is dead, the other may appoint a guardian of the person of his minor child. 21-102.	Custodial parents 16-4802, 16-4803.	Parent. 21-2301.	Parent or guardian. 16-4901.
How?	By will. 21-102.	Written designation before two witnesses, and signed acceptance by guardian. 16-4803.	Custodial power of attorney. 21-2301.	Any written form signed by parent or guardian may authorize an adult person, in whose care the minor has been entrusted to consent to medical care.[99] 16-4901.
Minor Selection?	If guardian is appointed, minor over 14 shall be entitled to select and nominate the guardian. Court shall pass upon character and competency of selected guardian. A minor of 14 or older, can select a new guardian notwithstanding earlier appointment. 21-108.			

99. Section 16-4901 includes a sample authorization form.

	Testamentary Guardian of the Person (D.C. Code §§ 21-101 et seq.)	Standby Guardianship (D.C. Code § 16-4801 et seq.)	General Delegation of Power (D.C. Code § 21-2301)	Examples of Medical Consent (D.C. Code § 16-4901)
Court Role?	If the person so appointed refuses or if no testamentary appointment, then court appoints on its own discretion or on application of next of friend of minor. 21-102, 21-103.	Court shall approve parent's designation if in best interest of child. 16-4806.		
For What Purpose?	For the care, custody and tuition of a minor child. 21-102.	To allow terminally ill, incapacitated or debilitated parent to plan for future of child without terminating or limiting parental rights. 16-4801.	Any of parent's rights and responsibilities regarding care, physical custody and control of child, including educational and medical matters. 21-2301.	Consent to medical, surgical, dental, developmental screening and/ or mental health examination or treatment, including immunization. 16-4901.
When Takes Effect?		Upon triggering event of parent's debilitation, incapacity, death, or written consent. 16-4804, 16-4802,16-4805, 16-4806, 16-4807.		
How Terminate?	Guardianship ends when minor becomes 18 or marries. 21-104.	Failure of guardian to file for court approval, or by revocation, repudiation, or rescission. 16-4805(e), 16-4810.		Parent can revoke authorization at any time. 16-4901.

FLORIDA

LEXIS updated for specified chapters with all legislation of the 2015 Session.

	Testamentary Guardian of the Person (Fla. Stat. Ann. §§ 744.101 et seq.)	Standby and Preneed Guardian (Fla. Stat. Ann. § 744.304 and § 744.3046)	Examples of Medical Consent (Fla. Stat. Ann. § 765.2035)	Examples of Medical Consent (Fla. Stat. Ann. § 743.0645)
Who Can Appoint?	Court. 744.3021.	Court, for standby guardian. 744.304. Parent may nominate for preneed guardian. 744.3046.	Natural guardian, legal custodian, or legal guardian may designate a surrogate. 765.2035 (effective Oct. 1, 2015, Fl. ALS 153, 2015 Fla. HB 889).	If person who has power to consent can-not be found, the power to consent, in order of priority is given to: a) person who possess a power of attorney b) stepparent c) grand-parent d) adult brother or sister e) adult aunt or uncle. 743.0645.
How?	Court shall give preference to appointment of person who is related by blood or marriage to ward and consider preference of minor over 14 and any person designated in any will in which the ward is a beneficiary. 744.312.	By petition to court for standby guardian. 744.304. By signed, written declaration before two witnesses for preneed guardian. 744.3046.	By written document with two witnesses. 765.2035. Suggested form at 765.2038.	
For What Purpose?	Exercise powers of plenary guardian. 744.3021, 744.361.		To make health care decisions for the minor. 765.2035.	To consent to medical care or treatment including blood testing, immunizations, tuberculin testing, but does not include surgery, general anesthesia, provision of psychotropic medications, or other extraordinary procedures. 743.0645.

	Testamentary Guardian of the Person (Fla. Stat. Ann. §§ 744.101 et seq.)	Standby and Preneed Guardian (Fla. Stat. Ann. § 744.304 and § 744.3046)	Examples of Medical Consent (Fla. Stat. Ann. § 765.2035)	Examples of Medical Consent (Fla. Stat. Ann. § 743.0645)
When Takes Effect?		Standby guardianship effective immediately on death, removal, or resignation of guardian, or upon death or incapacity of last surviving natural guardian, with subsequent court confirmation. 744.304. Preneed guardianship effective immediately upon incapacity or death of last surviving parent, with subsequent court confirmation. 744.3046.		After reasonable attempt, the treatment provider cannot contact a person who has the power to consent as otherwise provided by law. 743.0645.
How Terminate?	Terminated when ward becomes sui juris, ward not located, or ward deceased, or upon change of domicile of ward. 744.521, 744.524.		Unless document states time of termination, then effective until revoked by minor's principal. 765.2035.	

GEORGIA

	Testamentary Guardian of the Person (Ga. Code Ann. §§ 29-2-1 et. seq.)	Standby Guardian (Ga. Code Ann. §§ 29-2-9 et seq.)	General Delegation of Power (Ga. Code Ann. §§ 19-9-120 et seq.)	Examples of Medical Consent (Ga. Code Ann. § 31-9-2)
Who Can Appoint?	Parent. 29-2-4.	A designating individual including parent or legal guardian, 29-2-9, 29-2-10.	Parent may delegate authority to grandparent or great grandparent living in state. 19-9-121, 19-9-122.	Appointment not provided for by statute.
How?	By will. 29-2-4.	Designation shall be in writing and signed by designating individual and 2 witnesses, per sample form. 29-2-11. May be revoked as designated by statute. 29-2-12.	By written power of attorney before a notary, substantially like statutory sample form. 19-9-122, 19-9-127, 19-9-129.	Any of the following is authorized to consent to minor's treatment: parent or guardian, person temporarily standing in loco parentis, whether formally or not, for the minor under his care. 31-9-2.
Court Role?	Court hearing if objection filed but parental nomination prevails absent clear and convincing evidence that guardian is unfit. 29-2-4.			
For What Purpose?	Same rights, powers, and duties as permanent guardian appointed by court. 29-2-4, 29-2-21, 29-2-22.	Assume all rights, duties, and responsibilities of guardianship of the person of the minor. 29-2-10.	To care for child when hardship prevents parental care, including education, health care, food, lodging, recreation, travel, and other specified powers. 19-9-122, 19-9-123, 19-9-124.	Consent to surgical or medical treatment or procedures not prohibited by law. 31-9-2.

	Testamentary Guardian of the Person (Ga. Code Ann. §§ 29-2-1 et. seq.)	Standby Guardian (Ga. Code Ann. §§ 29-2-9 et seq.)	General Delegation of Power (Ga. Code Ann. §§ 19-9-120 et seq.)	Examples of Medical Consent (Ga. Code Ann. § 31-9-2)
When Takes Effect?		Upon the health determination being made, without necessity for judicial intervention. Standby guardian must file with the probate court of the county where minor resides notice of guardianship with a copy of designation and proof that health determination was made. 29-2-10.		
How Terminate?	Upon majority, adoption, emancipation, death of minor, or by court order. 29-2-30.	Except as otherwise stated, shall be automatically terminated 120 days after the making of the health determination, unless standby files petition for temporary guardianship. 29-2-13. If designating individual dies, standby guardianship terminates in favor of testamentary designation of a guardian. 29-2-13.	Written revocation by parent with notice to grandparent, or by order of court. 19-9-128.	

HAWAII

	Testamentary Guardian of the Person (Haw. Rev. Stat. Ann. §§ 560:5-201 et seq.) with Standby Clause (Haw. Rev. Stat. Ann. § 560:5-202(b))	General Delegation of Power (Haw. Rev. Stat. Ann. § 560:5-105)	Examples of Educational Consent (Haw. Rev. Stat. Ann. §§ 302A-481 et seq.)	Examples of Medical Consent (Haw. Rev. Stat. Ann. §§ 577-28)
Who Can Appoint?	Parent or court. 560:5-201.	Parent or guardian. 560:5-105.		
How?	By will or other signed writing confirmed by court. 560:5-202. Upon petition of a parent and finding that parent will become unable to care for child within two years, court may confirm parent's selection and terminate rights of others. 560:5-202(b).	By power of attorney. 560:5-105.	Related caregiver, residing with minor for six months or more, by valid affidavit. 302A-481, 302A-482.	Related caregiver, residing with minor for six months or more, by notarized affidavit. 577-28.
Objection?	A minor 14 or older, the other parent, or other caregivers may file objection, but does not preclude appointment of parent's selection. 560:5-203.			
Court Role?	Court may appoint guardian if parental rights terminated, minor objects, or appointee does not accept. Court shall appoint nominee by minor over 14, unless contrary to minor's best interest. 560:5-203, 204, 206.			

	Testamentary Guardian of the Person (Haw. Rev. Stat. Ann. §§ 560:5-201 et seq.) with Standby Clause (Haw. Rev. Stat. Ann. § 560:5-202(b))	General Delegation of Power (Haw. Rev. Stat. Ann. § 560:5-105)	Examples of Educational Consent (Haw. Rev. Stat. Ann. §§ 302A-481 et seq.)	Examples of Medical Consent (Haw. Rev. Stat. Ann. §§ 577-28)
For What Purpose?	All duties of parent for support, care, education, health, and welfare, including consent to medical care. 560:5-207, 208.	Care, custody, or property of minor, except consent to marriage or adoption, for period not exceeding one year. 560:5-105.	Consent to school enrollment and activities. 302A-482.	Consent to medical and dental care, diagnostic testing, and other medically necessary treatment. 577-28.
When Takes Effect?	Upon appointing parent's death, incapacitation, or written determination parent not able to care for child. Guardian eligible to act upon acceptance of appointment with court. 560:5-202.			
Guardian Compensation?	Reasonable compensation as approved by court. 560:5-209.			
How Terminate?	Upon minor's death, adoption, emancipation, majority, or court order. 560:5-210.		Rescinded by parent or guardian, or minor no longer resides with caregiver. 302A-482.	Rescinded by parent or guardian. 577-28.

IDAHO

	Testamentary Guardian of the Person (Idaho Code §§ 15-5-201 et seq.)	General Delegation of Power (Idaho Code § 15-5-104)	Examples of Medical Consent (Idaho Code § 39-4504)
Who Can Appoint?	Parent of unmarried minor. 15-5-202.	Parent or guardian of a minor. 15-5-104.	
How?	By will. 15-5-202.	By a properly executed power of attorney. 15-5-104.	Parent, guardian, relative, or other competent responsible person may consent to health care for minor. 39-4504.
Minor Objection?	Minor 14 or older may file objection before or within 30 days after notice of guardian's acceptance, but objection does not preclude appointment of parent's nominee. 15-5-203.		
Court Role?	Court may appoint if testamentary guardian failed to accept or was prevented by minor. Court must appoint person nominated by minor 14 or older unless contrary to best interests of minor. 15-5-204, 15-5-206.		
For What Purpose?	Guardian has powers and responsibilities of a parent; is empowered to facilitate ward's education and social activities, and to authorize medical care. 15-5-209.	Care, custody, or property including health and education except for consent to marriage or adoption, for period not exceeding 6 months, or 12 months for military out of country. Power delegated to grandparent, sibling, aunt, or uncle continues for 3 years or until specified. 15-5-104.	Consent to hospital, medical, dental or surgical care, treatment, or procedures. 39-4504.
When Takes Effect?	Upon filing acceptance of testamentary appointment in court in which the will is probated. 15-5-202.		
How Terminate?	Upon death, resignation (with court approval), or removal of guardian, or upon minor's death, adoption, marriage, or attainment of majority. 15-5-210. Ward if 14 or over, or other interested person, may petition for removal if in ward's best interest. 15-5-212.		

ILLINOIS

	Testamentary Guardian of the Person (755 Ill. Comp. Stat. Ann. 5/11-1 et seq.)	Standby Guardian (755 Ill. Comp. Stat. Ann. 5/11-5.3)	General Delegation of Power (755 Ill. Comp. Stat. Ann. 5/11-5.4)
Who Can Appoint?	Court. 5/11-5. Parent may designate person to be appointed.[100] 5/11-5.	Parent may designate a person to be appointed as standby guardian.[101] Court may also appoint. 5/11-5.3.	Parent.[102] 5/11-5.4.
How?	Parental designation can be made in any writing, including a will. Upon filing petition for appointment or on its own motion, court shall appoint guardian in best interest of minor. Court lacks jurisdiction if a living parent is willing and able to act. Minor 14 or over may nominate the guardian subject to approval of the court. 5/11-5.	Parent may designate by will or any signed writing before two witnesses. Court may appoint upon filing of petition for appointment of standby guardian. Court lacks jurisdiction if living parent willing and able to act. 5/11-5.3.	In written instrument signed by appointing parent and two witnesses. Person appointed must also sign. Appointment may be for a period up to 365 days. 5/11-5.4.
For What Purpose?	Under direction of the court guardian has custody, nurture and tuition of minor, including education of ward. 5/11-13.	Under direction of the court the guardian has custody, nurture and tuition of minor, including education of ward. 5/11-13.	Under direction of the court guardian has custody, nurture and tuition of minor, including education of ward. 5/11-13, 5/11-13.2
When Takes Effect?		Upon knowledge of death or consent of minor's parents, or inability of minor's parents to carry out day-to-day childcare. Standby guardian can act for 60 days without direction of court, but must file petition for appointment within that time.[103] 5/11-13.1.	Immediately upon date written instrument is executed, unless instrument provides that appointment effective upon later specified date or event. 5/11-5.4.
How Terminate?	Upon minor reaching age of majority (18), upon material change of circumstances, or upon death, incapacity, resignation or removal of guardian. 5/11-14.1, 5/11-1, 5/11-18.	Upon death, incapacity, resignation or removal of guardian, court may appoint successor. 5/11-18.	365 days from date appointment is effective. 5/11-5.4.

100. Whenever both parents of a minor are deceased, vitiation rights shall be granted to grandparents of minor, unless shown to be detrimental to best interests of minor. Reasonable visitation rights also may be granted to any other close relative. § 5/11-7.1.
101. Section 5/11-5.3 includes a sample form for "Designation of Standby Guardian."
102. Parent shall not appoint short-term guardian if minor has another living parent whose parental rights have not been terminated and who is willing and able to carry out day-to-day care of minor, unless non-appointing parent consents. § 5/11-5.4.
103. Guardian must take and file an oath or affirmation that standby guardian will faithfully discharge duties of the office. § 5/11-5.3.

INDIANA

	Testamentary Guardian of the Person (Ind. Code Ann. §§ 29-3-5-1 et seq.)	Standby Guardian (Ind. Code Ann. § 29-3-3-7)	General Delegation of Power (Ind. Code Ann. § 29-3-9-1)	Examples of Medical Consent (Ind. Code Ann. § 16-36-1-5)
Who Can Appoint?	Court. 29-3-5-3.	Parent or guardian may designate standby and alternate. 29-3-3-7.	Parent or non-temporary guardian. 29-3-9-1.	Appointment not provided for by statute.
How?	Any person can file petition for appointment of a person to serve as guardian. Court shall have a hearing and shall appoint person most suitable and willing to serve having due regard to: request contained in a will, or other written instrument, request made by minor 14 or older, relationship of proposed guardian to minor, best interest of minor. 29-3-5-1, 29-3-5-4.	By written declaration, signed before a notary. 29-3-3-7.	By properly executed power of attorney, for any period minor institutionalized, or period not exceeding 12 months. 29-3-9-1.	Any of the following can authorize medical care for minor: guardian, parent, a person in loco parentis, and adult sibling if parent not reasonably available. 16-36-1-5.
For What Purpose?	All responsibilities and authority of a parent unless court orders otherwise. 29-3-8-1, 29-3-8-2, 29-3-8-8.		Any powers regarding health care, support, custody, or property, except marriage or adoption, or as excluded in the power of attorney. 29-3-9-1.	Healthcare for a minor. 16-36-1-5.
When Takes Effect?		Death or incapacity of declarant. 29-3-3-7.	Immediately unless otherwise stated. 29-3-9-1.	

	Testamentary Guardian of the Person (Ind. Code Ann. §§ 29-3-5-1 et seq.)	Standby Guardian (Ind. Code Ann. § 29-3-3-7)	General Delegation of Power (Ind. Code Ann. § 29-3-9-1)	Examples of Medical Consent (Ind. Code Ann. § 16-36-1-5)
How Terminate?	Court shall terminate upon minor attaining 18 years of age, or minor's death. Court may terminate guardianship of minor upon minor's adoption, marriage, change in domicile, or other reason. 29-3-12-1. Guardianship not terminated at majority if ward incapacitated or recipient of financial aid through child services. 29-3-12-6. Court may extend guardianship to 22 or older for any ward if in best interest after notice and hearing. 29-3-12-7.	Terminates after 90 days unless standby files petition for guardianship with court. 29-3-3-7.	May be revoked in writing. 29-3-9-1.	

IOWA

	Testamentary Guardian of the Person (Iowa Code §§ 633.551 et seq.)	Standby Guardian (Iowa Code § 633.560)
Who Can Appoint?	Court. 633.556.	Court. 633.560.
How?	Any person may file petition for appointment of guardian for a minor. Burden of persuasion is on the petitioner to show by clear and convincing evidence that appointment is necessary. 633.551, 633.552. Preference given to person nominated as guardian in a will executed by custodial parent, and any qualified and suitable person requested by minor 14 or older. 633.559.	Petition pursuant to 633.560 for the appointment of a guardian on a standby basis follows same procedures for standby conservators in §§ 633.591 to 633.597.
For What Purpose?	Provide for care, comfort and maintenance of ward, including education and health care, subject to statutory conditions and exceptions. 633.635.	
When Takes Effect?		Upon verification of triggering event or condition set out in petition, court holds hearing for standby appointment. 633.595.
How Terminate?	Upon majority or death of ward, or court determination guardianship no longer necessary. 633.675.	Petition may be revoked prior to court appointment of guardian. 633.594.

KANSAS

	Testamentary Guardian of the Person (Kan. Stat. Ann. §§ 59-3051 et seq.)	Standby Guardian (Kan. Stat. Ann. § 59-3074)	Examples of Medical Consent (Kan. Stat. Ann. § 38-135 et seq.)
Who Can Appoint?	Court. 59-3054.	Court. 59-3074.	Parent. 38-136.
How?	A surviving natural guardian, by last will or inter vivos trust, may nominate guardian of a minor. 59-3054. Any person may file verified petition to appoint guardian. 59-3059, 59-3060. Among others, court must give priority to choice of natural guardian or minor over the age of 14. Court shall consider workload, capabilities, potential conflicts of interest, and number of other cases of proposed guardian. 59-3068.	Upon verified petition by individual that includes factual basis for the need of a standby guardian, or how appointment would be in best interest of ward. 59-3074.	Can delegate in written consent to: grandparent, adult brother or sister (or half-brother or half-sister), adult aunt or uncle, stepparent, another adult who has care and control of minor. 38-136. If parent is not reasonably available and no written consent was given, the following can consent: grandparent, adult brother or sister (or half-brother or half-sister), adult aunt or uncle, stepparent, another adult who has care and control of minor. A person cannot consent if they have actual knowledge that parent has expressly refused to give consent to the immunization. 38-137.
For What Purpose?	Custody and control of the minor, including minor's care, treatment, education, support, maintenance, plus other specified duties and exceptions, pursuant to written plan if required by court. 59-3075, 59-3076.	Responsibility to assume duties, responsibilities, and powers of a guardian upon temporary absence or impairment of the guardian. 59-3074.	Authority to allow immunization of minor. 38-136, 38-137.
When Takes Effect?	Before issuance of letters, guardian must file oath or affirmation, and complete basic instructional program. 59-3069.		
How Terminate?	Guardian may resign or be removed. 59-3088, 59-3089. Guardianship terminates if ward no longer needs guardian, or upon death or majority of ward. 59-3091, 59-3092.		

KENTUCKY

	Testamentary Guardian of the Person (Ky. Rev. Stat. Ann. §§ 387.020 et seq.)	Examples of Educational and Medical Consent (Ky. Rev. Stat. Ann. § 27A.095)
Who Can Appoint?	Court. 387.020. Last surviving parent may nominate guardian by will. 387.040. Minor over 14 may nominate own guardian. 387.050.	
How?	Court shall appoint any person in the best interest of the minor, taking into consideration the person nominated in a will and if the minor is over 14, a guardian nominated by the minor. 387.032, 387.040, 387.050.	The Administrative Office of the Courts shall develop a standard power of attorney. 27A.095.
For What Purpose?	Guardian has powers and responsibilities of a parent regarding the ward's support, care, medical care, and education, but is not personally liable for the ward's expenses. 387.065.	For the limited purpose of consent to a minor's medical treatment, as defined, and school-related decisions. 27A.095.
When Takes Effect?	Upon appointment and bonding with surety, if required. 387.070.	
Compensation	Guardians receive reasonable compensation for their services and reimbursement of expenses from the estate of the ward. 387.111.	
How Terminate?	Court shall remove guardian if guardian becomes insane, becomes incapable of discharging the duties of appointment, or fails to discharge duties of appointment, or leaves the Commonwealth. 387.090.	

LOUISIANA

	Testamentary Guardian of the Person (La. Civ. Code Ann. art. 250 et seq.)	Examples of Educational and Medical Consent (La. Rev. Stat. Ann. § 9:975)	Examples of Medical Consent (La. Rev. Stat. Ann. § 40:1159.4)
Who Can Appoint?	Last surviving parent. Art. 250. Must be confirmed by the court. By nature, by will, by the effect of law, by appointment of the judge. Art. 247.	Non-legal custodian, other than a foster parent, may consent to medical or educational services for child in his or her custody by executing affidavit described in the statute. Parent or legal custodian may supersede decisions of non-legal custodian. 9:975.	Appointment not provided for in statute. Any one of the following may authorize medical treatment for minor: parent, patient's sibling, patient's other ascendants, any person temporarily standing in loco parentis is for the minor. 40:1159.4.
How?	By will. Art. 257. By nature Art. 250, Art. 248. By appointment by the court Art. 248.		Signing and dating an acknowledgment form provided by hospital certifying that they meet criteria. 40:1159.4(A)(9).
Court Role?	If no will, then court shall appoint from among the qualified ascendants in the direct line the person whose appointment is in the best interests of the minor. Art. 263.		
For What Purpose?		Medical or educational services. 9:975.	Medical treatment. 40:1159.4.
When Takes Effect?	Upon court confirmation or appointment. Art. 248.		At the time medical treatment is suggested, recommended, prescribed or directed by a duly licensed physician. 40.1159.4(A).
How Terminate?		Affidavit not valid for more than one year. If child ceases to live with non-legal custodian, he or she shall notify all persons in possession of the affidavit. 9:975.	

MAINE

	Testamentary Guardian of the Person (Me. Rev. Stat. Ann. tit. 18-A §§ 5-201 et seq.)	General Delegation of Power (Me. Rev. Stat. Ann. tit. 18-A § 5-104)
Who Can Appoint?	Parent of an unmarried minor[104] or court. § 18-A, 5-202 and 5-204.	Parent or guardian of minor. 18-A, 5-104.
How?	By will or by the court. 18-A, 5-201.	By properly executed power of attorney. 18-A, 5-104.
Minor Objection?	A minor 14 or older may file a written objection to the appointment before it is accepted or within 30 days after notice of acceptance. 18-A, 5-203.	
Court Appointment?	Court may appoint guardian if all parental rights have been terminated or if testamentary guardian does not accept. Appointment of parent that has not been prevented by minor has priority over any appointment by the court but court can appoint upon a finding that the testamentary guardian failed to accept appointment. Court shall appoint person nominated by minor over 14 unless contrary to best interest of minor. 18-A, 5-204.	
For What Purpose?	Guardian must take reasonable care of ward's personal effects; is empowered to facilitate ward's education and social activities and to give consent to medical care. 18-A, 5-209.	Delegate any power regarding care, custody, or property of minor except consent to marriage or adoption for a period not exceeding twelve months. Automatic thirty-day extension applies to active national guard or reserves member, under certain circumstances. 18-A, 5-104.
When Takes Effect?	Subject to right of minor to object, becomes effective upon acceptance of testamentary or court appointment. 18-A, 5-201.	
How Terminate?	Terminates upon the death, resignation[105] or removal[106] of guardian or upon minor's death, adoption, marriage, or attainment of majority. 18-A, 5-210.	

104. If both parents are deceased, an effective appointment by the parent who died later has priority. § 18A-5-202.
105. A guardian may petition for permission to resign. § 18-A, 5-212.
106. Any person interested in welfare of a ward, or the ward if fourteen or over, may petition for removal of a guardian on the ground that it would be in the best interest of the ward. § 18-A, 5-212.

MARYLAND

	Testamentary Guardian of the Person (Md. Code Ann., Est. & Trusts §§ 13-701 et seq.)	Standby Guardian (Md. Code Ann., Est. & Trusts §§ 13-901 et seq.)	Examples of Educational and Medical Consent (Md. Code. Ann., Education § 7-101, and Md. Code Ann., Health-General § 20-105)	Examples of Medical Consent (Md. Code Ann. Health-General Code Ann. § 18-4A-01 et seq.)
Who Can Appoint?	Surviving parent of a minor may appoint. Guardian need not be approved by any court. 13-701.	Court. 13-903.		Parent or guardian. 18-4A-01, 18-4A-02.
How?	By will. 13-701.	Parent of minor can file for judicial appointment of standby guardian. Each person having parental rights over the minor must join petition. Petition must state that there is a significant risk that petitioner will become incapacitated or die within two years of the filing of the petition. Alternatively, parent can make a written designation before two witnesses; standby guardian shall file a petition for judicial appointment within 180 days of the date of the beginning of the standby guardianship.[107] 13-904.	If no court appointed guardian or custodian, a relative providing informal kinship care due to serious family hardship, verified by sworn affidavit, may make educational decisions and consent to minor's health care. 7-101, 20-105.	May delegate authority to consent to minor's immunization verbally or in writing to any of the following: grandparent, adult brother or sister, adult aunt or uncle, stepparent, any other adult who has care and control of the minor. If delegation is verbal, delegated person shall confirm in writing at time of consent. 18-4A-01, 18-4A-02. If parent not reasonably available, the same persons stated above, among others, could consent, absent knowledge that parent has expressly refused minor's immunization. 18-4A-03.

107. Section 13-904 includes a standby guardian designation form.

	Testamentary Guardian of the Person (Md. Code Ann., Est. & Trusts §§ 13-701 et seq.)	Standby Guardian (Md. Code Ann., Est. & Trusts §§ 13-901 et seq.)	Examples of Educational and Medical Consent (Md. Code. Ann., Education § 7-101, and Md. Code Ann., Health-General § 20-105)	Examples of Medical Consent (Md. Code Ann. Health-General Code Ann. § 18-4A-01 et seq.)
Court Appointment?	If no parent is serving as guardian and no testamentary appointment has been made, a court may appoint. If minor is 14 or older, court shall appoint person designated by the minor, unless not in minor's best interest. 13-702.	Court shall appoint standby guardian designated/petitioned by parent. 13-903(a).		
For What Purpose?		Petition for appointment/designation shall state the duties of the standby guardian. 13-903, 13-904. Authority of standby limited to express authority granted by court. 13-907.	Full range of educational decisions. 7-101. Health care of minor. 20-105.	Authority to consent to minor's immunization. 18-4A-02.
When Takes Effect?		Standby authority takes effect on determination of incapacity, death, debilitation, and/or written consent of parent before two witnesses. 13-903, 13-904, 13-906.		
Compensation?	None, unless will provides otherwise. 13-703.			
How Terminate?		Petitioner may revoke, or guardian may renounce, in written court filing with proper notice. Before filing of petition, parent may revoke verbally or in writing. 13-903, 13-904.		

MASSACHUSETTS

	Testamentary Guardian of the Person (Mass. Ann. Laws ch. 190B, § 5-201 et seq.) with Standby Clause (Mass. Ann. Laws ch. 190B, § 5-202(c))	General Delegation of Power (Mass. Ann. Laws ch. 190B, § 5-103)	Examples of Educational and Medical Consent (Mass. Ann. Laws, ch. 201F, § 1 et. seq.)
Who Can Appoint?	Parent or guardian of minor child, by will or other writing, or by appointment of the court. 190B, 5-202 and 190B, 5-201.	Parent or guardian of minor. 190B, 5-103.	Parent, legal guardian or custodian. 201F, 2.
How?	By will or other signed writing attested by at least two witnesses. 190B, 5-202. Upon petition of parent or guardian, and finding that parent or guardian will become unable to care for minor within two years or less, court may confirm parent or guardian's selection and terminate rights of others. 190B, 5-202(c).	In writing signed by, or at direction of parent or guardian, attested by two witnesses. 190B, 5-103.	Under caregiver authorization affidavit, designated caregiver, residing with the minor, may exercise certain parental rights relative to minor's education and health care. Parent or guardian may supersede caregiver's decision. 201F, 1 and 201F, 2. Requirements and form for affidavit set out in statutes. 201F, 5 and 201F, 6.
Objection by Minor?	Except for previously confirmed standby appointment, a minor 14 or more, among others, may file written objection before, or within thirty days' notice of acceptance. 190B, 5-203. Court shall appoint choice of minor 14 or more, unless contrary to minor's best interest. 190B, 5-207.		

	Testamentary Guardian of the Person (Mass. Ann. Laws ch. 190B, § 5-201 et seq.) with Standby Clause (Mass. Ann. Laws ch. 190B, § 5-202(c))	General Delegation of Power (Mass. Ann. Laws ch. 190B, § 5-103)	Examples of Educational and Medical Consent (Mass. Ann. Laws, ch. 201F, § 1 et. seq.)
For What Purpose?	Support, care, education, health and welfare. 190B, 5-209.	Temporary delegation of any power regarding care, custody, or property of minor except consent to marriage or adoption for a period not exceeding sixty days. 190B, 5-103.	Consent to medical, surgical, dental, and developmental or other treatment, and obtain records or insurance information. Make educational decisions regarding enrollment, disciplinary, curricular, special education, school activities, and other matters including access to school records. 201F, 3.
When Takes Effect?	Upon death, adjudicated incapacity, or written determination by physician that parent or guardian no longer able to care for minor. 190B, 5-202.		
How Terminate?	Upon death, resignation or removal of guardian or upon minor's death, adoption, marriage or attainment of majority. 190B, 5-210.	Parent or guardian may revoke or amend. Court may limit or alter. 190B, 5-103.	

MICHIGAN

	Testamentary Guardian of the Person (Mich. Comp. Laws Serv. § 700.5201 et seq.)	General Delegation of Power (Mich. Comp. Laws Serv. § 700.5103)
Who Can Appoint?	Parent[108] or court. 700.5201.	Parent or guardian of minor. 700.5103.
How?	Parental appointment can be made by will or other signed writing by the parent and attested by at least two witnesses. 700-5202.	By properly executed power of attorney. A guardian who delegates power shall notify court within seven days of executing the power. 700.5103.
Objection By Minor?	Minor 14 or older may file a written objection to the appointment before it is accepted or within 28 days after its acceptance.[109] 700.5203.	
Court Appointment?	If parental rights of both parents terminated, or the parents permit minor to live with another person and do not give them legal authority or maintenance. 700.5204.[110] Court shall appoint person nominated by minor, unless contrary to the minor's welfare. 700.5212.	
For What Purpose?	Same as parent, and must facilitate ward's education and social activities, and shall authorize medical care. A guardian may consent to a minor ward's marriage. 700.5215.	Delegate any power regarding care, custody, or property of minor except consent to marriage or adoption for a period not exceeding six months. For active military, delegation is effective until thirty-first day after end of deployment. 700.5103.
When Takes Effect?	Subject to objection by minor, becomes effective when guardian files acceptance in court. 700.5202(2).	
How Terminate?	Guardian's authority and responsibility terminate upon guardian's death, resignation[111] or removal[112] or upon the minor's death, adoption, marriage, or attainment of majority. 700.5217.	

108. If both parents are deceased, an effective appointment by the parent who died later has priority. § 700.5202.
109. Objection does not preclude appointment by the court of the parental nominee or another suitable person. § 700.5203.
110. Section 700.5204 identifies several other circumstances where a court may appoint a guardian.
111. Resignation does not terminate guardianship until it is approved by the court. § 700.5217.
112. A person interested in ward's welfare, or ward if fourteen or older, may petition for removal of guardian on the ground that removal would serve the ward's welfare. § 700.5219.

MINNESOTA

	Testamentary Guardian of the Person (Minn. Stat. §§ 524.5-201 et seq.) with Standby Clause (Minn. Stat. Ann. § 524.5-202(b))	Standby Guardian (Minn. Stat. §§ 257B.01-257B.10)	General Delegation of Power (Minn. Stat. § 524.5-211)
Who Can Appoint?	Parent or court. Minn. Stat. 524.5-202.	Parent can designate unless there is another legal parent whose parental rights have not been terminated, whose whereabouts are known, and who is willing and able to take care of child.[113] 257B.03.	Parent, custodian or guardian of minor. 524.5-211.
How?	By will or other signed writing. 524.5-202. Upon petition of parent, and finding that parent will be unable to care for minor within two years or less, court may confirm parent's selection and terminate rights of others. 524.5-202(b).	Must identify the standby guardian, the triggering event or events upon which standby becomes custodian.[114] Designator may also designate alternate. 257B.04.	By properly executed power of attorney, with copy to other parent within thirty days. 524.5-211.
Minor Objection?	Until the court has confirmed an appointee, a minor who is subject of an appointment by a parent and who is 14 or older can prevent appointment by filing a written objection with the court.[115] 524.5-203.		
Court Role?	Court can appoint if parental appointee has failed to accept or if appointment has been prevented by the minor. Court shall appoint guardian nominated by minor if over 14, unless contrary to the best interest of the minor. 524.5-203, 524.5-204.	Must get court approval after petition and filing with court. If triggering event has not occurred, only the designator may file for approval. If triggering event has occurred, standby named in designation may file. 257B.05.	

113. If parent appointed testamentary guardian and there is a conflict between designation in the will and duly executed standby designation, the document latest in date of execution prevails. § 257B.08.
114. Different standby custodians may be designated for different triggering events. § 257B.04.
115. Objection does not preclude an appointment of the appointee by the court. § 524.5-203.

	Testamentary Guardian of the Person (Minn. Stat. §§ 524.5-201 et seq.) with Standby Clause (Minn. Stat. Ann. § 524.5-202(b))	Standby Guardian (Minn. Stat. §§ 257B.01-257B.10)	General Delegation of Power (Minn. Stat. § 524.5-211)
For What Purpose?	Same as parent and must facilitate ward's education and authorize medical care. 524.5-207.	Act as co-custodian or custodian upon the occurrence of the triggering event. 257B.06(1).	Delegate any power regarding care, custody or property of minor except consent to marriage or adoption for a period not exceeding one year. 524.5-211.
When Takes Effect?	Subject to objection by minor, becomes effective upon the appointing parent's death, an adjudication that parent is incapacitated, or that parent unable to care for the child. Guardian can act upon filing of acceptance, which must be 30 days following effective date of appointment. 524.5-202.	Takes effect upon occurrence of triggering event and approval of designation by court. (If approval received before triggering event, then authority commences automatically upon occurrence of the triggering event. If designation made but no petition for approval was filed, takes effect upon court approval). Petition must take effect within 60 days of triggering event.[116] 257B.06.	
Compensation?	Guardian is entitled to reasonable compensation and reimbursement. 524.5-209.		
How Terminate?	Upon minor's death, adoption, emancipation, attainment of majority, or as ordered by court. 524.5-210.	If designator regains capacity, standby's authority becomes inactive. 257B.06. Designator may revoke prior to petition being filed. After petition filed, designator may revoke by written revocation filed with the court and notifying those designated of the revocation. 257B.07.	

116. Commencement of custodian's authority does not, by itself, divest parent of any parental rights. § 257B.06.

MISSISSIPPI

	Testamentary Guardian of the Person (Miss. Code Ann. § 93-13-7 et seq.)	Examples of Medical Consent (Miss. Code Ann. § 41-41-3)
Who Can Appoint?	Parent by written consent. 93-13-7.	Appointment not provided for in statute. Any one of the following persons, who is reasonably available, in descending order of priority, is authorized to consent: a) minor's guardian or custodian b) minor's parent c) adult brother or sister of minor d) minor's grandparent. 41-41-3.
How?	Signed writing, or attested by two or more credible witnesses, not including the person appointed as guardian if not written. 93-13-7.	Can consent orally or otherwise. 41-41-3.
Court Appointment?	If no parental designation, then court can appoint. Court may allow a minor over 14 to select a general guardian. 93-13-13.	
For What Purpose?	Control the person and tuition of the child, to manage the child's estate, real and personal, to receive the profits thereof, to prosecute suits and actions concerning the same. 93-13-11.	Authorized to consent to surgical or medical treatment or procedures not prohibited by law for minor. 41-41-3.
When Takes Effect?	Guardian must appear before court and declare acceptance in writing before exercising any authority. 93-13-9.	
How Terminate?	Any guardian may resign or be removed by the court. 93-13-23, 93-13-25.	

MISSOURI

	Testamentary Guardian of the Person (Mo. Rev. Stat. §§ 475.045 et seq.)	Standby Guardianship (Mo. Rev. Stat. § 475.046 et seq.)	General Delegation of Power (Mo. Rev. Stat. § 475.024)	Examples of Educational and Medical Consent (Mo. Rev. Stat. § 431.058 et seq.)
Who Can Appoint?	Court. 475.045, 475.079.	Court. 475.046.	Parent. 475.024.	
How?	Court shall appoint: (1) Parent or parents, (2) Person nominated by minor over 14, unless contrary to best interests of the minor, or (3) Where both parents are dead, any person appointed under this section or under 475.046 by the will of the last surviving parent. If none of these, court shall appoint most suitable person willing to serve in best interests of child. 475.045.	Custodial parent may designate standby in will complying with 474.320 or writing dated, signed or acknowledged by parent, before two witnesses. 475.046.	Properly executed power of attorney. 475.024.	Acting under affidavit complying with statutory form, a relative caregiver, living with a child, may consent to medical and educational services for minor, if parent so delegates in writing, or parent's consent not obtained after reasonable effort. 431.058. Generally, a parent, adult in loco parentis, guardian, or relative caregiver as described above may consent to minor's medical and surgical treatment. 431.061.
For What Purpose?	Custody and control of ward, including ward's education, support and maintenance. 475.120. Petition may be filed for sole purpose of school registration or medical insurance. 475.060.	Temporary care and custody of minor if parent becomes seriously ill, defined as likely to be incapacitated or dead within twelve months. 475.046, 475.010.	To delegate any powers of care or custody of minor, except marriage or adoption, for a period not exceeding one year. 475.024.	Medical treatment or procedures, including immunizations, and educational services. 431.058, 431.061.

	Testamentary Guardian of the Person (Mo. Rev. Stat. §§ 475.045 et seq.)	Standby Guardianship (Mo. Rev. Stat. § 475.046 et seq.)	General Delegation of Power (Mo. Rev. Stat. § 475.024)	Examples of Educational and Medical Consent (Mo. Rev. Stat. § 431.058 et seq.)
When Takes Effect?	Upon issuance of letters of guardianship. 475.055.	Upon granting of letters, or consent of custodial parent, order finding parent incapacitated, or death of parent, followed by timely court proceedings. 475.046.		
How Terminate?	When minor becomes 18, upon revocation of letters, upon acceptance by court of resignation of guardian, upon death of minor, upon expiration of appointment, or upon order of court terminating the guardianship. 475.083.	Same as testamentary guardian.		Contravening decision of parent may supersede caregiver's consent. Affidavit invalid if child stops living with relative caregiver. Affidavit expires in one year. 431.058.

MONTANA

	Testamentary Guardian of the Person (Mont. Code Ann. §§ 72-5-201 et seq. (West 2009 & Supp. 2016))	General Delegation of Power (Mont. Code Ann. § 72-5-103 (West Supp. 2016))	Examples of Educational Consent (Mont. Code Ann. §§ 20-5-501 et seq. (West 2009 & Supp. 2016))	Examples of Medical Consent (Mont. Code Ann. §§ 40-6-501 et seq. (West 2009))
Who Can Appoint?	Parent.[117] Court under some circumstances. 72-5-211, 72-5-223.	Parent or guardian of minor. 72-5-103.		
How?	By will. 72-5-211.	By properly executed power of attorney. 72-5-103.	Caretaker relative, under circumstances and affidavit under oath complying with statute, may enroll child in school, discuss progress of child, and consent to educational services and school-related medical care. 20-5-502, 20-5-503.	Caretaker relative, under circumstances and affidavit under oath complying with statute, has same authority as custodial parent to consent to medical care. 40-6-502.
Minor Objection?	Minor 14 or more may file a written objection to the appointment before it is accepted or within 30 days after notice of its acceptance.[118] 72-5-213.			
Court Role?	Court can appoint upon finding that the testamentary guardian failed to accept or was nullified by minor objection. Court shall appoint person nominated by the minor if minor is over 14 unless the court finds the appointment contrary to the best interests of the minor. 72-5-223, 72-5-222(2).			

117. If both parents are dead, an effective appointment by the parent who died later has priority. § 72-5-211.
118. Objection does not preclude appointment by the court of the testamentary nominee. § 72-5-213.

	Testamentary Guardian of the Person (Mont. Code Ann. §§ 72-5-201 et seq. (West 2009 & Supp. 2016))	General Delegation of Power (Mont. Code Ann. § 72-5-103 (West Supp. 2016))	Examples of Educational Consent (Mont. Code Ann. §§ 20-5-501 et seq. (West 2009 & Supp. 2016))	Examples of Medical Consent (Mont. Code Ann. §§ 40-6-501 et seq. (West 2009))
For What Purpose?	Unless otherwise limited by the court, guardian has powers and responsibilities of a parent; shall take care of ward's personal effects; is empowered to facilitate ward's education and consent to medical care. 72-5-231.	Delegate any power regarding care, custody, or property of minor except consent to marriage or adoption for a period not exceeding six months. The six-month limitation does not apply to certain military personnel. 72-5-103.	To protect rights of child by granting a caretaker relative limited authority for child left in relative's care. 20-5-501.	To protect rights of child by granting a caretaker relative limited authority for child left in relative's care. 40-6-501.
When Takes Effect?	Upon filing of acceptance of testamentary appointment if both parents are dead or the surviving parent is adjudged incapacitated. 72-5-211.			
How Terminate?	Guardian's authority terminates upon death, resignation[119] or removal[120] of guardian or upon minor's death, adoption, marriage or attainment of majority. 72-5-233.		Affidavit effective until end of school year, until revoked, or until child no longer resides with caretaker, whichever occurs first. 20-5-503.	Affidavit effective for six months, until revoked, or child no longer resides with caretaker, whichever occurs first. 40-6-502.

119. Resignation of guardian does not terminate guardianship until it has been approved by the court. § 72-5-233.
120. Any person interested in the welfare of a ward, or the ward if over fourteen, may petition for removal of guardian on the ground that it would be in the best interest of the ward. §72-5-234.

NEBRASKA

	Testamentary Guardian of the Person (Neb. Rev. Stat. Ann. §§ 30-2605 et seq. (LexisNexis 2016))	Standby Guardian (Neb. Rev. Stat. Ann. § 30-2608 (LexisNexis 2016))	General Delegation of Power (Neb. Rev. Stat. Ann. § 30-2604 (LexisNexis 2016))
Who Can Appoint?	Parent of unmarried minor. Court under some circumstances. 30-2605, 30-2606, 30-2608.	Court. 30-2608(c).	Parent or guardian of minor. 30-2604.
How?	By will. 30-2606.	By appointment for a minor whose parent is chronically ill or near death. 30-2608(c).	By properly executed power of attorney. 30-2604.
Minor Objection?	Minor 14 or older may file a written objection with the court before appointment is accepted or within 30 days after notice of acceptance.[121] 30-2607.		
Court Role?	Court may appoint if the testamentary guardianship is prevented by minor. 30-2607.	Court appoints. 30-2608(c).	
For What Purpose?	Powers and responsibilities of parent, including taking reasonable care of ward's personal effects, facilitate education and authorize medical care. 30-2613.		Delegate any power regarding care, custody or property of minor except consent to marriage or adoption for a period not exceeding six months. Parent or guardian of minor who is at least eighteen and not a ward of state, may delegate to minor power to consent to minor's own health care and medical treatment, for a period not exceeding one year. 30-2604.
When Takes Effect?	Upon filing of acceptance of testamentary appointment in the court or appointment by the court. 30-2606.	Take effect if minor is left without a remaining parent due to death, mental incapacity, or physical debilitation (with consent of parent). 30-2608(c).	
How Terminate?	Terminates upon death, resignation[122] or removal[123] of the guardian or upon minor's death, adoption, marriage, or attainment of majority. 30-2614.		

121. Objection does not preclude appointment by court of the testamentary nominee. §30-2607.
122. Resignation does not terminate guardianship until approved by the court. § 30-2614.
123. Any person interested in the welfare of the ward, or the ward if fourteen or older, may petition for removal of a guardian on the ground that removal would be in the best interest of the ward. § 30-2616.

NEVADA

LEXIS current including all legislation effective June 30, 2017 or earlier (not yet codified as of Nov. 3, 2017)

	Testamentary Guardian of the Person (Act of May 26, 2017, ch. 172, 2017 Nev. Legis. Serv. 693 (West))	Standby Guardianship (Act of May 26, 2017, ch. 172, 2017 Nev. Legis Serv. 693 (West))	Examples of Medical Consent (Nev. Rev. Stat. Ann. 129.040 (LexisNexis 2010))
Who Can Appoint?	Court. Sec. 34, 35 Parent can nominate in a will. Sec. 49.	Custodial parent of unmarried minor. Sec. 153.	Appointment not provided for in statute. Person standing in loco parentis can consent. 129.040.
How?	Court appointment. Sec. 34, 35). Guardian nominated in will must file a petition and obtain appointment by the court before exercising the powers of a guardian. 159.062.	By notarized writing, with written consent of minor 14 or older, and any qualified noncustodial parent. Sec. 153.	May give consent in emergency if, after reasonable efforts, the parents of the minor cannot be located. 129.040.
For What Purpose?	Guardian has the care, custody and control of ward and shall supply ward with food, clothing, shelter, and incidental necessaries including authorizing medical care and seeing that the ward is properly trained and educated. Sec. 61.	To establish short-term guardianship without court approval. Sec. 153.	Authority to consent to minor's emergency hospitalization or medical attention. 129.040.
When Takes Effect?	Takes effect upon taking an oath of office and filing appropriate documents with the court. Sec. 54. Guardian must file a bond unless will provides that no bond required. Sec. 50.	Effective immediately upon execution. Sec. 153.	
How Terminate?	(1) Death of ward, (2) ward's change of domicile out of state along with transfer of jurisdiction, (3) upon order of court, (4) in the event the ward is a minor and of 18 years. Sec. 144.	Guardian serves for six months unless written instrument specifies otherwise. May be terminated in writing by parent, or by order of court. Sec. 153.	

NEW HAMPSHIRE

	Testamentary Guardian of the Person (N.H. Rev. Stat. Ann. §§ 463:1 et seq. (2004)), As amended by Act of May 19, 2017, 2017 N.H. Legis. Serv. 39.
Who Can Appoint?	The court may appoint as guardian of the person of the minor any person or authorized agency whose appointment is appropriate. 463:10. Any person may nominate a guardian in a will, by petition, or by written consent to a petition by another. 463:5.
How?	Court may appoint as guardian any person or authorized agency whose appointment is appropriate and may, for cause, refuse to appoint a person nominated in a will, by petition, or by written consent to petition by another. 463:10, 463:5.
For What Purpose?	Guardian has powers and responsibilities of a parent regarding minor's support, care, and education, including power to consent to medical treatment.[124] 463:12.
When Takes Effect?	
How Terminate?	A guardianship of the person or of the estate of a minor shall terminate upon order of the court, the death of the minor, the minor's eighteenth birthday, a finding by the court that the minor has been emancipated under relevant state law, or upon the issuance of a final decree of adoption. 463:15.

124. Status of minors for whom guardianship has been granted shall be reviewed by court at six, twelve, and twenty-four months, and annually thereafter, except court may waive all reviews after twenty-four-month review upon good cause shown. § 463:17.

NEW JERSEY

	Testamentary Guardian of the Person (N.J. Stat. Ann. §§ 3B: 12-13 et seq. (West 2007 & Supp. 2017))	Standby Guardianship (N.J. Stat. Ann. §§ 3B: 12-67 et seq. (West 2007 & Supp. 2017))	General Delegation of Power (N.J. Stat. Ann. § 3B: 12-39 (West 2007))
Who Can Appoint?	Parent.[125] 3B:12-13.	Court. 3B: 12-72.	Parent or a guardian. 3B: 12-39.
How?	By will. 3B:12-13.	Upon petition of the parent, legal custodian or designated standby guardian. Petition shall state which triggering event shall cause the authority of the standby guardian to become effective, that there is a significant risk that the parent will die, become incapacitated, or debilitated, and the name of the proposed standby guardian. 3B: 12-72. Parent can also choose standby guardian by means of a written designation.[126] 3B: 12-74.	A parent, with consent of the other parent, still living and not incapacitated, or a guardian of the person, by a properly executed power of attorney, may delegate to another person, for a period not exceeding six months, any of his powers regarding care, custody, or property of the minor child except his power to consent to marriage or adoption of the minor. 3B: 12-39.
For What Purpose?	A guardian has the powers and responsibilities of a parent who has not been deprived of custody of his minor and unemancipated child. 3B:12-51, 3B:12-52(c).	Imperative need to create an expeditious manner of establishing a standby guardianship in order to enable a custodial parent or legal custodian suffering from a progressive chronic condition or a fatal illness to make plans for the permanent future care or the interim care of a child without terminating parental or legal rights. 3B: 12-68.	

125. Where parent appoints, and the other parent survives the appointing parent, the appointment shall be effective only when the surviving parent consents in writing and signs and acknowledges the consent in the presence of two witnesses. § 3B:12-14.
126. Section 3B: 12-74 includes a "Designation of Standby Guardian" form.

	Testamentary Guardian of the Person (N.J. Stat. Ann. §§ 3B: 12-13 et seq. (West 2007 & Supp. 2017))	Standby Guardianship (N.J. Stat. Ann. §§ 3B: 12-67 et seq. (West 2007 & Supp. 2017))	General Delegation of Power (N.J. Stat. Ann. § 3B: 12-39 (West 2007))
When Takes Effect?	Effective after posting bond with court (unless relieved from doing so by direction of will or by order of the court). 3B:12-16.	Upon occurrence of a triggering event set forth in decree appointing the standby, the standby is empowered to assume the duties of his office immediately. Standby must petition for court confirmation within 60 days. 3B: 12-73.	
How Terminate?	The authority and responsibility of a guardian of the person or estate of a minor terminate upon the death, resignation or removal of the guardian or upon the minor's death, adoption, marriage, or attainment of 18 years of age. 3B:12-55		

NEW MEXICO

	Testamentary Guardian of the Person (N.M. Stat. Ann. §§ 45-5-201 et seq. (2018))	General Delegation of Power (N.M. Stat. Ann. § 45-5-104 (2018))	Examples of Medical Consent (N.M. Stat. Ann. § 24-10-2 (2018))
Who Can Appoint?	Parental appointment or upon appointment by the court. 45-5-201.	Parent or guardian. 45-5-104.	
How?	Parent may appoint by will or other signed writing by the parent and attested by at least two witnesses.[127] 45-5-202. Court may appoint a guardian if all parental rights of custody have been terminated or suspended by circumstances or prior court order. 45-5-204.	Parent or guardian, by an acknowledged power of attorney, may delegate to another person, for a period not exceeding six months, any of the parent's or guardian's powers regarding care, custody or property of the minor, except the power to consent to marriage or adoption of the minor. 45-5-104.	In cases of emergency and when parents cannot be located, consent for emergency attention may be given by any person standing in loco parent is to the minor. 24-10-2.
Minor Objection?	Minor 14 or older who is subject to parental appointment may file a written objection to the appointment before acceptance or after its acceptance.[128] 45-5-203.		
Court Role?	Court can proceed with another appointment if parental nominee has failed to accept within 30 days or if prevented by minor. Court shall appoint person nominated by minor 14 or older unless contrary to best interest of minor. 45-5-204; 45-5-206.		

127. If both parents are deceased, an effective appointment by the parent who died later has priority.
128. Objection does not prevent appointment by the court of the parental nominee or any other suitable person.

	Testamentary Guardian of the Person (N.M. Stat. Ann. §§ 45-5-201 et seq. (2018))	General Delegation of Power (N.M. Stat. Ann. § 45-5-104 (2018))	Examples of Medical Consent (N.M. Stat. Ann. § 24-10-2 (2018))
For What Purpose?	Guardian has powers and responsibilities of a parent regarding ward's support, care, and education. A guardian may consent to medical or other professional, care, treatment, or advice. 45-5-209.		Authority to consent to emergency medical attention or surgery. 24-10-2.
When Takes Effect?	When guardian files acceptance in court. 45-5-202.		
How Terminate?	Terminates upon death, resignation[129] or removal[130] of guardian or upon minor's death, adoption, emancipation, marriage or attainment of the majority. 45-5-210.		

129. Resignation does not terminate guardianship until approved by the court. § 45-5-210.

130. Any person interested in the welfare of a ward, or the ward if 14 or over, may petition for removal of guardian on the ground that removal would be in the best interest of the ward. § 45-5-212.

NEW YORK

	Testamentary Guardian of the Person (N.Y. Surr. Ct. Proc. Act Law §§ 1710 et seq. (McKinney 2011))	Standby Guardian (N.Y. Surr. Ct. Proc. Act Law § 1726 (McKinney 2011))	Examples of Medical Consent (N.Y. Pub. Health Law § 2504 (McKinney 2012))
Who Can Appoint?	Court. 1710.	Court appoints; petition or written designation can be made only by a parent, legal guardian, legal custodian, or in limited situations a primary caretaker. 1726.	Parent or guardian. 2504.
How?	Parent can appoint by will, but it is not effective until will has been admitted and recorded in court and the court issues letters of guardianship. 1710. Parent can appoint by deed, but it is not effective until the deed has been acknowledged and recorded in the office for recording deeds in the county of domicile of the person making the appointment when the appointment was made. 1710. When no guardian by will or deed remains in office, the court may appoint unless appointment would be contrary to express provisions of the will or deed. 1712.	Petition shall state when the authority of standby guardian is to become effective (upon petitioner's incapacity, death, consent, or whichever occurs first); state that the petitioner suffers from a progressively chronic illness or an irreversibly fatal illness and the basis for such statement. Court shall make appointment. OR Parent, legal guardian, legal custodian, or primary caretaker can designate standby guardian in written designation. Standby must file a petition for appointment with the court when authority becomes effective.[131] Court will appoint if it finds petitioner was duly designated as standby. 1726.	Can give effective consent to any person. 2504.
For What Purpose?			Authority to consent to medical, dental, health, and hospital services for his or her child. 2504.
When Takes Effect?	When letters of guardianship have been issued. 1710.	Court decree states when authority of the standby guardian is effective. 1726.	Upon consent. 2504.
How Terminate?	Upon minor's marriage or attainment of majority or when the guardian is unavailable of unwilling to provide proper care and custody. 1707.		

131. Section 1726 includes a "Designation of Standby Guardian" form.

NORTH CAROLINA

LEXIS current; the final official version of statutes affected by the 2017 Regular Session will appear on Lexis.com and Lexis Advance in November 2017.

	Testamentary Guardian of the Person (N.C. Gen. Stat. §§ 35A-1213 et seq. (2015))	Standby Guardianship (N.C. Gen. Stat. §§ 35A-1370 et seq. (2015))	Examples of Education Consent (N.C. Gen. Stat. § 115C-366 (2015))	Examples of Medical Consent (N.C. Gen. Stat. §§ 32A-30 et seq. (2015))
Who Can Appoint?	Court. 35A-1224.	Court. 35A-1371.		Custodial parent. 32A-30.
How?	Recommendation of parent in a will is a strong guide, but court not required to follow if not in best interest of minor. 35A-1224.	By petition or designation. 35A-1372. Petition shall state that the authority of the standby guardian is to become effective upon the death, incapacity or debilitation of petitioner, and that the petitioner suffers from a chronic illness. 35A-1373. Designation shall identify person designated as standby guardian, indicate when guardianship becomes effective. 35A-1374.	A student who is not a domiciliary of a local school district may attend if the student resides with an adult who is a domiciliary as a result of death, serious illness, incarceration of parent or legal guardian. 115C-366. Adult must sign affidavit that confirms the qualifications establishing the student's residency, attests that student's claim of residency is not primarily related to attendance at a particular school within the unit, and attests that caregiver has been given and accepts responsibility for educations decisions for the student. 115C-366.	Written consent using "Authorization to Consent to Health Care for Minor" form. 32A-34.

	Testamentary Guardian of the Person (N.C. Gen. Stat. §§ 35A-1213 et seq. (2015))	Standby Guardianship (N.C. Gen. Stat. §§ 35A-1370 et seq. (2015))	Examples of Education Consent (N.C. Gen. Stat. § 115C-366 (2015))	Examples of Medical Consent (N.C. Gen. Stat. §§ 32A-30 et seq. (2015))
For What Purpose?	Guardian shall make provision for ward's care, comfort and maintenance and may give consent to medical treatment. 35A-1241.	Guardian shall make provision for ward's care, comfort and maintenance and may give consent to medical treatment. 35A-1378.	Adult that minor is living with must accept responsibility for educational decisions for the child, including receiving notices of discipline, attending conferences with school personnel, grant permission to school related activities. 115C-366.	Authorization to consent to health care for minor. 32A-31.
When Takes Effect?		Takes effect upon determination of incapacity, death, debilitation, or by signing a written consent by petitioner. Guardian must file with court within 90 days or authority will be rescinded. 35A-1373.		
How Terminate?	Upon court removal, resignation, when ward ceases to be a minor, or dies. 35A-1290, 35A-1292, 35A-1295.	If designator is subsequently restored to capacity or ability to care for child; if minor reaches 18, court revocation, or resignation. 35A-1382; 35A-1376.		

NORTH DAKOTA

	Testamentary Guardian of the Person (N.D. Cent. Code §§ 30.1-27-01 et seq. (2010))	General Delegation of Power (N.D. Cent. Code § 30.1-26-04 (2010))	Examples of Medical Consent (N.D. Cent. Code § 23-12-13 (2012))
Who Can Appoint?	Parent. Court under some circumstances. 30.1-27-01; 30.1-27-04.	A parent or guardian. 30.1-26-04.	Appointment not provided for in statute. · Persons in the following order of priority may provide informed consent care on behalf of minor: · Individual with durable power of attorney over minor · Appointed guardian or custodian · Parent, including stepparent who has maintained sufficient contact w/ minor or appointed guardian · Adult brothers and sisters · Grandparents · Close relative who has maintained sufficient contact. 23-12-13.
How?	Parent may appoint by will. 30.1-27-02.	A parent or guardian of a minor or incapacitated person, by a properly executed power of attorney, may delegate to another person, for a period not exceeding six months, any of the parent's or guardian's powers regarding care, custody, or property of the minor child or ward, except the power to consent to marriage or adoption of a minor ward. 30.1-26-04.	Before consenting person must determine that proposed health care is in patient's best interests. 23-12-13.

	Testamentary Guardian of the Person (N.D. Cent. Code §§ 30.1-27-01 et seq. (2010))	General Delegation of Power (N.D. Cent. Code § 30.1-26-04 (2010))	Examples of Medical Consent (N.D. Cent. Code § 23-12-13 (2012))
Minor Objection?	Minor 14 or older may file objection with the court before or within 30 days after notice of acceptance.[132] 30.1-27-03.		
Court Role?	Court can appoint if testamentary guardian failed to accept within 30 days or if prevented by minor. Court shall appoint guardian nominated by minor 14 or older, unless contrary to best interest of minor. 30.1-27-04; 30.1-27-06.		
For What Purpose?	Guardian must take reasonable care of ward's personal effects, facilitate ward's education, and can authorize medical care. 30.1-27-09.		Authorized to consent to health care for minor. 23-12-13.
When Takes Effect?	Upon filing of the guardian's acceptance of a testamentary appointment and upon court order or upon appointment by the court. 30.1-27-02.		
How Terminate?	Upon death, resignation[133] or removal[134] of guardian, or upon the minor's death, adoption, marriage, or attainment of the majority. 30.1-27-10.		

132. Objection does not preclude appointment by the court of the testamentary nominee.
133. Resignation does not terminate guardianship until it has been approved by the court.
134. Any person interested in welfare of ward, or the ward if fourteen or more, may petition for removal of a guardian on the ground that removal would be in the best interest of the ward. § 30.1-27-12.

OHIO

LEXIS current with Legislation passed by the 132nd General Assembly and filed with the Secretary of State through file 20 (HB 59) with the exception of file 14 (HB 49)

	Testamentary Guardian of the Person (Ohio Rev. Code Ann. §§ 2111.01 et seq. (LexisNexis 2016))	Standby Guardianship (Ohio Rev. Code Ann. § 2111.121 (LexisNexis 2016))	General Delegation of Power (Ohio Rev. Code Ann. §§ 3109.52 et seq. (LexisNexis 2015))
Who Can Appoint?	Court. 2111.02.	Court. 2111.121.	Parent, guardian, or custodian of child. 3109.52.
How?	Minor over 14 may select a guardian who shall be appointed if suitable. Parent can select guardian in will. Court may appoint person named in will, person selected by minor, or some other person. 2111.12; 2111.02.	Person may nominate in writing another person to be the guardian of the nominator's minor children. 2111.121.	By power of attorney. 3109.52.
For What Purpose?	Guardian has custody and maintenance of ward, charge of education, and can consent to medical care. 2111.06; 2111.13.		Allows the grandparent of the child with whom the child is residing any of their rights and responsibilities regarding the care, physical custody, and control of the child including educational and medical matters. 3109.52.
When Takes Effect?	Upon court appointment. 2111.04.		
How Terminate?	Marriage terminates guardianship of the person but not of the estate of the ward. § 2111.45. Guardianship otherwise normally terminates at age 18. § 2111.46.		Revoked in writing by person who created it, child ceases to reside with grandparent, by court order, death of child, or death of grandparent. 3109.59.

OKLAHOMA

	Testamentary Guardian of the Person (Okla. Stat. Ann. tit. 30, §§ 2-101 et seq. (West 2009 & Supp. 2017))	Examples of Education Consent (Act of May 15, 2017, ch. 254, § 5, 2017 Okla. Sess. Law Serv. 824, 843 (West) (to be codified at Okla. Stat. Ann. tit. 70, § 1-113))	Examples of Medical Consent (Okla. Stat. Ann. tit. 10A, § 1-3-101 (West 2009))
Who Can Appoint?	Court. 2-101.		Parent or legal guardian. 1-3-101.
How?	Guardian may be nominated by will or other written instrument; minor 14 or over may nominate own guardian. Court can appoint guardian if it doesn't approve minor's nominee. 2-101; 2-102; 2-103.	Residence of minor is school district in which parent or guardian holds legal residence. School has discretion to allow establishment of residency by affidavit when adult has assumed care and custody of child but does not have legal custody.[135] 1-113.	Parent can authorize, in writing, any adult person into whose care the minor has been entrusted to consent to medical care. 1-3-101.
For What Purpose?	Guardian shall have charge of education of minor. Court may also authorize guardian to provide for the care, treatment, education, and welfare of the minor. 2-107, 2-109.	Purpose of minor attending public school. 1-113.	Consent to: x-ray examination, anesthetic, medical, surgical, or dental diagnosis/ treatment, hospital care, or immunization, blood tests, and examinations to be rendered to minor. 1-3-101.
When Takes Effect?	Upon appointment. 2-101.		
How Terminate?	Removal of the guardian, marriage of ward, or ward attaining majority. 2-113.		

135. Section 1-113(A) also addresses residence in foster home, orphanage, state-operated emergency shelter, and so on.

OREGON

LEXIS updated with all legislation of emergency effect through the end of the 2017 Legislative Session with designated exceptions

	Testamentary Guardian of the Person (Or. Rev. Stat. Ann. §§ 125.300 et seq. (West 2016))	Examples of Educational and Medical Consent (Or. Rev. Stat. Ann. § 109.575 (West 2016))
Who Can Appoint?	Court. 125.305.	
How?	Shall make a guardianship order that is no more restrictive upon the liberty of the protected person than is reasonably necessary. 125.305.	A relative caregiver acting pursuant to an affidavit may consent to medical treatment and educational services for a minor child that the minor cannot legally consent to after reasonable efforts have been made to get the consent of the parent or legal guardian and the consent cannot be obtained. 109.575.
For What Purpose?	Promote and protect the well-being of the protected person. 125.300. Provide for the care, comfort, and maintenance of the protected person, in addition to making educational and medical decisions. 125.315.	
When Takes Effect?	After guardian files acceptance with the court and court issues of letters of guardianship. 125.310.	
How Terminate?	Upon death, resignation, or removal of the fiduciary, upon the minor's death, or when the minor reaches 18 years of age. The court may remove if in minor's best interests. 125.225, 125.230.	

PENNSYLVANIA[136]

LEXIS Pa. C.S. documents are current through 2017 Regular Session Acts 1-34; P.S. documents are current through 2017 Regular Session Acts 1-34

	Testamentary Guardian of the Person (20 Pa. Stat. and Cons. Stat. Ann. §§ 2519, 5111 et seq. (West 2005))	Standby Guardianship (23 Pa. Stat. and Cons. Stat. Ann. §§ 5602 et seq. (West 2010))	Examples of Medical Consent (11 Pa. Stat. and Cons. Stat. Ann. § 2513 (West 2016))
Who Can Appoint?	Court. 5111.	Court. 5612.	Parent, legal guardian or legal custodian of a minor. 2513.
How?	Parental selection in a will creates a presumption in favor of that person. Person of same religious persuasion as parents of minor is preferred. Person nominated by minor over 14 if suitable shall be preferred. 2519; 5113.	Upon petition for appointment. Parent may designate a standby guardian and triggering events upon which the standby shall become guardian.[137] Petition for court appointment of designation may be made at any time (before or after triggering event).[138] 5611; 5612.	Can confer upon any adult person the power to consent to medical care to the minor. § 2513 includes a "Medical Consent Authorization" form. 2513.
For What Purpose?		Standby has authority of parent. Commencement of standby guardian's authority does not itself divest parent of guardianship rights. 5613.	Consent to medical or mental health treatment. 2513.
When Takes Effect?		If petition filed and approved before triggering event, standby authority commences upon occurrence of triggering event. If designation has been made, but petition has not been filed, the standby has temporary authority to act as guardian of minor for 60 days and must file for approval within that time. 5613.	
How Terminate?			

136. Adaptation of chart originally prepared by Carmina Y. D'Aversa.
137. Section 5611 includes a designation form.
138. If parent has appointed a testamentary guardian and there is a conflict between that will and the written standby designation, the document latest in date of execution shall prevail. § 5615.

RHODE ISLAND

LEXIS current through Chapter 302 of the January 2017 Session but not including all corrections and changes made by the Director of Law Revision. The final official version of statutes affected by 2017 Legislation will appear on lexis.com and Lexis Advance in November 2017.

	Testamentary Guardian of the Person (33 R.I. Gen. Laws §§ 33-5-4, 33-15.1-1 et seq. (2011))
Who Can Appoint?	Court. 33-15.1-5.
How?	Minor 14 or over may nominate his/her own guardian and court shall appoint if approved. If minor over 14 does not choose guardian or chooses one whom the court does not approve, then the court may appoint. Court may appoint guardian for minor under 14.33-15.1-5; 33-15.1-6. Parent can make selection by will that court will approve, unless there is a good cause not to do so. 33-5-4; 33-15.1-7.
For What Purpose?	Same as parent, including power to make decisions regarding education of minor. 33-15.1-28; 33-15.1-30.
When Takes Effect?	Court approval.[139] 33-15.1-5.
Compensation?	Court may authorize guardian to receive reasonable compensation for his/her services. 33-15.1-38.
How Terminate?	Court may remove any guardian for absence, sickness, insanity, or other cause. Guardian may resign. 33-15.1-37.

139. The court can appoint a temporary guardian pending approval of the permanent guardian. § 33-15.1-14.

SOUTH CAROLINA

	Testamentary Guardian of the Person (S.C. Code Ann. §§ 21-21-25 et seq. (2007))	Examples of Educational Consent (S.C. Code Ann. § 59-63-32 (2004))
Who Can Appoint?	Court. 21-21-25.	
How?	Parent can appoint by will but is subject to approval by court. 21-21-25.	School district must require adult seeking to enroll child in public school to: accept responsibility for education decisions concerning child, attest that child's claim of residency is not primarily related to attendance at particular school within district. 59-63-32
For What Purpose?		Education decisions include: receiving notices of discipline, attending conferences with school staff, granting permission for school activities. 59-63-32.
When Takes Effect?		
How Terminate?		

SOUTH DAKOTA

	Testamentary guardian of the person (S.D. Codified Laws §§ 29A-5-201 et seq. (2004))
Who Can Appoint?	Court; 29A-5-201. Parent and/or minor over 14 may nominate. 29A-5-202.
How?	Minor 14 or older may nominate any individual to act as his/her guardian. Court may appoint the nominee if otherwise eligible to act. Parent of unmarried minor may nominate guardian by will or other signed writing.[140] Absent an effective nomination by minor, court may appoint parental nominee. 29A-5-202. Absent an effective nomination, court shall appoint person that will act in minor's best interest. Court shall consider guardian's geographic location, familial or other relationship with minor, ability to carry out powers of the office, commitment to promoting minor's welfare, any potential conflicts of interest, recommendations of parents or other relatives, and wishes of minor if of sufficient age to form an intelligent preference. 29A-5-202.
For What Purpose?	Guardian responsible for making decisions regarding minor's support, care, health, education, and act at all times in minor's best interest. 29A-5-401.
When Takes Effect?	Court must order appointment and guardian must file acceptance. 29A-5-208.
How Terminate?	Upon death, resignation[141] or removal[142] of the guardian, or upon minor's death or attainment of majority. 29A-5-501; 29A-5-505.

140. In the event that both parents are deceased and both made nominations, the court shall select the nominee which it believes best qualified. § 29A-5-202.
141. Guardian may petition for permission to resign; court may not grant permission unless there is a suitable successor willing to act, except for good cause shown. § 29A-5-503.
142. Court may remove upon petition by any interested person or on the court's own motion. § 29A-5-504.

TENNESSEE

	Testamentary guardian of the person (Tenn. Code Ann. §§ 34-1-101 et seq. (2015 & Supp. 2017))	Standby Guardianship (Tenn. Code Ann. § 34-1-119 (2015))	General Delegation of Powers (Tenn. Code Ann. §§ 34-6-301 et seq. (2015))	Examples of Educational Consent (Tenn. Code Ann. § 34-6-304 et seq. (2015))
Who Can Appoint?	Court. 34-2-105.	Regular fiduciary or the court. 34-1-119.	Parent or parents of the minor. 34-6-302(a)(1). If only one parent has custody, the noncustodial parent must consent in writing. 34-6-303.	The parent may authorize the caregiver through the power of attorney. 34-6-304
How?	Court determines what is in the best interests of the minor, with preference given to: (1) the parent or parents; (2) person designated by parent in will or other written document; (3) adult siblings; (4) closest relative of minor; (5) other persons. 34-2-103.	Petitioner may request; court may motion. 34-1-119.	By executing in writing a power of attorney for care of a minor child on a form provided by the department of children's services. 34-6-302(a)(1).	By authorization from the parent or parents. 34-6-304
For What Purpose?		To take the place of the fiduciary on a temporary or, if necessary, permanent basis. 34-1-119. The standby fiduciary shall have the same powers, rights and obligations as the fiduciary. 34-1-119.	To delegate temporary care-giving authority when hardship prevents the parent or parents from caring for the child. 34-6-302(a)(1).	(A) Enrolling the child in school and extracurricular activities; (B) Obtaining medical, dental and mental health treatment for the child; and (C) Providing for the child's food, lodging, housing, recreation and travel. 34-6-304

	Testamentary guardian of the person (Tenn. Code Ann. §§ 34-1-101 et seq. (2015 & Supp. 2017))	Standby Guardianship (Tenn. Code Ann. § 34-1-119 (2015))	General Delegation of Powers (Tenn. Code Ann. §§ 34-6-301 et seq. (2015))	Examples of Educational Consent (Tenn. Code Ann. § 34-6-304 et seq. (2015))
When Takes Effect?	After court order, guardian must take oath. 34-1-109.	After a court order. 34-1-119. The order shall state the duration of the standby fiduciary's authority and suspend the authority of the regular fiduciary. 34-1-119.	After properly signed by parent or parents and acknowledged before a notary public or signed by two witnesses. 34-6-302(b).	If authorized within, it takes effect at the time the power of attorney becomes effective under 34-6-302(b). 34-6-304
How Terminate?	When minor reaches 18 years of age. 34-2-106.	After duration of the time period set forth in the court order. 34-1-119.	By an instrument in writing signed by either parent with legal custody or by any order of a court of competent jurisdiction that appoints a legal guardian or legal custodian. 34-6-306.	Terminates when the power of attorney terminates. 34-6-306
Medical Consent? 34-6-403?				

TEXAS

LEXIS current through the 2017 Regular Session and 1st C.S., 85th Legislature

	Testamentary guardian of the person (Tex. Est. Code Ann. §§ 1001.001 et seq. (West 2014 & Supp. 2016))	Medical Consent (Tex. Fam. Code Ann. §§ 32.001 et seq. (West 2014 & Supp. 2016))
Who Can Appoint?	Court, if it accepts the petitioner's application. 1101.001(a); 1022.001(a). Surviving parent of a minor. 1104.053.	Guardian of child can consent to immunization of child. 32.101(a). If guardian not available and authority to consent not denied then consent can be given by: grandparent, adult brother or sister, adult aunt or uncle, education institution where child is enrolled if have written authorization, another adult who has possession of child and written authorization. 32.001.
How?	By application to the court in accordance with 1101.001 et seq. 1103.001. By will or written declaration of surviving parent of minor if the designated person is not (1) disqualified, (2) deceased, (3) unwilling to serve, or (4) court determines designated person would not serve the minor's best interests. 1104.053.	Consent must include name of child, name of parents, name of person giving consent and person's relationship to child, statement of nature of medical treatment/ immunization to be given, and date treatment/immunization to begin. 32.002.
Selection by Minor?	Before appointing a guardian, the court shall make a reasonable effort to consider the incapacitated person's preference of the person to be appointed guardian. 1104.002. If the minor is at least 12 years of age, the minor may select the guardian by a writing filed with the clerk, if the court finds that the selection is in the minor's best interest and approves the selection. 1104.054.	
For What Purpose?	Only as necessary to promote and protect the well-being of the incapacitated person. 1001.001.	Authority to consent to immunization of minor. 32.101.
When Takes Effect?	Court order. 1001.001.	
How Terminate?	Guardianship terminates when: (1) the ward dies, (2) the ward is found to have the capacity to care for his or herself and manage his or her property, (3) the ward is no longer a minor; or (4) the ward no longer needs a guardian appointed to receive funds from a governmental source. 1202.001(b).	

UTAH

LEXIS Statutes current through the 2017 First Special Session

	Testamentary guardian of the person (Utah Code Ann. §§ 75-5-201 et seq. (LexisNexis 1993 & Supp. 2017))	General Delegation of Powers (Utah Code Ann. §§ 75-5-401 et seq. (LexisNexis 1993 & Supp. 2017))	Educational Consent (Utah Code Ann. § 53A-2-202 (LexisNexis 2016))	Medical Consent (Utah Code Ann. § 78B-3-406(6)(c) (LexisNexis Supp. 2017))
Who Can Appoint?	Parent. 75-5-201(1)(a).	Court. 75-5-401.	Local board of education via policy. 53A-2-202	
How?	By will or other written instrument. 75-5-202(1).	Upon petition and after notice and a hearing. 75-5-401.	Submission to the school district of a signed and notarized affidavit by the child's custodial parent or legal guardian. 53A-2-202	Any person temporarily standing in loco parentis, whether formally serving or not for the minor under his care may consent to any health care not prohibited by law.[143] 78B-3-406(6)(c).
Minor Objection?	Minor over 14 or any person interested in the welfare of the minor can file a written objection to testamentary appointment before it is accepted or within 30 days of notice of acceptance. [144] 75-5-203.	Court gives consideration to the choice of the minor. 75-5-407(1).	Child must submit to the school district a signed and notarized affidavit stating that: (1) the child desires to be responsible to the named responsible adult. 53A-2-202	

143. Section 78B-3-406(6) lists other persons also authorized to consent.
144. Objection does not preclude appointment by the court of the testamentary nominee or any other suitable person. § 75-5-203.

	Testamentary guardian of the person (Utah Code Ann. §§ 75-5-201 et seq. (LexisNexis 1993 & Supp. 2017))	General Delegation of Powers (Utah Code Ann. §§ 75-5-401 et seq. (LexisNexis 1993 & Supp. 2017))	Educational Consent (Utah Code Ann. § 53A-2-202 (LexisNexis 2016))	Medical Consent (Utah Code Ann. § 78B-3-406(6)(c) (LexisNexis Supp. 2017))
Court Appointment?	Court may appoint if all parental rights have been terminated or suspended. Guardian appointed by will has priority over any guardian appointed by court, but court may proceed with appointment upon finding that testamentary guardian failed to accept or minor over 14 prevented appointment. 75-5-204. Court must appoint guardian in best interests of minor, taking into account the minor's physical, mental, moral, and emotional health needs. 75-5-206(1).			

	Testamentary guardian of the person (Utah Code Ann. §§ 75-5-201 et seq. (LexisNexis 1993 & Supp. 2017))	General Delegation of Powers (Utah Code Ann. §§ 75-5-401 et seq. (LexisNexis 1993 & Supp. 2017))	Educational Consent (Utah Code Ann. § 53A-2-202 (LexisNexis 2016))	Medical Consent (Utah Code Ann. § 78B-3-406(6)(c) (LexisNexis Supp. 2017))
For What Purpose?	Guardian has powers and responsibilities of a parent; is empowered to facilitate ward's education and authorize medical care. 75-5-209.	Managing money or property, managing business affairs which may otherwise be jeopardized or prevented by minority, managing funds needed for the minor's support and education. 75-5-401(1)(a).	To designate a responsible adult residing in the school district as legal guardian of a child whose custodial parent or legal guardian does not reside within the state. 53A-2-202	Any health care not prohibited by law. 78B-3-406(6)(c).
When Takes Effect?	When the guardian files acceptance in court or upon appointment by the court. 75-5-202(2); 75-5-204.	After court appointment and conservator acceptance. 75-5-407; 75-5-413.	Via guardianship letter to the applicant after determination by school board. 53A-2-202.	
How Terminate?	Terminates upon death, resignation,[145] or removal[146] of the guardian or upon minor's death, adoption, marriage, or attainment of majority. 75-5-210.	Court may remove for good cause or accept the conservator's resignation. § 75-5-415(1); 75-5-430.	May be terminated if school board believes applicant submitted false or misleading information. 53A-2-202.	

145. Resignation of guardian does not terminate guardianship until approved by the court. § 75-5-210.
146. Any person interested in welfare of ward, or ward if fourteen or over, may petition for removal of guardian on the ground that removal would be in the best interest of the ward. § 75-5-212.

VERMONT

LEXIS statutes current through the 2017 Session

	Testamentary guardian of the person (Vt. Stat. Ann. tit. 14, §§ 2621 et seq. (2010 & Supp. 2017))
Who Can Appoint?	Court. 14 § 2628. Parent can appoint by will. 14 § 2656.
How?	By granting a petition for guardianship and issuing a guardianship order stating: (1) the powers and duties of the guardian, (2) the expected duration of the guardianship, (3) a family plan approved by the Court Administrator, and (4) the process for reviewing the order. 14 § 2628.
Minor Nomination?	Minor 14 or over may choose guardian subject to approval of the court. 14 § 2650. When person appointed guardian by court, minor may choose to have another appointed after turning 14. 14 § 2652.
For What Purpose?	Custody and residence determination of minor, decisions related to health care, education, and contact with others, and receiving funds paid for support of the minor. 14 § 2629.
When Takes Effect?	After court issues guardianship order. 14 § 2628.
How Terminate?	Parent may file motion to terminate, and court may grant after hearing. 14 § 2632. When the minor marries or reaches the age of majority. If the guardian neglects to render an account, to perform a duty of the court, absconds or become mentally disabled or otherwise unable to discharge the trust, the probate division of the superior court may remove or may allow the guardian to resign. 14 § 3001.

VIRGINIA

LEXIS current through the 2017 Regular Session

	Testamentary guardian of the person (Va. Code Ann. §§ 64.2-1700 et seq. (2017))	Standby Guardian (Va. Code Ann. §§ 16.1-349 et seq. (2015))	Miscellaneous Medical (Va. Code Ann. § 54.1-2969 (2013))
Who Can Appoint?	The circuit court or the circuit court clerk of any county or city in which a minor resides. 64.2-1702. Parents. 64.2-1701.	Juvenile court. 16.1-350.	
How?	By court appointment. 64.2-1702. By parent's will. 64.2-1701.	Upon petition of any person. 16.1-350.	When minor separated from custody of parent or guardian and is need of medical treatment, authority to give consent is conferred upon: judges whose custody is within control of court, local director of social services in some cases, any person standing in loco parentis. 54.1-2969. When consent of parent or guardian of minor is unobtainable because whereabouts is unknown, authority to give consent to treatment is conferred upon judges of the juvenile. 54.1-2969.
Court Role?	The circuit court may hear and determine all matters between guardians and their wards, require settlements of guardianship accounts, remove any guardian for neglect or breach of trust and appoint another guardian for the ward, and make any order for the custody, health, maintenance, education, and support of a ward and the management, disbursement, preservation, and investment of the ward's estate. 64.2-1804.	Issue summons to child, proposed guardian, and interested parties, hold hearing if requested, and appoint an attorney as guardian ad litem for child. 16.1-350. Provide order specifying triggering event. 16.1-350.	

	Testamentary guardian of the person (Va. Code Ann. §§ 64.2-1700 et seq. (2017))	Standby Guardian (Va. Code Ann. §§ 16.1-349 et seq. (2015))	Miscellaneous Medical (Va. Code Ann. § 54.1-2969 (2013))
For What Purpose?	Possession, care, and management of the minor's estate, real and personal. To provide for the minor's health, education, maintenance, and support from the income of the minor's estate and, if income is not sufficient, from the corpus of the minor's estate. 64.2-1800.	To give the standby guardian the authority to act in a manner consistent with the known wishes of a qualified parent regarding the care, custody and support of the minor child. 16.1-349.	Consent to surgical or medical treatment. 54.1-2969.
When Takes Effect?	Upon court appointment and guardian filing bond, if applicable. 64.2-1704.	When standby guardian files with court documentation proving triggering event took place. 16.1-351. This must occur within thirty days of event. 16.1-351.	Whenever a minor has been separated from the custody of his parent or guardian and is in need of surgical or medical treatment. 54.1-2969.
How Terminate?	Unless guardian dies, is removed or resigns, he/she shall continue until minor is 18. In the event of a testamentary guardianship, the guardianship terminates according to the testator's will. 64.2-1803.	If standby guardian fails to file within thirty days, his or her authority is rescinded. 16.1-351.	

WASHINGTON

LEXIS Statutes current with effective legislation through the 2017 Third Special Session

	Testamentary guardian of the person (Wash. Rev. Code Ann. §§ 11.88.080 et seq. (West 2006 & Supp. 2017))	Standby Guardian (Wash. Rev. Code Ann. § 11.88.125 (West Supp. 2017))
Who Can Appoint?	Parent. 11.88.080.	Any individual or professional guardian appointed by the court as either guardian or limited guardian of the person and/or estate of an incapacitated person. 11.88.125.
How?	Will. 11.88.080. Court shall confirm parent's testamentary appointment unless court finds that individual appointed is not qualified to serve. 11.88.080.	File notice with court designating standby guardian. 11.88.125.
For What Purpose?		Powers, duties, obligations of a regularly appointed guardian, including to consent to medical procedures. 11.88.125.
When Takes Effect?	Guardian must take oath. 11.88.100.	Upon court issuing letters of guardianship and standby guardian filing oath. 11.88.125. & bond? See 11.88.125(2)(b)
How Terminate?	Upon minor's attainment of legal age, death. 11.88.140.	

WEST VIRGINIA

	Testamentary guardian of the person (W. Va. Code Ann. §§ 44-10-1 et seq. (LexisNexis 2014))	Standby Guardian (W. Va. Code Ann. §§ 44A-5-1 et seq. (LexisNexis 2014))
Who Can Appoint?	Parent.[147] 44-10-1.	Court. 44A-5-3.
How?	Will. 44-10-1.	Upon parental designation or petition. 44A-5-3.

Parent or any person acting on parent's behalf may file petition including name of proposed standby guardian, nature of triggering event, and whether there is a significant risk that parent will die or become incapable of caring for minor imminently.[148] 44A-5-3.

Parent can make written designation for standby guardian naming triggering event and person to be designated. 44A-5-5.

Standby must file with court no later than 30 days following parent's death in either case. 44A-5-4.

Court shall enter order approving designated/petitioned guardian. 44A-5-4(f). |
Minor Nomination?	Minor over 14 can, in writing or in the present of the circuit or family court, nominate his/her own guardian which must be approved by court. 44-10-4(a).	
For What Purpose?	Guardian responsible for making decisions and obtaining provision for minor's support, care, health, habilitation, education, etc. 44-10-7.	To temporarily assume the duties of guardian of the person or property, or both, of a minor child, on behalf of or in conjunction with a qualified parent. 44A-5-2(i)).
When Takes Effect?	Guardian must accept in court. 44-10-2.	Upon occurrence of stated triggering event.[149] 44A-5-4(c).
Review of appointment?		Child's parent or any person related to child by blood or marriage may petition court for review of whether continuation of standby guardian is in the best interest of the child. 44A-5-8.
How Terminate?	Until minor turns 18, or upon death, resignation or removal of guardian. 44-10-3(i).	Qualified parent may petition court for revocation. 44A-5-7(a).

Parent may revoke at any time before triggering event occurs. 44A-5-7(b).

Court finds the parent no longer meets the definition of "qualified parent." 44A-5-7(c). |

147. Where both father and mother have appointed guardians, only that guardian who is the appointee of the parent last living shall be entitled to custody. § 44-10-1.

148. Not a complete list of requirements for petition.

149. If triggering event was death of parent, standby shall file petition for appointment of a guardian for child within thirty days of death. § 44A-5-4(f).

WISCONSIN

LEXIS current through Act 58 of the 2017 Legislative Session

	Testamentary guardian of the person (Wis. Stat. Ann. §§ 54.01 et seq. (West 2015 & Supp. 2016))	Standby Guardian (Wis. Stat. Ann. § 48.978 (West 2017))
Who Can Appoint?	Court is given authority if individual is deemed a minor. 54.10(1). Parent may appoint by will. 54.15(6).	Court. 48.978.
How?	Court shall consider the opinion of the ward, the opinion of members of his or her family, and potential conflicts of interest when determining the best interests of the minor. 54.15(1). Parent may nominate a guardian by will unless the court finds that appointment would not be in the best interests of the minor. 54.15(6).	Upon petition for appointment by a parent.[150] If a parent cannot locate other parent, then parent can file without other parent joining in petition. If a parent can locate the other parent, but that other parent refuses to join petition, parent may file and submit proof to court of refusal. 48.978. Petition must include name of person nominated, a statement of when the duty becomes effective, and statement that there is significant risk that petitioner will become incapacitated or die within two years after date petition is filed. OR Parent can make written designation of guardian. 48.978.
For What Purpose?	To provide for the personal needs or property management of the ward in a manner that is appropriate to the ward and that constitutes the least restrictive form of intervention. 54.18(1).	Petition shall state the duties and authority that petitioner wishes standby to exercise. 48.978
When Takes Effect?		Written designation takes effect when standby files a petition and is appointed by the court. 48.978. Petition previously approved by court takes effect upon determination of incapacity or death of parent. 48.978.
How Terminate?	Guardianship shall terminate when minor: (1) reaches majority (unless minor is incompetent), or (2) lawfully marries. 54.64(3).	
Medical? § 54.25		

150. Petition can include alternate standby for court to appoint if the person nominated as standby guardian is unwilling or unable to serve as the child's guardian or if court determines appointment of person nominated is not in best interests of child. § 48.978(2)(a)(1).

WYOMING

LEXIS current through 2017 Legislative Session. Subject to revisions by LSO.

	Testamentary guardian of the person (Wyo. Stat. Ann. §§ 3-2-101 et seq. (2017))	Standby Guardian (Wyo. Stat. Ann. § 3-2-108 (2017))	Examples of Medical Consent (Wyo. Stat. Ann. § 3-2-202 (2017))
Who Can Appoint?	Court. 3-2-104.	Court. 3-2-108.	Court. 3-2-202.
How?	Any person may file a petition for appointment of a guardian. Court gives priority to: (1) person nominated as guardian in will of parent; (2) person requested by minor who has reached 14; and (3) any other person whose appointment would be in best interests of minor. 3-2-107.	Petition filed. 3-2-108.	Upon court order, the guardian may (1) commit the ward to a mental health hospital or facility, (2) consent to specified treatments, (3) relinquish the ward's minor child for adoption, and (4) execute any appropriate advanced medical directives. 3-2-202.
For What Purpose?	Determine residence for ward; facilitate ward's education, social and other activities; authorize medical care, etc. 3-2-201.	Guardian shall present and file report on activities of the ward every six months. Determine residence for ward; facilitate ward's education, social and other activities; authorize medical care, etc. 3-2-108.	
When Takes Effect?	Upon court order. 3-2-104.		Upon court order. 3-2-202.
How Terminate?			

APPENDIX 6-C

Internet Resources

This is list of some of the websites which provide further information on issues discussed in this chapter. There are many additional websites which may provide additional state-specific forms and information. Websites, of course, are reorganized from time to time; you may be able to find a document no longer precisely at the web link listed here by searching the home website of the organization if the document has moved since the publication of this book.

http://www.courts.ca.gov/documents/gc205.pdf (includes discussion of guardianship and possible alternatives to guardianship in California)

http://www.nclrights.org/our-work/family-relationships/family-relationships -resources/#parentingnational (parenting resources, including information on long-term planning for children, targeted toward same-sex couples)

http://www.purdue.edu/business/risk_mgmt/pdf/rm28.pdf (sample Indiana Medical Consent form used for Purdue University students)

https://projects.ncsu.edu/ffci/publications/1996/v1-n2-1996-spring/standby.php (North Carolina standby guardian information)

http://www.illinoislegalaid.org/index.cfm?fuseaction=home.dsp_content &contentid=246 (Illinois guardian of minor in general)

http://www.grandfamilies.org/Topics/Education (educational consent information targeted toward grandparents raising grandchildren; various states)

https://www.childwelfare.gov/pubPDFs/guardianship.pdf (resource on standby guardianships)

https://www.acep.org/medicalforms/#sm.000052rlxzuj2d54yap10cy9p2jy0 (consent to medical treatment form for minors provided by American College of Emergency Physicians)

http://www.nationwidechildrens.org/designation-of-another-person-to-consent-for -medical-care (consent to medical treatment form for minors provided by Nationwide Children's Hospital)

https://www.nycourts.gov/forms/surrogates/guardianship.shtml (New York guardianship forms, including standby guardianship)

http://www.co.marathon.wi.us/Portals/0/Departments/COC/Documents /rpoPOA-DelegatingParentalAuthority.pdf (Wisconsin form delegating pick-and-choose parental powers)

CHAPTER 7

Planning for the Disabled Minor Child

Cynthia Barrett

I. INTRODUCTION

If a minor child is significantly disabled, the estate planner knows that the simple "distributions for health, education, maintenance, and support"[1] (HEMS) trust, ending after the child becomes mature, will not address the client's concerns for his or her child. Some minor disabilities do not affect the ability of the child to become self-supporting. This chapter addresses planning for a significantly disabled minor child, who may *not* be fully self-supporting as an adult.

Parents of a disabled minor child in the United States worry about the child's access to

- medical care from private (or publicly funded) health plans,
- supportive in-home long-term care services, and
- public education services.

Estate planners are *not* experts in any of these areas—so parents of minor disabled children do not turn to their estate planners for day-to-day problem-solving or to develop a care plan for the child's medical, long-term care and education services.

Parents usually, however, have a care plan in mind, and need to communicate that plan to their designated fiduciaries and give them authority to act. Few parents document their care plans in writing—although special needs planners encourage that step. Some parents can articulate their care plan during their estate planning meetings; others shy from the subject.

While the disabled child is a minor, the parent is focused totally on improving function, and dealing with school and medical services. When seeing an estate planning lawyer, the parent confronts the fraught certainty of the parent's own death or disability. But the parent wants legal protection for the disabled child, and understands the need for the following:

- nomination of a guardian for the disabled child;
- a trustee to manage the child's share of the estate; and
- a trust document, instructing the trustee about use of funds.

This chapter addresses planning basics for both wealthy and less wealthy parents of disabled minors. The parents need to understand both public benefits, and how trusts affect those public benefits.

Most trusts for minors are typical "support trusts," instructing a trustee to make distributions for the "health, education, maintenance, and support" (HEMS distribution standard) of the minor. The trustee's authority to distribute income and/or principal may be discretionary or mandatory. Whether the trust is a discretionary or mandatory HEMS distribution trust, the trust language itself, as well as the actual trust distributions selected, can interfere with the disabled child's public benefits.

II. PLANNING BASICS

Parents are the primary care providers for their disabled minor children. The estate planning process forces the parents to contemplate one (or both) of them not being there to help.

If one parent dies, what help will the surviving parent need to keep the child at home? Would keeping the child at home even be feasible, if the surviving parent must work outside the home?

If both parents died, would the guardian of the person need to place the child in a facility? How would the guardian pay for needed help, from a trust (which may not name the guardian as trustee) or from public benefits?

A. While Disabled Child Is a Minor

While the child is a minor, the parent structures a care arrangement (likely in the home) and is the legal decider (natural guardian). While the child is small, the parent can structure interactions with the larger world to make the child safe and manage doctor and other medical appointments and transportation; care is usually home based. In a two-parent family, one parent typically is employed outside the home, and one parent takes primary responsibility for the disabled child.

1. If One Parent Dies

When a working parent dies, the surviving homemaker parent and minor disabled child lose not only the wage-earner's income but also the employer-paid group health coverage (after a thirty-six-month COBRA[2] insurance period).

(a) Health Coverage

If the deceased worker had an employer-paid group plan and the survivor can afford the premiums, then COBRA[3] coverage can continue for up to thirty-six months. Before the Affordable Care Act[4] (ACA) prohibited discrimination for preexisting conditions, disabled children could not get into new private health plans, so keeping a COBRA[5] plan for at least the child was critical.

Now, with the ACA marketplace plans and premium subsidies, private insurance is at least available for the decedent's disabled minor child However, the health care system is in flux. Perhaps lifetime limits on health coverage ($1,000,000 was a typical limit in pre-ACA private coverage) and discrimination based on preexisting conditions will return, so that keeping a COBRA[6] plan for the disabled minor will become critical.

When health coverage plans change after one parent's death, the surviving parent faces all the coverage problems: Will the child's specialist accept the new plan? What additional uninsured costs will be incurred (co-pays, privately paid services, deductibles, premiums)?

This health care private marketplace uncertainty will cause state by state variation in available coverage that the surviving parent will be forced to examine whether the child might qualify for publicly paid coverage—a Medicaid expansion plan, Child's Health Insurance Plan (CHIP) plan,[7] or some other state public plan offered for disabled minor children. Some families will move to a state offering better health coverage options for the disabled child.

(b) Income Replacement

Lack of regular household income is the real problem if the wage-earner dies. A family may have significant savings (and retirement plan accounts) to draw on for immediate needs after one parent dies. Perhaps the working parent participated in a traditional pension plan, providing income to a surviving spouse.

(c) Social Security Survivor and "Child in Care" Benefits

Social Security's "safety net" income will benefit the family: (1) a survivor benefit check monthly for a minor (until age eighteen) and a disabled adult child (for life, after age eighteen); and (2) a separate check monthly for the surviving parent of any age (the "child in care" benefit), if he or she is caring for the minor or disabled child. The two checks (i.e., the surviving child check and the separate "child in care" check for the parent), however, will not completely cover the family bills.

(d) Life Insurance

Life insurance is a critical element in planning for the loss of the wage-earner parent. The estate planner recommends

- maxing out any optional life insurance available as an employee benefit, and
- purchasing *substantial* additional coverage.

Human resources staff can help the family understand any employee group plan life insurance optional coverage. Private life insurance agents can review available whole or term life policies. Some insurance agents focus on helping families with disabled children, predicting lifetime costs of care and suggesting appropriate coverage for both the at-home and working spouse.[8]

(e) Replacement Homemaker Services

If the homemaker parent dies, the surviving wage-earner needs to replace those unpaid caregiving services. Temporarily, care for the child is cobbled together from willing relatives—but the wage-earner may need to quit work, consider facility care, or hire in-home caregivers.

If a working surviving parent must quit or reduce his or her work hours and forego promotion prospects because of caregiving responsibilities, this circumstance causes additional emotional strain. To increase the options available to a surviving wage-earner spouse, estate planners recommend *substantial* life insurance on the homemaker parent's life.

2. If Both Parents Die

If both parents are gone, what are the immediate needs?

(a) Daily Care Provider

The day to day rhythm of the disabled minor child will be disrupted by the loss of both parents. Daily care and supervision (known as "long-term care services and support" [LTSS]) needs to be arranged. Usually, the parents' wills nominate a guardian of the person to advocate for services and medical attention. The parents may have drafted a "statement of intent" describing what they intend for the disabled child. Often, family members step in temporarily to provide emergency care, but look to the parents' estate planning documents for a long-term solution.

(b) Guardian

(i) Guardian of the Person

In their wills or in stand-alone documents, the parents nominate a "guardian" (referred to, in some states, as a "guardian of the person")[9] to make medical/residential decisions for the child. The nominee must go to the local probate court, file a petition, and get appointed as legal guardian before his or her authority will be recognized. Some nominees advance the court costs and legal fees for this proceeding, and later seek reimbursement from the parents' probate or trust estate.

(ii) Guardian of the Estate

The guardian of the estate is a decision maker and advocate, but may not be able to provide home-based care. Whether or not the guardian takes the child into his or her home, the guardian needs help to understand care needs and payment sources for services. Securing the health coverage for the child is crucial—the first question the attorney should ask is whether a job-based health plan will provide coverage for the surviving child.

PRACTICE NOTE

> Parents can develop a written care plan to organize the health care coverage, school services, and social service information for their child. The parents' "statement of intent" might include some of this planning information.

(c) Quick Access to Cash

Getting funds flowing quickly for the needs of the disabled child (and to pay for the guardianship court proceeding) will be a priority. If the parent's estate goes to probate, getting access to cash must wait for appointment of the personal representative and establishment of the estate bank account. Court rules, in some states, may require filing a petition for an order to support dependents—and for some public benefit programs declaring the child a dependent opens the entire estate to claims for support of that disabled child.

Consider the advantages of having a stand-alone living trust drafted and naming that trust as beneficiary of life insurance.[10] The trustee can get the IRS tax ID number for the trust, apply for life insurance as soon as a death certificate is available, and have access to funds within a few weeks of a death.

3. *Minors and Public Benefits*

Parents of minor disabled children want to learn how to obtain needed medical and social services for their child. The parents hear the term "public benefits" but are not clear about what those benefits are, or when their child might access the help. The estate planner can help the parents wrap their arms about the basic structure of public benefits—without getting lost in acronyms and eligibility requirements for each program.

Breaking down the broad topic of "public benefits" in the following way, helps the parents develop a framework for understanding their child's access to taxpayer-funded help.

(a) Under Age Eighteen, School-Based Services and Medicaid Special Education School Services

Minor disabled children, under age eighteen and living with parents, receive local public school-based special education services, which are *not* needs-based. That is, the parents' income and resources cannot disqualify the child from the school's special education services.

Parents push the schools to improve offerings, and sometimes turn to litigation. In each state, there are a few dedicated lawyers who represent parents seeking better school-based services for their disabled children. Most estate planners refer their clients to the litigation lawyers offering special education services; a few estate planners have a special education litigation lawyer in-house.

Parents of disabled children know far more than their estate planning lawyers about school-based programs—which never completely satisfy the child's needs. The parents often home school the child for a while, and pay out of pocket for all sorts of specialized services to supplement what the public education system provides. When disabled children "age out" of the public school special education, they face the bleak prospect of under-funded adult disability services.

(b) Medicaid Health Plans and Special Services

Many disabled children receive basic health coverage through a parent's job-based group health plan. These children may have Medicaid wraparound coverage as well. Some Medicaid programs depend on family income, and some special Medicaid programs ignore the parents' income and resources.

Low-income families without good employer-based coverage qualify for basic health coverage through Medicaid-paid programs like the CHIP[11] or the ACA[12] Medicaid expansion program. All states offer some version of the CHIP program, and this health program for minors seems likely to survive the health care overhaul now being discussed in Congress at the time of this writing.

The ACA's Medicaid expansion program for low-income citizens may not survive the current health care overhaul in Congress. If Medicaid expansion exists in your state, there is no asset limit, and participants can join despite preexisting conditions, and with no prior determination of disability.

Before the ACA, minor children accessed health coverage through a parent's job-based group plan (which had no preexisting condition exclusions, but might have lifetime coverage limits), or parents shopped for an individual health plan (with lifetime coverage limits and preexisting condition denials).

The ACA Medicaid expansion program was a life-saver when both parents died, and the child could not afford (or missed the cutoff date for application for) the COBRA[13] premiums for a group health plan. Before the ACA, the only way to access Medicaid was through Supplemental Security Income (SSI). The SSI program has strict asset and income limits, and requires a "declaration of disability" from the Social Security agency. One could get health coverage for the child through the ACA without the SSI hurdles.

Medicaid-paid health plans cover more "long-term care services and supports" (LTSS) than private health plans. Private health plans greatly limit their LTSS, while Medicaid plans are designed to include many such services. Providers of both medical and LTSS care receive less from Medicaid than from private health plans. Because the reimbursement rates are low, certain specialists and programs will not accept Medicaid-only patients.

Obtaining (or keeping!) the disabled child's private health plan may be crucial for access to specialists and continuity of care. Most parents become experts at navigating between private and Medicaid health systems and providers. After the parents are gone, the guardian of the disabled child needs to become, or hire, a similarly skilled navigator.

Congress is expected to change the ACA in the next few years. A whole-sale repeal of the ACA will undo all the income-based Medicaid expansion programs.

Before the ACA, disabled children had difficulty finding health coverage because of preexisting condition exclusions and affordability. The available coverage had lifetime limits ($1,000,000 or $2,000,000 limits were common). Some states offered private High-Risk Pool policies to those with preexisting conditions—of course, these policies had lifetime limits just as regular health plan policies did. High-risk pool policies were oversubscribed in some states, like California, leading to wait times for coverage of over a year.

4. *Home Care Programs: Katie Beckett and K Plan*

Does the child's behavior or level of need bring the family to the brink of crisis? If the parents cannot care for the child at home safely, without medical equipment and trained hired caregivers, then they may need to send the child to an institution. No private health care plan pays for these costly long-term care services and supports, and only the wealthiest Americans can afford 24-hour in-home care.

Two Medicaid home care programs, the Katie Beckett option and the K Plan, might help keep the child in the home—and both programs disregard parental income and resources. Only the child's personal income and resources count in determining eligibility, making these programs available to both low-income and middle-class families.

Parents of severely disabled children need to see if their state participates in either program. Publicly paid programs for disabled children vary incredibly across state lines, and sometimes from county to county. State program names, origins, and eligibility requirements are impossible to summarize. Parents can simply google the phrase "Katie Beckett plan and [name of state]" to learn about their state's version of the plan.

In both the Katie Beckett program (enacted as a Medicaid option in 1982, at title XIX, Social Security Act, § 1902(e)(3)) and the K Plan option (enacted in 2010 as part of the ACA[14] Medicaid changes at 42 U.S.C. § 1396n(k)), the child must meet income and resource ($2,000) limits, but the parents' income and resources are disregarded.

The Katie Beckett Medicaid program provides funds to parents of severely disabled children for special in-home medical care and equipment and for in-home care providers. Few disabilities qualify for this waiver option—basically, the child must need nursing home levels of both medical care and supervision. All states, except Tennessee, adopted this pathway to Medicaid, but some states may cap enrollment.

The K Plan, known as the "Community First Choice" option, through the ACA, provides extra funding to help states cover severely disabled children in the home.[15] The Kaiser Family Foundation is keeping track of which states (eight as of March 2016) applied for this Medicaid plan option.[16]

This K Plan Medicaid pathway funds in-home care for developmentally disabled and mentally ill children who need custodial level care. The child's income and resources are considered, but the parents' income and resources are not deemed to the child. When the child has disqualifying resources (typically, a Uniform Transfers to Minors Act (UTMA) account[17] with contributions from grandparents or the parents), then the lawyer will recommend a payback special needs trust (see subsection E.2. of this chapter) for the disqualifying assets.

Estate planners who focus on special needs cases get to know local care managers and health/services navigators familiar with disabled child programs, and refer their clients to these on-the-ground experts. Some special needs estate planners have social workers on staff to assist parents.

Federal Medicaid programs stop deeming the parents' income and resources to the child at age eighteen, when the child becomes an adult. The parents of disabled minors hear about "Social Security" and "Medicaid health coverage" for disabled adults, but do not have the energy to focus on adult benefits until the child gets close to that age.

For the parents, dealing with the day-to-day challenges of running the family ship is almost overwhelming. The lawyer focusing on special needs planning is invaluable to the parents as, in the estate planning process, the plan for the adult life of the disabled minor takes shape.

B. Turning Age Eighteen

1. Adult Guardianship

Special education school services end as the child becomes an adult. The child becomes a legal adult at age eighteen, and receives transition services focusing on vocational rehabilitation and community college. The first time the parents hear the words "patient confidentiality" and "self-determination," they realize they should find out about guardianship.

In most states, both parents can be appointed co-guardians, but some courts actively discourage that practice. The courts hate to resolve disagreements between co-guardians. If the parents' marriage dissolves, the court might refuse to appoint either as sole guardian. The lawyer who represented both parents as co-guardian is usually "conflicted out" in the event of disagreements or marriage dissolution. The best practice might be to represent one parent as guardian of the person, but many lawyers feel comfortable representing both parents.

If the child has significant intellectual disabilities, or other developmental disabilities, or cannot communicate effectively because of a physical disability, then the parents will be able to become their child's guardian (known as "guardian of the person" in some states).[18] The guardian of the person can obtain medical information, make residential and treatment decisions, and advocate for better services.

A guardian of the person usually does not become a conservator (called "guardian of the estate" in some cases) unless the disabled adult has assets to administer. The guardian of the person can apply for private health coverage; waive confidentiality for insurance and medical providers; and seek publicly subsidized health plan coverage, SSI, housing benefits, and so on.

2. SSA Disability Determination

If the child's disability prevents him or her from working at substantial gainful employment, then he or she probably qualifies as "disabled" under Social Security Administration (SSA) rules. Even if the parents do *not* want to apply for any publicly funded benefits right away, they should apply for a "disability determination" through Social Security.

3. County Developmental Disabilities (DD) Assessment

If the child has intellectual or developmental disabilities (the acronym ID/DD includes both), the parents should contact the local county DD office to have a DD assessment completed. The Social Security and local DD disability determinations at age eighteen to nineteen are a precondition to many adult services.

4. SSI Program

The major Medicaid-funded programs for disabled adults often require the claimant be both "disabled" by Social Security standards and financially qualified for SSI. SSI has strict income and resource ($2,000) eligibility rules. Most disabled adults have no regular income, but some will have disqualifying bank or investment accounts or be beneficiaries of disqualifying trusts.

The SSI program has a monthly cash benefit ($750 in 2018) and links the recipient automatically with Medicaid health coverage (**Note:** This is the SSI pathway to Medicaid). For some families, the monthly cash benefit is very welcomed; for middle class or wealthier families, the cash benefit is immaterial. However, if you lose the SSI cash benefit, you lose the SSI-linked Medicaid coverage. Going through the SSI door also is necessary to qualify for many adult disability public services.

(a) Continuation of Social Security Benefits

Millions of minor children receive Social Security benefits on a parent's earnings account because a parent is disabled, retired, or deceased. The minor child's benefits begin when the parent's benefits commence, that is, at the parent's Social Security disability date, either at the parent's retirement (the parent can elect to claim Social Security at age sixty-two or above) or at the parent's death (at any age).

Social Security minor child benefits end when the child reaches age eighteen or finishes high school, but no later than age nineteen. The benefits, however, will continue into adulthood if the child became disabled while a minor. (Children who become disabled after age eighteen, but before age twenty-two, also qualify for this child's Social Security benefit on a parent's account.)

__PRACTICE NOTE__

The estate planner may encounter a family with a disabled minor child already receiving a Social Security check through a disabled, retired, or deceased parent, and should get a copy of the award letter for the file.

The parent of a minor disabled child manages the funds as a Social Security "representative payee," and files an annual report detailing how the money was spent. When the disabled child becomes an adult, then the parent will continue to manage the funds as a representative payee under Social Security rules. Minor disabled children *might* qualify for SSI program benefits, if the family income and resources are very low.

(b) Social Security Benefits for Disabled Adult Child

When one parent claims his or her own Social Security benefits (because of death, early disability, or retirement at or after age sixty-two), then a disabled adult child is entitled to 50 percent of the parent's check as a "Disabled Adult Child" benefit. These checks are on the deceased, disabled, or retired parent's own earnings record. If the low-earning parent retires first, the child receives one-half of his or her check; when the higher-earning parent eventually retires, the child receives only one check: the higher check on that parent's account. The first check from the low-earning parent's earnings record ends, replaced by the check from the higher earning parent.

5. ABLE Accounts

Special needs planners recommend that every parent of a disabled minor create ABLE accounts *now* for that child. In 2014, Congress enacted the Achieving a Better Life Experience Act,[19] adding section 529A of the Internal Revenue Code, to allow tax savings accounts for beneficiaries disabled before the age of twenty-six years.

Like the 529 education tax-savings accounts,[20] ABLE account contributions qualify as annual exclusion gifts,[21] and grow tax-free. Unlike the 529 educational tax-savings accounts, the balance in the ABLE account, at the beneficiary's death, is subject to a state claim for reimbursement of any Medicaid long-term care services and supports provided.

Before 2018, annual contributions to an ABLE account, *from all sources,* could not exceed the annual exclusion amount. Sections 11024 and 11025 of H.R. 1, "An Act to provide for reconciliation" (informally known as the Tax Cuts and Jobs Act) changed the ABLE account contribution rules in two respects:

- **Source of ABLE contributions broadened to include 529 rollovers.** Before January 1, 2026, a family can roll over funds (the annual total of all contributions to the ABLE account is $15,000 in 2018)[22] from an existing qualified tuition program (known as 529 educational accounts). The rollover must come from a 529 account for the disabled beneficiary or another member of his family to the disabled beneficiary's ABLE account.[23]

- **Annual ABLE contribution limit raised if compensation.** In addition to the annual contribution limit (no more than the annual exclusion, $15,000 in 2018), the disabled beneficiary can contribute the lesser of his compensation or the federal poverty level for a single person—up to an additional $11,770 in 2018—but only if he or she does not participate in an employer's retirement or deferred compensation plan.[24]

The ABLE law protects the disabled beneficiary from losing SSI and Medicaid eligibility by excluding the first $100,000 in the account as a countable resource. The new accounts, set up in at least thirty-five states, at the time of this writing, permit savings beyond $100,000 (up to $350,000 in Oregon, for example), but amounts over $100,000 will be countable assets to suspend an SSI cash grant (but not Medicaid!). Some states permit out-of-state residents to join their programs.

Each disabled individual can have only one ABLE account. The parent can create the account now, with a small contribution, and be the controlling person for the account. If the disabled person is an adult of any age, but the onset of disability was before age twenty-six, then he or she can establish and control the account on his or her own. Once established, any person, estate, or trust can contribute funds to the ABLE account—so long as the total contributed each year is no more than the annual contribution limit (annual exclusion amount, $15,000 in 2018, plus a limited amount of earned income contributed by the disabled beneficiary).

Distributions from the account for "qualified disability expenses" are not taxable income, or countable income in SSI and Medicaid programs. Qualified disability expenses are

> any expenses related to the eligible individual's blindness or disability which are made for the benefit of an eligible individual who is the designated beneficiary, including the following expenses: education, housing, transportation, employment training and support, assistive technology and personal support services, health, prevention and wellness, financial management and administrative services, legal fees, expenses for oversight and monitoring, funeral and burial expenses, and other expenses.[25]

Trustees of special needs trusts expect to coordinate trust distributions with ABLE account distributions to allow beneficiaries more noncountable income. ABLE account "qualified distributions" include housing costs. If a special needs trustee paid housing costs for the disabled child, the distributions would be SSI program "in-kind income," reducing the monthly SSI grant dollar for dollar.

The ABLE account can be linked to a debit card, so the person controlling the account has easy access to funds. If the disabled individual was the account control person, he or she could easily access funds. The account control person can be someone other than the disabled beneficiary, but the legislation was designed to work like a savings account for disabled individuals with capacity. Working disabled individuals can make account contributions from their wages and accumulate savings not subject to the usual $2,000 resource limit for SSI and Medicaid.

If the disabled beneficiary does not have the capacity to establish or manage the ABLE account, his parent, or another designee (e.g., an agent under a power of attorney) can establish the account and decide appropriate distributions. Special needs planners encourage parents of disabled minors to establish the accounts now, before the child reaches age eighteen, because funds saved in those accounts will not then disqualify the child from needed public benefits.

As a disabled minor reaches the age of eighteen years, the parents may realize he or she needs access to some public benefit program, but the disabled minor has disqualifying assets in his or her name. Usually, the disqualifying assets are gifts from the grandparents, or savings accumulated by the parent for the child in a UTMA account.[26]

Unfortunately, a guardian of the estate (called "conservator" in some states)[27] will need to be appointed for the now-adult child, seeking court authority to transfer the disqualifying asset to an ABLE account. If the resources are worth more than the ABLE account annual contribution limit (the annual exclusion amount, $15,000 in 2018), the balance of the disqualifying sum must be spent, or transferred by court order to a payback special needs trust (see subsection E.2. of this chapter). Nonetheless, the ABLE account is a perfect receptacle for disqualifying assets up to the annual exclusion amount.

III. LONG-TERM PLANNING

Estate planning by its nature is long-term planning. The will and/or trust that the parents create will be in place for many years. The estate lawyer helps the parents address the needs of their child over time, both as a minor and as an adult.

Will the child be able to work, and be self-supporting, and obtain health coverage through his or her job? Do the parents have sufficient wealth to provide all the additional services the disabled child will need for his or her lifetime?

The first need of the disabled is medical care—provided primarily by private health insurance or Medicaid. The second need, if the child's ability to function independently in activities of daily life is compromised, is long-term care services and supports—help with day-to-day chores, supervision if there are intellectual or developmental disabilities, and perhaps residential placement and custodial care. Long-term care services and supports are expensive, and most families cannot afford the costs, so Medicaid programs provide the bulk of the care.

Before ACA's ban on lifetime coverage limits and preexisting condition exclusions, the parents of a disabled child knew their child would someday be denied health insurance. Therefore, all parents, even the wealthy, had to consider public benefits simply to get medical care for their disabled child.

If the child's disabilities would lead to the need for custodial or institutional care, then even wealthy parents understood that their assets would not cover all foreseeable costs over the child's lifetime. If the funds available for a disabled child are modest, or the child is not expected to be self-supporting, the planning focus turns to the special needs trust, described later.

Estate planners working with parents of disabled minor children must realize that the parents hope for a positive, rewarding future for their child—and while the child is young, and the child's abilities are not yet known, the parents intensely cling to that vision. Parents may not recognize how the child's disability will affect his or her capacity for self-support.

Even if the parents do not acknowledge their anxiety and fears for the disabled child, the estate planner must help the parents put in place documents that increase the chance for the desired future. Residential peace, life quality, and kind caregiver options for the disabled adult in America are possible.

The parents must name surrogate decision makers (nominated trustees, guardians of the person, and guardians of the estate)[28] and protect the child's inheritance from exhaustion by uninsured medical and long-term care services and support.

A. Self-Supporting Disabled Adult Child

An adult is presumed able to manage funds, accept inheritances outright, and arrange his or her own life. If the disabilities do not interfere with an adult child's ability to be self-supporting, the parents might arrange outright gifts in the same manner as for nondisabled children.

A special needs trust is not always necessary! Some disabled children can work and earn enough to support their families. If ACA's protections against preexisting condition exclusions are not repealed, the disabled adult, without job-based health coverage, should be able to find private health coverage.

If the parents expect the child to be self-supporting but want funds available to help with expenses because the disability will reduce the child's earning capacity, the estate planning lawyer usually will suggest a mixture of outright devises, a long-term discretionary support trust, and/or a separate IRA conduit trust[29] (if an IRA or qualified plan is the parent's major asset for this child). The goal is to supplement a working disabled adult's earning capacity and help the disabled adult through economic "rough patches."

Restrictions on outright inheritance may not be necessary for a disabled child, if

- the disability is simply physical in nature, and the child is cognitively able to manage funds, and
- the child is not susceptible to undue influence from financial predators.

Where a child's susceptibility to predators or undue influence might be a problem, the estate planner usually suggests a long-term trust. Some disabled self-supporting children, like some children, simply need the creditor/predator/undue influence protection provided by a professionally managed trust.

Estate planners are familiar with the typical "ascertainable standard" *discretionary HEMS trust* distribution language: "The trustee may make distributions of income and/or principal, as the trustee may determine, in his or her sole and absolute discretion, for the health, education, maintenance and support [HEMS] of the beneficiary."[30] This is called a "discretionary support trust."

In disabled child estate planning, most lawyers avoid the typical *mandatory HEMS trust* distribution standard: "The trustee shall make distributions of income and/or principal for the health, education, maintenance and support [HEMS] of the beneficiary."[31] This is called a "full support trust."

Special needs planners avoid using the mandatory support trust distribution standard because public benefit agencies likely would consider mandatory HEMS trusts available resources and deny needs-based benefits.

Parent can include specific recommendations for distributions and care plans in a letter of intent for the trustee. The parents empower others to enforce their wishes about use of the trust funds by providing a copy of the "letter of intent" to a trust protector, relatives, or the disabled child.

The estate planner should explain how distributions from a HEMS trust help the employed disabled adult. For example, the trustee can make distributions during intermittent periods of unemployment for household expenses; pay for apartment security deposits, rent, and health coverage; or even purchase a home.

A disabled worker might be the first one laid off if an employer cuts payroll costs, and have difficulty finding a new job quickly. The child's disabilities could limit his or her lifetime earnings, and a trustee could make retirement plan contributions, or fund Roth and regular IRAs, or supplement retirement savings by purchasing a deferred annuity providing monthly payments when the child reaches a certain age.

The working disabled adult child may periodically need vocational counseling and assistance to find suitable work. The trustee can hire private vocational advocates and job coaches, rather than having the disabled adult rely on haphazardly funded public vocational services and inattentive, overworked publicly paid social service workers. The trust could pay for counseling, health plan premiums for the disabled adult's family, job search expenses, or moving expenses.

The parents' letter of intent to the trustee can describe these enhanced standard of living distributions. The trust document might give illustrations of intended distributions, such as job coaches and vocational education to develop the child's work skills, periodic income to pay some household expenses, and support during periods of unemployment.

B. Adult Disabled Child Will Not Be Self-Supporting

When a disabled minor child will *not* ever be able to support himself, then the parents must focus on public benefits, and leverage those benefits, unless they are very wealthy. Monthly support costs will vary, depending on whether the disabled adult can live alone in a private home or apartment, doing his or her own shopping and medication management, or needs full-time facility care.

The estate planning lawyer might suggest hiring an expert to develop a life plan and lifetime care cost estimate for the wealthy family's child. Each state's Medicaid agency publishes that state's average monthly cost of nursing home care. For example, in 2017, Oregon's average cost of care was $8,425 a month, and Pennsylvania's average cost of care was $321 a day, or about $9,630 a month.

The wealthy disabled child will need health insurance to pay for specialized medical care and treatment. The health plan marketplace is disrupted now by political uncertainty, and planning is difficult as insurers offering plans in the ACA marketplace decide whether to continue to participate. At the time of this writing, private ACA marketplace health coverage plans are available in most non-rural parts of the United States, and these plans have no preexisting condition exclusions and no lifetime limits on coverage.

The wealthy disabled child will need to access specialized medical services for his or her condition, and live where residential care and supervision services are offered—typically, an urban area with a regional medical center. If the family lives in a state where needed health coverage, specialized medical treatment, and in-home services are not provided, then the cost of a move will be included in lifetime cost of care projections.

Perhaps the wealthy parents of a disabled child conclude that adequate health insurance exists (without preexisting condition exclusions or lifetime limits to coverage), and private services can be engaged to provide in-home help. If these conditions exist, then very wealthy parents might ignore public benefit planning and substantially fund a HEMS discretionary support trust for the child.

Some disabled adults refuse to seek needed medical attention, refuse even to apply for a health insurance, or are incapable of doing so. Then, the parents' plan for the disabled child includes nomination of a guardian of the person[32] to secure health coverage and arrange in-home or facility care and supervision. Some mentally disabled adults refuse to live in one place, preferring to be homeless—arranging services for these individuals is a challenge for even the most skilled professional guardian.

C. Most Parents Rely on Public Benefits

Middle-class and low-income families are not able to fully fund a support trust to cover a severely disabled child's projected lifetime living costs and medical costs. Parents of disabled children and advocacy groups encouraged public policy makers (in agencies and in Congress and state government) to permit a limited benefit trust to pay for the child's "special needs."

For these less wealthy clients, the estate planner should be familiar with basic social safety net programs and recommend a "special needs trust." These trusts developed slightly differently in each state, but all deal with the federal SSI and state/federal Medicaid eligibility rules. Because the trusts are designed to "supplement but not supplant" public benefit programs for which the beneficiary might be eligible, special needs trusts are sometimes called "supplemental needs trusts."

As the social safety net programs change over time, special needs trust drafting also changes. Lawyers working with parents of disabled minor children should have a working knowledge of the basic programs.

Current social safety net programs can be briefly described as follows.

1. *Social Security Disabled Adult Child and Medicare Benefits*
If a working parent has a Social Security earnings record for forty quarters, he or she can claim a Social Security retirement check at age sixty-two or later, and if disabled before that age, collect a Social Security disability check. Linked to that retired or disability check for the worker are benefits for the worker's spouse, minor children, and disabled adult children.

When the retired or disabled worker starts receiving his Social Security check, then the disabled adult child also can file a Social Security claim for a check on the "retired or disabled worker's" (e.g., father's) earning record.

For example, a father of a developmentally disabled son, age thirty-eight, decides to retire at age sixty-six and collect Social Security retirement benefits. At that time, his developmentally disabled adult son will be eligible for a Social Security DAC (disabled adult child) check that is one-half of the father's check. If the son lives in the household with his father, then two checks from Social Security come to the home: the father's check and the disabled adult son's check.

Once the disabled adult child starts receiving his DAC Social Security, then after two years he will be eligible for Medicare as well. The DAC child may have been relying solely on SSI ($750/month in 2018) and its linked Medicaid health coverage for years. The DAC monthly check is usually higher than the $750 SSI check, and Medicare provides higher reimbursement to health care providers.

During the two-year waiting period for Medicare, the DAC child remains eligible for Medicaid health coverage; once Medicare starts, the DAC child is "dual eligible" and entitled to Medicaid as a wraparound.[33]

The state Medicaid program loves dual status beneficiaries. Medicaid is a state/federal program, and state general fund dollars pay a set share (the "match") of health costs. But Medicare is a federal program, 100 percent paid at the federal level. States save money when Medicare, not Medicaid, covers much of the expensive health care needed by a DAC child. State agencies work hard to identify "dual eligible" individuals and get them qualified for Medicare as soon as possible.

DAC Social Security checks *do not automatically begin when the child reaches age eighteen.* DAC checks commence when the parent dies (as a child survivor payment) or when the parent claims his or her own Social Security benefit. If the working parent dies while the disabled child is a minor, before claiming retirement or disability benefits, then the disabled minor child will collect child's survivor benefits before age eighteen, and then start DAC checks at age eighteen.

DAC benefits are paid without regard to the child's income or assets—unlike SSI and Medicaid, the DAC benefits are not "needs-based." The special needs trust (SNT) trustee rejoices to learn that a higher DAC Social Security check has replaced a beneficiary's lower SSI check. When the trust beneficiary no longer relies on the SSI link to Medicaid, the SNT trustee can loosen up the distributions, even paying for some in-kind support and maintenance.

2. Financial Screening for Disabled Adults

Most adult residential and social service programs for the disabled are funded by the taxpayer, with strict financial income and resource eligibility standards. If the parent wants the disabled adult child to live in a group home or access SSI and Medicaid, the child cannot have more than $2,000 in countable resources.[34] To qualify for SSI, the disabled adult child cannot have over $750 (in 2018) in countable income.

Public program funding is fragmented: Developmental disability funds are used for some programs; mental health funds for other programs; and physical disability funds for yet other programs. Eligibility criteria vary with each program, but, generally, if the adult disabled child qualifies for the SSI program, he or she is probably eligible.

3. Adult Residential Programs and Scarcity Crisis

Housing is a problem for all of America's low-income adults. When the adult suffers from severe mental illness or intellectual and developmental disabilities, the adult often needs either significant in-home supports or admission to a licensed care facility. Publicly supported residential living slots are hard to access and have strict eligibility requirements.

A few privately supported independent living apartment complexes and group living homes exist in every urban community. Some parents of disabled adult children work with their lawyers and hire nonprofit administrators to set up and run these private housing arrangements. Only those with a deep knowledge of the local parent and provider community ever learn about these private housing options.

Disabled but functional adults spend years on waiting lists for a HUD Section 8 voucher (subsidized independent housing) or developmental disability foster home placement. Only when a state-defined "crisis" exists will a residential slot open. Crisis adds "points" for the agency "needs assessment," qualifying the child for a crisis bed or placement slot.

The most common crisis is the medical decline or death of a care-giving parent. Another common crisis is the eviction of the adolescent or adult disabled person from the family home because the disabled child's chaotic (and perhaps aggressive) behavior can no longer be tolerated.

4. Chaotic, Explosive Adolescents/Adults

Parents who have adult children with behavioral problems find that few adult programs will accept them. Explosive, chaotic behaviors might arise in adolescence and continue for many years.

Parents will not usually "lead off" an estate planning discussion by telling the estate planner that they fear their adolescent or adult disabled child. The planner, however, should be alert to the potential problem, and plan for backup fiduciaries and eventual facility care. Family members will burn out from the emotional demands. If the child and parents live together, eventually the shared living situation will become unbearable.

Few residential homes are prepared to deal with aggressive young adults. Because the aggressive disabled adult is likely to have contact with the criminal justice system, an arrest is usually the trigger to entry in a specialized secure residential home, if one exists in the community.

Job or residential placements suitable for a sweet, calm, developmentally disabled young adult will be unsuitable for the young adult with an explosive combination of mental illness, autism, developmental, and cognitive disabilities. Residential care providers will simply refuse to take the young person with difficult behaviors or with "dual diagnosis" (e.g., drug and alcohol problems along with cognitive disabilities).

These chaotic young disabled people (whether minors or age eighteen and over) may live with the parents, causing incredible strain on the family, or live on the streets. Parents cannot rely on the overburdened haphazardly funded public case managers to find a home for a chaotic disabled child.

Many communities have trained care managers who can be privately hired to assist the parents to find residential placement for the disabled adult child. Private care managers are expensive, and prefer not to take on an engagement for an explosive adult disabled child. The special needs trustee might pay for a private advocate to advise the parents about any available services.

When the disabled adult child is aggressive or has frightening behaviors, family members might want to cut off or limit contact. The special needs trust is a critical payment source for private care managers and guardians where family members are "burned out." In these cases, only paid professionals will take on the responsibility of being a trustee, a trust protector, or guardian. In a few states, there may be a state-paid public guardian who can serve as the aggressive adult's guardian of the person or trustee.

D. Special Needs Trust or Support Trust?

Some wealthy parents are very wealthy and expect their wealth to support the disabled child during his or her entire life. The estate planner for these parents will draft full support trusts for the disabled minor child as a receptacle for the inheritance. These parents do not expect their child to apply for needs-based public benefits such as SSI and Medicaid.

Some less wealthy parents know that the child's disabling condition never will permit the child to be self-supporting. The estate planner for these parents always should draft a special needs trust as a receptacle for the inheritance, and thus leverage public benefits.

1. Support HEMS Trust and Disabled Minor Beneficiary

A support trust for a disabled beneficiary can be mandatory, requiring distributions for support, or discretionary, as shown later. In standard drafting, support trust distribution provisions mention "health, education, maintenance, and support"—hence the acronym "HEMS" trust.

- Drafting example (support standard—mandatory)

My trustee shall distribute to or for the benefit of the beneficiary those amounts of income or principal necessary for the beneficiary's health, education, maintenance, and support.

- Drafting example (support standard—fully discretionary)

My trustee may distribute to or for the benefit of the beneficiary those amounts of income or principal which my trustee may determine, in my trustee's sole, absolute and unfettered discretion, to be advisable for the beneficiary's health, education, maintenance, and support.

When the estate planner drafts a HEMS support trust for a disabled beneficiary, the parents need to be advised that there is a risk that state agencies administering publicly funded programs might consider these trusts "available resources," and deny eligibility to their child.

Mandatory support trusts *are* considered available to be spent down for care, because the disabled beneficiary can demand exercise of the trustee's discretion and, thus, has legal access to the funds.

In many states, discretionary support trusts, coupled with spendthrift provisions, are legally protected against beneficiary access and, thus, have not been considered available in all cases. That is, discretionary support trusts funded with inheritances may not automatically disqualify the beneficiary. The legal inquiry focuses on whether the beneficiary can force the trustee to exercise discretion to make support expenditures.

Even if the existence of a HEMS support trust is not per se disqualifying, the pattern of distributions from either the mandatory or discretionary support trust can be "countable income" and violate a program's income eligibility requirements.

2. *Special Needs Trust—Leverages Public Benefits*

The special needs trust (SNT) developed over the past fifty years, because parents of disabled children wanted to both (1) leave an inheritance to help their children and (2) not disqualify the child from needs-based social safety net programs. If the parents cannot afford to self-fund a trust to meet all the disabled child's foreseeable needs, the estate planner should recommend a special needs trust.

The current form of SNT, and state/federal SNT law, reflect the tension between the parents' goals and government's goal to be a good steward of limited taxpayer funds. The taxpayer expects government agencies to require the expensive needs of the disabled child be borne by the family, but the parent wants some funds set aside to give the disabled child a better quality of life.

(a) Testamentary or Inter Vivos Trust

A special needs trust set out in the parent's will is known as a "testamentary" special needs trust. A testamentary trust does not come into being until it is established by probate court order and funded by probate court-ordered distributions or survivorship account beneficiary designation. A better option is a stand-alone special needs trust created inter vivos during the estate planning process. The stand-alone special needs may be nominally funded during estate planning or exist unfunded until a funding event (perhaps the death of the grantor, perhaps an inter vivos gift).

I have come to prefer an inter vivos stand-alone unfunded special needs trust to receive the disabled child's share of the probate/trust assets, survivorship accounts, and life insurance, and attach an illustrative form of that trust at the end of this chapter (see Appendix 7-A). This trust is referred to as a "third-party receptacle trust" or "stand-alone third-party SNT."

When a trust is funded with assets of the individual beneficiary, it is called a "first-party" trust. In the special needs world of disabled minors or adults, if the disabled beneficiary has title or rights to the assets that are funding the SNT, the public agencies disqualify the disabled beneficiary from needs-based benefits unless the "first-party SNT" meets strict drafting rules. The estate planning goal for parents of disabled children is to *avoid* giving assets directly to the child, as then the child will be disqualified from needed public programs. The planner should advise the parent to bypass the disabled child, and send assets directly to the trustee of a properly drafted stand-alone third-party SNT (see, e.g., Appendix 7-A).

(i) North Dakota Prohibits Inter Vivos SNT While Child Is a Minor

However, one state—North Dakota—enacted legislation preventing all parents of minor children from using the third-party receptacle trust *until* the child is an adult.[35] In North Dakota, the parents of a minor beneficiary must use a testamentary special needs trust while their child is a minor. Once the child reaches the age of majority, the North Dakota parents can use a third-party inter vivos stand-alone special needs trust to receive the inheritance.

Both the testamentary and stand-alone special needs trusts direct the trustee to use the trust funds to improve the life of the disabled beneficiary. In the trust, the parents can include a list of the child's special needs. Alternatively, the parents can prepare a separate trustee letter of instructions to guide distributions.

During postmortem probate or trust administration, the trustee collects funds directed to the SNT; establishes a bank account; obtains a tax ID number; and provides a copy of the trust to public benefit agencies.

Public benefit agencies hold a copy of the trust in their files, and may (or may not) review the trust language and request periodic accountings from the trustee. If the beneficiary receives SSI, then the Social Security Administration does review the actual trust language for compliance with its rules. The state agencies and the Social Security Administration may periodically request an accounting for trust distributions from the trustee, to see if there have been disqualifying distributions.

3. *Third Party, Not Self-Settled Trusts*

The testamentary or stand-alone special needs trust are classic "third-party funded" trusts, funded with assets of the parents at death. When funds are directly transferred from the holder (i.e., estate, parents' revocable trust, financial institution, or life insurance company) of the assets to the trustee, the disabled adult child never has legal title or control of the assets. The third-party SNT is *not* a first-party self-settled SNT.

When the disabled child owns the funds going into a special needs trust, that trust is known as a "self-settled" SNT. If the disabled minor or adult child's own funds are transferred to a self-settled trust that is improperly drafted, the corpus remains a disqualifying resource.

Self-settled trusts for disabled minors (or for disabled adults less than sixty-five years of age) are permitted by federal statute but must include certain language and contain a "payback" provision to repay all state Medicaid benefits on termination. These first-party self-settled payback trusts are used as a "fix-it" technique to transfer otherwise countable resources to a protected payback trust.

Federal law[36] permits parents, grandparents, guardians, courts, and a capacitated beneficiary to establish these first-party payback trusts. Usually, these trusts are funded with a disabled person's personal injury settlement or unprotected inheritance. See subsection E, Fix-It Strategies.

4. *Possible Pooled Trust Account*

Some parents direct a disabled minor's inheritance to a pooled special needs trust for management. A pooled trust account may be the best option for the parent who has no suitable relative or friend to manage the disabled child's funds, or leaves an estate too small to interest local bank and professional trustees.

The parent should identify an appropriate pooled trust operated by a nonprofit in his or her community. Before the parent dies, he or she usually establishes a special needs account for the disabled child with that non-profit organization's "pooled trust." The estate planning documents direct the assets to the trustee of that pooled trust. Pooled trust staff are likely to keep up with public benefit program rules and provide expert management.

5. *If Parents Do Not Know (or Do Not Believe) the Child Will Need Benefits*
Some less wealthy parents do not know, one way or the other, whether the disabled minor will eventually support himself. These parents may hope the condition improves, or not expect the disabling condition to prevent the child from working. For the less wealthy parents who are not sure, the estate planner always should include a special needs trust but, perhaps, add a support trust with fiduciary instructions to fund one or the other or both trusts in some proportion.

6. *Three Drafting Suggestions*
All estate planners try to include flexibility provisions to deal with changing conditions. I encourage creating a "back door," allowing fiduciaries to make distributions to a newly created special needs trust, implemented at the time of the funding event. Some practitioners always include an optional special needs trust in all wills and trusts.

(a) Back Door to Create SNT

In all wills and trusts, there is a "manner of distribution" provision that allows the fiduciary (i.e., personal representative or trustee)[37] to choose to make distributions *for* a devisee, heir, or beneficiary who is a minor or disabled. Consider adding additional authority to make distributions to a special needs trust for the entitled person, as follows.

WILL PROVISION

5.3 CHOOSE MANNER OF MAKING DISTRIBUTION. My personal representative may make any distribution in any of the following ways to a devisee, heir, or beneficiary who is a minor, incapacitated, under legal disability, afflicted by a disabling condition, or considered by my personal representative to be unable to handle property if paid to the beneficiary directly, without liability to my personal representative:

5.3 (a) Directly to the beneficiary.

5.3 (b) To the extent permitted by Oregon law, to a custodian for that person under the Oregon Uniform Transfers to Minors Act until the person attains the age of twenty-five years.[38]

5.3 (c) To the beneficiary's guardian, conservator, or any other fiduciary for the beneficiary.

5.3 (d) To any person or organization furnishing health care, education, support, or maintenance.

5.3 (e) To the trustee of a receptacle trust for the lifetime benefit of a beneficiary with a disabling condition and receiving, or likely to receive, public benefits, so long as such trust is a special needs trust, to protect the eligibility of the beneficiary for needs-based public benefits. The remainder beneficiaries of the receptacle trust must be those persons set out in this instrument for that beneficiary's trust or estate distribution, had the beneficiary died before me. I anticipate that the receptacle third party special needs trust will be created at that time by an interested person and funded with the distribution.

TRUST PROVISION

7.8 CHOOSE MANNER OF MAKING DISTRIBUTION. Make any distribution in any of the following ways to a beneficiary who is a minor, incapacitated, under legal disability, or considered by my trustee to be unable to handle property if paid to the beneficiary directly, without liability to my trustee:

7.8(a) Directly to the beneficiary.

7.8(b) To the extent permitted by Oregon law, to a custodian for that person under the Oregon Uniform Transfers to Minors Act until the person attains the age of twenty-five years.

7.8 (c) To the beneficiary's guardian, conservator, or any other fiduciary for the beneficiary.

7.8(d) To any person or organization furnishing health care, education, support, or maintenance.

7.8(e) To the trustee of a receptacle trust for the lifetime benefit of a beneficiary with a disabling condition and receiving, or likely to receive, public benefits, so long as such trust is a special needs trust, to protect the eligibility of the beneficiary for needs-based public benefits. The remainder beneficiaries of the receptacle trust must be the remainder beneficiaries set out in this instrument for that beneficiary's distribution, had the beneficiary died. I anticipate that the receptacle third party special needs trust will be created at that time by an interested person and funded with the distribution.

(b) Both Support Trust and SNT in the Will/RLT.

Some estate planners recommend *always* including a full special needs trust as a distribution option in every will or trust. If this option is selected, the fiduciary needs authority to investigate the circumstances of beneficiaries and make otherwise disqualifying distributions to the special needs trust rather than outright or to a disqualifying support trust.

The fiduciary instructions permitting the personal representative or trustee to elect to send all of part of a distribution to a special needs trust might read as follows:

Authority to Fund Special Needs Trust. My trustee may consider the circumstances of a beneficiary of this Trust at time of distribution and exercise his or her discretion to place all or some portion of a beneficiary's distributive share in a Special Needs Trust for a beneficiary, as described in Article 10 OPTIONAL SPECIAL NEEDS TRUST, for administration according to its terms.

(c) Distribution Standard for Third-Party Special Needs Trust

The estate planner should consult local state bar resources for local "best practices" in drafting special needs trusts. Some states have statutes or administrative practices making a phrase or restriction mandatory for public program eligibility.

SNT distribution language twenty years ago prohibited any distributions that diminished any public benefit programs. Now, practitioners around the country prefer to use a special needs trust distribution clause, which allows the trustee broad discretion to reduce a benefit, such as:

> However, the Trustee may make distributions that diminish government benefits, if the Trustee determines that the distributions will better meet the beneficiary's needs, and are in the beneficiary's best interest, notwithstanding the consequent effect on receipt of benefits. For example, the SSI program rules contemplate that living arrangements where a third party provides in-kind support and maintenance of any value may be allowed, so long as the SSI recipient applies existing rules reducing the cash grant by one-third (the PMV[39] or VTR[40] rules).

For example, the SSI program rules permit a beneficiary to elect a one-third reduction in the monthly SSI check, opening a door to allow the special needs trustee to pay for all housing costs. If the trustee pays a beneficiary's household Internet/cable bill every month, this is not in-kind income in the SSI program, but will reduce the HUD housing Section 8 rent subsidy slightly. After careful investigation, these benefit reductions can be carefully crafted, if the trustee has discretion to reduce benefits, so the overall effect is not to lose the SSI and linked Medicaid completely, or the HUD housing voucher completely.

Article 7 of the illustrative special needs trust in Appendix 7-A contains this preferred flexible distribution authority.

E. Fix-It Strategies

1. Disqualifying Assets

A minor disabled child may own family limited partnership or limited liability corporation interests, or be the beneficiary of UTMA accounts, or have securities or bank accounts in his or her own name. Wealthy grandparents routinely make nontaxable annual exclusion gifts[41] to all grandchildren, including the disabled minor.

The estate planner also should review any wills or trusts that now, or in the future, are intended to benefit the disabled minor. Any outright distributions to the disabled minor will be disqualifying resources. A HEMS support trust, whether discretionary or mandatory, does not work well with a beneficiary's needs-based public benefits. Irrevocable gift or life insurance trusts will give the disabled child Crummey[42] withdrawal powers—and failure to exercise the withdrawal right is a disqualifying transfer by needs-based government program rules.

If the estate planner uncovers these accounts/gifts/trusts/Crummey powers for disabled minors, then ask whether these assets will disqualify the child from desired public benefits. If so, the planner should advise the family about fix-it strategies.

An UTMA account custodian cannot simply give away the disqualifying account to other family members. Gifts of the child's assets are a breach of fiduciary duty, and transfers or gifts by the child cause a gift disqualification period in both the SSI and Medicaid programs. Perhaps the UTMA account funds can be spent down before the minor child needs SSI and Medicaid or other needs-based programs. A court may permit the UTMA account custodian to transfer the funds (up to the annual contribution limit, $15,000 in 2018) to a new ABLE account.

When disabled minors are beneficiaries of irrevocable life insurance or gift trusts, the trustee can modify or amend the trust (if permitted by the instrument, or by state trust law) to (1) remove the disabled beneficiary from required Crummey notices, and (2) substitute a special needs trust for the existing discretionary or mandatory HEMS support trust.

Relatives can change their revocable trusts and wills to remove outright distributions to the disabled minor. They can add a special needs trust for the disabled minor's share to their revocable trust or will, or simply distribute the disabled minor's share to a new stand-alone special needs trust.

2. *Payback Special Needs Trust—42 U.S.C. § 1396p(d)(4)(A)*

The most common fix-it strategy is a payback special needs trust, employed where the beneficiary is already receiving needs-based public benefits and the disqualifying assets are discovered or the assets are about to be distributed to the disabled child. The payback special needs trust technique can maintain public benefit eligibility.

Federal and state laws permit otherwise disqualifying resources to be placed in a new special needs trust, created by the parent, guardian, disabled beneficiary (if he has capacity) or court, with required provisions including payback of Medicaid upon termination of the trust.[43] Because the disabled person's own assets are placed in the payback trust, it is sometimes referred to as a "first-party" or "self-settled" trust.

Many disabled minors are not yet receiving any needs-based public benefits. Most programs "deem" the parents' income and resources to the minor child until age eighteen, making the minor child ineligible for services. The estate planner for younger children flags the need for a payback trust at age eighteen, and brings the parents to establish the payback trust when the child nears age eighteen. Filing to appoint an adult guardian of the person is coupled with a petition to appoint a guardian of the estate to establish and fund the payback special needs trust.

The particulars of payback trust establishment and funding will vary from state to state. Most state bar associations have continuing legal education (CLE) materials describing how these trusts are created and funded. In many states, the parents petition the local probate court to appoint a guardian of the estate to establish and fund the payback trust, with notice to the local state Medicaid agency.

If the state bar resources are not up to date or clear, or no sample pleadings and form of payback trust are provided, then the estate planner can find excellent training and forms for payback special needs planning from ElderCounsel LLC, a membership organization; the Academy of Special Needs Planners, a membership organization; and the annual Stetson University's National Conference on Special Needs Planning.

3. Fixing Disqualifying Trusts

If existing trusts for which the child is a beneficiary will disqualify the child for public benefits, then those trusts should be fixed. If the minor receives no public benefits, the planner should warn the parents about the disqualifying mandatory distribution, withdrawal, and/or support standard problems, so they can determine whether (and when) to fix these disqualifying trusts.

Revocable trusts are easily amended or restated, if the grantor has capacity. But if the revocable trust grantor is incapacitated, and the trust instrument does not permit amendment by his or her agent under power of attorney, then fixing the trust will be more complicated. Irrevocable trusts are sometimes drafted with flexibility built in, to deal with changes in circumstances.

The trust may allow modification by an independent trust protector, or contain broad decanting authority, permitting the trustee or a trust protector decant the corpus to a trust better suited to the situation. But some trusts contain no such built-in flexibility, and then the clients must consider state law permitting trust modification or reformation, and if those do not work, trust termination.

Where the trust corpus is relatively modest, the quickest fix-it strategy might be to file a petition to terminate the trust and transfer the corpus to a newly established payback SNT. In some states, this will require two petitions: one in equity to terminate the trust, and a second in the probate court to establish the SNT and fund it with the corpus of the terminated trust.

(a) Trust Modification?—Transfer Penalty Problem

Under most state laws, modifying an irrevocable trust requires notice to, and consent by, the affected beneficiary. Public benefit programs analyze trust changes as disqualifying transfers, if the beneficiary consents to a change that makes the trust corpus suddenly unavailable. If your state's process for modifying trusts requires consent by the beneficiary, then by letting the trust modification proceed, the beneficiary incurs a disqualification period penalty for refusing to accept available resources.

The Medicaid program has a five-year lookback period to examine transfers. If the disabled minor applies for Medicaid benefits within five years of giving consent to a trust termination, then he will be asked about any transfers within the past five years. Failing to disclose the trust modification subjects him (or his authorized representative filling out the application) to criminal fraud charges.

The trust modification within five years before the Medicaid application will trigger a penalty disqualification period. The larger the trust corpus, the longer the penalty period will be. The penalty period begins when the applicant is otherwise eligible for Medicaid and goes forward.

If the disabled minor is currently receiving Medicaid or SSI (possible before age eighteen if the parents are low income or parental income/ resources are not deemed for some special program), then the minor's consent (usually through a parent or court-ordered representative) to trust modification causes an immediate disqualification penalty. A program recipient's failure to pursue an available resource is analyzed as a disqualifying transfer in most needs-based programs, including Medicaid.

(b) Trust Reformation for Unanticipated Circumstances or Scriveners Error

Most states permit trust reformation for unanticipated circumstances or scriveners error. The trustee petitions the court to change the trust, describing the testator's intent, the unanticipated circumstances (here, the disability of the beneficiary), or the error of the drafting lawyer in failing to include a special needs trust despite being told of the minor's disabling condition.

Trust reformation occurs without consent of the disabled beneficiary, so no transfer penalty should be imposed. But setting up the factual basis for the court to find unanticipated circumstances or an attorney error may not be easy.

(c) Trust Termination, Then Transfer Corpus to New Payback SNT

The simplest way to fix the disqualifying irrevocable trust is to seek court permission to terminate the trust, and then to transfer the corpus to a new payback 42 U.S.C. § 1396p(d)(4)(A) special needs trust. When this is done for trusts involving a minor, two petitions are filed: one to terminate the trust and one to appoint a guardian of the estate (conservator) for the minor to consent to the termination. The petition further requests the court permit establishment of a new payback trust and asks court authority to fund that new trust with the old trust corpus.

The minor's legal representative consents to the termination and the transfer to the payback trust, but this consent triggers no disqualification because the receptacle is the protected payback special needs trust. There is a no-penalty consent to change a trust, and no-penalty transfer to the new special needs trust.

F. Additional Drafting Suggestions

1. Nomination of Guardian of the Person and of the Estate
All parents of minor children nominate a guardian of the person and guardian of the estate (called a conservator in some states) in their estate planning documents. These fiduciaries manage the minor child's residential and medical care matters, and financial matters for assets outside a trust or custodial account arrangement, until a child becomes an adult. These

nominations are a routine part of a parent's will or trust. Often, but not always, the same person serves in both personal and financial roles.

Parents of *disabled* minor children may select different nominees for disabled and nondisabled children. Often, the same person is *not* able to handle both personal and financial decision making for the disabled child. The parents know that the person they select may serve for long after the child reaches age eighteen, if the child is cognitively disabled. Naming contingent guardians is wise, and the nomination should reference any formal written recommendations the parent has created describing how the child should live.

For example, the drafter can consider:

> Should a guardian be necessary for my disabled child [NAME OF CHILD] during minority or later during any period of adult incapacity, then I nominate [FIRST NOMINEE] to serve. If [FIRST NOMINEE] is unavailable or unwilling to serve, then I nominate [SECOND NOMINEE]. I have created Recommendations for the guardian, as allowed by ORS 125.425, to guide the guardian in the exercise of his or her fiduciary discretion.

> Should a guardian of the estate (conservator) be necessary for my disabled child [NAME OF CHILD] during minority or during any period of adult incapacity, then I nominate [FIRST NOMINEE] to serve. If [FIRST NOMINEE] is unavailable or unwilling to serve, then I nominate [SECOND NOMINEE]. I ask that the nominee heed my Recommendations, as required by ORS 125.425, in the exercise of fiduciary discretion.

(i) Parent's Recommendations for Disabled Child

Parents hope their disabled child has a good life. Most disability advocacy organizations encourage parents to set out their recommendations and expectations in writing.

Estate planners ask parents of disabled minors to write recommendations to guide guardians, and especially trustees. These parental recommendations are valuable guides for trustee discretion in administering mandatory support, discretionary or special needs trusts. Should a remainder beneficiary, financial service company, or corporate trust department perhaps prefer to keep funds under management, rather than make useful distributions, personal advocates for the disabled beneficiary can refer to the parent's recommendations when advocating for the child.

Oregon law requires that a court-appointed fiduciary consider "recommendations relating to the appropriate standard of support, education, care and benefit for the protected person made by any parent or guardian of the protected person." ORS 125.425 This statutory protection may be available in your state. To make sure fiduciaries *know* to look for recommendations, and pay attention, mention the recommendations in the will or trust, as shown below.

The following drafting suggestion, included in a full support trust for a disabled daughter, directs the trustee to be guided by the parent's written recommendations.

INTENT OF PARENT. My daughter is disabled, but capable of a high order of functioning, and can contribute to her community by volunteer work. After my death, I will not be there to watch personally over my daughter, so I have arranged this full support trust for her to be funded if my personal representative deems it appropriate, and the corpus is then to be spent down for her. I ask my trustee to exercise his or her distribution authority so that the beneficiary's everyday life includes companionship, stimulating activities, and quality experiences. I intend to leave written Recommendations to guide the trustee in understanding my daughter's character and needs, as the trustee exercises his or her discretionary distribution authority.

2. *Financial Power of Attorney—Parent of Disabled Child*

A parent's incapacity or decline disrupts the day-to-day routine of the disabled child. The parent's basic incapacity management document, his or her financial power of attorney, can be drafted to protect the disabled child. These provisions will vary, depending on the child's needs and the parent's wealth and resources, but usually include authority to

- support the parent,
- pay for special needs of the disabled child,
- create trusts for the disabled child, and
- fund trusts for the disabled child.

After incapacity, the parent's agent might be able to both pay for the parent's needed care and continue a prior pattern of special needs assistance to the disabled child. Some disabled adults can live outside facilities, using their Disabled Adult Children Social Security checks and limited earnings to support themselves with family help. If the parent can afford to both pay his or her own long-term care and fully support the disabled child, the power of attorney should so instruct the agent.

Consider the following circumstances: a widower client with two working adult developmentally disabled sons who shared an apartment. The elderly father met them weekly, helped with shopping, and gave them funds. There were no needs-based programs to be harmed by the father's support expenditures, so long as the brothers lived outside facilities and worked part-time, so this client's financial power of attorney provided authority to the agent as follows:

To make expenditures, in the event of my incapacity, for my care, maintenance, support, and general welfare, and for the support of my two developmentally disabled working sons, for so long as they can live independently outside a facility, and should they become unable to live independently, then to make expenditures for the supplemental needs of my two disabled sons RANDALL C. JONES and GEORGE W. JONES.

I consider the task of managing care and overseeing care/service providers to be very important to my quality of life, and to the quality of life for my two disabled sons, and I encourage my agent to hire a care manager who can both assist with my care and supervise the care and continued independent living of my two disabled sons."

Many elder law attorneys are familiar with the pre-Medicaid application "permitted transfer" to a disabled child. Should a client become so ill that he or she needs expensive facility-level long-term care, then family resources are quickly exhausted. The agent under power of attorney could, on the parent's behalf, transfer assets to the healthy spouse or a disabled child without triggering Medicaid transfer penalties.

The power of attorney can authorize both creation and funding of a special needs trust for the disabled child. An agent with specific authority to create and fund trusts for disabled children can consider a pre-Medicaid transfer strategy, should it seem the grantor might need long-term care and exhaust all resources on his or her own care, leaving nothing for the disabled child.

Your standard trust creation authority provision can be tweaked as in the following illustration for a single parent who gives his agent authority to create and fund a special needs trust:

Trust Powers.

(a) To amend or terminate any existing trust and to establish an irrevocable or revocable trust for my benefit, or for the benefit of my disabled son JOHN P. JONES, provided that the trust amendment, termination or establishment is consistent with my then existing estate plan to the extent reasonably possible, and also to transfer assets to any such revocable or irrevocable trust which may be then created, or which I have established prior to this time, or may establish in the future, or which at that time is established by my agent. If a trust is established and funded for my disabled son, I suggest the trust be a special needs trust to protect his public benefits.

(b) To withdraw assets from my revocable living trust for my benefit, and place those assets in my name, without breach of fiduciary duty and with my full prior consent to this exercise of my reserved power to withdraw assets from the revocable trust.

NOTES

1. *See* Reg. §§ 20.2041-1(c)(2), 25.2514-1(c)(2). *See also* Chapter 3.
2. COBRA is shorthand for "Consolidated Omnibus Budget Reconciliation Act." The Consolidated Omnibus Budget Reconciliation Act of 1985 (Pub. L. No. 99-272) amended certain acts of Congress "to require group health plans to provide a temporary continuation of group health coverage that otherwise might be terminated." *See* https://www.dol.gov/sites/default/files/ebsa/about-ebsa/our-activities/resource-center/faqs/cobra-continuation-health-coverage-consumer.pdf.
3. *See* note 2.
4. *See* 42 U.S.C. § 18001 *et seq.* The ACA is informally referred to as Obamacare.
5. *See* note 2.
6. *See* note 2.
7. *See* 42 U.S.C. § 1396 *et seq.*
8. *See also* Chapter 4.

9. *See* Chapters 6 and 9.
10. *See* Chapters 3 and 4.
11. *See* note 7.
12. *See* note 4.
13. *See* note 2.
14. *See* note 4.
15. *See* 42 U.S.C. § 1396n (k).
16. *See* www.kff.org/medicaid/state-indicator/section-1915k-community-first -choice-state-plan-option.
17. *See* Chapters 3 and 9.
18. *See* Chapters 6 and 9.
19. Pub. L. No. 113-295.
20. *See* Chapter 5.
21. *See* Chapters 1 and 3.
22. The rollover cannot exceed the annual exclusion amount. *See* I.R.C. § 529(c)(3)(C)(i) (flush language), referencing I.R.C. § 529A(b)(2)(B)(i). The annual exclusion amount is indexed for inflation. *See* Chapter 1.
23. I.R.C. § 529(c)(3)(C)(i)(III) (pertaining to qualified tuition programs).
24. *See* I.R.C. § 529A(b)(2)(B)(ii). The Internal Revenue Service announced it will be issuing proposed regulations clarifying the new contribution limits and providing guidance in the interim. *See* Notice 2018-62; 2018-34 I.R.B. 1 (Aug. 3, 2018), *available at* www.irs.gov/pub/irs-drop/n-18-62.pdf. *See also* www.irs.gov/government -entities/federal-state-local-governments/able-accounts-tax-benefit-for-people-with -disabilities.
25. I.R.C. § 529A(e)(5).
26. *See* Chapters 3 and 9.
27. *See* Chapters 6 and 9.
28. *See* Chapters 6 and 9.
29. *See* Chapter 8.
30. Restatement (Second) of Trusts § 154 (1959).
31. Restatement (Second) of Trusts § 128 cmts. d, e (1959).
32. *See* Chapters 6 and 9.
33. *See* 42 U.S.C § 1383c(c).
34. *See* SSA POMS SI 01110.003, Resource Limits for SSI benefits.
35. N.D. Cent. Code ch. 59-08, Trusts for Individuals with Disabilities, defines, in part, the "third party special needs trust" as a trust created and "funded by someone other than the trust beneficiary, the beneficiary's spouse, a parent of a minor beneficiary." *See* N.D. Cent. Code § 59-08-01.3.
36. N.D. Cent. Code § 1396p(d)(4)(A).
37. *See* Chapter 9.
38. *See* Chapter 9.
39. PMV, in social security parlance, is "presumed maximum value." *See* https:// secure.ssa.gov/poms.nsf/lnx/0500835200 (referring to PMV).
40. VTR, in social security parlance, is "value of the one-third reduction." *See* social security one-third reduction provision at https://secure.ssa.gov/poms.nsf /lnx/0500835200.
41. *See* Chapters 1 and 3.
42. *See* Chapter 3.
43. *See* 42 U.S.C. § 1396p(d)(4)(A).

APPENDIX 7-A

Illustrative Form:
Stand-alone Third-Party Special Needs Trust

THIS FORM IS PRESENTED FOR ILLUSTRATION ONLY AND IS NOT WAR-
RANTED FOR USE IN ANY PARTICULAR SITUATION.

THE PRACTITIONER DRAFTING SPECIAL NEEDS TRUSTS SHOULD BE FAMIL-
IAR WITH THE PUBLIC BENEFITS USED, OR REASONABLY EXPECTED IN THE
FUTURE, BY A PROPOSED TRUST BENEFICIARY, AND:

(1) DISTRIBUTION STANDARDS ACCEPTABLE TO PUBLIC BENEFIT AGENCIES
IN HIS OR HER STATE;

(2) ANY STATUTE, ADMINISTRATIVE RULES, or AGENCY PRACTICES REGARD-
ING SPECIAL NEEDS TRUSTS IN HIS OR HER STATE;

(3) SOCIAL SECURITY PROGRAM OPERATING MANUAL SYSTEM (POMS) PRO-
VISIONS ABOUT TRUSTS, AND ANY POMS TRUST SECTIONS SPECIFIC TO HIS
OR HER REGION;

(4) THE BUDGET-DRIVEN RESTRICTIONS BEING PROPOSED FOR PUBLIC
BENEFIT PROGRAMS IN HIS OR HER STATE.

JANET L. JONES GIFT SPECIAL NEEDS TRUST

DATE OF TRUST: December 12, 2017
[Date of Execution]

Paul J. Jones, Trustee
[Address]

For the Benefit of

JANET L. JONES, Beneficiary
Tax Identification Number
Of Trust: **Not to Be Obtained Until Trust Funded**
Until Funding, Tax Identification Number of Trust:
000 00 0000
SS# of Grantor Paul J. Jones

Prepared by:
[Name, Address, Telephone, Email of Attorney]

JANET L. JONES GIFT SPECIAL NEEDS TRUST

SETTLOR/GRANTOR OF TRUST: **PAUL J. JONES**
TRUSTEE: **PAUL J. JONES**
Date of Trust: December ____, 2017

THIS TRUST AGREEMENT is established by PAUL J. JONES for the benefit of JANET L. JONES, and the initial trustee will be PAUL J. JONES, hereinafter referred to as Trustee.

JANET L. JONES is a disabled person as defined in the Social Security Act [42 U.S.C. Section 1382c (a) (3)], and is hereinafter referred to as Beneficiary, and the beneficiary's Social Security Number is 111-11-1111. *Add reference to child's Social Security benefits, if any, at time trust executed: i.e. JANET L. JONES receives Supplemental Security Income (SSI) from the Social Security Administration.*

The effective date of this Trust Agreement shall be the date of execution, that is, December____, 2017.

ARTICLE 1
TRUST NAME; TRUSTEE; RELATIVES

1.1   NAME OF TRUST. This trust shall be known as the JANET L. JONES GIFT SPECIAL NEEDS TRUST. This trust is established by, and will be funded with, assets of the PAUL J. JONES, the settlor and grantor [*and may also receive gifts from other family members*].

1.2   DESIGNATION OF TRUSTEE. PAUL J. JONES is the initial Trustee of this trust, and is hereinafter referred to as Trustee. For purposes of transfers to trust, beneficiary designations, and formal correspondence, the trust shall be referred to as:

"PAUL J. JONES, TRUSTEE, JANET L. JONES GIFT SPECIAL NEEDS TRUST u/t/d December ____, 2017."

1.3   RELATIVES OF BENEFICIARY. The beneficiary, JANET L. JONES, is not married, and has no children or other descendants. The beneficiary's closest relatives are her father PAUL J. JONES and mother DORA A. JONES. Her sisters are KELLI D. JONES, YVONNE J. BOWMAN, and DOREEN J. JONES.

1.4   REVOCABLE TRUST; IRREVOCABLE AT PAUL J. JONES'S DEATH. This trust will be revocable during the lifetime of grantor and settlor PAUL J. JONES, but will become irrevocable at PAUL J. JONES' death. The trust may be funded during the settlor's life with his assets (and assets of the mother or other relatives), and at death of PAUL J. JONES or DORA A. JONES the trust will receive further funds from their estate or beneficiary/survivor accounts and insurance policies. **This trust is NOT intended to be funded with retirement account assets**.

ARTICLE 2
TRUST ESTATE

2.1   INITIAL FUNDING. **The Trust may be initially funded with $100.00 contributed by PAUL J. JONES, if he elects to set up a trust bank account now or at any time prior to his death. This trust is intended to be primarily funded at death of PAUL J. JONES**. Such property, together with any additions acceptable to the Trustee made by PAUL J. JONES and any other party for the benefit of the Beneficiary, together with any income and other accruals received on this corpus, shall constitute the Trust Estate. Any property acquired by the Trust must be titled solely in the name of the Trust.

2.2 ADDITIONAL PROPERTY. Should any person or the Beneficiary later wish to add additional assets to the Trust, such a transfer must be considered in light of the law on transfers at that time, and may or may not be accepted by the Trustee. The Trustee shall have sole discretion to accept, refuse or disclaim additions to the Trust from any source. Upon acceptance by the Trustee, the added property shall become subject to this agreement. Any property transferred to Trustee by PAUL J. JONES or a third party is a gift to the Trust and cannot be reclaimed by the third party. Any property acquired by the Trust must be titled solely in the name of the Trust.

2.3 QUALIFIED DISABILITY TRUST. The Settlor intends to create a qualified disability trust under 42 U.S.C. §1396p(c) (2) (B) (iv) and 26 U.S.C. §642(b) (2) (C) for the benefit of a disabled individual under the age of 65 years at time of establishment of the trust.

ARTICLE 3
PURPOSE OF TRUST

The sole beneficiary of this Trust shall be JANET L. JONES. The purpose of this Trust is to provide for the satisfaction of the disabled Beneficiary's special and supplemental care while still maintaining the Beneficiary's eligibility for public benefits such as the Supplemental Social Security Income program (SSI), the Medicaid program, and any additional, similar, or successor programs. In the administration of the Trust, Trustee shall make reasonable efforts to maintain the Beneficiary's eligibility for public benefits. The Trustee may supplement but may not completely supplant services, benefits, and medical care available to the Beneficiary through any governmental or private sources. In view of the vast costs involved in caring for a disabled person, a direct distribution would be rapidly dissipated.

ARTICLE 4
REVOCABLE INITIALLY, THEN IRREVOCABLE TRUST

This trust is revocable, and may be altered, amended, terminated, or modified by Grantor PAUL J. JONES during the Grantor's lifetime. These rights are personal to the grantor, and may not be exercised by any person other than an agent of PAUL J. JONES expressly authorized to exercise these trust powers under a financial power of attorney.

This Trust shall become irrevocable after the death of PAUL J. JONES.

The life beneficiary JANET L. JONES shall have no right or power, whether alone or in conjunction with others, in whatever capacity, to alter, amend, revoke or terminate this Trust Agreement, in whole or in part, or to designate the persons who shall possess or enjoy the Trust Estate. After the trust becomes irrevocable, the Trustee (who may never be the same person as the life beneficiary) is given the power to amend the Trust, as set forth below.

ARTICLE 5
COOPERATION REGARDING BENEFITS ELIGIBILITY

The Trustee should cooperate with the Beneficiary, the Beneficiary's conservator, guardian, or legal representative to seek support and maintenance for the Beneficiary from all available resources, including publicly funded programs and privately funded programs operated to benefit those with disabilities such as those disabilities experienced by this Trust beneficiary.

In determining whether the existence of this Trust has the effect of rendering the Beneficiary ineligible for any program of public benefits, the Trustee may in the exercise of his or her discretion initiate either administrative or judicial proceedings, or both, for determining eligibility, including initiating proceedings to modify this Trust. All costs relating thereto, including reasonable attorney fees, shall be charged to the Trust.

The Trustee is directed to defend, at the expense of the Trust, all contest or attacks of any nature against the Trust.

ARTICLE 6
PREFERENTIAL RIGHTS OF LIFE BENEFICIARY

The rights of the life Beneficiary, JANET L. JONES, are preferred to the rights of any Beneficiary who takes after the life Beneficiary's death. The Trustee may exercise his or her discretion so as to distribute all income and/or principal of the Trust to accomplish the purpose of providing for the supplemental care of the life Beneficiary, thereby giving preference to the interests of JANET L. JONES over the interests of the Remainder Beneficiary (ies).

ARTICLE 7
DISTRIBUTIONS DURING LIFE OF JANET L. JONES

7.1   DISTRIBUTIONS DURING BENEFICIARY'S LIFETIME

7.1.1 *Discretionary Distributions*: During the lifetime of JANET L. JONES, the Trustee may distribute from the principal or income, or both, of this Trust such amounts which the Trustee, in the Trustee's sole, absolute and unfettered discretion, may from time to time deem reasonable or advisable for JANET L. JONES's Special Needs. Any income of the Trust not so distributed shall be added annually to principal.

7.1.2 *No Control*: The Beneficiary shall have no control over the Trust pursuant to POMS SI 01120.200 B 10.

7.1.3 *No Trust Revocation or Termination*: JANET L. JONES shall have no right to revoke or terminate this Trust.

7.1.4 *Preference*: JANET L. JONES is the sole beneficiary and the beneficiary's interests shall be given priority over the interests of any remainder beneficiaries.

7.1.5 *Supplement but Not Supplant Assistance*: This trust is a supplemental fund for the benefit of the Beneficiary and is not intended to completely displace any assistance that might otherwise be available to the Beneficiary from any governmental and/or private program. The Trustee may supplement such other program sources, but the Trustee should not make distributions that completely supplant services, benefits or medical care that are otherwise available to the Beneficiary from the government programs for which my disabled child may be eligible. However, the Trustee may make distributions that diminish government benefits, if the Trustee determines that the distributions will better meet the beneficiary's needs, and are in the beneficiary's best interest, notwithstanding the consequent effect on receipt of benefits. For example, the SSI program rules contemplate that living arrangements where a third party provides in-kind support and maintenance of any value may be allowed, so long as the SSI recipient applies existing rules reducing the cash grant by one-third (the PMV or VTR rules).

7.1.6 *Supplemental Needs Savings Clause* In the event that the mere existence of the authority to make distributions that will impair or diminish receipt of, or eligibility for, public benefits, regardless of whether the Trustee actually exercises that authority, then that authority will be null and void, such authority will terminate, and the discretion of the trustee will be limited to distributions for supplemental needs in a manner that will not adversely affect public benefits.

7.2 DISTRIBUTION OF EXEMPT ASSETS AND TRANSFER TO BENEFICIARY

The Trustee may, in the Trustee's sole and absolute discretion, purchase and distribute to the beneficiary items that would be considered "exempt" assets for purposes of public benefit law, such as personal household items, transportation devices, medical equipment, or a home. Once distributed to the beneficiary, such items are free of trust and the Trustee need not further account for the distributed items; the Trustee should report such exempt asset distributions in the next regular accounting.

7.3 SPECIAL NEEDS

As used in this instrument, "special needs" refers to the requisites for maintaining JANET L. JONES' good health, safety and welfare when, in the discretion of Trustee, such requisites are not being provided by any governmental agency, office or department, non-profit organizations, or are not otherwise being provided by any other public or private source. While Trustee is authorized to consider these other sources, and where appropriate and to the extent possible endeavor to maximize the collection of such benefits and to facilitate distribution of such benefits for the benefit of JANET L. JONES, the Trustee may also, in the exercise of his or her discretion, disregard these other sources when making distributions to, or for the benefit of, JANET L. JONES.

ARTICLE 8
EXAMPLES OF SUPPLEMENTAL DISTRIBUTIONS

Examples of distributions for the benefit of JANET L. JONES which are not required, but which may be appropriate, as consistent with the terms of this Trust, and pursuant to 42 U.S.C. §1382a; 20 C.F.R. §§416.1100,1121, and 1141; POMS S.I. 01120.201.I, include:

- *Transportation including the cost of taxi, bus passes*
- *Clothing including good walking shoes*
- *Telecommunication and television expenses, including telephone, computer and/or cable equipment and services*
- *Cost of periodic outings and entertainment expenses (i.e., birthday, holiday celebration, movie tickets, musical events, video or DVD rental, etc.)*
- *Hair and nail care and supplies*
- *Private case management to assist the Beneficiary, or to aid the Trustee in the Trustee's duties*
- *Fees and costs for protective proceedings, including the existing guardianship and conservatorship, or criminal proceedings*
- *Drug and/or alcohol treatment*
- *Over-the-counter medications or personal care products helpful to relieve discomfort and/or increase the quality of life*
- *Nutritional supplements*
- *Computer equipment & supplies*
- *Furniture and household items including comfortable bed and bedding*
- *Tuition for classes; books and course materials*
- *Transportation costs, including bus passes*
- *Pet care and veterinary bills & medications*
- *Medical, dental or diagnostic treatment, including experimental treatment, for which there are not funds otherwise available (for example, the treatment may not be deemed "medically necessary" by the medical care review mechanisms in public or private benefit/insurance systems, or there may be too few providers willing to accept the Medicaid or Medicare reimbursement rate for their medical services, so that access to a provider is effectively impossible, or substantially delayed)*
- *Magazine or newspaper subscriptions*
- *Preparation of personal tax returns*
- *Eye exams and necessary treatment and glasses*
- *Travel expenses*

Prior to the death of JANET L. JONES, the Trustee shall give special consideration to paying any outstanding expenses of administration related to the Trust, including reasonable attorneys' fees, and should further consider purchasing a reasonable burial plan to pay expenses relating to the funeral of JANET L. JONES.

This list is intended to be illustrative and not inclusive of all kinds of non-support disbursements that may be appropriate for the Trustee, in his or her sole discretion, to make.

ARTICLE 9
SPENDTHRIFT/NONASSIGNMENT

9.1   PROTECTIVE PROVISIONS

This Trust is a purely discretionary non-support spendthrift trust. None of the principal or income of the trust estate or any interest therein shall be anticipated, assigned, encumbered, or subject to any creditors' claims or to any legal process. This Trust and its corpus are to be used only for the supplemental care of the Beneficiary. No part of the Trust Estate shall be construed to be part of the Beneficiary's estate, or be subject to the voluntary or involuntary creditors of the Beneficiary. No Beneficiary shall have the power to sell, assign, transfer, encumber, or in any other manner anticipate or dispose of the Beneficiary's interest in the Trust or the income produced thereby, prior to its actual distribution by the Trustee for the benefit of the Beneficiary in the manner authorized by this agreement. No Beneficiary shall have any assignable interest in any trust created under this agreement or in the income therefrom. Neither the principal nor the income shall be liable for any debts of the Beneficiary. The limitations herein shall not restrict the exercise of any power of appointment or disclaimer.

9.2   CLAIMS OF PROVIDER OF SERVICES

Because this Trust is to be conserved and maintained entirely for the special care needs of JANET L. JONES above and beyond what public benefits JANET L. JONES may receive, no part of the trust estate shall be construed as available to JANET L. JONES, or as part of the Beneficiary's estate, or be subject to claims for the provision of care and services, including residential care, by any private or public entity, office, department or agency of any state, or of the United States or any other governmental agency. The Trustee shall deny any request by any public or private entity to disburse trust funds for support or other care that such entity has the obligation to provide to the Trust Beneficiary.

9.3   NO SUPPORT OF DEPENDENTS

The Trustee shall in no event make distributions for the support of JANET L. JONES's dependents, and this Trust is not available for such dependent support.

ARTICLE 10
TERMINATION; DISTRIBUTION

10.1 TERMINATION

The Trust shall terminate upon the first to happen of the following events: the trust fund becomes too small to justify the expenses of administration, or the death of JANET L. JONES.

10.1 (a) TERMINATION OF UNECONOMIC TRUST/EARLY TER-MINATION. During the lifetime of the beneficiary JANET L. JONES, if the Trustee concludes that the trust fund no longer contains enough assets to justify its continued administration (an uneconomic trust), the Trust may be terminated.

Upon early termination of an uneconomic trust, Trustee may pay:

(i) All taxes due from the Trust to the State(s) or Federal Government due to the termination of the Trust,

(ii) Reasonable fees and administrative expenses associated with the termination of the Trust, and

(iii) After payment of aforementioned taxes, fees, and expenses, the Trustee shall distribute any remaining trust assets to or for the benefit of JANET L. JONES. No person or entity other than the Trust beneficiary may benefit from the early termination [after payment of taxes and administrative expenses outlined above.

10.1 (b) TERMINATION ON DEATH OF JANET L. JONES. On termination because of the death of JANET L. JONES, Trustee may pay:

(i) All taxes due from the Trust to the State(s) or Federal Government due to the termination of the Trust, or because of the death of JANET L. JONES, and

(ii) Reasonable fees and administrative expenses associated with the termination of the Trust, including legal fees and any costs or fees associated with the preparation of final accountings or making any distributions provided for herein. Such taxes, administrative expenses and costs attendant to terminating or settling this Trust shall be paid first out of the Trust's income and then out of principal.

10.2 ADMINISTRATION ON TERMINATION.

Trustee is encouraged to obtain professional help in terminating the trust and preparing any final account. The cost of such professional help shall be paid from the Trust assets as an administrative expense.

10.3 RESIDUARY TRUST ESTATE. After due administration, the remainder and residue of the trust estate, if any, shall be distributed to a group consisting of YVONNE J. BOWMAN, DOREEN J. JONES, and the trustee of the KELLI D. JONES GIFT SPECIAL NEEDS TRUST for the benefit of the disabled sister KELLI D. JONES, in equal shares, share and share alike, and if a sister does not then survive, to that sister's descendants by right of representation per stirpes. If a sister has died before distribution, leaving no descendants, then her gift lapses and her share passes to the other member of the group.

The remainder beneficiaries are referred to as "residual beneficiaries" in the Social Security Administration program operation manual system (POMS) regarding trusts.

10.4 DISTRIBUTION AND TAX ELECTIONS OF TRUSTEE. The Trustee has absolute discretion to make distribution in cash or in specific property, and to cause any share to be composed of property different in kind from any other share, and to make prorata and non-prorata distributions, without regard to any difference in tax basis of the property and without the requirement of making any adjustments among the remaindermen. The Trustee shall have the sole discretion to claim any tax deductions useful to the taxation of the Trust and to make any other election or decision available under any federal and state tax laws, regardless of the effect on any Beneficiary or on any interest passing under this Trust or outside this Trust, with or without adjustment between income and principal among beneficiaries.

10.5 TERMINATION IF NO TRUST BENEFICIARY. If at any time there remains no named or described Beneficiary of this Trust, the Trustee shall distribute the remainder of the Trust as provided in this article, as if JANET L. JONES had died.

10.6 RULE AGAINST PERPETUITIES. Despite any other provision of this instrument, 21 years after the death of the Grantor and the Grantor's lineal descendants, if any, living at the time this agreement is no longer amendable or revocable:

10.6 (a) All powers of appointment not irrevocably exercised shall terminate.

10.6 (b) All unsatisfied conditions precedent to the exercise of any power of appointment shall be deemed to have become impossible to satisfy.

10.6 (c) All interests and trusts created under the terms of this agreement, unless earlier vested or terminated, shall terminate. At the time of the termination, all trust property shall be distributed free of trust to those persons then entitled to distributions of income in the manner and proportions herein stated (equally if not stated), irrespective of their ages.

ARTICLE 11
TRUSTEE SUCCESSION AND REMOVAL

11.1 SUCCESSOR TRUSTEES. If the original Trustee, **PAUL J. JONES**, resigns, then **DORA A. JONES** shall serve as trustee, and if **DORA A. JONES** is not available to serve, fails to qualify as trustee, or ceases to act, then **YVONNE J. BOWMAN** shall serve as trustee, and if she is not available, then the person **YVONNE J. BOWMAN** nominates shall serve as trustee. Should none of the successor trustees named above be available or willing to serve, then MARTIN A. DISHMAN, the uncle of the beneficiary, may nominate a successor trustee (or elect to serve as successor trustee himself, and also nominate a successor). Any subsequent successor trustee may then nominate a successor following the procedure set out in Article 11.2 below.

11.2 NOMINATION OF SUCCESSOR TRUSTEE. In the event the Trustee after DORA A. JONES seeks to or finds it necessary to resign, the Trustee may nominate a successor trustee. Such successor trustee shall commence to serve as Trustee upon the Trustee submitting a written acceptance of the appointment. Should a trustee fail to nominate a successor trustee or should a trustee be unable to nominate such a successor trustee, then the probate court having jurisdiction of the Beneficiary's Trust shall appoint a successor trustee upon a petition of an interested person after twenty (20) days notice to the beneficiary and other interested persons, and after hearing on any objections presented and on consideration of any alternate candidate for trustee proposed by the beneficiary.

11.3 RESIGNATION OF TRUSTEE. A Trustee may resign the Trusteeship at any time. Any resignation shall be in writing and shall become effective only after thirty (30) days from the date of mailing or delivery of written notice to the Beneficiary, and the next successor trustee, if any. If notice is mailed, the thirty (30) day period begins to run upon deposit of the notice in the mail addressed to the person's address last known to the Trustee.

11.4 TRUSTEE NOTIFICATION UPON RESIGNATION. The Trustee shall give written notice of resignation to JANET L. JONES, the beneficiary's guardian and conservator, if any, and to the next nominated successor trustee. The Trustee may (but is not required to) give notice of the reasons for the resignation to any named successor trustee, the Beneficiary, the Beneficiary's guardian or conservator, if any, and any other interested person or public or private agency authorized to act for the protection of a Beneficiary.

11.5 REMOVAL OF TRUSTEE. Any interested person may petition a local probate court with jurisdiction over the trust for removal of any trustee, as allowed in Oregon law. The court shall apply general fiduciary law in determining whether to remove a trustee.

11.6 TRANSFER TO SUCCESSOR TRUSTEE. Upon acceptance of the trustee office in writing, and subject to the limitations set forth in paragraphs 11.2, 11.3, 11.4, and 11.5 of this Article 11, a successor trustee shall succeed to all rights, powers, and duties of the Trustee without any conveyance or transfer. All right, title, and interest in the trust property shall immediately vest in the successor trustee upon execution of the written acceptance of the office. The prior trustee shall execute any documents deemed advisable by the successor trustee to acknowledge transfer of the existing trust property to the successor trustee, and shall immediately transfer any property to the possession and control of the successor trustee without warranty. A successor trustee shall not have any duty to examine the records or actions of any former trustee and shall not be liable for the consequences of any act or failure to act of any former trustee.

ARTICLE 12
BOND, TRUSTEE LIABILITY

12.1 NO BOND. No bond would be required of the initial trustee, or of any successor trustee nominated as set out above. This trust does not contemplate joint operation with a conservator.

12.2 TRUSTEE LIABILITY. No Trustee shall be liable for any loss of trust assets, except for any loss caused by the Trustee's bad faith or gross negligence.

12.3 CONSULTATION WITH AGENCIES. The Trustee may seek the counsel and assistance of the Beneficiary's guardian or conservator, if any, and any public or private agencies that have been established to assist the handicapped or disabled person in circumstances similar to the trust circumstances of the Trust beneficiary. The Trustee may consult these entities to aid the Beneficiary, or the Beneficiary's guardian or conservator, as appropriate, in identifying programs that may be of social, financial, and/or developmental assistance to the Beneficiary. The cost, if any, of such consultation may be charged to the Trust Estate.

12.4 TRUSTEE DISCRETION ABSOLUTE. The Trustee's discretion in choosing among particular non-support disbursements is final as to all interested parties, even if the Trustee elects to make no distributions at all. No judge or any other person should substitute that person's judgment for the judgment of the Trustee.

12.5 INDEMNIFICATION. The Trustee may require indemnification to the Trustee's satisfaction, at the cost of the Trust, before accepting the Trust or taking any step authorized hereunder.

ARTICLE 13
AMENDING THE TRUST

13.1 TRUSTEE AMENDMENT. The grantor PAUL J. JONES may amend this trust during PAUL J. JONES's lifetime by written instrument accepted by the trustee. Also, the then-serving Trustee may amend the Trust to conform with later changes in federal or state law to better effect the purposes of the Trust, or so that it conforms with any laws or interpretations of laws by any agency administering public benefits available to the beneficiary, but may not amend the Trust in a manner so as to give the beneficiary access to or control over the funds such as would jeopardize public benefits. The Trustee shall disclose any trust amendment in the next regular accounting.

13.2 COURT AMENDMENT. An interested person may apply to an court with jurisdiction over the Beneficiary's trust for authority to amend the Trust to better effect the purposes of the Trust. The applicant shall give notice of the proposed amendment to other interested persons including the trustee.

ARTICLE 14
TRUST ADMINISTRATION

14.1 UNDISTRIBUTED INCOME. Income accrued or undistributed at the termination of a Beneficiary's interest in a trust shall be added to and become part of the principal of the trust.

14.2 PRINCIPAL AND INCOME. The Trustee may allocate items of income or expenditure to either income or principal and create reserves out of income, all as provided by law; and to the extent not so provided, may allocate to income or principal, or create reserves on a reasonable basis; and the fiduciary's decision made in good faith with respect thereto shall be binding and conclusive upon all persons.

14.3 ACCOUNT. There shall be no obligation to account should grantor PAUL J. JONES serve as trustee. But all trustees serving after PAUL J. JONES shall once each year account to the Beneficiary (and to the Beneficiary's legal representative or guardian, if any) in an account mailed or personally delivered to the entitled persons. In the account, the Trustee shall report any change in the Beneficiary's eligibility for public benefit programs. The statement of account shall include a description of the operations in the reporting period, showing all receipts, disbursements, investment transactions, distributions of both principal and income since the last statement of account, and an inventory of current trust assets. The statement of account shall be deemed to have been furnished to the person entitled thereto when it has been placed in the United States mail addressed to that person at the person's last known address, even if that person is under a legal disability. Copies of documents evidencing ownership of assets in the name of the Trust, and a copy of the most recently filed trust tax return, shall be attached to the accounting. The court may require the Trustee to submit to a physical inspection of the trust property in the control of the Trustee, which inspection may occur at any time and in any manner the court may specify.

14.4 AVAILABILITY OF RECORDS. A copy of the Trust and the financial records of the Trust shall be available for inspection by the Trust Beneficiary, the Beneficiary's legal representative (if any), and trust remainder beneficiaries during regular business hours upon five calendar days' notice to the Trustee.

14.5 ADMINISTRATIVE EXPENSES, TRUSTEE COMPENSATION. The Trustee may receive reasonable compensation for the Trustee services and expenses. The compensation allowed shall be reported in the subsequent account. If any Beneficiary or remainderman questions the amount of Trustee compensation, then the Trustee shall determine the compensation rate and average annual fees charged by professional and family Trustees in the Portland metropolitan area for similar responsibilities and notify the questioner of the rates and annual fees. If the Trustee's compensation rate and average annual fees are within the range shown in the survey, the Trustee's fees are deemed reasonable.

14.6 ANNUAL EVALUATION. When PAUL J. JONES, the initial trustee, is not serving as Trustee, then the next serving Trustee is requested (but not required) to arrange for an annual evaluation of JANET L. JONES addressed to the following topics:

(1)   Physical condition

(2)   Educational, residential and vocational and training opportunities

(3)   Recreational, leisure and social needs

(4)   Appropriateness of existing program services

(5)   Laws and administrative practices relating to various public benefit programs, because JANET L. JONES may not have a reasonable chance of earning sufficient income for support, so it is essential that these benefits be secured

(6)   Legal rights, treatment in accord with needs, payment of a fair wage for work performed (if working), and if deemed to have capacity, the right to vote and to marry.

ARTICLE 15
TRUSTEE POWERS

As to each trust created by this instrument, the Trustee shall have all powers conferred on a Trustee by Oregon law as now existing or later amended. In addition, the Trustee shall have the following authority:

15.1 MANAGE AND DISPOSE OF ASSETS. The Trustee may manage, maintain, improve, lease, grant options on, encumber, sell, exchange, or otherwise dispose of part or all of the trust estate in any manner and on any terms the Trustee considers beneficial to the trust estate.

15.2 RETAIN ASSETS. The Trustee may retain any property, including nonproductive property, for so long as the Trustee considers retention of potential benefit to the trust estate and the trust beneficiaries.

15.3 MAKE INVESTMENTS. The Trustee may invest and reinvest the trust estate in common or preferred stocks, bonds, mutual funds, common trust funds, secured and unsecured obligations, mortgages, and other property, real or personal, which the Trustee considers advisable and in the best interest of the trust estate, whether or not authorized by law for the investment of trust funds. The Trustee may seek professional investment advice, and the costs to the Trustee of this advice shall be a charge against the Trust. The Trustee shall not seek professional investment advice from persons related to the Trustee, by blood or by marriage, or if the Trustee has a financial interest in the company with whom the investment counselor is associated.

Further, any sale or encumbrance to a Trustee, the spouse, agent or attorney of the Trustee, or any corporation or trust in which the Trustee has a substantial conflict of interest is voidable unless the transaction is approved by the court after the filing of a motion with the court seeking approval of the transaction.

15.4 DISCLAIM, ABANDON VALUELESS ASSETS. The Trustee may disclaim an interest in a potential trust asset, or abandon an asset of the Trust, should the Trustee determine that the asset is valueless. Any abandonment or disclaimer shall be reported in the accounting for the period during which the disclaimer took place.

15.5 FIDUCIARY FOR OUT OF STATE PROPERTY. If the trust property includes real property located outside Oregon, the Trustee may, subject to prior court approval, convey title to that real property to a fiduciary qualified to serve in the jurisdiction where the real property is located. That fiduciary shall hold the real property as an asset of the Trust subject to all the terms of this instrument and subject to the further condition that the proceeds of any sale or disposition of that property shall be distributed to the Trustee in Oregon, to be held and distributed under the provisions of this Trust.

15.6 ENVIRONMENTAL AUTHORITY. The following provision shall apply notwithstanding anything in this Trust or applicable law to the contrary:

15.6 (a) The Trustee may in his or her absolute discretion periodically monitor or inspect any real estate or personal property, either directly or through any employee, agent or consultant, for the purpose of insuring the compliance with any and all federal or state environmental or other laws affecting such property or determining the presence of any substances considered to be hazardous or toxic wastes under such laws.

15.6 (b) Without limiting the generality of the foregoing, if for any reason the Trustee in his or her sole judgment determines that hazardous or toxic substances may be present, the Trustee is specifically authorized in his or her absolute discretion to conduct (or cause to be conducted) further investigations (such as so-called "Phase 1" and "Phase 2" site assessments) into the possible presence of hazardous or toxic substances.

15.6 (c) In the event the Trustee is informed or otherwise has reason to believe or suspect that any trust property may be contaminated with hazardous or toxic substances, the Trustee may in his or her absolute discretion take any and all action deemed necessary or appropriate to comply with federal, state, or local environmental laws, including any obligations to report, prevent, abate, or remediate environmental contamination. The Trustee may in his or her absolute discretion take (or fail to take) any such action whether or not requested or demanded to do so by any federal, state or local agency or governmental authority.

15.6 (d) Any and all costs and expenses incurred by the Trustee in connection with such monitoring, inspecting, investigating, and other action shall be charged against the Trust as a cost of administration, and any and all such costs and expenses advanced by the Trustee shall promptly be reimbursed from trust assets.

15.6 (e) The Trustee shall not in any event be liable to the beneficiaries or others for any loss or decrease in the value of assets resulting from compliance with environmental reporting and other obligations, or for any other actions or omissions taken or omitted in good faith and without gross negligence.

15.7 REAL ESTATE ASSETS; NO DUTY TO DIVERSIFY. The Trustee may choose to purchase real property, or may choose to purchase a residence outright for the Beneficiary if the same may be done without affecting public benefits. The Trustee has sole discretion to choose among the planning options, and if he or she decides to hold real estate as a trust asset, he or she is relieved of the obligation to diversify trust assets, at least with respect to the portion of assets representing the Trust's equity in the real property.

15.8 CHANGE SITUS OF TRUST. The Trustee may change the situs of the Trust from time to time.

15.9 ENGAGE PROFESSIONAL ADVISORS. The Trustee may engage professional advisors such as attorneys, accountants, and investment advisors to assist the Trustee in carrying out the duties of the office, and may charge the trust estate for the cost of their services.

15.10 LIFE INSURANCE. The Trustee is authorized to acquire every kind of property, real, personal or mixed, including insurance contracts, and every kind of investment, including but not limited to acquiring life insurance on the life of any person or persons in whom the Trust or any beneficiary shall have an insurable interest. With respect to life insurance policies held as part of the trust estate:

15.10 (a) The Trust may pay premiums, assessments or other charges with respect to such policies, together with all other charges upon said policies otherwise required to preserve them as binding contracts.

15.10 (b) In the event the Trustee intends not to pay any premiums, assessment or other charge with respect to any such policy held by the Trust, or otherwise intends to cancel, convert, or substantially modify such policy, the Trustee shall first give the insured, or the guardian and conservator of insured under disability, at least fifteen (15) days advance written notice of her intention to take such action.

15.10 (c) Any amounts received by the Trustee with respect to any policy as a dividend shall be treated as principal.

15.10 (d) Upon the receipt of proof of death of any person whose life is insured for the benefit of the Trust hereunder, or upon the maturity of any policy payable to the Trustee prior to the death of the insured, the Trustee shall collect all sums payable with respect thereto, and shall thereafter hold such sums as principal of the trust estate, except that any interest paid by the insurer for a period subsequent to maturity shall be considered as income. The Trustee shall use her best efforts to collect all sums payable by reason of the death of any person whose life is insured for the benefit of the Trust hereunder, or by reason of the maturity of any policy payable to the Trustee prior to the death of the insured, but shall not be required to initiate any legal proceeding until indemnified. The Trustee shall have no responsibility with regard to any such life insurance policies, or premiums thereon, except as herein provided.

15.10 (e) The Trustee may accept any payments due it under any settlement arrangement made both before or after the death of the insured and exercise any right available to it under such arrangements.

15.10 (f) The Trustee may compromise, arbitrate or otherwise adjust claims upon any policies, and may, but shall not be required to, exercise any settlement options available under such policies. The receipt of the Trustee to the insurer shall be a full discharge, and the insurer is not required to see to the application of the proceeds.

15.11 DO OTHER ACTS. Except as otherwise provided in this instrument, the Trustee may do all acts that might legally be done by an individual in absolute ownership and control of property and which in the Trustee's judgment is necessary or desirable for the proper and advantageous management of the trust estate.

ARTICLE 16
GENERAL ADMINISTRATIVE PROVISIONS

16.1 SURVIVORSHIP. A remainder Beneficiary (also known as a residual beneficiary, in the Social Security Administration POMS) under this instrument shall be considered to survive the lifetime Beneficiary only if the remainder/residual Beneficiary is living thirty days after the date of the lifetime Beneficiary's death.

16.2 DESCENDANTS. "Descendants" mean all naturally born or legally adopted descendants of the person indicated.

16.3 NONGRANTOR TRUST. For income tax purposes after funding, this Trust will be a nongrantor trust.

16.4 ELECTIONS, DECISIONS, AND DISTRIBUTIONS. The Trustee is authorized to make any election or decision available to the Trust under federal or state tax laws, to make pro rata or non-pro rata distributions without regard to any differences in tax basis of assets distributed, and to make distributions in cash, in specific property, in undivided interests in property, or partly in cash and partly in property. The good faith decisions of the Trustee in the exercise of these powers shall be conclusive and binding on all parties, and the Trustee need not make any adjustments among beneficiaries because of any election, decision, or distribution.

16.5 REPRESENTATIVE OF BENEFICIARY. A conservator of a Beneficiary under legal disability, or if none, the guardian of such person, or if none, the person having the right of custody for an incapacitated Beneficiary, may act for such Beneficiary for all purposes under the administrative provisions of this Trust.

16.6 CONSERVATORSHIP/GUARDIANSHIP. Should a conservatorship or guardianship of the estate be established for the benefit of JANET L. JONES, then the conservator shall be an interested person and the trustee may, in the trustee's discretion, file annual accounts or other reports in concert with that conservatorship, whether or not the same person serves as trustee or conservator. A guardianship of the person has been established for the benefit of the beneficiary, and that guardian (who determines residential and medical matters for the beneficiary) shall be consulted by the trustee not less than four times annually for suggestions about potential distributions. Should PAUL J. JONES have left a letter of intent about the living situation for JANET L. JONES, then the trustee shall include in his or her annual report whether, and how, the intentions of PAUL J. JONES are being addressed.

16.7 GOVERNING LAW. The validity and construction of this agreement shall be determined under Oregon law regardless of the domicile of any Trustee or Beneficiary, unless the Trustee has changed the situs of the Trust.

16.8 CAPTIONS. The captions are inserted for convenience only. They are not a part of this instrument and do not limit the scope of the section to which each refers.

16.9 INTERPRETATION. It is Grantor's primary intent that this Trust allow the Beneficiary to qualify for public benefits yet receive help through the Trust with supplemental care. All provisions in this instrument shall be interpreted consistent with this intent. All provisions are subordinate to that intent and to be so construed. Any ambiguities or apparent conflicts under any provisions of this Trust shall be resolved in favor of and consistent with the primary intent. In addition, all right, power and discretion of any fiduciary shall not be exercised or exercisable except in a manner consistent with the primary intent.

This agreement is executed this ___ day of_____, 2017.

SETTLOR/GRANTOR: **TRUSTEE:**

_____   _____

PAUL J. JONES   **PAUL J. JONES**

STATE OF OREGON)
) ss.

County of Multnomah)

On this ___ day of _____, 2017, personally appeared before me the above named PAUL J. JONES, and acknowledged the foregoing instrument to be his voluntary act and deed.

_____
Notary Public for Oregon
My Commission Expires: _____

STATE OF OREGON)
) ss.

County of Multnomah)

On this ___ day of _____, 2017, personally appeared before me the above named PAUL J. JONES, Trustee, and acknowledged the foregoing instrument to be his voluntary act and deed.

_____
Notary Public for Oregon
My Commission Expires: _____

ACCEPTANCE BY TRUSTEE

PAUL J. JONES, the initial Trustee in this instrument, accepts the office and responsibilities of Trustee.

Dated this ____ day of _____, 2017.

_____
PAUL J. JONES, Trustee

JANET L. JONES GIFT SPECIAL NEEDS TRUST

SCHEDULE A

PROPERTY TO BE TRANSFERRED TO TRUST

1. Funding at death of PAUL J. JONES or DORA A. JONES anticipated; client may elect to transfer assets earlier ($100 to set up the trust)
2. No retirement accounts intended to be placed in this trust
3. Relatives will be told of this trust, and may fund it during PAUL J. JONES's life or thereafter

CHAPTER 8

Transfer of Retirement Benefits

Svetlana V. Bekman[1]

I. INTRODUCTION

Qualified Retirement Plans (QRPs) and Individual Retirement Accounts (IRAs) are tax-advantaged investment vehicles. They are popular, and often represent a large proportion of an individual's total wealth.

In this chapter, the terms "account," "plan," "retirement plan," "retirement account," and "retirement assets"[2] are used interchangeably to refer to QRPs and IRAs (both traditional and Roth); the term "participant" is used to refer to an employee in the context of a QRP; and the term "owner" is used to refer to a participant and to an IRA account owner.

A retirement account owner may want to leave his or her retirement assets to one or more minors (e.g., children, grandchildren, or others). This chapter discusses the various issues pertaining to the testamentary transfer of a retirement plan to minors, including protecting the federal income tax benefits of the account and preventing the beneficiary from gaining control of the assets at an age when the beneficiary may not have the maturity or judgment to manage money.

II. TYPES OF RETIREMENT PLANS

A. Qualified Retirement Plans

QRPs typically are sponsored by the plan participant's employer and come in two flavors: a "defined benefit plan" and a "defined contribution plan."[3] A defined benefit plan is a traditional pension plan where the employer promises to pay a fixed monthly or annual benefit (calculated based on a formula specified by the plan) to the retiree or named beneficiary. For example, upon reaching normal retirement age, the participant may be entitled to receive a percentage of his or her average compensation calculated over a certain period of time, multiplied by the participant's total number of years of service. The promised benefits are funded through mandatory employer contributions to the plan. In contrast, under a defined contribution plan (e.g., a 401(k) plan), the employer's contributions to the plan are allocated to the participant's various accounts, usually based on the participant's relative compensation. The participant also may elect to make contributions to his or her account. Upon a participant's separation from service, death, disability, or at any other time specified in the plan documents, the participant (or beneficiary) becomes entitled to the vested account balance, including any net earnings or gains on previously contributed amounts, reduced by administrative expenses. Typically, the participant (or beneficiary) can elect to receive a lump-sum distribution.

For purposes of this discussion, the distinctions among the different types of QRPs are not material.

B. Individual Retirement Accounts (IRAs)

A traditional IRA is a trust or custodial account created for the exclusive benefit of an individual or her beneficiary. An IRA can be funded with "rollover" or annual contributions. A rollover contribution is a permissible transfer of assets from another tax-advantaged account (e.g., a QRP) to an IRA. A rollover does not trigger income tax.

Annual contributions to an IRA are limited. The maximum annual contribution is $5,500 for 2018.[4] The limit may be adjusted annually for inflation in $500 increments.[5] Also, individuals who have attained age fifty may make additional catch-up IRA contributions of $1,000 (not indexed for inflation).[6] No contributions to a traditional IRA may be made beginning in the year in which the owner attains age seventy and a half.[7] Annual contributions to an IRA may be deductible in whole or in part. An individual, who is an "active participant," in an employer-sponsored retirement plan may make a deductible contribution to an IRA only if the individual's adjusted gross income (AGI) for the taxable year falls below a certain threshold. If it does, then a full or partial deduction will be available depending on the individual's AGI.[8] Contributions and earnings are not subject to income tax until distributed.[9]

A Roth IRA is a special type of IRA. Contributions to a Roth IRA are not tax-deductible, and qualified distributions from a Roth IRA are not included in income.[10] In addition, contributions can be made to a Roth IRA after the account owner attains age seventy and a half.[11] Unlike in the case of QRPs and traditional IRAs, the distribution rules discussed later in the chapter do not apply to a Roth IRA during the owner's lifetime. After the owner's death, however, the Roth IRA generally must be paid in accordance with the same rules governing traditional IRAs, that is, as if the account owner died before his or her "required beginning date."[12]

III. DISTRIBUTIONS—DURING OWNER'S LIFE

Retirement plans described in section II are powerful investment vehicles because earnings (i.e., capital gains, dividends, interest, etc.) on contributions currently are not subject to federal income tax. Public policy, as reflected in relevant federal tax law, encourages preretirement savings. Eventually, however, the owner must begin receiving distributions from his or her retirement plan, and include distributions (other than from a Roth IRA) in taxable income. If the owner dies before withdrawing any or all assets from his or her plan, distributions to the beneficiary(ies) must continue or commence. The minimum distribution rules, contained in Code section 401(a)(9), provide (1) when distributions must begin and (2) the methodology by which the minimum required distributions (MRDs) are calculated.[13]

Distributions must begin no later than the account owner's "required beginning date" (RBD). For QRPs, the RBD is April 1 of the calendar year following the later of (1) the year the owner attains age seventy and a half and (2) the year the owner retires (except 5 percent owners of the employer).[14] For IRAs (and 5 percent owners of the employer), the RBD is April 1 of the calendar year following the year the owner attains age seventy and a half.[15] During the owner's lifetime, distributions are made with reference to the Uniform Lifetime Table.[16] The MRD is a fraction, whose numerator is the retirement account balance on December 31 of the calendar year immediately preceding the distribution calendar year, and whose denominator is the "applicable distribution period" found in the Uniform Lifetime Table and corresponding to the account owner's age in the year of distribution.[17]

EXAMPLE

Jane Gordon has an IRA the value of which was $500,000 on December 31, 2017, and attains the age of seventy-five years in 2018. According to the Uniform Lifetime Table, the applicable distribution period for a seventy-five-year-old is 22.9. Jane's 2018 MRD is $21,834.06, that is, $500,000 divided by 22.9.

With one exception, the identity of the designated beneficiary on the RBD does not matter to the preceding method. If the retirement plan owner's spouse is the sole designated beneficiary of the account and is *more than* ten years younger than the owner, however, then the applicable distribution period found in the Joint Life and Last Survivor Table[18] can be used, resulting in a smaller MRD.[19]

After the owner attains age seventy and a half and, generally, after the owner dies, the deadline for withdrawing the MRD is December 31 of any distribution year.[20] If the deadline is missed or an insufficient amount is withdrawn, the owner is subject to a 50 percent penalty, which may be waivable. The owner should report the failure to distribute or under-distribution on the IRS Form 5329,[21] and request a penalty waiver. The grounds for waiver are (1) the shortfall in the withdrawal was due to reasonable error and (2) appropriate steps have been taken to remedy the shortfall.[22]

IV. DISTRIBUTION—AFTER OWNER'S DEATH

After the retirement plan owner dies, the beneficiary becomes the retirement plan's new owner and the party responsible for payment of any income tax related to plan distributions. If the deceased owner was receiving MRDs at the time of his or her death, and had not taken the entire MRD for the year of death, the plan beneficiary must take the balance.[23] The deadline for the beneficiary to withdraw the MRD balance is December 31 of the year of death.[24] Missing the deadline (or withdrawing less than the MRD) will result in the 50 percent penalty, the waiver of which can be sought in the same manner as described earlier.

A. Inherited IRA

United States federal tax law does not mandate that the plan beneficiary open a new account for the inherited retirement assets after the owner's death. The QRP beneficiary can take distributions from the deceased participant's QRP. Likewise, an IRA beneficiary can take distributions from the deceased owner's IRA. However, the employer is unlikely to want to administer the QRP after the employee's or retiree's death, and probably will insist that the beneficiary withdraw the assets in a lump sum or over a short period of time. Similarly, in the case of a deceased owner's IRA, the financial institution, holding the IRA account, will want to avoid administrative confusion, and will request the beneficiary to enter into a new IRA contract, thus allowing for retitling of the decedent's IRA. In the past, a QRP beneficiary was forced to accept one or several large taxable distributions from the employer. The Pension Protection Act of 2006[25] allows non-spouse beneficiaries to direct a trustee-to-trustee transfer of the QRP proceeds to an IRA, thus avoiding forced acceptance of a large taxable distribution. The transfer is treated, for federal tax purposes, as an "eligible rollover distribution."[26] Distributions from the beneficiary's IRA, also called an "inherited IRA," are made in accordance with the MRD rules.

NOTE: Although the Pension Protection Act of 2006[27] and commentators refer to the movement of the inherited retirement assets as a "rollover," the provision should not be confused with a spousal rollover. After a spouse "rolls over" inherited retirement assets, the spouse is able to withdraw distributions in accordance with the MRD rules applicable to the prior living account owner. The non-spouse beneficiary cannot do this. Instead, the non-spouse beneficiary must use his or her life expectancy for purposes of distributions as described in the following sections.

A non-spouse beneficiary of a QRP or IRA customarily will establish an inherited IRA at a financial institution of his or her choice. The beneficiary then must direct that the retirement assets from the decedent's account—whether QRP or IRA—move to the inherited IRA in a direct trustee-to-trustee transfer.[28] If the beneficiary accidentally withdraws the assets from the decedent's account, and then attempts to deposit them in the inherited IRA, the beneficiary will be out of luck! The withdrawn amount is fully taxable, and no relief is available.

PRACTICE NOTE

There is no IRS-prescribed convention regarding the titling of an inherited IRA. However, when reporting the value of and distributions from inherited IRAs to the IRS, the IRA custodian must show the name of the decedent, as well as the name and taxpayer identification number of the beneficiary.[29] Therefore, the name of an inherited IRA should reflect that the IRA originally was owned by the decedent and that it is now owned by the beneficiary.[30]

EXAMPLE

If Gabby Gordon inherits an IRA from her grandmother, Jane Gordon, Gabby's inherited IRA can be titled as follows: "Gabby Gordon as beneficiary of Jane Gordon" or "Jane Gordon (deceased) Inherited IRA fbo [for benefit of] Gabby Gordon, XYZ Financial, as custodian."

Recall, if the deceased owner of a retirement plan was receiving MRDs at the time of the deceased owner's death, and had not taken the entire MRD for the year of death (Year 0), the plan beneficiary must take the balance. If the deceased owner died before the deceased owner's RBD, no MRD would be required in Year 0. In the year following the year of the account owner's death (Year 1), the beneficiary again will have to withdraw an MRD. Ideally, the beneficiary will establish and fund the inherited IRA before taking the Year 1 MRD. However, the timing may not work out, and the establishment and transfer of funds to the inherited IRA may not occur until Year 2. Nevertheless, even if the assets are held in the decedent's retirement account, the deadline for the Year 1 MRD is December 31 of that year and must be calculated correctly, and withdrawn *irrespective of the account title*.

B. Distributions from Inherited IRA

The federal income tax rules governing distributions from an inherited IRA rely on the concept of "designated beneficiary" (DB). If the deceased account owner leaves his or her retirement plan to an individual, that beneficiary is a DB.[31] Regardless of the deceased account owner's age at death, a DB is allowed to "stretch" distributions from the inherited IRA over the DB's life expectancy.[32] If the retirement account has a DB, distributions from the account are computed as follows. The Year 1 MRD equals (1) the fair market value of the account as of December 31 of the year of the account owner's death divided by (2) the "applicable distribution period" from the Single Life Table.[33] The "applicable distribution period" is based upon the age of the DB in the year following the year of the deceased account owner's death. In each subsequent year, the "applicable distribution period" must be reduced by one.[34]

EXAMPLE

Jane died in 2018, leaving her IRA, with a fair market value of $500,000, to her granddaughter, Gabby. Gabby turns fifteen years of age in 2019. Under the IRS Single Life Table, the "applicable distribution period" for a fifteen-year-old is 67.9. That is, a fifteen-year-old has sixty-seven years of income tax deferral with modest distributions in the early years. Assuming the relevant fair market value of the IRA remains $500,000, MRDs, payable to Gabby, in years 2019, 2020, and 2021 and then 2054, 2055, and 2056 are calculated as follows:[35]

Year	Age	ADP	MRD	
2019	15	67.9	$500,000÷67.9	$7,363.77
2020	16	66.9	$500,000÷66.9	$7,473.84
2021	17	65.9	$500,000÷65.9	$7,587.25
***	***	***	***	***
2054	50	32.9	$500,000÷32.9	$15,197.57
2055	51	31.9	$500,000÷31.9	$15,673.98
2056	52	30.9	$500,000÷30.9	$16,181.23

Because a minor has a long life expectancy, Gabby's MRDs will be very modest compared to, for example, the MRDs of her parent, if the parent had been named as the DB. The deceased account owner's retirement plan (albeit, in the form of an inherited IRA), thus, can remain intact, and continue to grow on a tax deferred basis longer.

EXAMPLE

In contrast, suppose that Jane, in the preceding example, left her IRA with a fair market value of $500,000 to Gabby's mother, Ginger, who attained age forty-five in the year following Jane's death. Under the IRS Single Life Table, the "applicable distribution period" for a forty-four-year-old is 38.8. Assuming the relevant fair market value of the IRA remains $500,000, the following comparison chart of MRDs payable to Gabby and those payable to Ginger illustrates why leaving a retirement plan to a minor is beneficial from federal income tax perspective.

	GABBY			GINGER		
Year	Age	ADP	MRD	Age	ADP	MRD
2019	15	67.9	$7,363.77	45	38.8	$12,886.60
2020	16	66.9	$7,473.84	46	37.8	$13,227.51
2021	17	65.9	$7,587.25	47	36.8	$13,586.96
***	***	***	***	***	***	***
2054	50	32.9	$15,197.57	80	5.8	$131,578.95
2055	51	31.9	$15,673.98	81	4.8	$178,571.43
2056	52	30.9	$16,181.23	82	3.8	$277,777.78

1. Multiple Beneficiaries—General Rule

Under the Treasury Regulations, the general rule is that, if there are two or more individual beneficiaries, the oldest beneficiary will be treated as the DB.[36]

EXAMPLE

Jane leaves 50 percent of her IRA with a fair market value of $500,000 to the fifteen-year-old Gabby and 50 percent to the forty-five-year-old Ginger. Gabby will have to use Ginger's life expectancy (38.8 years) for purposes of calculating MRDs. When a minor is named as a beneficiary together with significantly older individuals, the general rule prevents the minor from realizing maximum income tax benefits by not allowing the minor to stretch distributions over the minor's longer life expectancy.

2. Separate Accounts

An exception to the general rule—knowns as the "separate accounts" rule—can assist the minor beneficiary in maximizing securing federal income tax deferral. If each beneficiary is entitled to a separate account, then each beneficiary should be able to use his or her own individual life expectancy to determine MRDs.[37] "Separate accounts" are defined as separate portions of the owner's retirement plan, reflecting separate interests of the beneficiaries under the plan as of the date of the owner's death for which separate accounting is maintained.[38] "The separate accounting must allocate all post-death investment gains and losses, contributions, and forfeitures for the period prior to the establishment of the separate accounts on a pro rata basis in a reasonable and consistent manner among the separate accounts."[39]

To be effective, separate accounts must be "established" by the end of the calendar year following the calendar year of the account owner's death.[40] What does it mean to "establish" a separate account? It does not appear to be sufficient to designate fractional shares of an account as payable to different beneficiaries. In the foregoing example, Gabby and Ginger must each open a separate inherited IRA account and fund it with her respective 50 percent share by December 31 of the calendar year following Jane's death.[41]

EXAMPLE

Suppose Jane's beneficiary designation provides as follows: "$250,000 to Gabby, if she survives me, and the balance to Ginger, if she survives me." The pecuniary designation probably will not satisfy the definition of a "separate account" because post-death investment gains and losses, contributions, and forfeitures will not be allocated on a pro rata basis between Gabby's and Ginger's shares of the IRA. Gabby and Ginger will each have an opportunity to open a separate inherited IRA account. Gabby, however, will not be able to use her life expectancy for purposes of calculating MRDs from her inherited IRA. Hence, for maximum income tax deferral, a beneficiary designation must divide retirement assets among multiple beneficiaries on a fractional or percentage basis. The following are examples of beneficiary designations.

EXAMPLE

I leave my IRA as follows: one-fourth to my grandson, Daniel Doe; one-fourth to my grandson, David Doe; one-fourth to my granddaughter, Sarah Doe; and one-fourth to my granddaughter, Julia Doe. If one or more of my grandchildren do not survive me, I leave his, her, or their shares proportionately to those who do survive me.

Or

EXAMPLE

I leave my IRA in equal shares to such of my grandchildren, Daniel Doe, David Doe, Sarah Doe, and Julia Doe, who survive me.

Or

EXAMPLE

I leave my IRA as follows: 25 percent to my grandson, Daniel Doe; 25 percent to my grandson, David Doe; 25 percent to my granddaughter, Sarah Doe; and 25 percent to my granddaughter, Julia Doe. If one or more of my grandchildren do not survive me, I leave his, her, or their shares proportionately to those who do survive me.

3. Multiple Beneficiaries—Beneficiary Is Not DB

If the account owner names multiple beneficiaries, the general rule is that, unless all beneficiaries are individuals, the account does not have a DB.[42]

EXAMPLE

Jane leaves 50 percent of her $500,000 IRA to Gabby and 50 percent to her favorite charity. A charity does not qualify as a DB. Thus, the account does not have a DB. If the account does not have a DB, then the distribution rule for MRDs depends on the owner's age at death. If the owner reached his or her RBD at death, then the MRDs must be distributed over the owner's remaining life expectancy.[43] If the owner had not reached his or her RBD, then the inherited IRA will be subject to the five-year rule and must be distributed in full by the end of the calendar year which contains the fifth anniversary of the owner's death.[44]

The "separate accounts" exception can help the fifteen-year-old Gabby achieve maximum income tax deferral in the foregoing example. Gabby and the charity must establish separate inherited IRAs by December 31 of the year following Jane's year of death. Subsequently, Gabby will be allowed to take MRDs from her inherited IRA over her life expectancy of sixty-seven years. If the charity were to receive its share of the IRA by the BDD, Gabby would likewise be able to stretch distributions from her inherited IRA over her life expectancy.[45]

EXAMPLE

Suppose Jane leaves $250,000 of her IRA to Gabby and the balance to her favorite charity. Because the pecuniary designation probably will not satisfy the definition of a "separate account," the only way to preserve federal income tax deferral for Gabby is to distribute the charity's share to it by the BDD.

If, on the BDD, the charity continues to be a beneficiary, Jane's retirement account will not have a DB. Therefore, if Jane died after her RBD, Gabby's MRDs will be calculated based upon Jane's remaining life expectancy determined in the year of her death. The "applicable distribution period," which is the denominator of the MRD fraction, will be reduced by one for each year of distribution, starting with the first year of distribution.[46] According to the Single Life Table, a seventy-five-year-old individual has a life expectancy of 13.4 years. The applicable distribution period for Gabby's first MRD will be 12.4. Assuming the fair market value of the IRA remains $500,000 at all relevant dates, the following table shows Gabby's MRDs from her inherited IRA established under these facts:

Year	Age	ADP	MRD
2019	15	12.4	$40,322.58
2020	16	11.4	$43,859.65
2021	17	10.4	$48,076.92
2022	18	9.4	$53,191.49
2023	19	8.4	$59,523.81
2024	20	7.4	$67,567.57
2025	21	6.4	$78,125.00
2026	22	5.4	$92,592.59
2027	23	4.4	$113,636.36
2028	24	3.4	$147,058.82

Year	Age	ADP	MRD
2029	25	2.4	$208,333.33
2030	26	1.4	$357,142.86
2031	27	last withdrawal	Balance

If Jane died before her RBD and assuming that her date of death was November 1, 2018, Gabby will have to deplete her inherited IRA no later than December 31, 2023. In the interim, Gabby may withdraw as much, as little, or none of her inherited IRA.

V. OPTIONS FOR BENEFITING MINORS

As demonstrated earlier, there are compelling federal income tax reasons for naming a young person as beneficiary of a retirement plan. The younger the beneficiary, the longer the period over which MRDs may be withdrawn, thereby increasing federal income tax deferral and the overall value of the retirement plan. Importantly, the early years' distributions will be small, giving the vast majority of the assets plenty of time to grow tax-free. In addition, for the period when the beneficiaries are in their twenties and even thirties, they are likely to be in a lower tax bracket than their parents or a trust.

On the negative side, if the testamentary transfer of retirement benefits will be a direct skip for purposes of the generation-skipping transfer (GST) tax, naming a minor as beneficiary will use the account owner's GST exemption (or will be subject to the GST tax).[47] Retirement assets may not be the best assets to shelter with the GST exemption, especially if the taxpayer's GST exemption is limited, given that retirement benefits have imbedded income tax liability which will diminish their value overtime.

A. Designating Beneficiaries, Generally

Before discussing specific methods for leaving retirement assets to minors, a few general comments regarding beneficiary designations are warranted. First, the only way to transmit retirement assets posthumously is through a beneficiary designation. If the account owner provides one thing in the beneficiary designation and something else in the estate planning documents, the former will control and the latter disregarded.

EXAMPLE

The beneficiary designation might provide that the account is payable to the account owner's child, while the account owner's revocable trust might provide that the retirement assets pass to a trust for the child benefit. In this case, the child will inherit the retirement account outright.

If the account owner fails to complete the beneficiary designation, the default provisions under the documents governing the retirement account will control, Default provisions might provide that the retirement assets pass "to the account owner's spouse, if living; otherwise to the account owner's then living descendants, per stirpes, otherwise to the account owner's estate." Second, the IRA custodian or QRP trustee (or administrator) might impose restrictions on the beneficiary designation. An IRA custodian, especially if the product is relatively inexpensive, is likely to insist that the beneficiary designation fit into the custodian's form. For example, such forms might preclude division on a per stirpes basis. Third, federal law may limit a beneficiary designation. In fact, a QRP is subject to the ERISA[48] spousal consent requirement so that, if the account owner is married, the surviving spouse is entitled to the QRP unless the spouse consents to someone else being named as beneficiary.[49]

PRACTICE NOTE

The practitioner is advised to confirm with the IRA custodian or QRP trustee that the beneficiary designation is acceptable and was, in fact, received and made part of the account records.

B. Naming Minor as Beneficiary

Naming a minor as a primary or contingent beneficiary of a retirement plan is not advisable. The account owner may name someone, other than the minor, as primary beneficiary and the minor, as contingent beneficiary. In such case, a minor is not the intended beneficiary of a retirement plan, but inherits it because a prior beneficiary (1) predeceased the retirement account owner or (2) decided to disclaim.

EXAMPLE

An IRA owner with two adult children and several minor grandchildren might name his or her "descendants per stirpes" as beneficiaries. One of the children might predecease the account owner (or disclaim after the account owner's death), causing that child's 50 percent of the IRA to pass to the child's minor children.

Since a minor may not have legal capacity to contract,[50] the IRA custodian or QRP trustee must identify a party who can act for the minor. The parent, as such, does not have legal authority to act for the child. However, if the parent is appointed by a court as guardian of the child's estate or already is acting as custodian under a particular state's Uniform Transfers to Minors Act (UTMA), the parent has legal authority to receive distributions, otherwise direct administration of the account, and execute an inherited IRA agreement.

If a UTMA account already is in existence, the IRA custodian or QRP trustee probably will accept a direction by the custodian to deposit MRDs in the UTMA account. The title of such an account would look like the following: "Rachel Doe, as custodian under the [state] UTMA for Richard Roe, minor." If a UTMA account already does not exist, then the parent (or other adult) must decide whether to serve as a UTMA custodian, thereby assuming fiduciary duties and obligations relative to the minor's account. Different states have different UTMA rules, including the maximum value of the property that a custodian can control.[51] The parent should be encouraged to consult with his or her attorney. The foregoing process will likely take time and may cost money.

C. Naming Custodian under UTMA as Beneficiary

Whether the minor is a primary or contingent beneficiary, a better approach than naming the minor directly is to leave the account to a specified individual who would act for the minor as custodian under a UTMA. Illinois UTMA authorizes

> [a] person having the right to designate the recipient of property transferable upon the occurrence of a future event [to] revocably nominate a custodian to receive the property for a minor beneficiary upon the occurrence of the event by naming the custodian followed in substance by the words: "as custodian for (name of minor) under the Illinois Uniform Transfers to Minors Act."[52]

EXAMPLE

The beneficiary designation for an IRA might therefore look something like this:

> My IRA is payable (i) to my grandson, Daniel Doe (Daniel), if he survives me; provided, however, that if Daniel is under the age of eighteen years or is otherwise disabled at the time of distribution, then (ii) to Daniel's then living parent who is my child, otherwise to Daniel's then living parent, as custodian for Daniel under the applicable Uniform Transfers to Minors Act or similar law. Such custodian shall be authorized to act for Daniel in all respects with regard to the benefits payable to Daniel hereunder.

or

> My IRA is payable (i) to my descendants per stirpes; provided, however, that if any descendant is under the age of eighteen years or is otherwise disabled at the time of distribution, then (ii) to that descendant's then living parent who is my child, otherwise to that descendant's then living parent, as custodian for the descendant under the applicable Uniform Transfers to Minors Act or similar law. Such custodian shall be authorized to act for the descendant

in all respects with regard to the benefits payable to such descendant hereunder.

To the best of the author's knowledge, to date, the IRS has not opined as
to whether, when a retirement plan is distributed to a UTMA custodian, the
plan is deemed to have a DB. If given an opportunity to rule on the issue,
the IRS hopefully would conclude that the minor, not the custodian, is the
DB for purposes of the MRDs.[53]

If the retirement plan is left to a custodian for the minor's benefit, then,
depending on state law, the young person will have unfettered access to the
assets upon attaining the age of eighteen or twenty-one years.[54] The major
drawback of naming a custodian as beneficiary of a retirement plan is that
the young person, although over eighteen or twenty-one years,[55] is unlikely
to be financially mature to handle the assets responsibly.

D. Trust

Recognizing the downsides of giving a young person unfettered access to
assets, the owner of a retirement plan should consider ways to benefit the
minor without giving complete control to the minor. Trusts are the most
common means of accomplishing this objective.[56] An account owner can
create a trust to benefit a particular minor and would then, in turn, name
the trust as beneficiary of the retirement account.

1. *"Look-Through" Requirements*

As previously discussed, if an inherited IRA has a DB, MRDs will be computed based upon the life expectancy of the DB. A trust, not being an individual, does not qualify as a DB. However, federal income tax deferral is
available to a trust if it satisfies the "look-through" requirements.[57] If the
trust meets the look-through requirements, then the IRS, in effect, looks
through the trust to its beneficiaries and treats them, for most purposes, as
if the account owner named them directly as beneficiaries of the retirement
plan.[58] The look-through requirements are the following: (1) the trust is
valid under state law; (2) the trust is irrevocable or will, by its terms, become
irrevocable upon the death of the retirement account owner; (3) the trust
has identifiable individual beneficiaries; and (4) a copy of the trust instrument (or a list of all trust beneficiaries, including contingent and remaindermen beneficiaries) is provided to the IRA custodian or QRP trustee by
October 31 of the year following the death of the account owner.[59]

A typical trust prepared for estate planning purposes has multiple beneficiaries (i.e., current, remainder, contingent, and appointees (or donees) of
a lifetime and testamentary powers of appointment). The issue is whether
all trust beneficiaries are countable for purposes of the look-through rules.
If none can be disregarded, the risk is high that a typical trust structure will
not meet the look-through rules or, even if it does, the trust will qualify for
only limited federal income tax deferral.

2. Count or Disregard Beneficiary?

To determine whether a beneficiary will be counted for purposes of the look-through rules and the MRD calculation, the following Treasury regulatory provisions (in a question and answer format) are applicable:

Q-7. If an employee has more than one designated beneficiary, which designated beneficiary's life expectancy will be used to determine the applicable distribution period?[60]

***

A-7.

***

(b) Contingent beneficiary.

Except as provided in paragraph (c)(1) of this A-7, *if a beneficiary's entitlement to an employee's benefit after the employee's death is a contingent right, such contingent beneficiary is nevertheless considered to be a beneficiary for purposes of determining whether a person other than an individual is designated as a beneficiary* (resulting in the employee being treated as having no designated beneficiary under the rules of A-3 of [Section] 1.401(a)(9)-4) and which designated beneficiary has the shortest life expectancy under paragraph (a) of this A-7.[61]

(c) Successor beneficiary.

(1) A person will not be considered a beneficiary for purposes of determining who is the beneficiary with the shortest life expectancy under paragraph (a) of this A-7, or whether a person who is not an individual is a beneficiary, merely because the person could become the successor to the interest of one of the employee's beneficiaries after that beneficiary's death. However, the preceding sentence does not apply to a person who has any right (including a contingent right) to an employee's benefit beyond being a mere potential successor to the interest of one of the employee's beneficiaries upon that beneficiary's death. Thus, for example, if the first beneficiary has a right to all income with respect to an employee's individual account during that beneficiary's life and a second beneficiary has a right to the principal but only after the death of the first income beneficiary (any portion of the principal distributed during the life of the first income beneficiary to be held in trust until that first beneficiary's death), both beneficiaries must be taken into account in determining the beneficiary with the shortest life expectancy and whether only individuals are beneficiaries.[62]

No definitive legal authority exists on where to draw the line between a *contingent* beneficiary who is countable for purposes of MRD and the *mere potential successor* beneficiary who can be ignored.

3. Accumulation Trust

A very common estate planning technique is a revocable (or "living") trust, which functions as a will substitute. An owner of a retirement plan frequently will name a revocable trust as beneficiary of his or her retirement plan. A revocable trust may have multiple beneficiaries, and the trustee will have discretion to accumulate assets and to distribute them to one or more beneficiaries.

EXAMPLE

Upon Jane's death, her revocable trust might direct the trustee to

(a) pay death taxes and expenses;
(b) distribute $10,000 to Jane's friend, Robert;
(c) distribute $100,000 to Jane's alma mater, the University of Illinois;
(d) distribute the balance to a trust whereby the trustee could make distributions of income and principal to or for the benefit of Gabby and her descendants for their respective health, support, and education;
(e) upon Gabby's death, distribute trust property to such of Gabby's spouse and descendants as she appoints;
(f) in default of appointment, distribute trust property to Gabby's then living descendants, per stirpes;
(g) if no descendant of Gabby is living, to distribute trust property to Jane's then living heirs-at-law.

Conservative application of the Treasury regulations[63] and the principles outlined in the private letter rulings[64] to most revocable trust structures would cause the trusts to flunk the look-through test.

If, in the preceding example, Gabby's spouse[65] or Jane's heirs-at-law[66] cannot be ignored as beneficiaries for MRD purposes, the IRS might argue that the "identifiable beneficiaries" prong of the look-through test is not satisfied because "it is [not] possible to identify the class members with the shortest life expectancy" who might receive a portion of Jane's IRA.[67] Even if the appointees under the power of appointment and the remote contingent beneficiaries can be ignored, the University of Illinois is countable because, under the look-through rules, all trust beneficiaries are viewed as having been named directly as beneficiaries of the retirement plan. The presence of the University of Illinois, among the beneficiaries, means that Jane's retirement plan has no DB.

Robert, if an eighty-year-old individual, also cannot be disregarded. As the oldest beneficiary of the revocable trust, his life expectancy will be the applicable distribution period of 10.2 years. Even if Jane's revocable trust meets the look-through rules, MRDs will have to be calculated on the basis of the life expectancy of the oldest trust beneficiary, Robert. This result will be a significant sacrifice of income tax deferral as compared to using Gabby's life expectancy of 67.9 years.

A recent private letter ruling 201633025 appears to be willing to disregard remote beneficiaries for purposes of MRDs. An IRA owner named a trust as beneficiary. Under the terms of the trust, the decedent's daughter is to receive net income and, along with her children, the decedent's daughter is eligible to receive principal under an ascertainable standard. The trust document further provides that the trust terminates, and will distribute to the daughter upon attaining age fifty, or, if she does not survive, to her children. If the children are under age twenty-one, their shares are to be held in trust, and paid to their estates in the event of death. If no descendant of the IRA owner are living, the trust property passes to the IRA owner's siblings, otherwise to various charities.

Although the daughter's age is not specified, it would seem unlikely that she would be older than the decedent's siblings. Nevertheless, the IRS ruled that the daughter's life expectancy would be used to calculate the MRDs. IRS disregarded the siblings, the charities, and the fact that the children's estates could potentially benefit from the IRA, stating that these "potential recipients of the funds in the Trust are *mere successor* beneficiaries within the meaning of the regulations" (emphasis added). Perhaps, one can be hopeful the foregoing is a signal of where the IRS is heading rather than an anomaly.[68]

4. Postmortem Fixes

As discussed, the IRS will make the determination as to which trust beneficiaries are countable for purposes of determining MRDs on BDD, which is September 30 of the year following the year of the retirement account owner's death.[69] Accordingly, between the date of death and the BDD, "problematic" beneficiaries (e.g., charity, estate, older individual), however, may be removed via disclaimer[70] and/or via full distribution of such beneficiaries' interests.

For achieving the best federal income tax result, the trustee of Jane's revocable trust may want to make a full distribution of assets (other than of Jane's IRA) to the University of Illinois and to Robert by September 30 of the year following the year of Jane's death. If assets other than Jane's retirement account are insufficient to satisfy the gifts to Robert and/or the University of Illinois, perhaps Robert and/or the university may be persuaded to disclaim.

NOTE: Lastly, the private letter rulings are somewhat inconsistent on this issue, but a recent ruling suggests that, if a trust does not meet the look-through test, retroactive reformation, even via a court order, may not be effective.[71]

5. Additional Drafting Fix

Certain drafting and postmortem planning techniques can help a trust achieve maximum possible federal income tax deferral. For example, many drafters are worried that, if retirement assets can be used to pay estate debts, expense, and taxes, the retirement plan's owner's estate would be deemed a beneficiary for MRD purposes. To avoid this result, practitioners might include a provision that prohibits the use of retirement assets for the foregoing purposes.[72] Such a provision also can be used to preclude non-individuals (e.g., charity or estate) and persons older than a specified individual from ever benefiting from the retirement assets.[73] In determining (1) whether a trust satisfies the look-through rules and (2) the identity of the oldest beneficiary of that trust, the IRS apparently respects such "savings clauses."[74]

NOTE: In summary, the MRDs distributable to the trust will be computed based upon the life expectancy of the minor if (1) an accumulation trust meets the look-through rules, (2) all countable beneficiaries are individuals, and (3) the minor is the individual with the shortest life expectancy. If the minor's life expectancy is not the shortest, the life expectancy of the oldest beneficiary will be used for purposes of computing the MRDs. If the trust does not meet the look-through test, the retirement account will be deemed to have no DB, and the MRDs will be distributed over the life expectancy of the deceased account owner or will have to be withdrawn no later than December 31 of the year containing the fifth anniversary of the deceased account owner's year of death.

6. *Conduit Trust*

The Treasury regulations expressly endorse one particular type of trust that passes the look-through test and, thus, certain of its beneficiaries can be disregarded. Practitioners have dubbed this structure a "conduit" trust. A conduit trust provides that all distributions (including MRDs and all other distributions) the trust receives from the inherited IRA must be paid to a particular individual beneficiary of the trust.[75] Accordingly, a conduit trust for the benefit of Gabby would include the following provision:

> If the trust is beneficiary or owner of an individual account in any employee benefit plan or individual retirement plan, during Gabby's lifetime, all distributions and withdrawals from the individual account to the trust shall be paid to Gabby upon receipt by the trustee of the trust.

If Jane named a conduit trust as beneficiary of her IRA, the IRS would consider Gabby to be

> the sole designated beneficiary of [Jane's IRA] for purposes of determining the designated beneficiary under section 401(a)(9)(B)(iii) and (iv). No amounts distributed from [Jane's IRA to the trust] are accumulated in [the t]rust . . . during [Gabby's] lifetime for the benefit of any other beneficiary. Therefore, the residuary beneficiaries of [the t]rust . . . are mere potential successors to [Gabby's] interest in [Jane's IRA].[76]

Accordingly, any beneficiaries (including appointees under a power of appointment) whose interests succeed Gabby's interest would be disregarded for purposes of the look-through rules. Instead, Gabby's life expectancy would be used for purposes of calculating MRDs, and the trust would enjoy sixty-seven years of income tax deferral.

As just demonstrated, a conduit trust can have non-individuals and older individuals as successor beneficiaries and appointees under a power of appointment and still allow the use of the younger primary beneficiary's life expectancy. Therefore, the retirement account owner should consider naming a conduit trust for the benefit of a minor as beneficiary.

There is disagreement among commentators as to whether an effective conduit trust can be structured for *multiple* beneficiaries.[77] However, if a retirement plan owner wants to benefit several minors, he or she can divide the plan among multiple conduit trusts—each for the benefit of one minor—on a fractional or percentage basis within a beneficiary designation.[78]

There are drawbacks, however, to a conduit trust. A conduit trust does not fulfill many of the reasons for having a trust in the first place—conferring on the trustee discretion to accumulate assets and to distribute them to the beneficiary (or beneficiaries) pursuant to a standard such as "health, support, and education" or "best interest"—while an accumulation trust does. The structure of a conduit trust may be inconsistent with the account owner's goal of preventing the young person from gaining access to the assets.[79] The trustee of a conduit trust will be required to distribute, at a minimum, MRDs to that young person.

NOTE: The foregoing discussion applies to IRAs and QRPs. In the case of a QRP, however, the creation and funding of an inherited IRA from a decedent's QRP is available only to trusts when the application of look-through rules yields a DB.[80]

E. Trusteed IRA

An IRA owner who does not wish to leave the assets outright to a minor beneficiary might consider using a "Trusteed IRA," an alternative to a freestanding trust (just discussed) or to a custodial IRA.[81] Many financial institutions that provide custodial IRAs also offer Trusteed IRAs. For income tax purposes, custodial IRAs and trust IRAs (Trusteed IRAs) are treated identically.

The document governing a Trusteed IRA must comply with the MRD rules and other requirements of section 408 of IRC.[82] Otherwise, it can confer a variety of trustee powers on the institution administering the IRA. For example, the IRA trustee can have investment discretion over the Trusteed IRA, whereas a custodial IRA is entirely self-directed. Unlike an IRA custodian, the IRA trustee can be authorized to use assets for the benefit of the IRA owner and/or beneficiary. Under a custodial IRA, the beneficiary will have complete control over the inherited IRA assets. By contrast, the IRA owner can restrict the beneficiary's ability to withdraw any IRA assets over and above the MRDs.

Consistent with Code requirements, the Trusteed IRA mandates distribution of MRDs consistent with the applicable income tax rules. Whether or not the Trusteed IRA limits what the beneficiary can withdraw from the account beyond the MRDs, it will satisfy the requirements of a conduit trust discussed earlier. This is because, during the lifetime of the beneficiary, no accumulation for the benefit of someone other than the beneficiary can occur. Therefore, MRDs can be calculated using the life expectancy of the beneficiary regardless of who or what is designated as the successor beneficiary.

If an owner of a retirement account wishes to use a Trusteed IRA to benefit a minor, the owner will have to establish the Trusteed IRA during lifetime, and name the minor as beneficiary. Within the beneficiary designation, the IRA owner will have the opportunity to restrict the beneficiary's access to the IRA assets by, for example, providing that, in addition to the MRDs, the beneficiary can withdraw the IRA only at a certain age (e.g., one-third at age twenty-five, one-third at age thirty, and one-third at age thirty-five). In addition, the trustee of the IRA can be given authority to supplement withdrawals with discretionary distributions for the beneficiary's health, support, and education or the beneficiary's best interests.

The Trusteed IRA governing instrument will require MRDs to be distributed to the beneficiary. During minority, the beneficiary's UTMA account will be set up to receive the MRDs. After the beneficiary attains the age of majority, the beneficiary will receive MRDs directly. Given the absence of restrictions built into the beneficiary designation, the beneficiary, upon retaining the age of majority, will have complete control over the entire IRA.

A Trusteed IRA will be more expensive than a custodial IRA, and will not permit accumulation of MRDs inside the trust. On the other hand, this arrangement will be cheaper than a custom-drafted conduit or accumulation trust. By design, the distributions from the Trusteed IRA will stretch over the life expectancy of the minor beneficiary, allowing assets to continue to grow on an income tax deferred basis. Further, if the minor beneficiary's parent/custodian does not have money management skills, the trustee of the Trusteed IRA will provide professional investment services.

F. Grantor Trust Status

Change of ownership—from a minor to a grantor trust—may not trigger federal income tax consequences. For example, in private letter ruling 200826008, the taxpayer requested a ruling pertaining to the federal income tax consequences of a transfer of a IRA share to a trust. Specifically, a minor was one of two designated beneficiaries of an IRA. Following the owner's death, the IRA custodian set aside the minor's share in a separate IRA of which the minor is the sole beneficiary. The court-appointed conservator wanted to secure court authorization for the creation of a trust, and transfer, with court authorization, the minor's share of the IRA to the trust. Trust provisions would include, but not be limited to, (1) naming the minor as sole beneficiary, (2) allowing the trustee to make discretionary distributions of income and principal to the minor, and (3) allowing the minor to make withdrawals upon attaining a certain age. The Internal Revenue Service concluded the trust would be a grantor trust,[83] treated as owned by the minor under Code sections 671 and 677(a). In addition, the transfer of the IRA share to the trust would not be a sale or disposition for federal income tax purposes or a transfer for purposes of Code section 691(a)(2).[84]

> **PRACTICE NOTE**
>
> If the inherited IRA is sufficiently large and the circumstances otherwise warrant, a private letter ruling request should be considered notwithstanding its expense and time.

VI. ESTATE AND GST TAXES

The value of an IRA or QRP, payable to a minor beneficiary at the account owner's death, is includible in the account owner's gross estate for federal estate tax purposes.[85]

As previously discussed, leaving retirement benefits to a minor beneficiary will use the account owner's GST exemption (or will be subject to the GST tax) if the minor is a skip person.[86]

VII. ESTABLISHING IRAS FOR WORKING MINORS

Sometimes, a parent may wish to open an IRA (traditional or Roth) for his or her minor child. All persons who are under age seventy and a half and also earn compensation are eligible to establish a traditional IRA.[87] Young actors or models, for example, may have sufficient earnings to justify establishing an IRA. The preamble to the final Treasury regulations pertaining to Roth IRAs specifically provides that a parent or guardian of a minor may establish a Roth IRA on behalf of the minor child.[88] The financial institution providing the IRA will have to identify an adult who is legally authorized to act for the minor. That adult—a court-appointed guardian or a UTMA custodian, both discussed earlier[89]—will execute the IRA contract, designate a beneficiary, and exercise other powers vested in the account owner.

The UTMA custodian, who establishes the IRA, is the financial institution's client. The institution will not have duties to the minor (the "ward") for whom the adult is acting. For example, the financial institution will not have an obligation to inform the ward that an account for her benefit exists when the ward attains an age at which the custodianship terminates under the applicable state law. Likewise, the financial institution does not have an obligation to advise the custodian of his or her duties under UTMA including, for example, that the custodian is required to retitle the IRA in the name of the ward who has attained the age when the custodianship terminates.

VIII. CONCLUSION

An owner of an IRA or QRP may wish to leave retirement assets to one or more minors (e.g., children, grandchildren, or other relatives), or a minor may inherit retirement assets due to a disclaimer by a beneficiary or as the result of an unexpected death of a beneficiary. With a minor as beneficiary of a retirement account, the assets can grow on a tax deferred basis for a long time after the account owner's death because a minor has a long life expectancy and the minor's MRDs will be very modest in the early years.

Before the minor reaches the age of majority, the minor's guardian (typically, a parent) will exercise ownership rights over retirement assets on the minor's behalf.[90] Upon attaining the age of majority, the young person will have unfettered control of and access to the assets.[91] Access to substantial sums of money without financial maturity could create problems for the youth. There is no perfect solution for this problem. The best approach is to create a trust for the minor and name the trust as beneficiary of the retirement plan. However, a typical trust, designed for estate planning purposes, is likely to interfere with the income tax deferral. The income tax result can be improved through expert drafting, postmortem planning, and/or the possible use of a Trusteed IRA.

In the final analysis, the retirement account owner must confront a trade-off—maximum income tax deferral versus protection of a young person from the adverse consequences of "getting too much too soon."

NOTES

1.   While the author is a member of the Legal Department of The Northern Trust Company (Northern Trust), she is not an official spokesperson for the company. The ideas and observations expressed in the chapter reflect the author's day-to-day experiences but do not necessarily reflect official policies and procedures of Northern Trust.

2.   As a general matter, the term "retirement assets" may include IRAs, defined contribution plans, private and public defined benefit plans, and annuities.

3.   QRPs include plans that meet the requirements under sections 401(a), 403(a), or 403(b) of the Internal Revenue Code (I.R.C. or Code). An in-depth discussion of QRPs and the rules governing them is beyond the scope of this chapter. The reader is referred to Louis A. Mezzullo, *Estate and Gift Tax Issues for Employee Benefit Plans (Portfolio 814)*, Bloomberg, https://www.bna.com/estate-gift-tax-p7466/ (last visited Dec. 21, 2018) and Natalie Choate, Life and Death Planning for Retirement Benefits (8th ed. 2019). Updates to Ms. Choate's book are available at www.ataxplan.com/life-and-death-planning-for-retirement-benefits.

4.   https://www.irs.gov/retirement-plans/retirement-plans-faqs-regarding-iras-contributions.

5.   I.R.C. § 219(b)(5)(C).

6.   I.R.C. § 219(b)(5)(B).

7.   I.R.C. § 219(d)(1).

8.   I.R.C. § 219(g).

9.   I.R.C. § 408.

10.   I.R.C. §§ 408A (c)(1), 408A(d)(1).

11.   I.R.C. § 408A(c)(4).

12.   I.R.C. § 408A(c)(5). The concept of "required beginning date" is discussed later in the chapter.

13.   I.R.C. §§ 401(a)(9), 408(a)(6), 408(b)(3).

14.   Reg. § 1.401(a)(9)-2, A-2(a). A participant is considered a 5 percent owner if the participant owns more than 5 percent of the employer. In determining the 5 percent ownership, the attribution rules of Code section 318 apply.

15.   Reg. §§ 1.401(a)(9)-2, A-2(b), 1.408-8, A-3.

16. Reg. § 1.401(a)(9)-9, A-2.

17. Reg. § 1.401(a)(9)-5, A-1. The Uniform Lifetime Table is based on the account owner's age (beginning at age seventy) and the age of an individual ten years younger than the account owner in each distribution calendar year. Reg. § 1.401(a)(9)-9, A-2. The Uniform Lifetime Table and other tables are included in appendix B of IRS Publication 590-B, Distributions from Individual Retirement Arrangements (IRAs). IRS publications are available on the IRS website, www.irs.gov.

18. The Joint Life and Last Survivor Table and other tables (see note 17) are included in appendix B of IRS Publication 590-B, Distributions from Individual Retirement Arrangements (IRAs). IRS publications are available on the IRS website, www.irs.gov.

19. Reg. §§ 1.401(a)(9)-5, A-4(b), 1.401(a)(9)-9, A-3.

20. Reg. § 1.401(a)(9)-5, A-1(c).

21. Form 5329 and its instructions are available on the IRS website, www.irs.gov.

22. Reg. § 54.4974-2, A-7(a).

23. Reg. § 1.401(a)(9)-5, A-4(a).

24. Reg. § 1.401(a)(9)-5, A-1.

25. Pub. L. No. 109–280, 120 Stat. 780.

26. I.R.C. § 402(c)(11).

27. *See* note 25.

28. IRS Notice 2007-7, 2007-1 C.B. 395, V.

29. Instructions for 2016 IRS Forms 1099-R and 5498, p. 20. Forms and instructions are available on the IRS website, www.irs.gov.

30. IRS Notice 2007-7, 2007-1 C.B. 395, A-13.

31. Reg. § 1.401(a)(9)-4, A-1.

32. I.R.C. § 401(a)(9)(B)(iii).

33. Reg. § 1.401(a)(9)-5, A-5(a), (b).

34. Reg. §§ 1.401(a)(9)-5, A-5(c)(1); 1.401(a)(9)-5, A-6.

35. For convenience sake, the intermediary years are not illustrated.

36. Reg. § 1.401(a)(9)-5, A-7(a)(1). The determination of the identity of DB (or DBs) occurs on the so-called beneficiary determination date (BDD), which is September 30 of the year following the year of the retirement plan owner's death. Reg. § 1.401(a)(9)-4, A-4(a).

37. Reg. § 1.401(a)(9)-5, A-7(a)(2).

38. I.R.C. § 401(a)(9)(B)(iii).

39. Reg. § 1.401(a)(9)-8, A-3.

40. Reg. § 1.401(a)(9)-8, A-2(a)(2).

41. The discussion of the mechanics of how a minor establishes an inherited IRA is found later in this chapter.

42. Reg. § 1.401(a)(9)-4, A-3.

43. Reg. § 1.401(a)(9)-5, A-5(a)(2).

44. Reg. § 1.401(a)(9)-3, A-2.

45. There are ways that the identity of one or more DBs can be changed after the account owner's death, but before the BDD. *See* note 36 (explaining BDD). For example, one or more beneficiaries may be cashed out, that is, each receives the entire amount of the retirement account to which each is entitled. Another method involves a qualified disclaimer before the BDD. Reg. § 1.401(a)(9)-4, A-4(a). *See also* I.R.C. § 2518.

46. Reg. § 1.401(a)(9)-5, A-5(a)(2) and (c)(3).
47. *See* Chapter 1.
48. Employee Retirement Income Security Act of 1974, Pub. L. No. 93-406.
49. I.R.C. §§ 401(a)(11), 417.
50. *See also* Chapter 9.
51. *Id.*
52. 760 ILCS 20/4(a).
53. Choate, *supra* note 3, ¶ 6.4.05(G).
54. Some states have extended the age to twenty-five in limited circumstances. *See* Chapter 9.
55. *See* note 54.
56. *See* Chapter 9.
57. Reg. § 1.401(a)(9)-4, A-5.
58. Reg. § 1.401(a)(9)-4, A-5(a).
59. Reg. § 1.401(a)(9)-4, A-5(b) & A-6(b). The term "identifiable" means that, on the date of the IRA owner's death, it must be possible to determine the identity of the oldest individual who could receive the retirement account. Reg. § 1.401(a)(9)-4, A-1.
60. Reg. § 1.401(a)(9)-5, Q-7.
61. Reg. § 1.401(a)(9)-5, A-7(2)(b) (emphasis added).
62. Reg. § 1.401(a)(9)-5, A-7(2)(c).
63. *See* Reg. § 1.401(a)(9)-5, A-7(c)(3), ex. 1.
64. While only the taxpayer who requests the ruling may cite it as precedent, existing private letter rulings warrant examination because they provide insight into the IRS's thinking.
65. *See, e.g.,* PLR 200438044 (disclaimer of power to appoint to descendants and their spouses allows trust to qualify as a look-through trust).
66. *See, e.g.,* PLR 200228025 (IRS based MRDs on the life expectancy of a sixty-seven-year-old contingent beneficiary; PLR 200843042 ("heirs at law" cannot be ignored).
67. Reg. § 1.401(a)(9)-4, A-1.
68. *But see* note 66.
69. *See* Reg. § 1.401(a)(9)-4, A-4(a); PLR 2012203033 (despite execution by child of partial release of testamentary power of appointment so that only appointees would be individuals younger than surviving spouse, IRS ruled that surviving spouse's life expectancy would be used to calculate MRDs).
70. The disclaimer must be qualified for purposes of Code section 2518.
71. *See, e.g.,* PLR 201623001 (IRS denied spousal rollover notwithstanding court ruling that surviving spouse was entitled to retirement assets under community property law; IRS treated transfer as taxable distribution to surviving spouse).
72. *See* Exhibit 8-A.
73. *See* Exhibit 8-B.
74. *See, e.g.,* PLR 200537044 (trust protector limited beneficiary's power of appointment and takers-in-default to person not older than beneficiary; IRS ruled MRDs could be stretched over beneficiary's life expectancy); PLR 200235038 (power of appointment donees limited to individuals younger than beneficiary; IRS ruled MRDs may be calculated using beneficiary's life expectancy); PLR 200235041 (same).
75. *See* Exhibit 8-C.
76. Reg. § 1.401(a)(9)-5, A-7(c)(3), ex. 2.

77. *See*   http://www.morningstar.com/advisor/t/42990628/conduit-trusts-for -multiple-beneficiaries.htm?&ps=9.

78. *See* Exhibit 8-D.

79. *See* Chapter 9.

80. *See* section IV of this chapter. *See also* IRS Notice 2007-7, 2007-1 C.B. 395.

81. IRAs can be established in one of two legal forms: a custodial account or a trust account. *See* I.R.C. §§ 408(h), 408(a).

82. An IRS prescribed model document entitled Form 5305, Traditional Individual Retirement Account, is available on the IRS website, www.irs.gov.

83. *See* also Chapter 1.

84. *See also* PLR 200620025 (retirement assets left to a disabled beneficiary outright were transferred to special needs trust for the individual's benefit without adverse income tax consequences).

85. I.R.C. § 2039(a).

86. *See also* Chapter 1.

87. I.R.C. § 219(d)(1)

88. 84 Fed. Reg. 5597 (Feb. 4, 1999).

89. *See also* Chapter 9.

90. *See* Chapter 9.

91. *Id.*

EXHIBITS*

Notice and Disclaimer: Although the following provisions are the product of thought and effort, the attorney advising a particular client must make an independent determination as to whether and to what extent a provision is appropriate for his/her client and, further, how the provision may need to be modified to meet any special circumstances and objectives of the client.

Northern Trust does not guarantee that any of the following provisions effectively accomplish their purpose, and assumes no responsibility for any provision or its use. By using any of the following provisions, the attorney acknowledges that he or she (and not Northern Trust) is responsible for any document the attorney prepares which incorporates the provision.

EXHIBIT 8-A

Notwithstanding anything herein to the contrary, if any retirement plan benefits are payable to this trust, then the trustee shall not use any retirement plan benefits to pay any debts, taxes, or administration and other expenses due upon my death.

The term "retirement plan" means any qualified pension, profit-sharing, stock bonus, Keogh plan, or individual retirement account, as those terms are defined in the Code, or any other retirement arrangement, subject to the "minimum distribution rules" of Code section 401(a)(9) and regulations thereunder. The term "retirement plan benefits" means assets distributed to any trust hereunder from a retirement plan and any assets traceable to any such distribution.

---

* These exhibits are modified from iterations originally prepared by Northern Trust and repurposed in this chapter of *Tax, Estate, and Lifetime Planning for Minors, Second Edition,* with Northern Trust's express permission.

EXHIBIT 8-B

Notwithstanding anything herein to the contrary, if one or more of my spouse and my descendants survive me and any retirement plan benefits are payable to this trust, then (1) the trustee shall make no distribution or payment of any retirement plan benefits to a Disqualified Person (defined later in this paragraph), and (2) no power of appointment granted by me hereunder with respect to retirement plan benefits may be exercised in favor of a Disqualified Person. If necessary to carry out this intent, the class of beneficiaries of such trust or objects of any such power of appointment, in either case with respect to such retirement plan benefits, shall be narrowed to the largest class consistent with the terms of the trust instrument and the foregoing limitation. "Disqualified Person" means (1) any individual born in the calendar year prior to the calendar year of birth of (a) my spouse, if my spouse survives me, or, if my spouse does not survive me, (b) my oldest living descendant at the time of my death; (2) any recipient other than a noncharitable trust or an individual; or (3) any trust that may have as a beneficiary, with respect to retirement plan benefits, anyone described in (1) or (2) above that is not subject to the restrictions of this paragraph.

The term "retirement plan" means any qualified pension, profit-sharing, stock bonus, Keogh plan, or individual retirement account, as those terms are defined in the Code, or any other retirement arrangement, subject to the "minimum distribution rules" of Code section 401(a)(9) and regulations thereunder. The term "retirement plan benefits" means assets distributed to any trust hereunder from a retirement plan and any assets traceable to any such distribution.

EXHIBIT 8-C

Conduit Trust for Minor Grandchild

Each trust named for a grandchild of mine shall be administered as follows:

A. If the grandchild for whom the trust is named is living when the trust is created, then commencing as of that date and during the life of that grandchild, the trustee shall distribute to the grandchild:

1. The entire net income of the trust, except that if the trustee so elects, any portion or all of the net income otherwise distributable to the grandchild before the grandchild has reached the age of twenty-one years may be retained by the trustee and added to principal, as from time to time determined by the trustee;

2. As much of the principal of the trust, even to the extent of exhausting principal, as the trustee determines from time to time to be required for the health, support, and education of the grandchild, and as the independent trustee, if any, believes to be desirable for the best interests of the grandchild, without regard to the interest of any other beneficiary;

3. If any retirement plan benefits (as defied under this instrument) (the "plan") are payable to this trust, then each year, beginning with the year of my death, the trustee shall withdraw from the plan the Minimum Required Distribution for the plan for such year, and such additional amount or amounts as the trustee deems desirable in its discretion. The trustee shall distribute all such withdrawn amounts to the grandchild for whom the trust is named during the grandchild's lifetime; and

4. Upon the grandchild's death for whom the trust is named before complete distribution of the trust, the trust shall terminate, and the trustee shall distribute the remaining principal of the trust as follows:

   a. To such one or more of the grandchild's descendants, the grandchild's surviving spouse, and one or more charitable organizations and as the grandchild may appoint by will; or

   b. In default of effective appointment, to the then living descendants of the grandchild, per stirpes, or, if none, to my then living descendants, per stirpes.

EXHIBIT 8-D

Beneficiary Designation

My IRA account shall be allocated among my grandchildren who are living at my death, in equal shares, provided, however, that each grandchild's share shall be held in a separate trust named for such grandchild created under my revocable trust agreement in effect at my death.

CHAPTER 9

Nontax Considerations in Testamentary Transfers to Minors

Susan N. Gary and Nancy E. Shurtz

In addition to providing for the personal care of a child (see Chapter 6), an estate plan should address the management of property received by a child after the death of a parent, grandparent, or other adult. Decisions about how property will be managed, when the child will receive the property, and who will manage the property will have significant effects on the child. The manner in which a child receives property can have a positive influence on a child's development and choices, but it also has the potential to affect the child negatively. An estate planner can help clients think through potential choices and weigh the advantages and disadvantages of each option.

Estate planners who focus on tax planning to the exclusion of personal and family issues do not serve their clients well. Nontax issues always deserve attention; for some clients the nontax issues may take precedence over tax concerns. Through thoughtful planning, parents can provide adequate resources for a child's care and development, encourage or discourage particular behaviors or activities, and create mechanisms to help the child learn to manage money as the child matures.

In addition to discussing the how, when, and who of property management for a minor child, this chapter considers issues that arise in defining family relationships for purposes of testamentary documents. Adopted children, stepchildren, illegitimate children, and posthumously conceived children may require special planning. An estate planner must take care to draft definitions that include or exclude family members according to a client's wishes. For a sample "Client Questionnaire," see Appendix 9-A. Please see Chapter 10 for a focus on children born using assisted reproductive technology, including drafting suggestions.

I. HOW THE PROPERTY IS MANAGED: ASSESSMENT OF THE TRANSFER MECHANISMS

In most situations, property left to a minor child should be managed under a fiduciary arrangement—a guardian or conservator appointed by a court, a custodian under a custodianship, or a trustee under a trust. The costs, flexibility, and ease of administration of each of these arrangements vary, as does the age at which the fiduciary arrangement must terminate. The best choice for a particular client will depend on the type and amount of property involved; on the child's abilities; and on family relationships, values, and goals.

A. Outright Transfers to a Minor

Generally, states permit a child to hold title to property. However, state law usually restricts the child's abilities to deal with the property. A minor is incompetent to sell, invest, rent, mortgage, exchange, or otherwise administer the property, and transactions with third parties are voidable at the election of the minor. In many states a minor cannot make a will, thus if the child dies during minority, the property will go by intestate succession—contrary to any intended estate plan. In addition, outright transfers to minors result in the minor obtaining full control of the property when the child reaches age eighteen, whether or not the child is ready to manage the property.

Conclusion: Transferring property to a minor to hold in the minor's own name is almost always undesirable.

B. Transfers Directly to Minor's Parents or Other Responsible Adult

For small amounts of money or for transfers of tangible personal property, a will often authorizes the personal representative to transfer the property to a parent or other adult relative of the child. Relying on a "facility-of-payment" provision may be appropriate for small amounts, if an appropriate adult can receive the payment, and this approach has the advantage of no administrative costs. However, unless the provision creates a trustee-beneficiary relationship between the adult and the child, the direct-payment approach does not give the child legal recourse if the adult misuses the property. For this reason, facility-of-payment clauses typically direct payment to the adult as a custodian or trustee.

1. Sample Facility-of-Payment Clause

If a beneficiary has not attained age twenty-one at the time any property becomes distributable to him or to her, the property shall vest in the beneficiary, but the personal representative may distribute any part or all of the property to a custodian for the beneficiary under any Uniform Transfer to Minors Act (and the personal representative shall not be liable for any act or failure to act of any such custodian) or to a parent or adult relative of the beneficiary, or to any person having custody of the beneficiary, as trustee, against such person's receipt and upon such person's written under taking to hold the property in trust, to use the property for the benefit of the beneficiary, and at the time the beneficiary attains age twenty-one to deliver the then remaining property to the beneficiary. The distribution to such a custodian or such receipt and written undertaking shall discharge the personal representative.

If the will does not contain a facility-of-payment provision, statutes in some states permit payment to the person who has custody of the minor. The Uniform Probate Code (UPC) includes a facility-of-transfer provision but limits the amount that can be transferred to $5,000.[1]

Conclusion: Direct transfers work well for personal property of limited value and when the adult who is the transferee can be trusted. Requiring a conservatorship, guardianship, custodianship, or trust in these circumstances may not be necessary.

C. Conservatorships

If a will fails to create a trust to manage a minor's property or if nonprobate assets, such as life insurance proceeds, retirement assets, and bank accounts, will be distributed to a minor, a conservatorship may be necessary. The personal representative, other transferor, or another person interested in the child's welfare can petition the court for the appointment of a conservator to manage the child's property. A conservator's duties are to manage the property for the benefit of the child and to distribute the property after considering the needs of the child and the best interests of the child. The conservator must file an inventory of the assets subject to the conservatorship with the court. The conservator must keep accurate records and must file an accounting with the court annually. The court can appoint a visitor to monitor the reports, interview the minor, and otherwise investigate the conservatorship. A conservatorship usually terminates when the minor child reaches the age of majority—eighteen in most states.

The need for a conservatorship usually arises due to a lack of planning, and a conservatorship is rarely part of the intended estate plan. If a decedent failed to plan for the distribution of property to a minor, then a conservatorship will be necessary unless a court will permit the distribution to a custodian (see subsection I.E., Custodial Accounts) or outright to a parent or other responsible adult (see subsection I.B.).

Advantages:

- A conservatorship provides court supervision of the fiduciary's management of the minor's assets.
- A conservatorship serves as a mechanism for managing property for a minor if the decedent did not plan for a trust or custodianship.

Disadvantages:

- The cost of the initial court proceeding to appoint the conservator and the costs of preparing the inventory and annual accountings can be significant.
- The conservator may be required to post a bond or surety on the bond.
- The requirement to report to the court every year may be an unnecessary burden.
- Conservators are restricted in their investment and disbursement opportunities.
- The conservatorship usually terminates when the child reaches age eighteen, and the child may not be ready to handle the property at that age.

Conclusion: Because conservatorships require strict court supervision and end when the child reaches the age of majority, they should be used for minors only when there has been no planning.

D. Guardianships

Some states lack updated conservatorship statutes and instead provide for guardians of the property to manage property for minors. These guardianship statutes tend to be more limiting than the conservatorship statutes.[2] Like conservators, guardians are court supervised, but the supervision is more restrictive. For example, guardians may be required to obtain court orders to sell property or change investments. In states that lack conservatorship statutes, planning for an alternative to guardianship is even more important.
Advantages:

- Because of the close court supervision, the requirement to post a bond, and the limits on the guardian's investment powers, guardianships ensure that the minor's property is protected.
- Guardianships, like conservatorships, serve as a mechanism for managing property for a minor if the decedent did not plan for a trust or custodianship.

Disadvantages:

- Guardians do not have title to the property and cannot sell the property or change investments without a court order.
- A guardian's actions may be voidable for lack of authority, making third parties reluctant to deal with the guardian.

- In a guardianship, the ward is likely to end up with less property than in a conservatorship.
- Like conservators, guardians may be required to post a bond.
- As with conservatorships, the costs of guardianships may be significant.
- As with conservatorships, guardianships require strict court supervision.
- As with conservatorships, guardianships usually terminate when the child reaches age eighteen.

Conclusion: Guardianships offer the most conservative approach to the protection of a minor's assets. However, because the guardians lack title and their transactions are voidable, guardianships are even less desirable than conservatorships.

E. Custodial Accounts

Every state has enacted statutes that authorize the transfer of property to a custodian to hold for the benefit of a minor. Only one state, South Carolina, still follows the Uniform Gifts to Minors Act (1956, revised 1966) (UGMA).[3] The other states, the District of Columbia, and the U.S. Virgin Islands have adopted the Uniform Transfers to Minors Act (1983, revised 1986) (UTMA).[4] A custodianship is somewhat like a statutory trust, with the terms of the arrangement established by statute. Because state statutes vary, a counselor should review the applicable state statute. (For a state-by-state comparison chart, see Appendix 9-C.)

The revision of UGMA in 1966 expanded the types of property covered. UGMA, as revised, can be used for securities, bank deposits, and insurance. The 1983 changes to UTMA went further, permitting any type of property to be transferred to a custodian. This could include real estate and tangible property, as well as limited liability company and limited partnership interests. Furthermore, UTMA places no limit on the dollar amount of the property that can be transferred.

A transfer to a custodianship can be made as a lifetime gift or after the donor's death, for example, through a life insurance designation or under a will or trust provision. Even if the transferor has not authorized the creation of a custodianship, if a personal representative, trustee, or conservator decides that a transfer to a minor would best be handled through a custodianship and determines that doing so is not inconsistent with the will or trust that directs the transfer of property to the minor, the fiduciary may create the custodianship.[5] If the transfer involves an amount greater than $10,000, the fiduciary must seek court approval.[6] Someone who owes a debt to a minor, for example a tortfeasor, can, if a conservator has not been appointed for the minor, transfer the amount owed to the minor to a custodian.[7] The provision authorizing transfers from estates, trusts, conservatorships, and third-party obligors was added to UTMA and may not be the law in South Carolina under UGMA.

A custodianship account must be set up for each beneficiary; UTMA does not permit multiple beneficiaries in one account.[8] This limitation can be particularly problematic if the transferor wants the use of the property to vary based on the needs of the family. Another problem is that the case law as to rights and duties under custodianships is not substantial, which could lead to uncertainty.[9]

1. Custodian

Generally, any person age twenty-one and older or a trust company can serve as custodian.[10] Only one custodian can act at a time,[11] in contrast to a trust, which can have multiple trustees. Nonresidents and foreign citizens may serve as custodians.[12] As with a trust, the custodian need not post a bond.

The transferor can name successor custodians, to act one at a time if the original custodian resigns.[13] A custodian can resign by giving notice to the minor, if the minor is over age fourteen, and to the successor custodian and by transferring the property to the successor custodian.[14] UTMA provides that a minor who has attained the age of fourteen, the transferor, an adult member of the minor's family, the minor's guardian, or the minor's conservator may petition the court to remove the custodian and appoint a successor custodian, or require the custodian to post a bond.[15]

2. Duties of the Custodian

As a fiduciary, a custodian must keep the property separate from the custodian's own property and from other property. Custodianship property is not to be commingled, placed in joint tenancies,[16] or otherwise disposed of for less than adequate consideration.[17] The custodian has a duty to take control of the property and to manage and invest the property.[18] The custodian must maintain records of all transactions and make the records available to the minor's legal representation or to the minor, if the minor is fourteen or older.[19] The custodian need not report to the court.

The custodian may retain the property in the form originally received.[20] However, if the custodian intends to actively manage the custodial property, then UTMA requires the custodian to exercise the "standard of care that would be observed by a prudent person dealing with property of another."[21] Thus, UTMA adopts the prudence norm that is used throughout fiduciary law. The standard continues to evolve, and any fiduciary, including a custodian, should stay abreast of developments in prudent investing, including the Uniform Prudent Investor Act.[22] Analyses of the prudence standard in other areas of fiduciary law can be used to interpret the UTMA standard.[23]

Although a UTMA custodianship can hold property such as real estate, automobiles, and business interests, liability issues suggest caution in using a custodianship to manage those assets. UTMA limits liability arising from property held in a custodianship to the property itself, unless the minor or the custodian is personally at fault.[24] However, a trust may be a better way to manage assets where potential liability is a concern.

3. *Costs of Custodianships*

A custodian may serve with or without compensation. However, in no event can a transferor who serves as custodian receive compensation.[25] All custodians are entitled to be reimbursed for all reasonable expenses incurred in the performance of their duties.[26]

4. *Use of the Property*

A custodian has broad discretionary powers to use the property for the benefit of the minor. UTMA directs the custodian to use such amounts as the custodian "considers advisable for the use and benefit" of the minor.[27] This includes support, education, and maintenance but also includes such things as paying tort claims, child support, and taxes. If a custodian uses property improperly, the custodian may be liable to the minor for breach of fiduciary duties.

5. *Jurisdictional Issues*

Jurisdictional issues become important if the minor moves out of the state or if the donor wants to choose a law for the custodianship account other than that of the donor's state of residence. Under UTMA the transferor may designate which state law should control.[28] The only restriction is that at the time of the transfer, the transferor, minor, or custodian must be a resident of the designated state or the custodial property must be located in that state.[29] The law of the state in which the account was initially established or the state chosen in the custodianship account will apply if the beneficiary later leaves the state. Even if the custodian relocates, the custodian remains subject to personal jurisdiction in the state in which the account was created.[30]

6. *Asset Protection*

Ownership of the custodianship account is vested in the minor beneficiary, so the account can be reached to pay any personal debts of the minor that are nonvoidable obligations. Generally, creditors of the custodian cannot reach assets in the account.[31] However, if the donor is also the custodian, the property may not be protected from creditors.[32] For example, when the custodian improperly uses the custodianship assets, the custodian's creditors may be able to reach the account.[33] If a parent is negligent with respect to UTMA funds, creditors will not be able to reach the funds, but "when a custodian's use of such funds appears to be more than merely negligent, creditors may, depending on the circumstances, have a right to levy on such funds which would otherwise not be attachable."[34] Of course, if the donor established the account to defraud creditors, the account will not be protected.

7. *Federal Tax Consequences*

Generally, income in a custodianship account is taxed to the minor, regardless of whether the custodian distributes any income to the minor. The kiddie tax would tax any unearned income of a beneficiary who has not attained the age of nineteen by the end of the year or who is a full-time student under the age of twenty-four at the tax rates of trusts and estates for tax years after December 31, 2017, and before January 1, 2026.[35] Long-term capital gains or "qualified dividends" would be subject to current favorable rates (which could be zero), but with modified income thresholds.[36] If, on the other hand, any unearned income actually is used to satisfy the support obligation of the parent, it will be taxed to the parent.

Transfers to custodianship accounts during the life of the donor will qualify for the annual exclusion for federal gift tax purposes, as long as the transfer qualifies under section 2503(c) of the Internal Revenue Code (hereinafter IRC or Code). Code section 2503(c) requires that the property held in a trust or a custodianship be distributed to the minor at age twenty-one. A custodianship established to continue until age twenty-five, now permitted in a few states, will not qualify for the annual exclusion. Any failure to qualify under IRC section 2503(c), however, has no effect on testamentary transfers.

With respect to the federal estate tax, if the beneficiary dies during the term of the custodianship, the account will be included in the beneficiary's estate. If a donor acts as custodian, the custodianship assets will likely be included in the donor's estate if the donor dies while serving as custodian.[37] If a donor-parent creates a custodianship for the donor's child and acts as custodian, IRC section 2036(a)(1) causes inclusion, because the custodian could use custodianship property to satisfy the custodian-parent's duty of support.[38] Even if the donor is not the child's parent, if the donor acts as custodian, the assets may be included in the donor's estate under IRC section 2038 due to the custodian's control over the timing of disbursements to the child.[39] A possible risk of making a nondonor parent the custodian is that the custodian could be viewed as having a general power of appointment under IRC section 2041, because the property could be used to discharge the legal obligation to support the child.

If the donor names his or her spouse as custodian, the assets should not be included in the spouse's estate because the power over the assets is not a retained power. However, if two donors create custodianships for their children and name each other as custodian, the reciprocal trust doctrine may cause inclusion if one of the donors dies.[40]

If the minor is assigned to a generation more than one generation from the donor, the transfer could be a direct skip and be subject to federal generation-skipping transfer tax. Whether a tax is owed will depend on the donor's other taxable transfers. These transfers might be sheltered by the applicable exclusion amount.[41]

Advantages:

- A custodianship is simple and inexpensive to create and manage.
- In contrast with a trust, the transferor does not need to hire a lawyer to draft a trust instrument.

- In contrast with a conservatorship or guardianship, no court approval or supervision is required.
- A custodian need not post a bond.
- A nonresident can be custodian and the donor can select as the state that controls the custodianship the state in which the donor, custodian, or beneficiary resides or the state in which the property is located.

Disadvantages:

- The terms of a custodianship, unlike those of a trust, cannot be tailored to fit the needs of a particular family.
- Unlike a trust, a custodianship cannot have multiple beneficiaries.
- Unlike a trust, substantial case law does not exist as to the rights and duties under custodianships.
- Unlike a trust, there can be no spendthrift provisions to protect the donee against creditors.
- The property must be distributed to the minor at the age of majority, at age twenty-one, or in some cases age twenty-five.
- If the custodianship continues until the child is twenty-five, the transferor will not be entitled to a gift tax annual exclusion for transfers to the custodianship.
- Adverse federal income tax consequences may arise when the donee is under the age of nineteen or the income from the account is used to support the minor.
- If the donor is custodian, the assets may be includable in the donor's estate if the donor dies while serving as custodian.
- If the parent is not the donor but acts as custodian, the assets may be includable in the parent's estate.
- If the minor dies during the custodianship, the property will be includable in the minor's estate.
- Property in the custodianship account will be considered owned by the minor for purposes of need-based scholarships or financial aid.

Conclusion: Custodianships are a simple and inexpensive alternative to establishing conservatorships, guardianships, or trusts for gifts of property to minors. They work well for modest transfers of property. In some circumstances a custodianship can be used to avoid a conservatorship. For larger estates, however, a trust provides greater flexibility and can continue until the child is older.

PRACTICE NOTE

Typically, in a custodianship, the property is placed "[in the name of the custodian] as custodian for [name of minor] under the [name of enacting state] Uniform Transfers [or Gifts] to Minors Act."[42]

F. Trusts

A trust is the most flexible way to hold and manage property for a minor because a trust can be drafted to fit the specific needs of a family or a child. The trust instrument establishes the rules for the distribution of the property, so the transferor can decide when and how the minor should receive income and principal from the trust. A trust is a private arrangement and requires no court supervision.

1. Trustee

A trustee holds legal title to the trust property and has authority to deal with third parties. Unlike a custodianship, a trust can have more than one trustee. The trust document should name successor trustees or give someone (the acting trustee or the income beneficiaries) the power to name a successor trustee. If no trustee named can act, a court proceeding will be necessary to appoint a new trustee. The trust document can waive the posting of a bond.

2. Trust Protector

A trust protector is a person authorized by the settlor to exercise one or more powers over the trust. For example, a trust protector might be given the power to remove and replace the trustee, to make investment decisions, or to make decisions about distributions to beneficiaries. A trust protector's authority supersedes that of the trustee, to the extent of the specified powers. In most states a trust protector is treated as a fiduciary with respect to the specified powers, but the law in some states remains unclear. The Uniform Directed Trusts Act (2017) uses the term "trust director."

3. Duties of the Trustee

State trust law—either the common law or the Uniform Trust Code[43] or other state trust statutes—requires that a trustee act under strict fiduciary duties, similar to those required for conservators and custodians. Basic fiduciary duties, such as the duty "to act in good faith and in accordance with the purposes of the trust,"[44] are mandatory. The trust instrument can modify other duties, such as duties associated with investment decision making. For example, if the trustee is a family member, the trustee may be permitted to buy property from the trust or to vote shares of stock in a family business the trustee controls. Also, state law may permit the transferor to direct that the trustee report to one but not all beneficiaries or even to a third party who will protect the interests of the beneficiaries.[45]

With respect to investments, trustees are subject to the prudent investor standard. Most states have adopted the Uniform Prudent Investor Act (UPIA),[46] and in the handful of other states, an understanding of the prudence norm would be influenced by UPIA. UPIA requires a trustee to "invest and manage trust assets as a prudent investor would" considering factors relating to the trust, the investments, and general economic conditions.[47]

The prudent investor standard gives trustees more flexibility than the older "prudent person" rule and permits investing on a total-return basis rather than requiring that the prudence of investments be considered on an asset-by-asset basis.[48] UPIA also permits trustees to delegate to investment advisors and permits a trustee to determine that due to special circumstances the purposes of a trust will be better served without diversifying the investments.[49] Thus, trustees will have greater flexibility in making investment decisions than do conservators or custodians.

4. Costs of Trusts

Like a custodian, a trustee may serve without compensation. However, the trust usually provides for reasonable compensation. Because of the initial cost of drafting the trust document and the cost of ongoing administration, trusts can be more expensive than other transfer mechanisms. When the trustee is a corporation, the expenses and fees can be quite high.

5. Use of the Property

The person creating a trust—the settlor—has complete control over the timing of and reasons for distributions. The trust instrument can require mandatory distributions at specified times. For example, a trust might provide that after a child reaches age twenty-one the trustee will pay all the trust income to the child. The trust might provide that the trustee must distribute one-half of the corpus of the trust when the beneficiary reaches age twenty-five and the remaining corpus of the trust when the beneficiary reaches age thirty.

The trust instrument can provide for discretionary distributions and should provide directions to guide the trustee in making the distributions. The standard of distribution in the trust instrument creates legally binding rules governing the trustee's actions. To promote flexibility, however, the standard usually leaves a substantial amount of discretion in the hands of the trustee. The standard may be non-ascertainable—for the child's welfare and best interests—or ascertainable—for the child's health, support, maintenance, and education. The trust instrument also may provide instructions—for example a direction that distributions be made "after first considering" or "without regard to" any other income and assets then available to the child.

The trust instrument may include precatory language, describing the transferor's primary purpose in creating the trust but leaving the actual determinations of distributions up to the trustee. For example, the trust document might provide: "It is my hope that the trust will be used primarily to pay for my grandchild's college education." A trust instrument could limit distributions to provide for educational expenses, but usually giving the trustee greater discretion is appropriate, so that the trust property will be available if unexpected situations arise. *See* Appendix 9-D, Document 1, Sample Education-Related Incentive Provisions.

A trust also might provide for distributions for specific purposes. The trust could direct the trustee to distribute funds to a beneficiary to assist in the purchase of a car or a residence or to help the beneficiary start a business. *See* Appendix 9-D, Document 2, Sample Provisions for Distributions to Assist in Purchase of Automobile and Residence, and Document 3, Sample Provision for Distributions to Assist in Starting a Business.

In some circumstances, permitting distributions to a child's guardian may be appropriate, even if the guardian is not otherwise a beneficiary of the trust. A trustee might be authorized to make distributions to the beneficiary's legal guardian, to assist the guardian with financial burdens associated with raising the child. *See* Appendix 9-D, Document 4, Support of Guardian Provision.

The settlor can incorporate values into a trust and use the distribution provisions to encourage or discourage behaviors. For example, distributions could depend on the child's graduating from college, demonstrating maturity and the ability to manage money, or abstaining from drug abuse. Adequate guidance to the trustee is essential if the settlor limits distributions based on the conduct of the beneficiary.

A parent who wants to provide an incentive to a child not to use drugs might include a provision that requires the beneficiary to submit to random drug tests. Under terms spelled out in the trust, the trustee would choose a contact person. The contact person would notify the beneficiary and immediately accompany the beneficiary to a medical laboratory for testing. Distributions from the trust could depend on compliance and negative test results. *See* Appendix 9-D, Document 5, Sample Provision for Distributions to Substance Abusers.

Some parents become concerned that children who receive a substantial inheritance will be disinclined to work productively. A trust might include an incentive provision that matches trust distributions with income earned by the beneficiary. Alternatively, the trust could provide for distributions to beneficiaries who work in lower-paid but altruistic jobs, for example by working as missionaries, teachers, or Peace Corps volunteers.[50] *See* Appendix 9-D, Document 6, Sample Provision for Withholding Distributions to a Beneficiary Not Engaged in Productive Activities.

6. Sample Incentive Provision

The following is an example of a sample incentive provision:

> The trustee shall pay to Alex the sum of $50,000, upon his graduation with a bachelor's degree from an accredited college or university.

7. Jurisdictional Issues

The settlor of a trust can select the law that will govern the trust. Unlike a custodianship, a trust need not have a connection with the state whose law is selected.[51] The settlor also can designate the principal place of administration for the trust if the trustee is located in the jurisdiction or all or part of the administration occurs in the jurisdiction.[52] Furthermore, the trustee can change the situs of the trust to any other state, even to a jurisdiction outside the United States, as the trustee determines to be in the best interests of the trust estate and beneficiaries.[53]

8. *Multiple Beneficiaries*

Unlike a conservatorship or a custodianship, one trust can have multiple beneficiaries. For a family with several minor children, creating one "basket" or "pot" trust for all the children may be a good way to manage the property for the children if their parents both die. When the youngest child reaches a specified age, perhaps twenty-five, the trust property can either be distributed outright to the children or be divided into separate trusts, one for each child. The concept of a basket trust is that the parents' property will be used for the family, as the parents would use their property if they were alive. The trust assets are divided after the youngest child reaches age twenty-five, because by then the children are likely to have finished college.

A basket trust has the advantage of minimizing administrative duties and expenses, as compared with creating a separate trust for each child. However, a basket trust may lead to dissatisfaction if the trustee makes unequal distributions among the children. The trustee may view distributions to the child who needs them most as fair, but the other children may think that only equal distributions are fair. If children are of significantly different ages, a basket trust may not work well because the older children will be much older than the younger ones when the children receive their inheritances.

9. *Asset Protection*

Creditors of the settlor should not be able to reach assets in a trust if the transfer to the trust was a completed gift, unless the transfer was intended to defraud creditors. With respect to creditors of the beneficiary, trusts typically contain a spendthrift provision that will protect trust property from most creditors.[54] A spendthrift clause prohibits the child-beneficiary from alienating his or her interests so that the child cannot sell the trust interest (voluntary alienation) and the creditors of the child cannot reach the interest (involuntary alienation). When a trust terminates, creditors can attach distributions to be made to the beneficiary.

During the administration of the trust, a few exceptions to spendthrift protection may apply. Some states have created exceptions for claims for child support or spousal support. In some of the states, a child or former spouse of a beneficiary can reach property subject to mandatory distribution but not property subject to discretionary distribution, until the trustee exercises the discretion.[55] The Uniform Trust Code (UTC) provides that these creditors may attach both mandatory and discretionary distributions and may compel distributions if the trustee has not complied with a standard of distribution or has abused the trustee's discretion.[56] Another exception under the common law is for creditors who have supplied "necessaries"—services or support necessary for the beneficiary.[57] The UTC does not include this rule.

Under the common law, creditors cannot reach the assets subject to a general power of appointment until the donee of the power exercises the power.[58] Several states have changed this common law rule.[59] Thus, if a trust creates a power of withdrawal for federal gift tax reasons (e.g., a Crummey power to allow the transferor to obtain the annual exclusion for a transfer to the trust), then until the power lapses, in some states the beneficiary's creditors may be able to reach the property subject to withdrawal.

Settlors increasingly worry that a trust created for a child or grandchild may end up in the hands of the beneficiary's former spouse after a divorce. Even if the trust does not name the spouse as a beneficiary, the spouse may argue that the trust should be considered in dividing the spouses' marital assets on divorce. If the settlor creates the trust during the marriage, the spouse may argue that the transferor intended to benefit the spouse as well as the child. A strategy for the settlor is to include language in the trust instrument establishing the settlor's intent to benefit only the child. Evidence that the spouses commingled distributions from the trust also may support the inclusion of the trust in calculations of marital property. The settlor may want to include language directing the trustee not to distribute income or principal if the trustee determines that the beneficiary is commingling trust distributions with marital assets. Such an instruction may encourage the child to keep nonmarital assets segregated. These tactics do not guarantee that the trust will be ignored when the couple divides their assets, but the additional language may help.

10. Spendthrift Clause

The following is an example of a spendthrift clause:

The interest of beneficiaries in principal or income is not subject to claims of their creditors or others, nor to legal process, and may not be voluntarily or involuntarily anticipated, alienated, or encumbered.

11. Disability Planning

If a child qualifies for state aid due to a disability, a trust for that child must be structured carefully to avoid having the inheritance disqualify the child from benefits. Planning is critical if needs-based government benefits are an issue, because an outright transfer to the child, through a will or by intestacy, or property held for the child in a conservatorship or custodianship, will be deemed available to the child and will cause the child to lose benefits. If the transferor instead creates a supplemental needs trust, the trust assets will be available to pay for extra needs of the child but will not prevent the child from receiving government benefits.[60]

12. *Federal Tax Consequences*

Unlike custodianships, the federal income tax consequences of trusts can be complex. The settlor, the trust, or the beneficiary may be the taxpayer. Any income retained in the trust and not taxed to the grantor or the beneficiary is taxed to the trust at tax brackets that become very high, very quickly.

Like custodianships, transfers to a trust are generally considered gifts of a future interest and will not qualify for the annual exclusion from gift tax. Two exceptions allow a donor to obtain the federal gift tax annual exclusion. A trust can be set up to qualify under IRC section 2503(c) if the trust has only one beneficiary, the trust instrument does not impose substantial restrictions on the trustee's discretion, and the beneficiary will receive the trust assets at age twenty-one. An alternative exception involves giving the beneficiary the power to withdraw amounts transferred to the trust, a so-called Crummey withdrawal power, named after the case that established this technique.[61]

When the trustee dies, the value of the trust will be in the trustee's estate only if the trustee is the donor and retains certain powers or interests, either individually or as trustee. If the minor dies, whether the trust will be taxed in the minor's estate will depend on the minor's beneficial rights in the trust. Like custodianships, if the minor is assigned to a generation more than one generation from the donor, the transfer to the trust or distributions from the trust could be subject to federal generation-skipping transfer tax.[62]

Advantages:

- Trust property need not be distributed to a child at an early age, before the child is ready to manage the property.
- A trust may have more than one beneficiary, thus providing for the specific needs of the particular family.
- The transferee can establish the terms for distribution of the property.
- A trust can be perpetual in states that have abolished the Rule Against Perpetuities.
- A trust may include a spendthrift provision that protects the assets from the beneficiary's creditors.
- A trust can be drafted so as not to disqualify the beneficiary from needs-based benefits.
- A trustee has legal title and can deal with third parties.
- A trustee need not post a bond.

Disadvantages:

- A trust is more expensive to create than a custodianship.
- A trust may be more expensive to administer than a custodianship, particularly if a corporate trustee is used.
- The income of trusts can be taxed in high tax brackets.

- The transferor may not be entitled to a gift tax exclusion for transfers to the trust.
- The value of trust assets and/or income could be considered the minor's assets or income for purposes of needs-based scholarships or financial aid.

Conclusion: For transfers of substantial amounts of property and when there are multiple beneficiaries, the trust is the most desirable transfer mechanism. Although the trust may cost more than other types of transfers, the benefits of controlling the age and terms of distribution, as well as asset protection and planning for disability, make it well worth the cost.

II. WHEN SHOULD THE PROPERTY BE DISTRIBUTED?

As mentioned earlier in this chapter, conservatorships and guardianships will most likely end when the minor becomes an adult, which is eighteen years old in most states. Custodianship, on the other hand, can end when the minor turns twenty-five. The advantage of a trust is that it is flexible and can assure that distributions of the property occur only when the child has matured.

A. Conservatorships and Guardianships

By statute, most states have lowered the age of majority to eighteen for most purposes. Thus, in most states a conservatorship or guardianship will end when the minor reaches the age of eighteen. Under the Uniform Guardianship and Protective Proceedings Act (UGPPA), a conservatorship created for a protected person terminates when the minor attains the age of eighteen or is emancipated. However, state law must be checked. For example, under Colorado law, a conservatorship does not terminate until the protected person attains the age of twenty-one.[63]

B. Custodial Accounts

States vary as to when a custodianship terminates. Under UTMA, a custodianship of property transferred by gift, through the exercise of a power of appointment, or by specific authorization under a will or trust, will terminate when the minor reaches age twenty-one. For a custodianship created by a personal representative or trustee without specific authorization in a will or trust or by an obligor, such as an insurance company or a tortfeasor, the age of termination is eighteen. A number of states have modified these rules, permitting the transferor to designate a later termination date, *but only if the transferor does so* **in the original document creating the UTMA account**. Some states permit termination to extend to twenty-one and others to twenty-five.

In a few states, the statutory age for termination is twenty-one, but the transferor can direct an age between eighteen and twenty-one for termination. Appendix 9-C, State-by-State Comparison Chart, lists the ages for termination. In at least one state, Illinois, a custodian can terminate a custodianship early by transferring the assets into a trust that qualifies as a section 2503(c) trust.[64]

The appropriate age for distribution will depend on the amount of property involved and the likelihood that the child will be ready to handle the property. In states that permit the donor to set the age of distribution earlier or later than the age fixed by the statute, the designation must be made when the donor creates the custodianship. The donor should consider whether to designate a different age for distribution, keeping in mind that choosing an age later than twenty-one may have gift tax consequences.

C. Trusts

The trust instrument directs the termination of the trust, and the settlor has nearly complete flexibility in deciding how long the trust should continue. A trust for a minor may continue until the child reaches the age the parent believes appropriate, possibly twenty-five or thirty. The trustee can be directed to distribute the principal all at once or in two or three stages. For example, the child could receive one-third of the principal at age twenty-five, one-third at age thirty, and the remaining property at age thirty-five. The options are many.

Although oftentimes children receive their inheritances after attaining a specified age, some families may decide to hold the property in trust for a longer period. One reason for doing this is that a trust with a spendthrift provision protects the assets from creditors. A second reason is that federal transfer tax savings may be possible if the transferor uses the transfer tax exemption and the generation-skipping transfer tax exemption to protect the trust from transfer taxes. A properly drafted trust can continue for multiple generations without paying transfer tax, if the trust is entirely exempt when created. In some states, the Rule Against Perpetuities prevents a trust from continuing indefinitely, but even in a state with the common law Rule Against Perpetuities, the trust can continue until the death of the transferor's child. Thus, a transferor may choose to structure a trust to continue for the life of the child, protecting the property from creditors and keeping the trust property from being taxed in the child's estate when the child dies.

D. Comparison Chart

For a concise comparison of features of transfer mechanisms in chart form, see Table 9.1 on the next page.

Table 9.1 Transfer Mechanism Comparison Chart

Feature	Conservatorships	Custodianships	Trusts
Asset Protection Possible	Yes	No, exposure to child's creditors but not parent's creditors unless parent/custodian more than "merely negligent"	Depends on terms of trust
Bond Required	Yes	No	No
Costs and Fees	Court costs, accounting fees, possible bond or surety	No fee for drafting document, no court costs	Drafting document, financial reporting and administration expenses
Court Supervision	Yes	No	No
Federal Estate Tax: Donor's Estate	No	Yes, if donor is custodian and owes duty of support	Not unless donor retains interest or powers
Federal Estate Tax: Minor's Estate	Includable in estate	Includable in estate	Depends on terms of trust
Investments: In General	Restricted	Liberal under UTMA, more restrictive under UGMA	Very flexible, duty to diversify unless trust provides otherwise
Jurisdictional Issues	Where the property is located or beneficiary resides	Choice of law where connection to donor, donee, custodian, or property	Unrestricted (subject to public policy) choice of state law
Multiple Beneficiaries	No	No	Yes
Only One Fiduciary	Yes	Yes	No
Periodic Accounting	Yes	No, unless requested by interested party	Depends on direction in trust agreement
Planning to Protect Government Benefits	No	No	Yes
Standard of Care for Investments	Prudence	Prudence	Prudent Investor Rule
Successor Fiduciary	Court appoints	Document can provide or donor, custodian, or 14-year-old-minor can appoint	Trust can provide for successor, otherwise court must appoint
Termination Age	18	Usually 21	Anytime, depends on trust
Unequal Distributions	No	No	Yes

III. WHO SHOULD SERVE AS TRUSTEE OR CUSTODIAN?

In some families, the person who serves as guardian of the person of the minor can serve as the custodian or trustee of the property. Making one person (or two people acting together) responsible for both personal decisions and for decisions involving the child's property is efficient and will make caring for the child easier. Naming one person to handle both roles will also avoid conflicts between the guardian and the trustee. Resentment may develop if the guardian, who has day-to-day responsibility for the child, must ask the trustee for distributions from the trust to pay for the child's care.

In other families, however, one person may be more appropriate to serve as guardian and another more appropriate to serve as custodian or trustee. The qualities necessary to raise a child are not the same as those necessary to manage assets and in some families may not reside in the same person. Adequate planning and good communication between the guardian and the trustee should minimize any potential conflicts. The two people can consult each other in making decisions for the child and can also monitor each other's performance.

If a trust is used, the transferor may want to consider using a corporate trustee. A corporate trustee can provide management and investment expertise for large trusts and may be a good option if no family member is available or appropriate to serve as trustee. Corporate trustees generally have minimum requirements and will handle only trusts valued above a certain amount. Thus, a corporate trustee is not an option for many trusts. The fees and expenses charged by a corporate trustee should be reviewed before appointment so that the transferor is satisfied that the cost is justified.

For smaller trusts, a professional fiduciary may be an option. Professional fiduciaries are available in some locales to serve smaller trusts and estates for transferors who have no family members who can serve.

A. Federal Tax Considerations

If a parent of the child or the transferor of the property serves as trustee or custodian, various tax issues must be considered. The grantor trust rules may cause the income of the trust to be taxed to the transferor-fiduciary. In addition, certain controls the fiduciary may hold over the trust or custodianship may cause the assets, for federal estate tax purposes, to be included in the estate of the transferor as interests retained by the transferor-fiduciary.[65] Finally, a parent serving as trustee or custodian may face federal income tax consequences if the property can be used to fulfill the parent's legal obligation of support.

B. Successor Trustee

The transferor should name successor trustees or custodians in the transfer document. Doing so gives the transferor input as to who should serve. In a trust, the transferor also can include a mechanism for selecting a successor trustee. The trust instrument can give the initial trustee, anyone serving as trustee, or beneficiaries who are not minors the right to name successors. Building flexibility into a trust instrument is of particular importance in trusts that will continue for a long time.

If no successor trustee is named, a court proceeding will be required for the appointment of a successor. If no successor custodian is named, the acting custodian can appoint a successor, a minor over the age of fourteen can name a successor, or the child's conservator will become the successor. Only if the child is too young to name a successor and has no conservator will it be necessary to go to court to have a successor appointed.

IV. DEFINING THE FAMILY

A. Who Are the Beneficiaries?

Special planning may be required in certain family situations. Children may be born into a family or may be adopted. Children may be created "the old fashioned way" or by using assisted reproductive technology. Parents may raise children who are not their legal children, and grandparents may raise their grandchildren when the biological parents are unable to do so. Biological parents may maintain relationships with children who are adopted into another family—or they may cut all ties after the adoption. Given all these possible permutations, estate planners cannot rely on definitions of family that come from state statutes. Careful drafting should carry out a transferor's wishes and be neither over inclusive nor under inclusive.

1. Legal Definitions

The legal definition of parent and child does not always match a transferor's own definition, and the use of terms like "children" and "descendants" typically will be interpreted to use the legal definition of the parent-child relationship. A transferor can direct the distribution of property to whomever the transferor wishes, so an estate planner must ask specific questions about family relationships and about the client's wishes. The estate planning documents may need to include definitions of "children" and "descendants" that differ from the legal definitions.

The intestacy rules and related probate statutes provide legal definitions of parent and child that are used not only for intestate distributions but also to interpret terms used in wills and trusts. An estate planner must understand the application of these rules both to apply them when someone dies intestate and to draft documents that carry out the intent of clients.

In general, intestacy statutes define as children those who are legal children, related to their parents biologically or by adoption. The statute may refer to the state parentage statute, so that a determination of legal parenthood under the parentage statute will serve as a determination for probate purposes. New reproductive technologies have made the determination of legal parenthood based on biology more complicated. A new Uniform Parentage Act, approved by the Uniform Law Commission in 2017, addresses these issues but has not yet been widely adopted.[66] These rules vary by state and continue to change, so an advisor should be familiar with the current rules in the state where the document will be executed.

Assisted reproductive technologies (ART) raise a variety of issues addressed in Chapter 10. Leaving ART issues aside, a biological parent will generally be a legal parent for inheritance purposes unless parental rights are terminated. However, a father who is not married to the child's mother and does not recognize the child—hold the child out as his child—may not be considered a parent for inheritance purposes if a determination of parental status is not made under family law. Although the marital status of the parents does not limit a child's ability to be considered an heir of the biological parents, statutes in many states create a rebuttable presumption that the husband of a woman who gives birth to a child within the marriage is the father of the child. Now that same-sex couples can marry, states are grappling with the question of whether the birth of a child to a married woman creates a presumption that her female spouse is the child's parent.

2. Adopted Children
An adopted child is treated as the child of the adoptive parent for purposes of inheritance, both for intestacy and in interpreting documents.[67] In most states, an adoption cuts off rights to inherit from the parents who were the legal parents before the adoption, with an exception for stepparent adoptions.[68] For example, if a stepfather adopts a child, the child's mother, who is married to the stepfather, continues to be a legal parent of the child. In addition, the child can inherit from and through the child's biological father, even though the biological father is no longer a legal parent. In some states the child's right to inherit through the former parent (i.e., to inherit from the biological father's relatives) continues only if the adoption occurred after the death of the former parent.

If the unmarried partner of a child's legal parent adopts the child, that adoption will cut off inheritance rights between the child and the child's legal parent. For example, if a biological mother has a child by artificial insemination using an anonymous donor and the mother's unmarried partner intends to be the child's other parent, adoption by the unmarried partner will have unintended consequences. Unless the biological parent adopts her own child, the statute terminates inheritance rights between the child and the biological parent. Of course, if the unmarried partner does not adopt the child, then no inheritance rights exist between that person and the child, regardless of the fact that they treat each other as parent and child.

A child usually will be treated as a child of his or her adopted parent for purposes of interpreting documents created by another transferor, with some exceptions. If a grandparent creates a trust, with the remainder to "descendants," the question becomes whether the grandparent-settlor intended to include adopted children as remainder beneficiaries. Issues arise under two circumstances. With respect to documents created many years ago, the legal definition of descendants may have changed between the time the settlor executed the document and the time for distribution. In the early part of the twentieth century some statutes did not include adopted children as descendants; now all intestacy statutes treat adopted children the same as biological children. Thus, in trying to determine the meaning of "descendants" as used in a trust, interpreting the term under the law from 1920 when the settlor established the trust may result in excluding an adopted child from the group of beneficiaries. Increasingly, states simply use current law, under the assumption that the settlor would want to include the adopted child.

A second issue is whether the settlor intended to include as descendants persons adopted as adults who did not have a parent-child relationship with the adoptive parent. A husband in Kentucky adopted his wife in an effort to make her a descendant for purposes of taking as a beneficiary under a trust created by the husband's mother. The court in *Minary v. Citizens Fidelity Bank & Trust Co.*[69] refused to treat the adopted wife as an heir of the deceased settlor of the trust. Some states have addressed this problem by statute. For example, Oregon states that an adopted person will be treated as a descendant for purposes of interpreting documents only if the person was adopted as a minor or was a member of the adopting parent's household as a minor.[70]

3. Children Born Posthumously

For inheritance purposes, a child born after a decedent's death will be considered the decedent's child (or descendant) if the child was in gestation at the time of the decedent's death and is later born alive. States often presume that a child was in gestation if the child is born within 280 or 300 days after the decedent's death.

With advances in ART, a child may be conceived posthumously, using gametic material (sperm or eggs) deposited and stored before a prospective parent's death. Whether the child will be the deceased parent's child for inheritance purposes depends on state law. Cases and statutes in some states have created rules for determining whether a posthumously conceived child will be considered the child of the deceased parent for inheritance purposes. The statutes or cases typically required proof of a genetic relationship between the parent and child, consent of the deceased parent (the requirement may be for written consent or testimony as to verbal consent or consent may be presumed), and conception or birth within some period of time (e.g., two or three years) after the decedent parent's death. Some states have rules that preclude posthumously conceived children from inheriting and other states have yet to address the issue.

Cases brought to determine the status of posthumously conceived children primarily have been brought to determine whether the child qualified for social security benefits through the deceased parent. The Supreme Court ruled in 2012 that determination of parentage for social security purposes will depend on the state's intestacy law,[71] so more states will likely address the issue by statute, one way or the other.[72]

4. *Stepchildren*

Stepchildren are generally not treated as children under intestacy statutes regardless of the relationship between the stepparent and stepchild. California's intestacy statute includes a provision for stepchildren, but the statute's application is limited.[73] The statute creates an intestate share for a stepchild only if the stepparent would have adopted the child but for a legal impediment to the adoption. The impediment is usually the legal parent's refusal to permit the adoption, so the statute will not likely apply to a stepchild who has reached the age of majority and can consent to an adoption. For purposes of interpreting documents, a stepchild might be included in the term "children" if the court is willing to look at evidence that the transferor intended to include a stepchild in the meaning of the term. Because courts usually construe terms like "children" and "descendants" by referring to their meanings under intestacy statutes, using those terms when stepchildren are involved is risky. Proper planning requires careful attention to definitions and specific identification of all known family members to avoid later questions about intended meanings.

B. Disinheriting or Omitting a Child

Sometimes a parent or grandparent wants to disinherit a child or grandchild who would otherwise take a gift as a "descendant." Careful drafting can ensure the result the transferor intends.

1. *Unintended Disinheritance*

Statutes protect children from unintended disinheritance that may occur when a child is born or adopted after the parent executes a will. The statutes create a share for the omitted child, but usually under limited circumstances. UPC section 2-302 provides that if the testator had no children when he or she executed a will, the after-born child will take an intestate share of any amount not going to the child's surviving parent. Thus, if the child's father dies leaving his entire estate to the child's mother, the child receives nothing. If the testator had one or more children when he or she executed the will, the after-born child will share in amounts going to the other children. If the decedent's will left nothing to other children, then the statute does not create a share for the after-born child.

2. *Intended Disinheritance*

Only Louisiana creates a forced share for children. In all other states a parent can completely disinherit a child, even if the child is a minor. If a parent intends to disinherit a child, the parent must effectively give all property to someone else. Few states permit negative disinheritance—simply stating the intent to disinherit a child or other heir. In addition to giving his or her property to others, the parent may want to indicate that the parent has intentionally not provided for the disinherited child. The parent must exercise caution in doing so. Stating the parent's intent to disinherit the child

prevents a later question about whether the disinheritance was uninten-
tional. However, the document should not use language that could be considered libelous in explaining why the parent decided to disinherit the child.
Otherwise the child may have a cause of action for testamentary libel after
the parent's death.

V. DRAFTING CONSIDERATIONS

When an estate planner prepares a will or trust leaving property to "children" or "descendants," the planner may need to define those terms in the
documents to carry out the client's wishes. Using those terms is a good idea
because the terms will include children born or adopted after the date of the
document, but a definition in the document can address the client's own
views of who should be included—or excluded. Without a personalized definition, the interpretation will likely be the one used by the intestacy statutes. The planner may need to probe a bit to determine the client's intent,
and helping the client think about potential issues can be tricky.

One area to discuss is adoption. Many clients will want to include
adopted children but only those who are adopted into a parent-child relationship. An option would be to include in the definition a requirement
that a parent-child relationship existed, but then someone (the personal representative or trustee) will have to make that determination, and litigation
could result. Other options would be to require that the adoption occur
before the child reached a specified age or after having lived as a member of
the household of the adoptive parent. Age requirements are becoming more
common, but the planner may want to consider whether too young an age
will exclude a child raised by a stepparent who adopts the child as an adult.
When the child is an adult that child can give consent to the adoption.

Another issue is the possibility of a child conceived after the death of
the client's descendant using gametic material of the descendant. The planner should discuss with the client whether and under what circumstances
the client would want a posthumously conceived child treated as the client's
descendant. Standard drafting language that includes as descendants those
"born before or after my death" should be reexamined.

Appendix 9-B, Discussion Questions about Children, lists questions the
planner can ask clients to help the planner develop the appropriate definitions for children and descendants. Appendix 9-E, Definition of Family,
provides a few sample definitions.

VI. CONCLUSION

Whether outright or in trust, an extensive range of transfer mechanisms
are available for testamentary transfers to minor children. In determining
which mechanism is best, the age of distribution, the costs, and investment
flexibility are all relevant factors. Custodianships can be useful for small
amounts of property. Conservatorships serve as a back-up mechanism when
an adult transferor does not plan adequately. In general, trusts work best

when there is a sizeable estate or multiple beneficiaries. No matter what the mechanism, choosing the proper fiduciary is crucial, for nontax as well as for tax reasons. Lastly, properly identifying the family members who should inherit requires careful drafting.

NOTES

1. Uniform Probate Code, § 5-104 8 U.L.A. 171 (amended 2003) [hereinafter UPC].

2. *See* Peter Mosanyi, II, *A Survey of State Guardianship Statutes: One Concept, Many Applications,* 18 J. Am. Acad. Matrim. Law. 253 (2002).

3. Uniform Gifts to Minors Act, 8A U.L.A. 375 (1956, rev. 1966) [hereinafter UGMA].

4. Uniform Transfers to Minors Act, 8B U.L.A. 497 (1983, amended 1986) [hereinafter UTMA].

5. § 6.

6. UTMA § 6(c).

7. UTMA § 7.

8. UTMA §§ 10, 12(d).

9. *In re* Levy, 412 N.Y.S.2d 287 (Surr. Ct. Nassau Cty. 1978).

10. UTMA §§ 1, 9. A custodian under the age of twenty-one may be possible for certain types of property.

11. UTMA § 10.

12. UTMA/UGMA do not contain any residency requirements for custodians. In Estate of Mantzouras, 589 N.Y.S.2d 724 (N.Y. Surr. Ct. 1992), the court held that absent "a specific requirement in the UGMA that a custodian must be a resident or citizen of the United States, a nonresident alien may be named custodian." *Id.* at 726.

13. UTMA § 3.

14. UTMA § 18(c).

15. UTMA § 18(f).

16. UTMA § 12(d). A custodian may receive property in joint tenancy and may retain property as tenants in common.

17. *See* Hinschberger, By and Through Olson v. Griggs County Soc. Ser., 499 N.W.2d 876 (N.D. 1993); Fogelin v. Nordblom, 521 N.E.2d 1007 (Mass. 1988).

18. UTMA § 12(a); *see also* Estate of Baldwin, 442 A.2d 529 (Me. 1982).

19. UTMA § 12(e).

20. UTMA § 12(b). The custodian may retain a joint tenancy interest received by the custodian. UTMA § 12(b) cmt.

21. UTMA § 12(a) & (b). The UTMA standard of care mirrors the UPC's standard for fiduciaries, and the case law interpreting UPC § 7-302 may be used to interpret the UTMA standard.

22. *See infra* notes 44–47 and accompanying text.

23. Restatement (Third) of Trusts § 1 (2003) states that custodianships are "substantively so similar to express private trusts in their characteristics, applicable legal principles, and role in the donative transfer of family property that, as 'virtual trusts,' they are treated as trusts within the meaning of this Restatement." Thus, the prudent investor standard from trust law may apply to custodians.

24. UTMA § 7.

25. UTMA § 15(a) & (b).

26. UTMA § 14, cmt.

27.   UTMA § 14(a). The UGMA standard is different—the custodian may use the property for the support, maintenance, education, and benefit of the minor. UTMA § 4.

28.   UTMA § 2(a). Under UGMA there is no such provision.

29.   UTMA § 2(c).

30.   *See* James R. Ledwith & Mary Ann Robinson, *Expanded Opportunities Available Under Uniform Transfers to Minors Act,* 13 Est. Plan. 258, 260 (1986).

31.   *See* Friedman v. Mayeroff, 592 N.Y.S.2d 909, 912 (N.Y. Civ. Ct. 1992).

32.   *See* Ryiz v. First Bankers, N.A., 516 So. 2d 1069 (Fla. Dist. Ct. App. 1987); Dubisky v. United States, No. 93C 4505, 1994 WL 861127, at *1 (N.D. Ill. Sept. 13, 1994).

33.   *Dubisky,* 1994 WL 861127, at *1 (1994); Marshall v. United States, 831 F. Supp. 988, 1005 (E.D.N.Y. 1993).

34.   *Marshall,* 831 F. Supp. at 1004.

35.   *See* I.R.C. § 1(j)(4) (cross-referencing I.R.C. § 1(j)(2)(E)), added by Pub. L. No. 115-97, § 11001(a). *See also* Rev. Proc. 2018-18, 2018-10 I.R.B. 392, § 3.01. For tax years before January 1, 2018, see I.R.C. § 1(g)(1) and (3) (child's unearned income generally taxed as if parent's income). *See also* Chapter 1.

36.   *See* I.R.C. § 1(j)(h)(4)(C), 1(j)(5), added by Pub. L. No. 115-97, § 11001(a). *See also* § 1(h). For tax rates and corresponding brackets and income thresholds, *see* Chapter 1, note 118 and accompanying text.

37.   I.R.C. §§ 2036, 2038.

38.   Reg. § 20.2036-1(b)(2).

39.   Lober v. U.S., 346 U.S. 335 (1953).

40.   Estate of Grace, 395 U.S. 316 (1969); Exch. Bank & Trust Co. of Fla. v. U.S., 694 F.2d 1263 (Fed. Cir. 1982).

41.   *See also* Chapter 1.

42.   UTMA § 9. *See also* Chapter 3.

43.   The National Conference of Commissioners of Uniform State Laws adopted the first comprehensive codification of trust law in 2000. As of July 2018, thirty-two states plus the District of Columbia have adopted the Uniform Trust Code (Alabama, Arizona, Arkansas, Colorado, Florida, Kansas, Kentucky, Maine, Maryland, Massachusetts, Michigan, Minnesota, Mississippi, Missouri, Montana, Nebraska, New Hampshire, New Jersey, New Mexico, North Carolina, North Dakota, Ohio, Oregon, Pennsylvania, South Carolina, Tennessee, Utah, Vermont, Virginia, West Virginia, Wisconsin, and Wyoming). Bills were introduced in Connecticut and Illinois in 2018.

44.   UTC § 105(b)(2).

45.   *See, e.g.,* D.C. Code Ann. § 19-1308.12 (2004).

46.   Uniform Prudent Investor Act (1994), 7B U.L.A. 286 (2000) [hereinafter UPIA]. As of July 2018, forty-four states plus the District of Columbia have enacted UPIA, and Maryland has enacted a "substantially similar" statute. Delaware, Florida, Georgia, Kentucky, and Louisiana have not enacted UPIA.

47.   UPIA § 2(a) (1994).

48.   UPIA § 2, cmt.

49.   UPIA § 9.

50.   *See* Howard M. McCue III, *Planning and Drafting to Influence Behavior,* 2000 Inst. on Est. Plan. 6–22.

51.   UTC § 107.

52. UPIA § 108(a).

53. UPIA § 108(c).

54. *See* Restatement (Third) of Trusts § 58 (2003) (explaining that a clause that restrains both voluntary and involuntary alienation by the beneficiary is valid).

55. *See, e.g.,* Shelley v. Shelley, 223 Or. 328, 354 P.2d 282 (1960).

56. UTC § 504.

57. *See* Austin W. Scott, 2A The Law on Trusts, § 157.2 (William Fratcher, 4th ed. 1987).

58. Restatement (Second) of Property: Donative Transfers § 13.2 (1986).

59. *See id.,* Stat. Note to § 13.2.

60. *See* Chapter 7.

61. Crummey v. Comm'r, 397 F.2d 82 (9th Cir. 1968).

62. *See also* Chapters 1 and 3.

63. C.R.S. § 15-14-431(1). *See also* Chapter 6.

64. 760 Ill. comp. Stat. 20/15.

65. *See also* Chapter 3.

66. As of July 2018, the act has been adopted in two states, Vermont and Washington, and introduced in two more, California and Rhode Island.

67. UPC § 2-114(b).

68. *Id.* In Texas, however, adoption does not cut off the child's right to inherit from and through the child's biological parents, unless the adoption occurs when the child is an adult. Tex. Prob. Code Ann. § 40 (West 2005).

69. 419 S.W.2d 340 (Ky. Ct. App. 1967).

70. Or. Rev. Stat. § 112.195 (2003).

71. Astrue v. Capato, 132 S. Ct. 2021 (2012).

72. *See also* Chapter 10.

73. Cal. Prob. Code § 6454 (West 2004).

APPENDIX 9-A

CLIENT QUESTIONNAIRE

A typical client questionnaire requests detailed information about the client and the client's assets. In addition, a questionnaire should include questions designed to identify children and those whom the client considers his or her children. The questionnaire can raise questions to be discussed at the first meeting between the client and the lawyer, so that the client can begin thinking about some of the issues involving the children and can better inform the lawyer about the client's views as to appropriate distributions. The following portion of a client questionnaire would be used in connection with questions about the client and the client's property.

CHILDREN

In listing your children, please include children from a prior marriage and any other child who is your legal child (because you are the child's birth parent or because you adopted the child).

Full Name   Date of Birth   Address
[space for names]

Do you have any stepchildren or other children who live with you or lived with you in the past who are not your legal children?
Full Name   Date of Birth   Address
[space for names]

In thinking about who should inherit your property after your death, which of the children you have listed should be considered your "children." For example, a stepparent may have a close relationship with a stepchild and may want the stepchild treated as a child for inheritance purposes or may have a close relationship but choose not to leave property to a stepchild who will inherit from another parent. Another parent may have no real relationship with a child and may prefer that the child not inherit the parent's property. As we plan the distribution of your property, identifying those who should inherit will be important.

Notes for discussion
[space for notes by client]

GRANDCHILDREN AND FUTURE GENERATIONS

Do you have any grandchildren, step-grandchildren, or other children in the next generation?

Full Name   Date of Birth   Name of Parent Address (if different)
[space for names]

Are additional grandchildren possible? What are your feelings about distributions to the next generation? About adopted grandchildren? About step-grandchildren? About grandchildren born using reproductive technologies that could mean a step-grandchild could be born after your child's death?'

Notes for discussion
[space for notes by client]

GUARDIANS AND TRUSTEES

If you should die while your children are still minors, the court will appoint someone to make decisions about their care. In your Will you can nominate someone to make decisions about the personal care of your children, and the court will usually appoint that person as the children's legal guardian. Your Will can also name the person who will make decisions about managing the property you leave to your children. If we decide to create a trust for your children, this person will serve as trustee of the trust until the children are ready to handle their property. If no trust is created for the children, this person will be nominated as "conservator," the person appointed by the court to manage property for the children. The guardian and the trustee or conservator can be the same person or they can be different people, and you can have more than one guardian and trustee.

Who should be the guardian(s) for your children? List as many people as you wish, in the order of your preference in appointing them.

Name   Relationship to You   Address
[space for names]

Who should be the trustee(s) of the trust for your children or the conservator? List as many people as you wish, in the order of your preference in appointing them.

Name   Relationship to You   Address
[space for names]

DISABILITIES

Do any of your children have any mental or health-related disabilities that may require special planning? Do any of your children receive government benefits due to disabilities or have disabilities that may make qualification for government benefits important in the future?

Notes for discussion
[space for notes by client]

PERSONAL PROPERTY

Usually personal property (household goods, furniture, jewelry, pictures, etc.) will be divided among family members and not held as part of a trust for the children. If the children are young, property may be held in trust until they are older. Do you have any personal items that should go directly to your children? How should decisions about dividing your personal property be made? Do you have specific items that should go to particular children, grandchildren, other relatives or friends?

Notes for discussion
[space for notes by client]

VALUES AND GOALS—TRUST FOR CHILDREN

If your spouse/partner survives you, should any property be set aside for your children?

If neither you nor your spouse/partner is alive, property held for your children will probably be held in a trust or trusts. You have a great deal of control over how the trust(s) will operate. We will talk about the specifics at our meeting, but thinking through the following questions before our meeting will be helpful.

When do you think the children should have control of their inheritance? Would it be helpful if they received the property in stages and not all at once? A trust can provide creditor protection as long as it continues. Would it be helpful to continue to hold the property in trust during a child's life? Would you like to include incentives in the trust, to encourage particular behaviors? Does any child have problems that make managing property a problem?

If a child does not survive you or dies while the child's property is still held in a trust, to whom should the property be given?

Notes for discussion
[space for notes by client]

APPENDIX 9-B

DISCUSSION QUESTIONS ABOUT CHILDREN

The client questionnaire asks some questions about children and descendants, but the estate planner may want to have a broader conversation with the client. These questions provide ideas about ways to engage the client in that conversation. These questions could be incorporated into a questionnaire but might be perceived as overwhelming and confusing by the client.

- Who are your children?
- Is there a child who is legally your child but should be excluded from your estate plan? If so, should the child's children be excluded?
- Is there someone who is not a legal child who should be included? This could include a child raised in the home who was never adopted.
- Do you have any stepchildren? How should they be treated?
- Have you stored gametes (eggs or sperm) that could be used after your death? If so, how should any resulting child be treated?
- Who should be treated as your descendants?

The following questions relate to your grandchildren and other descendants beyond your own children. If a child of yours dies before you do, that child's "descendants" may take that child's share. Or you may decide to put property into a trust for the life of your child and then distribute the property to the child's descendants. These questions relate to decisions about children that your children and later descendants will make and how you want their children treated.

- What if a child is born outside marriage? What if the parents are in a long-term committed relationship but chose not to marry? What if the child is the result of a brief sexual encounter?
- What if a child is conceived after your descendant's death, using stored gametic material?
- Should a stepchild who is not adopted by your descendant be included as a descendant?
- Should an adopted adult be included? Would you like to limit inclusion to children adopted before a specified age, such as eighteen, twenty-one, or twenty-five? Would you like to limit inclusion to children who have lived in a parent-child relationship with your descendant?
- Would you like to include a child of a descendant of yours who was adopted by someone other than your descendant's spouse or domestic partner?
- What if your descendant dies and the child is adopted by the person the surviving parent marries (a stepparent adoption)?

APPENDIX 9-C

State-by-State Comparison Chart on UTMA and UGMA

State	UTMA	UGMA	STATUTE	Age of Termination for Transfers	
				By Gift, POA, or Authorized by Will or Trust	By Life Insurance, Other Obligor, or by Personal Representative or Trustee Without Authorization
Alabama	X		Code of Ala. §§ 35-5A-1 to 35-5A-24	21	19
Alaska	X		Alaska Stat. §§ 13.46.010 to 13.46.999	21	18
Arizona	X		Ariz. Rev. Stat. §§ 14-7651 to 14-7671	21	18
Arkansas	X		Ark. Stat. Ann. §§ 9-26-201 to 9-26-227	18–21[1]	18
California	X		Cal. Probate Code §§ 3900–3925, 6341–6349	18–25[2]	18–25
Colorado	X		Colo. Rev. Stat. §§11-50-101 to 126	21	21
Connecticut	X		Conn. Gen. Stat. Ann. §§ 45a-557 to 45a-560b	21	21

---

1. Twenty-one is the default age. The transferor can direct an earlier age, between eighteen and twenty-one.
2. Eighteen or twenty-one is the default age. The transferor can direct a later age, but no later than age twenty-five.

State	UTMA	UGMA	STATUTE	Age of Termination for Transfers	
				By Gift, POA, or Authorized by Will or Trust	**By Life Insurance, Other Obligor, or by Personal Representative or Trustee Without Authorization**
Delaware	X		Del. Code tit. 12, §§ 4501 to 4523	21	18
District of Columbia	X		D.C. Code §§ 21-301 to 21-324	18	18
Florida	X		Florida Statues ch. 710	21	18
Georgia	X		Ga. Code Ann. §§ 44-5-110 to 44-5-134	21	18
Hawaii	X		Haw. Rev. Stat. §§ 553A-1 to 553A-24	21	18
Idaho	X		Idaho Code §§ 68-801 to 68-825	21	18
Illinois	X		Ill. Comp. Stat. 20/1 to 20/24	21	18
Indiana	X		Indiana Code Ann. §§ 30-2-8.5-1 to 30-2-8.5-40	21	21
Iowa	X		Iowa Code ch. 565B	21	21
Kansas	X		Kan. Stat. §§ 38-1701 to 38-1726	21	18
Kentucky	X		Ky. Rev. Stat. §§ 385.012 to 385.252	18	18
Louisiana	X		La. Rev. Stat. Ann. §§ 9:751-9:773	18	18

State	UTMA	UGMA	STATUTE	Age of Termination for Transfers	
				By Gift, POA, or Authorized by Will or Trust	**By Life Insurance, Other Obligor, or by Personal Representative or Trustee Without Authorization**
Maine	X		33 M.R.S.A. §§1651 to 1674	18–21[3]	18
Maryland	X		Md. Est. and Trusts Code Ann. §§ 13-301 to 13-324	21	18
Massachusetts	X		Mass. Gen. L. ch. 201A, § 1-24	21	18
Michigan	X		Mich. Comp. Laws Ann. §§ 554.523 to 554.551	18–21[4]	18–21
Minnesota	X		Minn. Stats. ch. 527 §§ 527.21 to 527.44	21	18
Mississippi	X		Miss. Code Ann. §§ 90-20-1 to 91-20-49	21	18
Missouri	X		Mo. Ann. Stat. §§ 404.005 to 404.094	21	18
Montana	X		Mont. Code Ann. §§ 72-26-501 to 72-26-803	21	18
Nebraska	X		Neb. Rev. Stat. §§ 43-2701 to 43-2724	21	19

---

3. Eighteen is the default age. The transferor can direct a later age, but no later than age twenty-one.
4. Eighteen is the default age. The transferor can direct a later age, but no later than age twenty-one.

State	UTMA	UGMA	STATUTE	Age of Termination for Transfers	
				By Gift, POA, or Authorized by Will or Trust	**By Life Insurance, Other Obligor, or by Personal Representative or Trustee Without Authorization**
Nevada	X		Nev. Rev. Stat. §§ 167.010–167.100	18–25[5]	18–25
New Hampshire	X		N.H. Rev. Stat. Ann. §§ 463-A-1 to 24	21	18
New Jersey	X		N.J. Stat. Ann. §§ 46:38A-1 to 57	18–21[6]	18
New Mexico	X		N.M. Stat. Ann. §§ 46-7-11 to 34	21	18
New York	X		N.Y. Est. Powers & Trusts Law §§ 7-6.1 to 7-6.26	18 or 21[7]	18
North Carolina	X		N.C. Gen. Stat. §§ 33A-1 to 33A-24	18–21[8]	18
North Dakota	X		N.D. Cent. Code §§ 47-24.1-01 to 47-24.1-22	21	18
Ohio	X		Ohio Rev. Code §§ 1339.31 to 39	21	18

---

5. Eighteen or twenty-one is the default age. The transferor can direct a later age, but no later than age twenty-five.

6. Twenty-one is the default age. The transferor can direct an earlier age, between eighteen and twenty-one.

7. Twenty-one is the default age, but the transferor can direct age eighteen.

8. Twenty-one is the default age. The transferor can direct an earlier age, between eighteen and twenty-one.

State	UTMA	UGMA	STATUTE	Age of Termination for Transfers	
				By Gift, POA, or Authorized by Will or Trust	By Life Insurance, Other Obligor, or by Personal Representative or Trustee Without Authorization
Oklahoma	X		Okla. Stat. Ann. tit. 58, §§ 1201 to 1225	18	18
Oregon	X		ORS §§ 126.805 to 126.886	21–25[9]	18
Pennsylvania	X		20 Pa. Cons. Stat. Ann. §§ 5301 to 5321	21–25[10]	21
Rhode Island	X		R.I. Gen. Laws §§18-7-1 to 18-7-26	21	18
South Carolina		X	S.C. Code Ann. §§ 20-7-140 to 20-7-240	18–21[11]	18–21
South Dakota	X		S.D. Compiled Laws §§ 55-10A-1 to 55-10A-26	18	18
Tennessee	X		Tenn. Code Ann. §§ 35-7-201 to 35-7-226	21–25[12]	21–25

9. Eighteen or twenty-one is the default age. The transferor can direct a later age, but no later than age twenty-five.

10. Eighteen or twenty-one is the default age. The transferor can direct a later age, but no later than age twenty-five.

11. Twenty-one is the default age but the custodian, in the custodian's discretion, can distribute assets any time after age eighteen.

12. Eighteen or twenty-one is the default age. The transferor can direct a later age, but no later than age twenty-five.

State	UTMA	UGMA	STATUTE	Age of Termination for Transfers	
				By Gift, POA, or Authorized by Will or Trust	By Life Insurance, Other Obligor, or by Personal Representative or Trustee Without Authorization
Texas	X		Texas Property Code § 141.001, et. seq.	21	18
Utah	X		Utah Code Ann. §§ 75-5a-101 to 75-5a-123	21	18
Vermont		X	Vt. Stat. Ann. tit. 14, §§ 3201 to 3209	18[13]	18
Virginia	X		Va. Code §§ 31-37 to 31-59	18 or 21[14]	18–21
Washington	X		Wash. Rev. Code Ann. §§ 11.114.010 to 11.114.904	21	18
West Virginia	X		W. Va. Code §§ 36-7-1 to 36-7-24	21	18
Wisconsin	X		Wis. Stat. Ann. §§ 880.61 to 880.72	21	18
Wyoming	X		Wyo. Stat. §§ 34-13-114 to 34-13-137	21	18
Puerto Rico	*Not Enacted*				
Virgin Islands		X	Tit. 15, pt. III, ch. 62, §§ 1251a to 1251x	18	18

13. At the time of publication, the Vermont legislature was considering H.0043, a bill to adopt UTMA.

14. Eighteen is the default age. The transferor can direct a later age, but no later than age twenty-one.

APPENDIX 9-D

(With permission from *Managing the Benefits and Burdens of New Wealth with Incentive Trusts* by Nancy G. Henderson from 47 PRACTICAL LAWYER 60, 62, 63, Sept. 2001 and 21, 22 Oct. 2001)

DOCUMENT 1—SAMPLE EDUCATION-RELATED INCENTIVE PROVISIONS

The following does not address all of the concerns raised in this article, but are a few relatively typical education-related incentive provisions:

A. Distribution Upon Entering College. At any time after a beneficiary has commenced a course of study at an accredited college or university with the objective of obtaining a bachelor's degree in a subject which the trustees, in their discretion, deem reasonably likely to prepare the beneficiary for financial self-sufficiency, the trustees may make a single, lump-sum distribution to the beneficiary for financial self-sufficiency, the trustees may make a single, lump-sum distribution to the beneficiary from his or her trust of an amount not to exceed $5,000. The trustees may also make this one time distribution to a beneficiary who does not satisfy the foregoing requirements, but who has commenced a course of study of training which the trustees, in their discretion, determine to be reasonably equivalent to the pursuit of a bachelor's degree in light of all of the facts and circumstances, including the beneficiary's abilities or disabilities and the beneficiary's career goals. The distribution described in this paragraph may be made to the beneficiary no more than once during his or her lifetime.

B. Annual Award for Academic Performance. At the end of each academic year that a beneficiary is engaged in a course of study at an accredited college or university with the objective of obtaining a bachelor's degree in a subject which the trustees, in their discretion, deem reasonably likely to prepare the beneficiary for financial self-sufficiency, if such beneficiary has maintained a grade point average of at least 3.0 on a grading scale that provides a 4.0 for an "A" average (or the equivalent on a different grading system), and if such beneficiary is pursuing his or her education on a full time or substantially full time basis, the trustees may make a lump-sum distribution to the beneficiary of an amount not to exceed TEN THOUSAND DOLLARS ($10,000). In determining the amount distributed under this paragraph, the trustees may take into consideration, for example, the quality of the educational institution, the difficulty of the beneficiary's curriculum, and any special challenges the beneficiary may have faced during the academic year.

C. Distribution Upon Receiving a Bachelor's Degree. At any time after a beneficiary has received a bachelor's degree from an accredited college or university, or such other degree or certification as the trustees, in their discretion, shall deem reasonably equivalent to the attainment of a bachelor's degree in light of all of the facts and circumstances, including such beneficiary's abilities or disabilities, or the beneficiary's career goals, and if the beneficiary has completed his or her education with a final grade point average of at least a 3.0 on a grading scale that provides a 4.0 for an "A" average (or the equivalent on a different grading system) the trustees may make a single, lump-sum distribution to the beneficiary from his or her trust of an amount not to exceed TWENTY-FIVE THOUSAND DOLLARS ($25,000). In determining the amount to be distributed under this paragraph, the trustees may take into account, for example, the degree of difficulty of the beneficiary's curriculum, the beneficiary's grade point average, any academic honors received by the beneficiary. The distribution described in this paragraph may be made to the beneficiary no more than once during his or her lifetime.

D. Distribution Upon Receiving an Advanced Degree. At any time after a beneficiary has received an advanced degree (such as a master's degree, a PhD, and MBA or a professional degree) from an accredited university, or such other educational achievement as the trustees, in their discretion, shall deem reasonably equivalent thereto in light of all of the facts and circumstances, including such beneficiary's abilities or disabilities, the trustees may make a single, lump-sum distribution to the beneficiary from his or her trust of an amount not to exceed THIRTY-FIVE THOUSAND DOLLARS ($35,000). The distribution described in this paragraph may be made to the beneficiary no more than once during his or her lifetime.

E. Indexing for Inflation. Wherever a specified dollar amount is referred to in this Article in connection with a distribution to or for the benefit of a beneficiary, such amount shall be increased by the same percentage as the percentage of increase, if any, shown by the All Items Consumer Price Index for Urban Wage Earners and Clerical Workers published by the U.S. Department of Labor, Bureau of Labor Statistics, for the San Diego Area for the month in which this trust agreement is executed, as compared with the most recently published index on the first date that such gift takes effect or such distribution becomes permissible. If such index is no longer published, the trustees, in their discretion, shall select an appropriate index for the purpose of adjusting such amounts for the effect of inflation since the date this trust agreement was executed.

DOCUMENT 2—SAMPLE PROVISIONS FOR DISTRIBUTIONS TO ASSIST IN PURCHASE OF AUTOMOBILE AND RESIDENCE

Distribution to Assist in the Purchase of an Automobile. At any time after a beneficiary has attained at least twenty (20) years of age, upon the request of the beneficiary, the trustees may contribute to the beneficiary's maintenance and support, but are not required to do so, by making a down payment for the purchase of an appropriate automobile for the beneficiary, provided such payment shall in no event exceed TWENTY THOUSAND DOLLARDS ($20,000) or fifty percent (50%) of the value of the automobile, whichever is less. Before making any such distribution to or for the benefit of the beneficiary, the trustees, or persons selected by the trustees, shall meet or otherwise confer with the beneficiary to determine what constitutes an appropriate automobile for purposes of this Section based upon the beneficiary's needs and his or her ability to pay expenses related to such automobile (including insurance, loan or lease payments, maintenance, and taxes) from resources outside of the trust. The trustees are discouraged from making a distribution authorized under this Section to any beneficiary who fails to cooperate with the trustees in performing this analysis.

DOCUMENT 3—SAMPLE PROVISION FOR DISTRIBUTIONS TO ASSIST IN STARTING A BUSINESS

Distributions to Assist in Starting a Business. At any time after a beneficiary has attained at least twenty-seven years of age, upon the request of the beneficiary, the trustees may contribute to the beneficiary's maintenance and support, but are not required to do so, by assisting the beneficiary to commence a business or profession in which the beneficiary will be employed on a full-time or a substantially full-time basis, alone or with others. Such assistance may be in the form of a loan (with or without interest or security), an outright distribution, an investment by the trustees in the proposed endeavor, or any combination thereof. Before making a distribution to or for the benefit of the beneficiary, the trustees, or persons selected by the trustees, shall meet or otherwise confer with the beneficiary to establish a realistic business plan in order to determine the likelihood that the beneficiary will become financially self-supporting through the proposed endeavor, the timing and amounts of distributions from the beneficiary's trust that would be required to insure the success of the proposed endeavor, the remaining assets of the trust, and any other factors which the trustees deem reasonable under the circumstances. The trustees are discouraged from making a distribution under this Section to or for the benefit of any beneficiary who fails to cooperate with the trustees in establishing a realistic business plan for the proposed endeavor.

DOCUMENT 4—SUPPORT OF GUARDIAN PROVISION

"If any beneficiary is a minor, and if such beneficiary is being raised by a legal guardian who is not the beneficiary's natural parents, the trustees may distribute to such guardians such sums form the net income and principal of the trust as the trustees shall determine necessary or appropriate to ease the financial burden on the guardian resulting from the presence of such minor beneficiary in the guardian's household."[80]

DOCUMENT 5—SAMPLE PROVISION FOR DISTRIBUTIONS TO SUBSTANCE ABUSERS

In making distributions to or for the benefit of any beneficiary whom the trustee believes may have substance abuse problems, we request that the trustees limit distributions to such beneficiary to those which the trustees deem necessary to insure that such beneficiary's basic living requirements are met. In making distributions for the basic health and maintenance needs of a beneficiary with substance abuse problems, the trustees are requested, to the extent practicable, to make payments directly to persons or organizations who are furnishing housing, utilities, health care (including health care insurance), and other basic goods and services to the beneficiary, rather than make distributions directly to the beneficiary.

DOCUMENT 6—SAMPLE PROVISION FOR WITHHOLDING DISTRIBUTIONS TO A BENEFICIARY NOT ENGAGED IN PRODUCTIVE ACTIVITIES

The following is a sample provision, the purpose of which is to give the trustee *the flexibility* to withhold distributions to beneficiaries who are not productive or who have problems with creditors or ex-spouses.

Withholding Distributions to a Beneficiary Not Engaged in Productive Activities. Notwithstanding any provision of this trust agreement to the contrary, the trustees may withhold any distributions of income or principle to, or for the benefit of, any beneficiary which are authorized or required under the terms of this trust agreement, if the trustees determine such beneficiary as not engaged in productive activities. In reaching such a determination, the trustees may consider for example:

a) Whether the beneficiary is seriously pursuing an education which will enable the beneficiary to obtain gainful employment commensurate with his or her goals and abilities;

b) Whether the beneficiary is working to support himself or herself in a manner commensurate with his or her abilities (even if such beneficiary's chosen career does not produce substantial income but makes a productive contribution to the community);

c) Whether the beneficiary is working in the home as a parent in the care of such beneficiary's children or other family members.

---

80. "Managing the Benefits and Burdens of New Wealth with Incentive Trusts"

d) Whether the beneficiary is free of substance abuse or other negative addictive behavior;

e) Whether the beneficiary is capable of managing money in a responsible manner as demonstrated by past conduct;

f) Whether distribution to the beneficiary would serve to benefit such beneficiary's creditors, including former spouses, rather than the beneficiary; and

g) If the circumstances warrant, whether the beneficiary is involved in activities which promote the welfare of others or of the community as a whole.

The trustee's determination as to whether distributions should be withheld as to a particular beneficiary pursuant to the provisions of this Section shall be final and binding upon all persons interested in the trust estate. The trustees shall not be liable to the beneficiary or to anyone else for the trustees' decision to make or withhold any distribution to a beneficiary on the basis of the trustees' determination under this Section.

APPENDIX 9-E

Definition of Family: Drafting Examples

The following are alternative paragraphs that can be used where appropriate. Providing birthdates for children is helpful if the children are minors or below the age at which they will receive trust assets.

Basic paragraph:

I am the [husband/wife/partner] of _____ (herein my spouse/partner). I am the [father/mother] of _____, born _____; _____, born _____; and _____, born _____.

Basic paragraph if all children are adults and will receive trust property outright (or have only life estates):

I am the [husband/wife/partner] of _____ (herein my spouse/partner). I am the [father/mother] of _____, _____, and _____. My children are all adults.

Option for including a stepchild and the descendants of the stepchild:

My spouse/partner is the parent of _____, born _____. Although I am not a legal parent of [child's name], for purposes of this will [child's name] shall be considered a child of mine and [his/her] descendants shall be considered descendants of mine.

Option for excluding a grandchild:

My son, _____, is the legal father of _____, born _____. For purposes of this will [name of grandchild] shall not be considered a descendant of mine and no descendant of [name of grandchild] shall be considered a descendant of mine.

Option for including children born after the execution of the will whether conceived before or after death:

As used in this will, "children" shall mean my children named above and any other child born to or adopted by me hereafter. A child in gestation at the time of my death shall be considered a child of mine for purposes of this will if the child is born alive and lives at least 120 hours. A child conceived after my death shall be considered a child of mine for purposes of this will if the child is born within a reasonable time after the date of my death and lives at least 120 hours. Three years following the date of my death shall be conclusively presumed to be a reasonable time, but a longer period may be reasonable under the facts and circumstances connected with the conception.

Option for including children born after the execution of the will but only if con-ceived before death or for whom an adoption process began before death:

As used in this will, "children" shall mean my children named above and any other child born to or adopted by me hereafter. If I have begun the process of adopting a child but have not completed the process before my death, the child shall be considered a child of mine for purposes of this will. If a genetic child of mine is conceived before my death but born after my death, the child shall be considered a child of mine for purposes of this will. A child conceived after my death shall not be considered a child of mine for purposes of this will.

CHAPTER 10

Special Considerations in Transfers to Minor Beneficiaries Born as a Result of Reproductive Technologies

PART I: LEGAL OVERVIEW AND PRACTICAL POINTERS

Lisa Milot and T.J. Striepe

The use of technology to assist human reproduction has become common-place in the United States, with tens of thousands of children born annually through sperm donation, in vitro fertilization, egg donation, gestational surrogacy, and the like.[1] Use of this technology can complicate estate planning, as the legal roles of mother, father, and child are no longer based on genetic relationship or who gave birth to a child. Instead, statutes and courts look to (1) the intent of each party to the process, (2) whether the intended parents are married to each other, (3) the exact procedure used, and (4) who may perform the procedure. While many states have now dealt with these issues at least in part through statutes, some have remained silent so that parent-child relationships are determined under more general statutes enacted without consideration of the unique issues posed by these technologies.

Some of the technology, such as artificial insemination using sperm from a man who intends to become the father of any resulting children, is fleeting in its involvement and does little to complicate matters. However, when materials from individuals other than those intending to become parents are used or there is a lag in time between the retrieval of genetic material and its use, technology and practices have outpaced the law.

This part of the chapter discusses the interpretation of intestacy statutes and testamentary instruments when a potential heir or beneficiary was born with the use of reproductive technology: With whom does he have a parent-child relationship? Moreover, it discusses the special estate planning concerns raised when body materials are frozen for future use. Along the way, it provides best practice pointers for working with clients utilizing the technology. The appendices provide citation to the relevant state statutes and case law and summarize the points discussed.

I. TERMINOLOGY

In many cases, the type of reproductive technology used determines the legal relationships of mother, father, and child. Reproductive technologies are classified based on (1) the aspects of reproduction assisted (sperm production, egg fertilization, and/or gestation) and (2) where the technological intervention occurs (within the intended mother's body, in a laboratory, or within a surrogate's body).

A. Artificial Insemination

Artificial insemination is the least invasive form of reproductive technology, as sperm is medically introduced into the uterus or cervix of the woman who intends to be the mother of any resulting children (the "intended mother"). The sperm can either be from the "intended father" or from a "donor" who does not plan to have a parental role with respect to any resulting children. While medication is often used to increase the number of mature eggs the intended mother produces, the technological portion of the procedure is fleeting: Once the sperm is produced by the intended father or donor and transferred to the intended mother, nature takes its course.

B. In Vitro Fertilization

By contrast, in vitro fertilization (IVF) involves the removal of eggs from the biological mother before fertilization. The eggs are then fertilized in a laboratory setting. Several days after fertilization, the resulting embryo is transferred to the intended mother's uterus (or that of a surrogate) for gestation. Eggs used in IVF can either be from the intended mother or from a donor, and sperm may be from the intended father or a donor.

C. Surrogacy

Surrogacy involves an arrangement in which a woman other than the intended mother carries the child to term. Surrogacy arrangements can either use the surrogate's egg (traditional surrogacy)[2] or an egg from the intended mother or a donor (gestational surrogacy). The sperm used comes from either the intended father or a donor.

D. Cryopreservation

The body materials used for reproduction can be fresh or frozen. Cryopreservation refers to the freezing of eggs, sperm, or embryos for use at a future time. IVF and surrogacy may use fresh or cryopreserved material; artificial insemination always involves fresh eggs but the sperm used may be either fresh or frozen. Embryos produced by IVF can either be used fresh or can be cryopreserved for later use. Use of cryopreserved material in reproduction after the death of an intended parent results in "posthumous conception" and complicates estate planning matters further.

E. Authors' Summary Note

Depending on the technology employed, there may be as many five individuals—two intended parents, two donors, and a surrogate—with relationships to a child at birth, and the legal effects may not be effectuated for years after the body materials are produced. Part II of this chapter reviews state laws with respect to determining with whom a child has a legal parent-child relationship for estate planning purposes.

II. LEGAL PARENTAGE OF CHILDREN WHEN SURROGACY IS NOT INVOLVED

Inheritance or taking under a class gift[3] often turns on the establishment of a parent-child relationship between a decedent and a potential heir or beneficiary. Thirty-eight states[4] and the District of Columbia have enacted statutes that specifically address the steps necessary to establish a parent-child relationship in instances in which a child is conceived using reproductive technology other than surrogacy.[5] By case law, Indiana has done the same.[6] Where a state has not enacted a specific provision concerning parentage with respect to assisted reproduction, or existing statutes or case law do not cover a particular situation, general parentage provisions apply to determine kinship.

While not widely enacted, the Uniform Probate Code (UPC)[7] and Uniform Parentage Act (UPA)[8] have been influential in this area. As a result, the following discussion includes the relevant provisions from these acts where helpful.[9]

A. Establishing a Mother-Child Relationship

As a general rule, an intended mother who gives birth to a child conceived through assisted reproduction is the legal mother of that child, whether the egg was hers or provided by a donor. Establishing a second parent-child relationship, though, is more complicated.

B. Establishing a Second Parent-Child Relationship

Depending on the jurisdiction, a second parent-child relationship may be determined under a probate code; a parentage act provision, specifically applicable to reproduction using technology; a more general parentage act provision; or case law. Appendix 10(I)-A provides citations and a summary of relevant terms for each state and the District of Columbia with respect to the legal status of donors and the establishment of a second parent-child relationship where the child is conceived during that parent's lifetime.

1. A Donor Usually Is Not a Legal Parent

In most instances, someone providing sperm or eggs for use in reproduction without intending to be a parent to any resulting child is not a parent of the child. To this end, the UPC provides that "[a] parent-child relationship does not exist between a child of assisted reproduction and a third-party donor."[10] Similarly, the current UPA provides that "[a] donor is not a parent of a child conceived by means of assisted reproduction."[11] Fifteen states have adopted similar language.[12]

The primary variation on this approach is based on the 1973 UPA, which provides that "[t]he donor of semen provided to a licensed physician for use in artificial insemination of a married woman other than the donor's wife is treated in law as if he were not the natural father of a child thereby conceived."[13] There are three major differences between this approach and that found in the current UPC/UPA.

The first difference is the application of the section only to a donor of sperm for use in artificial insemination.[14] At the time of the 1973 UPA, artificial insemination was the only option for assisted reproduction, and sperm was the only gamete subject to donation. More recently, IVF, egg donation, and other technologies have become possible and commonplace. Courts that have reviewed this language recently have interpreted it to apply to donors whose body materials are used for assisted reproduction more generally.[15] Thus, it seems likely that statutes referring to artificial insemination would extend the treatment to other forms of assisted reproduction if the issue arose.

The other two differences are more substantive. First, to shield a donor from claims of parentage, the assisted reproduction must occur under the supervision of a licensed physician. This excludes home inseminations or those performed by a midwife or nurse without physician participation. Second, a married woman must be the intended recipient of the material; donors to single women may still be found to be a parent of any resulting child. Four states have enacted statutes with both of these limitations.[16]

Variations on these approaches exist. Some statutes incorporate the "licensed physician" limitation of the 1973 UPA without requiring that the intended mother be married,[17] while Massachusetts requires that the mother be married but not that the gametes be provided to a licensed physician. Minnesota employs the UPC language with respect to defining a parent-child relationship for purposes of intestacy, but the 1973 UPA formulation in its generally applicable parentage provision. Oklahoma only specifically covers parentage of children conceived through egg donation, establishing that the birth mother and her husband are the parents.

In summary, jurisdictions that have addressed the relationship of a donor to a child born from assisted reproduction have decided that someone acting merely as a donor is not a legal parent, although the marital status of the mother and the context in which the donation occurs may limit the applicability of a particular statute to protect a donor from a claim of parentage.

2. *The Spouse of the Mother Who Intends to Be a Parent Is Usually a Parent*

Every statute on point provides that the husband of the mother of a child born from assisted reproduction is the child's legal father so long as he consented to the procedure. Older versions of the UPA and twenty states draw the line here; only the *husband* of the child's mother is expressly covered by statute.[18] While South Carolina has no statute on point, its state supreme court has held that the husband of a woman who is artificially inseminated with his consent is the father of any resulting child.[19]

The 2002 UPA employs gender-neutral language so that a consenting *spouse* of the mother who intends to be a parent is a legal parent, regardless of sex. Ten states and the District of Columbia have adopted this language[20] and three others that use gender-specific language ("husband" and "his") in their statutes have, by case law, extended the treatment to any lawful spouse of the mother.[21] Indiana has no statute on point, but case law establishes that the consenting spouse of the mother is the parent of a resulting child.[22]

The statutes that use gender-specific terms require reconsideration in light of *Obergefell v. Hodges*.[23] In *Obergefell*, the Supreme Court held that the right to marry is guaranteed to same-sex couples as well as opposite-sex ones by the Due Process Clause and Equal Protection Clause. In light of this holding and in combination with *Skinner v. Oklahoma*,[24] which previously recognized a fundamental right to procreate, it seems likely that the same parentage rules should apply regardless of whether the spouse of the legal mother is male or female, even in states with statutes specifically referring to "husband" of the mother and the "father" of any resulting children. At least one New York appeals court decision has explicitly recognized this extension.[25]

Thus, parentage for a woman who consents to her wife's use of assisted reproduction to produce a child they both intend to parent is not as definite under existing statutes as where the consenting spouse is a man. However, recent developments make it likely that a consenting spouse, regardless of sex, would be considered a parent of a child resulting from assisted reproduction if the spouse so intends, regardless of the specific language of a governing statute.

3. An Intended Parent Who Is Not Married to the Mother May Be a Parent

If the mother of a child born from assisted reproduction is not married, the child will have a second legal parent only if an applicable assisted reproduction statute expressly provides for one or if the intended father (or the child) can establish paternity through the jurisdiction's more general parentage statute.

As with the statutes concerning the establishment of a second parent-child relationship where the mother is married, some of the statutes concerning reproduction outside of wedlock are gender-specific and by their terms only provide for the establishment of a *father*-child relationship. The 2002 UPA, which has not been widely adopted on this point, provides that "a man who provides sperm for, or consents to, assisted reproduction by a woman . . . with the intent to be the parent of her child, is a parent of the resulting child."[26] Texas's formulation is narrower, providing that an unmarried man who provides sperm to a licensed physician and consents to its use in assisted reproduction by an unmarried woman is the father of any resulting child if he so intends.

Others allow for the possibility that the second parent could be either a father or a mother. The current UPC provides that "a parent-child relationship exists between a child of assisted reproduction and an individual other than the birth mother who consented to assisted reproduction by the birth mother with intent to be treated as the other parent of the child."[27] This has been the most common formulation where a state has addressed the issue.[28] Colorado takes this approach for class gifts,[29] but requires the mother to be married to the intended father for intestate succession purposes.

For intestate succession purposes, Minnesota provides that a man who consents to a birth mother's assisted reproduction is the father of the resulting child if he so intends. However, a similar presumption only applies for class gift[30] purposes if the consenting man is the birth mother's "husband." As a result, under Minnesota law, as written, a father for intestacy purposes does not need to have been married to the child's mother at the time of the procedure but, for all other purposes, marriage is a necessary prerequisite for paternity to be determined under the state's assisted reproduction statute.

While maternity of a child born using assisted reproduction other than surrogacy, and establishing a parent-child relationship with the mother's spouse, is fairly straightforward, establishing a second parent-child relationship where the mother and intended parent are not married requires a closer analysis. Absent specific authorization under an assisted reproduction statute or qualification under a more general parentage provision, the child will have only one legal parent.

C. Posthumous Conception and Parentage

Assisted reproduction involving fertilization that occurs, or gestation that begins, after the death of an intended parent presents special issues with respect to the establishment of a parent-child relationship with the decedent. This issue generally only arises where one intended parent stores his sperm or her eggs, or where they jointly store embryos, for possible use in the future. After the death of one intended parent, the other decides to have a child using the material.

Some jurisdictions specifically authorize establishment of a parent-child relationship where the decedent-parent has clearly expressed intent to become a parent under these circumstances; others disallow establishing a relationship in this instance, while still others are silent on the point. Appendix 10(I)-B provides citations and a summary of the terms under which a parent-child relationship may be established, if any.

Fourteen jurisdictions do not address the issue.[31] A majority of those that do address it allow a parent-child relationship to be established under certain circumstances,[32] while the remainder require that conception occur before death for a relationship to be established.[33] Hawaii's statute allows that posthumous children inherit on the same basis as other children, but provides no guidance as to whether this includes only afterborn children or also posthumously conceived ones. Kentucky requires that a child be born within ten months of the intended parent's death but does not address whether conception may occur after death.

The primary variations between states that allow the establishment of a parent-child relationship between a decedent and a child born of posthumous conception are (1) whether the decedent must have expressly consented to posthumous conception; (2) whether the decedent must be genetically related to the child; (3) whether the decedent must have been married to the child's surviving parent at the time of his death; and (4) whether there is a timeframe within which the conception or birth must occur.

The UPC provides that a parent-child relationship exists where a decedent has provided consent and expressed the requisite intent. This consent must either be in a signed document mentioning posthumous reproduction or there must be clear and convincing evidence that the decedent had the specific intent to be the parent even if conception were to occur posthumously.[34] For purposes of intestate succession and class gifts,[35] the child must be in utero within thirty-six months of the decedent's death or born within forty-five months.[36] For states that have adopted the UPA but not the UPC on this point, a proponent of the relationship must provide a "record" evidencing consent by the "spouse" to posthumous conception.[37]

As with the UPC, many states allowing a parent-child relationship to be established in instances of posthumous conception require that the decedent have provided signed consent,[38] although some require only written consent.[39] Some states impose additional requirements: Florida requires that the consent be in the decedent's will; Oregon requires both a written consent and a specification in the decedent's will; Alabama and Texas both require that the signed consent be kept by a licensed physician; and New York requires that the consent not have been given more than seven years before the decedent's death. Meanwhile, Massachusetts and New Jersey require proof of consent without specifying the form. Finally, if the gift in question is created under a trust, Maryland requires that the decedent must also be the trust grantor and the trust must have become irrevocable on or after October 1, 2012.

States are fairly evenly divided on whether a parent-child relationship can be established if the decedent is not genetically related to the child. Twelve states require a genetic relationship;[40] Arizona likely does as well, but its authorization is in case law and the point is not directly addressed.[41] Eleven states do not require a genetic relationship.[42]

Approximately two-thirds of states that recognize parent-child relationships between a decedent and a posthumously conceived child do not require that the decedent and the child's surviving parent be married to each other at the time of the decedent's death.[43] Only seven states follow the UPA in requiring marriage.[44] (Arizona and New Jersey likely do as well but, as with the genetic relationship point, the question is not addressed directly in the opinions authorizing the relationship.)

Only ten states have adopted a time constraint on posthumous conception.[45] Of those that have, the time limits have for the most part been shorter than under the UPC; only Colorado and New Mexico enacted timing provisions equivalent to the UPC's and no U.S. jurisdictions allow for a longer gap between death and gestation or birth. New Jersey case law provides that there is likely a time limit, but that there was no reason to hold that twins born eighteen months after their father's death should not be found to be his heirs.[46] In addition to limiting the time period during which conception may occur, California and Oregon require that the person designated to control a decedent's genetic material provide written notice of existence of the material to the decedent's personal representative within four months of the decedent's death; New York allows seven months. Virginia allows for parentage to be established between a decedent and child born of assisted reproduction where implantation occurs after death but before notice could reasonably be conveyed to the attending physician.

Because the issue of posthumous conception is a relatively recent one and has arisen only infrequently, the variations in approaches among states that have adopted statutes on point are fewer than with respect to establishing a second parent-child relationship more generally. However, fewer states allow the relationships at all in the first instance.

D. Best Practices

Before an assisted reproduction procedure, anyone other than the birth mother who intends to establish a parent-child relationship with any resulting child should indicate his or her intent and consent to the procedure in a writing signed by both the mother and the second intended parent. The birth mother, intended second parent, and physician all should receive copies of the consent. Any revocation of consent by the second parent should be in writing and delivered to the birth mother and physician before the procedure. Divorce before the procedure generally acts as a revocation of any consent previously given but, to be safe, written notice of the divorce and revocation of consent should be delivered to the physician before insemination or embryo transfer. Once the procedure has been performed, consent may not be withdrawn.

If the mother and second intended parent will not be married to each other at the time of the procedure, they should verify that, under applicable law, the second intended parent can be considered the parent of any resulting child. If the law of the jurisdiction in which the parents are resident does not allow for this, the parents should consider, to the extent they are able, having the child born in a jurisdiction that does allow for this relationship. Otherwise, the second parent will need to adopt the child in order to establish the parent-child relationship, if allowable under applicable law.

To the extent insemination or embryo transfer will or might occur after the death of an intended parent (as with frozen gametes or embryos), the intended parents should provide for the possibility in their estate planning documents and prepare a written statement of intent to be a parent, or not, in such instance.

III. SURROGACY

In surrogacy, the intended parent or parents enter into an agreement with a woman to carry a child for whom she does not intend to be the legal mother. Because surrogacy explicitly attempts to overturn the usual presumption that the woman giving birth to a child is his legal mother, assisted reproduction using a surrogate problematizes maternity unlike the other forms of assisted reproduction.

Early surrogacy arrangements involved fertilization of the surrogate's egg with the sperm of the intended father. However, this approach quickly lost favor within the legal and assisted reproduction community once gestational surrogacy was a possibility because courts were loathed to enforce agreements that stripped a genetic mother of her legal rights in cases where the surrogate changed her mind about surrendering custody.[47] As a result, the UPA and UPC both contemplate use of a gestational surrogate.

Surrogacy agreements cover the roles of each of the parties (intended parent(s), surrogate, and any donors) as well as any expense reimbursement or compensation for the services provided. Approximately one-third of the states do not have law or other clear authority on point with respect to gestational surrogacy agreements.[48] Where this is the case, these agreements will be enforced, or not, based on general contract principles, including public policy considerations that militate against enforcement. If not enforced, maternity and paternity will be determined based on general parentage provisions under state law.

Jurisdictions that address these agreements generally take one of three approaches: (1) enforce the agreements if all requisites are followed, (2) allow the agreements but make them unenforceable in the case of dispute, or (3) prohibit the agreements. However, a number of jurisdictions take positions that do not fit neatly into any of these categories.

A. Jurisdictions Where Surrogacy Agreements Are Enforceable

Approximately one-third of U.S. jurisdictions explicitly enforce surrogacy agreements in at least some cases.[49] Where surrogacy agreements are enforceable, the intended parents do not need to adopt the resulting child to become the legal parents. Instead, the intended parents are listed as the parents on the child's birth certificate from the start. This is the surest approach to establishing a parent-child relationship between the intended parents and the child.

Jurisdictions that enforce surrogacy agreements have specific and varied requirements for doing so. The UPA requires that a surrogacy agreement be validated before conception and that the husband of the gestational surrogate, if any, be a party to the agreement. Analogous to the process for adoption, a home study is required before validation unless the court waives this requirement. Under this approach, the surrogate may be compensated a reasonable amount.

Other somewhat more common requirements are that (1) the intended parents be married to each other,[50] (2) that one or both have a genetic relationship to the child,[51] and (3) that no compensation be paid in exchange for the surrogacy services.[52] Because the variation in requirements is so great, though, no general overview can capture the diversity of the specific requirements for an enforceable agreement.

Massachusetts and South Carolina both have case law recognizing intended parents as the legal parents of a child born through surrogacy.[53] However, neither case was contested by the surrogate and it is unclear whether a similar outcome in one or both states would hold if there was a dispute. Pennsylvania has no statue or published case law on point, but its Office of Legal Counsel (Department of Health) has provided a letter to the judges of the Courts of Common Pleas detailing the department's policy in favor of allowing intended parents to file a pre-birth petition with the court and obtain an order with respect to parentage of a child carried by a gestational surrogate. The letter recites the existence of successful petitions in more than thirty Pennsylvania counties, including by same-sex couples and by single parents.

B. Jurisdictions Where Surrogacy Agreements Are Allowed but Unenforceable

Kentucky, Michigan, and Washington allow parties to enter into surrogacy agreements but refuse to enforce them in court if one or both parties contest the arrangement. Where this is the law, intended parents will be named as the legal parents in cases where the gestational surrogate does not contest parentage but would have no assurance that this will occur until after the child is born. In addition, Washington prohibits the payment of compensation in connection with a surrogacy arrangement.

Where an agreement is not enforced, the surrogate will be named the mother with her husband, if any, the legal father.

C. Jurisdictions Where Surrogacy Agreements Are Void

Idaho, Kansas, New York, Oklahoma, and Oregon invalidate or prohibit surrogacy agreements. Clients entering into arrangements in these jurisdictions will need to adopt the child for whom they intend to become parents, after a release of parental rights by the surrogate.

D. Other Approaches

A handful of states take unique or uncertain approaches. Statutorily, Arizona bans surrogacy agreements. However, a state appeals court held that the statute is unconstitutional.[54] Yet no other court in the state has ruled on the issue so, for now, the statutory approach remains in all but Appellate Division I.

West Virginia allows fees and expenses to be paid for a surrogate, and Nebraska and New Mexico prohibit the payment of compensation. All three jurisdictions, though, are silent on all other related points, including the requirements for and enforceability of surrogacy agreements outside of this realm.

New Jersey and Tennessee might recognize intended parents as legal parents where there is a genetic connection, but the case law is not developed enough in either state to be clear. Similarly, while the Maryland Supreme Court held that a gestational carrier could disprove that she was the mother of a child she bore,[55] applicable state law provides no mechanism to require a surrogate to do so or for naming someone else as mother. Instead, the intended father, who provided the sperm for the assisted reproduction, was recognized as the legal father with no mother legally recognized.[56]

E. Best Practices

Any client intending to have a child using a gestational surrogacy needs to enter into a comprehensive surrogacy agreement in which all interested persons—the intended parent(s), donor(s), the surrogate, and the surrogate's spouse (if any)—are party. It is important to choose a jurisdiction that permits and enforces these agreements to govern the relationship.

While the specifics of what is required differ, the jurisdictions open to enforcing surrogacy agreements provide the best option for clients intending to build a family in this way. They also provide the best treatment of surrogates: Their rights are respected as well and child support is generally available in instances of breach by the intended parents. Thus, any surrogacy agreement should be entered into and performed in one of these jurisdictions.

Surrogacy agreements and arrangements should be avoided in the jurisdictions that do not enforce or that invalidate agreements. For the intended parents to become the legal parents in these jurisdictions, the surrogate would need to relinquish her maternal rights (and, if married, her spouse would need to release all parental rights as well) a reasonable period of time after birth of the child, and the intended parents would need to adopt the child. Because of the high likelihood of complications, these jurisdictions should be avoided.

IV. SPECIAL ISSUES WITH CRYOPRESERVATION

Cryopreservation is the freezing of sperm, eggs, and embryos for future reproduction. Because the materials are stored, often for years, it is important to understand the role of these materials in a well-crafted estate plan. Little case law and no statutory law has developed around these materials, so clear planning is necessary.

In general, clinics that provide cryopreservation services require that intended parents specify what should be done with any excess reproductive materials. For unmarried clients, clinics often require a letter from an attorney asserting that there is an agreement between the parties as to who is to have control over the materials; that is, who can direct them to be disposed of or used. The general practice is to bill the female (or a female) partner for the annual storage fee—often $500 per year or more—unless the stored material is sperm.

Because human body materials are not legally property, disposition upon divorce (or other dissolution of a relationship) or death can become problematic.[57] On divorce, the issue arises when embryos have been stored. Because neither partner has a better claim to the materials, conflicts over how to handle the materials often arise in the absence of a clear advance agreement. Courts in general are loathe to allow the use of frozen embryos absent agreement from both intended parents. Thus, directions for disposal made at the time of cryopreservation are generally followed, while those assigning possession to one party are ignored if objected to by the other party.

If your clients have cryopreserved materials, any agreement about their disposition needs to take into account the possibility that the parties will divorce and disagree about the use of the materials. If both are willing to have the materials used even under these circumstances, they need to be aware that there are risks with respect to child support and visitation rights, even if the materials are not used until after divorce.

Upon the death of a client with cryopreserved materials, there are several possible problems. First, any directions given to the clinic may not cover this scenario. Second, extended family may not know the materials exist and thus fail to notify the clinic. In this case, an annual storage fee would continue to be charged despite no possibility the materials would be used.

Finally, a family member may have wishes with respect to the materials that are contrary to any instructions previously given.

To the extent a client dies with cryopreserved materials, fiduciaries should comply with any instructions about their disposition. Because body materials are not legally property, they cannot be disposed of by will.[58] However, it is prudent to mention them and the intended disposition in a will so that family members and the personal representative are aware of them and the directions given concerning their disposition. Moreover, courts have at times upheld intended dispositions under a will in the face of contest. However, this is not something on which a client should rely.

Cryopreserved material also can become an issue should your client become incapacitated. A conservator may need to decide how long it is reasonable to continue paying the storage fees for the material. Covering this issue in both a durable power of attorney and a Living Trust in a consistent way is important to ensure your client's wishes are followed.

V. CONCLUSION

While no longer particularly novel, assisted reproduction continues to present estate planning issues not well-covered under the laws of many U.S. jurisdictions, making this an area where careful planning is particularly important. Clear drafting that defines the terms "child" and "descendant" in ways consistent with your client's wishes remains the best way to protect your client and ensure his or her wishes are followed with respect to children born through the use of reproductive technologies.

For specific drafting and additional planning suggestions for clients using assisted reproduction to build their families or intending to include posthumously conceived children in their estates, see Part II of this chapter.

NOTES

1. *See 2014 Assisted Reproductive Technology National Summary Report*, CENTERS FOR DISEASE CONTROL & PREVENTION, AMERICAN SOCIETY FOR REPRODUCTIVE MEDICINE, SOCIETY FOR ASSISTED REPRODUCTIVE TECHNOLOGY (Oct. 2016), *available at* https://www.cdc.gov/art/pdf/2014-report/art-2014-national-summary-report.pdf.

2. However, because of the legal complications with traditional surrogacy arrangements, use of gestational surrogates is now generally encouraged. *See* discussion in section III of Part I of this chapter.

3. The UPC does not define class gift. The Restatement of Property defines it as:

> [A] disposition to beneficiaries who take as members of a group. Taking as members of a group means that the identities and shares of the beneficiaries are subject to fluctuation. A disposition is presumed to create a class gift if the terms of the disposition identify the beneficiaries only by a term of relationship or other group label. The presumption is rebutted if the language or circumstances establish that the transferor intended the identities and shares of the beneficiaries to be fixed.

RESTATEMENT (THIRD) OF PROPERTY: Wills and Donative Transfers § 13.1 (2011).

4.   Alabama, Alaska, Arizona, Arkansas, California, Colorado, Connecticut, Delaware, Florida, Georgia, Idaho, Illinois, Kansas, Louisiana, Maine, Maryland, Massachusetts, Michigan, Minnesota, Missouri, Montana, Nevada, New Hampshire, New Jersey, New Mexico, New York, North Carolina, North Dakota, Ohio, Oklahoma, Oregon, Tennessee, Texas, Utah, Virginia, Washington, Wisconsin, and Wyoming.

5.   Surrogacy is covered in section III of Part I of this chapter.

6.   Gardenour v. Bondelie, 60 N.E.3d 1109 (Ind. App. 2016).

7.   UPC (2008), https://www.uniformlaws.org/HigherLogic/System/Download DocumentFile.ashx?DocumentFileKey=af0af595-c596-4663-8426-e21b1e2435 46&forceDialog=0; UPC (2010), https://www.uniformlaws.org/HigherLogic/System /DownloadDocumentFile.ashx?DocumentFileKey=ea041355-39bc-42cb-b9f3-563f 14bd7539&forceDialog=0.

8.   UPA (2002) http://www.uniformlaws.org/Act.aspx?title=Parentage%20Act. *See also* Chapter 9.

9.   Where provisions of the UPA and UPC conflict, UPA (2002) § 203, in combination with its comments, provides that the provisions of the UPC govern for probate purposes. Thus, this chapter discusses the UPC provisions exclusively in such instances.

10.   UPC § 2-120(b) (2008 & 2010).

11.   UPA § 702 (2000 & 2002). *See also* note 66 of Chapter 9 and accompanying text.

12.   Colorado, Connecticut, Delaware, Illinois, Maine, Nevada, New Hampshire, New Mexico, North Dakota, Texas, Utah, Virginia, Washington, and Wyoming. Florida specifies that covered donors include those of eggs, sperm, and pre-embryos. Oklahoma indirectly provides that egg donors are not mothers by specifying that any resulting child is deemed to be a naturally conceived child of the intended parents.

13.   UPA § 5(b) (1973).

14.   Washington DC, Idaho, Kansas, Minnesota, Missouri, Montana, New Jersey, Ohio, Oregon, Wisconsin, and Massachusetts by case law.

15.   *See, e.g.*, Sieglein v. Schmidt, 136 A.3d 751 (Md. App. 2016) and *In re* Adoption of a Minor, 29 N.E.3d 830 (Mass. 2015).

16.   Alabama, Minnesota, Missouri, and Montana.

17.   Kansas, New Jersey, and Wisconsin. California requires that the body materials be provided to a licensed physician, surgeon, or sperm bank, or pursuant to an agreement between a sperm donor and the intended mother that the donor not be a parent of any resulting child.

18.   Alabama, Arkansas, Connecticut, Florida, Idaho, Kansas, Louisiana, Maryland, Michigan, Missouri, Montana, New Jersey, New York, North Carolina, Ohio, Oklahoma, Tennessee, Texas, Utah, and Virginia. The 1973 UPA and 2000 UPA take this approach as well. Minnesota's parentage statute similarly refers to the "husband" of the intended mother, however the more general language of "man" is used in the intestacy statute, implying that for intestacy purposes only, marriage to the mother is not required. *See* text accompanying note *infra*.

19.   *In re* Baby Doe, 353 S.E.2d 877 (S.C. 1987).

20.   Arizona, California, Colorado, Georgia, Illinois, Maine, Nevada, New Hampshire, North Dakota, and Washington.

21.   Massachusetts, Oregon, Wisconsin.

22.   Gardenour v. Bondelie, 60 N.E.3d 1109 (Ind. Ct. App. 2016).

23.   Obergefell v. Hodges, 576 U.S. 1 (2015).

24.   Skinner v. Oklahoma, 316 U.S. 535 (1942).

25.   *See* Matter of Christopher YY. v. Jessica ZZ, 2018 N.Y. Slip Op. 004495 (AD 3d).

26. UPA § 703 (2002). Delaware, Minnesota (for intestate succession), and Wyoming take this approach.

27. UPC § 2-102(f) (intestacy) & § 2-705(b) (class gifts) (2010).

28. California, DC, Illinois, Maine, Nevada, New Hampshire, New Mexico, North Dakota, and Washington.

29. *See* note 3.

30. *Id.*

31. Alaska, DC, Kansas, Mississippi, Montana, Nevada, North Carolina, Oklahoma, Rhode Island, Tennessee, Vermont, West Virginia, and Wisconsin.

32. Alabama, Arizona, California, Colorado, Connecticut, Delaware, Florida, Illinois, Iowa, Louisiana, Maine, Maryland, Massachusetts, New Hampshire, New Jersey, New Mexico, New York, North Dakota, Oregon, Texas, Utah, Virginia, Washington, and Wyoming.

33. Arkansas, Georgia, Idaho, Indiana, Michigan, Minnesota, Missouri, Nebraska, Ohio, Pennsylvania, South Carolina, and South Dakota.

34. UPC § 2-120(f)(1) & (2)(C) (2010).

35. *See* note 3.

36. UPC § 2-120(k) (2010).

37. UPA § 707 (2002).

38. Alabama, California, Connecticut, Delaware, Iowa, Maine, Maryland, New Mexico, Virginia, and Washington.

39. Illinois, Louisiana, New Hampshire, North Dakota, Utah, and Wyoming.

40. California, Connecticut, Florida, Illinois, Iowa, Louisiana, Maryland, Massachusetts, New Jersey, New York, Oregon, and Virginia.

41. Gillett-Netting v. Barnhart, 371 F.3d 593 (9th Cir. 2004).

42. Alabama, Colorado, Delaware, Maine, New Hampshire, New Mexico, North Dakota, Texas, Utah, Washington, and Wyoming.

43. California, Colorado, Delaware, Florida, Illinois, Maine, Maryland, Massachusetts, New Hampshire, New Mexico, New York, Oregon, Virginia, Washington, and Wyoming.

44. Alabama, Connecticut, Iowa, Louisiana, North Dakota, Texas, and Utah.

45. California, Colorado, Connecticut, Illinois, Iowa, Louisiana, Maryland, New Mexico, New York, and Oregon.

46. *In re* Estate of Kolacy, 753 A.2d 1257 (N.J. Super. Ct. Ch. Div. 2000).

47. *See, e.g., In re* Baby M, 109 N.J. 396 (1988).

48. Alabama, Alaska, Georgia, Hawaii, Minnesota, Mississippi, Missouri, Montana, North Carolina, Rhode Island, South Dakota, Vermont, Wisconsin, and Wyoming.

49. Arkansas, California, Colorado, Connecticut, Delaware, DC, Florida, Illinois, Iowa, Louisiana, Maine, Nevada, New Hampshire, North Dakota, Ohio, Texas, Utah, and Virginia.

50. Florida, Louisiana, Texas, Utah, and Virginia.

51. Florida, Illinois, Iowa, Louisiana, North Dakota, Utah, and Virginia.

52. Florida, Louisiana, and Virginia.

53. Culliton v. Beth Israel Deaconess Med. Ctr., 756 N.E.2d 1133 (Mass. 2001); Mid-S. Ins. Co. v. Doe, 274 F. Supp. 2d 757 (D.S.C. 2003).

54. Soos v. Super. Ct for Cty. of Maricopa, 897 P.2d 1356 (Ariz. App. Div. 1 1994).

55. *In re* Roberto d.B., 923 A.2d 115 (Md. 2007).

56. *Id.*

57. UPC (2010) § 1-201(38).

58. *Id.*

APPENDIX 10(I)-A

General Rules of Parentage for Children Born of Assisted Reproduction (Other Than Surrogacy)

(page intentionally left blank)

	DONORS ARE USUALLY NOT PARENTS			WHO CAN BE A PARENT?			
	Authority	Must the mother be married?	Physician Required?	Authority	Must the Intended Parents be Married?	Sex of Second Parent	Physician Required?
Alabama	Ala. Code § 26-17-702	Yes	Yes	Ala. Code §§ 26-17-201(b)(5); 26-17-702 & 26-17-703	Yes	Male	Yes
Alaska	None	N/A	N/A	AS § 25.20.045	Yes	Male	Yes
Arizona	None	N/A	N/A	A.R.S. § 25-501(B)	Yes	Any	No
Arkansas	None	N/A	N/A	A.C.A. § 9-10-202	Yes	Male	Yes
California	Cal. Fam. Code § 7613(b)	No	Yes or surgeon/sperm bank or agreement	Cal. Fam. Code § 7613(a)	No	Any	No
Colorado	Colo. Rev. Stat. §§ 15-11-120(3) (intestacy) & 19-4-106(2)	No	No	Colo. Rev. Stat. § 15-11-120(6) & (intestacy)	No	Any	No
				Colo. Rev. Stat § 19-4-106	Yes	Male	Yes or advanced practice nurse
Conn.	Conn. Gen. Stat. § 45a-775	No	No	Conn. Gen. Stat. §§ 45a-772(b); 45a-774 & 45a-777(a)	Yes	Male	Yes
Delaware	13 Del. C. § 8-702	No	No	13 Del. C. § 8-703(1)	No	Male	No
D.C.	D.C. Code § 16-909e(2)	No	No	D.C. Code § 16-909e(1)	No	Any	No

	DONORS ARE USUALLY NOT PARENTS			WHO CAN BE A PARENT?			
	Authority	Must the mother be married?	Physician Required?	Authority	Must the Intended Parents be Married?	Sex of Second Parent	Physician Required?
Florida	Fla. Stat. § 742.14	No	No	Fla. Stat. § 742.11	Yes	Male	No
Georgia	None	N/A	N/A	O.C.G.A. §§ 53-2-5 & 19-7-21; *Patton v. Vanterpool*, 2017 WL 4582398 (Ga. 2017) (§ 19-7-21 does not apply to children conceived by IVF)	Yes	Any	No
Hawaii	None	N/A	N/A	None	N/A	N/A	N/A
Idaho	Idaho Code Ann. § 39-5405(1)	No	No	Idaho Code Ann. § 39-5405(3)	Yes	Male	No
Illinois	750 ILCS 46/702	No	No	750 ILCS 46/103(m-5) & 750 ILCS 46/703(a)	No	Any	No
Indiana	None	N/A	N/A	*Gardenour v. Bondelie*, 60 N.E.3d 1109 (Ind. App. 2016)	Yes	Any	No
Iowa	None	N/A	N/A	None	N/A	N/A	N/A
Kansas	K.S.A. § 23-2208(f)	No	Yes	K.S.A. § 23-2302	Yes	Male	No
Kentucky	None	N/A	N/A	None	N/A	N/A	N/A
Louisiana	None	N/A	N/A	La. Civ. Code Art. 188	Yes	Male	No
Maine	M.R.S.A. § 1922(1)	No	No	M.R.S.A. § 1923	No	Any	No

	DONORS ARE USUALLY NOT PARENTS			WHO CAN BE A PARENT?			
	Authority	Must the mother be married?	Physician Required?	Authority	Must the Intended Parents be Married?	Sex of Second Parent	Physician Required?
Maryland	None	N/A	N/A	Md. Code Ann., Est. & Trusts § 1-206(b) & *Sieglein v. Schmidt*, 136 A.3d 751 (Md. App. 2016)	Yes	Male	No
Massachusetts	*In re Adoption of a Minor*, 29 N.E.3d 830 (Mass. 2015)	Yes	No	Mass. Gen. Laws ch. 46, § 4B; *In re Adoption of a Minor*, 29 N.E.3d 830 (Mass. 2015)	Yes	Any	No
Michigan	None	N/A	N/A	MCL §§ 700.2114 (intestacy) & 333.2824(6)	Yes	Male	No
Minnesota	Minn. Stat. § 524.2-120(1) (intestacy)	No	No	Minn. Stat. § 524.2-120(5) (intestacy)	No	Male	No
	Minn. Stat. § 257.56(2)	Yes	Yes	Minn. Stat. § 257.56(1)	Yes	Male	Yes
Mississippi	None	N/A	N/A	None	N/A	N/A	N/A
Missouri	Mo. Rev. Stat. § 210.824(2)	Yes	Yes	Mo. Rev. Stat. § 210.824(1)	Yes	Male	Yes
Montana	MCA § 40-6-106(2)	Yes	Yes	MCA § 40-6-106(1)	Yes	Male	Yes
Nebraska	None	N/A	N/A	None	N/A	N/A	N/A
Nevada	NRS § 126.660	No	No	NRS §§ 126.041 & 126.670	No	Any	No

	DONORS ARE USUALLY NOT PARENTS			WHO CAN BE A PARENT?			
	Authority	Must the mother be married?	Physician Required?	Authority	Must the Intended Parents be Married?	Sex of Second Parent	Physician Required?
New Hampshire	NHRSA § 168-B:2(III)	No	No	RSA § 168-B:2(II)	No	Any	No
New Jersey	N.J.S.A. § 9-17-44(b)	No	Yes	N.J.S.A. § 9-17-44(a)	Yes	Male	Yes
New Mexico	N.M. Stat. Ann. §§ 45-2-120(B) & 40-11a-702	No	No	N.M. Stat. Ann. §§ 45-2-120(F) (intestacy) & 40-11a-703	No	Any	No
New York	None	N/A	N/A	N.Y. Dom. Rel. L. § 73(1)	Yes	Male	Authorized to practice medicine
				Matter of Christopher YY. v. Jessica ZZ., 2018 N.Y. Slip Op. 004495 (AD 3d)	Yes	Any	No, as long as spouse consents.
North Carolina	None	N/A	N/A	N.C. Gen. Stat. § 49A-1	Yes	Male	No
North Dakota	N.D. Cent. Code §§ 30.1-04-19(2) & 14-20-60	No	No	N.D. Cent. Code §§ 30.1-04-19(6) (intestacy) & 30.1-04-05(2) (class gifts)	No	Any	No
				§ 14-20-61	No	Male	No
Ohio	Ohio Rev. Code Ann. §3111.95(B)	No	No	Ohio Rev. Code Ann. §§ 3111.95(A) & 3111.97(B)	Yes	Male	No

	DONORS ARE USUALLY NOT PARENTS			WHO CAN BE A PARENT?			
	Authority	Must the mother be married?	Physician Required?	Authority	Must the Intended Parents be Married?	Sex of Second Parent	Physician Required?
Oklahoma	10 Okla. St. Ann. § 554 (only applies to egg donation)	Yes	No	10 Okla. Stat. Ann. §§ 552 & 556(B)(1)	Yes	Male	No
Oregon	ORS § 109-239	No	No	ORS § 109.243 & *Shineovich and Kemp*, 214 P.3d 29 (Or. App. 2009), *rev. den.* 222 P.3d 1091 (Or.)	Yes	Any	No
Pennsylvania	None	N/A	N/A	None	N/A	N/A	N/A
Rhode Island	None	N/A	N/A	None	N/A	N/A	N/A
South Carolina	None	N/A	N/A	*In re Baby Doe*, 353 S.E.2d 877 (S.C. 1987)	Yes	Male	No
South Dakota	None	N/A	N/A	None	N/A	N/A	N/A
Tennessee	None	N/A	N/A	Tenn. Code Ann. § 68-3-306	Yes	Male	No
Texas	Tex. Fam. Code § 160.702	No	No	Tex. Fam. Code § 160.7031(a)	No	Male	Yes
				Tex. Fam. Code § 160.705(a)	Yes	Male	No

	DONORS ARE USUALLY NOT PARENTS			WHO CAN BE A PARENT?			
	Authority	Must the mother be married?	Physician Required?	Authority	Must the Intended Parents be Married?	Sex of Second Parent	Physician Required?
Utah	Utah Code Ann. § 78B-15-702	No	No	Utah Code Ann. § 78B-15-703	Yes	Male	No
Vermont	None	N/A	N/A	None	N/A	N/A	N/A
Virginia	Va. Code. Ann. § 20-158(A)(3)	No	No	Va. Code. Ann. §§ 64-2-102(2) (estates generally) & 20-158(A)(2)	Yes	Male	N/A
Washington	RCW § 26.26.705	No	No	RCW § 26.26.710	No	Any	No
West Virginia	None	N/A	N/A	None	N/A	N/A	N/A
Wisconsin	Wisc. Stat. § 891.40(2)	No	Yes	Wisc. Stat. § 891.40(1) & Torres v. Seemeyer, 207 F. Supp. 3d 905 (W.D. Wis. 2016)	Yes	Any	Yes
Wyoming	Wyo. Stat. Ann. § 14-2-902	No	No	Wyo. Stat. Ann. § 14-2-903	No	Male	No

APPENDIX 10(I)-B

Can a Posthumously Conceived Child Be the Child of the Decedent?

(page intentionally left blank)

	Authority	Yes or No?	Form of consent needed from decedent	Genetic relationship required?	Must decedent and living parent have been married?	Required timeframe for conception or birth
Alabama	§ 26-17-707	Yes	Signed & kept by licensed physician	No	Yes	N/A
Alaska	None	N/A	N/A	N/A	N/A	N/A
Arizona	*Gillett-Netting v. Barnhart*, 371 F.3d 593 (9th Cir. 2004)	Yes, at least in context of Social Security	N/A	Probably	Maybe	N/A
Arkansas	*Finley v. Astrue*, 270 S.W.3d 849 (Ark. 2008)	No	N/A	N/A	N/A	Must be conceived before death
California	Prob. Code § 249.5	Yes	Signed	Yes	No	In utero within 2 years of death
Colorado	§ 15-11-120(b)	Yes	None	No	No	In utero within 36 months of death or born within 45 months
Connecticut	§ 45a-785	Yes	Signed	Yes	Yes	In utero within 1 year of death
Delaware	§ 13-8-707	Yes	Signed	No	No	N/A
District of Columbia	None	N/A	N/A	N/A	N/A	N/A
Florida	§ 742.17	Yes	In his will	Yes	No	N/A
Georgia	§ 53-2-1(b)	No	N/A	N/A	N/A	Conceived before death
Hawaii	None	N/A	N/A	N/A	N/A	N/A

	Authority	Yes or No?	Form of consent needed from decedent	Genetic relationship required?	Must decedent and living parent have been married?	Required timeframe for conception or birth
Idaho	None	N/A	N/A	N/A	N/A	N/A
Illinois	750 46/705	Yes	Written	Yes	No	Born within 36 months of death
Indiana	§ 29-1-2-6	No	N/A	N/A	N/A	Begotten before death
Iowa	§ 633.220A	Yes	Signed	Yes	Yes	Born within 2 years of death
Kansas	N/A	None	N/A	N/A	N/A	N/A
Kentucky	N/A	None	N/A	N/A	N/A	N/A
Louisiana	§ 9:391.1	Yes	Written	Yes	Yes	Born within 3 years of death
Maine	§ 1927	Yes	Signed	No	No	None
Maryland	Est. & Trusts § 1-205	Yes	Signed; for a trust, decedent is grantor & trust became irrevocable on or after 10/1/2012	Yes	No	Born within 2 years of death
Massachusetts	*Woodward v. Comm'r of Soc. Sec.*, 760 N.E.2d 257 (Mass. 2002)	Yes	Proof of consent & intent to support	Yes	No	None
Michigan	*Mattison v. Soc. Sec. Comm'r*, 825 N.W.2d 566 (Mich. 2012)	No	N/A	N/A	N/A	In gestation before death
Minnesota	§ 524.2-120(10)	No	N/A	N/A	N/A	In gestation before death
Mississippi	None	N/A	N/A	N/A	N/A	N/A

	Authority	Yes or No?	Form of consent needed from decedent	Genetic relationship required?	Must decedent and living parent have been married?	Required timeframe for conception or birth
Missouri	*Vogel v. Mercantile Trust Co. Nat'l Ass'n*, 511 S.W.2d 784 (Mt. 1974)	No	N/A	N/A	N/A	Conceived before death
Montana	None	N/A	N/A	N/A	N/A	N/A
Nebraska	*Amen v. Astrue*, 284 Neb. 691, 822 N.W.2d 419 (2012)	No	N/A	N/A	N/A	Conceived before death
Nevada	None	N/A	N/A	N/A	N/A	N/A
New Hampshire	§ 168-B:2(IV)	Yes	Written	No	No	None
New Jersey	*In re Estate of Kolacy*, 332 N.J. Super. 593, 753 A. 2d 1257 (Ch. Div. 2000)	Yes	Proof of intent	Yes	Maybe	Child born 18 months after father's death is potential heir where no reason to cut off inheritance
New Mexico	§ 40-11A-707 & § 45-2-120(K)	Yes	Signed	No	No	In utero within 36 months of death or born within 45 months
New York	Est. Powers & Trusts L. § 4-1.3	Yes	Written no more than 7 years prior to death	Yes	No	In utero within 24 months of death or born within 33 months
North Carolina	None	N/A	N/A	N/A	N/A	N/A
North Dakota	§ 14-20-65	Yes	Written	No	No	None
Ohio	§ 2105.14	No	N/A	N/A	N/A	Begotten prior to death
Oklahoma	None	N/A	N/A	N/A	N/A	N/A

	Authority	Yes or No?	Form of consent needed from decedent	Genetic relationship required?	Must decedent and living parent have been married?	Required timeframe for conception or birth
Oregon	§ 112.077	Yes	Written and specified in will	Yes	No	In utero within 2 years of death
Pennsylvania	Seaman v. Colvin, 2015 WL 5112975 (E.D. Pa. 2015)	No	N/A	N/A	N/A	Begotten prior to death
Rhode Island	None	N/A	N/A	N/A	N/A	N/A
South Carolina	None	N/A	N/A	N/A	N/A	N/A
South Dakota	None	N/A	N/A	N/A	N/A	N/A
Tennessee	None	N/A	N/A	N/A	N/A	N/A
Texas	Fam. Code § 160.707	Yes	Written and kept by a licensed physician	No	Yes	None
Utah	§ 78B-15-707	Yes	Written	No	Yes	None
Vermont	None	N/A	N/A	N/A	N/A	N/A
Virginia	§ 20-158	Yes	Signed	Yes	No	None
			None	Yes	No	Implantation after death but before notice conveyable to physician
Washington	§ 26.26.730	Yes	Signed	No	No	None
West Virginia	None	N/A	N/A	N/A	N/A	N/A
Wisconsin	None	N/A	N/A	N/A	N/A	N/A
Wyoming	§ 14-2-907	Yes	Written	No	No	None

APPENDIX 10(I)-C

Who Are the Legal Parents of a Child Born from Gestational Surrogacy?

(page intentionally left blank)

	Authority	Can Intended Parent(s) be Parents?	Must the Intended Parents Be Married?	Is a Genetic Relationship Required?	Other
Alabama	§ 26-17-201 (comment)	Unclear	N/A	N/A	Courts decide based on existing legal principles.
Alaska	None	No	N/A	N/A	N/A
Arizona	§§ 25-218 & *Soos v. Cty. of Maricopa*, 182 Ariz. 470 (Ariz. App. Div. 1 1994)	Unclear	N/A	N/A	Statute bans surrogacy contracts; an appeals court found the statute unconstitutional but no other court has addressed it.
Arkansas	§ 9-10-201	Yes	No	No	Parent-child relationship based on whether sperm donor is known or anonymous and married or not.
California	§ 7960 & § 7962	Yes	No	No	Requires valid assisted reproduction agreement and court filing.
Colorado	§ 15-11-121	Yes	No	No	Requires validated gestational agreement.
Connecticut	§ 7-36 & § 7-48a	Yes	No	No	Requires court order approving the gestational agreement.
Delaware	§§ 8-801–8-813	Yes	No	No	Compensation permitted.
District of Columbia	§§ 16-401–16-412	Yes	No	No	N/A
Florida	§§ 742.13–742.16	Yes	Yes	Yes	Requires binding gestational surrogacy contract and court petition; compensation prohibited.
Georgia	None	No	N/A	N/A	N/A
Hawaii	None	No	N/A	N/A	N/A

	Authority	Can Intended Parent(s) be Parents?	Must the Intended Parents Be Married?	Is a Genetic Relationship Required?	Other
Idaho	*Matter of Doe*, 160 Idaho 360 (2016)	No	N/A	N/A	Surrogacy contracts are void; termination of parental rights and adoption required.
Illinois	750 §§ 47/1–47/75	Yes	No	Yes	Gametes of at least one intended parent must be used; compensation permitted.
Indiana	§ 31-20-1-1	No	N/A	N/A	N/A
Iowa	Admin. § 641-99.15(144)	Yes	No	Yes	Only an intended parent that provided gametes is recognized; in other cases, adoption is required.
Kansas	§ 59-2116 & Kan. Atty. Gen. Op. No. 82-150	No	N/A	N/A	Adoption may not be agreed to until the child is born; surrogacy contracts are void.
Kentucky	*Surrogate Parenting Assoc., Inc. v. Com. ex. rel. Armstrong*, 704 S.W.2d 209 (Ky, 1986)	Yes but not enforceable	N/A	N/A	Surrogate mother may change her mind; custody aspects of a surrogacy agreement will not be enforced against her.
Louisiana	§ 9:2718–§ 9:2720.15	Yes	Yes	Yes	Compensation prohibited.
Maine	19-A §§ 1931–1939	Yes	No	No	At least one party must be a resident of Maine.
Maryland	*In re Roberto d.B.*, 399 Md. 267 (2007)	Unclear	No	Yes	A surrogate may disprove maternity using genetic testing, but provides no authority for mandating it or for naming another person as mother.
Massachusetts	*Culliton v. Beth Israel Deaconess Med. Cent.*, 435 Mass. 285 (2001)	Yes but possibly not enforceable	N/A	N/A	Pre-birth declaration of parenthood permissible where gestational surrogacy was used and there was no contest.

	Authority	Can Intended Parent(s) be Parents?	Must the Intended Parents Be Married?	Is a Genetic Relationship Required?	Other
Michigan	§§ 722.851–722.863	Yes but not enforceable	N/A	N/A	Compensation prohibited; surrogacy agreements are unenforceable.
Minnesota	None	No	N/A	N/A	N/A
Mississippi	None	No	N/A	N/A	N/A
Missouri	None	No	N/A	N/A	N/A
Montana	None	No	N/A	N/A	N/A
Nebraska	§ 25-21,200	Unclear	N/A	N/A	Compensation prohibited; no other authority.
Nevada	§§ 126.710–126.810	Yes	No	No	Compensation permitted.
New Hampshire	§§ 168-B:1–168-B:22	Yes	No	No	Compensation permitted.
New Jersey	*In re T.J.S.*, 212 N.J. 334 (2012)	No	N/A	N/A	Birth mother is the legal mother, at least where intended mother is not biologically related to the child.
New Mexico	1978 §40-11A-801 & § 32A-5-34	Unclear	N/A	N/A	New Mexico law does not authorize or prohibit surrogacy arrangements and does not permit payment for surrogacy.
New York	Dom. Rel. L. § 121–§ 124	No	N/A	N/A	Surrogate parenting contracts are void; compensation prohibited; proposed legislation to allow both but not in effect as of 7/31/2017.
North Carolina	None	No	N/A	N/A	N/A
North Dakota	Civ. Code § 14-18-01 & § 14-18-08	Yes	No	Yes	N/A

	Authority	Can Intended Parent(s) be Parents?	Must the Intended Parents Be Married?	Is a Genetic Relationship Required?	Other
Ohio	*J.F. v. D.B.*, 116 Ohio St.3d 363 (2007)	Yes	No	No	Gestational surrogacy agreement enforced; compensation permitted.
Oklahoma	Okl. Op. Atty. Gen. No. 83-162 (Sept. 29, 1983)	No	N/A	N/A	Compensation prohibited; only married women may be artificially inseminated, and resulting child is the legal and natural child of the birth mother and her spouse.
Oregon	Ore. Rev. Stat. § 163.537(d)	No	N/A	N/A	References "adoption pursuant to a surrogacy agreement."
Pennsylvania	PA Dep't of Health Policy and Procedures for Assisted Conception Birth Registrations	Yes, but possibly not enforceable	No	Unclear	Provides procedure for "assisted conception birth registration"; requires court order. More than 30 counties have issued orders.
Rhode Island	None	No	N/A	N/A	N/A
South Carolina	*Mid-South Ins. Co. v. Doe*, 274 F. Supp. 2d 757 (2003)	Yes, but possibly not enforceable	N/A	N/A	Gestational surrogacy agreement not struck down, but the court did not rule on its enforceability and child was adopted by intended parents.
South Dakota	None	No	N/A	N/A	N/A
Tennessee	§ 36-1-102(50A) & *In re Amadi A.*, 2015 WL 1956247 (Tenn. Ct. App. Apr. 24, 2015)	Probably	Probably	Probably	Surrogacy explicitly is not accepted? compensation prohibited. Cases express approval for recognizing intended parents where there is a genetic relationship and reference "husband" and "wife."

	Authority	Can Intended Parent(s) be Parents?	Must the Intended Parents Be Married?	Is a Genetic Relationship Required?	Other
Texas	Fam. Code § 160.751–§ 160.763	Yes	Yes	No	Gestational agreement must be validated.
Utah	1953 § 78B-15-801–§ 78B-15-809	Yes	Yes	Yes	Compensation permitted; gestational agreement must be validated.
Vermont	None	No	N/A	N/A	N/A
Virginia	§ 20-156–§ 20-165	Yes	Yes	Yes	Compensation prohibited; gestational agreement must be approved by a court. If agreement is not approved, parenthood determined based on relationship to the child and marital status.
Washington	§§ 26.26.210–26.26.260 & § 26.26.735	Yes but not enforceable	No	Unclear	Compensation prohibited; superior court will decide on custody in the event of a dispute; surrogacy agreement must be filed.
West Virginia	§ 61-2-14h(e)(3)	Unclear	N/A	N/A	Fees and expenses for surrogacy are authorized.
Wisconsin	In re F.T.R., 349 Wis.2d 84 (2013)	Unclear	N/A	N/A	Portion of a traditional surrogacy agreement requiring relinquishment of maternal rights was unenforceable.
Wyoming	None	No	N/A	N/A	N/A

PART II: PLANNING AND DRAFTING CONSIDERATIONS

Cynthia L. Barrett

> PRACTICE TIP
>
> Avoid archaic terms!
>
> A law of "intended" parental relationships is developing to deal with all intended parents of children born using artificial reproductive techniques (ART). If your clients or their descendants have, or intend to have, children using ART, be wary of these archaic terms:
>
> "Lawful issue"
> "Heirs of his body"
> "Natural issue"
> "Children of this marriage"

If your client intends to benefit descendants born using artificial reproductive techniques, then your estate planning documents should define "descendants" to include those intended devisees. Each state has both statutes and court decisions defining how parent/child status comes to be. In a will or trust, the definition of descendants need not mirror any particular state law.

The following section deals with parent/child status for the same-sex couple. Some advocates use the phrases "same-gender couple" or "opposite-gender couple" instead of "same-sex couple" or "opposite-sex couple." The concept of gender is quite fluid, and a full discussion of that topic is beyond the scope of this chapter.

I. SAME-SEX COUPLES WITH CHILDREN

Same-sex couples who want to have a child typically will use some form of assisted reproduction technique. Lesbians usually (but not always!) enter into formal agreements with sperm donors; gay men usually (but not always!) enter into formal surrogacy arrangements with an egg donor and a gestational mother (an egg donor may bear the child, or not—the woman who bears the child is the gestational mother.)

In a gestational surrogacy, the surrogate bearing the child need not be related genetically to the child she bears. The embryo is created at the fertility clinic from the intended parent's egg or sperm, or from a donated egg and donated sperm, and transferred to the surrogate via in vitro fertilization.

If egg or sperm donation or gestational surrogacy are arranged through a reputable agency in the United States, one of the intended parents usually donates egg or sperm. An intended parent who is a donor is thus biologically related to the child; an intended parent who contributes no genetic material is not biologically related to the child.

Using formal gestational surrogacy and anonymous donors is a very expensive process, and during that process the intended parents usually establish legal parentage by both pre-birth and post-birth court orders. Some intended parents take an informal approach. A male friend may donate sperm to a lesbian couple. A gay man's female friend may offer to bear a child for him.

The intended parents of the child resulting from an informal arrangement may not consult an attorney and may not reach agreement about parentage orders, donor rights or waivers, visitation, support, and custody. Should donor, gestational surrogate, or intended parent later disagree about the child, their disputes are decided in state family court.

PRACTICE NOTE

An estate planner should document the marriage or non-marital legal relationship (some couples have both). Copies of the marriage or other relationship certificate should be in the file, along with birth certificates and parentage orders or adoption decrees.

The careful estate planner also will document a nonbiological parent's intent: to recognize the child, or not; to include the child in the estate plan, or not. If informal arrangements resulted in a child, and no court orders of adoption or parentage exist, the careful estate planner certainly can include the child by name in the estate plan—but declaring a child as yours in a will does not establish legal parentage for other purposes.

Parent/child status determines rights outside the four corners of a will or trust, such as wrongful death, workers compensation survivor benefits, intestate succession, Social Security benefits, and so on.

To protect the child's legal status rights, the estate planner should recommend that intended parents consult with a family law attorney about an adoption decree or parentage order. If a nonbiological intended parent has no court order of parentage or second parent adoption decree, then the laws of both state of domicile and state of the child's birth should be reviewed to determine how best to proceed.

The same-sex couple's own legal status (marriage, civil union, registered domestic partnership) will affect the nonbiological parent's legal relationship to minor children in the home. The nonbiological intended parent might be a step-parent, or be deemed a legal parent if a state's "presumption of legitimacy" can be invoked.

If one partner/spouse came to the relationship with children, the nonbiological parent will become a legal "step-parent" *after they marry*. If the couple lives in a state that recognizes civil union or registered domestic partnership, then after the couple enters the civil union or registers as partners, the nonbiological parent will be deemed a "step-parent." Their estate planning attorney might recommend the nonbiological intended parent consider a step-parent adoption.

If ART children were born to the same-sex couple during their marriage or registered domestic partnership or civil union, then the state law "presumption of legitimacy" should be considered as a basis for legal parentage. If an out-of-state civil union or other non-marital legal relationship is not recognized in the state where the couple resides, then the state court might refuse to apply a presumption of legitimacy.

PRACTICE NOTE

Asking "what happens if the nonbiological parent dies" will help the client focus on a murky parentage problem. Will the child qualify for federal Social Security survivor benefits, workers compensation survivor or wrongful death benefits should the nonbiological parent die? The child's financial security is threatened if the nonbiological intended parent is not legally recognized.

II. ESTABLISHING PARENT/CHILD STATUS

Nonbiological parent/child status is established in several ways: (1) court orders (second parent adoption, parentage orders pre-birth and after birth, step-parent adoption); (2) presumption of legitimacy for children born during a marriage; and (3) de facto parentage.

A lesbian couple intending to become parents decides which partner will bear the child or donate the egg, and then obtains sperm from a donor. Either lesbian may donate the egg, and one lesbian is usually the gestational mother. Less commonly, a lesbian couple may have a surrogate implanted with an embryo, and the surrogate bears the child.

A gay male couple may enter into a surrogacy arrangement with a gestational surrogate (who may or may not donate the egg) and use the sperm from either man to fertilize the egg. That is, either gay man may be the biological parent. In some cases, both donate sperm and they do not want to know which man is the biological parent. Gay men are more likely than lesbians to secure parent status with formal second parent or step-parent adoption, pre-birth orders, and/or parentage orders.

A. Second Parent Adoption and Parentage Orders

Before legalization of gay marriage, the nonbiological parent filed a petition to adopt the child of her or his partner. Same-sex couple adoption came to be known as "joint adoption" or "second parent adoption." Some states did not allow gay parents to adopt, and refused to recognize out of state adoption decrees.

The estate planner should obtain copies of the child's birth certificate, and of any same-sex couple adoption decree or parentage order. Adopted children are included in the definition of "descendants" in most states for intestate succession purposes.

Gay and lesbian parents without a second parent adoption decree may have some other form of court order (such as California's declaratory judgment of parentage) establishing parent/child status. These declaratory decrees and court orders may—or may not—be considered the equivalent of adoption in hotly contested inheritance litigation outside the state where the decree or order was granted.

DRAFTING SUGGESTION

After second parent adoption, the parent's will or trust simply declares the parental relationship:

> I have one child at this time, namely JOHN STEVENS.

B. Step-parent Adoption

After gay marriage became accepted in each state, if the gay or lesbian couple married *after a child was born*, then the nonbiological parent would file for step-parent adoption—a simpler, more straightforward method of establishing parentage if a second legal parent is not in the picture (or if the second legal parent gave consent).

Some couples elect not to marry, but have entered a civil union or registered as domestic partners and live in states recognizing that status. These recognition states should permit the partners to do a step-parent adoption.

PRACTICE NOTE

Some states have been slow to accept step-parent adoption for same-sex couples, so the estate planner may find that a second parent adoption decree was obtained even though the couple had married before the birth. Estate planners should get a copy of the adoption decree, whatever it is, for the file!

DRAFTING SUGGESTIONS

If no step-parent adoption has been done, then consider inserting the following sample language in the will or trust of the nonbiological parent:

> I consider my step-son JOHN STEVENS, the son of [NAME OF SPOUSE], to be my son for all purposes under this instrument, and the terms "child" and "descendants" in this instrument shall be construed to include him.

If a step-parent adoption was done, the nonbiological parent's will or trust will include the following sample language:

> I have one child at this time, namely JOHN STEVENS, who is the son of my spouse from before our marriage. I have adopted JOHN STEVENS.

C. Presumption of Legitimacy: Birth during Marriage

After gay marriage became accepted in each state, if the gay or lesbian couple married *before a child was born*, then parent/child status could be based on each state's statutory presumption that a child born during marriage is the child of both spouses. Formerly known as the "presumption of paternity" in same-sex couple parentage analysis, this common law evidentiary rule is referred to as the "presumption of legitimacy."

Because of resistance to same-sex couple family formation in some states and countries, cautious lawyers are reluctant to rely on the presumption of legitimacy, and still recommend parentage orders as well as second parent and step-child adoption.

Does the law of the state of the child's birth recognize the marital presumption of legitimacy for gay and lesbian parents, and will the law of the state of domicile follow suit? What state law will your estate planning instrument apply to interpretation of your will or trust. The estate planner should flag this as an issue for the parents. If the estate planner is unfamiliar with same-sex couple parentage, suggest a consultation with a local family formation lawyer about whether parentage orders or a step-parent/ second parent adoption is advisable.

DRAFTING SUGGESTION

Because all states do not have binding authority applying the statutory presumption of legitimacy for children born to same-sex couples during marriage, the estate planner might recommend language such as the following:

> My [wife] [husband] [NAME OF SPOUSE] and I have the following children, namely KAREN STEVENS and JOHN STEVENS, born during this marriage, and the terms "child" and "descendants" as used in this instrument shall be construed to include them for all purposes.

D. Emerging Law of Intended or De Facto Parentage

For years, family law courts have been resolving custody and visitation disputes between unmarried couples (both heterosexual and gay/lesbian) with ART children, creating a body of law about "intended" or "de facto" parentage. This body of family court parentage law will be relevant in future inheritance disputes.

Unmarried gay/lesbian clients open the door to these inheritance disputes when they lack adoption decrees, parentage orders, and/or carefully drawn legal agreements between a surrogate mother, egg donor and/or sperm donor. Those who rely on concepts of intended or de facto parentage in a parentage or survivor benefits dispute always wish they had done more to cement parentage status.

Estate planners can counsel clients to clear up murky parent/child relationships and refer them to a family formation/adoption firm.

DRAFTING SUGGESTION

In the will or trust, the careful estate planner identifies by name any minor child intended to benefit, and might describe the intended relationship in the will or trust as follows:

> I intend to benefit JOHN JACKSON's son MATTHEW JACKSON in this [Will] [Trust], and I consider him to be my child, and the terms "child" and "descendant" as used in this instrument shall be construed to include him for all purposes.

III. RELATIVES OF SAME-SEX COUPLES: CLASS GIFT

Are the children of same-sex couples included as beneficiaries in the estate planning documents of their relatives? When relatives draft estate planning documents, typically they leave assets to the gay/lesbian partner, and if the partner predeceases the relative, to the "descendants" or "issue" or "children." The estate planning document may contain the following language:

> If [NAME] does not survive me, then the share of [NAME] shall be distributed to her descendants by right of representation per stirpes.

If the deceased lesbian was the biological mother, the child takes the class gift as described in the foregoing provision. Likewise, if the deceased gay man was the biological father of the child, with the customary surrogacy/egg donor agreement and adoption decree, the child takes the class gift.

> If the deceased lesbian or gay man is the nonbiological parent, what is the child's legal status as a descendant?

Because there are many ways to create the gay/lesbian parent/child relationship (and some states may resist parentage recognition unless a formal adoption decree has been entered), the careful drafter for relatives of same-sex couples can broaden the standard definition of "descendants" or "issue" to allow these children to inherit.

DRAFTING SUGGESTIONS

In the illustrative "definition of descendants" that follows, be cautious to inquire about the client's actual intent about which descendants inherit.

- Include **section (e)** of the following illustration only where the client consents explicitly to this very broad sweeping parentage inclusion.
- Include **section (f)** of the following illustration if the client is focused on having family wealth pass only with a genetic link to the person indicated.

"DEFINITION OF DESCENDANTS" ILLUSTRATION

9.1 "Descendants" of the person indicated include those children whose parent/child status arose by virtue of one or more of the following events:

(a) Natural child birth, regardless of whether the woman giving birth contributed genetic material, unless the woman giving birth was a gestational surrogate under a written contract;

(b) Legal adoption, including second parent, joint and post-mortem adoption;

(c) Court declaratory judgment of parentage, including pre-birth order;

(d) Parent/child status granted by state law to children born during a registered domestic partnership, civil union, reciprocal beneficiary (Hawaii) or designated beneficiary (Colorado) relationship, or same-sex marriage;

(e) Parent/child status granted by state law by any means permitted under law; [Alternative provision]

(f) Child conceived through assisted reproductive technology with the consent of the person indicated, who intends to be the ART child's parent. [Alternative provision]

All children or descendants deemed children or descendants of the person indicated by any of the above methods are children or descendants for the purpose of this instrument.

IV. POSTHUMOUS CHILD AND STORED GENETIC MATERIAL

When your client (gay, lesbian, or heterosexual) has stored genetic material (eggs, sperm, or frozen IVF eggs known as pre-embryos), ask for a copy of the clinic storage agreement.[1]

Clinic storage agreements describe (1) the cryopreservation techniques used; (2) the material (semen, eggs, and/or IVF pre-embryos); (3) the reasons for cryopreservation; and (4) what the client wants done with unused genetic material after his or her death.[2]

Oregon law treats stored genetic material and the possible posthumously conceived child as matters to be dealt with by will.[3] Provisions in the will or trust should not conflict with the storage contract. If there is a conflict between the contract and the client's estate plan, explore whether the genetic material can be transferred to another clinic willing to follow the client's wishes.

Hoping a child will be born using the material, the estate planning client may want to give the stored material to a spouse, partner, or other relative. The client may want the material destroyed or donated (to prospective intended parents or for research). State law may restrict destruction of a stored IVF egg (known as a pre-embryo, when implanted in the uterus of the gestational mother, it becomes an embryo).

Your state may have recently passed legislation defining when posthumously born children are deemed "descendants." For example, Oregon law requires a written declaration of intent, giving control of the material to a designated person, that the child be in utero within a period of time after the decedent's date of death, and that notice be given to the personal representative within a short time after death.[4]

Check recent and pending probate code revisions in your state for posthumous children definitions. Your instrument's CHOICE OF LAW provision will select which state laws govern construction of the will or trust, as in:

> CHOICE OF LAW. The laws of the State of *California* shall govern the validity, construction, and administration of this *Trust.*

If the client lives in a state with no laws governing the posthumous child/parent relationship, the terms of the will or trust should be very specific about disposition of the genetic material.

If the clients with stored genetic material intend to move to another state, in your closing letter suggest the posthumous child provisions be reviewed by a lawyer in the new state.

When a client has stored genetic material, the will and/or trust should address both (1) ownership and use of the stored genetic material and (2) the possibility of a posthumous child.

Local state bar and estate planning groups are including posthumous child issues in their drafting seminars.

Beneficiary designations for federal agency (like NASA, U.S. Department of Justice Public Safety Officers Benefits, Federal Employees Compensation) survivor benefits are beginning to include references to "posthumous children" as permissible beneficiaries.

All financial service industry survivorship account contracts use generic terms such as "issue" or "children of the beneficiary" or "descendants," and include a "choice of law" provision declaring which state's law governs construction of the contract.

PRACTICE NOTE

The estate planner can help the client include a posthumous child in the client's estate plan for assets governed by the will or trust. Inclusion in the estate plan, however, does not guarantee that the posthumous child qualifies (1) for a survivorship account; (2) as a descendant of a class gift by someone other than the client; or (3) as a legal child for government survivor benefits (Social Security, workers compensation, and veterans' benefits).

A. Specific Devise of Genetic Material

Ownership and use of stored genetic material can be addressed in the specific devise section of the will or trust.

DRAFTING SUGGESTION

Consider the following language if (1) the clients are married, (2) the testator wants to give complete discretion to the surviving spouse, (3) posthumous children are *not* intended to inherit, and (4) the material will be donated if the spouse does not survive. This provision does *not* give posthumous children status as a child of the testator:

> **Specific Devise of Stored Genetic Material** I have stored genetic material for possible use in the future for artificial reproductive techniques, and I leave any right title and interest in said stored genetic material, wherever located, to my spouse, for disposition as my spouse may determine, in my spouse's sole and absolute discretion. **I do not intend that a posthumous child inherit under my estate plan.**

> If my spouse does not survive me, then I leave any interest I may have in stored genetic material to my sister, JANE JONES, for disposition as she may determine, but express my preference that the stored material be donated to prospective parents if possible, and not used for research.

B. Posthumous Child in Gestation

A client whose wife or partner is pregnant at the time of his or her death probably wants to include that posthumous child in the estate plan. This issue, the posthumous child in gestation, affects all couples, even those with NO stored genetic material.

DRAFTING SUGGESTION

This posthumous child in gestation problem is addressed easily in the will or trust, as shown in sample article 2.5:

> 2.5 DEFINITION OF CHILD and DESCENDANTS. For the purposes of this instrument, any reference to "my child" or "my children" shall include any biological or adopted child of mine, and any biological child born after my death who was conceived before my death.
> Distribution to a person's descendants by "right of representation" means a division into equal shares, counting one share for each living or posthumous child and one share for each deceased child who leaves one or more then surviving descendants or descendants born posthumously and conceived before the person's death as described in ORS 112.077(3). Each living or posthumous child receives one share. The share of each deceased child passes by right of representation to his or her then surviving or posthumous descendants.

C. Planning for ART/Posthumous Conception

If the client expects his or her stored genetic material to be used to attempt to have a posthumous child after the client's death, then the will or trust should address the posthumous conception issue. If no state law governs these issues, the client simply can set up a trust to hold the rights to the genetic material and designate a trustee. If the clinic storage agreement does not allow the client to transfer ownership at death to his or her trustee, suggest the client change clinics!

The client can set up a special purpose, limited duration trust in the estate plan. The client appoints a trustee and distributes to the trustee both the genetic material and those funds intended for both birth costs and the posthumously conceived child. The trust will be for a limited duration, as the genetic material retains its viability for a limited number of years.

If birth attempts are successful, and a child is born during the limited duration of the trust, then the trustee can be ordered to terminate the trust and distribute the remainder to the usual child's health, education, support, and maintenance trust.

If birth attempts are not successful, and no child is born during the trust term, then the trustee can be ordered to terminate the trust and dispose of remaining genetic material and distribute the trust remainder to the trust's contingent beneficiaries.

The drafting attorney's standard definition of "descendants" should be broadened to include posthumous children, as defined in any applicable state law, if posthumous descendants are intended to inherit.

For illustrative purposes in an ART/posthumous conception situation, consider the following sample article 2. Timelines from both Oregon law and the Uniform Probate Code are alternative approaches in the illustration.

ILLUSTRATION 10(II)-A

ARTICLE 2
ART and POSTHUMOUS CHILDREN PROVISIONS

2.1 DECLARATION OF INTENTION. MARY DOE, my spouse, and I plan to have children through assisted reproduction technology and/or a gestational carrier ["ART"], and any child so born before my death, or conceived before the date of my death, or posthumously conceived but [**in utero within two years of my death—ORS 112.077**] [**born within 45 months after the date of my death—Uniform Probate Code Article II, Section 2-120**] shall be deemed for all purposes a child of mine.

2.2 DEVISE OF STORED GENETIC MATERIAL TO CONTROL PERSON. If my spouse survives me, I grant to MARY DOE the right to control the disposition and use of my stored genetic material, and specifically devise all such stored material to her, for disposition as she may determine, in her sole and absolute discretion.

2.3 DISPOSITION IF NO CHILD IS BORN. I hope, and intend, that MARY DOE can conceive a posthumous child of ours, who can inherit a share of my estate. But if she is unable to arrange for a child to be conceived within the time required under applicable state law, then she can dispose of the material as she then determines, in her sole and absolute discretion. I express my preference that the material be donated to prospective intended parents rather than to research.

2.4 DISPOSITION IF SPOUSE DOES NOT SURVIVE. If MARY DOE does not survive me, then I do not intend that the stored genetic material be used to create a posthumous child to inherit under my estate. I give the stored genetic material to my brother, JOHN PAUL JONES, who will have the right to control the disposition and use of the material, for disposition as he may determine in his sole and absolute discretion, with due regard to any regulations or laws governing such disposition but express my preference that the material be donated to prospective intended parents rather than to research.

2.5 DEFINITION OF CHILD and DESCENDANTS. For the purposes of this instrument, any reference to "child" or "children" or "descendants" shall include those children whose parent/child status arose by virtue of one or more of the following events:

(a) Natural birth;

(b) Legal adoption, including second parent or joint adoption;

(c) Court declaratory judgment of parentage;

(d) Parent/child status granted by state law to children born during a same-sex domestic partnership, civil union, or same-sex marriage;

(e) All children born of ART arrangements MARY DOE and I may have entered into during my lifetime, or which MARY DOE enters into after my death using my genetic material or her genetic material, whether the child was conceived before or after my death, so long as the child is [**in utero at my death or within two years of my death—ORS 112.077**] [**born within 45 months after the date of my death—Uniform Probate Code Article II, Section 2-120**].

Distribution to a person's descendants by "right of representation" means a division into equal shares, counting one share for each living or posthumous child and one share for each deceased child who leaves one or more then surviving descendants or descendants born posthumously but either (1) in utero at the time of the person's death or (2) in utero within 2 years of the time of the person's death and the product of artificial reproductive techniques as described in ORS 112.077. Each living or posthumous child receives one share.
The share of each deceased child passes by right of representation to his or her then surviving or posthumous (within the meaning of ORS 112.077) descendants.

NOTES

1. *See* Chapter 10, Part I, section II.B. (discussing state approaches in permitting a parent-child relationship after posthumous conception). *See also* Appendix 10(I)-B (eighteen states are silent on this issue).

2. *See* Chapter 10, Part I, section IV. (discussing special issues pertaining to cryopreservation).

3. *See* ORS 112.077.

4. *See* ORS 112.077 (2015 c. 387 sec. 27).

CHAPTER 11

Management of a Minor's Digital Assets in the Event of Incapacity or Death

Naomi Cahn, Matt Savare, and John Wintermute[1]

Talia Joy Castellanos, a thirteen-year-old YouTube and Instagram star, passed away on July 16, 2013, after a six-year battle with neuroblastoma and leukemia. Talia's social media postings on makeup and fashion, and her battle with cancer, connected with fans worldwide.[2] In addition to accumulating millions of YouTube and Instagram followers, Talia appeared on *The Ellen DeGeneres Show* and was named an honorary face of CoverGirl cosmetics.[3] At the time of her death, the videos on Talia's YouTube channel had accumulated tens of millions of views and were valuable assets.[4]

Talia's social media following created extensive and lucrative digital assets that raise a special set of questions about how these assets should have been managed before and upon her death. Who owns Talia's videos and other postings? Who has the right to control her accounts?

Talia's popularity is part of a growing trend among minors: 92 percent of teens report going online daily, and more than half of children use social media by the age of ten.[5] Popular websites like Facebook, Instagram, and YouTube provide platforms that are unparalleled in their ability to give a voice to billions of minors across the world.

The widespread use of these platforms allows for the monetization of popular content, accounts, and persona rights. YouTube's most watched user, *PewDiePie* (with over twelve billion views on his channel), reportedly earned $12 million in 2015 alone.[6] The growing importance of digital media and value of digital content means that parents must consider how a child's digital assets might be handled if the parents are no longer able to be involved. They must also help a child plan for the succession of his or her own digital assets if something were to happen to the child.

Yet digital asset rights carry important consequences for even the average social media user. In Germany, a fifteen-year-old girl died tragically after being struck by a subway train.[7] After her heartbreaking death, her parents sought to access her Facebook account to determine if this accident was actually suicide.[8] Ultimately, the German Federal Court of Justice ruled that user agreements could be inherited.[9]

This chapter addresses the new world of digital assets, including both online accounts that range from social media to e-mail to online photo storage and also digital data stored on a local device. The first part of the chapter reviews the context for digital asset planning before turning to specific steps that minors can take to plan, and then to the steps that parents can take both with respect to advance planning and to accessing a minor's assets.

Although there are persuasive analogies to traditional brick-and-mortar forms of property, federal and—increasingly—state laws distinguish digital assets from other types of assets. Consequently, it is important to consider planning for these assets separately. Note that this is a newly developing area of the law, so there are few legal certainties on just what constitute the appropriate planning steps for minors or their parents.

I. THE DIGITAL WORLD

As this section discusses, digital assets are affected by myriad state and federal laws that protect privacy, and criminalize unauthorized access to computers and data. In addition, Internet providers' terms of service/term of use agreements (TOS) and privacy policies govern digital accounts.

A. Accessing Digital Assets and Data at Death

The disposition of digital assets is governed by federal and state laws concerning Internet privacy as well as by a growing number of specific laws in the trusts and estates area. Although parents typically have access to most of a minor's property, this is not true for digital assets, which have a distinct set of privacy protections. If a minor is incapacitated or dies, a parent may not be able to access the child's Internet accounts in the absence of specific authorization from the child or a state law that provides access once the parent is appointed as a fiduciary.[10] Even if the parent has become a court-appointed fiduciary, such as the executor of the estate, access to digital accounts is not guaranteed as either a legal or a pragmatic matter.

For example, most online accounts are password protected, and the passwords generally can be reset only with access to the account holder's e-mail account and, as discussed later, the Internet service provider (ISP) may have restriction on third-party access. Even if the fiduciary is able to find a password, most TOS forbid account access by anyone except the account holder,[11] thereby barring the fiduciary from access. Online TOS may say nothing about postmortem options; they may explicitly prohibit postmortem transfer; or they may explicitly grant only a lifetime license.

TOS, especially ones that require the user to click through to accept them, are generally held to be enforceable, even though very few people read them and even a fewer number understand them.[12] Nonetheless, in *C.M.D. v. Facebook, Inc.*,[13] the Ninth Circuit ruled that Facebook's TOS was enforceable against minors under California law, which does not void all contracts entered into by minors.[14]

Online service providers and websites also post privacy policies that govern the collection, use, and distribution of the data of their users. Privacy policies can be terms within a larger TOS, linked to the TOS, or incorporated by reference.

B. Federal and State Statutes Affecting Fiduciaries

At the federal level, the Computer Fraud and Abuse Act (CFAA) creates civil liability for (and, in some cases, criminalizes) the unauthorized access of computer hardware and devices and the data stored thereon.[15] It was designed to prevent hacking, and it covers two different kinds of computer trespass: (1) access "without authorization" and (2) access that "exceeds authorized access." A fiduciary who accesses e-mails or Internet accounts from a computer protected by the CFAA—which effectively includes any computer connected to the Internet—may face liability.[16] Moreover, the CFAA may cover violations of a website's or mobile app's TOS.

If the minor expressly authorized the fiduciary to access the minor's computers, it is unlikely that such *computer* access violates the CFAA. Even with authorization, however, the fiduciary may still be breaking the law. Access to a user's online account requires accessing the provider's or another vendor's computers, which requires the service provider's further authorization. Thus, the CFAA is potentially violated when a TOS prohibits third parties from accessing the account; the fiduciary has exceeded authorized access to the service provider's system.

This means that while the CFAA might not preclude the fiduciary from accessing the hard drive, it can affect fiduciary access to the account holder's digital accounts or assets, which implicate third parties.

Each state has an analogous statute, which varies in coverage, but typically prohibits "unauthorized access" to computers.[17]

Until Congress amends and clarifies the CFAA, its impact on fiduciaries trying to perform their statutory duties will remain unclear.

C. The Stored Communications Act

Privacy protection begins with the Fourth Amendment, which prohibits the government from searching homes unless it can show probable cause.

Although we may expect the same privacy protections when we use our laptops, the computer network is not physically located or even being accessed within our computers or in our homes, so it is outside the coverage of the Fourth Amendment. Based on concerns about potential breaches of privacy, Congress enacted the Stored Communications Act (SCA) in 1986, as a part of the Electronic Communications Privacy Act (ECPA).[18] The privacy protections of the SCA are directed at certain providers of *public* communications services: They are prohibited from disclosing the *contents* of a user's communications to a government or nongovernment entity, except under limited circumstances, which are similar to the "warrant" required under the Fourth Amendment.

Providers are allowed to divulge *non-content* information, such as the user's name, address, connection records, IP address, and account information, because the SCA prohibits only the disclosure of the *contents* of communications. That is, protections extend only to information in the body of an electronic message that is not readily accessible to the public; if the information were readily accessible to the public, it would not be subject to the privacy protections of federal law under ECPA.[19] Social media account contents (e.g., photos, videos, and posts) not readily accessible to the public are probably all "communications" protected by the SCA; public posts are not protected.[20]

There are two types of restrictions, depending on whether the fiduciary seek log-type information or the contents of an electronic communication. First, providers are permitted, but not required, to divulge non-content information, such as the user's name, address, connection records, IP address, and account information to a nongovernmental entity.[21] The statute permits disclosure of "customer records" that do not include content, either with lawful consent from the customer or "to any person other than a governmental entity."[22] This catalogue (or list) of the user's electronic communications shows the addresses of the sender and recipient, and the date and time the message was sent.

Second, a provider may disclose the contents of communications to a fiduciary, but only if an *exception* to the SCA's blanket prohibition against disclosure applies.[23] There are two exceptions that are relevant for fiduciaries. The first allows disclosure to the recipient/addressee or to the recipient/addressee's agent. The second exception allows disclosure to third parties with the "lawful consent" of either the sender or the recipient/addressee.[24] Thus, in contrast to its restrictions on the release of content, the electronic-communication or remote-computing service provider is permitted to disclose the catalogue of electronic communications to anyone except the government.

Note that the SCA applies different rules to government entities (mainly law enforcement) requesting information, versus all others (such as fiduciaries). Under the SCA, law enforcement officials can force or compel a provider who is otherwise covered by the SCA to divulge account contents.[25] A fiduciary, however, can never compel the provider to divulge the same information.

Although the drafters tried to cover future developments, at the time of the SCA's enactment, the Internet did not yet exist; the development of Facebook was still almost two decades away, the founding of Google was more than a decade in the future, and even the large-scale use of e-mail was still a few years distant. The drafters were focused on privacy, not on how the SCA might affect fiduciary property management and distribution, and the SCA has not been amended since its original enactment. The resulting uncertainty affects anyone with an e-mail account. It hampers fiduciaries, including personal representatives, conservators, agents acting pursuant to a power of attorney, and trustees who want to obtain access to any type of electronic communication, although it does not affect the ability of a fiduciary to distribute the assets held in the underlying account—once the fiduciary has been able to identify and access it.

On the other hand, ECPA does not provide privacy protections for private e-mail service providers, such as educational institutions.[26] Thus, if a student's account is established by an educational institution, then that institution cannot use ECPA to defend against a fiduciary's request for copies of communications or access to an account. However, the institution may have other, legitimate grounds for refusing fiduciary access, so a parent may not be able to demand access if an educational institution hosts the student's e-mail account.

D. Copyright Law

Much of the content posted to Facebook, YouTube, Instagram, or similar social media sites/apps is protected under U.S. copyright laws. Copyright law affords users of these services a bundle of exclusive rights to their content, such as the right to use, distribute, create derivative works of, copy, perform, and display the content.

However, although copyright protection vests in each piece of copyrightable content upon its creation, the user's posting of such content to a digital platform will be subject to that service's TOS. On virtually every such digital service, users retain ownership of all content they post or upload, but they grant broad licenses to the platform and its other users. In order to understand the ownership and the value of any content created and posted online, fiduciaries must understand the rights that have been granted and retained pursuant to the applicable TOS.

Copyright law affords protection to an author's copyrighted material for seventy years following the author's death. This postmortem right is fully descendible and transferable, and thus copyrighted digital content can retain value for decades following its inclusion in a deceased author's estate.

E. Children's Online Privacy Protection Act

The rising popularity of social media is driven, in large part, by easy access to the Internet and connected devices. For example, approximately 95 percent of teens have, or are able to access, a smartphone.[27] But this easy access leads to privacy concerns as well. In response to concerns over the safety and privacy of minors on the Internet, Congress passed the Children's Online Privacy Protection Act (COPPA) in 1998.[28] COPPA requires, among other things, that website and mobile app operators take certain steps to protect personal information of children under thirteen, including obtaining verifiable parental consent before collecting the personal information from a child under thirteen and enforcing certain minimum levels of data security.

Rather than subjecting themselves to COPPA, many online service providers "age gate" and prohibit minors under thirteen from using their service. Fiduciaries must be attuned to such terms. For example, if a minor under thirteen was using a social media site in violation of its TOS, this could potentially impact the ability of the fiduciary to secure such minor's digital assets in the event of the minor's death. In such a case, the minor's violation of the TOS could result in invalidating the minor's contractual relationship with the website provider and place at risk the minor's ownership or rights to any content created using the website's tools.

F. Right of Publicity

The right of publicity is the "inherent right of every human being to control the commercial use of his or her identity,"[29] which is violated when an individual or entity "appropriates the commercial value of . . . [the] person's identity by using without consent the person's name, likeness, or other indicia of identity for purposes of trade."[30] Although there is no federal statute in the United States governing the right of publicity, thirty-one states, including New York and California, as of this writing recognize the right (nineteen by statute, twenty-one by common law, and nine by a combination of the two).[31]

Whether—and for how long—a deceased persona can be protected is a particularly controversial and fluid area of publicity law. Many states recognize a postmortem right of publicity, ranging from ten years in states like Tennessee (although this term can be extended if commercial use continues) to 100 years in states like Indiana.[32] Other states, however, such as New York, do not afford any postmortem publicity rights at all.[33] Adding to the complexity, some courts have held that publicity rights survive death only if the individual exploited the right during his or her lifetime. At least one state statute affords longer postmortem protection—seventy-five years—if the person's identity has "commercial value" versus only ten years for those whose identity does not.[34]

Parents should determine whether applicable state laws dictate that postmortem publicity rights should be considered at all and, if so, the scope of rights that a minor possesses. In addition to length of postmortem protection, states vary in defining the elements of publicity rights—statutes and courts from various states have extended protection to, among other things, name, voice, signature, photograph, likeness, "look-alikes," "sound-alikes," catchphrases, nicknames, performance characteristics, and biographical data. No registration or other formal measures are required to protect a right of publicity. As a common law right, the right of publicity is enforced through the courts.[35] Protection of a postmortem right consists of identifying and prosecuting misuse.

II. AN OUNCE OF PREVENTION: PLANNING WITH THE MINOR

The first piece of advice is to talk to the minor about planning. As difficult as this may be, minors often appreciate the importance of making decisions about access to their digital accounts; they may have friends or relatives who have died whose online presence still haunts their computers.

A. Existing ISP Options

Several of the online service providers, beginning with Google's Inactive Account Manager (IAM) in 2013, permit the account owner to designate a contact who will have certain rights concerning the account through "online tools." The minor can choose anyone: a sibling, a parent, a friend, and so on. Under the Google system, the contact will have access to e-mails, photos, and other documents stored through Google (e.g., Gmail, Google+, and YouTube).[36] With the IAM, the user sets a period of time after which the account will be deemed inactive. Once that time period runs out, Google will notify the contact[s] whom the user specified and, if the user so indicated, share data with these contacts. Alternatively, the user can request that Google delete the account's contents. Note that, even if a minor does designate a parent as a trusted contact, that parent will not know until the account has become inactive (of course, the minor also may confide in the parent).

Facebook was the next large provider to set up such a system, establishing the possibility of creating a "legacy contact" to look after an account if it is memorialized. Once the account is memorialized, the legacy contact has the option of writing a final message, providing information about a memorial service, responding to new friend requests, and updating the profile picture and cover image. Memorialization itself is a fairly straightforward process, with directions available on the Facebook website. Facebook warns, however (at least as of mid-2016), that it cannot provide login information: "It's always against Facebook's policies to log into another person's account."[37] That precludes the self-help option of the minor simply providing a parent with a login. A joint account, with the child and a third party, would permit the third party to login.

B. Other Advance Measures

In an entirely separate document, a minor also could designate third parties to have access to his or her accounts, such as through a power of attorney. The following provides some sample language, but here, as in all other contexts of this chapter, the technology and the law are changing quickly, so this provision will need to be updated based on those changes.

<u>DRAFTING ILLUSTRATION</u>

Digital Assets. My personal representative/trustee/agent has the authority to: (i) access, use, and control each of my digital devices, such as my laptop, tablet, storage devices, phones, and any comparable items; (ii) access, modify, delete, control and transfer my digital assets, including but not limited to, any accounts and related content access digitally, such as e-mail, music, photographs, videos, software licenses, social network accounts, file sharing accounts, financial accounts, domain registrations, online stores, any other online accounts and similar digital items; and (iii) access, modify, delete, control, and transfer any personal files in a digital format that may contain medical records, school records, personal e-mail, correspondence, diaries, writings, images, photos or videos, hobby or game websites, or other files.[38]

One potential issue is the "infancy" doctrine, which allows minors to void contracts before they reach the state age of majority or are emancipated.[39] This doctrine does not seem relevant when it comes to minors granting authority to a fiduciary; presumably, by the time the fiduciary acts, the minor is no longer able to disaffirm the grant of authority because the minor is either incapacitated or dead.

III. POSSIBILITIES FOR PARENTS

Parents may interact with minors and their digital assets in two distinct ways. First, parents may want to plan for their own incapacity or death; second, parents may need to take control of their children's digital accounts when their children are incapacitated or have died.

A. Parental Planning

Parents may have strong preferences on how their children should approach the digital world around them if the parents are no longer able to direct their children's access. Moreover, parents may want to leave a digital legacy for their children, such as through an online memory book. Because of the special laws concerning digital assets, the planning process, however, differs from the additional planning options described in Chapter 6.

<u>PRACTICE NOTE</u>

Estate planners might recommend that parents draft a letter to their children's guardian setting out the parents' approach to their children's access to digital devices and to the material on those devices. Such a note would be relevant whenever a guardian is appointed because the parents are unable to act; for example, a parent's will might nominate a guardian to care for a child after the parent's death, as discussed in Chapter 6. In such a note, for example, a parent might write: "I wish there to be no restrictions on my child's access to the digital world," or might instead write, "I wish my child to access digital content subject to the strictest controls available through parental guidance programs."

B. Parental Access

Regardless of whether a minor has engaged in advanced planning, a parent may want to access the minor's assets for several reasons: (1) to prevent identity theft; (2) to collect mementos, contact friends; or (3) to even sort through financial records (a minor's bank account, for example).

States increasingly have adopted legislation that allows an individual's legally appointed representative to access that individual's digital assets, although few states explicitly address the rights of fiduciaries to access minors' accounts upon incapacity or death. A growing number of states have enacted the Revised Uniform Fiduciary Access to Digital Assets Act (Revised UFADAA), which was promulgated by the Uniform Law Commission in 2015.[40] Revised UFADAA addresses agents acting pursuant to a power of attorney, personal representatives, conservators (sometimes called "guardians of the estate" under state law),[41] and trustees. Although the model Revised UFADAA does not specifically address minors, it does cover all "users," or anyone who has an account with a custodian of Internet accounts.[42] It thus presumptively would cover minors, although, to date, there have been no reported cases under Revised UFADAA concerning users who are minors.[43]

Under Revised UFADAA:

- Where a parent has been legally appointed as a fiduciary on behalf of the minor (or the minor's estate), the parent would have the access permitted by the statute.
- If the parent is dead or incapacitated, then a court-appointed guardian also would have the access permitted by the statute.

Indeed, in enacting Revised UFADAA, a few states explicitly have addressed "minors" when they define guardian, as discussed later.

The scope of access depends on whether the fiduciary is trying to access the content of an electronic communication (which may be protected by the SCA), the log or catalogue for that communication (which is not protected in the same way by the SCA), or another type of digital asset. The term "content of an electronic-communication" is defined in Revised UFADAA as "information concerning the substance or meaning of the communication" which has been sent or received by a user, is not readily accessible to the public, and is in electronic storage by a custodian providing an electronic-communication service to the public.[44] A fiduciary cannot access the contents of SCA-covered communications without the user's consent.

If a minor has not engaged in any advance planning, then the TOSA for that particular account will determine whether a fiduciary may access the minor's digital assets. If the terms of service are silent on the issue, then Revised UFADAA allows the fiduciary to access the catalogue under the circumstances spelled out in the act. If, for example, the minor has died, then Section 8 of Revised UFADAA requires the Internet custodian to disclose all other digital assets, unless prohibited by the decedent or directed by the court, once the personal representative provides the requisite verifications.

Here's a concise description of Revised UFADAA's three-tiered system of priorities:

1. If the Internet company provides its own online tool,[45] and the teen has named someone to have access to the teen's digital assets or to direct that the company delete the teen's digital assets (think of Facebook's Legacy Contact option), then these online instructions are binding.

2. If the Internet company didn't provide this option, or if the teen did not use the tool, and assuming the teen did not use a will, trust, or another writing to set out what should happen to the digital assets, then the TOSA for the account controls just what the fiduciary can access.

3. However, many TOSAs are silent as to what happens when the user dies. If that's the case, then Revised UFADAA can allow the fiduciary access to digital material other than the content of certain electronic communications. So a fiduciary would be able to go into the teen's account to find e-mail addresses, for instance, or to look for the date and time that the teen sent an important e-mail. But you couldn't look at what the e-mail itself said (or even the subject line, technically).[46]

Only a few states explicitly have addressed fiduciaries' rights to minor's accounts. Virginia's is the most extensive, and it was enacted because of the campaign of Ricky Rash[47] to obtain information from his son's Facebook account, which he hoped would explain why his son committed suicide. In 2013, Virginia granted the personal representative of a deceased minor access to the minor's digital accounts, such as those containing e-mail, social networking information, and blogs. The personal representative can obtain this access unless a will, trust instrument, power of attorney, or court order provides otherwise.[48] Virginia thus appears to permit a minor to create a document, such as a will, that prevents digital access.[49]

In order to gain access, a personal representative may make a written request to a provider. The provider then must provide access to the minor's online communications within sixty days of receiving the request, including a copy of the death certificate of the minor.[50] If the provider has notice of a dispute about access to the account, the provider does not have to provide any access until a final judgment is obtained.

Other states have addressed this issue in the limited context of guardianship for minors, generally within the definitional section of their fiduciary access legislation.[51] North Carolina, for example, provides that a guardian of a minor ward may take access of any digital assets and digital accounts owned by the ward.[52] The North Carolina statute broadly provides that a guardian of a minor ward may "access, take control of, handle, conduct, continue, distribute, dispose of, or terminate" the digital accounts or assets, appearing to give more control to the guardian to access content, not just the catalogue. The custodian is not permitted to destroy the digital account or asset for two years following the guardian's request.[53]

The Florida version of the Fiduciary Access to Digital Assets Act defines "guardian" to include a fiduciary who is responsible for the property of a minor.[54] Although the law does not set out explicitly a law for deceased minors' digital assets, it grants personal representatives (including guardians) the right to access the content of the deceased's electronic communications if the representative provides a written request for disclosure, a death certificate, and a court order.

When Nevada passed legislation in 2013 on the power to direct termination of certain electronic or digital accounts or assets of the decedent, although the statute itself did not explicitly mention "minors," there was testimony concerning the privacy needs of minors.[55] In the minority of states that have not enacted legislation clarifying access, a fiduciary's ability to obtain digital assets is unclear. There are, however, various new start-up companies that will help in this task and that also will walk the parent through the steps necessary to gain access.[56]

Once the parent gains access, then there is the decision on what to do with the accounts. A parent often will want to close the account, and most service providers have instructions on how the account owner can do so.

IV. CONCLUSION

Given the pervasiveness of digital assets and children's involvement in the digital world, children themselves must consider the future of their digital lives. And parents must be aware of their rights—or lack of rights—with respect to their children's digital assets.

NOTES

1. We thank Mohammad Zaheerudin for his research assistance.
2. Carolina Moreno, *Talia Joy Castellano Dead: Inspirational YouTube Star Dies After 6-Year Battle With Cancer,* HUFFPOST (July 17, 2013), http://www.huffingtonpost.com/2013/07/16/talia-joy-castellano-dead_n_3606118.html.
3. *Id.*
4. *Id.*
5. Amanda Lenhart, *Teens, Social Media &Technology Overview 2015*, PEW RESEARCH CENTER (Apr. 9, 2015), http://www.pewinternet.org/2015/04/09/teens-social-media-technology-2015/.
6. Michael Thomsen, *PewDiePie Doesn't Make Anywhere Close To What He Should Be Making*, FORBES (July 11, 2015), https://www.forbes.com/sites/michaelthomsen/2015/07/11/pewdiepie-doesnt-make-anywhere-close-to-what-he-should-be-making/#529f08fb7add.

7.   Elizabeth Armstrong Moore, *Parents Denied Access To Dead Teen's Facebook Account,* FoxNews (June 1, 2017), http://www.foxnews.com/tech/2017/06/01/parents-denied-access-to-dead-teens-facebook-account.html.

8.   *Id.*

9.   Global Legal Monitor, *Germany: Federal Court of Justice Rules Digital Social Media Accounts Inheritable* (Sept. 7, 2018), http://www.loc.gov/law/foreign-news/article/germany-federal-court-of-justice-rules-digital-social-media-accounts-inheritable/?loclr=eaglm.

10.   A parent may be appointed by a court as a conservator during the child's lifetime, or as an estate administrator or personal representative at the minor's death. *See* Chapter 9. After the parent's death, a [third-party] guardian might be appointed by the court to care for the minor. *See* Chapter 6.

11.   Each TOS is different, and there is no standard form. While, as a practical matter, the providers are unlikely to sue parents for a breach, it is possible. *See e.g.,* Yahoo!, Yahoo Terms of Service, https://policies.yahoo.com/us/en/yahoo/terms/utos/index.htm (last updated May 12, 2017) ("Yahoo grants you a personal, non-transferable and non-exclusive right and license to use the object code of its Software on a single computer . . . .").

12.   *But see* Ajemian v. Yahoo!, Inc., 478 Mass. 169, 84 N.E. 3d 766 (2017), *cert. denied sub nom,* Oath Holdings, Inc. v. Ajemian, 138 S. Ct. 1327 (Mar. 26, 2018) (state supreme court set aside summary judgment favoring Yahoo!, Inc. given that record was inadequate to establish whether TOS had been communicated to and accepted by the deceased account holder).

13.   *C.M.D.*, 621 F. App'x at 488 (9th Cir. 2015).

14.   *Id.*; *see* Age Restrictions and Contracts with Minors, 2 E-Commerce and Internet Law 22.05[2][N] (2d ed., 2014).

15.   18 U.S.C. § 1030(a)(2)(C) (2012).

16.   *See id.* § 1030(e)(2); *see also* Charles Doyle, Cong. Research Serv., RL97-1025, *Cybercrime: An Overview of the Federal Computer Fraud and Abuse Statute and Related Federal Criminal Laws* 18 (Oct. 15, 2014), https://www.fas.org/sgp/crs/misc/97-1025.pdf (explaining the scope of the CFAA).

17.   *Computer Crime Statutes,* Nat'l Conf. of St. Legislatures, http://www.ncsl.org/research/telecommunications-and-information-technology/computer-hacking-and-unauthorized-access-laws.aspx (last updated Dec. 5, 2016).

18.   18 U.S.C. §§ 2701–2711; *see* Richard M. Thompson II & Jared P. Cole, Cong. Research Serv., R44036, *Stored Communications Act: Reform of the Electronic Communications Privacy Act* (ECPA) (May 19, 2015), https://www.fas.org/sgp/crs/misc/R44036.pdf (emphasis added).

19.   *See* S. Rep. No. 99–541, at 36, 99th Cong., 2d Sess. (1986) (enacted).

20.   *See* Rudolph J. Burshnic, *Applying the Stored Communications Act to the Civil Discovery of Social Networking Sites,* 69 Wash. & Lee L. Rev. 1259, 1260 (2012).

21.   18 U.S.C. § 2702(c)(6).

22.   *Id.* § 2702(c)(2) & (c)(6).

23.   *Id.* § 2702(b).

24.   *Id.* § 2702(b)(3). It prohibits an electronic-communication service or a remote-computing service from knowingly divulging the content of an electronic communication that is stored by or carried or maintained on that service unless disclosure is made (among other exceptions) "to an addressee or intended recipient of such communication or an agent of such addressee or intended recipient"

or "with the *lawful consent* of the originator or an addressee or intended recipient of such communication, or the subscriber in the case of remote-computing service." *Id.* §§ 2702(b)(1), (b)(3) (emphasis added). *See also, e.g.,* Ajemian v. Yahoo!, Inc., 478 Mass. 169, 84 N.E.3d (2017), *cert. pending* (2018) (in setting aside summary judgment favoring Yahoo!, Inc., state supreme court interpreted "lawful consent" to include consent of personal representative of estate). For updates, the reader is directed to the map's current location at https://www.uniformlaws.org/committees/community-home?CommunityKey=f7237fc4-74c2-4728-81c6-b39a91ecdf22.

25. *See* 18 U.S.C. § 2703.

26. *See* 18 U.S.C. § 2702(a)(2); *see also* James D. Lamm, Christina L. Kunz, Damien A. Riehl & Peter John Rademacher, *The Digital Death Conundrum: How Federal and State Laws Prevent Fiduciaries from Managing Digital Property*, 68 U. Miami L. Rev. 385, 404 (2014).

27. Monica Anderson & Jingjing Jiang, *Teens, Social Media & Technology 2018*, (May 31, 2018), http://www.pewinternet.org/2018/05/31/teens-social-media-technology-2018/.

28. 15 U.S.C. §§ 6501–6506 (1998).

29. J. Thomas McCarthy, The Right of Publicity and Privacy 1:3, at 3 (2d ed. 2012).

30. Restatement (Third) of Unfair Competition § 46 (Am. Law Inst. 1995).

31. *See* Cal. Civ. Code. § 3344 (2016); N.Y. Civ. Rights § 51 (2014); C.B.C. Distrib. & Mktg., Inc. v. MLB Advanced Media, 505 F.3d 818, 822 (8th Cir. 2007); and *see also* Matt Savare, *Image Is Everything*, Intellectual Property (Mar. 2013), https://www.lowenstein.com/files/Publication/82dfd7a2-5eec-41a0-8412-bd65931a19af/Presentation/PublicationAttachment/f915b2ea-515e-472f-b2e0-be8e7ce33451/Publicity%20Rights.pdf.

32. *See* Savare, *supra* note 31. *See also* Tenn. Code Ann. §§ 47-25-1101–08 (2016).

33. N.Y. Civ. Rights § 51 (2014).

34. *See* Wash. Rev. Code §§ 63.60.020, .040 (2016). (If there was commercial value at the time of an individual's death, the duration of the right extends to seventy-five years after death). *See also* Savare, *supra* note 31.

35. *See* Kevin L. Vick & Jean-Paul Jassy, *Why a Federal Right of Publicity Statute Is Necessary,* 28 Comms. Law. 1, 2 (2011).

36. *About Inactive Account Manager,* GoogleGoogle, https://support.google.com/accounts/answer/3036546?hl=en (last visited May 24, 2017) (note that Internet addresses may change; a simple search for google inactive account manager will lead to this information).

37. *What will happen to my Facebook account if I pass away?* Facebook, Help Center, https://www.facebook.com/help/ (last visited May 24, 2017).

38. *See* Lamm et al., *supra* note 26, at 417.

39. Cheryl B. Preston, *Cyberinfants*, 39 Pepp. L. Rev. 225, 231 (2012); Megan Diffenderfer, Note, *The Rights of Privacy and Publicity for Minors Online: Protecting the Privilege of Disaffirmance in the Digital*, 54 U. Louisville L. Rev. 131, 147 (2016).

40. Uniform Fiduciary Access to Digital Assets Act, Revised (2015), Uniform Law Commission, https://www.uniformlaws.org/HigherLogic/System/DownloadDocumentFile.ashx?DocumentFileKey=112ab648-b257-97f2-48c2-61fe109a0b33&forceDialog=0 (last visited Mar. 18, 2019) [hereinafter Revised UFADAA]. See Appendix 11-A for a map of states that have enacted the law as of Feb. 2018.

41. *See* Chapter 9.

42. Revised UFADAA § 2(26) (Unif. Law Comm'n 2015).

43. As of Feb. 16, 2018, a search for "uniform /2 fiduciary /3 access /5 digital /40 minor" did not yield any federal or state cases.

44. *See* Revised UFADAA § 2(6) (2015), https://www.uniformlaws.org/Higher Logic/System/DownloadDocumentFile.ashx?DocumentFileKey=112ab648-b257-97 f2-48c2-61fe109a0b33&forceDialog=0 (last visited Mar. 18, 2019).

45. "A user may use an online tool to direct the custodian to disclose to a designated recipient or not to disclose some or all of the user's digital assets, including the content of electronic communications. If the online tool allows the user to modify or delete a direction at all times, a direction regarding disclosure using an online tool overrides a contrary direction by the user in a will, trust, power of attorney, or other record." *Id.* § 4(a).

46. *See* Naomi Cahn, *The Digital Afterlife Is a Mess*, SLATE (2017), http://www.slate.com /articles/technology/future_tense/2017/11/the_digital_afterlife_is_a_mess.html.

47. Fredrick Kunkle, *Virginia Family, Seeking Clues to Son's Suicide, Wants Easier Access to Facebook*, WASH. POST (Feb. 17, 2013), https://www.washingtonpost.com /local/va-politics/virginia-family-seeking-clues-to-sons-suicide-wants-easier-access-to -facebook/2013/02/17/e1fc728a-7935-11e2-82e8-61a46c2cde3d_story.html; Tracy Sears, *Local Parents Win against Social Media Giants*, CBS 6, WTVR–TV (Feb. 6, 2013, 12:17 AM, last updated 6:16 AM), http://wtvr.com/2013/02/06/facebook-sons -suicide/.

48. VA. CODE ANN. §§ 64.2–109; 110 (West 2015) (repealed 2017) (current versions at §§ 64.2–116; 117 (2017)); *see also* H.B. 1068, 2017 Reg. Sess. (Va. enacted Feb. 17, 2017).

49. *See* VA. CODE ANN. §§ 64.2–118(A)–(C) (West 2017); *see also* Matthew D. Glennon, Note, *A Call to Action: Why the Connecticut Legislature Should Solve the Digital Asset Dilemma*, 28 QUINN. PROB. L.J. 48, 65–66 (2014).

50. *See* VA. CODE ANN. § 64.2–130(A) (West 2017); H.B. 1068.

51. *See* Florida Fiduciary Access to Digital Assets Act, FLA. STAT. ANN. §§ 740.001 & 740.002(14) (2016) (guardian is inclusive of "an original guardian, a co guardian, [] a successor guardian, [and] a person appointed by the court as an emergency temporary guardian of the property"); IND. CODE ANN. §§ 32–39–2–11; 32–39–2–12(c)–(e) (West 2016) (guardian is deemed an "authorized user"); *see also* TENN. CODE ANN. §§ 35–8–102(15); (17) ("limited guardian" has "partial, restricted, or temporary powers"); *id.* § 35–8–114(c) (guardian has "general authority" for formally requesting a custodian to "suspend or terminate [the minor's] account"); N.C. GEN. STAT. § 36F–14(a)–(c) (West 2016) (same language as Tennessee law). As of May 2017, the following states explicitly define guardian in their fiduciary access statutes to include an individual acting on behalf of a minor: Florida, Indiana, Tennessee, and North Carolina.

52. N.C. GEN. STAT. §§ 35A–1252; 1254 (West 2016).

53. *See id.* at § 35A–654.

54. S.B. 494, 118th Reg. Sess., (Fla. 2016) (enacted) (codified as Florida Fiduciary Access to Digital Assets Act, FLA. STAT. § 740.002 (State of Florida definitions), and FLA. STAT. § 740.006 (F.S., Disclosure of content of electronic communications).

55. S.B. 131, 77th Sess. (Nev. 2013); STAFF OF ASSEMB. COMM. ON JUDICIARY, 77TH CONG., Minutes, 17, 32–36, 41, 43–44 (Comm. Print 2013), http://www.leg .state.nv.us/Session/77th2013/Minutes/Assembly/JUD/Final/1118.pdf (testimony of Elisa Caffereta, "a young person who is gay or lesbian may have a Facebook

account or other social media accounts . . . if one of those young people dies, they no longer have a right to privacy, but their friends and followers certainly still do have a right to privacy").

56. *See, e.g.*, WebCease, http://www.webcease.com/ (last visited Feb. 16, 2018); Directive Communications Systems, http://www.directivecommunications.com/ (last visited Feb. 16, 2018) (provides planning tools for attorneys).

APPENDIX 11-A

Legislative Enactment Status Fiduciary Access to Digital Assets Act, Revised (2015)

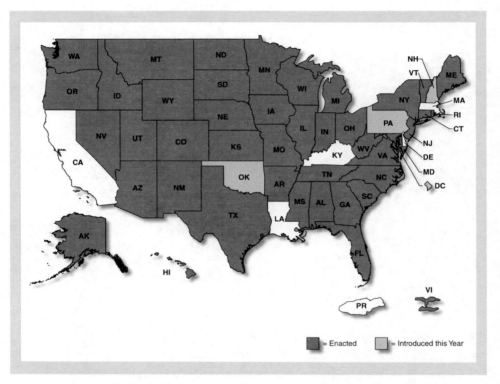

Generated on Friday, February 16, 2018, 1:17 PM

Used with permission of the Uniform Law Commission, © ULC, 2018

APPENDIX 11-B

Websites*

- Complying with COPPA: Frequently Asked Questions, https://www
  .ftc.gov/tips-advice/business-center/guidance/complying-coppa
  -frequently-asked-questions
- Children's Online Privacy Protection Rule: A Six-Step Compliance Plan
  for Your Business (2017), https://www.ftc.gov/tips-advice/business
  -center/guidance/childrens-online-privacy-protection-rule-six-step
  -compliance
- Uniform Fiduciary Access to Digital Assets Act, Revised (2015),
  https://www.uniformlaws.org/HigherLogic/System/DownloadDocu
  mentFile.ashx?DocumentFileKey=112ab648-b257-97f2-48c2-61fe109
  a0b33&forceDialog=0
- Useful digital asset websites include Digital Passing, http://www.digi
  talpassing.com/ (blog coverning estate planning and digital assets);
  Directive Communications, http://www.directivecommunications.
  com/ (services for estte planners and personal representatives); Ever-
  plans, https://www.everplans.com/#/?_k=emqmrm ("secure, digital
  archive" for estate planning documents and digital asset information, etc.); and the Digital Beyond, http://www.thedigitalbeyond
  .com/ (provides digital asset information).

---

*Useful (not endorsed) websites compiled by Naomi Cahn

Index